Boris Pasternak
VOLUME 1

Boris Pasternak
A Literary Biography

❧✣❧

VOLUME 1
1890–1928

❧✣❧

CHRISTOPHER BARNES

CAMBRIDGE
UNIVERSITY PRESS

Published by the Press Syndicate of the University of Cambridge
The Pitt Building, Trumpington Street, Cambridge CB2 1RP
40 West 20th Street, New York, NY 10011–4211, USA
10 Stamford Road, Oakleigh, Victoria 3166, Australia

First published 1989
Reprinted 1992

Transferred to digital printing 1999

Printed in the United Kingdom by Biddles Short Run Books

British Library cataloguing in publication data
Barnes, Christopher, *1942–*
Boris Pasternak; a literary biography.
Vol. I, 1890–1928.
1. Fiction in Russian. Pasternak, Boris, 1890–1960.
Biographies
I. Title
891.73'42

Library of Congress cataloguing in publication data
Barnes, Christopher
Boris Pasternak: a literary biography / Christopher Barnes.
p.   cm.
Bibliography.
Includes index.
Contents: v, 1. 1890–1928.
ISBN 0-521-25957-6
1. Pasternak, Boris Leonidovich, 1890–1960.
2. Authors. Russian – 20th century – Biography.
I. Pasternak, Boris Leonidovich. 1890–1960.
II. Title.
PG3476.P27Z56   1989
891.71'42 – dc 19   88-39638   CIP

ISBN 0 521 25957 6 hardback

Contents

Illustrations

Illustrations

Preface

Despite the power of his writing and the fascination of his career, Pasternak is no easy subject for the biographer. He offered little encouragement to speculate or inquire about the circumstances and personality underlying his published works. One of his poems states that 'Time will preserve my handwriting from the historians' curry-combs', and he himself endeavoured to enforce this announcement. What survived of his archive did so despite his best efforts, and another poem written in 1956 had the force of a programmatic statement in recommending that

> One should not bother keeping archives
> Or fussing over manuscripts

The destruction of drafts and manuscripts was an almost daily event with Pasternak; those which survived were often handed freely and generously to friends and colleagues, and many such items are now so widely distributed that they can never be traced.

There is a further aspect in which the biographer has been forestalled by his subject. Pasternak produced two autobiographies – *Safe Conduct* which appeared in 1931, and an *Autobiographical Essay*, written in 1956 and published posthumously. The former in particular is marked by a brilliance and originality of perception far beyond the powers of any pedestrian chronicler. Yet its oblique narrative viewpoint and laconism disguise keen observation and precision of judgement and often themselves posed new conundrums. Pasternak also referred to *Safe Conduct* as an 'essay in autobiography', yet the designation is strange in view of his remarks in its early pages:

I am not writing my biography. I turn to it when somebody else's requires me to. Together with its main character I believe that only the hero merits an actual account of his life, whereas the story of a poet is utterly inconceivable in such form [...] The poet imparts to the whole of his life such a steep incidence that it cannot exist in the vertical axis of biography where we expect to find it. It cannot be found under his name and has to be sought under someone else's, in the biographical column of his followers.

Thus, in the case of Rilke, to whom *Safe Conduct* is dedicated, Pasternak announced that his recollections were not so much 'in memory of Rilke' as a gift from him. *Safe Conduct* also contains some strangely cavalier treatment of the reader:

I am not going to describe this. The reader will do it for me. He is fond of stories with plots and horrors and he regards history as an endlessly continuing tale [. . .] Only those places beyond which he has never ventured on his walks appeal to him. He is completely taken up with prefaces and introductions, whereas for me life has only revealed itself at the point where he is inclined to start summing up.

If such readers' expectations were unacceptable, life itself often created situations that were beyond Pasternak's grasp. *Safe Conduct* thus paid scant attention to his dealings with Mayakovsky and other poets in the 1920s. Regretting his own involvement with the Left Front of Art and unable to fathom a poet's surrender to ideological commitment, Pasternak simply offered no account of a period in which he 'ran up against the limits of [his] comprehension'. There were several other such examples of a reluctance to offer narrative details.

The purpose of *Safe Conduct* lay in a quite different quarter both from Mayakovsky's commitments and from our own interests. The book is a detailed, evocative account of those episodes in Pasternak's life which helped reveal his authentic voice in poetry and assisted the growth of his artistic personality. As an account of the forty-year period it spans, however, it is bafflingly incomplete, and despite the virtuosity of style and naked emotion of some confessional passages it leaves much unsaid. But the book was the man. Many people who knew Pasternak noted in his conversation an unusual exuberance combined with waywardness, and in both speech and writing he suppressed numerous thoughts and memories or gave them a highly subjective illumination. The reasons were various and they included modesty and injured pride, as well as a healthy delight in paradox and mystification.

A further frustrating imponderable must be borne in mind when reading Pasternak's autobiographical writings. Post-revolutionary official censorship (or else the author's self-preservatory internal censor) discouraged candid narration and the naming of certain names, promoting sometimes an almost impenetrable Aesopic obliqueness. Inhibited narration in *Safe Conduct* and elsewhere was partly therefore the result of objective restraints. But the latter also prevented the proper distillation of experience into *art*, and thus, again, both the suppressant and the things suppressed were excluded from Pasternak's artistic purview.

Pasternak's later *Autobiographical Essay* was produced in a period of post-Stalinist liberalism and a mood of mature reflective self-assessment. It might therefore have been expected to follow more conventional norms of autobiographical writing. But it too shows certain eccentricities. Apart from factual errors (some of which are corrected in the pages that follow) many of the *lacunae* left in *Safe Conduct* still remain unfilled. In a disappointingly premature conclusion, Pasternak points out that he 'never intended writing a history of half a century in several volumes and with many characters'. He ends when he has 'written enough to give an idea of how in my individual case life has been transformed into art, and of how art was born of fate and experience'. A later (1957) version of the *Autobiographical Essay* that reached the galley-proof stage before being withdrawn has a more abrupt conclusion:

To continue further would be immeasurably difficult. In order to maintain the sequence, one would have to go on to speak about years, circumstances, people and destinies contained in the frame of revolution – about a world of aims and aspirations, tasks and feats previously unknown, about a new restraint, a new severity and about new trials which this world set for the human personality, honour, pride, industry and endurance [...]

One should write of it in such a way as to make hearts falter and hair stand on end. To write of it in a routine and commonplace manner, to write less astonishingly, or less vividly, than Gogol's and Dostoevsky's depictions of Petersburg would not only have no sense or purpose. To write in such a manner would be base and shameless.

But part of the literary biographer's concern must be with those 'stories with plots and horrors' and with the 'prefaces and introductions' that Pasternak himself never composed. He must also reconstruct some of history's 'endlessly continuing tale', which will doubtless emerge in a paler account than his subject would have condoned. Pasternak would have resented the intrusive genre of biography applied to himself. 'Life initiates very few people into the secret of what it is doing with them', he wrote in *Zhenya Luvers' Childhood*, and among the many distractions designed to prevent man from involving his own stupidity in the formation of his immortal essence Pasternak identified religions, general concepts, human prejudices, and psychology. Had he extended the list of such misguided, self-defeating activities, he might well have included the writing of biography. Nevertheless, the latter, like theology or psychology, remains a legitimate field of inquiry and can reveal things of value and interest even if the creative artist has limited use for them. It is, in fact, difficult either to discard or wholly to accept Pasternak's own sketchy summary of so many decades of life and experience. He would have maintained that the finest essence of his creativity was contained in his final verses and in the novel *Doctor Zhivago*. Yet even the patently autobiographical or confessional quality of these later books leaves many questions still unanswered. Also, it seems to me, despite the fact that some of Pasternak's very earliest writings contain character and situational prototypes for *Zhivago*, there is risk of losing perspective on his earlier life and work if one adopts his own retrospective view that they were nothing more than a preparation for the later novel.

Inevitably there are texts and matters of fact and private experience that defy investigation. Yet almost all Pasternak's literary output unmistakably draws on and points back to his own biography. Scarcely a page of his writing is a purely invented fiction. The close connection between life and art was indeed a point of conscience with him. The realism towards which he strove in later years, for instance, was to him a token of 'the depth of biographical impact which has become the artist's chief motive force, driving him towards originality and novelty'. In reconstructing Pasternak's biography below, I have therefore tried to make careful use of belletristic texts at such points where these seem a reliable indicator of their author's experiences and attitudes. But I have avoided any wanton 'fictionalising'; where my own or others' surmise is involved, or when literary evidence is our only source, this has usually been made clear in the text.

A systematic destroyer of his own archive, Pasternak kept no diaries or notebooks, and his natural reticence has been reinforced by other circumstances: by a partly sought, partly imposed, withdrawal from official literary life in the oppressive 1930s and postwar years, and by the shadow cast over his last years and posthumous reputation which only now seems to be clearing. It is true that since his death several individuals and institutions in the USSR and abroad have preserved letters, manuscripts and other papers relating to his life and work. Yet, although he is recognised, rehabilitated, and selectively published and discussed in Soviet and Western journals, the complete editions, monographs and documentation that Pasternak deserves have not yet appeared. In this respect his near contemporaries, Blok, Esenin, Mayakovsky and others have fared better. Their literary canonisation in the USSR has not been exclusively beneficial, yet their tragically premature deaths have encouraged the publication of commentaries and memoirs by almost anyone who had any significant contacts with them.

Pasternak's situation is thus still one of relative neglect. For the various reasons given above, as well as those intended by the author, one is frequently thrown back upon his own suggestion in *Safe Conduct* that the facts of his life must be sought not under his name, but 'in the biographical column of his followers'. Pasternak's studied passivity and acute receptivity to outward impressions meant that the 'depth of biographical impact' from other men and women was in his case particularly great. Like the lyric hero of his verse who dissolves into the surrounding imagery, so the story of his life becomes at certain points in effect not the story of what he did and achieved, but of what he witnessed, what happened to him and what changes he underwent as his existence was dominated by a changing sequence of events and person-alities. This is nowhere more true than of Pasternak's childhood (the 'ladle of the soul's profundity', as he called it in one poem of *Themes and Variations*). For this reason the present biography devotes a perhaps greater than normal proportion of attention to the artist's earlier years. These were spent in the happily creative home atmosphere of a family of artists. His father was one of Russia's foremost painters, and his mother was a uniquely gifted concert pianist. Physically, temperamentally and artistically, Pasternak owed his origins to them, and it is with their story that this book commences.

The chapters that follow describe in detail the life and literary work of Boris Pasternak, and the reflection of the one in the other. It is not the first book on this subject, and certain aspects of the theme have been impressively covered in some recent monographs. However, it adds to what is already known, partly through its wider use of archival sources and through personal contacts with many people who knew Pasternak. I have benefited greatly from the investigations of earlier monographers, notably Lazar Fleishman, Henry Gifford, Ronald Hingley, Olga Hughes and Guy de Mallac, and I have had at my disposal the valuable harvest of Pasternak materials that have appeared in the last five years. Another advantage I have enjoyed is the scope and detailed treatment that are possible in the present two-volume format; for this much credit goes to Professor Henry Gifford and to Terence Moore of Cambridge University Press for their initial enthusiasm in pursuing a venture of this size.

On occasion I have attempted to allow the author's voice to sound independently, and not merely as a source of factual evidence or material for commentary. Although only a pale reflection of the originals, the translated poetry and prose passages at the head of each chapter afford examples of Pasternak's art which at the same time relate in some way to the chapters that they preface.

The many pages of literary discussion in this study are mainly descriptive, and although they contain some original interpretative insights the excellent full-length monographs by Gifford, Hughes and Livingstone and many other scholarly articles and dissertations probe textual depths and details that could not be discussed here. Also beyond the aim and scope of this study is the minute exploration of Pasternak's specifically literary activities in the 1920s and 1930s such as Lazar Fleishman has undertaken in his two recent books.

The proportion and subdivision of the present biography may arouse surprise and disagreement. More than normally generous space has been allotted to Pasternak's early life, reflecting his own insistence on the importance of these years (and the contents of his own autobiographies). This, and the fact that the period up to the late 1920s was more artistically prolific than the 1930s and 1940s, explains an apparently premature cut-off date in this first volume. Strictly speaking, it was 1929 or 1930 that marked the end of an era both personally for Pasternak and in the cultural and political history of Russia. But the events of those years were perhaps more vital as an adumbration of the period ahead than as a summing-up of the past. I have therefore deliberately made an arbitrary and 'unclean' break and have allowed various threads to remain hanging in order to weave them together at the start of the forthcoming second volume.

The rendering of Russian names in the main text below is a compromise between accepted (though not necessarily English) transcription (e.g. Tchaikovsky, Koussevitsky, etc.), the need for elegance and consistency, and an approach that gives phonetic guidance to non-Russian readers. In the case of some Russian names that have obvious French, German or other antecedents, the original pre-Russian version has been restored (e.g. Rubinstein, or Gay – instead of Ge); but usually such names (e.g. Fokht, Vilyam, or Shtikh) are given in Russified versions and can be traced to their originals via the index. Actual Russian quotations in the text, however, as well as the bibliographical and reference sections, adhere to the transliteration system adopted in the journal *Oxford Slavonic Papers*.

Christian names in Russian often exist in one or more familiar diminutive forms. But except in the case of 'Shura' Shtikh, Aunt 'Asya', Cousin 'Olya', 'Zhenya' (Pasternak's son) and of quoted passages, I have refrained from using diminutives so as not to 'overpopulate' the account for English readers unfamiliar with this practice. Pasternak's sisters Zhozefina and Lidiya are referred to throughout as Josephine and Lydia, since they have resided in Britain for nearly half a century and have published and become known under these English forms of their names.

Institutions, hotels, streets, etc. have sometimes been translated, sometimes transliterated, depending on what seemed appropriate. Consistency throughout the text has been followed, however, and 'first mention' translations and Russian versions are given in brackets. Titles of books and literary miscellanies are given in English, with original versions indicated in brackets on their first occurrence. Conversely, foreign-language journals and newspapers retain their Russian titles. One consistent divergence from normal practice is the italicising of titles of all Pasternak's major works – i.e. short stories, cycles of poems, longer poems (*poemy*), articles and essays – regardless of whether they were actually published as separate books. Shorter items, such as lyric poems, appear with an English title or first line between quotation marks, and a Russian version in parenthesis. Except where otherwise indicated, all translations are my own. The omission of passages from quotations is indicated by [. . .].

Dates given for Russian events up to the end of January 1918, when the country switched to the Western European calendar, accord with the 'Old Style' Julian calendar. The latter ran twelve days behind the modern Gregorian one in the nineteenth century, and thirteen days in the present one.

The collected (although not complete) prose and verse of Pasternak is available in three standard editions. The first was the Michigan University Press collection of *Sochineniya* (Ann Arbor, 1961) in three volumes. Pasternak's verse appeared in the 'large series' of the Soviet 'Biblioteka poeta' under the title *Stikhotvoreniya i poemy* (Moscow–Leningrad, 1965). A good Soviet edition of prose writings is *Vozdushnye puti: Proza raznykh let* (Moscow, 1982). These editions have recently been followed up by the two-volume *Izbrannoe* (Moscow, 1985). Where direct quotation from standard editions occurs in the present study, page references are given in brackets in the main body of the text. Reference to *Sochineniya* is made with the volume number in Roman numerals followed by the page; where this is duplicated in *Stikhotvoreniya i poemy* or *Vozdushnye puti*, a reference appears consisting of *SP* or *VP*, followed by the page number. Citations from *Izbrannoe* (*Izbr.* followed by a page reference) are not given unless the text exists only in this edition. References to *Doktor Zhivago* are indicated by *DZh* and page number, referring to the 1957 Russian-language edition by Feltrinelli of Milan.

There are several people to whom I am irredeemably indebted for help in preparing this biography. First and most of all, I thank various members of the Pasternak family in Moscow and Oxford, who not only themselves figure in the story but have over many years given generous time and attention to my queries. More specifically: the late Aleksandr Pasternak on several occasions gave me the benefit of his reminiscençes, his knowledge of his brother's writings, and his warm personality. Evgenii Borisovich and Elena Pasternak have spent countless hours answering my questions, correcting misunderstandings, and inspíring me with their devoted and encyclopaedic knowledge of Boris Pasternak's life and work. Josephine Pasternak and her late husband, and Lydia Pasternak-Slater have also willingly submitted to numerous gruelling interviews about their life in Russia and Germany and their memories of their family and friends; they have also read through substantial sections of this biography in an earlier draft and have helped me avoid many errors. I am further greatly indebted to Ann Pasternak-Slater for numerous kindnesses and ready help with answers to my queries about the Pasternak family archive of documents and photographs.

Among many others whose help I gratefully acknowledge, special thanks go to the following: Professor Dame Elizabeth Hill and the late Dr Nikolai Andreyev who supervised my postgraduate research and laid the foundations of my present knowledge and enthusiasm; Geoffrey Hosking who shared my first discovery of Pasternak's verse; the late Anna Akhmatova, Sergei Bobrov, Konstantin Bogatyryov, Pyotr Grigoryevich Bogatyryov, Kornei Chukovsky, Evdoksiya Fyodorovna Nikitina, Zelma Ruoff, Irina Nikolayevna Vilyam and Boris Zaitsev, who during the 1960s and 1970s allowed me to consult them and provided much inspiration and information. From Riga, Jerusalem and Stanford, Lazar Fleishman has sent me invaluable commentaries, off-prints, bibliographic materials and other information; lengthy sections of the manuscript have been read and helpfully criticised by my wife Alexa, Henry Gifford, Rima Salys and Gabriel Superfin; to my colleague Roger Keys I am deeply indebted for a huge number of critical annotations and stylistic suggestions; to Rima Salys I am also immensely grateful for her answers to many queries in both the literary and artistic field, and for her invaluable assistance with illustrations; and Richard Davies has generously shared with me his knowledge of relevant holdings in the Leeds Russian Archive.

In addition to the above, the following friends and colleagues have frequently, and in ways too various to detail, rendered me assistance, and I wish here to thank: Valerii Alekseyev, Nicholas Anning, Michel Aucouturier, Per Arne Bodin, Leonid Chertkov, Neil Cornwell, Martin Dewhirst, Renate Döring-Smirnov, Victor Erlich, Peter France, Maria Gonta, Jane Grayson, Peter Haworth, the late Max Hayward, Ronald Hingley, Olga Raevsky Hughes, Robert Hughes, Vyacheslav Vsevolodovich Ivanov, Bengt Jangfeldt, Simon Karlinsky, Yurii Levin, Evgenii Levitin, Angela Livingstone, Anna Ljunggren, Gordon McVay, Guy de Mallac, John Malmstad, Zoya Maslennikova, A. I. Metchenko, Elliott Mossman, Georges Nivat, Katherine O'Connor, Aleksandr Parnis, Harvey Pitcher, the late Alexis Rannit, Iwanka Rebet, Ivan Rozhansky, Dmitry Segal, Daša di Simplicio, Gerald Stanton Smith, Ada Steinberg, Valerii Voskoboinikov, the late Anatolii Yakobson, and Aleksandr Zholkovsky.

Needless to say, I take upon myself responsibility for the errors and omissions that this work no doubt contains, and also for several judgements which are not shared by all those who have offered their advice and assistance. The fact that the second volume is still in preparation affords a certain comfort, and I would be grateful for any comments which may help to correct errors in the present volume, and for any information that may assist in improving the forthcoming one.

During the preparation of this volume I have been the fortunate recipient of several grants for study in the USSR, Germany and various parts of Britain, and I am happy to acknowledge help from the following bodies: the British Academy, the British Council, the Carnegie Trust, the Hayter Fund, and the St Andrews University Research and Travel Funds.

The staff of various libraries and archives have lent invaluable support on various occasions, notably: Cambridge University Library, the Bodleian and Taylorian Institute Libraries in Oxford, the Leeds Russian Archive, the British Museum, the St Andrews University Library, the State Lenin Library and Gorky Institute of World Literature; in Moscow I have also on several occasions had welcome assistance from the Foreign Department of Moscow State University.

For their typing skills I wish to thank my wife, and particularly Norma

Porter who undertook the ungrateful task of deciphering and typing up my much corrected and nearly impenetrable final manuscript. Finally, my warm thanks go to Terence Moore, and Katharina Brett and Con Coroneos of Cambridge University Press, for their patience, advice and careful work in preparing this book for publication.

Acknowledgements

Leonid Pasternak: sketch of Boris Pasternak as a boy (20 July 1898), is reproduced by courtesy of the Ashmolean Museum, Oxford. All other illustrations are by courtesy of The Pasternak Trust. The poem 'Black spring! Pick up your pen . . .' translated by Lydia Pasternak-Slater, is reproduced by courtesy of George Allen and Unwin, London. The frontispiece portrait of Pasternak appears thanks to a generous supporting grant from the Carnegie Trust.

1

Origins and infancy

Thus you begin. To a mass of melody
From nurse's arms aged two you surge.
You twitter, squeak . . . eventually
In the third year words emerge.

As the rotating turbine roars,
Thus you begin to understand.
It seems your mother is not yours,
You are not you, your home's a foreign land.

And perched on a bench of lilac,
Can awful beauty then do otherwise
That straightway captivate a child? And
Thus suspicions may arise.

Thus terrors ripen. Can he resist
The chance to catch at every star?
When he is a Faust, a fantasist?
That is how the gypsies start.

Thus over trellises soaring high,
Where houses ought to be, there roll
Oceans sudden as a sigh.
Thus iambic verses will unfold.

Thus you fall into the summer corn,
Mouthing the prayer 'So let it be!' And in
Your gaze the night-time threatens dawn.
Thus quarrels with the sun begin.

To live by verse thus are you born.

෨෨෨෨

In Pasternak's novel, *Doctor Zhivago*, the central hero is described as a man who had 'studied ancient history and the Scriptures, legends and poets, the sciences of the past and of nature, as though they were the family chronicle of his house, his family tree' (*DZh*, 88). Pasternak's picture of Yurii Zhivago was in fact partly an exercise in self-portrayal, depicting a man who felt at one with nature, art and history, and who saw himself as inheritor of a broad Russian and European culture. Although Zhivago did not share Pasternak's Jewish descent (indeed, Pasternak always played down the importance of his racial origins), his portrait nevertheless seems to hint obliquely at the legend of the author's ancestry. Through many generations the Pasternak family had traced their origins to Don Isaac Ben Yehuda Abravanel, the fifteenth-century Jewish philosopher and theologian, one time treasurer in the court of Alfonso V of Portugal and later a minister in the Republic of Venice. And Abravanel in turn had claimed descent from the royal house of David, his ancestors having moved to the Spanish peninsula after the fall of the First Temple.[1]

The father of Boris Pasternak recalled having seen a written account of the family tree during his childhood. But all trace of it was subsequently lost, and today there are no means of confirming those legendary origins. By the nineteenth century the Pasternak family's fortunes had changed beyond recognition. They lived in poverty and obscurity. Further migrations had brought them to the Ukrainian city of Odessa, inside the Pale of Settlement where most of the Russian Empire's Jewish citizens were confined. There was little to distinguish them with their Sephardic origins from the majority of Russia's Ashkenazim Jewry. The surname they had acquired further obscured their descent. Pasternak – meaning 'parsnip' – was a mild example of the grotesque family names sometimes imposed upon Jews in central and eastern Europe, and its etymology reflected a very different migration of language and people. (The term was in fact a loan-word from Polish, which in turn derived it via German from the Latin *pastinaca*, itself a word that spawned numerous variants among the Romance languages.) Boris Pasternak's grandfather Osip and great uncle Evgenii were the first in their family to bear this surname. Probably tsarist functionaries forced it on them in place of their Jewish name some time in the reign of Nicholas I.

Odessa has sometimes been titled the 'Palmira of the South', and, less glamorously, the 'Russian Marseilles'. Thanks to Black Sea and Mediterranean trade as well as to the movement of peoples within the Russian Empire, the city acquired a colourful population of Tatars, Greeks, Italians, Turks and Jews, as well as Russians and Ukrainians. By the late nineteenth century it was an exotic, vital centre of commerce and culture, with around 300,000 citizens. Some of the modern world's finest musicians were to spring from its Jewish community, and several Russian literary celebrities, including Babel, Olesha, and poets such as Bagritsky and Kirsanov were born there. Among the artists who came from Odessa, Kishinyovsky, Kostandi, Rubo and Braz made firm reputations within Russia, and Leonid Pasternak, the father of Boris, achieved international celebrity.

In the mid nineteenth century the Pasternaks must have seemed unlikely contributors to any flowering of the arts. Leonid Osipovich Pasternak was born on 22 March 1862. He was the youngest of a large family whose modesty and limited horizons betrayed nothing of their fabled ancestry. Although Odessa was a centre of Jewish culture, the Pasternaks were becoming assimilated and losing their religious and national identity. They only nominally observed Jewish rituals; Leonid Pasternak had the Jewish name Isaak but hardly ever used it except in official documents, and the language spoken at home was neither Ladinu nor Yiddish, but Russian. Leonid's father, Iosif, or Osip, Pasternak, scraped an income by renting a small guest-house with an adjoining coach-yard. Most of his patrons were old-style landowners who drove up in clumsy Gogolian carriages. The courtyard with its quaint clientele, vehicles and animal life first awakened Leonid's artistic imagination, and eventually the whole city began to excite his gaze. Strangely, when he first journeyed to Venice many years later, he recognised the Italianate quality of his native city, and pictures by Italian masters often revived certain impressions of his own Odessa childhood.[2]

Apart from a colourful environment and inborn gift, however, there were few encouragements towards a career in the arts. Earnings were meagre and there were many mouths to feed. Osip and Lea Pasternak had nine children of whom three had died in infancy while David, another artistically gifted son, died in his late teens. Without being grimly tyrannical, Osip Pasternak matched their spartan family life with his own moral severity. His children's upbringing was designed to prepare them for hardship and to teach self-discipline and independence. Success was viewed in terms of the security and social position which he and his wife had failed to achieve. He could afford a complete education only for his sons Aleksandr and Leonid whom he intended for respectable careers in medicine or the law. Of three surviving daughters, Anna (known in the family as 'Asya') was the only one to attend secondary school. Roza and Ekaterina received only primary education. (The latter probably also had some latent artistic talent: her grandson was to become the celebrated artist, Philippe Hosiasson.)

3

Despite his ascetic philosophy, Osip Pasternak evidently had an amusing talent for mimicry and acting, and his wife was a lyrical, affectionate and sensitive soul. She was brought up in the countryside, responded keenly to flowers and nature, and was virtually illiterate. But neither of Leonid's parents did anything to encourage his serious artistic gifts. His early signs of talent aroused only their alarm. They angrily destroyed some of his first pictures and he was directed towards more practical pursuits. As he later recalled, in his family's circle painting was associated only with domestic decorating and distempering, jobs that were always done by poorly paid, grimy, bespattered workmen.[3]

Eventually, Leonid cajoled his parents into paying for occasional art lessons, and his gifts were fostered by outsiders – an elderly janitor who commissioned some hunting scenes, a French teacher from his school, and especially Mikhail Fyodorovich Freidenberg. The latter was a brilliant and versatile actor, journalist and inventor. He remained a lifelong friend of Leonid's and eventually married his sister Asya. At this early stage he helped place some of Leonid's work in local Odessa journals and, as an inspired freelancer, encouraged him by his own example. Their most extravagant collaboration involved Freidenberg's ascent over Odessa in a home-made calico balloon, an event for which Leonid designed the publicity posters.[4] At the age of seventeen, while still at secondary school, Leonid began attending the Odessa Fine Art Society's School of Drawing. It was there that his foreign-born instructors probably imparted a Germano-Italian bias to his artistic sympathies, and these eventually provided a pretext for the vivid German and Italian cultural experiences that enriched the biography of his son Boris.[5]

After Leonid Pasternak left school, art remained only a spare-time pursuit. In 1881, to placate his self-sacrificing parents, he signed on to study medicine at Moscow University. He evidently coped well with the courses in myology and osteology, and this insight into muscle and bone structure was later of direct use in figure drawing. But an aversion for the dissecting room forced him in 1882 to transfer to the Law Faculty. The change both carried parental blessing and afforded more time for painting. He had little interest in the law course and attended few lectures on the subject. Apparently his most vivid university memories were of Professors Chuprov and Klyuchevsky with their brilliant disquisitions on political economy and Russian history. It was Leonid Pasternak's ambition to study simultaneously at the University and as an extramural student at the Moscow School of Painting, Sculpture and Architecture. But for two successive years these hopes were dashed, first by a late application and then by the award of the one free place to a daughter of the author Lev Tolstoy. To avoid wasting time he took private painting lessons from Academician Evgraf Sorokin and also published some work in the prestigious art journal *Svet i teni* (*Chiaroscuro*). But this was no compensation for his exclusion from the School of Painting, and he ruled out the St Petersburg Academy, since it was a stronghold of conservative academic classicism. Instead, Leonid Pasternak turned his gaze towards Western Europe.[6]

Returning to the south, he registered in Odessa at the Law Faculty of the University of Novorossiisk. This institution allowed students to study *in absentia* and return merely to sit their examinations. While thus nominally pursuing his legal studies, Pasternak was able to set out in autumn of 1882 for Munich, a leading European artistic centre, where he enrolled at the Bavarian Royal Academy of Art. By frugal living he was able to survive on the slender funds provided by his father and with occasional advances from Karl Evgenyevich Pasternak, a wealthy cousin some years his senior. He evidently studied diligently and Herterich, his mentor in the Naturschule, could hardly fault an already masterly charcoal technique.

Having won a medal for draughtsmanship, Leonid Pasternak intended to turn his attention to painting, and curiosity about French impressionist techniques attracted him towards Paris. In spring of 1885 he returned to Odessa, planning to cram for his law examinations and serve his obligatory year in the Russian Imperial Army. Thereafter, with filial and civic duties dispatched, he would be free to continue studying in France. In the autumn he duly gained a second-class diploma in law and enlisted in the army. But in late 1885 the carefully laid plans were diverted. While serving in the artillery he met and fell in love with the young woman who was to become his wife.[7]

Like Leonid Pasternak, Rozaliya Isidorovna Kofman (or Kaufman*) was a native of Odessa. Her family's comfortable middle-class existence and intellectual and artistic interests contrasted with the austere Pasternak household. Her father, Isidor Kofman, was a soda-water manufacturer who also enjoyed local repute as a chess-player and mathematician, while Berta, her mother, combined practicality with a love of music and singing. Rozaliya ('Roza' to family and friends) evidently showed

* Kofman seems to have been the version in currency in Odessa, while Kaufman was the more accurately Germanic form adopted by various members of the family who moved to Moscow and other cities.

unusual precocity. She could talk when only one year old, and after sitting under the grand piano during a cousin's music lessons at the age of five, she one day reproduced his pieces perfectly without tuition. Regular piano lessons were then started with a local teacher called Tsvet, and at the age of eight she gave her first recital. Her second concert, three years later in April 1878, was a major triumph greeted by enthusiastic press notices. Among her audience was Ignác Amadeus Tedesco, an eminent pianist, composer, conductor and teacher. Born in Czechoslovakia and once internationally hailed as 'Hannibal of the Octaves', Tedesco had lived in Odessa since 1840. His pupil Pachman was already a rising international star, and in 1878 he undertook to teach Rozaliya Kofman further.[8]

Rozaliya displayed both flair and industry, as well as a maturity of musical insight well beyond her years. In 1880 she made a much acclaimed tour of Southern Russia, and the following year came to the attention of Anton Rubinstein. Having heard her play in Odessa, he recommended that she present herself in the musical centres of Moscow and Petersburg. Another tour followed, taking in Kiev and Poltava as well as the two capitals. However, after a warm reception from Rubinstein and an appearance as accompanist for Sarasate, the Spanish violinist, Rozaliya's visit to Petersburg was cut short by illness. Her frail constitution failed to withstand the combination of nervous and physical strain and the northern climate.

When Tedesco in 1882 proclaimed his pupil ready for a foreign tour, this venture too was interrupted. Hardly had she left Odessa in November when news of Tedesco's sudden death induced such a state of shock and delirium that meningitis was suspected and the tour was cancelled. Both these incidents suggested that, despite her prodigious gifts, Rozaliya Kofman was ill-equipped for the rigorous life of a touring artiste, and as an adult she was for many decades troubled by a nervous heart condition. Her early experience of triumph curtailed or snatched away also led to her permanent distrust of celebrity – and there was a coincidence here (if not a causal connection) with the later experience of her son Boris. But in the 1880s there was no immediate halt to her developing career. A tour of major cities in Russia and Poland was an unqualified success and in 1883 on Rubinstein's advice she went to Vienna to further her studies with Theodor Leschetitzky.[9]

The three years in Austria were happy and successful. A review of her recital shortly after arriving announced her as 'the equal of our most illustrious and laurel-crowned masters of the pianoforte', and flattering comparisons were drawn with Rubinstein and Liszt.[10] Each spring in the company of her mother she undertook tours of Poland and southern Russia and was everywhere greeted with acclaim. Further tangible proof of rising stardom was the publication in Odessa in 1885 of a book in German containing a biographical sketch of her together with several press reviews.[11]

On her final return to Odessa in 1886, Rozaliya Kofman was offered a professorship at the Odessa Music School, eventually incorporated as a branch of the St Petersburg Conservatoire. Soon after returning, she also attended a soirée given by a local littérateur named Semyon Vinogradsky, and it was there that she met the young artist Leonid Pasternak.[12]

Leonid Pasternak recalled how Rozaliya Kofman captivated him by her obvious musical gifts as well as her 'intelligence, rare kindness and spiritual purity'. A warm friendship quickly sprang up between them. But despite common artistic interests, their diverse commitments inevitably raised problems. Pasternak had expected to complete his military service and then resume his studies, envisaging for himself a life of almost monastic dedication to art. His new emotional commitment seemed likely to impede Rozaliya's career and to require a total revision of his own plans. But despite a period of depression at his dilemma, Leonid's bond with Rozaliya grew and their courtship continued. It was planned that they should eventually marry and settle in Moscow, a city which he already knew and which offered professional opportunities for both of them.[13]

Leonid Pasternak initially went to Moscow on his own in 1888, and occupied modest rooms in Lubyansky Passage near the city centre. One of his close neighbours there was Mikhail Nesterov, another young artist destined for fame but as yet undiscovered and struggling to survive. The first months in Moscow brought many new contacts, especially with younger artists and students from the Moscow School of Painting. Some of them he met through the artist Vasilii Polenov's drawing circle, and several new friends, including Arkhipov, Golovin, Sergei Ivanov, Korovin, Levitan, Serov and Vrubel, were to figure prominently in the history of Russian art.[14]

In his furnished lodgings Pasternak worked on his first large original canvas, a genre painting entitled 'Letter from Home' and based on impressions of life in the army. Even before its completion, connoisseurs were admiring its fresh realistic execution, and it was quickly purchased for two thousand roubles by Pavel Tretyakov, founder of the famous Moscow gallery collection. This sale of his work brought both celebrity and an injection of finance which, as cousin Karl Pasternak pointed out, removed all obstacles to Leonid's marriage plans. The transaction with Tretyakov was actually concluded on the eve of his fiancée's arrival with her parents in Moscow. The wedding was on 14 February 1889, and after the synagogue there was a gathering with food, wine and dancing at the Moscow home of Karl Pasternak. The honeymoon journey took them to Petersburg to see the first public showing of 'Letter from Home' in an exhibition mounted by the Itinerant (Peredvizhniki) exhibition group. Then, in April, the couple returned to Odessa where Rozaliya carried out various examining and concert commitments. In Odessa they lived with her parents on Meshchanskaya Street and also had a seaside holiday at a nearby resort; during July Leonid paid a visit to the Paris World Exhibition. In the autumn of 1889, however, they moved back to Moscow, by which time Rozaliya was expecting their first child.[15]

The late phase of Alexander III's reign was a period of political reaction, chauvinist nationalism, censorship, repression and stultifying bureaucracy. Indeed, if Leonid Pasternak had followed a legal career, he might well have fallen foul of a ruling which in 1889 forbade non-Christians from practising at the bar except by special permission. Nevertheless, the Moscow ambiance was congenial. While ranking as second capital, the city retained a colourful provinciality quite different from the cultivated Western European aspect of Petersburg. The Pasternaks were to stay there for over thirty years, and they and their family came to regard themselves not as wandering Jews from the south, but as Muscovite and Russian. In the artistic intelligentsia circles where they moved, nationality and religion were not crucial factors. Dissociated from official attitudes and prejudice, the intelligentsia viewed themselves partly as the nation's cultural trustees; their ranks included men and women of very different stations, from poor students and bohemians to some of the social élite, and among them the life of the arts and intellect transcended social barriers.

The Pasternaks lived in straitened circumstances in the early years of their marriage. Tretyakov's bounty was soon spent, and their life was almost devoid of luxury. Rozaliya Pasternak was able to boost the family income. Both before and after the birth of their first child Boris, she continued to practise and occasionally perform and she also tutored piano students delegated to her from the Moscow Conservatoire. With her pianistic credentials she was immediately accepted and colleagues regularly visited to hear her play and to make music together. Moscow had plenty to offer to any pianist. Another Leschetitzky pupil, Vasilii Safonov, was director of the Conservatoire and among many recent and brilliant students, Aleksandr Scriabin and Sergei Rachmaninov were on the threshold of their careers as pianist-composers.

Despite the attention he commanded among colleagues and cognoscenti, Leonid Pasternak found no easy road to financial security. He and his wife made their first home in apartment 3 of Vedeneyev's house near the site of the old Triumphal Gateway on Tverskaya (now Gorky) Street. This building, which like many residential blocks of the time was referred to by the surname of the owner, still stands with its adjoining carpentry workshops next door to what is now the 'Sofia' Restaurant. The Pasternaks' six small rooms, rented at fifty roubles per month, afforded no proper studio space, and in this cramped accommodation Leonid confronted the inevitable: poverty, constant anxiety, and a heavy sense of debt to his family. When they engaged a wet-nurse for their child their material cares were even reflected in the lullaby which she was once overheard to improvise. 'There, there, my darling,' she sang to Boris. 'When you're older your father won't need to work any more. He'll have hired hands to paint for him...'![16]

Fortunately help was at hand. Rozaliya and the wife of Leonid's friend and colleague Serov, who was also in dire straits, frequently assisted one another with small loans – by mutual agreement never exceeding three roubles. Leonid also enjoyed the support of his cousin Karl. As a successful merchant, the latter had already helped finance Leonid's studies. Now, after several years' residence in Vienna, he had brought his Austrian wife and their family to Moscow, where they maintained a fine apartment at Chistye Prudy (Clear Pools). Karl Pasternak now worked as assistant to Protopopov, a prominent figure and *inter alia* head of the Russian wax and candle trade. In Moscow Karl Pasternak became known as a charitable benefactor, and it was he who founded the blind school where Leonid picked up an idea for his second major canvas. Until his death in 1915 Karl remained his cousin's close ally and admirer.[17]

In the 1880s the life of Moscow was still rooted firmly in the nineteenth century. Social and commercial life was not deeply affected, as it was soon to be, by the rise of a prosperous entrepreneurial middle class. The arts too were not yet in a state of prolific ferment – Russian Symbolist culture, which began as a literary movement born of Western Decadent trends, was launched only in the 1890s. The blossoming of visual arts to which Leonid Pasternak helped point the way had also hardly begun, and collectors were only starting to acquire the French Impressionist works that were eventually to make a deep impact. It was true, Pasternak's 'Letter from Home' showed a certain 'pre-Impressionist' luminosity and lyricism, but it was basically realistic and matched the tastes of the popular and influential 'Peredvizhniki' or Itinerants. (So named because of their touring exhibitions, this group emerged in the 1870s, reacting against the stereotyped classicism of academy art and promoting the idea of art as a realistic 'genre' commentary on contemporary Russian life.) In the early 1890s, however, Pasternak's work began displaying an awareness of modernist trends thoughtfully and organically assimilated. While still convinced that sound draughtsmanship was the foundation of all good art, he absorbed Impressionist techniques and in effect began practising a controlled form of innovation.[18]

In the 1890s the conservatism of the once innovatory Itinerants thus began to irk Pasternak. His second major picture, 'The Blind Children's Prayer', with its unusual interior lighting effect, was rejected by the Itinerant jury in 1890. Together with some younger Moscow colleagues, he founded a new Group of Thirty-Six Artists which dispensed with artistic programmes and juries and had a more progressive outlook. Almost at the same time a group called The World of Art came into being in Petersburg, fertilising Russian national material with Western European modernist techniques; Pasternak and other Muscovites joined this group and from 1898 onwards contributed to their exhibitions in the capital. Despite disagreements, however, Pasternak did not break altogether with the Itinerants, and still occasionally coexhibited, enjoying with them a certain mutual appreciation. Moreover, as the 1890s wore on his success depended less and less on the Itinerants – his 'Students Before the Examinations' was almost rejected by the Itinerant jury but won a gold medal in Munich in 1895, and at the Paris Exhibition of 1900 was acquired by the Musée du Luxembourg.[19]

A key to Leonid Pasternak's success and gradually improving finances in the early 1890s was his mastery of several different media. His skill with pencil, pen and charcoal earned him rapid recognition as an illustrator, portraitist, and sketcher with an unusual ability to seize fleeting actions and impressions 'on the wing'. He was able to market a number of his drawings and charcoals produced while a student in Munich. For a short time he was art editor of the prominent monthly *Artist* for which, *inter alia*, he created the illustrations to Chekhov's story

The Swansong (*Lebedinaya pesnya*). In 1891 he was also commissioned by the publisher Pyotr Konchalovsky to organise illustrations for the jubilee edition of Lermontov. Among the artists he recruited for this work was Mikhail Vrubel, whose brilliant, sensual and faintly cubist illustrations to 'The Demon' later achieved an independent fame. The following year the magazine *Sever* (The North) invited Pasternak, along with Repin, Kivshenko and Vereshchagin, to help illustrate Tolstoy's *War and Peace* (*Voina i mir*). In a different medium, Pasternak also assisted in creating sets for Arensky's new opera *Raphael*. A further lucrative sideline during his early years in Moscow was the offering of art instruction to various individuals, including some relatives of the prominent lawyers Garkavi and Shaikevich. Such was the success of this that he and his colleague, Viktor Shtember, eventually set up their own private art school. New social contacts brought an increasing flow of portrait commissions, and also invitations to Prince Golitsyn's, where interesting models were provided and high society regularly came to observe the various artists at work.[20]

There was another chapter in Pasternak's career which involved all his family and ultimately had important consequences for his son Boris. At the preview of the Itinerants' 1893 summer exhibition, his canvas entitled 'The Débutante' was admired by none other than Lev Tolstoy, and Pasternak and the venerable author were immediately introduced by colleagues. A warm friendship quickly sprang from their meeting. Pasternak was frequently invited to visit Tolstoy at his Moscow and country residences. Tolstoy was full of admiration for his series of *War and Peace* illustrations, and the two men collaborated in the late 1890s, working concurrently on the text and illustrations for the novel *Resurrection* (*Voskresenie*). On his very first visit to Yasnaya Polyana, Tolstoy's country estate south of Moscow, in June 1893 Pasternak started making sketches and pictures of his host. Apart from the artist's own family, Tolstoy in fact became his most frequent model and was depicted in a variety of settings and media. In later life Leonid Pasternak wrote a touching memoir about their friendship.[21]

During family visits to the Tolstoys, Rozaliya Pasternak had her own role to play. Notwithstanding the implications of his story *The Kreutzer Sonata* (*Kreitserova Sonata*) and his sometimes perverse views on certain composers, Tolstoy was a lifelong music-lover. Musicians often visited and played to him, including such celebrities as Chaliapin, Goldenweiser and Rachmaninov. Rozaliya Pasternak too was often invited to present programmes of Lev Tolstoy's favourite piano music, and the Yasnaya

1 View of Vedeneyev's house, where Pasternak was born
(photograph taken in 1986)

2 Rozaliya Pasternak, Feona the nurse, baby Boris (1890)

Polyana house concerts in which she played were usually attended by the entire Tolstoy family.[22]

Surviving family correspondence establishes the Pasternaks as still resident in Vedeneyev's house in early 1890. It was there that their son Boris was born on Monday, 29 January. (The erroneous account of his birth-place in the *Autobiographical Essay* was based on his fleeting perusal of family albums and some of his father's pictures in the mid-1950s.)[23] The birth was apparently a difficult one and during it Rozaliya was assisted by her mother who came up from Odessa for the occasion. Shortly after the birth a wet-nurse called Masha was engaged. It was common practice for even families of modest means to employ such assistance, and it in no way reflected a lack of parental devotion, which was never in question in the Pasternak family.

Little is known about Masha, and her successor Feona, who took over in autumn of 1891, is known only from a family photograph. In a letter written later in life Pasternak claimed that he had been baptised in early infancy by one of his nurses. This may have been no more than a private fantasy which took root during his childhood, since it was never expressed and therefore never contradicted. There was even a hint to this effect when he wrote that 'the fact was somewhat complicated and remained half-secret, half-intimate, the object of a rare and exceptional inspiration rather than of serene habit'.[24] When questioned on the subject more recently, Pasternak's brother and sisters have been unable to confirm his statement and there is no written record of such an event. It is Pasternak's claim to have knowledge of it, rather than the possibility of such an occurrence, which is open to doubt. If in fact it was an early nurse who baptised him in this manner (rather than the nanny who arrived in 1892) it may have been a simple Christian woman's response to an Imperial ukase of 29 March 1891 requiring the eviction of most of Moscow's Jewish population. This repealed a law of 1865 allowing Jewish artisans to work outside the Pale of Settlement and it was one of several discriminatory legislations in Alexander III's latter years. Because he had higher education, Leonid Pasternak and his family were exempted, but twenty thousand Jewish artisans left Moscow as a result of the ruling.[25]

A second son was born to the Pasternaks on 12 February 1893. His name was Aleksandr – or 'Shura' in its traditional affectionate contraction. Rozaliya Pasternak herself breast-fed Aleksandr, but a new nurse had been engaged in the autumn of 1892 to take care of both children.

13

Like her predecessor and most of her kind, Akulina Gavrilovna Mikha-
lina was a modest woman of peasant background. She had little
education and was prone to humorous malapropism, but she was a
person of integrity and gentle firmness and was trusted by both parents
and children. She had a deep Christian faith, was a regular churchgoer
and in her younger days had visited the Holy Land with a party of
Russian pilgrims. She stayed with the Pasternaks for several years, and
after an interval was re-engaged to look after the Pasternak daughters
who were born in the early 1900s. She appeared on many family
photographs, and her plump bespectacled figure was brilliantly caught
by Leonid Pasternak in several charcoals and in a watercolour that
depicted her sewing by lamplight.[26]

After the birth of Boris it was clear that the apartment in Vedeneyev's
house was too cramped for family life and the music-making, painting
and art tuition that Rozaliya and Leonid wished to pursue. But financial
straits prevented immediate removal to better quarters. For a summer
holiday in 1900 they stayed as guests of the Protopopovs at Pok-
rovskoye-Streshnevo and with Shaikevich at Petrovsko-Razumovskoye
(the large Petrovsky Park area which has now been engulfed by the
expanding city and is situated close to the 'Dinamo' metro station). Only
a furious bout of work by Leonid in summer of 1891, living in a cheap
room at Petrovsko-Razumovskoye while his wife and son were dispatched to Odessa, eventually produced earnings (from the Lermontov
illustrations) which solved their debts. In September 1891 the Pasternaks were able to move to a larger four-roomed apartment on the upper
floor at number 37 in the house owned by one Svechin. This building,
which the following year changed hands and became known as Lyzhin's
house, stood in Oruzheiny (Armoury) Lane in the north of Moscow,
just off the Garden Ring (Sadovoye Koltso), the outer of two broad
avenues encircling the city centre. The two-storey stone-built house
stood opposite the gates of a theological seminary. The Pasternaks'
apartment was on the upper floor over the arched entrance to a
courtyard that was used as a base by the local cab-drivers. (In the early
twentieth century a third storey was added, and the whole building was
demolished in 1977 as part of a scheme for widening Sadovo-Karetnaya
Street.)[27]

Some of Pasternak's earliest memories were of 'walks in the autumn
with my nurse through the seminary park, sodden pathways covered in
fallen leaves, ponds, artificial mounds and the painted railings of the
seminary, and the games and fights and merry laughter of the seminarists

14

3 View from Lyzhin's house towards the seminary and park, Oruzheiny Lane
(photograph taken in 1966)

in the break between classes' (II, 1; *VP*, 414). Another early recollection
was of Konchalovsky the publisher, a gruff and shaggy giant who invited
the Pasternaks to stay at Davydkovo (near Kuntsevo) in 1893, and
whose home was crammed with pictures including several by Leonid
Pasternak. Boris also retained half-frightening fairytale memories of
stuffed bears in display windows, including one great specimen with its
raised paw in the window of Echkin and Sons, the Karetny Row
coachmakers, as well as cut-glass lanterns and huge carriages displayed
on the cleanly swept floors of the coachmakers' sheds.[28]

Boris Pasternak later recalled the whole area where they lived as
'disreputable'. It embraced the side-alleys of Tsvetnoi Boulevard, the
Tverskie-Yamskie Lanes where coaches and cabs were serviced, Trub-
naya (Pipe) Street with its flea-market, and the nearby Znamensky
Barracks where mounted dragoons could be watched through the
railings as they exercised their horses. The neighbourhood was the home
of a flourishing trade in vice, and there were many sights and sounds not
meant for children, although Boris innocently observed and remembered them. Among the local residents and street tradesmen roamed
beggars, prostitutes, drunkards and wandering holywomen – inhabitants of a hysterical, woe-beset world in which he later claimed that he

15

had first learned compassion for the weakness and vulnerability of women. Here, as he said in a poem called 'Women in My Childhood', he first sensed the 'presence of the female element' and learned to 'fathom passion as a science, and adoration as heroic feat' (III, 104–5; *SP*, 485). To rescue and save all these folk by some unprecedented shining deed, so he maintained, became an early serious concern. Maybe this was initially a reflection of Akulina Gavrilovna's pious homilies; later it was reinforced by adult understanding and embodied as a theme in several of Pasternak's writings. Features of his home area figured in some of the earliest prose extracts, in prose fragments of the 1930s and *Doctor Zhivago*; a plan to redeem the women of Moscow's streets formed part of a prose *Story* (*Povest'*) written in the late 1920s.[29]

A sharp ear and eye, imagination and retentive memory were maybe natural complements of the shyness and sensitivity that Boris Pasternak showed in early infancy. At the age of four, according to his father, he was extremely timid with strangers. The only person he immediately approached without fear was the genial elderly artist Nikolai Gay, a regular guest at the Pasternaks' until his death in the summer of 1894. On that occasion Boris had entered the room during dinner, stared at Gay, then without a word settled on his knee where he remained throughout the meal. Perhaps this reserve was inherited from Leonid Pasternak, and as in his case it was a permanent trait only partially offset by his later acquired self-assurance.[30]

From a combination of intelligence and introversion there doubtless sprang also a tendency in Boris to fantasise. The reported tale of his baptism was probably one of its products. Other childhood fantasies, as he recounted them, strike one as almost morbid in one so young. His early desire to assist the suffering humanity of his neighbourhood seems to have grown soon into a general craving for some romantic act of self-sacrifice. 'How often at the age of six, seven and eight I was close to suicide!' the *Autobiographical Essay* records. Other childhood fixations conflicting with common sense also left their trace in Pasternak's writings. A memory of the first smocks he wore caused him to imagine that once, in earlier times, he 'had been a girl, and that this more charming and delightful quality must be regained by pulling in my belt to the point where I felt faint' (II, 11–12; *VP*, 424). Was it mere coincidence that some twenty years later, in a novel that contained other autobiographical features, Pasternak made the central character a girl, a female *alter ego* figure endowed with his own sensitivity and perceptiveness? A further, more commonplace fantasy that haunted him as an infant was the conviction that he was not his parents' son but an adopted foundling. This too found expression in his books: Patrikii, the little hero of his 1930s prose, and Yurii Zhivago both had this imagined orphan state attributed to them.[31]

During the 1890s the family's improving circumstances brought important changes in Boris' childhood world. Testimony to Leonid Pasternak's increasing recognition came in May of 1894, when Prince Aleksei Lvov, Director of the Moscow School of Painting, visited him with an invitation to join his staff. Leonid readily accepted. It meant for the first time a sound material basis for their existence. The starting salary was only fifty roubles a month. But after Lvov's representations on behalf of his staff this sum was soon tripled, and within a couple of years Leonid Pasternak was made head of the Life-Drawing Section. He was to remain at the School of Painting for over quarter of a century, and along with colleagues such as Korovin and Serov he did much to enhance its reputation.[32]

Along with his post Leonid Pasternak received a free apartment, with studio facilities which for the first time provided proper working conditions. At the age of four, Boris Pasternak was thus brought with his infant brother to live on the premises of the Moscow School of Painting. The School stood at 21 Myasnitskaya (now Kirov) Street, which was one of Moscow's main radial thoroughfares running north-east to the Garden Ring and whose extension led out to the Nikolaevsky (now Leningradsky), Kazansky and Yaroslavsky railway stations. The tree-lined and cobbled Myasnitskaya was electrically lit already in the 1890s, when most of Moscow's streetlighting was of the gas or kerosene type, and the street boasted sophisticated foreign shops and elegant apartment houses. Along Myasnitskaya passed the procession transferring the body of Emperor Alexander III from Moscow to Petersburg on 30 October 1894, and two years later it was the scene of ceremonial to honour the coronation of Nicholas II. Boris Pasternak clearly recalled both events, which he watched from his mother's arms up on the balcony of the School's main building. But much more often he observed pomp and ceremony within the School itself, which was administered directly by the Ministry of the Imperial Court, enjoyed the patronage of Grand Duke Sergei Aleksandrovich, Governor of Moscow, and regularly entertained important visitors.[33]

In contrast and close proximity to the modern street and the formality of the School of Painting was the colourful, spontaneous life of the local population. The seedy elements of Oruzheiny Lane were here less in evidence. Yet even close to its centre, Moscow had some qualities of a 'large village' (a title, *bol'shaya derevnya*, by which it was sometimes known) where town and country mingled and coexisted, Pasternak himself recalled in his *Autobiographical Essay*:

Moscow in the nineties still retained its old appearance of picturesque, fairytale provinciality, with the legendary features of the Third Rome or capital city of old epics, and with all the splendour of its 'forty times forty' belfries. Ancient customs were still practised. In the autumn in Yushkov Lane where the School courtyard emerged, they used to carry out the blessing of horses in the churchyard of St Florus and St Laurus, who were regarded as the patron saints of horse-breeders. And the whole lane right up to the School gates was filled with horses and the coachmen and grooms who brought them, just like a horse fair.

(II, 6; *VP*, 419)

The School of Painting was an imposing eighteenth-century building. Slightly Italianate and with four storeys, it had an impressive facade with a pillared rotunda at the corner of Myasnitskaya and Yushkov (now Bobrov) Lane. The Pasternaks' actual home, however, was a four-roomed apartment on the first floor of an annexe which stood in the courtyard behind the main building. The annexe stood opposite the gate leading to a garden laid out with lawns, red gravel pathways, bushes and ancient poplars. In other parts of the courtyard were various outhouses and stables, together with a shed which housed a cow belonging to the Director. This courtyard and garden formed a playground for Boris, Aleksandr and their companions, mostly children of the School's janitors and handymen. There was also a convenient hummock in the yard down which the children could slide in winter on improvised toboggans of wood and bast.[34]

The Pasternak boys witnessed many of the School's daily activities. In the basement of their annexe students were served hot lunches, and the vapours of pasties and cutlets constantly hung on the staircase leading to their apartment. From the nursery window they watched pictures for the Itinerants' spring exhibition being delivered, and later on had a preview of work by Repin, Makovsky, Surikov, Polenov and others as the lush canvases in gilt frames were unloaded and brought from storage sheds to the exhibition hall. From their kitchen and dining-room in the later 1890s the boys also had a bird's-eye view into the recently constructed studio of the eminent sculptor Trubetskoi. Pavel, or Paolo, Trubetskoi returned to Moscow in 1897 after many years in Italy. With him came his Italian assistant Robecchi, who was an adept at trick-cycling and often amused the children by practising on the asphalt roof of the underground studio. When neither he nor his master were there, the Pasternak boys would sometimes go down to the studio to watch or talk to Mikhail Agafyin, the mould-maker, and there they could inspect the various wild animals Trubetskoi sometimes kept as his models – dogs, horses, deer, and on one occasion even a dromedary.[35]

Although Leonid Pasternak had a studio in the main building of the School, he did some of his work in the family apartment. The smell of oil and turpentine, and the sight of paint, pastel and charcoal and of their father at his easel or with sketching block were an everyday experience for Boris and his brother. Sometimes their mother was also drafted in to assist – one such occasion recalled by both brothers was in 1899, when they watched Leonid working against time to complete his brilliant ink and wash illustrations for Tolstoy's *Resurrection*, while Rozaliya mounted and dispatched the pictures to Petersburg in time to meet each weekly deadline of the journal *Niva* (The Cornfield).[36] The whole family were also involved in Leonid Pasternak's work in another way: he constantly produced sketches, watercolours, charcoals and oils of all of them (and of many relatives, colleagues and friends), and few families have ever been so meticulously recorded in art works as they. A particularly fine sketch of Boris as a boy, dated 20 July 1898, shows him barefoot and with one leg crossed behind the other as he sits on a wooden bow-backed chair at the table, absorbed in writing or drawing. (See figure 9.) But there were many others too – of Boris at the piano, Boris and Aleksandr together, and so on – showing every stage of their lives from infancy to early manhood. Later Leonid Pasternak made an even more complete artistic chronicle of the lives of his daughters born at the start of the new century.[37]

Not surprisingly, one of the first games Boris and Aleksandr played together was 'exhibitions'. The boys drew and painted their own pictures and then invited guests to the *vernissage* held in their nursery. Sketching and painting were in fact one of Boris' major interests in the 1890s and early 1900s, and although it was Aleksandr who eventually showed more graphic skill and went on to become an architect, Boris as a boy drew well enough to persuade his father that he had inherited some artistic talent[38] (see figures 11a–e).

Other popular children's games which Boris played with his brother and which the latter recalls in his memoirs were 'Cossacks and Brigands', 'chemist's shop', 'tip-cat' (*chizhiki*) and a variety of table and parlour games. Of special interest in view of his later development was Boris' idea of putting out his own magazine containing stories, riddles and various news items, with illustrations by his brother. Aleksandr Pasternak later recalled having been ill with diphtheria, and for a certain quarantine period Boris was exiled to the dacha of family friends. From his country retreat he evidently wrote telling Aleksandr about the stories he planned to write. They included one about Japanese fishermen, based on a children's book about life in Japan, and another about Iroquois Red Indians. A third story, though, seems to have had a moral theme, indicating already a boyish compassion and a concern with 'redemption' which figured in some of his adult writings; it was a naïvely appealing tale about stray dogs which were caught and locked up, but then released thanks to a young boy's kind intervention.[39]

In 1927, looking back on his childhood, Boris Pasternak wrote:

I am the son of an artist, I have observed art and important people from my earliest days, and I have become accustomed to treating the sublime and exclusive as something natural, as a norm of life. And since my birth, in everyday social life, it has existed along with my daily routine.[40]

The daily creativity which Pasternak observed included also his mother's piano playing, an act of artistry no less striking than his father's painting. Although she gave up her full-time concert career when she married, Rozaliya Pasternak was a woman of uncommon energy and dedication; still possessed by music, she practised regularly and the sound of her playing was a constant feature of family life. In Moscow she stayed in touch with Sofya Rubinstein, the sister of her one-time champion, and sometimes took her sons to visit the elderly lady's photograph- and picture-lined apartment on Sobachya Square. Like her husband, though, Rozaliya was happier to receive guests at home than to go visiting, and she was an enthusiastic hostess. With the exception of Nikolai Gay, Leonid Pasternak found most of his artist colleagues to be less sociable. But musical celebrities, local and national, some from the staff of the Moscow Conservatoire, were constant visitors. Over many years they included violinists Grzhimali (Hřimalý), Krein, Mogilevsky, and Michael Press, and cellists Brandukov, von Glen, Anna Luboshitz, Zisserman and Josef (brother of Michael) Press. The celebrated contralto Deisha-Sionitskaya was a frequent visitor, and pianists of the stature of Rachmaninov and Scriabin also occasionally appeared. In the early 1900s, after moving to a larger apartment, the Pasternaks held a regular *jour fixe* and supper followed by music-making became a weekly routine. And of course, apart from musicians, they entertained many from the world of theatre, literature, medicine, the law and Academe, as well as relatives and visitors from abroad.[41]

From infancy the Pasternak children were thus exposed to music. As soon as Boris was old enough, he was taken to matinée concerts at the Moscow Hall of Columns and the Conservatoire, and received basic piano tuition from his mother. Despite a natural aptitude, he did not take happily to the routine of scales and exercises, and when he preferred to follow his own bent for improvising and playing by ear, he was not coerced into practising. In due course his brother and sisters also had piano lessons. Aleksandr was an enthusiastic pupil but had to give up owing to a congenital defect in the right wrist which made playing painful; later in his teens and early twenties he also attempted the violin but having started so late he mastered no more than the rudiments.[42]

Boris' first intense and indelible experience of music preceded any instruction, however, and occurred at the age of four. It was an altogether unusual occasion, recorded as such in his father's memoirs and pictorially in a water-colour. For Boris, it had special private meaning bound up with his developing personality. On 23 November 1894, soon after the Pasternaks' removal to the School of Painting, Lev Tolstoy attended a musical evening at their home. The invitation came at the request of his daughters Tatyana and Maria: their father normally avoided public concerts and other functions but was anxious to hear Tchaikovsky's piano trio in A minor, 'On the Death of a Great Artist' (Tchaikovsky had himself died the previous year, and his trio commemorated the passing of Nikolai Rubinstein, brother of Anton, in 1881).[43] A vegetarian supper, for Tolstoy's benefit, was followed by the music. Rozaliya Pasternak played the piano, partnered by Brandukov and the Czech-born violinist Grzhimali. (The latter had played in the première in October 1882 and all three musicians had recently performed the work in the Hall of Columns in December 1893.) Pasternak later recalled the events in his *Autobiographical Essay*:

In the middle of the night I was aroused by a sweet and oppressive torment, more intense than I had ever experienced before. I cried out and wept with anguish and fear. But the music drowned out my tears, and they only heard me when they reached the end of the movement that had wakened me. Then the curtain that divided the room where I lay parted. My mother appeared, bent over me and quickly calmed me. Probably I was carried out to see the guests, or perhaps I saw the drawing-room through the open door. The air was full of tobacco smoke. The candles seemed to blink their eyelashes, as though it stung their eyes. The

21

piano loomed black, and the men's suits were also black. The women's heads and shoulders emerged from their dresses like birthday bouquets from flower baskets. The grey hair of two or three old men merged in with the rings of smoke. One of them I later got to know and saw often. It was the artist Nikolai Gay.[44] The image of another man has gone with me throughout life, as it has for most people – especially since my father illustrated his work, visited him and revered him, and since our whole household was permeated with his spirit. This was Lev Nikolaevich Tolstoy.

Boris Pasternak attempted in his *Autobiographical Essay* to explain the cause of his alarm. He had been used to his mother's masterly piano-playing already:

The voice of the piano seemed to me an integral part of music itself. But the timbre of the strings, especially in a chamber ensemble, was unfamiliar to me and alarmed me like the news of some disaster, or like heartfelt appeals for help carrying in through the window from outside.

There was another special reason for Pasternak's recollection of that occasion:

That night was for me like a boundary between the unconsciousness of infancy and my later childhood. From that point onwards my memory functioned and my consciousness worked without significant gaps and intervals, as in an adult.

(II, 4–5; *VP*, 416–17)

Memories of that November night in 1894 had a further biographical significance which Pasternak may have appreciated but never explicitly commented on. The name of Tolstoy at first played for him a merely 'brain-racking role', hidden in his father's clouds of tobacco smoke as he painted:[45] it was just the puzzling name of an old man recalled from conversations and occasional visits to Khamovniki and Yasnaya Polyana. But that first recollection of Tolstoy as part of a painfully intense musical experience at the dawn of conscious life drew together two elements that figured vitally in Pasternak's personality and artistic biography; in an interview in September 1980, Aleksandr Pasternak characterised the whole 'spiritual atmosphere' of his parents' home in terms of a 'Tol-stoyan element' combined with the experience of music.

Tolstoy was keenly aware within himself, and discussed and drama-tised in several of his writings, how moral imperatives conflict with the absolute and elemental claims of art. He himself personified that established nineteenth-century Russian tradition of art conceived as a form of service to humanity, expressing morality through artistic creati-vity. This for him was the loftiest aim of the artist and a deeply spiritual

act. Later, in a retrospective assessment in 1950, Boris Pasternak
described his own existence as founded on 'the transcendent feature of
Tolstoy which is greater than his preaching of good, and broader than
his immortal artistic originality ... *a new kind of spiritualisation* in his
perception of the world, life and reality, the new element that Tolstoy
introduced into the world which enabled him to advance the history of
Christianity'. Pasternak went on to claim that 'despite all appearances,
this historical atmosphere of the first half of the twentieth century
throughout the world is a Tolstoyan atmosphere'.[46]

But it was not so much the conscious memory of Tolstoy as an
individual that so deeply influenced Pasternak from early childhood. It
was, rather, the extent to which Tolstoyan example had been perceived
and absorbed by his parents and become a tutelary presence in their
home. Unlike some of their acquaintances (including Nikolai Gay
junior, eldest son of the artist), the Pasternaks did not subscribe to
Tolstoy's entire sectarian cult of communal living, simple rural virtues,
and non-violent resistance to evil. It was Tolstoy's austere moral idealism
and integrity as man and artist that made the deepest impact on Leonid
Pasternak. And as Aleksandr his son later observed, 'Doubtless all this
floated in the atmosphere, and people that came to see us sensed it as an
emanation of the Tolstoyan spirit.'

It was also not merely conscious imitation that brought the Pasternaks
close to Tolstoy. Leonid and Rozaliya had themselves at an early age
realised what sacrifices art required of them, and in their marriage they
had also learned to accommodate these demands to the dictates of
morality, concern for others, and parental duty and affection. In one
form or another, these problems and their resolution were therefore part
of the very fabric of family life. And heredity, daily awareness and
half-conscious emulation brought out many of the parents' qualities in
the children.

In the veneration which Leonid and Rozaliya Pasternak inspired in all
their children there was more than a routine filial piety. In a short
autobiographical sketch written at the age of thirty-four, Boris Pasternak stated that 'Much, if not everything, I owe to my father, Academician L. Pasternak, and to my mother, a magnificent pianist.' Ten years
later, he wrote to his father, recalling what the latter had achieved at his
own age, back in 1906:

You were a real man [...] a colossus, and before this image, large and wide as the
world, I am a complete nonentity and in every respect still a boy, as I was then.

To both his parents at about the same time, in the mid-1930s, he also wrote: 'All that I am I owe to you – education and influence, as well as intellectual heritage.'[47]

Surprisingly, though, Boris Pasternak left no detailed verbal portraits of his parents, and they are in fact strangely unprominent in both his autobiographies. But some of their cardinal traits are apparent from Leonid Pasternak's reminiscences and from sympathetic memoirs left by Aleksandr, Josephine and Lydia.

Lydia Pasternak has described her father as a man of 'unquestionable loyalty and integrity, with an exaggerated sense of responsibility and duty which made his personal life more austere and difficult than it need have been'. For all his talent, Leonid Pasternak worked hard to achieve success. He persevered in the face of his parents' bourgeois prejudice against the arts, yet there was nothing of the bohemian or rebel in his make-up. Lydia records further:

My father was a man of dreamy, gentle disposition, kind and altruistic, slow and uncertain in anything but his work, modest, retiring, and with a genuine dislike of being in the limelight, which at times it was not easy for him to avoid. He also had a wonderful sense of humour, and an ability for impersonation; observing and drawing were for him a natural necessity, like sleeping and breathing [...] It was fascinating to watch him at work: when painting a portrait [...] the speed, the ease and decisiveness with which he worked were truly amazing, and in direct contrast with his usual bearing.[48]

In childhood and adult life Boris was not unlike his father with his retiring nature and discomfort in public situations, and with a rapt engrossment in his thoughts which sometimes suggested naive impracticality or 'otherworldliness'. Furthermore, speed, accuracy and originality of perception, and the ability to record sensations at an almost pre-conscious stage were to emerge as a quality of Boris' literary talent. And like his father's lightning draughtsmanship and painting technique, it was to be designated as a form of impressionism.[49]

From observing his father, Boris Pasternak could have learned something even as a boy about the toll exacted by the pursuit of art. After the gruelling pressures to complete his *Resurrection* illustrations in 1898–9, Leonid Pasternak had fallen ill for several weeks with nervous exhaustion. Earlier in his career, though, he had made an even more fundamental sacrifice in deciding to marry and abandoning a hitherto single-minded dedication to art. The consequence of this and the need to raise a family caused neither him nor his wife to relinquish their integrity as artists. Their mutual admiration and affection also withstood all the difficulties of early married life, and they both provided their family with an absolute emotional security. Yet there was a tragic aspect which Boris later discerned in all this and he described it to his father in a letter of 23 January 1928:

Over and above the concessions which you made, to the detriment of your strength, to the eternal promptings of simple cordiality, were you able to fight against that silent demon of a desire for solitude which is *indissoluble* from the work of an artist? I am not saying that you did not receive or go visiting. On the contrary, in your work and behaviour you were more humane and sociable than you could be. But you could not conceal the attraction of solitude, its *preferability*, however hard you tried. And is it your fault that this always hung in the air and that the children were infected with this sickness emitted best of all by artistic work itself? What could you, or ought you to have done? Live away from people? In order that your tendencies did not infect the household? So that the girls would never smell that drying-oil and become soaked in it? But it was precisely a concern for your family that caused you to part with this treasure of belonging completely to yourself. And is it your fault, too, that the latter, its spirit, its smell, you shared with the family? And that to their sorrow they were brought up with it? No, all the principles and all the foundations were splendid, and you have nothing to grieve about.

Boris Pasternak would emerge, if anything, as an even more uncompromising servant of his art than his father, and in more morally testing times and conditions. When he addressed that letter to his father, he had already endured years of not 'belonging to himself'; the conditions of his domestic life were about to ruin his first marriage, and there were even harsher ordeals ahead. But the resilience and vitality which he and his art demonstrated must in some measure have been prefigured by the achievement of his father.

Perhaps Rozaliya Pasternak had a no more natural concern for mundane affairs than her husband. But when Boris and the other children were born, it was she who shouldered the burden of organising the family, household and finances. Evidently Leonid always handed to her his entire earnings – and then continuously turned to her for even minor expenses, tramfares and visits to the barber. Rozaliya was an untiring assistant in her husband's work. She handled much of his correspondence and arrangements for exhibitions, and she was often called in to play music or talk to his portrait models in order to animate and prevent them from 'freezing'. To all these tasks she brought the same devotion that she had earlier applied to music. And at heart, and in her limited spare time, she still remained an artist. According to those who heard her under concert conditions, she had few rivals – not so much technically as in her sensitive penetration of even the most standard repertoire. And in domestic music-making, too, her playing showed the same absorption and surrender to the composer, with no trace of conscious bravura or display. Her normal radiant energy made it · difficult to assess what the sacrifice of music to marriage and mother-hood meant for her. But her gifts continued to exact a tribute. Aleksandr Pasternak later spoke of the 'strange and cruel fate' of his mother – like Boris in the case of their father, he was aware of a nostalgia and sorrow which their mother usually concealed from the family. She never had robust health, and while her sons were small the first signs appeared of what doctors diagnosed as a cardiac neurosis. From the mid-1890s she suffered 'rare but frightening crises which involved numerous to-ings and fro-ings between the kitchen and her bedroom where several cold moist cloths were required'. It was Aleksandr's conviction that these bouts and his mother's subsequent heart trouble were caused largely by anxiety at her inability to perform publicly and take occasional concerts in her stride as once she had, without nervous exhaustion.[50]

Few children, and even fewer adults, are wholly fathomable in terms of heredity, upbringing and environment. And in accounting for the personality of a genius such as Boris proved to be, no facile 'derivations' are applicable. For all the family similarities, inherited and acquired, Boris Pasternak emerged in many respects as the most untypical of the Pasternak children, and as the most difficult. As a child, youth and adult, he could be uncooperative, uncommunicative and inscrutable in a way that perplexed the rest of his family. It was Josephine's opinion that Boris was temperamentally more akin to their mother, although this was not always an opinion Boris himself shared. 'You are closer to me than mama,' he told his father in a letter of 10 May 1916, 'but I am much more like you than like her.' Nevertheless, in early childhood he appeared like her to be a natural if less prodigiously gifted musician. And later on, as his mother had done, he made a conscious and agonising decision to abandon a professional career in music. Unlike her he had the good fortune to discover another eloquent medium of expression.[51]

Tolstoy once quipped to Leonid Pasternak that he, Tolstoy, was more of a Jew than Pasternak, and he claimed that the artist as a 'worshipper of form' was obviously an utter heathen![52] In fact, though a defender of principles and spiritual values, Leonid Pasternak was an uncommitted 'liberal' in religious matters. His Jewishness was not a source of concern to him. In Russian surroundings he attempted neither to integrate more than was natural nor, conversely, to cultivate specifically Jewish interests. Both he and his wife regarded themselves to all intents as Russian. Officially, though, they continued to be registered as Jews, and Leonid showed a strange acceptance of this. On racial grounds he would normally have been ineligible for an academic post, and it was only the unprejudiced views of Grand Duke Sergei Aleksandrovich and Prince Lvov which secured his appointment to the Moscow School of Painting. But as he said in his memoirs:

Although I believed in God, but did not in practice belong to any religious denomination, I would never have considered baptism as a means of facilitating my progress in life or of raising my social status.[53]

Coming from Odessa, Leonid Pasternak doubtless understood some Yiddish and retained a rudimentary knowledge of Hebrew. But it was only in later life, after 1910, that he showed some interest in Jewish or Zionist affairs, and in 1923 he published a book on Jewish elements in the work of Rembrandt, and the following year visited Palestine. Nevertheless, as he explained in a letter of that period to the Hebrew poet Chaim Nakhman Bialik, he had 'grown up in Russian surroundings, received a Russian education, and developed under the influence of Russian tendencies in the eighties, i.e. tendencies towards assimilation, and *with a debt of service to the Russian people*. And I have given my whole life to this duty [...] Art is a fountain, and any thirsty person, regardless of nationality, can quench his thirst at it.'[54]

It was thus a broad, non-denominational religiosity and a sense of Russian nationality that Boris Pasternak and his brother and sisters imbibed from their parents. His playmates in the School of Painting courtyard were Russian children. Those Jewish professional and guilded mercantile families with whom the Pasternaks did associate, such as the tea-trading Vysotskys, were relatively few in number and, like themselves, Russified. The Pasternak parents raised no objection when Akulina Gavrilovna took the children to Orthodox church services – at St Florus and St Laurus in Yushkov Lane, the 'Menshikov Tower' church of the Archangel Gabriel, or other nearby places of worship. The sumptuous church decorations, the pageantry of Orthodox rite, the piety and emotively surging choral singing were vivid ingredients of Boris' childhood, and later on he went of his own accord to listen to the magnificent choirs of Moscow's churches. Although excused from Christian religious instruction at school, the Pasternak children attended the inaugural services at the start of the school year along with other pupils, and nobody saw anything unusual in this. Symptomatic too was Boris' Marburg University matriculation note in 1912 which stated his religion as 'Mosaic' (i.e. Jewish), whilst his own recollection was that 'I lived most of my life in Christian thought in the years 1910–1912, when my roots were formed.'[55] Another letter of 21 December 1917 announced to Boris' friend Aleksandr (Shura) Shtikh that 'By blood I am a Jew, but in everything else and with that exception I am Russian.' In his younger days, seemingly, Pasternak was not overly concerned by his racial and religious status. It was only in middle life, and in changed circumstances, that he became more self-conscious about his position. The dilemmas and complexes he then suffered will be discussed at a later point in this biography.

If not in religion, then certainly on other moral issues the Pasternak parents had firm convictions which were applied to the education of their children. In everything except artistic commitment they themselves exercised, and expected from their children, restraint and moderation. Some aspects of Decadent *fin de siècle* culture smacked of amorality and it was a period when necromancy, erotic, narcotic and other irregular experiences were cultivated in some circles. But none of this impinged on the Pasternaks' world. Their life style was modest, conservative, well-ordered and tasteful, and – in the best sense of the word – middle-class. The same was true, evidently, of the majority of their acquaintances. Leonid Pasternak smoked *papirosy* heavily at times, but he was a non-drinker and hated the inebriating entertainment that was occasionally pressed on him. Moreover, he and his wife had no truck with artistic bohemianism.

Inevitably there were certain subjects which decency suppressed and left unmentioned. 'Not exactly puritanical, but strict and "Victorian"' was how Josephine Pasternak later described her own upbringing. Being boys, Boris and Aleksandr maybe enjoyed a less sheltered and more liberal régime. Symptomatically, they were on familiar *ty* terms with their parents, while Josephine and Lydia were trained by their nanny to address mother and father always with the respectful and formal *vy*.[56] Of the four Pasternak children, it was only Boris who later rebelled against his upbringing and in his twenties cultivated friendships and habits that were unacceptable at home. Prior to that, however, he and his brother enjoyed a well-regulated boyhood which might have been flatly conventional but for the cultural atmosphere and stimulating conversations, to which at first they responded only with half-comprehending fascination.

2

School and Scriabin

Darkness fell, and even before the first peal of thunder the sound of the grand piano started up indoors.

He took as his theme the night sky as when it emerges from the bathhouse decked in a cashmere cloud down and in the sulphate and incense vapour of a wind-tattered copse, with a mighty spread of stars rinsed through to their last fissure and seemingly enlarged. Above the instrumental thicket he had already strung up the glitter of these droplets that were simply inseparable from the space they occupied, no matter how they tried to detach themselves. Now, running his hands over the keyboard, he abandoned what he had done and returned to it, he committed it to oblivion and instilled it in his memory. The window panes were rolled smooth by streams of mercuric chill. In front of the windows the birches moved around with armfuls of immense air, scattering it everywhere and strewing shaggy waterfalls, and all the while the music went on bowing now right now left and still promised something from the road.

And the extraordinary thing was that every time anyone thought to express doubt at the honesty of musical statement, the player drowned that doubter in some unexpected, persistently returning miracle of sound. It was the miracle of his own voice, that is, the miracle of how people would feel and recollect on the morrow. The strength of this miracle was such that it could quite easily have split open the belly of the piano, crushing the bones of the merchants and the Viennese chairs as it did so – and yet it scattered as a silvery tongue-twister and sounded gentler, the more frequent and rapid its return.

from *The Story*

ૐૐૐૐ

In his *Autobiographical Essay* Pasternak describes various changes occurring around him as he approached the age of ten. In a transformation

29

process which started in the 1890s Russia was gradually shunted into the modern era. The Ministry of Finance under Sergei Witte attracted foreign investment and technology and encouraged capitalist enterprise, and in the years leading up to the First World War building programmes were initiated, industry and commerce expanded, new railways were opened, urban populations grew, and flourishing entrepreneurs appeared. As Pasternak recollected:

With the advent of the new century everything seemed transformed as though at the wave of a magic wand. Moscow was seized by the commercial frenzy of the world's leading capitals. They began furiously constructing tall buildings for rental, speculating on making a rapid profit. On every street brick-built giants reared suddenly up into the sky.   (II, 6–7; *VP*, 419–20)

This transformation was particularly striking against the backcloth of Moscow's many older wooden buildings, genial grass-grown courtyards as depicted in Polenov's pictures, and the red-brick, white and golden splendour of the Kremlin and its cathedrals. In this setting a new, specifically Muscovite urban awareness was born, and Boris Pasternak was eventually to help capture it in his early poems and prose.

The changes had an immediate effect on the Pasternaks' family life. Prince Lvov did much to modernise and improve the School of Painting and his efforts, so Leonid Pasternak believed, made it a leading European centre of art education. At the turn of the century when treasury grants proved inadequate, approaches were successfully made to the world of commerce to finance a modernisation programme. In consequence the annexe and sheds in the School courtyard together with Trubetskoi's studio were all demolished. The garden area became the site of a clay mould-making studio and the Pasternaks' annexe residence was replaced by a glass-roofed exhibition hall, the first of its type in Moscow, which could be used by the School itself as well as hired out to external organisations.[1]

In the autumn of 1902 the Pasternaks were therefore re-housed on the top floor of the School's main building. Their new quarters were reached by a formidably steep staircase with an iron balustrade; the stairwell itself provided shelter and flying space for numerous pigeons which found their way in through broken panes. At fourth floor level a dim corridor served as an anteroom to the Pasternaks' flat, and a telephone of the type with separate ear- and mouthpieces was eventually installed there. The spacious apartment itself was made up of several converted former classrooms. Through one wall the Pasternaks would still occasionally hear Professor Chaplin[2] lecturing to architecture students on heating and plumbing techniques. The actual apartment had a somewhat bizarre configuration. Situated at the rotunda end of the building, the bathroom and storeroom were half-moon shaped, the large kitchen was an indeterminate oval, the dining-room had a jutting semi-circular prominence, and the toilet pedestal stood on a raised dais to impart a proper slope to the drainage pipe. This for the next ten years was their family dwelling. Despite its geometry it was a comfortable and spacious home, furnished in good taste and without ostentation. Rozaliya Pasternak's black Bechstein grand piano stood in the drawing-room and she had another upright piano in her bedroom. The appearance of the apartment and its homely atmosphere with comfortable chairs, settees and pictures, is well conveyed in surviving photographs and in Leonid Pasternak's many pictures with a domestic setting.[3]

Even among the larger edifices appearing at the turn of the century, few of the city's buildings were then taller than the School of Painting, and the Pasternaks' apartment commanded a fine view of central Moscow. From their dining-room they saw close at hand the huge cupola of the Polish Catholic Church. On the Myasnitskaya side there was a bird's-eye view of the street and Central Post Office, and beyond it the church of the Archangel Gabriel. The drawing-room windows looked over towards the School's inner courtyard and the neighbouring house at number 19. These were the premises of S. V. Perlov and Sons, the well-known tea-traders. Their shop had an elaborate Chinese-style facade which survives to this day, and when windows were open in the spring and summer various herbal aromas of the Orient wafted up and could be smelt in the apartment.[4]

In pre-Revolutionary Russian homes one or more house servants were not unusual, even in families of moderate means. With their move to more spacious quarters the Pasternaks had room for a cook and for two maid-servants, in addition to Akulina Gavrilovna. The latter had been re-engaged in 1900 to take charge first of an infant daughter Josephine (Zhozefina in its Russian form, usually abbreviated to 'Zhonya') who was born on 6 (19) February 1900, and then of Lydia ('Lida' or 'Lidok') born on 8 (21) March 1902.

Boris and his brother had meanwhile started their schooling. Although initially they began lessons with mother, most of their instruction came from hired tutors. Normal school entry was at the age of seven, but it was not uncommon for parents to engage governesses or private instructors for the early stages in reading, writing, arithmetic and languages. Boris retained a specially affectionate memory of his first such teacher, Ekaterina Ivanovna Boratynskaya who taught him reading, writing, basic arithmetic and French from very first principles, starting with how to sit and hold a pen. She was a friend of the artist Kasatkin and of the Tolstoys, and was well known as an authoress and translator of children's books. Her dark, book-crammed room Pasternak later recalled as smelling of 'cleanliness, austerity, boiled milk and roasted coffee' (II, 8; *VP*, 420–1).

Initially it was planned to send Boris to the Peter and Paul High School, a private institution attached to the Moscow Lutheran Church. Originally established for children of the local German community, it was favoured by many Jews (including the family of Karl Pasternak) and attracted a certain number of Russian pupils. From their studies in Austria and Germany both Pasternak parents had an affinity with German culture and in the late 1890s they engaged a German Fräulein and arranged for Boris and his brother to take German lessons and work through the preliminary school subjects in that language in preparation for the High School.[5]

Plans for Boris' schooling were changed, however, for reasons evidently connected with the family's Jewish status. For Jews entry to all places of higher education was restricted, and only a gold medal class award from a state rather than a private school ensured eventual admission to university. But even at state secondary schools Jewish places were limited to three per cent, and for this reason Boris was obliged to continue with private tuition for an extra year before going directly into the second form at the age of eleven. In the autumn of 1901 he therefore donned the traditional Russian schoolboy's uniform of grey trousers and jacket, with metal buttons, black leather belt, and a cap with a tinplate cockade of oak-leaves surrounding the characters 'M.5.G.', which stood for the Moscow Fifth Classical Gymnasium, or High School. The school itself occupied two adjacent buildings near Arbat Square, on a corner of Povarskaya (now Vorovsky) Street and Bolshaya Molchanovka. In close proximity stood several fine private houses on the tree-lined Povarskaya, as well as the seventeenth-century church of Semeon Stylites. To reach the school from Myasnitskaya it was a brisk half-hour walk, or a somewhat shorter tram-ride. The route took Boris, and later also his brother, across the centre of Moscow: down Myasnitskaya to Lubyanskaya Square, past the Bolshoi Theatre and University, then turning right up Vozdvizhenka Street. An alternative route was via the Kremlin precinct where a free ride could sometimes be had:

horse-cabs were allowed to pass through the Kremlin only if carrying passengers, and drivers were occasionally glad to take a schoolboy on his way as an excuse for the short cut![6]

The Fifth High School was for boys only. Lessons began at nine in the morning and for junior classes ended at one o'clock; for older pupils they sometimes continued longer. In later life Pasternak talked and wrote very little about his schooling, and its cursory treatment in his two autobiographies suggest that he saw more important formative experiences as having occurred elsewhere. Nevertheless, his school was important in providing a sound and broad-based education. The Fifth Classical High School had survived Education Minister Vannovsky's recent reform programme which shifted the stress from classics to modern science and, as its title suggested, it retained the ancient languages while adding certain modern subjects to the curriculum. Perhaps it was this feature that led the Pasternaks to choose that particular school, despite its distance from home. Their Jewish status exempted the boys from religious instruction (*zakon Bozhii*) but in other respects they followed the standard syllabus. Boris' school leaving certificate is still preserved in the family and shows that he qualified with top marks of 'five out of five' in all subjects: Russian language and literature, Latin, Greek, mathematics, mathematical geography, physics, history, geography, German, French, and 'philosophical pro-paedeutics'.[7]

According to witnesses and on his own admission, Boris Pasternak did not relish the conformity and routine of school life. One of his class-mates, Georgii Kurlov, recorded that mathematics aroused little sympathy in him, and his enthusiasm was sparked by subjects with some aesthetic appeal. In general Pasternak appears not to have been specially diligent. However, he had an outstanding intellect and aptitude which usually made laborious effort unnecessary. As a result, at school he already developed a certain vanity and a tendency to spurn both academic subjects and other tasks which could not be mastered quickly. Nevertheless, for most of his schooldays he was among the top half-dozen pupils in his class, and in his final year in 1908 he was awarded a gold medal.[8]

One of the stimulating younger teachers at Pasternak's school was Aleksandr Barkov, who later became a distinguished geographer and Academician. With his encouragement, both Boris and Aleksandr Pasternak at one point made a collection of palaeontological exhibits. It was also under Barkov's influence that Boris acquired an interest in botany, although his note in *Safe Conduct* suggests its aesthetic rather than scientific appeal: the various names looked up in a manual 'in response to the fixed and five-petalled gaze of a plant, brought calm to those fragrant pupils, which rushed without question to Linnaeus, from obscurity to glory' (II, 204; *VP*, 193). Pasternak apparently put much time and energy into collecting samples for his herbarium. But his passion for botany was short-lived, and another philatelic enthusiasm quickly fizzled out. As his later life demonstrated, he did not have the mentality of a collector; he was much more a forgetter and discarder – of objects, experiences, and relationships.[9]

Lev Tolstoy's youngest daughter, Aleksandra, who recalled the Pasternaks' visits to her father, described Boris as 'a thin and dark-eyed boy who spoke rarely and had the gift of vanishing among shadows'. His reserve seems to have stemmed more from a serious, pensive nature than from unsociability. Kurlov, who went on to be an advocate at the Moscow bar, entered the High School one year later than Pasternak, and after a predictably bantering reception by other class-mates he specially recalled Boris' earnest handshake, offer of help, and his use of formal address rather than the casual second-person singular current among other boys. Kurlov had further detailed recollections of Pasternak:

In his movements he was clumsy, which was particularly noticeable in gymnastic lessons, where we had a number of very good gymnasts. He rarely took part in pranks, but he always took the part of the pranksters whenever they were threatened with some form of punishment.

As a schoolboy already, Pasternak's outward appearance was slightly unusual:

In his whole appearance there was a certain mixture of fastidiousness and carelessness – but more of the latter. For instance, the parting in his thick, bluish-black hair was never straight.

Contemporary photographs confirm Kurlov's observation of Pasternak's ample lips and other features. But his most remarkable trait was the dark, vitreous gaze of his eyes – more prominent than in his brother and sisters, who also inherited this feature from their mother. As a young teenager Pasternak was thus assuming the striking and slightly equine appearance (something both of the Arab and of his stallion, as Tsvetaeva put it) which distinguished him through life.[10]

Pasternak became no special friend of Kurlov, and in fact he probably caricatured him as 'Koka' Kornakov, the socialite and party-goer in the novel *Doctor Zhivago*. But he had a small circle of companions who

4 Leonid and Rozaliya Pasternak (Odessa, August 1896)

5 Aleksandr, Iosif (Leonid's father), Boris (Odessa, 1895)

6 Berta Kofman (Rozaliya's mother), Rozaliya, Boris, Leonid's mother,
Aleksandr (Odessa, 1896)

7 Boris and his parents (Odessa, 1896)

8 Aleksandr and Boris (Moscow, 1897)

sometimes came to visit and play with him and his brother at home or at their summer dacha. One close pre-school friendship which survived into adulthood was with Aleksandr (Shura) Shtikh, the son of an ear, nose and throat specialist whose whole family were friendly with the Pasternaks and lived in nearby Bankovsky Lane. Like Boris, Shura Shtikh had a brother, Mikhail (Misha), who was about ten years his junior, and a sister, Anna (Anyuta). During summer holidays for several years running Boris was sometimes invited to stay at the Shtikhs' rented dacha at Spasskoye near Moscow. Later on, Shura Shtikh showed some poetic talent which Boris tried to foster, but although he published some poetry he eventually followed a legal career.[11]

Another slightly older companion of Boris' schooldays was Mikhail Romm. His family too enjoyed a long-standing friendship with the Pasternaks. His uncle, Yakov Romm, was an excellent amateur pianist who often came to play duets with Rozaliya. They were recorded so doing, with Boris looking on, in a pencil sketch by Leonid Pasternak in 1905.[12]

Almost every year up to 1902, Leonid Pasternak took his family for an annual summer holiday to Odessa. They travelled by train, taking with them their nanny and some domestic help. Meanwhile, relatives in Odessa arranged for rental of a villa by the sea. Usually the Pasternaks holidayed at the popular resort of Srednii Fontan, where they lodged successively at Bortnevsky's, Olgino, and at Vuchin's dacha at Bolshoi Fontan, where they stayed in 1901. Both resorts were a short ride by steam tram from Odessa city centre. Sometimes during these family holidays Leonid had made trips to Western Europe – to Paris in 1895, and Vienna, Munich and Paris in 1898 – where he visited museums and art centres while his wife and children stayed by the Black Sea.[13]

Apart from the pleasures of sun, sand and sea, the annual vacation was an opportunity for renewed contacts with relatives and friends. In addition to their parents, both Leonid and Rozaliya had many brothers, sisters and cousins. Some of them resided in or near Odessa, while others eventually removed to other areas. Rozaliya's brother Osip, who was a doctor, finally settled in the town of Kasimov to the east of Moscow and worked for the district *zemstvo*.* Her sister Klara had in 1902 married a railway official, Aleksandr Margulius, who was based in Petersburg and managed the freight office on the Nikolaevsky Railway which connected the capital with Moscow. Their daughter Maria, known as 'Mashura' in the family, was about the same age as Boris' brother Aleksandr.[14]

* *zemstvo* – a local and district government body in pre-Revolutionary Russia.

On Leonid's side there was his hunchback elder brother Aleksandr – 'Uncle Sasha' or 'Indidya' – who pursued a professional career in his home town. Of the three sisters Rozaliya (Roza), Ekaterina (Katya), and Anna (Asya) it was the latter with whom Leonid was on closest terms. Aunt Asya had married the wayward but gifted Mikhail Freidenberg, who earlier helped promote Leonid's talents in Odessa. The Freidenbergs had two sons born in the 1880s and a younger daugher Olga – or 'Olya' – who was Boris Pasternak's exact contemporary. Cousin Olya shared with Boris a similarity of character and interests, and their childhood summers together laid the foundations of a lifelong friendship. In 1900 Olya's brother Evgenii died of peritonitis aged fourteen. His mother took a long time to recover from this tragedy, and a year or so after his death Mikhail Freidenberg took his whole family to make a fresh start in Petersburg, a move which required their nominal conversion to Christianity. After their summers in Odessa in the 1890s, it was therefore in Petersburg or at holiday villas near Moscow and on the Baltic that Boris' main reunions with relatives took place in the second decade of his life.[15]

The Odessa summers were also bound up with another event in Pasternak's childhood whose significance went unrecognised at the time. In summer of 1900 he was granted his one and only fleeting glimpse of the Austrian poet Rainer Maria Rilke. A description of the encounter later appeared at the opening of *Safe Conduct* as symbolic testimony to Rilke's significance in his own growth as an artist.

Rilke was paying his second visit to Russia in 1900 and his companion was the Russian-born German authoress Lou Andreas-Salomé. He had been hypnotised and marked for life by his first Russian journey in 1899. On that occasion he had called on Leonid Pasternak, bringing him a note of introduction from some common friends in Munich. Thereafter they had remained in contact and Rilke sent him a signed edition of his first book of verse. Their friendship was renewed on Rilke's return in 1900, and after meetings in Moscow a further chance encounter was witnessed by Boris on a hot day in late May. The Pasternaks were travelling south for their vacation when Rilke and Lou Salomé turned up on the same train, heading for Yasnaya Polyana in the hope of visiting Tolstoy. Leonid Pasternak had in fact introduced them the previous year and was now able to direct them to a Mr Boulanger, a director of the Moscow-Kursk Railway who was travelling in the train and helped bring about what emerged as an uncomfortable meeting between Rilke and the elderly Russian writer.[16]

Boris Pasternak retained only a fleeting memory of Rilke as a figure

10 Leonid and Rozaliya Pasternak, Akulina Gavrilovna and baby Josephine; with Boris in school uniform, and Aleksandr (photograph taken by the entrance to the annexe, Moscow School of Painting, 1901)

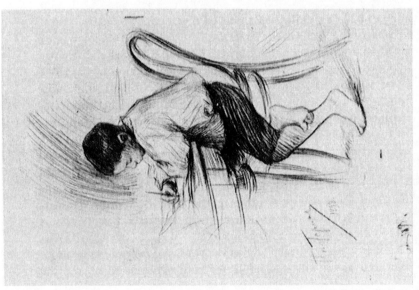

9 Leonid Pasternak: sketch of Boris as a boy (20 July 1898), photograph by courtesy of the Ashmolean Museum, Oxford

dressed in Lodenmantel and speaking German with an unusual Austrian lilt before he and Salomé were shortly whisked away from Kozlovka Zaseka rail-halt by carriage and pair. Some recollected details – the red-sleeved coachman and the vehicle flitting from the copse – were maybe superimposed memories from other family visits to Yasnaya Polyana. At the time, as *Safe Conduct* records, 'the face and the incident were forgotten, so it seemed, forever'. Pasternak never saw Rilke again in the flesh, and his father set eyes on him only rarely thereafter although they met again by chance in Italy in 1904 and some correspondence passed between them. Yet, for Boris, more important would be Rilke's role as a spiritual and artistic entity, and within a few years of their meeting this assumed a reality that effaced the mere physical encounter and became a vital formative influence.[17]

In the summer of 1903 the Pasternaks broke their tradition of annual vacations on the Black Sea and visits to Odessa. Leonid had already begun mortgage payments on a plot of land near the city where he hoped eventually to build a house and studio for his retirement. But both of his parents were now dead and Rozaliya's father too had died in the spring of 1903, and the journey for a family of six plus nanny and baggage became a too daunting prospect. Instead they rented a dacha in the vicinity of Moscow for the duration of the school and academic recess, from early May until mid-August. This was the first of several summer holidays in the country. Over a short distance by local train they could move most of the household with them, and they usually took the cook, the maid and Akulina Gavrilovna too. They also brought items of food, bed-linen and cooking utensils, so that some domestic routine was maintained and all the family could rest and relax. Their rented accommodation was usually large enough to house visitors too, and friends from Moscow and further afield frequently came to stay. Among the summer visitors in 1903 was Aunt Asya with cousins Aleksandr (Sasha) and Olya.

During these country holidays the Pasternak children could walk, explore, play, read, and above all see more of their father. For nearly three months Leonid Pasternak, so preoccupied during the academic year, was free to enjoy the company of his family. Although he continued to sketch and paint at leisure, he was available for family outings, games of croquet, *gorodki** and other entertainments with the children.

* *gorodki* – a Russian game in which small cylindrical blocks of wood are knocked out of a marked area using a stick.

(a) Landscape with church

(b) Man walking, Petrovsko-Razumovskoye, 2 April, 1903 (date supplied by Leonid Pasternak, who kept several of Boris' youthful sketches)

11 Sketches by Boris Pasternak, 1903

(c) Girl seated

(d) Josephine Pasternak, Boris'
sister, 6 April 1903

(e) Horse's head, sketched at
Obolenskoye, 8 July 1903

12 Christmas Party at the Pasternaks', Moscow School of Painting (1901):
Rozaliya and Leonid Pasternak, Akulina Gavrilovna and baby Lydia are on the
right; Josephine is sitting immediately above and between Aleksandr and
Boris who are on the floor

13 In the dining-room, apartment in the School of Painting (1905):
Boris, Rozaliya Pasternak, Lydia and Josephine in the foreground. In the
background are: unidentified lady, Aleksandr, a maid, Shura Shtikh

Their first holiday in the countryside around Moscow, or Podmosko-vye, was marked by some events with far-reaching consequences. The dacha which they rented was one of three at a place called Obolenskoye, an estate formerly owned by the princely family of Obolensky. It lay close to the towns of Obninsk and Maloyaroslavets, some hundred kilometres south-west of Moscow down the Bryansk (now Kievan) Railway. The timber-faced villa stood in open ground. It was flanked by woodland and a hill with parkland which had run wild and was overgrown by pines, and there was a profusion of mushrooms, ant-hills and squirrels. In the further distance were the swift-flowing river Protva, meadows, cropfields and the railway.[18]

Boris Pasternak's main recent interest had been sketching, and his father believed that this talent might flourish if only the boy applied himself. Boris' earliest surviving sketches date from 1902, and thirty-four of his drawings in a little album titled 'I am Thirteen' ('Mne 13 let') have been preserved among Leonid Pasternak's papers; some of these pictures Boris produced in April and May of 1903 at the park in Petrovsko-Razumovskoye, while others dated from June–July in Obolenskoye. (See figures 11a–e.) In summer of 1903, though, Boris abandoned this interest along with his herbarium, a school holiday assignment on which he had at first worked enthusiastically. Aleksandr had often accom-panied his brother on botanical expeditions which were sometimes combined with games of tracking, Red Indians, and so on. On one such occasion, amid birdsong and squirrels' chattering, the brothers suddenly caught the sound of piano music coming in bursts from the neighbour-ing dacha. Advancing through the thickets, they heard what Boris correctly identified as someone actually composing at the piano. Having had piano lessons from his mother and mastered the rudiments, he strummed and improvised for his own amusement. But what he now heard transformed a smouldering interest into a blazing passion, and the power of that music drew him back several more times to his woodland hiding-place.[19]

And just as light and shadow alternated in the woodland and birds called and flew from bough to bough, so the pieces and fragments of the Third Symphony, or 'Divine Poem', carried and reverberated through it as they were composed at the piano in the neighbouring dacha.

Lord, what music that was! The symphony constantly collapsed and fell in ruins like a city under shell-fire, and then it was built up and grew again from its own fragments and destruction. (II, 9; *VP*, 421–2)

Soon afterwards Boris met the creator of that music. Leonid Pasternak returned from one of his strolls down the nearby Kaluga highway and reported seeing an eccentric man with waxed moustaches and beard who moved with a peculiar skipping gait and flapped his arms as though attempting to fly. They struck up an acquaintance; the strange man turned out to be their neighbour and was the Moscow pianist and composer Aleksandr Scriabin. It was not long before his family and the Pasternaks became friends.[20]

This was Scriabin's second summer in Obolenskoye, and it was proving a particularly inspired and prolific one. Apart from working on his Third Symphony, he completed not less than thirty piano pieces including his Fourth Sonata. He aimed to use the sale of these to finance his removal to Switzerland, having decided (at about the same time as both Grechaninov and Rachmaninov, incidentally) that conditions for creative work were better in Western Europe than in Russia. That summer was also a time of crisis and domestic troubles for Scriabin, however. With him at Obolenskoye were his four children and the wife from whom he was about to separate; he intended his forthcoming residence abroad to precipitate their estrangement and promote his new liaison with Tatyana Schloezer. However, their marital upheaval did not prevent the Scriabins' friendship with the Pasternaks, although back in Moscow Scriabin and his wife eventually began calling to visit them separately. Vera Ivanovna Isakovich-Scriabina was herself a fine pianist and well-known champion of her husband's work; a woman of impressive gentleness and kindness, she became close friends with Rozaliya Pasternak.[21]

In the summer of 1903 Leonid Pasternak and Scriabin often walked together at Obolenskoye. Sometimes Boris went with them, and he was able to confirm his father's observation:

Scriabin liked to take a run and then continue skipping along under the impetus like a stone sent skimming across the water [. . .] In general he cultivated various forms of inspired airiness and untrammelled movement verging on actual flight. Among these were the spellbinding elegance and urbanity with which he avoided seriousness in society and tried to appear banal and superficial. All the more astonishing were his paradoxes on those walks at Obolenskoye.

(II, 9; *VP*, 422)

Scriabin's whole character quickly held Boris in the same thrall as his music. He was the first of several spectacular romantic personalities who infected his youthful imagination and prompted attempts at emulation. Even allowing for the difference in their ages, Scriabin's flamboyant brilliance was a complete contrast to Boris' withdrawn nature, and maybe this was partly the secret of his allurement. Scriabin's advocacy of the Nietzschean philosophy of the *Übermensch*, which during 1900–3 he had also incorporated in an operatic libretto with a youthful 'philosopher-musician-poet' as its hero, was the subject of constant disputation with Leonid Pasternak during their walks. It was the antithesis of the Tolstoyan spirit that reigned in the Pasternak household, and this too was doubtless part of its attraction for Boris.[22]

Scriabin's philosophical beliefs were part of a personal artistic drama, and they marked the beginning of a self-exalting psychotic state which would in a few years' time verge on insanity. On the other hand, the personality cult of the creative artist in music and literature and his appearance as prophet in various eschatological scenarios figured generally at that time in the aesthetic programme of Russian Symbolism. As Pasternak later realised, Scriabin's self-absorption and egocentricity were a luxury that only a man of maturity and genius could afford. Picked up superficially and mistaken by an impressionable teenager, they could only have an unhealthy, negative influence. Indeed the vanity which they encouraged in Pasternak ultimately undermined the musical value of Scriabin's impact. In the short term though, Pasternak could do nothing but worship that overpowering music and its creator, who after a day's composing was 'as light and clear, luxuriantly tranquil as God resting from his labours on the Seventh Day'.[23]

That autumn and winter there were opportunities to see more of Scriabin and hear him play in the intimacy of the Pasternaks' drawing-room. His manner at the instrument was unique and inimitable. He sat unusually far from the piano and held his head thrown back. As with his airborne gait, he seemed to produce sound not by downward pressure on the keys; on the contrary, his hands appeared to draw sonorities forth by fluttering and hovering over the surface of the keyboard. But the appeal of his music alone can readily be understood. His sonatas and other pieces were standard repertoire by the turn of the century, and Rozaliya Pasternak played many of his études, preludes and impromptus. Demanding rubato, romantic eloquence and refinement, these earlier works of his were cast in an idiom best described as a blend of Chopin and Wagner, with traces of Lyadov, César Franck, Liszt and Tchaikovsky. Often set in remote tonalities, they explored the limits of the emotional spectrum, Dionysian frenzy alternating with passages of exquisite, languid serenity. The textures and rhythm of Scriabin's work were also often highly intricate and presented great technical difficulties in execution. A further engrossing feature was Scriabin's dual competence as both creator and interpreter; he was one of several illustrious composer-pianists who in Russia alone numbered such figures as Balakirev, Rubinstein, Rachmaninov and Medtner. The result of his encounter at Obolenskoye was that Pasternak returned to Moscow in the autumn of 1903, set on becoming a composer and emulating his new idol.[24]

In the course of the summer in 1903 fate also intervened at Obolenskoye in less propitious ways. There were two deaths by drowning in the Protva; one of these victims was a student who perished while trying to rescue the daughter of family friends, and the daughter's horror at this tragedy caused her own dementia and a suicide attempt. Shortly afterwards, the nearby house of other friends, the Goldinger family, was burnt down. Seeing the smoke and glow as he returned on horseback from Maloyaroslavets, Leonid Pasternak thought his own family were the victims, and the shock of this caused him suddenly to go grey.[25]

Prior to all this, however, a mishap occurred on the evening of 6 August which had important long-term effects for Boris. Having admired the intrepid young peasant horsewoman from the nearby village of Bocharovo, he was convinced he could copy them and attempted himself to ride bareback. As his horse jumped a stream he was thrown and fell, breaking his right thighbone. Fortunately, their neighbour, Dr Goldinger, was on hand to assist; he applied a temporary setting and made Boris comfortable. But since the patient was delirious and the injury required expert attention, Leonid Pasternak rode off to Maloyaroslavets to fetch a surgeon and nurse. The outcome for Boris was a six-week spell of lying with his leg in plaster and a consequent delay in the family's return home. Back in Moscow, since he was unable to attend school, several of his classmates called and kept him *au fait* with school activities until he was able to return. Sadly, this accident had also interrupted Leonid Pasternak's preliminary work on a potential masterpiece – an ambitious, natural-size canvas depicting the 'peasant Valkyries' of Bocharovo against a sunset landscape. His one surviving pastel sketch was later lost and the picture itself was never completed.[26]

When Boris' right leg healed it remained slightly shorter than the other, and in later life he still suffered occasional pain and discomfort. For a few years, until such custom-built items vanished after the Revolution, he wore shoes with a built-up sole. Apparently by practice, he eliminated almost all trace of a limp, but in his younger years he was self-conscious about his slightly awkward movement, and later events reminded him of it. His lameness caused his exemption from military service in both the First and Second World Wars, and it figured as an attribute of some characters in his verse and prose writings.[27] In a later imaginative reconstruction of that summer's events his limping gait was linked up with the musical rhythms it seemed to engender in his fevered thoughts:

Through his delirium there passed the triple-time syncopated rhythms of galloping and falling. From now on rhythm would be an event for him, and conversely events would become rhythms. And melody, tonality and harmony would become the setting and substance of an event . . .[28]

One further echo of the mishaps of the summer of 1903 was later to find a place in Pasternak's writings. In the late afternoon of 7 June a passenger train had pulled up on the stretch of line adjoining Obolenskoye estate and sounded several alarm blasts after one of the passengers had fallen to his death on the track. In Pasternak's novel this appears as the incident in which the hero's father meets his death by suicide. The rural setting of 1903 was recognised later by all readers who recalled the events of that summer in Obolenskoye.

The Pasternaks were delighted by Boris' musical ambitions and did their best to encourage him. Lessons in musical theory were arranged for him with the well-known Moscow musicologist, critic and teacher, Yulii Engel, and during the next three years he worked through the basics of structure, harmony and counterpoint with his young pupil. Some of Boris' notebooks still survive in the family archive and contain exercises in four-part writing and fugal expositions, most of them skilfully worked out but with occasional corrections by a tutor's hand.[29]

During the first months of his musical apprenticeship Boris had the stimulus of Scriabin's personal visits to his parents' home. But on these occasions there took place not so much communication as the giving and receiving of embarrassed adoration. 'Seeing him, I turned pale, in order then to blush deep red in shame at this pallor', Pasternak recalled:

He would address me and I would lose the ability to think and would hear myself give a quite irrelevant answer – to everyone's amusement – though I did not hear *what* I said. I knew that he had guessed everything, but he never once came to my assistance. That meant he was not sparing me, and that was precisely the unresponsive, unrequited feeling that I thirsted for. That alone. And the more fiercely that blazed, the more it protected me from the ravaging effects of his indescribable music. (II, 206; *VP*, 194)

In February 1904 Scriabin finally departed for Switzerland, where he installed himself at Vézenas by Lake Geneva. He was followed there by

Vera and the children; soon after came Tatyana Schloezer, his new partner who eventually became his second wife. Scriabin's absence from Russia lasted five years. As he departed, he left at the Pasternaks' copies of his latest études and a thirteen-year-old disciple who rushed, even as he left, to catch one last glimpse of his idol walking away down Myasnitskaya.[30]

It was generally assumed that Boris would become a composer. And because of this, every indulgence was shown to his quirks and omissions both at home and in school, where he was sometimes discovered working at musical problems during lessons. But the one aspect of musical training that Boris overlooked, or wilfully neglected, was regular piano practice. This was partly the common story of a child failing to learn properly when taught by a parent, even though his mother was a first-rate instructor and both parents were intolerant of dilettantism and alert to the need for disciplined technique, without which no artistry is possible. But Boris had only the end goal in mind and ignored the fact that successful emulation of Scriabin, even as composer, required pianistic accomplishment as well as inspiration. Time that might have been spent on piano drill was instead squandered on improvisation, in which ideas flowed thick and fast and were realised, however infelicitously, in spontaneous outpourings. Pasternak, in fact, displayed a genuine flair for such music-making. His sister Josephine recalls how he would hum as he played, and 'it was as if by his voice he tried to force the instrument to follow his design'. To Pasternak this was genuine creativity, the centre of all his attention and ambition. Only later did he admit his 'adolescent arrogance and nihilistic contempt of the half-taught for everything that seemed attainable and earnable by ordinary effort'.[31]

I despised everything uncreative and technical, and had the audacity to think that I understood these matters. In real life, I imagined, everything has to be miraculous, predestined from on high. There must be nothing deliberate, intentional, no wilfulness.   (II, 11; *VP*, 424)

This was the reverse side of Scriabin's influence. nevertheless Pasternak apparently worked with great concentration at his composing. To his brother, who shared a room with him and was a close witness, it seemed that he was almost excessively demanding on himself. Frequently Aleksandr observed how he 'sat in a state of great animation, irritation, and complete distraction over some manuscript paper covered length and breadth with notes'. At other times when the two were in their room, 'Boris seemed to fill the whole of it from one corner to another. Humming something and even apparently conducting, he would keep sitting down and jumping up again in a state of anger, and he said nothing to me, as though I was simply not there in the room.'[32]

Yulii Engel was under the circumstances probably the ideal tutor. He was a kind, friendly man (and so he emerges in Leonid's sketch of him in 1906 and the portrait of 1910). He was young in heart and got on famously with young people, as Aleksandr Pasternak observed on two summer holidays which the Engel family shared with them in 1906 and 1910. But in matters musical he was serious and demanding. By the time he taught Boris Pasternak he was a regular music correspondent for the important Moscow paper *Russkie vedomosti* (Russian News) and a contributor to the journal *Muzykal'ny sovremennik* (Musical Contemporary). Engel's own schooling and sympathies were in the classical tradition, but he was a keen follower of new music and a careful admirer of Scriabin's talent. His various critiques showed some misgivings at the psychological and emotionally excessive 'content' of Scriabin's music, and his reactions to his later works in particular were cautious rather than rapturous. No doubt in some measure he was able to temper Boris' indiscriminate worship.[33]

Best evidence of the extent to which Pasternak allowed himself to be taken over by Scriabin emerges in a handful of his teenage compositions which have come down to us. All his finished pieces are cast in a Scriabinesque mould and display the hallmarks of his style: tumbling polyrhythms in the melody, nervously intrusive bass motifs, climaxes sustained by rapidly pulsating chordal accompaniments, whole episodes and pieces constructed from repetition of a single motif at gradually rising pitch, and in general a chromatic harmonic language and piano style clearly derived from Scriabin's earlier manner. In short, Pasternak showed a mastery of Scriabin's style which, even if derivative, was nevertheless proof of an unusual gift. His original compositions and several unfinished sketches also reflected Scriabin's almost exclusive interest in the piano as his medium. As a concert-goer too, according to his brother, Pasternak was stirred not so much by choral, chamber, or orchestral music, but by the solo pianoforte, whether in recital or concerti with orchestra.

The musical models Pasternak adopted are recognisably those of the earlier Scriabin. The latter's fine D sharp minor étude, opus 8, no. 12, is the unmistakable source for Pasternak's imitative attempt in the same key, composed in October 1906. Marked 'Con moto' this piece inhabits the same emotional region as its model and actually develops a motif taken from Scriabin's étude. Moreover, the Roman figure IV at its head suggests a (probably unrealised) plan to write a cycle of étude-type compositions. A further response to Scriabin's preludes, opus 11, comes in Pasternak's own 'Prélude' in G sharp minor, his most distinguished surviving composition, dated 8 December 1906, which reveals itself as a virtual compendium of Scriabinesque themes and devices.[34]

When writing in his *Autobiographical Essay* about Scriabin's earlier works of the 1890s and early 1900s, which he himself took as his models, Pasternak described them as 'totally contemporary, completely full of musical correspondences with the world around them, with the way in which people then lived, thought, felt, travelled and dressed' (II, 13; *VP*, 425–6). Had he been able to read this, Scriabin would doubtless have been gratified that his work had caught so well the atmosphere of that historical epoch. In his works he was primarily concerned to wreak an aesthetic revolution, and although the social disturbances of the early twentieth century struck a sympathetic chord with him, he had only a vague and romantic understanding of them. Nevertheless, he was able in 1906 to convince the Marxist émigré Plekhanov of a revolutionary spirit that animated his musical inspirations and reflected recent external events. Drozdov, a young pianist and critic of that time, also recorded that the famous D sharp minor étude of Scriabin's opus 8 sounded to contemporaries 'like an analogue of Gorky's "Stormy Petrel", like a new and unknown musical element, a rebellious whirlwind'. Were Pasternak's piano pieces of 1906, composed within a year of the 1905 Revolution also perhaps a form of musical response to the storm and stress of the age, expressed in a borrowed idiom? Certainly, he and his family were direct witnesses of the troubles that shook Russia in 1905, and their lives were radically affected by them.[35]

3

Revolution and Berlin

Lulling, trailing, flattening
Snow-cloaks of poplars and of gutterspouts,
The alarm blew out of future time
Like a sirocco from the south.

It hurled and flung the saffron torches
From noble palace and pediments,
And with its blazing tow it scorched
And lashed the foul grey elements.

So shall it be or never be,
That distant future age? . . .
We seem to glimpse through smoke, uncertainly,
The brazen witches of Macbeth.

. . .

Under arms the stormclouds stood –
Troops in their barracks, waiting till
The order came to fire. What good
Were human moans then to the cramped chill?
Snow – lovingly caressed by firing,
Amazingly innocent the roadway,
Guiltless as a prayer rising,
Inviolate as something holy.
The ice was shattered by the cavalry
Then covered by the snow again.
December stood eternal memory
To all the hero-martyrs slain.
Houses bared blank windows –
At that late hour no sign of light –
For all the world like horsecloths
With incisions for the creatures' eyes.
       from *The Tenth Anniversary of Krasnaya Presnya*

In January 1904 war broke out between Russia and Japan. Arising from a clash of imperial ambitions in the Far East, it aroused little patriotic enthusiasm in European Russia and it unfolded as a series of military and naval disasters for which the blame fell squarely on the tsarist government. Waves of civil unrest swept the Empire. After the assassination of Interior Minister Plehve, half-hearted concessions by his successor failed to quell the discontent, and despite the favourable terms of the Peace of Portsmouth in August 1905, the disturbances which began while the war was in progress continued to spread. Apart from the ruling élite, most sections of the population had long-standing grievances against tsarist autocracy, and these found expression in a nationwide agrarian rebellion, naval mutiny, workers' strikes, student demonstrations, political rallies, and agitation by reformist and revolutionary parties. None of this formed a coherent revolutionary movement, but it voiced the nation's discontent and gravely disrupted routine and civic order.

A relatively limited circle of schoolfellows and those of his parents' friends and colleagues known to Pasternak were described in *Safe Conduct* as 'apolitical' (II, 268; *VP*, 259). The family were never at any time involved with political parties, and as members of the liberal intelligentsia they remained idealist humanitarians and reformists, opposed to violent change. In his youth, Leonid Pasternak had seen life at the lower end of the social ladder both in Odessa and Moscow. As a Jew he knew well the flaws, discriminations and injustices of autocratic rule, and he shared the widely felt hatred of gendarmes, Cossacks, and other soldiery used to suppress freedom and maintain order. Professionally, his early association with the Itinerants implied a concern with the unvarnished depiction of an often ugly social reality, but he was never happy even with the mild pamphleteering that underlay their aesthetic programme and he believed that the honest service of art accorded ill with any political engagement.

On the eve of the Revolution, however, Leonid Pasternak made the acquaintance of Maksim Gorky and was invited with several artist colleagues to visit the controversial left-wing author with a view to establishing a new satirical journal.[1] With Serov and others he subsequently contributed to a number of such editions which adopted an openly dissident political stance. In June 1905 Leonid Pasternak wrote to his friend Pavel Ettinger expressing horror at the number of victims already claimed by the Revolution, remarking that he himself '[could] not help envying those whose fate it has been to participate in the movement to liberate our land and its future happiness' (*sic*). The sight of Boris' keen interest in events and sympathy with the protest had in fact forced his father to ponder his own behaviour, and he found it impossible to refrain from stating his own views.[2] Already in February 1905 Yulii Engel had drawn up a resolution signed by many artists and musicians which was published in the newspaper *Nashi dni* (Our Days),[3] and in May Leonid Pasternak joined with 112 colleagues in signing an 'Artists' Resolution', printed in the newspaper *Pravo* and calling for government reform and for 'full freedom of conscience, of expression, and of the press, freedom of assembly and meeting, and personal immunity'.[4] There were many such declarations by various professional and other liberal groups. And against the background of violent protest Leonid Pasternak's moderate position even enhanced his official standing. Together with Vrubel, Ivanov, Korovin and Malyutin, he was in 1905 elected a member of the St Petersburg Academy of Arts. Pasternak accepted the distinction, although two years later he declined when offered an Academy professorship in succession to Repin.[5]

Boris Pasternak was fourteen when the Russo-Japanese War began. Up till then he had been busied by academic pursuits and distracted from the outside world by a stimulating home life and his musical studies. But he could not fail to observe and ponder recent events. The Fifth Classical High School staff tried to discourage pupils from open discussion of the war. But the talk continued. Buoyant official placards promoting an image of national armed might could not conceal the ferment of public discontent, and even the junior classes heard and spread the rumours of Russian military ineptitude.[6] Apart from this, there was evidence on many a Moscow street of widespread social malaise and in ensuing years the signs of this increased. *Safe Conduct* later recorded some of these scenes of misery and decadence in which

the fragile squalor of a vegetating drudgery was fingered by gentle, drunken pluckings of guitars, and stately ladies, flushed and hardboiled from the bottle, emerged with their swaying husbands into the nightly wave of horse-cabs [. . .] People took poison and were burnt by fire, they threw acid at their rivals, drove out to weddings wearing satin and pawned their furs. Winks were exchanged by the lacquered smirks of a way of life that was cracking apart.

(II, 216; *VP*, 203–4)

In the early 1900s Pasternak had also glimpsed some of the wretchedness of rural Russia. In 1904 and again the following year, the family rented a summer dacha near Safontyevo on the small estate of the advocate I. I. Rukavishnikov. It stood sixty kilometres south-east of

55

Moscow, in a wild setting on the river Istra near the small town of Voskresensk; the closest rail station was several kilometres away at Novoierusalimskaya, which took its name from the important nearby Monastery of New Jerusalem. As always, the weeks at their summer villa were spent agreeably enough in the company of family and friends. But the Pasternaks were forcefully struck by the misery of the local peasantry. The poverty-stricken villagers lived in filthy, dilapidated thatched huts and appeared listless and indifferent to their plight. Their children stared in fear at the holiday guests from town, and Aleksandr Pasternak was particularly haunted by a memory of the deaf mute who lived by begging from the local inhabitants and any compassionate strangers.[7]

When revolution came in 1905, in many cities of the Empire even schoolboys joined the student rallies and demonstrations, and the Fifth Classical High School in Moscow had its own contingent of junior radicals. Although not among the orators or activists, Boris Pasternak sympathised with many of their progressive views, believing in the liberal ideal of reform. Like the later hero of his novel, he understood the revolution 'in the sense in which it was accepted by the middle classes, and in the interpretation that young students, followers of Blok, gave to it' (*DZh*, 162). His reaction, spontaneous and untainted by practical considerations, was typical of his age and milieu and it aroused the envious approval of his father. The most engaged member of the family, surprisingly, was twelve-year-old Aleksandr. He was persuaded by one of his mother's Marxist suffragette friends to help copy out revolutionary literature for distribution. Later on the woman was arrested, but Aleksandr's activities were never discovered and he used the wages from this clandestine copywork to expand his foreign stamp collection![8]

Initially it was the more distant revolutionary events of 1905 which shaped the Pasternaks' attitudes. All the family shared the horror and anger that swept the country after 'Bloody Sunday'. On 9 January in Petersburg, just after Boris' own Christmas visit there, a peaceful procession of workers and their families was fired on by the Winter Palace guards. The massacre further polarised public opinion. For some weeks Moscow was spared the armed violence that occurred in other cities, but eventually it too was affected. On the bright morning of 4 February, residents on Myasnitskaya heard a distant explosion: Grand Duke Sergei Aleksandrovich, Governor of Moscow, patron of the School of Painting and a personal admirer of Leonid Pasternak, was assassinated by a Socialist Revolutionary bomb as he rode out through the Kremlin's Nikolsky Gate. Only four months later his successor

Count Shuvalov also fell victim to a terrorist attack. These and many similar acts of revolutionary violence were repugnant to all members of the Pasternak family.[9] Nevertheless, although Boris remained a passive witness, as he did also in 1917, he could not escape being infected by the atmosphere and 'spirit of revolution', and by a whirling awareness of history in action at close quarters. The impressions and events of those weeks were later captured in the galloping anapaests of his poem *The Year Nineteen-Five*:

> And those days were a diary.
> You could read it
> Wherever you opened.
>
> We played at snowballs and
> Rolled them from soldiers
> And snowflakes
> And reports of the time
> As they fell from the sky.
> This landslide of kingdoms,
> This drunken snow falling
> In the yard of the school
> On the corner of Povarskaya
> In January.
>
> Every day blew a blizzard.
> And those in the Party
> In senior classes
> Had the stern look of eagles,
> While we went unpunished
> And defied the Greek master.
> We moved desks to the wall
> And played parliament in the classes
> And soared in our dreams
> To outlawed Gruziny.*
>
> And a third day – snow fell,
> And it snowed till the evening
> Then cleared in the night.
> The following morning there came
> From the Kremlin a thunderous peal ...
> Done to death –
> The Art School's own patron,
> Prince Sergei Aleksandrovich! ...

* Gruziny – an area of Moscow near Krasnaya Presnya, a centre of revolutionary disturbances.

In those first days of February
I fell in love with the storm.   (I, 118; *SP*, 253–4)

As the year 1905 wore on, reports reached Moscow of further nationwide upheavals: clashes between strikers and troops in Lodz, mutiny on the Black Sea Fleet battleship Potemkin in June, and in November Lieutenant Shmidt's naval uprising at Sevastopol. All of these formed major episodes in Pasternak's narrative verse of the 1920s.

The agitations of early 1905 had caused the Moscow School of Painting to close its doors in February and they stayed shut for the rest of the academic year. The early summer months in the Moscow region were relatively calm, however, and the Pasternaks again took a dacha at Safontyevo; surviving family photographs show them there with the Margulius family who came as guests from St Petersburg. But total escape from the outside world was not now so welcome; the Pasternaks regretted being cut off from events, and newspapers arrived only after several days' delay. At various points Rukavishnikov turned up bringing news, and in June came first rumours of a promised constitution. Concerned for his own family's safety at Safontyevo, Rukavishnikov carried a revolver in case of trouble with the locals, and when he and his family finally left for Moscow he pressed the weapon on Leonid Pasternak. For a short time Leonid and his sons used it for target practice. Fortunately, as it turned out, their bouts of competitive shooting were the only thing that disturbed the rural calm.[10]

When they returned to Moscow in mid-August, however, the city was in uproar. The announcement of election procedures for a consultative assembly had been met with public derision and votes of no confidence. And in the renewed wave of unrest Boris and Aleksandr's schooling was now affected. After allegations that propaganda was being conducted among pupils, several schools including their own were closed in September for a cooling-off period. Later that month Moscow was hit by a strike of bakers and printers, and a rail strike in early October rapidly spread and affected industry nationwide (some personal impressions of these events were later incorporated in the second chapter of *Doctor Zhivago*). Finally, faced with a general strike in St Petersburg, the Tsar on 17 October issued a Manifesto proclaiming a new constitution with civil liberties and universal suffrage. As well as reading newspaper reports of all this the Pasternaks received eyewitness accounts in Aunt Asya's frequent letters from the capital. Muscovite reactions to the news of a constitution echoed those in St Petersburg. Exultant throngs filled the streets, harassed on the one hand by still hostile police and Cossacks, and harangued and manipulated by left-wing militants still pressing for more radical change.[11] The Pasternaks saw all this with their own eyes. But it was a concessionary ruling announced on 27 August which most directly affected them. On that date universities and other higher education institutions were granted their autonomy. The result was immediately to turn lecture rooms into public forums. No longer threatened by police intervention, revolutionary rhetoric flowed from their platforms for weeks on end. Though officially closed, the School of Painting together with the University and Technical College became a centre of agitation, and the speeches attracted not just students, but drew large mixed audiences of clerks, workmen, soldiers, schoolboys, women and children. Boris Pasternak heard several of these debates which took place almost literally on his doorstep, and impressions of them were later worked into his narrative prose. From the balcony of the School he also watched in October as thousands turned out for the funeral procession of Nikolai Bauman, a revolutionary activist murdered by police. With other members of his family and School staff he saw mourners process for hours along Myasnitskaya, in silence apart from choruses of the funeral anthem 'Eternal Memory' and the revolutionary song 'You fell as a victim'. Later came reports that as the procession returned from the cemetery, it had clashed outside the University with the forces of law and order. The latter, helped by members of the right-wing league of Black Hundreds and by troops and self-appointed vigilantes, harassed the crowds until they finally scattered.[12]

Not unnaturally, Boris Pasternak was infected by the classroom rhetoric he heard, and awareness of the reprisals faced by the speakers from those waiting outside in ambush increased his sympathy for their cause. Unable to enter the premises themselves, the police recruited mobs to take summary revenge on any institutions harbouring trouble-makers. The *Autobiographical Essay* records as follows:

The rabble from Okhotny Ryad [Hunters Row] went on the rampage, smashing up institutes of higher education, the University and Technical College. The School of Painting was also threatened with attack, and on instructions from the Director heaps of cobblestones were made on the front staircase landings and hoses were screwed into fire nozzles to repel any insurgents.

From the passing street processions demonstrators turned off into the School and organised meetings in the assembly hall, took over the premises and went out on to the balconies and made speeches to those standing below in the street. The students of the School formed militant organisations and at night mounted their own guard inside the building. (II, 14; *VP*, 427)

This militant guard of *druzhinniki* was made up of armed students and workers, who established headquarters on the lower floor of the School while political meetings went on in classrooms and lecture halls in other parts of the building.[13]

The course of public events could be observed by the Pasternaks from their apartment. During daylight hours their windows on the top floor provided a perfect view of happenings in the street, and at night their sleep was frequently disturbed by distant gunfire. Much of what he observed in the autumn of 1905 later found its way into Pasternak's writings. His novel in particular recalled a frosty, leaden-skied November and its demonstrations: 'faces, faces, and more faces, quilted winter coats and sheepskin hats, old men, girl students, children, railwaymen in uniform, workers from the tramway depot and telephone exchange in kneeboots and leather jackets, secondary schoolboys and students' (*DZh*, 35). On his sorties into the street Pasternak sometimes joined other processing schoolboys, and he later recalled his own 'twopenny-halfpenny revolutionism which never went further than a show of bravado before a Cossack stockwhip and a lash received across the back of my quilted overcoat' (II, 267; *VP*, 259). This incident outside the Myasnitskaya post-office railings was apparently a source of pride to Boris at the time, although his parents heard his gleeful account of it with some alarm. His later dismissive retail of it, however, perhaps underplayed the serious social awareness which the 1905 revolution aroused in him.[14]

'Moscow in December' was the title and setting of the final section of Pasternak's poem devoted to the events of 1905, and it reconstructed the last, violent phase of the Moscow revolution. After the arrest of the Petersburg Workers' Council on 3 December, strikes broke out in the capital. Then Moscow too was gripped by a general strike leading to ten days of fighting at the barricades which began on the 9th. Although the armed uprising was centred some distance away in Krasnaya Presnya, there was an increase in student revolutionary activity on Myasnitskaya. Pasternak probably saw little actual fighting, but he doubtless heard direct reports of a huge public rally at the Aquarium Pleasure Garden, and tales of street barricades, stranded tramcars, demonstrations by railwaymen, and of dragoons, gendarmes, and soldiers of the Semyonovsky Regiment called in to deal with them. Armed clashes involved the use of sabres, rifles and heavier artillery; injuries and fatalities were many.

60

Though uninvolved in the December fighting the Pasternaks were not entirely unscathed. Any building used by armed revolutionaries was liable to be shelled by government troops. In nearby Mashkov Lane, schoolboy protesters at the Fiedler Institute were forced out under an artillery barrage and set upon by waiting dragoons; many were arrested and imprisoned, including Mikhail Kasatkin, the son of Leonid's artist colleague. The troops then turned their attention to the School of Painting.[15] The director, Prince Lvov, came up to the Pasternaks' apartment with news of an ultimatum from the Governor General, stating that the School would be fired upon if the insurgents had not vacated it by nightfall. For their own safety the Pasternaks were advised to leave. This disturbing news was made even more terrible since three-year-old Lydia lay gravely ill with pneumonia and could not be moved. All other resident staff had left, the central heating no longer functioned, and the sole source of heat and light was a kerosene lamp in Lydia's room. The only other comfort was the constant presence of the doctor who while visiting Lydia was cut off by the fighting and for several days was unable to return to his home in the Tverskaya district. When the ultimatum came, Leonid and his wife set out on a frantic search for accommodation nearby. But on their return they discovered that a senior *druzhinnik* on duty was Leonid's own student from the Department of Architecture. He promised his assistance and soon returned with news that their revolutionary headquarters was moving to a new, secret location. Disaster was thus averted. The Pasternak parents wept with relief, Dasha the maid turned up with food and tea, and on the ninth day Lydia began to improve.[16]

Surprisingly, throughout the upheavals Leonid Pasternak managed still to work. Though unable to concentrate on any major project, he continued sketching and produced a pictorial record of several scenes he had witnessed. One picture which still survives was vividly recalled by Boris and depicted a woman agitator fired on by dragoons as she spoke from a balcony; although wounded, she grasped a pillar in order to support herself and still continued speaking. At Gorky's instigation Leonid Pasternak also produced various art work for satirical journals such as *Zhupel* (The Bugbear) and *Bich* (The Scourge). In general, though, he found it difficult to engage in serious creative work. Tuition at the School had ceased in February, and with no likelihood of its immediate resumption he and his wife decided to take their family away from the unrest.[17] Their reaction was shared by many, including relatives in other towns. After the revolutionary agitation and pogroms of 1905, Leonid's eldest sister Ekaterina and her husband Leon Yakobson left Odessa and moved their family permanently to Riga in Latvia.

At the end of 1905, when Lydia was fit to travel, and when calm had been restored and railways reopened, Leonid Pasternak took his family to Berlin. The prospect of a prolonged stay in Germany was a congenial one to both parents. It promised renewed contact with German cultural life, and particularly since organising the Russian section of the Düsseldorf Exhibition in 1904, Leonid Pasternak enjoyed increasing renown in Germany.[18] Meanwhile the unpleasantness of life in Russia was driven home by Leonid's last joyless impressions before departure, recorded in a letter of 3–4 January 1906 to Pavel Ettinger:

What is enviable is the fact that I no longer see those beasts – the soldiers and police, those ugly faces which in Moscow haunted me till I started seeing things. You should have seen them at the Nikolaevsky Station when we left! Worse than a military camp! Carousing Cossacks and gendarmes everywhere, the stink of the barracks and the spirit of the *oprichnina** – I shall never forget it.[19]

By the time of their trip to Berlin, Boris Pasternak had had several years of German tuition and was familiar with the language. But as they crossed from Verzhbolovo (Wirballen) and entered East Prussia at Eidkuhnen, the train journey itself was a revelation:

Everything was unusual and different. It was not real life but a dream, as though you were taking part in some invented theatrical entertainment which nobody was compelled to involve himself in. There was nobody you knew, and nobody to give you orders. Down the whole length of the coach was a long row of doors swinging open and slamming to, with a separate door for each compartment ...

Memorable too were the novelties of Berlin:

Four railtracks on a circling flyover that towered over the streets, canals, racing stables and backyards of the gigantic city; trains that caught up and overhauled one another, ran side by side and diverged; lights on the streets that divided, crossed and intersected beneath the bridges; lights burning on first and second floors on a level with the raised railtrack; automatic vending machines in the station buffets which were lit with multicoloured lamps and disgorged cigars, sweetmeats and sugared almonds.   (II, 18–19; *VP*, 432)

---

* *oprichnina* – a subdivision of the Muscovite state created by Ivan the Terrible in 1565 and also the title of a special corps of servants responsible for its government; one of the latter's main functions was that of a political police force designed to exterminate any opponents of the Tsar.

Within a few years, some of these features of Western urban life and gadgetry were to appear in Russia too, but in their original foreign setting they made a specially indelible impression.[20]

It was early January by the Western calendar when the Pasternaks arrived in the German capital and for a few days their home was the Fürst von Bismarck Hotel in the south-western suburb of Charlottenburg. The weather was intensely cold and they shivered in their three upper-storey hotel rooms, despite the management's provision of extra gas-stoves. Soon, however, more modest but cosier lodgings were found. The parents and daughters moved into Fräulein Gebhardi's boarding house at 112 Kurfürstenstrasse, and since finances were limited a cheaper room was rented for Boris and his brother in the house of the shopkeeper next door.

Apart from minor irritations, such as the Teutonic regularity of boarding-house mealtimes (about which Leonid complained in his correspondence), the Berlin interlude was a happy one. Rozaliya Pasternak resumed piano playing and regularly made music with a Scandinavian woman violinist residing at Gebhardi's. Their playing eventually came to the notice of the Berlin Conservatoire and they were invited to play for the staff and students. This renewal of concert activities prompted Rozaliya to think of returning to the concert platform when once they were back in Moscow.[21]

Leonid Pasternak also resumed work in Berlin. He painted several portraits and under the influence of Heinrich Eickmann, who had a well equipped studio nearby, he became interested in etching. He established contacts with German artists such as Corinth and Slevogt and also got to know Max Liebermann, leader of the Berlin Secessionist School, whose work, like his own, showed impressionist leanings grafted on a realist foundation. Some of Pasternak's work was reproduced in important magazines such as *Meister der Farbe* (Masters of Colour) and in the autumn of 1906 with the encouragement of local friends he held a successful joint exhibition at the Galerie Schulte together with Finnish artist Akseli Gallén-Kallela.[22]

Outside the professional sphere, other friendships also flourished including one with the family of businessman Julius Rosenfeld. He and his wife Rozaliya Aleksandrovna (*née* Geduld) were old friends from Odessa and had moved to Germany some years previously. The Pasternaks were often entertained at their home on the Kurfürstendamm, and their family friendship was to last for several decades. In Berlin there were also large numbers of Russian students, and the regular community of expatriates had greatly expanded following the recent unrest at home. The Pasternaks thus met up with several old acquaintances in Berlin. Among these was artist Elizaveta Kruglikova; Mikhail Freidenberg passed through en route for southern Europe; and Maksim Gorky was staying at a holiday home in Zehlendorf in the south of Berlin where Leonid Pasternak visited him and cemented a friendship with this 'likeable, genuinely Russian type'.[23]

Boris Pasternak accompanied his father on several visits to Gorky. These were important encounters since he was eventually to inherit and continue his father's acquaintance. He recalled one of his father's pictures of Gorky offending the author's secretary and companion Maria Andreyeva: 'You haven't understood him – he is Gothic', she protested, in the somewhat affected manner of the time (II, 19; *VP*, 432). At Zehlendorf, Leonid Pasternak presented Gorky with his recent engraving of Tolstoy depicted against a stormcloud background. The hinted symbolism was not lost on the author of 'The Song of the Stormy Petrel', and an inevitable subject of conversation was the recent upheaval in Russia. As a man of the people, Gorky understood the anarchic traits of the Russian character better than any artistic intellectual. He maintained to Leonid Pasternak that the present submissiveness was a temporary illusion; the day of reckoning would come, and it was part of Gorky's purpose to ensure that it did so. An abhorrence of the evils of autocracy, if nothing else, was certainly something the Pasternaks could share with the radicals, and in due course it was to condition their initial reaction to the revolutions of 1917.[24]

Boris and Aleksandr Pasternak were meanwhile absorbed by their new surroundings. Living apart from their parents and sisters, they were in close contact with the daily life of Berlin. In their excursions through the city, Boris enjoyed his new semi-independence and acted as an attentive yet discreet guardian and guide to Aleksandr. The two of them rapidly mastered the local geography and enjoyed walking the busy streets and breathing the un-Muscovite atmosphere – 'a mixture of engine smoke, coal-gas and beer fumes', Boris later recalled (II, 19; *VP*, 432). The brothers also visited the Tiergarten, and sometimes they sat and read in some quiet corner of this park which reminded them slightly of Moscow's Sokolniki. Prolonged daily practice quickly improved their German. Boris was particularly proud of his fluency and tried cultivating the local Berlin dialect until he was one day mocked by a street urchin, after which he abandoned the habit. It was at this time that Boris began reading widely in German. In this too he played the role of tutor to his brother, often recommending books which Shura avidly read in an effort to keep up with him. Boris regularly brought home cheap, brown-backed Universal-Verlag editions of the classics. His chief enthusiasms were E. T. A. Hoffmann and Jean Paul. Shura recalled him saying that he had never read a better book than the latter's *Dr Katzenberger's Spa Journey (Dr Katzenbergers Badereise)*. Of the two authors, though, it was to be Hoffmann who had the stronger influence on Pasternak's own early writing.[25]

The Pasternak boys' lessons continued in Berlin on a nominal basis and probably suffered no more than in the recent months of disrupted schooling in Moscow. Instead of attendance at a German school, a Russian émigré student with the unusual name of Maibardyuk and a thick crop of black hair and whiskers was engaged to supervise them. This tuition was particularly needed by Aleksandr who showed less intellectual aptitude than Boris (although he too was to collect a gold medal when he left school in 1911).

Boris and Aleksandr shared a modest room above a fruiterer's shop advertising 'Obst und Südfrüchte' on the Kurfürstenstrasse. Parodying Dickens, they referred to it as 'The Old Spicery Shop' and enjoyed the ready supply of mandarins, oranges and pineapples. (In Moscow these were still an expensive luxury to be had only from Eliseyev's exclusive foodstore on Tverskaya.) The shopkeeper (known to them just as 'Frau Witwe' – Mrs Widow – since they forget her real name) had two daughters. The elder was close to Boris in age and she sometimes played on the family piano. Boris was delighted to find an instrument in the house, and it was arranged that he should give the elder daughter lessons in return for the chance to play himself. The piano was duly tuned in his honour and he often played and improvised for hours on end.[26]

Of all the fresh impressions Berlin offered, the most absorbing for Boris Pasternak were the musical ones. He encountered several new composers, among them the Russian Vladimir Rebikov, who had studied in Germany and had an established reputation there. Probably it was in the company of musicians that Pasternak heard Rebikov play excerpts from his popular opera score *The Christmas Tree (Elka)* which had been premiered in Moscow three years earlier. Perhaps he already knew some of Rebikov's piano pieces. Using whole-tone scales, parallel fifths and a few other impressionist devices erected on a Tchaikovskian foundation, Rebikov was often seen as a pioneer and bracketed with Scriabin as a leading Russian modernist. The equation now strikes one as absurd, and probably Pasternak saw through Rebikov's claims. At any rate, his later memoirs highlighted the only feature where Rebikov genuinely rivalled Scriabin – his vanity. Musical history for Rebikov was divided into three phases: bestial up to Beethoven, human in the period following, and the music of the future beginning with Rebikov![27]

Pasternak was already a Wagner enthusiast by the time he arrived in Germany and he possessed a fine bound set of piano scores from which his mother frequently played. But in Berlin there was opportunity to hear Wagner in plenty; his impact was probably enhanced by the fact that Scriabin had already assimilated several features of his harmonic style. And although Scriabin remained first in Pasternak's affection, there were some touches in the piano 'Prélude' of December 1906 which suggested a direct influence of orchestral Wagner.[28]

Symphonic poems by Richard Strauss, and the symphonies and concerti of Beethoven and Brahms also featured in the many concerts Pasternak attended in Berlin. Among the artists he heard were conductors such as Nikisch, Mengelberg and Bruno Walter, and pianists Leopold Godowski and Arthur Schnabel. Usually Pasternak went to the matinée concerts, popular with students and young people (and where refreshments were served during the music at tables at the back of the hall), rather than the evening performances which attracted the social élite. Occasionally Pasternak would also take his brother or the landlady's elder daughter to these concerts.

Another musical treat in Berlin was the opportunity to hear fine church organ music. The Pasternak brothers made regular pilgrimages to the Gedächtniskirche where they attended Sunday services and sometimes also went during the week to hear the organist practising. The finest moments came at the end of the Sunday services, with the all-engulfing sonorities of J. S. Bach. Impressions of this went into Boris' Hoffmannesque *Suboctave Story* (*Istoriya odnoi kontroktavy*),[29] but Aleksandr Pasternak has also left an evocative account of that music and its effect:

It seemed that everything all around vanished in a general infinity of worlds, but still something held us in its powerful embrace and sustained us in the mighty roar of the organ's bass. At last, as it sounded out the final chords, now beyond all earthly force, the organ suddenly and abruptly fell silent, listening in to the reverberation of its own sound in the walls, windows and arches of the suddenly regenerate church. Drained of all strength, we were the last to leave and were surprised that the houses and streets still existed. We slowly made our way home in complete silence.[30]

In the first few months of his stay in Berlin Boris continued his musical studies with Yulii Engel by correspondence. He had with him Karl Riemann's standard textbook and a volume of musical exercises, and he worked through these, sending regular dispatches to Engel who returned them corrected and with comments. In summer of 1906, however, music lessons could be resumed on a personal basis. The Pasternaks left Berlin for a holiday and travelled via the Stralsund train ferry to the Baltic island of Rügen. There they settled in the Villa-Pension Wilhelmshöhe at Goehren on the island's north-east coast. Goehren at that time was a small resort town with its own Kursaal and a town-cryer who announced forthcoming attractions to the guests. The brothers swam in the sea and often left the official beach with its sunshades and wickerwork beach-chairs in order to explore the cliffs and rocks. Meanwhile Leonid Pasternak drew and painted on the beach, in the garden, and on the balcony, while Rozaliya had a chance to continue playing and practising at the guest-house.[31] At first the Pasternaks were the only Russians at Goehren, but they were eventually joined by Yulii Engel and his family. Josephine and Lydia were already friends with the Engels' two daughters Ala and Vera and were glad of their company. Engel himself was an excellent companion for adults and children alike. He willingly joined in the fun, organised beach games, helped the children sail their model yacht, and arranged woodland walks and expeditions. Between swimming and sunbathing he also gave Boris further tuition, often there and then while sitting on the beach. According to Aleksandr Pasternak, at such times neither of them seemed fully aware of their surroundings and their talks resembled the animated discussion of professionals rather than exchanges between master and pupil.[32]

The Pasternaks stayed on for a short time after the Engels' departure, but they too left after a thunderstorm signalled the break-up of the summer weather. For a few weeks more they stayed in Berlin, this time at a different guest-house. Leonid's exhibition opened at the Galerie Schulte on 15 (2) September, and before their autumn departure he received a tempting offer from England for an exhibition in Kensington. However, the Pasternaks decided to pursue their original plans and the whole family returned to Moscow.

The turbulent birth of Russia's new constitutional order had seen dismissal of the First State Duma and the violent suppression of a new revolutionary upsurge. But by the autumn of 1906 a relative calm had settled. At the Moscow School of Painting normal teaching recommenced in November, Boris and Aleksandr Pasternak returned to their interrupted schooling at the Fifth Classical High School, and Boris resumed his musical studies under Yulii Engel. Along with this, however, he now pursued another important, though still secondary, interest – the reading of Russian and European literature.[33]

4

Youth's impressions, literature and music

'The Muse of 1909'

From showers' family descended,
Thunderstorm's youngest offspring,
You are dusted by thunder
Till black as peacock moth's wing.

Lightnings of teeming events,
Darkness of thoughts at devotion,
Antiquity churned by excess,
Your sheen is now rusted, corroded.

Towers collide and sound tocsins,
Veins swell up in the gallop,
Heavens in craters wash and
Meridian hour's at the sap-head.

Sunrays give tinplate fine lustre,
A mouth is choked and turns mad,
Suggestions of midday are gusting
Like simoom-driven sands.

By your speech these are vanquished,
But the world's crunching sandgrains
Like dust 'tween the teeth
Smack still of the duel.

❧❧❧❧

In his mid-twenties Pasternak wrote a review of some verse by Mayakovsky. In it, while recalling the sensations allegedly experienced by
several adolescents of his generation, he described what was in some
ways peculiar to his own world of perception:

It is increasingly rare for people to be born into the world as musicians, painters
and poets. But the childhood of some takes place in towns that are totally unlike
everything that those forming their population say about them. Yet on entering

the brains of a few young people, actual impressions begin to resemble their most distant neighbours within the brain. Ultimately, there is no phenomenon surrounding such a youth which does not ache with its own particular obviousness and is not visible within the memory at an eternally present moment, that is, at the critical instant of some acute inflammation of colour.

The most obvious thing to such a young man, Pasternak claimed, was the brilliance of his impressions. Much less binding or obvious was the mode of expression for which they called: 'A brain pregnant with them will sooner or later impose some self-limitation [...] a youth who in this way becomes a poet will be sufficiently complex and sharp-witted to allow himself to bid farewell forever to the paradoxes of painting and music.'[1]

In his youth Pasternak had already come to realise the potential multi-valency of his talents, even if the moment of 'self-limitation' had not yet arrived. (Perhaps he thought it was behind him in view of his commitment to music.) Strangely, and unlike Scriabin, however, Pasternak showed virtually no interest in combining musical and literary inspirations and seemingly made no settings of literary texts. (His partsong version of the opening of Lermontov's 'Lonely white sail' is clearly a harmony exercise rather than an original composition.) His total dedication to instrumental music, the one art form least bound up with cognition or the transfer of 'information', probably avoided any youthful perplexities at the non-congruity of language and inner experience. Pasternak did record in *Safe Conduct* that his 'awareness of the city never corresponded to the place where my life was going on. An emotional pressure always thrust it away into the depths of the perspective described' (II, 216; *VP*, 203). But the psychological and literary implications of this realisation were only explored later, in Pasternak's first attempts at verse and prose. His adolescent awareness, akin to the pre-linguistic state of the infant, was later magically evoked in the story *Zhenya Luvers' Childhood*, and his ability to express such experience partially explained Akhmatova's comment on his endowment with 'a certain eternal childhood'.[2]

Pasternak's youthful lack of ambition to seek verbal outlets for inner experience seemed to complement his natural reticence. Unlike his music, his literary attempts were initially an almost clandestine activity, and for most of his youth he inhabited a world of emotions that were sublimated in the wordless utterance of music. Not, of course, that Pasternak was incapable of verbal communication: raised in a highly cultured milieu, he was more than averagely articulate on all issues except those affecting the core of his emotional being. As he said in his Mayakovsky review, 'There are no such epidemics of imagery which people cannot give a name to: names of seasons, localities, feelings and passions, terms denoting states of the soul.'[3] But whatever its objective accuracy, the 'naming' of such states of the soul in the language of everyday communication was a lame form of expression far removed from the power of poetic statement.

Another aspect of Pasternak's mentality was revealed in his later correspondence with the English poet Stephen Spender. In the summer of 1959 he wrote to him the following in his own idiosyncratic English:

I also from my earliest years have been struck by the observation that existence was more original, extraordinary, and inexplicable than any of its separate astonishing incidents and facts. I was attracted by the unusualness of the usual. Composing music, prose or poetry, I was driven by definite conceptions and motifs [...] But the top pleasure consists in having hit the sense or taste of reality, in having been able, in having succeeded in rendering the *atmosphere of being*, the surrounding whole, the total environment, the frame where the particular and depicted thing is having been plunged and floating.[4]

Another letter of Pasternak's old age, written in French, went further in describing what formed the basis of all his artistic endeavours, both musical and literary:

En parlant des données de la conscience, faudrait-il sentir mieux la saveur verbale, dynamique de ce mot (de ce que c'est un acte de donation, un don) [...] La réalité du monde j'ai perçue toujours (et je cherchais toujours à représenter) comme l'effet d'un élan inconnaissable, comme la venue, l'arrivée du monde lancé, envoyé de l'abîme du mystère.[5]

(Talking of the data of consciousness, one should have a better sense of the verbal, dynamic savour of this word [of the fact that it is an act of giving, a gift] [...] I have always perceived [and always sought to represent] the reality of the world as the effect of some unknowable impulse, as the advent and arrival of a world, launched and sent from the mysterious abyss.)

Yet another letter, written in May 1959 to Jacqueline de Proyart, revealed the emotional impact of an apparently dynamic world on the acute senses of the artist:

J'aimais l'aspect de mouvements de toute sorte, les phénomènes de force, d'action, j'aimais à saisir ce monde agile de la turbulence universelle et de le rendre. Mais l'image de la réalité qui consistait de tous ces mouvements et les

71

renfermait, ce 'tout' qu'on nomme 'monde' ou 'univers' ce n'était pas un cadre pour moi, une donnée ferme.[6]

(I loved the appearance of movement of every sort, phenomena of force and action, I loved to grasp and convey this world that was moved by a universal turbulence. But the image of reality which consisted of all these movements and enclosed them, this 'entirety' which one calls the 'world' or 'universe', was not a [rigid] frame for me, something given and fixed.)

Pasternak claimed, however, that animated *perceptions* should not be confused with the mere *physical* characteristics of the empirical world: 'Toute cette réalité (le tout du monde) était à son tour animée d'agitation de toute autre sorte que les mouvements visibles organiques ou matériels'. (All this reality [the world's entirety] was in its turn enlivened by an agitation quite different from visible movements of an organic or material sort.)[7] The animation of observed reality was for Pasternak a quality of personal vision. Maybe it was partly a predisposition inherited from his father, a master at recording the impression of a fleeting instant in his impromptu sketches. Possibly too it was a sensitive youth's barometric reaction to the 'historical atmosphere', reflected in the impetus of his own and Scriabin's music as in other contemporary art forms. To some extent, though, turbulent movement was an objective characteristic of the modern age. Social upheaval in 1905 had evoked Pasternak's animated response, while machinery and rapid movement were generally typical of the contemporary urban environment – so much is evident from the memoirs of Aleksandr Pasternak, a helpfully sympathetic recreator of his brother's and his own early experiences.

Both Pasternak boys apparently took special delight in a gift from Vienna from their uncle Karl Pasternak – a set of photographic albums whose pages when steadily flicked through reproduced the motion of a galloping horse, soldiers marching, or a modern street scene. Another of Boris' 'dynamic' pleasures was the magic lantern acquired by his family around the turn of the century, and the first moving cinema. Both brothers were regular patrons of Hermans, the chemist on Turgenev Square, where a Pathé cinematograph on the first floor showed short film-strips, including news shots of the Russo-Japanese War. Meanwhile, the first motor cars were appearing in Moscow, although they seemed to arouse no special interest in Pasternak; despite his responsiveness to new experience, the 'poetry of the machine' evidently passed him by, and he was later to scorn the naïve forms it assumed for some Russian Futurist poets.[8]

Something equally dynamic but more traditionally poetic which left a deep imprint on Pasternak's youthful sensibility (and something which was characteristic of Moscow) was the interaction of climate, nature and the seasons with the modern townscape. Much of Pasternak's early verse was to register seasonal realia at such moments of transformation – at dawn, or in the changing light of evening, in storms and showers, at the onset of winter, or the spectacular spring thaw. At the start of winter, for instance, thicker rugs and carpets were laid in the apartment, dutch stoves were lit, fur-coats, hoods and felt boots were unpacked, and the double-glazed windows were sealed and rolls of cotton-wool and pots of acid placed between the panes to prevent condensation. Moscow in winter was dominated totally by the snow. The main form of transport was by sleigh, and the few early automobiles could not cope with a snow cover constantly replenished by further falls and shovellings from the courtyards. Specially memorable were night sleigh-rides to visit friends, or to concerts and the theatre, along streets lit mainly by kerosene lamps and with moonlight glowing blue upon the snow. Then came the sudden miracle of the Russian spring, observed and admired by many, and specially welcome to the Muscovite. In the words of Pasternak's close contemporary and friend, Ilya Ehrenburg, 'Spring in Moscow is extraordinary. Residents of the blessed south know nothing of it. It is not a change of season but an exclusive event in the life of any man ... life's noisy resettlement in a new abode.'[9] In spring on the way home from school Boris would often go down with his brother to the Moskva River to see the winter ice break up – an awe-inspiring spectacle enhanced by the crunch of the floes and by the fact that the river was still unhemmed by artificial embankments apart from a short stretch between the Great Stone and Krasnokholmsky Bridges. Then in late March or early April, water would suddenly become the dominant element. Sleighs stuck on the bared roadway and horses strained, iron-rimmed cab wheels rumbled through the slush, windows were unsealed and opened, the noise of the town flooded suddenly into the apartment, and a favourite pastime was floating matchbox boats down the streaming gutters. Such sights and sounds were an integral part of the Muscovite boy's life, and it was they which produced many 'epidemics of imagery' which eventually found their way into verse and prose.[10]

Pasternak's absorption by his surroundings and his venting of emotion in music may have diverted him from the dilemmas of verbal expression. But an equally potent diversion was the opulence of contemporary art, musical, visual and belletristic. In the early 1900s this became almost more vivid and fascinating than the real world.

A force kept watch behind the trees along the boulevards which was fearfully tested and experienced and which followed people with its intelligent gaze [...] Behind the trees it stood and bore an awful resemblance to real life.

(II, 266; *VP*, 256)

First of all there was the artistic creativity witnessed in his father's own studio and at the Itinerant and World of Art exhibitions where his work was often displayed. Then there were exhibitions sponsored by the impressionist Blue Rose group in 1907, and by Ryabushinsky's Symbolist journal *Zolotoe runo* (The Golden Fleece) the following year. At these 'along with Russian names like Somov, Sapunov, Sudeikin, Krymov, Larionov and Goncharova, one could glimpse the French names of Bonnard and Vuillard. At the "Golden Fleece" exhibitions, in halls shaded by curtains where arrays of potted hyacinths exuded a greenhouse smell of earth, one could see the works of Matisse and Rodin sent from abroad' (II, 22; *VP*, 435).

But the art of whose intelligent gaze Pasternak was most aware was 'the youthful art of Scriabin, Blok, Komissarzhevskaya and Bely, advanced, enthralling and original'. This music, drama and literature was so striking that 'not only did it excite no thoughts of replacing it, but on the contrary, for its even greater stability, one wished to repeat it again from the very foundations, yet even more speedily, fervently and wholly' (II, 266–7; *VP*, 256). The repetitions urged on Pasternak by the example of Scriabin have been mentioned already, and they continued almost throughout his brief musical career. While this lasted he made no literary attempts of his own, but he absorbed plenty of Russian Symbolist literature as well as writings by contemporary Western Europeans.

The early works of Andrei Bely, in fact, formed an interesting bridge between literary and musical culture and included several prose poems with 'symphonic' titles: the *Northern* or *Heroic Symphony* (1903), the *Second* or *Dramatic Symphony* (1902), a third entitled *The Return* (*Vozvrat*) (1904), and a fourth that was later revised and published as *The Goblet of Blizzards* (*Kubok metelei*) in 1908. These, together with a volume of lyrics on a mixture of mystical and Nietzschean themes – *Gold in Azure* (*Zoloto v lazuri*) (1904) – doubtless aroused Pasternak's initial enthusiasm for Bely. Their impact was reinforced by subsequent works and a personal acquaintance with Bely at the time of Pasternak's 'conversion' to literature around the year 1910.

As he wrote in his *Autobiographical Essay*, Pasternak and several of his contemporaries 'spent their youth with Blok' (II, 15; *VP*, 429). The discovery of his poetry and of Komissarzhevskaya's theatre, a major centre for Symbolist and contemporary drama, was bound up with Pasternak's growing familiarity with the city of St Petersburg. As a schoolboy he had paid a Christmas vacation visit there to see his relatives during the winter of 1904–5.[11] As head of the Petersburg-Moscow freight station, his uncle Aleksandr Margulius could organise free travel warrants. Using one of these, his nephew journeyed alone on the overnight express, supervised by the conductor who had been suitably briefed. He stayed with Aunt Asya and Uncle Mikhail Freidenberg, who lived on the Ekaterininsky (now Griboedovsky) Canal behind the Kazan Cathedral, but he also visited the Marguliuses, whose home was near the station, on Ligovsky Prospect.

Pasternak spent almost a fortnight absorbing new impressions of the capital:

I wandered for whole days through the streets of the immortal city, as though with my feet and eyes I was devouring some book in stone written by a genius. And in the evenings I was engrossed in the theatre of Komissarzhevskaya.

(II, 18; *VP*; 431)

Cousin Olya accompanied Boris to the theatre on free tickets obtained from her father who worked for the paper *Peterburgsky listok* (Petersburg Leaflet), and together they saw Ibsen's *Hedda Gabler* and Hoffmansthal's *Marriage of Sobeide* (*Die Hochzeit der Sobeide*). Evidently Boris was disgusted when his Uncle Mikhail enthused to him about these productions and then proceeded to follow his paper's policy by publishing a negative critique of them.

Aleksandr Blok was born in 1880 and was at the height of his celebrity and creative powers when Pasternak, as a teenager, first read his work. The importance of this revelation can be gauged from the generous account of it in the *Autobiographical Essay*. Of all contemporary poets, Blok had the greatest charisma and most strikingly perpetuated the literary 'myth' of Petersburg established in the previous century. Pasternak could not recall what it was that he first read by Blok – the poems 'Darkened pale-green nursery...' (1904) or 'Pussy Willow' (1906), or something else on an urban, revolutionary theme, but he evidently first discovered Blok at about the age of sixteen. By that time Petersburg was already an independent reality for him which enriched, and was subsequently itself enriched by, his reading of Blok's cycles such as 'The

City' and 'The Terrible World'. These verses presented not merely a haunting cityscape, they contained also 'an absorbing display of a remarkable inner world' (II, 17; *VP*, 430). Blok's poetry was a model of what Pasternak later identified as a form of 'realism', incorporating a physically observed reality which at the same time reflected a poetic psychological landscape.

Recalling the quality of his initial impressions of Blok's work, Pasternak later cited examples which had particularly struck him: 'Deception', 'The Last Day', 'Legend', 'The Meeting', 'The Stranger', and so on.[12] These were not products of Blok's early, bright prophetic phase; they registered darker aspects of the Russian 'ville tentaculaire' whose maladies and neuroses figured in the work of Gogol and Dostoevsky. Blok's celebration of urban vice and misadventure perhaps held a special fascination for Pasternak, whose faintly morbid awareness of women's suffering had been jolted in childhood by scenes observed near Oruzheiny Lane, and later by the 'naked ranks and serried suffering' of a troupe of 'Dahomey amazons' – forty-eight horsewomen from modern Benin who put on a display in Moscow's Zoological Gardens in April 1901 as part of a current vogue for exotic circus-style entertainments (II, 204; *VP*, 193).[13] But aside from such details, it was Blok's Petersburg as a whole which for Pasternak became 'the main hero of his story and the central character of his biography':

It seemed as if the page was covered not by verses about wind, puddles, street-lamps and stars, but the street-lamps and puddles themselves were chasing their wind-blown ripples across the pages of the journal.   (II, 15; *VP*, 428)

Pasternak's youth coincided with the flowering of Russian Symbolist culture in all its varieties. Although primarily a literary movement, it had musical ramifications in the cult of Wagner. Scriabin too, with his music and heaven-storming artistic philosophy, was increasingly becoming a cult figure for contemporaries, and several Symbolist poets associated with him, including Balmont, Bryusov, Baltrušaitis and Vyacheslav Ivanov, addressed verse to him or wrote about him. Dialogue between artistic genres was also maintained, for example, in the painting and musical compositions of Čiurlionis, and in the artist Vasilii Milioti's graphic 'symphonies' illustrating the music of various composers. The specifically literary horizon of Symbolism embraced not just native figures such as Blok, Bryusov, Bely, and others, but European figures, among them Friedrich Nietzsche, Oscar Wilde, Stefan George, Emil Verhaeren, and the French *symbolistes*. Scandinavian and Polish theatre also enjoyed considerable vogue in Russia, and in an account of his 'intoxication with the newest literature' Pasternak mentioned two other figures who excited his special enthusiasm – Knut Hamsun and Stanisław Przybyszewski.[14]

Of Hamsun's books accessible to the Russian reader, Pasternak probably read and was most impressed by *Hunger* (1890), *Mysteries* (1892) and *Pan* (1894) with their sometimes Dostoevskian psychological explorations and challenge to the traditional novel's social preoccupations. He might also have seen Hamsun's *Drama of Life* at the Moscow Art Theatre in 1907. Przybyszewski was a Nietzschean, and his aesthetic programme of 'art – and life – for art's sake' was also redolent of the Russian Symbolist Bryusov. Some of Przybyszewski's German writings could have been read by Pasternak in the original, but his contributions to the 'Young Poland', or 'Moderna', movement also enjoyed renown in Russia, where a complete translated edition of his works appeared in the late 1900s. Pasternak may also have seen or heard about productions of his tormented psychological dramas at Moscow theatres – *The Golden Fleece* in 1905, or *For the Sake of Happiness*, *Snow*, and others in the years that followed.[15]

Despite this rich diet of reading and other artistic experiences, until the age of nineteen Pasternak's heart remained set on a composer's career. Indeed, he 'could not imagine a life outside music' (II, 208; *VP*, 196). His studies under Engel were followed, in 1907, by instruction from a new teacher. Reinhold Glière was already making a name for himself both as composer and teacher. (From 1902 to 1904 he was the young Sergei Prokofiev's first music instructor.) Unlike Engel, Glière was on the staff of Moscow Conservatoire and he was thus entitled to tutor Pasternak and present him as an external candidate for the Conservatoire examinations. It was anticipated that Boris could thus eventually graduate in music in 1911. Under Glière Pasternak advanced his studies of form and counterpoint and by the age of eighteen had completed the Conservatoire composition course apart from orchestration. Like his schooling, his Conservatoire studies are virtually unmentioned in his autobiographies and little is known of this episode. Evidently, he was sufficiently established among musicians to make friends with some of the more outstanding Conservatoire pupils, including such fine pianists and composers as Samuil Feinberg and Isai Dobrovein. These friendships were to last for many years. Until his emigration Dobrovein in particular remained on good terms with all the Pasternaks and was a frequent visitor. Both he and Glière appeared at several of the intellectual gatherings which Pasternak attended during his student years.[16]

Details of the expert verdicts on Pasternak's talent are not available, but certainly until the end of 1909 everything seemed to favour his successful career in music. The prospect delighted both him and his parents, his mother in particular, who had resumed concert activity in 1907 and was pleased that Boris was to follow her own profession.

In the summer of 1908 Pasternak had completed his schooling at the Fifth Classical High School and he planned to study music intensively but on a part-time basis while attending Moscow University. Jewish holders of a school class medal qualified for university entrance and overcame the restriction permitting them only three per cent of the available places. Moreover, unless engaged in university study, a Jew upon coming of age could risk losing his entitlement to reside in Moscow and could be liable for immediate army conscription. Therefore, when the academic year began in autumn of 1908, Pasternak signed on at the Moscow University Faculty of Law. His father before him had pursued this study as an easy option that allowed time for artistic activities and Boris may well have followed his advice on choice of subject.[17]

Pasternak's baptism of fire as a composer was planned for early 1909, when he was to show himself to Scriabin. The latter had been abroad since 1904, and now on his forthcoming triumphant return to Russia he was to present some major new compositions, his Third Symphony, the *Poème de l'Extase* and the Fifth Piano Sonata. Of particular interest was the *Poème de l'Extase* which was scored for enormous orchestral forces and marking a significant advance in Scriabin's development.[18] Its completion had been preceded by publication in Geneva in 1906 of Scriabin's Russian verse text, *Poem of Ecstasy* (*Poema ekstaza*), a literary companion piece to the orchestral work and evoking the same mystic dionysian creative frenzy. The Fifth Sonata was a spark from the same anvil; its manuscript carried an epigraph from the verse poem, cited in both Russian and French:

> Je vous appelle à la vie, ô forces mystérieuses!
> Noyées dans les obscures profondeurs
> De l'esprit créateur, craintives
> Ébauches de la vie, à vous j'apporte l'audace.[19]
>
> (I summon you to life, o mysterious forces!
> Drowned in the obscure depths

Of the creator-spirit, timorous
Flickerings of life, to you I bring boldness.)

After two performances of the *Poème de l'Extase* in Petersburg and the Sonata's première in the second half of January, Scriabin came on to Moscow on 4 February together with his new consort Tatyana Schloezer, and lodged in an apartment on Glazovsky Lane (now Lunacharsky Street) as guest of the conductor Koussevitsky. Shortly after arriving he took up with the Pasternaks again, and some results of this were Leonid's new portrait sketches of him. For his part, Aleksandr Pasternak noted that Scriabin 'struck our parents, and us too, as somehow different – new, or at least renewed. Probably he showed the clear signs of his newly established artistic and philosophical, theosophic thoughts, new views on the art of the future and a clear picture of his own future works.'[20]

The first of two concerts of Scriabin's works was fixed for Saturday 21 February in the Large Hall of the Conservatoire, and the programme conducted by Emil Kuper (or Cooper – he was of English origin) was to consist of the Third Symphony, the Fifth Sonata played by the composer, and the *Poème de l'Extase*. Rehearsals began on Scriabin's arrival. Together with his mother and brother and Sergei Durylin, who was his regular concert companion, Pasternak attended all of them. Other musicians and visitors were also present and their numbers increased each day as news spread of a forthcoming spectacular event. Rehearsals were held in the mornings and afternoons in a hall transfixed by slanting shafts of winter sunlight which fell on the large oval portraits of Russian composers lining the side-walls. And 'in those constantly moving beams', Aleksandr Pasternak recalled, 'there danced sparkles of illuminated dust. The play of light and those sunbeams belonged both to the music and to the hall.'[21] As rehearsals proceeded, the interruptions became rarer and from the chaotic fragments a musical edifice was erected which exceeded even Scriabin's expectations. To Yulii Engel's remark that this was 'the end of music', Pasternak's rejoinder was, 'This is its beginning', and he described the work in a vivid episode of his autobiographical *Safe Conduct*:

The music was let loose. Multi-coloured, boundlessly shattering, and multiplying like lightning, it teemed and leaped across the platform. It was set in tune and rushed with feverish haste towards concord. And suddenly rising to a roar of unprecedented unanimity, with a whirlwind raging in the bass, it would break off, dying away entirely and flattening out along the footlights.

This was man's first settlement in those worlds discovered by Wagner for fantasies and mastodons. And on this land was erected a quite unfantastical lyrical dwelling-place, equal in material to the entire universe which had been ground down to make its bricks. Over the wattle fence of this symphony glowed the sun of Van Gogh. Its window-sills were covered with the dusty archive of Chopin. Yet the inhabitants did not poke around in this dust, but with their whole being fulfilled their forerunner's brightest behests.

(II, 207–8; VP, 195–6)

That music brought tears to Pasternak's eyes, and from the rehearsals and première performances in Moscow (the concert was repeated on 8 March) it became indelibly etched on his memory. In later years he found the title of the *Poème de l'Extase* pretentious and ill-matched to the music's profundity. Yet it accurately reflected the spirit of the Symbolist epoch and that native Russian 'striving for the superlative' which Pasternak identified as typical of Scriabin.[22]

An arrangement was made for Pasternak to present himself to Scriabin and show him some of his compositions. His impressions of that occasion had all the incisive clarity of stage-fright, and many years later he gave a detailed account of the tramcar ride along the Arbat, the sensations in each muscle of his face, details of his host and hostess and of the sunlight, samovar steam and cigar smoke in their drawing-room. Confidence apparently returned slightly as he settled down to play a handful of his pieces (probably including some of the items that have come down to us) and Scriabin was no doubt flattered to detect Pasternak's appropriation of his own manner. As he listened he made a characteristic 'elevated' response: 'He raised his hand, then his eyebrows, and finally standing up with a beam that gently ebbed and flowed with the melodic inflections of the music, he floated towards me down its rhythmic perspective' (II, 209–10; *VP*, 197–8).

Scriabin was more than politely complimentary about what he saw to be a genuine talent. Then, as he discussed his impressions in more detail, he sat down at the instrument and reproduced a phrase of Pasternak's – faultlessly but transposed into another key. If he was not already aware of it, Pasternak was probably astounded to find that Scriabin shared his own lack of perfect pitch. And in the same instant he evidently made a private wager with himself: if Scriabin were to reply 'Why, Borya, even I do not have it', this would be a sign that Boris was not imposing himself and could in some way hold his own in the practice of music. But any reference to Wagner or Tchaikovsky (a composer Scriabin detested) and to the countless piano-tuners with perfect pitch would be an implicit admission of Scriabin's non-exclusivity and, more importantly, a sign that Pasternak was not destined for a life in music. Alas, Scriabin gave the second kind of answer, and Pasternak interpreted this as fate's signal that he was not one of music's chosen. From that moment he evidently began suppressing the idea that music should be his life's profession.[23]

Such was the setting and motivation for abandoning music as described in *Safe Conduct*. Lack of perfect pitch in itself was not a fatal flaw. Although most professional musicians, including Pasternak's mother, possessed it, the examples of Scriabin, Wagner, Mussorgsky, Borodin and Cui might well have convinced him that it was a dispensable asset. Nevertheless, the opinions of their scientist family friend Professor Samoilov about the close statistical links between musical genius and absolute pitch had already caused Pasternak considerable upset when he was trying to weigh up his musical prospects, and he took a fatalistic view of his defect, seeing it as a humiliation and 'evidence that my music was unpleasing to fate and to heaven' (II, 12; *VP*, 424). Staking everything on the chance of Scriabin's reply was merely a sign of Pasternak's 'preference for the hazards of divination to the eloquence of actual facts' (II, 210; *VP*, 198). This belief in portents and predestination was a childhood legacy of which he never totally rid himself; had he not received a sign from fate just then, he might well have sought it elsewhere, for as he later admitted to his friend Shura Shtikh, 'the absence of perfect pitch was only an expedient argument'.[24]

In fact, a fancifully random motivation for Pasternak's decision disguised more substantial, well-founded doubts about his musical future. External evidence as well as Pasternak's later *Autobiographical Essay* points to a deficient piano technique and poor fluency in reading music as serious grounds for abandoning music as a profession. All this was the sad result of neglected piano study and overindulgence in improvising, and it undermined any hopes of ultimate success as a pianist-composer – or even as a composer *for* the piano. But until 1909 Pasternak had never revealed his doubts:

Nobody knew my secret trouble, and had I talked of it to anyone, nobody would have believed me. Although my composing had progressed successfully, I was still helpless on the practical side [. . .] And this cleft between a new musical idea of uninhibited complexity and its deficient technical support turned a gift of nature that could have been a source of joy into the subject of constant torment, which I was finally unable to bear.   (II, 11; *VP*, 423–4)

Yet despite these defects, Pasternak's promise as composer was apparent enough to others as well as Scriabin. Even in the 1930s the eminent pianist Genrikh Neigauz (Heinrich Neuhaus) tried persuading Pasternak to let him play his compositions in public. One wonders, indeed, why he might not have been content with such directly creative (rather than interpretative) musicianship. The reason maybe lay in the character of his enthusiasm for music and for Scriabin, and it reflected deep-rooted psychological traits that revealed themselves several times in Pasternak.

Pasternak's attitude to music was largely shaped by his initial desire to emulate Scriabin, and it carried traces of Scriabin's own vanity and craving for the absolute, tolerating no half-measures or compromise. As Pasternak himself wrote, 'music was a cult, that is, the destructive point at which everything in me that was most superstitious and self-abnegating was focussed' (II, 208; *VP*, 196). The realisation of his professional shortcomings which dawned on him at the age of nineteen might in others have led to suicide. Pasternak decided not to kill himself but instead to throttle his musical urge, which he later described as 'a direct act of amputation, cutting off the most vital part of my existence'.[25]

Revelations by Pasternak's brother throw further light on the character features underlying his decision to abandon music. Temperament and talent brought Pasternak success in almost everything he undertook in his youth and 'confirmed in him a strong faith in his own powers, in his abilities, and in his destiny'. He was used to leading or coming first in any game or competition. But the habit of success encouraged his vanity and made him a poor loser. Whenever frustrated, his reaction was not revolt or anger, but abject silence and a refusal ever to pursue or even mention that particular activity again. Family and friends eventually got used to his sullen bouts concealing an injured self-esteem. Among the topics which became unmentionable during his youth were the pursuit of philately, a game of 'Battle at Sea', and aping the Berlin dialect when in Germany. A propos of Boris' accident in 1903 (after his vainglorious insistence on riding bareback), Aleksandr Pasternak noted that from childhood his brother 'had a remarkable, unbridled passion for mastering things that were obviously beyond his powers, or else quite out of keeping with his ideas and character'.[26] These characteristics all persisted even in later life. Although Pasternak did not attempt to present his life as a sequence of infallible choices, his autobiographies several times drew a veil over episodes and personalities when his interest in them had been exhausted or disappointed.

In the case of music Pasternak had quite justly believed in his talent, and neither in real life nor in his autobiographical account could he gainsay what had been successfully cultivated over several years. The personal impact and influence of Scriabin in particular were not readily annulled, and it was many years before Pasternak achieved critical detachment from the idol of his youth. When he left Scriabin's residence on that February evening of 1909, he experienced a feeling that 'something was tearing and trying to free itself. Something was weeping. Something was exulting' (II, 211; *VP*, 199). But he made no mention to Scriabin of abandoning music and in fact carefully heeded the composer's advice about his future. Scriabin warned him – too late – against excessive improvising, and counselled him when, why, and how to compose:

As models of the simplicity one should always strive for he cited his own new sonatas, notorious for their brain-racking difficulty. He cited examples of reprehensible complexity from the most banal song literature.

(II, 210; *VP*, 198)

(When writing *Safe Conduct* Pasternak's memory was perhaps somewhat hazy: in February 1909 there was only *one* sonata that was *new* – the Fifth – and despite its formidable technical difficulty, the work had a clearcut structural design.)

Pasternak's final conversation with Scriabin touched on other topics, including his future education. Following his own penchant, Scriabin urged him to give up law and take up the study of philosophy. The suggestion was not altogether misplaced: Pasternak's tendency to philosophise had led him already in 1907 to sign a letter to his parents with the name 'Baruch Spinoza'. So Scriabin's advice fell on fertile ground. No doubt, too, Scriabin discerned a rapport between his own ideas and the school of thought represented at Moscow University by his now deceased friend and admirer Professor Sergei Trubetskoi, who until 1905 had been head of the philosophy department. (The wife of another philosophy don, Professor Grushka, was owner of the house in which Scriabin was to live his last years in Moscow.) Pasternak accordingly transferred to the Faculty of History and Philology under whose aegis philosophy was taught. Academic philosophy thus became his main pursuit at Moscow University in 1909, and the way was prepared for his life to follow a new course.[27]

Pasternak was often to be tormented by a yearning for the life of a composer. But his resolve was firm and he was later capable of rationalising the decision both to himself and to others. In 1915 he told Shura Shtikh: 'It was important for me to give up music: I now realise how I would have constricted myself had I stayed with it.' Probably this was another issue over which Pasternak could not bear to lose face, and he displayed the same jaunty self-assurance when discussing the topic with members of the family. Many years later, in late 1929, he wrote to his parents telling them of his recent meeting with Prokofiev and offering some thoughts on his own abandonment of music. 'All the dots,' he wrote, explaining the inconclusive end of his account, 'are because it would take a long time to tell. But there is no deep significance or sorrow behind them. I did splendidly to give it up. I would have been a pianist and not a natural diamond. Had I not given it up, I would now be a homeless cripple . . .'[28]

But the gates to a musical future did not close irrevocably in 1909. As Pasternak told his student friend Konstantin Loks, his change of course was an exercise of youth's privilege, 'when one makes decisions about one's fate then cancels them, still sure of the possibility of restoring them'.[29] Even had he so wished, he would have found it hard to isolate himself from the sound of music. His two sisters were learning the piano, his brother was an ardent music-lover, and his mother had in 1907 resumed public playing and practised at home for her recitals and chamber music concerts. And Pasternak still remained friends with Feinberg and Dobrovein, who themselves showed the indelible mark of Scriabin on their compositions.[30] In such company Pasternak could not present his last encounter with Scriabin as anything but a triumph and he made no immediate mention of a ripening resolve to abandon music. Indeed, he continued his custom of many years and for a while continued to compose and play. Exactly when he voiced his doubts and announced his change of heart is uncertain. The news evidently caused shock and consternation to his family, but perhaps parental exhortations helped delay implementation of his decision, for despite his later account in *Safe Conduct*, there is evidence that he continued serious musical pursuits until the summer of 1909.

Starting in 1907, the Pasternaks spent three successive summer holidays at Raiki, an estate situated near Fryazino, north of Moscow, and reached from Shchelkovo station on the Yaroslavl railway line. Raiki belonged to a well-known sportsman and horse-owner, N. V. Putyata, and its array of white villas was set in pleasant parkland with a view over the River Klyazma to the village of Gorodishche. The Pasternaks' dacha (now a Ministry of Foreign Affairs sanatorium) had large rooms,

14 Leonid Pasternak: drawing of Boris at the piano (April 1909)

regency furniture and several console mirrors that reflected the candle-light. For part of the summer of 1907, the Pasternak parents were away on a trip to Holland, Belgium and England. Matriarchy was maintained in the interlude by Rozaliya's mother Berta Samoilovna, assisted by the Fräulein and nanny, while Boris acted as his father's secretary, forwarding and handling his mail.

Several letters from Boris to his parents convey a fairly full picture of the company and activities at Raiki. Apart from unidentified names such as Timkovsky, Nerses, Panov-Rubtsov and Ginzburg, there are mentions of time spent with the neurologist Professor Samoilov and his wife and their children Lyova and Alya. Samoilov's wife was a close relative of some other guests at Raiki, the wealthy American-Swiss contractor Aleksandr Bari and his wife and their children. (One daughter was a pupil of Leonid's.) Also mentioned in Boris' letters was Aleksandr Ivanovich Ugrimov, married to a daughter of the advocate Garkavi; their children Aleksandr and Vera were slightly younger than Josephine and Lydia Pasternak. (The Ugrimovs had no special role to play in Pasternak's life at this stage but they were important in that their family and household served as partial models for the Gromekos, adoptive parents of the central hero of *Doctor Zhivago*. Ugrimov was of a noble and wealthy family, a professor of agriculture and vice-president of the Moscow Agricultural Society. He and his wife Natalya Vasilyevna and family lived in a house at the corner of Sivtsev Vrazhek and Plotnikov Lane. The site of their home, their cultural ambiance and various other details passed recognisably into Pasternak's novel.)[31] A further guest at Raiki in 1907 was Boris' second cousin Fyodor or Friedrich (Fedya), the son of Karl Evgenyevich Pasternak. Photographs also show that the Margulius family came to visit from Petersburg, and some of Boris' school friends paid visits to Raiki; other friends holidaying nearby were the family of the Pasternaks' physician, Dr Lev Grigoryevich Levin. Among the summer's attractions mentioned in Pasternak's correspondence with his parents in 1907 were group outings to Kozhino by boat, and to the so-called Bear Lakes (Medvezhi Ozera), as well as a celebration with fireworks on the nameday of a local woman artist, Olga Davydova.[32]

The following summer of 1908, Raiki echoed to the sound of Rozaliya Pasternak's music-making, sometimes together with the violinist Aleksandr Mogilevsky who occupied one of the neighbouring villas. (That autumn, on 3 November, they gave a highly-acclaimed duo recital in the Small Hall of the Noble Assembly.)[33] Boris himself spent only a short time at the end of summer 1908 in Raiki. He had complained the previous year of a lack of kindred spirits among the dacha community, and he stayed on alone in the Myasnitskaya flat. Having just finished school, he felt independent and preferred his own choice of friends and entertainment. But Summer 1909 again saw all the Pasternaks in residence at Raiki, apart from Leonid who spent part of the time in Vienna and Italy.

The estate of Raiki was the setting for Pasternak's last serious bout of musical compostion early in the summer of 1909. The memory of an excited inspiration that produced a complete sonata for painoforte was later captured in the vivid impressionistic imagery of a poem titled 'The Muse of 1909' (printed at the head of this chapter). According to the date on the manuscript, Pasternak completed his sonata on 27 June. Like earlier pieces it bore the strong imprint of Scriabin and showed how he had absorbed the advice given in February about the best models to follow. Like Scriabin's Fifth Sonata, it was cast in a single continuous movement. It also showed a response to Scriabin's own recent harmonic exploration, making wide use of 'viscous' tritone harmonies and suggesting a harmonic system based not on the traditional interval of a third but on perfect, diminished and augmented fourths. The results were some passages of opaque sonority with intriguingly modern harmonic 'crunches' reminiscent of Scriabin's own later period. Scriabinesque, too, were some of Pasternak's indications for the manner of performance: 'sordo', 'occulto', 'profundo', 'imperativo e fiero'. But the sonata clearly displayed its origins in a mediocre pianist's improvisations. Unlike his model, Pasternak relied too much on facile repeated bass motifs to float a melody, and on sequential passages in lieu of developing a musical argument. All this was the stock-in-trade of the improviser rather than the thoughtful composer, and the resulting work which contained some awkwardly unpianistic episodes lacked both professionalism and the emotional tension which it strove to create. If Pasternak's sonata of 1909 is in fact the best work he could produce at the age of nineteen, one wonders indeed whether he would have scaled the summits of musical achievement.[34]

It is uncertain whether the sonata was Pasternak's very last composition. Nikolai Vilmont's memoirs refer to a 'Ballade in Ninths' which Pasternak played to interested listeners in the early 1920s. From its title this must have been a harmonic and technical curiosity of the sort composed by Scriabin in his opus 67 études of 1912, but there is no further information on the work and its manuscript (if it was ever committed to paper) has been lost. In any event, the sonata of 1909 was Pasternak's last serious gesture towards the musical career he was now forsaking. Thereafter, he tended to avoid meetings with professional musicians, except close friends like Feinberg and Dobrovein, and he usually absented himself from the family 'jour fixe', or when colleagues were invited back after his mother's concerts. Like Tolstoy, though, he never lost his love of music. There is evidence that he continued piano playing in the 1910s and 1920s in letters, photographs and several pictures by his father, as well as in accounts by friends and family. Only later did he become more severe in his abstinence and for some time in the 1930s he avoided touching the piano altogether.[35]

Perhaps Pasternak's gradual escape from the profession of music was assisted during 1909 by Scriabin's absence. Shortly after the Moscow concerts and their February meeting Scriabin departed for Brussels and remained away for the rest of the year. When he took up permanent residence in Moscow in early 1910 he resumed his friendship with the Pasternaks, and with his second wife Tatyana he was a not infrequent visitor. Leonid Pasternak produced several further pictures of him, including a particularly fine pastel of the Moscow première of *Prometheus* on 2 March 1911, with Koussevitsky conducting and the composer as soloist.[36]

But whenever Scriabin came to visit, Boris avoided appearing. He was absent, for instance, from a luncheon still recalled by Josephine Pasternak, at which Leonid Pasternak and Scriabin hotly disputed the legitimacy of combining different art forms – a problem to which Scriabin devoted much attention in his final years and which was already adumbrated in the use of coloured light in *Prometheus*. Pasternak seemingly failed to attend the 1911 performance of *Prometheus*, but he wrote a dismissive letter shortly afterwards to Shura Shtikh:

Nyuta [Shtikh's sister Anna] has started talking about a new musical theory built on [...] the association of sound and colour sensations [...] Can you fathom it? C, for instance, is red! [...] I think, Shura, that you too must share my dislike of such theories which imagine that reflections on art are made more profound by analysing individual 'rich' elements of its material, and which completely lose sight of the fact that [...] the core of art lies not in its creator nor in what is created, but in the supreme method of creativity in general (in its idea).[37]

The whole concept of the *Gesamtkunstwerk* to which Scriabin was aspiring in his last and uncompleted work, the *Preliminary Action* (*Predvaritel'noe deistvie*) for a cosmic mystery, was also in due course rejected by Pasternak as a set of 'ideas revealing in a tired artist the dilettante latent within him [...] a distraction of the soul in a wrongly chosen profession'.[38]

If he could reject Scriabin's later works, it was more difficult for Pasternak to distance himself from the non-musical aspect of Scriabin's legacy. Although Pasternak's eventual enthusiasm for Neo-Kantianism did not reflect Scriabin's philosophical interests, many of the latter's eclectic thoughts on art and history featured in the cultural purview of the Symbolist circles in which Pasternak moved upon entering university. Some of the leading Symbolist poets with whom he came in contact – Balmont, Baltrušaitis and Ivanov – belonged to Scriabin's coterie in 1912–15.[39] Indirectly therefore Pasternak continued imbibing ideas from the same springs as the man whose influence he consciously sought to escape.

It is typical of Pasternak's long-term attempt to rid himself of music's domination and to lay the ghost of Scriabin that *Safe Conduct* made no mention of the composer's later work or of his untimely death in 1915. Although he was then away from home and living in as tutor with the Philipp family on Prechistenka Street, it seems scarcely credible that he failed to attend Scriabin's funeral in April of that year. His parents were among the many mourners, but neither Josephine nor Aleksandr, who were also there, could recall Boris' presence. The literary tributes and obituaries were left by him to others, including the Symbolist elders, and it was almost a year before Pasternak wrote to his parents from the Urals, on 19 March 1916, to tell them of plans for an article on Scriabin and to ask for biographical details about him. But nothing came of this project, and it was decades before he recorded an appraisal of what Scriabin had meant to him, in the *Autobiographical Essay* of 1957.[40]

The Scriabin whom Pasternak always admired was the composer he had known in his youth, the creator of the Third Symphony (or 'Divine Poem'), the *Poème de l'Extase*, and the Third, Fourth and Fifth Sonatas, written mainly between 1897 and 1905. He had little affection for the later innovatory works:

The harmonic summer lightning flashes of *Prometheus* and his last works seem to me to be only evidence of his genius, but not daily food for the soul. I do not require such evidence, because I believed in him without needing proof.

(II, 12; *VP*, 425)

It was left to a fictional character in *Doctor Zhivago* to dismiss finally the cosmic and mystical aspirations of Scriabin's last period of creativity, and to personify a more complex summing-up of his significance. In section 10 of the second chapter there is an unmistakable allusion to the pretentious Apocalyptic libretto which Scriabin composed for his *Preliminary Action*;[41] Nikolai Vedenyapin, Yurii Zhivago's uncle, notes in his diary:

Upset all day because of that stupid Schlesinger woman. She came this morning and sat through till dinner-time and for two solid hours tormented me by reading out that nonsense – a text in verse by Symbolist A for the cosmogonic symphony by composer B with the spirits of the planets, voices of the four elements, and so on and so forth.   (*DZh*, 43)

Despite this dismissal, there seems nevertheless to be a certain parallel between Scriabin's later half-paranoid identification of creative subjectivity with actual divinity and the association in *Doctor Zhivago* of the main hero with the figure of Christ. Scriabin's belief that 'music and death are incompatible, and anyone capable of profound musical expression is immortal', is comparable with Zhivago's view of art and immortality and a conviction that 'art has two preoccupations: it is always meditating upon death and is always thereby creating life' (*DZh*, 91).[42]

Ideas such as these were common currency among the Symbolist generation in Russia. But *Doctor Zhivago* contains specific and also more positive hints of Scriabin in the character of Vedenyapin. The latter is not a musician, but a former priest and a man of ideas, yet just as Scriabin once dominated Pasternak's imagination, so Vedenyapin is the idol of Yurii Zhivago's youth. Both Scriabin and Vedenyapin have the same penchant for philosophical speculation, and the first encounter with Vedenyapin as a thinker occurs on a country estate in summer of 1903 and in a setting similar to that in which Pasternak discovered Scriabin. Like his real-life antecedent, Vedenyapin is 'close to certain writers of the Symbolist school' and believes that 'for centuries man was raised above the beast and borne upwards not by the cudgel but by music' (*DZh*, 42). Later, both Vedenyapin and Scriabin go for several years to Switzerland, and in both cases their return (Vedenyapin in 1917) marks the liberation of their young admirers from their dominant influence.[43] Thus, in an indirect and not immediately obvious way, Pasternak in later life finally came to terms with memories of the artist whom he had worshipped in his youth.

5

Literature, love and creativity

'Enseignement'

I shall teach to you that bliss
Which no caress replaces.
Rule me therefore as you wish.
Mine – the obedient herdsboy's anguish.

And when foul weather with stray tress
Sanctifies fatigue,
Then arise, be resurrected
From any movement now asleep.

And waking tell the deceived echo
To your supposed sadness. More
Wild than laughter the response's sorrow –
For all glib orators a crown.

The instant passed. Obedient hound,
It waits still now you're gone.
Come as a moon to the constellation of your days.
Turn on the axis of their song.

I shall teach to you the ecstasy
That satisfies all thirst.
Do not forsake the morgue erected.
Abide forever with what's past.

৶৶৶৶

Many musicians have hankered after philosophy [...] Yet they have not realised
that one of the postponed tasks of philosophy also involves a revenge against
music. If exacted, this vengeance would have the imprint of lofty nobility. It
would not be a selfish act of spite. Poetry has always loved philosophy. But not
everyone realises that this is not a love of equals. Philosophy is jealous of poetry
and often imagines that music has perpetrated an insult against its divinity. So
one can therefore have revenge on music. This should not be understood
personally. The devastations wrought within the soul by music give no grounds
for indignation. Such displeasure would be base and pusillanimous.

91

But music must be called to order. The 'musicality of the lyric' is a definition which does honour to poetry, but at the same time contributes to a general fund of prejudices which support the illegitimate primacy of music among the arts . . .[1]

It was in these terms that Pasternak once attempted as a student to define the complexion of music, philosophy and poetry which occupied him in the latter half of 1909. Though abandoned as a profession, music left its ineradicable trace and trauma. In some fragments of fiction written during his time at Moscow University, music and musicians cast as *alter ego* figures played a prominent role; a sharp musical sense also shaped both the acoustic profile and the content of his early lyrics. But another important ingredient in Pasternak's early writings was philosophy – not so much the academic discipline pursued at Moscow University as the adventurous theorisings which animated conversations with student friends and the younger literary intelligentsia.

A ready arena for such discussions was the small 'salon' which Pasternak began frequenting in the autumn of 1908. This company, which called itself 'Serdarda', consisted of a dozen or so young poets, musicians and artists, and was a 'tipsy confraternity' (according to Pasternak's later account) which met in the home of Yulian Anisimov in the Razgulyai area of Moscow. In the interior courtyard at 4 Elokhovskaya (now Spartakovskaya) Street stood a traditional old wooden house owned by Yulian's father, Lieutenant-Colonel Anisimov, a retired army engineer. Yulian Anisimov was one year older than Pasternak and possessed a similarly versatile talent. He painted and had studied in France with Matisse; he knew several languages and had a broad knowledge of modern European poetry, some of which he translated. Pasternak was impressed, for example, by his renderings of the German poet Richard Dehmel although much less taken with his original verse; Anisimov 'embodied poetry to a degree that reflected an amateur's enchantment and which made it difficult to be a strong artistic personality' (II, 22–3; *VP*, 436). Anisimov wore a pince-nez and had an aristocratic burr in his speech. His family was well-off, and since he had a weak chest he usually escaped the Moscow winters and travelled abroad. In the autumn and spring evenings of 1908–9, however, his mezzanine apartment under the poplars with its background noise of rook calls was the Serdardans' meeting place. Here he entertained his friends in the 'bohème galante' of his spartan studio full of easels and paint and furnished with nineteenth-century cupboards and a bow-front desk.[2]

Serdarda's activities included verse recitations and readings of prose and translations, sketching and exhibiting, music making, intellectual discussion, and the consumption of wine and endless glasses of tea laced with rum. Pasternak's first entrée to the circle was as a musician, and he improvised musical portraits of various members as they arrived. Another contribution which he made, and later recalled in *Safe Conduct*, was to introduce the poetry of Rilke. This appealed instantly to Anisimov, who began translating it and displayed Rilke's influence in some of his own original verse.[3] The motley assembly described in Pasternak's memoirs also included Arkadii Guryev, a homespun but gifted actor, singer and poet from the Volga, whose clowning and artistic gifts evidently provided regular amusement. Guryev also provided the title 'Serdarda'; an evocative word he had heard in Volga regional dialect, it hinted at the Russian *serdtse*, meaning 'heart', but its precise meaning seems to have been unclear to any members of the gathering.[4] Other characters in attendance whom Pasternak later recalled were the composer Boris Krasin, the visiting Petersburg poet, critic and art expert Sergei Makovsky, and Aleksandr Kozhebatkin, secretary of the 'Musaget' (Musagetes) publishing house and owner of 'Altsiona' (Halcyon) its musical subsidiary.

In addition to the above, Pasternak made several closer associations at Serdarda which played a significant part in his life over the next few years. Sergei Durylin, born in 1881, was the eldest member of the company. Known since 1906 as a publishing poet and belletrist, he later made a distinguished name as a literary and theatrical scholar and author. Deeply religious and with a strong interest in philosophy and patristics, he struck Pasternak even at the time of their first meeting by his 'burning integrity and fanatical conviction'. More importantly, as Pasternak later claimed, 'It was he who enticed me over from music to literature and in his kindness managed to find something worthy of attention in my first experiments' (II, 23; *VP*, 436).[5]

Another early mentor and supporter of Pasternak's talent was Konstantin Loks, an erudite melancholic nobleman from Surazh in Belorussia who was slightly older than Pasternak. He too was a Moscow University student and eventually became a professional literary historian and critic. After the Revolution he held professorships in Bryusov's literary institute and the State Institute of Theatrical Art (GITIS); his later memoirs contain the most detailed known account of Serdarda's membership and activities.[6] Loks began his studies in August 1908 and for some time he and Pasternak knew one another only by sight from the corridors of the University. Their first proper encounter was at a crowded meeting of the Moscow Society of Free Aesthetics in patroness

Margarita Morozova's house on the Vozdvizhenka, when Andrei Bely lectured on 'The Tragedy of Creativity in Dostoevsky'. Loks well recalled their meeting on Monday, 1 November 1910: 'At that moment I saw only the eyes of the man standing next to me. They had a kind of joyous and ecstatic freshness, something wild, childish and exultant.'[7]

In and around Serdarda there were other figures with whom Pasternak associated, but who for various reasons were virtually unmentioned in his autobiographies. Vera Stanevich was an educated and forceful character with a penchant for erotic mysticism. 'A sort of amazon and gentleman-killer' was how Loks described her. Apparently she was infatuated with Andrei Bely, who mockingly referred to her as '*Sh*tane-vich' (from *shtany*, meaning 'trousers'). Eventually, however, she turned her attention to Yulian Anisimov and married him in the autumn of 1911. For some time Loks lodged with them at their Molchanovka apartment which in 1912 became the new Serdarda headquarters. For a short time prior to that the circle had gathered at some bachelor quarters which Anisimov maintained in Maly Tolstovsky Lane.

The Serdardans also met together outside Anisimov's home. Not infrequently Pasternak went with Loks, Anisimov and Stanevich to visit the poet Boris Sadovskoi, who lived in seedy furnished accommodation on the corner of the Arbat and Kaloshin Lane. Unlike most of their circle, Sadovskoi was no supporter of Symbolist 'questings' and maintained that 'everything has been found already. In the country of Pushkin and Fet it has been established once and for all what poetry is.' Nor did Sadovskoi appreciate hearing Pasternak recite some of his earliest poetic attempts, probably some time in 1910. Pasternak took offence at the negative reaction and promptly left, which may partly explain why Sadovskoi merited no more than a mention in his autobiographies. It was Loks who probably first perceived what others in Anisimov's circle had missed: 'They did not suspect that there before them was a great poet, and meanwhile treated him as an intriguing curiosity without ascribing any serious importance to him'. And Loks himself was not always certain about Pasternak's first verses: 'So unlike the dominant style of the epoch, they lay quite outside the usual contemporary canon that was always taken for granted.'[8]

As Loks eventually realised, Pasternak's poetic emergence was one of the general signs of the end of Symbolism and the start of a new era. Yet for the time being, although associating with a few quasi-classical figures such as Sadovskoi and Khodasevich, Pasternak was surrounded mainly by practitioners and adherents of Symbolist culture. Apart from Serdarda, he attended meetings of the Society of Free Aesthetics, which had links with Bryusov's 'Skorpion' Symbolist publishing house, and he was an active participant in 'something like an academy' which formed around the Musaget publishing concern when it opened in the autumn of 1909. A special attraction of the Musaget gatherings was their Germanic bias: topics such as the history of German Romanticism and the aesthetics of Goethe and Wagner were discussed and debated there, as well as more general problems of Russian lyric verse, Baudelaire and French Symbolism, pre-Socratic philosophy, and so forth. Under the aegis of Musaget more specialised discussion groups were also created. Pasternak regularly attended a philosophical circle led by Fyodor Stepun (a disciple of Rickert's Neo-Kantianism), and a 'Circle for the Investigation of Problems of Aesthetic Culture and Symbolism in Art' which was run by the Symbolist poet Ellis. In 1913 Pasternak himself was to deliver a paper to this group which met in the studio of sculptor Konstantin Krakht.[9]

Through Musaget and other circles Pasternak brushed shoulders with some leading figures of Russian Symbolism. Apart from those already mentioned, these included the poets Vyacheslav Ivanov, Valerii Bryusov, Lithuanian-born Jurgis Baltrušaitis, the critic and philosopher Emilii Medtner who was brother of the composer and better known under his pen name of 'Volfing', Grigorii Rachinsky who was a philosopher and chairman of the Society of Free Aesthetics, the literary scholar Vladimir Shenrok, and Aleksei Petrovsky who was an erudite literary scholar and translator.[10] But the brightest star in the Musaget constellation was Andrei Bely. Bely had enthralled Pasternak as a schoolboy and went on to reveal his 'profundity and charm' both in their personal dealings and in his novels *The Silver Dove (Serebryanyi golub')* (1909) and *Petersburg (Peterburg)* (1912–13). Like Scriabin, Bely was an example of eccentric brilliance, bearing 'all the hallmarks of genius' and an 'excess of inspiration', typical of the Symbolist cultural hothouse. In a broad-ranging quest to establish a scholastic and philosophical basis for the movement, Bely's current enthusiasm was the rhythmic analysis of lyric verse in what proved to be a pioneering of statistical and Formalist critical methods. Within the Musaget academy he directed a 'rhythmic seminar' for the study of Russian classical iambics.[11] To Pasternak, however, this appeared to have little connection with actual creativity and he attended only a few times before dropping out, convinced, in his own words, that 'verbal music is not an acoustic phenomenon and consists not in the euphony of vowels and consonants on their own, but in the relationship of the sound of speech to its meaning' (II, 25; *VP*, 438).

Although shaped mainly by academic and literary pursuits, Pasternak's life as a student in the years 1908–13 was marked also by some notable family and personal events. A telling passage in his *Autobiographical Essay* concerned the death of Tolstoy at Astapovo in November 1910. When his father was summoned to the scene by telegram, Pasternak went with him, travelling by the night train from Paveletsky Station. Next day Leonid Pasternak produced his final pictures of Tolstoy laid out on his deathbed in the Astapovo station-master's cottage. What they saw there was a small wrinkled figure lying on a bed surrounded by fir saplings and lit by the setting sun, as in Leonid Pasternak's picture – a strange contrast with Tolstoy's living spiritual presence which could still be sensed in the room, towering like Mount Elbrus.[12]

Tolstoy's death was linked with another sad milestone in the Pasternak family history. One year later, on 10 November 1911, Rozaliya Pasternak, who now suffered from a permanent heart condition, gave her last important public concert. This was at a Tolstoy memorial celebration organised by Koussevitsky in the Large Hall of the Conservatoire. Following a programme of literary readings, some of Tolstoy's favourite music was played, including the Tchaikovsky trio he had first heard at the Pasternaks' in 1894.[13] That same year of 1911 they were robbed of two other close friends: the historian Klyuchevsky, who had been a visiting lecturer at the School of Painting and a regular family guest, and the artist Valentin Serov, whose death was a sad blow for Leonid Pasternak, his colleague and comrade of many years' standing.[14]

Symptomatically, it was cultural events such as these and his own artistic and intellectual involvements which, much more than current social issues, dominated Pasternak's life and later figured in his auto-biographies and fiction set in that period. Although after 1905 some radicals were roused to increased political activity, many of the intelligentsia sought a solution in some form of individual spiritual regeneration, or inward renewal, as preconditions for social reform. The focus for this tendency was the 'Landmarks' (*Vekhi*) intellectual group, which in 1909 published a widely discussed collection of articles affirming the primacy of spiritual values and opposing the nihilistic strain in Russian thought. 'Landmarks' philosophy had a strong following in Symbolist circles, and in Pasternak's view the apoliticism which was its corollary reflected the general state of the Empire:

It was an apoliticism highly typical of the [...] order, because it was a fading reign which by its doomed nature amplified all the fatal features of a hereditary system. Finally, in order to be historically exact, it was the apoliticism of a feigned simplicity in which two waves met and combined – a wave of natural democratisation that in 1905 permeated society and gripped it ever increasingly, and a wave of artificial simplification which originated demagogically from above. Simple Simon was in fashion, and it was not society but the Empire itself which chattered over English-style sandwiches, wore fancy dress in everyday life and posed as an illiterate and stupid peasant woman.[15]

This cavalier and clever dismissal was part of the political innocence Pasternak cultivated in the 1920s, but its very schematism suggests the degree of his earlier uninvolvement in public issues. His university reminiscences, for instance, make no mention of the protest and resignation of several eminent professors and widespread student unrest in 1910–11 at the repressive policies of the Ministry of Education, all of which he must have witnessed.

Russian universities of Pasternak's day differed in many respects from their Western counterparts. Although university autonomy was restored in 1905, there had been no rescindment of a charter of 1884 which deprived students of the right to any corporate activities, including even innocent clubs and cultural societies. Consequently, Pasternak's main contacts and friendships formed and flourished extramurally. But he was still partly governed by student caste instinct and by behaviour patterns which were more narrowly channelled than in universities abroad. Manual work, for example, was almost excluded as a means of income while studying (and sports were even regarded by some as a desecration of the scholastic temple). At the turn of the century, half of Moscow University's 4,000 students had no adequate means of support and their tuition fees were waived; less than 1,000 received a very modest stipend. The tradition was to live in cheap and often squalid lodgings and to earn a frugal existence by tutoring or occasional office work. Some of Pasternak's friends, such as Dmitrii Samarin, had private means and were unaffected. But others, like Durylin who lived on the outskirts of town and had an elderly mother and aunt to support, lived in extreme poverty.[16]

Pasternak's own circumstances were fairly comfortable and in his first few years as a student he lived at home. But a sense of duty learned from his father, as well as his own vanity, emotional privacy and self-sufficiency made him anxious not to exploit his parents' generosity. To avoid taking money from his parents he thus followed tradition and gave private lessons 'for a mere pittance'. His pupils were either children receiving their education at home or, more commonly, schoolchildren who had 'countenances saffron-bright with unintelligence' and had been kept back and needed remedial coaching. Another, more grateful task he shared with fellow undergraduates in cheap furnished rooms was to help supervise the work of various mature students – clerks, workers, butlers and postmen – all anxious to improve their lot in life and prepared to study in order to do so.[17] With Pasternak however, personal reasons weighed more than economic necessity in pursuing this semi-independence. Even during the summer holidays in 1908 and after, when the rest of the family and several friends were away, he preferred to stay on in the Myasnitskaya apartment at his own expense. And 'the illusion of independence was achieved by such moderation in eating that there was hunger too, on top of everything else, and it finally turned night into day in the empty apartment' (II, 214; *VP*, 202).

Pasternak's experience as a tutor began in the spring of 1908, before he left school, and the sense of responsibility which this involved became linked with another aspect of his emotional ripening. It was his pupil, Ida Vysotskaya, who became the first object of his emotional attention. She was the eldest of four daughters in a wealthy local family who lived in a large wooden house between Myasnitskaya and Chudovskoi Lane (now Stopani Street). David Vysotsky and his wife Anna had been friendly with the Pasternaks for several years. He was a tea-trader and art connoisseur who encouraged several modern painters, and he had almost a score of Leonid Pasternak's works displayed in his gallery at the top of the house. Boris and Aleksandr Pasternak were in the same age group as Ida and her sister Elena. Two younger sisters, Revekka (or 'Bébé') and Rakhail – also known as 'Reshka' (or 'Rachel', pronounced as in French) – were friends and near contemporaries of Josephine and Lydia who in 1910 joined them as pupils at Mansbach's Gymnasium.[18]

Boris' first calf-ish attachment to Ida had begun, so he claimed, at the age of fourteen. In his final year at school he was therefore delighted when her parents invited him to help her prepare for the school-leaving examination. Neglecting his own studies (though with no detriment to his own excellent performance), he went regularly to the Vysotskys, where tutorial sessions were a ready pretext for endless conversations with his pupil. However, Ida's doting elderly French governess (a prototype, evidently, for Mademoiselle Fleury in *Doctor Zhivago*) suspected that Pasternak's geometry lessons were 'more Abélardian than

Euclidian' and she attended all their evening sessions and ushered the tutor away at a decorously early hour. Thus no improprieties or confessions ever took place.[19]

When Pasternak entered university, he and Ida continued to visit one another. In later years she told Jacqueline de Proyart something of the content of their conversations and saw them reflected partly in the discussions between Tonya and Yurii Zhivago on such topics as the vulgarity of modern society and its views of sexuality. (It was the age of both Victorian attitudes and the unorthodox 'progressive' ideas of Rozanov, as well as of the cult of Sanin and Peredonov, heroes of two novels by Artsybashev and Sologub that appeared in 1907.) Perhaps some of Pasternak's ideas elaborated in conversation with Ida later found their way also into his story of *Zhenya Luvers' Childhood* and *Safe Conduct*. His relationship with Vysotskaya, however, remained a totally platonic affair, limited to visits, conversations, and various social events and outings. The strange, emotionally taut atmosphere of their walks together in Sokolniki park was later probably reflected in Sergei Spektorsky's similar promenades with Anna Arild in the prose *Story*.[20] But as with his fictional hero, Pasternak's upbringing and natural diffidence tended to stifle any self-revelation.

Both Ida and her parents were aware of his affection for her; they also recognised his talents and were fond of him despite his occasional farouche brusqueness. Ida herself was an engaging companion, and although she failed to appreciate his early poetry she had certain cultural interests. But her feelings never matched the intensity of his and she accepted her parents' view that Boris lacked firm prospects – an agreeable friend maybe, but definitely not a partner for life. Ultimately it is clear that their personalities, tastes and life-styles were ill-matched. At that age he was not entirely at ease in society, and his serious and sometimes abstracted air must have appeared incongruous. It was probably largely for her sake that as a youth and student he attended parties and soirées (some impressions of these occasions were incorporated in early prose fragments and in chapter three of his novel).[21] But without any declarations to precipitate a change in their relations their friendship continued. No doubt she was happy with the status quo, and with his inflamed imagination Boris still clung to hopes and illusions.

A reading of *Safe Conduct* might suggest that Ida Vysotskaya was Pasternak's only real emotional attachment in early manhood. In fact, his attitude to women was multivalent, complicated and complex-ridden. As he stated in his first autobiography:

There is on this earth a so-called elevated attitude towards women [...] a boundless circle of phenomena which in adolescence lead to suicides [...] a circle of mistakes made by the infant imagination, childish perversions, youthful fastings [...] I have been in that circle and tarried there a shamefully long time.

(II, 233; *VP*, 221)

Pasternak's 'elevated attitude towards women' and consequent mis-judgement of their characters probably stemmed from his infantile fantasies and compassion for womankind in general. He never com-pletely overcame this proclivity, and in addition to personally directed affections he was in love with femininity as such and thus with all who personified it. As he later told Raisa Lomonosova, 'I have never experienced not just friendship, but even *attention* without an admixture of love'![22] Pasternak therefore indulged freely in heroine-worship, forming and expressing exaggerated views of individual women as people. The eventual results were self-delusion and disappointment. Some women, such as Akhmatova and Tsvetaeva, were irritated; others (like Ida Vysotskaya and Elena Vinograd) brushed his admiration aside or took it for granted without responding; yet others, to their cost, found themselves almost accidentally wooed and beguiled. Symptomatic of all this was the fact that the rapturous poem, 'Enseignement', printed at the head of this chapter was not dedicated to Ida Vysotskaya but inscribed with the initials of her sister Elena, who seemingly was at one time more sympathetic to Boris. Whether either of the girls read the poem, and how they reacted, is unknown.

During his student years Pasternak had other amorous attachments which went unmentioned in his autobiographies. In the summer of 1909 on a visit to the Shtikh family dacha at Spasskoye he met Elena Vinograd, Shura's second cousin, who was then still a schoolgirl. Although too young to inspire any flare of passion, she appealed to Pasternak enough for him to enquire after and send greetings to her in his letters to Shura. Eventually in 1917 she was the addressee of some of his finest love poetry.[23]

Another recipient of Pasternak's affections in 1910 was his own cousin, Olya Freidenberg. In some ways she was perhaps the most compatible of his early loves. She was dark, neatly attractive and intelligent. They were the same age and had a close friendship based on several family holidays spent together. Their exchange of letters, which lasted over half a century, reached a peak of intensity and frequency in 1910, when their relations came closest to blossoming.

Lacking a gold medal from school, Olya did not enrol at St Petersburg

15 Boris Pasternak on completing
his schooling (1908)

16 Olya Freidenberg
(about 1910)

17 Autograph MS of one of Pasternak's earliest poems, 'Kak bronzovoi zoloi
zharoven'' ('Like bronze ash from braziers')

University. She attended a few lectures at the 'Women's Higher Courses' on an informal basis but disliked the atmosphere and eventually followed her father's example and used the next few years to read and educate herself independently. She sometimes discussed her reading with Boris, and in their letters of spring 1910, for example, they exchanged views on Jacobsen and his novel *Niels Lynne*. In addition, Olya devoted time to assisting her father in his journalistic and bookbinding activities. Unfortunately, like his scientific work these produced poor and irregular income. Mikhail Freidenberg's brilliant inventions were only recognised posthumously; they included an early automatic telephone exchange, and a linotype machine, and in the 1910s he was working on plans for a submarine.[24]

By 1910 Boris was already a familiar guest with the Freidenbergs. His gushing enthusiasm for the splendours of Petersburg and other topics caused amusement to Olya's family and friends, and she was already used to his 'love and tenderness, his exaggerated praise, admiration and his confessions'. But on a visit to Petersburg in early 1910 he was 'excessively attentive and entranced', she recalled, 'although our daily life gave him no pretext for this', and he had followed her around 'like one in love'. In March she paid the Pasternaks a return visit. Her own impression of Boris at the time was that

In everyday respects he was 'not of this world'. He bumped into curb-posts, was absent-minded and wrapped up in himself. His Pasternakian nature emerged in his virgin purity, which he preserved until quite late in life. Perhaps Borya's most distinguishing feature was his rare spiritual nobility.[25]

Olya was one of the first to be initiated into Boris' new literary endeavours. She quickly and correctly perceived how vital this was to him, and she encouraged him despite his disquiet at yet another change of career and her own benign envy of his artistic gifts.[26]

In June 1910 all the Pasternaks apart from Boris went to the Baltic coast for a summer holiday. The family of Yulii Engel already knew the area and especially recommended it after Zhonya's recent bout of malaria and a recurrence of Lydia's pneumonia. The Engels had gone up to the Estonian coast in early summer and they found accommodation for the Pasternaks nearby, at dacha 42 in the little resort of Mereküla. (Its Russian name, Merekyul', was a rendering of the Estonian 'sea village', and the place was described in guide books of the time as a charming group of villas on the wooded shores of the Gulf of Finland, with two churches, a *Kurhaus* and restaurant.) Here the Engels and Pasternaks were also joined by Berta Kofman and Aunt Asya Freidenberg, who came from Petersburg to spend a few days with them. At Mereküla they all enjoyed a traditional family seaside holiday, with cycling and a children's fancy-dress parade for Josephine and Lydia. Boris meanwhile stayed on in the Moscow apartment with occasional trips out to Tarasovka to see Sergei Durylin and a couple of days spent with the Shtikhs at Spasskoye in June. It was Boris' intention to join his family at Mereküla later in July and he sent Olya Freidenberg a pressing invitation to join him on the trip. She at first resisted but eventually came independently and spent a few days with her relatives during Boris' stay there.[27]

Although Boris revealed nothing of his feelings to Olya directly, their time together in Mereküla and afterwards in Petersburg saw an emotional climax in their relations. Olya recalled that their previous light-hearted banter gave way to a new solemnity, and Boris was 'restrained, serious and over-scrupulous in his treatment of me'. Most of the time he had in fact talked, for hours on end and in a dry, abstract and philosophical manner, while she listened in silence. But the two of them were drawn together by a common romantic strain that continued as they journeyed back together to Petersburg, and when Boris stayed on for a few days at the Freidenbergs' he and Olya were 'unable to tear themselves away from one another'.[28]

When he finally went back to Moscow, it was left that Olya should come and see him there in August, and he would later pay another visit to Petersburg. Immediately on arriving home, on 23 July, he wrote to Olya an immense, original love-letter. A fine and complex piece of finished prose, it began with a description of the content and thought behind a poem called 'Turnpikes' ('Zastavy') on which he had started and which was based partly on impressions of Mereküla and their walks. The letter also told of Pasternak's perceptions of the city, the surrounding world of objects, and of the birth of poetry among them.[29] Only towards the end did he mention his feelings for Olya and present his earlier descriptions as the reflection of an intense shared experience:

But you know, there has grown and grown and become clear to me another tormenting feeling for you. When you walked at my side so impassively I could not express it to you. It is some rare closeness, as though we together – you and I – loved one and the same thing which was equally indifferent to us both, almost abandoning us in its unique unadaptedness to the rest of life. I have been telling you about a certain activity that replaces observation, about an experience of life that has become a quality of objects which have left behind the objectivity of life...[30]

Pasternak probably half-suspected that his feeling was unrequited and that he was the victim of an inspired self-deception. 'Probably I shall not quickly get used to being the only one to love and think of all this,' he commented; then, drawing to a close:

Oh, Olya, I have written many, many words here. By this artillery barrage I wanted to defend myself from a misunderstanding that would be painful. Yet you might think differently if I were to say only that everyone has become alien, that I trembled when I saw in the window a scrap of *Petersburg* newspaper, and that I beseech you to write to me, even a postcard (!!!) But rather come to Moscow immediately! Olya, write and tell me whether I may write to you like *this*? And don't be afraid to upset me. If you are different you must say so. After all, I have rather spoken out, and perhaps it is easier for you to write. Perhaps all this has been a confession – a confession that I am in love with Mereküla, with our journey, with the first evening, with Uncle Misha's day (when I asked for your help),* with the Spit,† with Petersburg, with you amidst all this, with the station, with everything that confronted *you and me together* – and here only at the end the full weight of the confession, the whole confession.[31]

This important letter was probably the first of many similar ones Pasternak wrote in his lifetime – similar not in their amorous content, but in that they formed a natural extension of his creative writing. In this example his declaration of love was interwoven with philosophical discourse, reminiscence, self-analysis and description, which combined in a piece of typical Pasternakian prose with many features in common with the belletristic fiction he began writing at about the same time.

Olya's long reply, written two days later, was not the one Pasternak had hoped for as he waited alone in Moscow, in places that were 'specially hateful and alien through their lack of knowledge about you, their lack of relation to you.'[32] Olya's answer conveyed her fear of confirming his own worst suspicions, and her clear awareness of his delusion:

I fear that you are approaching me with some ready mould – never mind what sort – and you want me to fit into it. Oh, what a mistake this is, for, I repeat, whatever idea you may form about me, I shall not live up to it, and some time, somewhere, you will see something jutting out which will not fit into the mould.

Olya Freidenberg also affirmed and confessed her own strength, independence and desire for freedom. Overwhelmed by the flood of his feelings, she pleaded with him to view her more dispassionately:

* Presumably a reference to a day spent with Mikhail Freidenberg.
† The Spit (*Strelka*) – a promontory with esplanade at the eastern end of Petersburg's Vasilyevsky Island.

I have always been alone, and now suddenly you have arisen in front of me and have started talking and require an answer. There must be no mirages – that would be the only piece of stupid vulgarity still missing. But you must get to know me, and then I shall cease to attract you. I know anyway that you are attracted by an 'unfathomed character'. So just you try and fathom it – here I stand before you. And then you'll go away, and I can then get 'distracted' and begin 'generalising'. Jokes apart – I have no fears, but don't you try and embellish me. You mustn't.[33]

For the next three weeks there were further exchanges of letters, although less intense ones than the first two. Olya prevaricated, and meanwhile there was discussion of her possibly coming to Moscow and of Boris' scraping together a Petersburg fare by some hastily organised Latin tuition to a girl from Irkutsk.[34] By mid-August, though, Olya had adopted a more detached view of affairs and peremptorily informed him (as though 'by the way', in a message to be passed to a friend) that she would not be coming to Moscow.

Her retreat and rejection of Boris' advances were a shattering blow to him. On a visit to the Shtikhs at Spasskoye in August he recounted the whole affair to his friend Shura and described plans to take himself in hand in order to avoid further such occurrences. One or two more exchanges with Olya followed in the later summer – curt and barbed messages from her, and an attempt by him to cover his injury in a jaunty account to Aunt Asya of his latest academic undertakings.[35] Thereafter contact between the cousins lapsed for over a year.

Eventually the cousins' long-standing friendship helped to repair their relations, but without any repeat of 1910. When Olya went to Moscow in one of the following winters, Boris had recovered his equilibrium and was his affectionate self again, and he too resumed his visits to the Freidenbergs. Olya ultimately regretted that things ended so prosaically, and she later assessed the affair of the summer of 1910 as follows:

All that happened with Boris and myself during July was a great passion of two people, connected by blood and the spirit, to come close and meet. With me this was a passion of the imagination, but not of the heart. Borya never ceased to be a cousin to me, however warmly and tenderly I loved him [. . .] I could never fall in love with him. And when this appeared in him, I found it difficult [. . .] unpleasant, and – I don't like saying this of him – repulsive, unconsciously of course, even against my own awareness and volition, but somewhere inside, in the darkness of emotions, in my blood. . . I was passionately dedicated to him, but still his cousin.[36]

Olga Freidenberg's emotional independence was probably a barrier to any serious liaisons at the age of twenty, and her later attachments to others were all unhappy, although for different reasons. She never married, and over the years remained close to her mother. Typically after personal failure, Pasternak never publicly recalled this misadventure. Olya was never named and made only a peripheral appearance in his autobiographies. This may have been a protective gesture towards her. (By contrast – and strangely perhaps – the story with Vysotskaya was recounted in *Safe Conduct*; there Ida, who had emigrated by the time of writing, was identified by her initial 'V-' and the climax of their affair in 1912 was presented as a turning point in Pasternak's artistic fate.) But, occurring when it did and in epistolary form, his passion for Olya Freidenberg established a new and powerful link between the agony of unexpressed and unrequited emotion and the mental condition that produced inspired poetry.

From the time of his disaffection with professional music in the spring of 1909, Pasternak's family noticed his increasing distance from them. This was more than a young man's natural desire for independence and suggested there was something he was attempting to conceal. The family were not unused to his bouts of diffidence and silence, but his new and prolonged emotional withdrawal caused puzzlement and sadness, especially to his parents. To his sisters he remained an affectionate elder brother, and he admitted to Aleksandr that his self-imposed detachment pained him and he assured him his love for them all was undiminished. But no explanation was offered, and although the brothers still shared the same room, reading and writing at the same table, there was no observable reason for Boris' secretiveness.[37]

In retrospect, it is clear that all this was a sign of Pasternak's vulnerability at a time when he was seeking to escape from music, evaluate his first literary experiments and rededicate himself. Withdrawal from his family was perhaps unavoidable. As his sister Josephine later commented, 'For Boris art was supreme and he would sacrifice everything for it.' Artistic impulse and commitment thus took precedence over filial affection, and in this respect his order of priorities perhaps differed from his parents' own.

In *Safe Conduct* Pasternak called his first poetic experiments the 'signs of a new immaturity' (II, 219; *VP*, 207). They probably began in the winter of 1909–10 and the results were shown initially to sympathetic outsiders such as Durylin, Loks, Shtikh and Olya Freidenberg. It was only after gaining confidence in his efforts that he showed or recited his first poems to members of the family. The first to be initiated were not his parents (a wise decision: when he eventually read Boris' early verse Leonid Pasternak was sceptical about its worth and neither liked nor understood its modernistic traits). It was Josephine, ten years his junior, with whom Pasternak enjoyed the closest kinship, and she clearly recalls her brother sitting on her bed in the evening and reading his first poems to her, an interruption of the bedtime routine which their mother did not welcome. In 1912, too, when he was studying abroad, it was mainly to his 'dear, pensive Zhozefina' that he wrote letters, detecting some of his own sensitivity in her 'love of conjecturing about colours, freshness, silence and occasional sounds, and about how all these are intertwined in the human soul'.[38]

Pasternak's entry into literature was thus not the confident adoption of a new career that his first musical enthusiasm had been. Nor, unlike his philosophy, did it have any formal academic status. Although aware of his new interests, his parents still hoped that he might yet opt for a musical career. The critic Kornei Chukovsky recalled meeting Leonid Pasternak in 1909 or 1910 at the home of Repin where he learned that Boris was still 'tossing back and forth between poetry and music', and it was unclear to his father whether he would become a poet or a composer.[39]

The summer of 1911 was an eventful time for all the Pasternaks and it marked a new stage in Boris' literary pupation. In a letter he described to Shura Shtikh the 'vivisection' of the School of Painting, which involved extensive rebuilding and the construction of a new gateway. The Pasternaks chose that moment with its inevitable upheaval in order to move house. The removal should have taken place in spring, but it was delayed so as not to disrupt Aleksandr's school-leaving examinations. (For similar reasons to Boris' in 1908, Aleksandr now enrolled to study physics and mathematics at the University, despite his pronounced artistic and architectural skills.)[40] Rozaliya Pasternak with her daughters and servants spent a spring holiday down in Odessa and Boris himself joined them for a week in June. Then, while Leonid Pasternak and the rest of the family rented a dacha at the Black Sea resort of Bolshoi Fontan, Boris and his mother packed up in Moscow and supervised the removal, before themselves travelling to Odessa to rejoin the family.[41]

In the few summer weeks in Moscow Boris saw something of Ida Vysotskaya, who continued to react diffidently to his own intense monologues and finally went abroad with her sister Elena. Absorbed with his literary plans, Pasternak did not relish the prospect of a boring stay in the south. As he told Shura Shtikh in a letter dated 31 July, 'By now I know my own nature: I am terribly lacking in independence. I need some inspiring agent.' Moreover relations with his father were strained, apparently because of his casual approach to his studies and unsociability. In the few days spent with his family at Bolshoi Fontan Boris in fact stayed most of the time closeted upstairs in their seaside dacha. He was evidently busy writing but offered no explanations and finally he made an abrupt departure, leaving the room strewn with scraps of paper. His brother picked up these drafted fragments of verse and prose and presented them to him back in Moscow. Boris was entirely ungrateful and told him to dispose of them as he saw fit; fortunately Aleksandr had the presence of mind to preserve them, and they now form one of the bases of our knowledge of Pasternak's earliest writing.[42]

The Pasternaks' address as of August 1911 was 14 Volkhonka Street, apartment 9. Their new home was on the upper floor of a two-storey house at the corner of Maly Znamensky Lane and the Volkhonka, a main road leading south-west from the Moscow Kremlin. The house itself belonged to the School of Painting; it was part of a distinguished old architectural complex and at various times had housed a number of notable Russian artists. Next door to the Pasternaks' home was the Knyazhii Dvor (Princes Court) Hotel, and on the other side of the house in 1912 the new Museum of Fine Arts was opened. (Aleksandr Pasternak's photographs of this Imperial ceremony still survive.) The windows of the Pasternaks' apartment looked out over the Volkhonka to the Moskva River and the Zamoskvorechye area beyond. In the foreground could be seen part of the vast Temple of Christ Saviour, built to celebrate Russia's delivery from Napoleon, together with the smaller Church of Praise to the Holy Virgin. Family life was thus regularly punctuated by pealing churchbells.[43]

The apartment interior was slightly unusual, forming an enfilade of five interconnecting rooms with double doors along the house facade, and a hallway, dining-room and kitchen that faced back into the courtyard. At the front were various bedrooms and Leonid Pasternak's studio adjoining the music-cum-drawing room. In view of the family's size Boris still had to share a study-bedroom with his brother. Konstantin Loks described it as 'unremarkable, very clean and neat with two small tables, two beds, and a sort of sterilised tedium in the air'.

Loks and Boris' other friends were regular visitors to the Volkhonka apartment, but the irksome lack of privacy caused them eventually to prefer other meeting places – at the University, the Anisimovs', or their favourite stamping ground at the Café Grec on Tverskoi Boulevard.[44] Pasternak now usually turned up to their meetings bringing his latest poems, and Loks recalled often being allowed to take them away to read. This, together with his brother's observations in summer 1911, suggests that prose and verse composition were by then a regular activity. Aleksandr Pasternak later described 1911 as 'the breakthrough year' in which Boris 'reconstructed the whole of his life', and at about the same time Loks came to realise that poetry was for Pasternak 'one of the manifestations of a still unrealised and developing spiritual world . . . not just a happiness, but also a tragedy'.[45]

It was in the company of Loks and the Serdardans, and probably in 1911, that Pasternak met up with Sergei Bobrov. Bobrov had studied at the Moscow School of Painting and was friendly with the modernists Lentulov, Goncharova and Larionov. He also wrote verse, had published since 1908, and was known already as a brilliant young littérateur, 'a freshly hatched Russian Rimbaud' (II, 24; *VP*, 437). Pasternak's dealings with Bobrov were to be crucial in the orchestration of his literary début in 1913. Recalling their first meeting, Bobrov wrote:

Hardly had a few days passed before we became already bosom friends – and on familiar *ty* terms. We walked along the deserted snowy lanes of Moscow [. . .] We loafed around for hours on end, working out and expressing to one another our pet ideas that we had kept concealed [. . .] I constantly kept reciting my own verses to him [. . .] and he listened as though straining his ears.[46]

More than other members of Serdarda, Bobrov was an ambitious, practical professional, and doubtless his dedication and sense of purpose rubbed off on to Pasternak. Partly thanks to him Pasternak's certainty about his choice of a literary future hardened during 1911, and with it the desire to cut loose from his family. Within a year, by the autumn of 1912 on returning from study in Germany, Pasternak was to reinforce his emotional exile from them by moving out and living for most of the next few years in cheap lodgings in the Volkhonka area.

Symbolist convention had from the outset recognised the primacy of the lyric genre, and like his Serdarda confrères, Pasternak at that time usually referred to himself specifically as a 'poet' rather than a writer of prose. Nevertheless, there were artists such as Andrei Bely who made no fundamental distinction between the lyric and prosaic modes; Pasternak himself began writing poetry and prose almost concurrently and inspirational impetus tended to break down rigid distinctions of genre. Not only did his early manuscripts show a free ebb and flow of material between verse and prose, but his bewildering poise between music, philosophy and literature caused a further blurring of boundaries between belletristic and other writing. In his student notebooks and papers, poems and prose sketches were interspersed – sometimes on the same sheet – with lecture and seminar notes; drafts of letters, philosophical essays, phrases of musical notation and academic notes blended with discourses on such subjects as artistic creativity, the Greek concept of immortality, human subjectivity, dreaming and wakefulness, and so forth.[47]

Probably no single motivation prompted Pasternak's first literary endeavours. His inchoate yet deeply felt desire for artistic self-expression was channelled by a successive abandonment of drawing and music, and fertilised both by reading modern literature and by the example of those artists he had met while a student. In addition to Russian Symbolist literature, which seemed to invite impassioned repetition, an identifiable stimulus was the poetry of Rilke. He had first lighted on Rilke's *My Celebration* (*Mir zu Feier*) in his early teens while helping his mother to tidy a bookshelf. He took the volume away to read, and the faded memory of a cloaked figure on a railway platform in 1900 was suddenly linked with the discovery of a unique poetic personality. Soon afterwards Pasternak also read his father's inscribed gift copy of Rilke's *Book of Hours* (*Das Stundenbuch*), a work which fed partly on the poet's Russian experiences and attempted to recreate something akin to Russian religious piety, discovering God not in the transcendental, but substantiated in the objects of this world.[48] According to Vera Stanevich, Pasternak could regularly be seen immersed in this book during his student days, and he introduced Rilke to Serdarda members. Evidently at some point between 1911 and 1913 he also wrote to Rilke but then failed to send the letter;[49] their only direct communication took place in the mid-1920s.

Among the papers containing Pasternak's earliest poetic drafts are several renderings of part or the whole of Rilke's 'Die Stille' ('Stillness'), 'Musik', 'Der Schutzengel' ('The Guardian Angel'), and 'Die Engel' ('The Angels') from *The Book of Images* (*Das Buch der Bilder*) and 'Jetzt reifen schon die roten Berberitzen...' ('Now the red barberry ripens...') from *The Book of Hours*.[50] Of these poems, perhaps 'Musik' with its reference to the anguish of musical artistry had some special meaning for Pasternak:

Was spielst du, Knabe? Siehe deine Seele
verfing sich in den Stäben der Syrinx.

Was lockst du sie? Der Klang ist wie ein Kerker,
darin sie sich versäumt und sich versehnt;
stark ist dein Leben, doch dein Lied ist stärker,
an deine Sehnsucht schluchzend angelehnt...

(What are you playing, boy? See, your soul / Has become ensnared in the rods of the syrinx. // Why do you entice it? The sound is like a prison / in which it slows and languishes; / Strong is your life, but your song is stronger, / sobbing as it leans upon your yearning...)

In a letter of 1959 to Michel Aucouturier, Pasternak recalled his earlier perceptions of Rilke and confessed:

J'avais toujours pensé que, dans mes tentatives originales, dans toute mon activité artistique, je ne faisais que traduire ou diversifier ses motifs, que je n'ajoutais rien à son originalité et que je nageais toujours dans ses eaux.[51]

(I had always imagined that in my original efforts, in the whole of my artistic activity, I was only translating or diversifying his own motifs, I was adding nothing to his originality, and swimming always in his waters.)

This admission had particular relevance to Pasternak's earliest poetic endeavours. In addition to direct translations, some of his first original verse approached Rilke in structure and choice of imagery; one piece bewailed 'how much torment the monk endured to tread more disembodiedly',[52] using self-projections similar to the ones found in *The Book of Hours*. Echoes of Rilke were also to appear in Pasternak's first published books of verse in the early 1910s, and later in the 1920s he produced more Rilke translations and registered a further kinship in the prose of *Safe Conduct*.[53]

Along with traces of Rilke, Pasternak's earliest verse displayed a familiarity with the Symbolist poetic urbanism of Verhaeren, Bryusov and Blok, while Konstantin Loks noted certain traits of the Silver Age impressionist Innokentii Annensky. Yet very little of Pasternak's early verse could be dismissed as palely imitative, whatever else its shortcomings. True, no wholly consistent poetic voice was yet discernible. His philosopher friend Aleksandr (Sasha) Gavronsky commented on his 'excess of content at the expense of form' and proved his point by producing a poetic parody, which upset Pasternak and somewhat clouded their relations.[54] Nevertheless, Pasternak's earliest verse showed mastery of an impressive variety of diction, orchestration, and formal

111

experiment. There were signs too of his highly charged temperament, exhilarated by, if not yet in control of, a rich array of expressive devices. Pasternak suggested in *Safe Conduct* that his early originality stemmed partly from the sheer novelty of the literary medium after 'fifteen years of abstinence from verbal expression sacrificed to sound', which now condemned him to originality 'as other sorts of injury doom one to perform acrobatics' (II, 214; *VP*, 202). However, Loks discovered in Pasternak's verse a more positive organic originality that was reflected also in his speech:

I realised that his manner of conversation [. . .] was unceasing creativity, not yet cast into a mould and therefore just as brilliant and incomprehensible as his verses. This torment consisted in the need not to express himself within the limits of established meanings, but past them, and in despite of them.[55]

The main token of originality in these early verses was the extent to which they arose not from literary prototypes, but from deeply personal, autobiographical observation and experience. Even an attempt to describe to Olya Freidenberg the perceptions underlying the poem 'Turnpikes' produced what was virtually a *poème en prose*:

I wanted to tell you a tale about turnpikes, about that gate where I was at the instant when the street – such an ordinary street, used to itself and simply buried under the stone-flagged habitude of pavements, such a simple and conventional street in the town centre – experiences a profound upheaval at the point when it bids farewell to the highroads as the city ends; where it waves agitated billows of dust to the horizon on its green tether; where it betrays itself and, while remaining as the same peals of city sound, starts turning sentimental with single storeys and houses of wood, the elements of a noble tenderness . . . [I wanted to tell you a tale] about the turnpike of the spirit, where streets come together, where they owe their meeting to the frontier which starts these spiritual spaces unpaved with words, and where the streets become an ultimate limit, signboards fixed on the lawns with their empty tin-cans, signboards that descend from the outskirts of the town into a kitchen-garden nature to meet the sky like John the Baptist; and about the turnpikes where the pealing thunder of colossal bulk is embraced by the tenderness of communication with one and the same frontier.[56]

The actual poem described here was unfortunately lost, but the turnpikes and characteristic Muscovite confluence of town and country figured in several other verse and prose sketches of Pasternak's student period. Such descriptions of suburban approaches revealing the character of the city and countryside exemplified a general proclivity with Pasternak for things (and people) to define their essence in terms of their physical extremities and limits, or even via contiguous objects. This was a regular and major feature of what could be termed Pasternak's 'impressionism' in the 1910s and 1920s, a tendency to deal in outlines, limits, or 'surface phenomena' bearing analogy with visual art – not only with the swift draughtsmanship of such as Leonid Pasternak, but also with modern painting techniques, both Impressionist and post-Impressionist.[57]

The definitive role of extremities or contiguities in Pasternak's early writing applies not just to space, but also to time. It explains why so many early poems contained evocations of nature or the city, dynamised metaphorically or else witnessed at moments of transformation – at morning or evening twilight, in the spring thaw, or the onset of autumn or winter – i.e. when some state or quality is ceasing or else coming into being. The predominantly sad and dark moods of this student verse were perhaps hallmarks of a *young* man's emotional world; and almost all of them were expressions of an experience resulting from change rather than constant state, or from an awareness (as Loks suggested) that emotion and 'established meanings' inhabited discrete and exclusive realms. A typical transformation scene, with emotion refracted as 'atmosphere' and metaphorically attributed to surrounding objects, can be seen in 'Sounds of Beethoven in the Street', a poem of Pasternak's student period:

> How eloquent the sky-glow where
> Through melt-holes flares the stone.
> Above the roadway someone else
> Blows out the evening flame.
>
> Sometimes beneath the joists a tenant
> Resonating shifts the floor,
> And suddenly Beethoven hauls
> Sonatas' shackles on the square.
>
> Above one's temples hangs the spring.
> The window's shut, the flight erased.
> A cleft in throngs of stone is cut
> By music's philharmonic test.[58]

In Pasternak's novel one reads the following of Yurii Zhivago:

Almost from his school years, he had dreamed of writing prose, a book of a biographical sort into which he would introduce the most stunning things he had seen and thought over in the form of concealed explosive charges. But he was still too young for such a book, so instead he made the best of it by writing

113

verses, just as a painter might all his life produce studies for the large picture he had conceived. (*DZh*, 65–6)

Pasternak, however, was slightly bolder than his *alter ego* Zhivago. Initially he published only verses, but as a young man he produced several prose sketches that were in no way inferior. Although fragmentary or episodic, some of these pieces were carefully polished, suggesting that in themselves they were almost finished pieces of work – akin perhaps to Leonardo's cartoons, as Nikolai Vilmont suggested in his memoirs. Perhaps, indeed, they were not part of any larger scheme and were written simply to explore and record a vivid short segment of experience. For all their lyrical qualities, though, a narrative ingredient distinguished most of them from earlier 'poems in prose' by Turgenev, Annensky, and others.

Stylistically Pasternak's early prose sketches are also hard to describe by any ready-made terminology. Through their metaphor and their hints of a fracture between experience and expression the reality they record is subjectively transformed, but Pasternak still probably viewed these works as a novel form of realism. In Odessa in the summer of 1911, he drafted an essay for the centenary of the death of the German author Heinrich von Kleist, who was a kindred spirit in his own triple pursuit of music, literature and philosophy. Pasternak wrote of him in terms applicable to himself, describing his inspiration as 'an ascetic act, a breach with the natural, a long or short stretch along the road to death', and representing Kleist's work as a model of artistry worth reviving in a new dispensation of realism:

In the face of oblique and flat naturalism, which falls upon culture because it lacks the lyrical impetus to transfer its nature to the symbolic sphere of culture, the revival of the name of Kleist has a special, almost exclamatory significance [...] And if this renaissance, the renaissance of realism as tonality, is only in the structure of culture in general, it is nevertheless called upon to gag the mouth of a certain importunate pretender, the self-styled realism of the South – simple naturalism.

Perhaps such 'realism as tonality' is a good term for describing Pasternak's earliest prose sketches – as well as his later works, which he himself described in terms of a 'realism' that underlay all manifestations of genuine art.[59]

A permanent essential of the realistic mode for Pasternak was its autobiographical imprint, in verse as well as in prose; writing of a purely fictitious sort was rare for him. One of his early prose sketches has a mediaeval chivalric setting, and a few other items with foreign characters and situations may have resulted from reading or discussions with Loks, who was a Stendhal enthusiast. One sketch describes a character called Taglioni as he tells a story to his lady friend; another describes the state of mind of one Legendre, a theatrical party and the stage entrance of a character called Blafard; a longer fragment introduces dialogue between the Russian Pyotr and Henri Crispé and the latter's dream of his first love's marriage to Frédéric Goursat in Geneva; in a further item of romantically tinged narrative, a German from Hamelin alludes to the Pied Piper legend (a recurrent motif in Pasternak's early verse exemplifying the Hoffmannesque theme of the enthralling power of music).[60] Some early prose sketches are populated by characters with fanciful Italianate names in the manner of German Romantic prose. There are also a number of celebrities, who may have been namesakes, *Doppelgänger*, or imagined reincarnations.[61] Thus, Kanadovich and composer Salieri meet at night to talk in a tavern by Moscow's Dorogomilovo Gate; in another Muscovite conversation piece one Relinquimini appears together with his friends Mozart and Aleksandr Makedonsky (Alexander the Great). Slightly different are appearances by a musician with the name Shestikrylov (sometimes Shestokrylov), recalling the 'six-winged [*shestikrylyi*] seraphim' who visited Pushkin's 'Prophet' in the wilderness and endowed him with divine powers. But most of these fanciful or 'literary' names do not lend symbolic significance so much as colouration to what are otherwise realistic settings drawn from Pasternak's own experience. In one piece Shestikrylov and a friend are reminded of a former love by the smell of mandarin, first scented long ago in the 'batiste petal' of her handkerchief at a New Year's Dance – and the same configuration of images occurs later in a poem of 1917 and in *Doctor Zhivago*, obviously stemming from a social occasion attended by Pasternak with Ida Vysotskaya's coterie.[62] Elsewhere in the sketches there are pianists and music students; Kanadovich is described as 'a grand-nephew of the Königsberg philosopher' (Immanuel Kant) whom Pasternak studied at Moscow University; and there are further references to schoolboys, such as he continued to encounter in the course of his peripatetic tutoring.

Perhaps surprisingly for a lyric poet, there were few examples of first person narrative in Pasternak's early prose. Instead, the author's personality was objectified as a figure who 'began waving in my direction as to some stranger' and 'evidently required from me someone, or something unknown to him'. In at least a dozen fragments, the poet's *alter ego*

115

bore the name Reliquimini (or Relinquimini, the more correct Latin version meaning 'you will remain'). This odd surname may suggest an affirmation of the power to live and endure through art, but it could equally suggest a cast-off skin, an incarnation that has now been outlived and abandoned – thus, a form of self-distancing. This character appeared as an observer of landscapes, as a partner in encounters and dialogues, and in ruminations where almost all distinction between his and the author's consciousness disappeared. In several places he was also immediately identifiable with his creator as the son of an artist, a musician, poet, or else as a generalised sensitive personality reflecting Pasternak in his characteristic role as observer, contemplator and dreamer, rather than as an active agent.[63]

Pasternak used his early prose sketches as a testing ground for some of the central points of his aesthetic system. Frequently met was his idea of the artist's need to rescue inanimate objects and memories of the past from their dead or empirical state by 'reanimating' them. This was also elaborated in *Safe Conduct*, which refers to a 'hiss of nostalgia' issuing from *nature morte* asking to be launched in pursuit of emotion' (II, 215; *VP*, 203). An early prose sketch speaks of the very presence of the objective world as a command to create, the 'order for a drama'. In an item with this latter title, composer Shestikrylov is likened to 'a surgical thread which had to sew together the operated world order', while the other elements involved are 'pure music, the duty of something unthinkable to become reality and life', and life itself which 'also performs but does not notice itself and only suggests itself as a caryatid for an unrealised lyricism'.[64] Another prose extract likens reality and art to the stressed and unstressed syllables in a feminine poetic line-ending:

Reality gave only the heavy syllable, the first half of the foot – a certain melodic sense demanded the second part, evening, twilight, in which past event or its bandages would slacken.[65]

The image of twilight, a characteristically Pasternakian transitional setting, was in itself an accessory and simile for artistry. 'What is creativity if not a sympathy for the twilight?' Pasternak asks in one of his prose fragments. 'The artist is there to provide a new outline for objects which by twilight have lost their contours.' This description of the artist's function seems to complement the author's religious views at the time as they emerge in these unpublished notes. Even God apparently ceases to be Himself and becomes absorbed in His own created world. 'I do not experience any need for God in life, in morality and truth,'

Pasternak writes. 'Even here I understand him as a great outline, as a contour.' Whatever homilies Pasternak may have heard from his pious friend Sergei Durylin, his religious awareness at this time seems to have been entirely shaped by his artistic sensitivities. Like the artist, God is an entity deducible only from the results of His creation. And both of their intangible, evanescent personalities seemingly cannot be experienced directly, but only through the meaning and order they have infused in an otherwise pain-racked, inarticulate objective world.[66]

When he turned to writing, Pasternak had clear memories of a youth spent in a city where intense experience defied expression in plain speech. He described this sensation to Olya Freidenberg in terms of the cessation of objects to be 'definite': 'verbs and nouns of the experienced world [...] have become adjectives, a sort of whirlpool of *qualities*'. And for their expression the latter require metaphor or simile whose aim is 'to liberate objects from belonging to the interests of real life or science [...] Pure creativity [...] transfers bonded phenomena from one owner to another. From ownership by causal connection, destiny or fate, as we experience them, it transfers them to another realm.'[67] Pasternak registered all this as a specifically urban experience, and in the early prose sketches it was attributed to Reliquimini whose youth was 'marked by the dawning town':

The town too often became different. Or rather, it became nothing. It escaped from itself, ceased to be itself [...] This led to a craving to enumerate all these individual objects which had all the time been betraying themselves, pouring like a melody and bearing undeservedly constant names. As one named them one wanted to liberate them from words [...] in similes.[68]

Ultimately there was nothing in the world surrounding Pasternak-Relinquimini which was immune to 'transfer to another realm'. His anguished inability to articulate an intensely perceived and experienced world was closely akin to the yearning associated with passionate musical expression. As the narrator in one prose sketch recorded, 'Two years ago I wrote my last piece, the finale of a sonata. And the town itself is now performing it.' And this same anguish was cognate with the sense of unrequited love, and its effects were the same:

There was a girl in his life. All the dawns sounded an alarm for her. But then the childish middays dried out the alarm of the March roadways. When she had left, or begun appearing only in the afternoon, or started denying the alarm as a signal only apposite at an early hour and which had now become comical – in a word, when she became lost to Reliquimini, he was startled to see what she had done!

She had replaced the whole town stone by stone. She had substituted other winters and springs.[69]

Urban observations, the experience of love, a recent engagement with music and a new involvement with literary self-expression thus combined to occupy a central thematic place in Pasternak's earliest poetry and prose writing. It remains to show the relation of all this to his main official activity in the years 1909–13, the study of philosophy.

6

Philosophy in Moscow and Marburg

The day was harsh, the tone was too.
Harsh the tone, and harsh the day.
No, pardon me, the curtains' hue
Was yellow – chiton-fine your négligé.

And there in tulle July's caress
Splashed, against the ceiling beat.
Above your head were hands and chairs,
Behind – a cushion for your feet.

How late you rose. You dressed in fashion.
I knocked, went in, and was taught how to dance
By the prancing linoleum squares that high passion
Had cast underfoot and laid like wood planks.

And what did you do? Or to put it more gently: So cold
Blows the blizzard of lace in your white matinée?
But why this surprise? In a form slightly bold:
    I'm in pain. Enough! Let's call it a day.
    Pull – not too hard, though, the string must not break –
    I'm in pain. That's enough.
                My heart moans and aches
Within me, my friend in your white matinée . . .

                         from *Marburg*

ᏜᏜᏜ

Although enrolled as a law student at Moscow University in the autumn of 1908, Pasternak seems never to have seriously concerned himself with jurisprudence. Georgii Kurlov, his schoolmate who eventually graduated in law and became an advocate at the Moscow bar, reported that neither he nor Pasternak were at all diligent in attending lectures, and Pasternak's legal studies left no memories worth recording in his autobiographies. In fact, by February of 1909 there was no further reason for studying law, which he had only pursued as an easy option

119

while concentrating on music. According to *Safe Conduct*, he went to inquire about a transfer to the Philosophy Department of Moscow University on the very next day after his fateful meeting with Scriabin, although he formally commenced philosophy studies only in the autumn of 1909.[1]

Until 1905 the professor of philosophy at Moscow (and also University Rector since 1904) had been Prince Sergei Nikolaevich Trubetskoi, whose brand of thought was a blend of Hegelian objective idealism with the mysticism of Vladimir Solovyov. His zoological appearance ('tall, and gaunt, with stilts in place of legs and a short trunk and camel's head framed by a yellowish-red beard' was how Andrei Bely described him) was shared by his brother Evgenii who came from Kiev to succeed him in his post. Pasternak vividly recalled the latter's frock-coated elephantine ascent of the dais and his remarkable lectures 'delivered in a tone of appeal, in a droning whine and with an aristocratic lisp'. The historian Klyuchevsky, familiar already from the School of Painting and his visits to the Pasternaks, was another fine teacher whose lectures he attended. Pasternak also evidently liked the historians Vipper and Savin for their 'dryish factuality', and the latter specially impressed him with his ability to draw an audience – and time itself, so it seemed – back into mediaeval Britain or to the Paris of Robespierre in search of example and illustration. Other mentors who engaged Pasternak's sympathy were the younger philosophy lecturers Kubitsky, Samsonov and Gustav Shpet. Shpet was a follower of Husserl and not just accepted among academics but eagerly received in Symbolist circles, where he showed keen interest in modern literature, and where his easy manner and wit made a ready appeal. (His grand-daughter was to become the wife of Pasternak's elder son Evgenii.) Loks' memoirs also recall that Pasternak and he together attended and enjoyed Sobolevsky's course on Aristotle and Grushka's on Lucretius.[2]

The actual contents of the course which Pasternak followed consisted of preliminary classes in psychology, logic, Greek and Latin set authors, and an introduction to philosophy. These studies eventually led on to final examinations in the history of Greece, history of ancient philosophy, history of mediaeval philosophy, history of modern Russian literature, modern history, modern Russian history, the history of modern philosophy, history of modern Western literature, and an essay. In all of these, according to his degree diploma issued in June 1913, Pasternak performed to a 'highly satisfactory' standard and was awarded first class honours. Beyond this, however, he himself recorded few details of his studies or his reaction to them. From correspondence with the Freidenbergs we know that in his first year he performed well in Shpet's seminars and wrote him an essay on 'The Psychological Scepticism of Hume'. His capacity for abstract thought was remarked upon and he was apparently warned off the subject option in experimental psychology taught by Chelpanov, since this might come as a disappointment after his success in pure logic. In fact, Pasternak did try out Chelpanov's lectures but made little headway: absorbed as he was in Neo-Kantianism, his conclusion voiced to Loks was that 'this man Chelpanov hasn't the slightest connection with philosophy'. Pasternak's student jottings also contained a snide verse lampoon aimed at Theodor Lipps, the exponent of logical psychologism who was opposed by both the Moscow Neo-Kantians and the Husserlians.[3]

In general, it seems, the official syllabus was not much to Pasternak's taste. He was not alone in this attitude. A few years earlier Andrei Bely had studied philosophy in Moscow and he remarked on the grey company of rank and file lecturers who provided seminars on established figures but catered little for the more exciting modern thinkers, Neo-Kantians Otto Liebmann and Hermann Cohen, or Alois Riehl. In retrospect Pasternak described the course in general as 'a strange mixture of antiquated metaphysics and unfledged enlightenmentism', in which 'the history of philosophy became a matter of belletristic dogmatism, and psychology degenerated into vague and empty journalese'. Part of the blame he placed on a huge increase in student numbers from 1890 onwards, and on new trends towards simplification and accessibility which were perhaps an unconscious concession to official policies aimed at eradicating illiteracy and offering universal education. But none of these reservations dampened Pasternak's enthusiasm. After mastering the rudiments of a subject, he and his like-minded companions worked semi-independently in the University library and pursued their private philosophical enthusiasms. In Pasternak's case this included attending the Musaget philosophical circle run by Fyodor Stepun, who was a follower of the Freiburg Neo-Kantian, Heinrich Rickert.[4]

Through their coincidence in time (and juxtaposition in Pasternak's notebooks and manuscripts) one might have assumed that philosophy and literary creativity were a happy and mutually fructifying combination. In fact there were elements of conflict. After the shock of his failed romance with Olya Freidenberg in 1910, he told Shura Shtikh that her refusal to come to Moscow required of him 'a radical self-reeducation in order to approach the classical world of Olya and her father', and he

121

resolved to use the rationality and mental discipline of academic philosophy to suppress those qualities which he believed had caused her to reject him. Philosophy thus became a means of his 'removal from romanticism and from a creative and ever more creative fantasy, an objectivisation and strict discipline'.[5]

Given Pasternak's artistic leanings, there was even a grim perversity in the school of philosophy for which he developed a special enthusiasm. The main trends that enjoyed a following among students and younger lecturers were the teachings of Henri Bergson, German Neo-Kantianism, and the phenomenology of Edmund Husserl. Husserl's writings gained ground with young Muscovite thinkers especially when his major work, *Philosophy as Strict Science* (*Philosophie als strenge Wissenschaft*) appeared in German and in a Russian translation published by Musaget in the journal *Logos* in 1911.[6] Of these various schools the most artistically congenial were those of Bergson and Husserl. Some recognisable features of them could be discerned in Pasternak's aesthetic theory as it emerged in his writings of the 1910s and 1920s. Bergson, for instance, described experience as a form of spontaneous vitalism defying rational scientific analysis, which by its very operation destroyed or distorted the object of investigation,[7] while Husserl described the intuition of phenomena in terms of a process called *Wesensschau*, which eliminated the sharp divide between perceiver and object perceived. In Lazar Fleishman's paraphrase of Husserl: 'Intuitive cognition preserves the object in its authenticity. Man does not perform the act of cognition but lives within it. It is not I who must speak about the object, about existence – the object and existence must speak about themselves.'[8]

Several of Pasternak's writings demonstrate a familiarity with these principles. The story of *Zhenya Luvers' Childhood* echoes Bergson in a refutation of any probings by psychology and 'all general concepts' (including those of philosophy, no doubt), which are described as benignly negative influences that have diverted man's harmful attention away from the formation of his immortal essence. In his second year at University, Pasternak studied Husserl's work under Gustav Shpet, and there was a sympathetically Husserlian ring in a letter to Olya Freidenberg in the summer of 1910, where he says that creativity

does not notice what is characteristic, does not observe, but only in one way or another ascertains the fact that both the verbs and nouns of the experienced world, the embodied nouns and verbs, have become adjectives, a sort of whirlpool of *qualities* which you have to relate back to a supreme bearer, to the object, to the reality which is not disclosed to us. And not to the object of religious feeling, but to the object of a lyrically creative ecstasy or sorrow.[9]

In *Safe Conduct*, too, there is an element of Husserl in Pasternak's appreciation of 'what it is like for the visible object when it begins to be seen', and in his description of the painter's 'identity with this pictorial element, and it becomes impossible to tell which of the three is most actively manifest upon the canvas and for whose benefit: the painter, the painting, or the thing painted' (II, 262; *VP*, 250).

The first years of the twentieth century until the First World War were the high point in the development of German Neo-Kantian thought, which enjoyed a reputation throughout Eastern Europe and the Western philosophical world. Its various schools had gone beyond probing separate elements of Kant's *Critique of Pure Reason* (*Kritik der reinen Vernunft*) and they used his teaching as a whole and proceeded to build up a complete subjective-idealist philosophy, often incorporating objective motifs from the world of culture or applying Kantian thought to current ethical and aesthetic problems, or else (as Paul Natorp did increasingly) bringing Kantian ethics to bear on contemporary political and social problems. Research into problems of values and ethics was the chief occupation of the school based in Freiburg, whose main spokesmen were Windelband, Rickert, Lask, Bauch and Cohn. Meanwhile, the Marburg school, headed by Hermann Cohen, concerned itself primarily with Kantian 'transcendental deduction'. It viewed cognition as a conceptual, almost mathematical process and saw the outer world as a web of logical relationships for apperception by human consciousness. Philosophy's prime object was *Wissenschaft*, knowledge viewed as a cognitive science.[10]

Among Moscow University's Neo-Kantians allegiances were divided between the Rickertian philosophers of culture, Professor Kistyakovsky and Doctors Rubinshtein, Gessen, and Stepun, and the more rigorously scientific Marburgians, represented by lecturers such as Fokht (Vogt), Kubitsky, Savalsky, Gordon, Delektorsky, Trostyansky and Polivanov. As Andrei Bely commented, there were literally 'cohorts of Kantians':

Cohen and Rickert ruled within the walls of the University without ever even coming to Moscow, for their 'pupils' supplied them from Moscow with youths for all manner of processing. A regular export of young men to Marburg and Freiburg was organised, where the worthy Minotaurs gobbled them up without trace and disposed of them.[11]

There is no doubt that Bely's jaundiced assessment of Moscow's Neo-Kantians was known to Pasternak through their meetings at Musaget. But despite the Mephistophelian Fokht and his traffic to the 'one-eyed Moloch' (Hermann Cohen), it was precisely the Marburg school which caught Pasternak's interest as a student. His first awareness of it came through reading and perhaps also from Aleksandr Gavronsky. Gavronsky was related to the Vysotskys and was a younger brother of Dmitrii Gavronsky, who was already an established philosopher and pupil of Hermann Cohen. In the spring of 1911, while Pasternak was recovering from a severe bout of scarlet fever, Aleksandr Gavronsky visited and regaled him with accounts of his own recent studies abroad. But Pasternak ascribed his more active enthusiasm for Marburg to other student friends – to the postgraduate historian Sergei Mansurov and two of his undergraduate relatives whom Pasternak knew already from the High School: Nikolai Trubetskoi (son of the late Rector and eventually to become a celebrated philologist at Vienna University) and Dmitrii Samarin. (The latter was the eccentric, cantankerous descendant of a noble line who 'carried philosophy, dialectics and Hegelian scholarship in his blood as a hereditary gift' and had visited Marburg already and was a convinced devotee.) His friends' zest quickly sparked Pasternak's own interest, and as he later recalled, he found his attention shifting from Kant and Hegel to Plato and to the modern Neo-Kantians Cohen and Natorp.[12]

It was a sleeting windy day in February 1912 when Pasternak first heard an account of Marburg's splendour as a town, as distinct from an 'abstract' philosophical school. He was sitting over coffee in the Café Grec with Loks and Samarin, and when conversation turned to Marburg Samarin gave such a graphic and vivid account of it, reinforced with flourishes of a biscuit, that by the time the latter made his eccentric exit Pasternak was left a total convert, incapable of following Loks' routine discourse on Stendhal. His new ambition to go to Marburg became a matter of special urgency since in July of 1912 Hermann Cohen was seventy and was due to retire. In April, however, came the sudden promise of a dream's fulfilment. Pasternak's mother offered him a couple of hundred roubles saved from household expenses and piano teaching and suggested he use the money to travel abroad. The choice of destination was obvious. He quickly assembled the various papers needed from the University, avidly consulted the lecture programme announced for the Marburg summer semester, made his explanations to Chelpanov and others, and on Friday 21 April set out for Germany. Determined to spin out his mother's gift to the limit, and to include also a trip to Italy if funds allowed, he resolved on a programme of maximum austerity – third or fourth-class rail travel, the slowest trains, cheapest lodgings, and a basic diet of sausage, bread and tea.[13]

The letters Pasternak wrote to his parents from the journey were full of understandable rapture. They described 'a gorgeous day in Smolensk' with folklore figures besieging the railcoaches and himself wearing his father's frockcoat lying on the top bunk. 'It will be clear to you of course that I am fit, am full of joie de vivre, am studying Cohen up here under the ceiling, and that I send you my love.' Further stages of the trip were charted in successive letters and in later autobiographical recollections of a Russian thaw and Polish apple-blossom. The train reached Berlin at half-past midnight, and Pasternak went straight to a hotel where his family's friends, the Rosenfelds, were attending a silver wedding celebration. However, the Berlin stopover was brief and the city later only fleetingly remembered for its frock-coated youths with their broadswords, helmets, canes, pipes and bicycles, and also for the volume of Natorp's *Logical Bases of the Exact Sciences* (*Die logischen Grundlagen der exakten Wissenschaften*) acquired in anticipation of meeting its author. The rail journey then continued via the Harz mountains, Goslar and Göttingen. Standing at night by the open window, Pasternak was buffeted by a 'hurricane redolent of dew and roses' and 'spattered with a cluster of sparks from the hands of the rapturously rushing night'. It was also a voyage of discovery in time as well as space:[14]

The Middle Ages immemorial were revealed to me for the first time. Like any original object their authenticity was fresh and terrible. Clanging familiar names like naked steel, the journey took them one by one from descriptions I had read, as though from the historians' dusty scabbards. (II, 223; *VP*, 210)

Pasternak's Marburg pilgrimage was his response to a call felt already by two centuries of Russian students. One of the most distinguished had been Mikhail Lomonosov, who at the dawn of the Russian Enlightenment had gone to Marburg to study with Christian Wolff, and it was there in 1739 that he wrote his celebrated 'Letter about the Rules of Russian Prosody'. Since that time other universities too had made their appeal to Russian writers – Radishchev, for instance, studied in Leipzig, and Turgenev in Heidelberg. In the nineteenth century, though, the chief magnet had been Berlin, where Hegel taught. At the start of the new century student numbers expanded hugely, and by 1912 there were about five thousand Russian students in Germany. But Neo-Kantian scholars were a small minority among a wave of mainly lower middle-class students who came to study science, law and engineering and often brought left-wing ideas that caused many Germans to view all Russian students with distrust.[15]

When Pasternak went to Marburg the university's school of philosophy was one of Europe's most prestigious academic centres. Made famous already by Lange, author of a celebrated *History of Materialism* (*Geschichte des Materialismus*), it achieved a pinnacle of prominence with his successor Hermann Cohen. In the first decade of the century Cohen's pupils from the Russian Empire included Petersburgian Wilhelm Sesemann, and Gabriel Gordon and Boris Fokht from Moscow. There was also Nikolai Hartmann from Riga. He had studied in Marburg and then stayed on as a lecturer in modern philosophy; according to Pasternak he was already slightly halting in his Russian.[16]

Marburg was a strikingly lovely town. It had around twenty-five thousand inhabitants and two thousand students. Set by the quietly flowing river Lahn and grouped in a semicircle round the approaches to the towering Schlossberg, it has a picturesque and dramatic quality to which many have responded. In the early 1900s, for instance, Rilke described it as 'beautiful and carefully located on a summery elevation, dignified but without severity, dominating its clear surroundings with a calm vigilance', a town with 'roads that recede, sending out a call and summoning up the rapid streets from the vesperal valley' and where 'the old is not cold and dilapidated, but simple, tall and strong, just like old trees that still live and bear fruit'.[17]

Alighting from the train on 8 May (25 April by the Russian calendar), Pasternak made his way to the town centre. There he stood with his head thrown back, gasping at 'a vertiginous hillslope on which the stone models of the university, Rathaus and 800-year-old castle stood in three tiers'. The streets he compared to Gothic dwarfs clinging to the hillside. The cellars of one row of houses overlooked the attics of neighbours below, and between houses whose upper storeys and gables almost met in mid-air ran the quaint, narrow, shaded gorges of streets and alleyways. Marburg was steeped in history and had links with Giordano Bruno, Martin Luther, Zwingli and the brothers Grimm; St Elizabeth of Hungary was buried in the lovely Elisabethkirche, a perfect example of early Gothic and hallowed by pilgrims. The university was founded in 1527 by Philipp the Magnanimous of Hesse, and the town boasted a fifteenth-century Lutheran church and an early sixteenth-century Rathaus. The castle above the town, once residence of the Princes of Hesse and later a prison, had a fine Gothic chapel and Rittersaal and housed the archives of the Land of Hesse. Apart from Marburg's architecture, lush gardens and the banks of the Lahn added their own beauty. All this was registered later on in *Safe Conduct*, and it is no surprise that Pasternak's letters to family and friends were full of enraptured descriptions:

If only this were merely a town! But it is a sort of mediaeval fairytale. If only there were just professors here! But sometimes in the middle of a lecture a stormy Gothic window opens, the tension of a hundred gardens fills the darkened lecture-room, and down from on high gazes an eternal mighty Reproach. If only there were just professors here! But there is God here too![18]

God in fact manifested himself to Pasternak at the start of his stay in Marburg in the form of new access of religiosity and church-going. Evidently Pasternak also for a short time considered taking church-organ lessons, but his religious and musical enthusiasms soon lapsed under pressure of his academic and other commitments.

On first arrival Pasternak had sought temporary lodging at a 'mediaeval hostelry' recommended by Samarin and identified later by Guy de Mallac as the Gasthof zum Schützenpfuhl. Shortly afterwards he found accommodation on the outskirts of town, at 15 Gisselbergerstrasse. His landlady, Frau Elise Ort, was the widow of a veterinarian;[19] both she and her daughter had pronounced goitres that irresistibly attracted his furtive glance. The second-floor room which he occupied had a squalid little balcony with a view of the neighbour's garden where a converted horse-tram did duty as a hencoop. On the far side, in the distance, flowed the river Lahn flanked by bushes and with the railway line beyond.[20]

Pasternak threw himself wholeheartedly into his Marburg experience and eagerly absorbed student behaviour patterns. The town by night became almost as familiar as the daylight scene; he often took a latchkey with him and found himself at late-night discussions on the hillside terrace of the Café Vetter, a favourite haunt of philosophy students. The company he kept there included his Moscow friend Aleksandr Gavronsky, who helped him out with the loan of several books. Another Muscovite was Mitrofan Gorbunkov, and as Lazar Fleishman has recently shown, his circle also included the Russian-born American scholar Henry Lanz and the colourful Spanish revolutionary Fernando de los Rios – these were only some of a cosmopolitan company of Danes, English ladies, Japanese and others who had come to sit at Cohen's feet.[21] On his way to such evenings of conviviality at the Café Vetter, Pasternak would go past the 'fluvial oil of the Lahn' and through an operatically illuminated town in which 'streetlamps suspended from wall to wall above the roadway had nowhere to disport themselves. Their light crashed down with full force on to the sounds, drenching the ring of receding footsteps and salvoes of loud German speech with fleur-delis highlights. It was as though even electricity knew the legend of this place' (II, 229; *VP*, 217).

On his first day in Marburg Pasternak was overawed by his impending meeting with Cohen. His thoughts were later relayed in a letter to Shura Shtikh, when he recalled asking himself:

Where have you come to, clueless idiot? What are you doing here? [...] I was shy then of all those Russians who were already long established pupils of his, and I almost started apologising for my impudence.[22]

Nevertheless, Pasternak paid his five Deutsche Mark registration fee, leaving a whole fifty to live on – 'quite a decent sum by local standards' – and on 9 May duly matriculated, an act completed by ceremonial handshake, as he reported to sister Josephine. Thereafter he presented himself regularly for lectures and seminars. He attended Hermann Cohen's classes on ethics, and perhaps also Natorp's on logic and Dr Hartmann's course on the history of modern philosophy. He may also have attended some of Professor Georg Misch's lectures on the philosophy of history;[23] one of the Marburg school's attractions for Pasternak was its review of history 'through both Hegelian eyes' (II, 225; *VP*, 212).

Paul Natorp's appearance was remarkable mainly for his large white beard and rapid speech. Pasternak had brought a letter of recommendation to him from his Moscow tutor Gabriel Gordon, and his own ideas were probably more congruent with Natorp's world of thought than with other members of the Marburg school. Cohen was a shockheaded, bespectacled, deaf, tetchy and daunting Teutonic professor of the old school, pedantic, rarely and reluctantly approving, and often caustically dismissive. Pasternak's first impression was recorded in a letter home:

Cohen is really just what I anticipated. Outwardly he resembles Ibsen, Schopenhauer, and those old men in general with large heads. The bitter experience of a great life, aware of his own value yet insufficiently valued, renders his speech mournful and tragic when he speaks of great men.[24]

Safe Conduct also includes a striking pen portrait of Cohen:

He would lift his head and step back as he talked about the Greek concept of immortality, flourishing a hand towards the Marburg fire station as he interpreted the image of the Elysian fields [...] On some other occasion he would make a stealthy approach to pre-Kantian metaphysics and coo away in a show of paying court to it, before suddenly uttering a rasp and giving it a frightful scolding with quotations from Hume.   (II, 231; *VP*, 219)

In another passage Pasternak described Cohen as 'to a certain degree filled with that precious essence which in days gone by was bottled up in the heads of Galileos, Newtons, Leibnitzes and Pascals'. Cohen 'refused to tolerate not only vagueness but also any approximation to the truth instead of the actual truth' (II, 248, 245; *VP*, 236, 233).

Cohen's forbidding presence made it difficult for Pasternak to approach him about a special request from his father. 'Of course, I haven't been able to speak to him yet,' Pasternak told his parents on 15 May. 'Why should one cause offence to great subjects!! But I know *I shall work my way through to him*'. Although Cohen appeared 'very unfriendly and wound up', Pasternak's third approach was successful, even though one misunderstanding still remained to be corrected. Pasternak's mention of his father's urgent desire to visit Marburg and paint Cohen's portrait was interpreted by the latter as part of some dubious commercial venture. In fact, the initiative had come from two of Cohen's other Russian pupils, Dmitrii Gavronsky and Sergei Rubinshtein.* They wished Leonid Pasternak to make a lithograph portrait as their seventieth birthday gift to Cohen, and the latter was mollified only when Rubinshtein himself reassured him of the artist's fame, Jewish blood, and desire to honour him.[25]

In addition to this assignment, however, Boris Pasternak cherished a 'delirious novice's ambition' to come to Cohen's attention as a philosopher and perhaps qualify for the Sunday lunch invitation that usually signalled the start of a new academic career. His first seminar paper for Cohen, delivered on Tuesday 2 July, dealt with an aspect of Kant's *Critique of Practical Reason* (*Kritik der praktischen Vernunft*) and was an unmistakable success. So too was an essay in textual analysis. He was patted on the shoulder and asked in mid-delivery where he came from, how long he had been in Marburg, and so forth. And the rest of his answers were punctuated with approbation: 'Sehr richtig, sehr richtig. Sie merken wohl? Ja, ja. Ach, ach der Alte!'† (the last remark referring to Kant) (II, 246; *VP*, 233). As Pasternak later wrote to Shtikh:

Cohen was very pleased with me. I did a second paper for him. With an analysis of Kant. Cohen was really astounded [. . .] You can imagine how nervous I was in front of all the doctors from every corner of the earth who filled the seminar room, and in front of the ladies.[26]

* Gavronsky became a permanent émigré after 1917; in the period 1923–29 he lectured at Berne University and thereafter went to the USA. Rubinshtein later became a celebrated Soviet psychologist.
† 'Just so, just so. Do you note that? Yes, yes. Oho, the old fellow!'

On the strength of this success Pasternak was invited to pursue his ideas in a further paper at the end of the semester. Meanwhile, Thursday 4 July was Cohen's seventieth birthday celebration, at which his pupil Cassirer gave a marvellous speech, Pasternak reported in a letter the next day. It turned out to be an expensive affair too, despite his vow of austerity: the hire of evening dress, starched shirt, and the cost of flowers and a banquet consumed 25-30 Deutsche Mark. In a further letter of 9 July, however, he told his parents of Cohen's compliments and announced that the coveted invitation would be forthcoming, which indeed it was – for Sunday 14th.[27]

But despite his apparent progress towards a successful philosophical career, Pasternak already discerned signs of his unsuitability for the academic world. One of the first Marburg letters to his parents talked about a tormenting awareness that 'here in Marburg I can only see how little there is of the philosopher in me', an admission he repeated in a letter to sister Josephine. This feeling persisted, despite the stimulation and enjoyment of his studies and the conviction that, if he actually set his mind to it, he might have a future in philosophy.[28] The fact that he had favourably impressed Cohen certainly allays any suspicions of dilettantism, yet the actual degree of his enthusiasm for the subject at the time seemed a barrier to success. As part of his preparations for his first seminar paper on Leibniz for Dr Hartmann, he later recalled the arboreal fern-like accumulation of materials which spread across the floor of his room in Gisselbergerstrasse – a work method by which, he claimed, 'an experienced observer could have told that I would never make a scholar':

I *lived* my academic studies more intensely than the subject itself required. I had rooted within me a vegetable way of thought. Its special peculiarity was that any secondary idea would unfold endlessly in my interpretation and begin demanding nourishment and attention. And whenever under its influence I referred to any books, I was drawn to them not by a selfless interest in knowledge but by a search for literary references in support of my idea.   (II, 239; *VP*, 227)

The plant-like progress of Pasternak's argument across his room seemed to offer tangible evidence of an artistic (rather than academic) mentality, which worked discursively by intuition and random association rather than by logical deduction. The 'living' of academic philosophy 'more than the subject required' also contrasted with the staid mentality of Cohen and his faculty colleagues. Had he followed in their footsteps, Pasternak might have settled down to a respectable, disciplined and unspontaneous scholarly existence. Marburg held up a mirror to this potential future and the prospect dismayed him. As he wrote on 19 July to Shura Shtikh:

I have seen these married academics. Not only are they married. They sometimes also take pleasure in the theatre and in lush green meadows. I believe the drama of a thunderstorm also appeals to them. But can one talk of such things in three lines? They do not exist. They never conjugate in the passive voice. They do not collapse in bouts of creativity. These men are intellectual cattle.[29]

Small wonder that the company of men with a consumer attitude to some of life's greatest revelations filled a future poet with distaste; by the end of June 1912 he had confessed to Shtikh that he could never now become Cohen's pupil.[30]

Pasternak was justified in choosing the Neo-Kantian school for special attention, in preference to Bergsonian or Husserlian thought, if he was genuinely searching for a system that gave least opportunity to indulge – or even describe – pernicious irrationalisms or fantasies. Neo-Kantian pursuits meant not only a negation of qualities Pasternak had supposedly over-indulged in his dealings with Olya Freidenberg, but also contrasted with his other recent aberration – music, the one art form least bound up with cognition. In fact, among the three main philosophic trends at Moscow University, the Neo-Kantian one provided not even a satisfactory description of artistic perception. Several commentators and philosophically inclined artists (including some German Romantics and Samuel Taylor Coleridge, as well as Bely and Pasternak) have suggested that artistic intuition forestalls or falls outside the process of cognitive apperception described by Kant.[31] Similarly, there was little of Marburgian thought that a poet could take with him into his art, whether as a description or embodiment of the 'creative process'. Significantly, in his autobiographies Pasternak avoided expounding or discussing the epistemological framework of Cohen's school; those features which *Safe Conduct* presented as its main attractions were secondary yet artistically congenial ones.

First of all, the Marburg school made a point of investigating everything from first principles. It retested basic procedures and primary sources, and 'was interested in how science thought throughout twenty-five centuries of continuous authorship'. Secondly, Pasternak admired the Marburg school's 'discriminating and exacting treatment of the heritage of history' and the fact that 'they never tired of hauling treasure after treasure from the archives of the Italian Renaissance, French and Scottish rationalism, and other little-studied schools' (II, 224–5; *VP*, 211–12). Such diverse cultural interests inevitably appealed to someone reared on Russian Symbolist culture; writers of that generation regularly raided the world's cultural vaults in order to present Symbolism as (in Bryusov's words) 'a radiant crown to the history of literature',[32] and Pasternak had inherited their broad-ranging cultural appetite. The appeal of Marburg was thus understandable, and when he moved on to Italy in the later summer of 1912, his sense of communion with world culture was further reinforced:

The main thing that everyone take away with him from an encounter with Italian art is a sense of the tangible unity of our culture [...] I realised, for instance, that the Bible is not so much a book with a ready, hard and fast text, as notebook of humanity, and that everything long-lasting is like that. It is vital not when it is enforced but when it is amenable to every comparison drawn in the retrospective review of later ages. I realised that the history of culture is a chain of equations in the shape of images which form pairs linking the already known with the next unknown. And this known element which remains constant for the whole series, is the legend underlying the tradition, whereas the unknown which is new each time is that actual moment in the stream of culture. (II, 263; *VP*, 252)

Despite what has been said, however, it would be wrong to view Pasternak's exposure to Neo-Kantian thought as totally irrelevant to his formation as an artist. The trained philosopher's mental habits and vocabulary were not easily discarded. Both as a student and in later years he often resorted to the Kantian notions of 'category', 'concept', 'cognition' and 'a priori' to elucidate his ideas on creativity. It was typical of his constantly questing alertness to treat other men's pronouncements as catalysts for his own thought, and analogies were revealed and sympathetic chords struck in some unexpected quarters. An interesting instance was the Neo-Kantian Paul Natorp. His cultural purview was akin to Pasternak's in its breadth (his publications included works on Beethoven, Dostoevsky, Pestalozzi and Plato, religion, sociology, politics, history, education, and so forth), and his *General Psychology through Critical Method* (*Allgemeine Psychologie nach kritischer Methode*) published in Tübingen in 1912 was the subject of a long paper which Pasternak wrote at Moscow University in 1913 'On the Object and Method of Psychology'. Pasternak's paper included the following Bergsonian propositions:

From the subjective quality to an objective concept of it there is a reflex following the same path as leads from sensory assessment of space or time to an objective measurement of it [...] A scientific explanation of psychic phenomena can mean nothing other than their objectification as processes of nature [...] Immediate data will not submit – without damage to this immediacy – to immediate definition [...] Can one go directly to the *phenomenon*, the *manifes-tation*, as the *object* of one's judgement? ... Direct judgement, even if descriptive, creates or places a construction upon the object.[33]

Natorp's thought contained many notions that seem compatible with a shared exploration of reality by both philosophy and art: 'freedom of creativity', a 'poietic' content that removed the opposition between being (*Sein*) and imperative (*Sollen*), and so forth. 'Art', Natorp claimed, 'is not an arbitrary invention, not a series of random products of the fantasy. It consists of revelations, or visions, as it were, objective contemplations, i.e. in a certain sense, genuine objective formations'.[34] Pasternak's own paper of 1913 dealt with this process of 'formation', with the role of consciousness and of the subconscious as 'potential consciousness', with their realisation in an act of volition, sensation and imagination, with the contents of consciousness in time and the role of apperception, with the 'unfathomable miracle of consciousness' whereby the identical becomes non-identical, and with the interconnection between subjective and objective in the act of creation. Specially notable were Natorp's identification of a dynamic element in perception and of consciousness as energy (*Energie*): these ideas figured importantly in the account of creativity that Pasternak later provided in *Safe Conduct*.[35]

The ideas developed in his paper of 1913 were closely bound up with Pasternak's other early non-fictional writings on subjects such as immor-tality, human subjectivity, dreaming, etc., and with his discourse on 'Symbolism and Immortality' delivered to members of the Musaget 'academy' in 1913. All these writings helped form the bridge between philosophy and art which Pasternak actually resolved to cross while still in Marburg in 1912.

If his pianistic limitations had earlier posed an obstacle to musical ambitions, so a temperamental unsuitedness to academic philosophy now erected an equally formidable psychological barrier. However, just as the immediate pretext for rejecting music had hung, as it were, on the throw of a dice, so in Marburg chance played a part in precipitating this new fateful decision. Again fate was put to the test, and the wrong answer to a question was used as poetic justification for a change. An emotional jolt was required to prompt a re-embracing of the irrational.

Towards the end of the summer semester, in the third week of June, while Pasternak worked on the first of his papers for Cohen, two visitors arrived. While spending the summer in Belgium, Ida and Elena Vysotskaya were summoned to a family gathering in Berlin, and they

133

decided to visit Boris in Marburg on the way. They appeared, as always, dressed in the smartest fashions and put up at the best hotel in Marburg, the Europäischer Hof, opposite the Elisabethkirche. Ida had just spent several months in England at Cambridge University, where she had discovered English poetry for herself and she had conveyed her enthusiasm to Boris in several letters; she now turned up with a Shakespeare volume as a gift for him.[36]

For a few blissful days Pasternak enjoyed Ida and Elena's company. 'Constantly telling them things, I was intoxicated by their laughter and by signs of understanding from those who happened to be around us. I took them to places, and they both appeared with me at university lectures' (II, 235; *VP*, 223). The feelings unleashed by renewed contact with Ida in such entrancing surroundings finally overcame Boris' reticence. On the morning of their departure he went to their hotel and spoke to Ida briefly and alone in her room, where he gave vent to a passionate but confused statement of his feelings for her. This much emerged from his later account of the incident in a letter of 6 February 1915 to Shura Shtikh:

My Marburg adventure was, after long years of fruitless dreaming and timid drifting, my first vital action, which was accomplished only with extreme pain. The meaning of it was as follows: the girl who was the protagonist in that three-day interlude was for the first time made by me to give answer on all the basic paragraphs of the heart that cannot be talked about or 'shared', and which, in short, cannot be joked about. She turned out to be a most refined interpreter of femininity while still being uninformed as to what it was I wanted of her [. . .] If at that time I wrote about femininity, then only because I was badly deluded: I did not realise that an access of passion is nobler than any unrecognisably ornate phrases about it.

The verses which Pasternak later wrote under the impact of this incident and the autobiographical account in *Safe Conduct* later presented the story as a declaration of love, a proposal which Ida refused. Whether in fact his phraseology was so explicit or clear at the time is uncertain, but the tenor of her reply to his declarations was quite unambiguously conveyed:

In awful agitation I told her things could not go on like this and that I wanted her to decide my fate. Apart from my insistence, there was nothing new in any of this. She rose from her chair and retreated from the manifest agitation that seemed to advance upon her. But when she reached the wall, she suddenly realised that there was an immediate way of putting an end to all this . . . and she refused me [...] Although as I discussed matters with V- nothing occurred to alter my situation, our discussion was accompanied by some unexpected element resembling happiness. I was filled with despair and she consoled me. Yet her mere touch was such bliss that a wave of exultation swept away the distinct bitterness of what I had just heard and what could not be altered.

(II, 236, 241–2; *VP*, 224, 229)

If Pasternak's story was coloured by a storm of recollected feelings, the basic accuracy of his account of events and their romantic circumstances were later confirmed by Ida Vysotskaya herself.[37]

Their private drama was interrupted by the arrival of porters to remove the young ladies' cases. Boris quickly gathered himself and walked with them to the station. However, unable to say farewell, he boarded the train as it left and the sisters rescued him from the conductor's wrath and bought him a ticket to Berlin, thus procuring a few hours' continuation of that 'fairytale holiday'. In the capital, though, they parted. The sisters were being met and Boris, still in disarray, retreated discreetly among the crowd. The next train to Marburg left only the following morning. Abandoned in Berlin without luggage or documents and unequipped against the drizzle, he was turned away by all decent hotels. Finally he found room in a cheap guest-house, paid in advance, and spent the night slumped over a table and sobbing uninterruptedly. The following day he left early and returned to Marburg, paying his fare with money borrowed from Ida.[38]

What Pasternak experienced was perhaps a fairly commonplace young man's amorous misadventure. Nor was he altogether secretive about it – even at the time, at any rate not on paper. A message to Shura Shtikh on returning to Marburg contained some slightly affected sighing: 'O triste, triste était mon âme / À cause, à cause d'une dame...'[39] At about the same time a letter to his parents who were also staying in Berlin implored them not to mention his 'excess' to the Vysotskys and included a special address to his mother:

Mama! They stayed here five days. I found it hard to part with them and so I went to Berlin [...] And Ida – she is so brilliantly profound, impenetrable and incomprehensible to herself, and so aphoristically unforeseen, and so gloomy and uncommunicative – and so ... so sad.[40]

Pasternak's behaviour and correspondence following the incident revealed that he was almost suicidal. Shura Shtikh was implored to offer support and consolation, just as Pasternak himself had evidently done for Aleksandr Gavronsky the previous year;* probably Pasternak's recent bout of religiosity and church attendance in Marburg imparted a further dimension to this anguish.

But the 'Marburg incident' unleashed some more striking consequences. From the morning following his disappointment he noted a transformation in his vision, which lent an even more acute slant to his earlier sensation that emotional experience eluded the descriptive grasp of language. In *Safe Conduct* he described how he emerged from his overnight lodgings in Berlin:

> I was surrounded by things transformed. Something never before experienced had invaded the substance of reality. The morning had recognised my face and appeared precisely in order to be with me and never leave me.
>
> The mist dispersed, promising a hot day in store. Little by little the city began to move. Carts and bicycles, vans and trains began to slip in all directions. Above them human plans and desires snaked like invisible plumes. They moved and vapoured with the terseness of parable, familiar and fathomed without explanation. Birds, dogs, houses, trees and horses, men and tulips became shorter, more abrupt than I had known in childhood. Life's laconic freshness was revealed to me. It crossed over the road, took me by the hand and led me along the pavement. (II, 238; *VP*, 226)

Later that day he 'failed to recognise Marburg on arrival. The hill had grown taller and drawn in. The town was blackened and weazen' (II, 240; *VP*, 228). This emotionally distorted vision was a prime instance of the state described in *Safe Conduct* as giving birth to poetry: 'Focussed on a reality dislocated by feeling, art is a record of this dislocation which it copies from nature' (II, 243; *VP*, 231). Shortly afterwards Pasternak set down memories of this incident in a handful of lyrics, and later, in 1916, a more ambitious composition called 'Marburg' contained graphic examples of how 'passion like a witness turned grey in the corner', while 'every detail/Came alive and, reckoning me of little worth,/Rose up in its ultimate significance' (I, 220–2; *SP*, 107–9). The fact that over the next few years Pasternak returned obsessively to the experience in his verse is evidence of its special importance to him. In due

* Prior to his reappearance in Marburg in 1912, Gavronsky had shown himself as an intelligent but feckless dilettante and reprobate. After his uncompleted studies at several European universities, he had married then abandoned his wife Zhenya. Returning to Moscow from Switzerland in the spring of 1911, he had 'disappeared' and Boris had discovered him in some cheap lodgings, Vorobyov's rooms, on Malaya Lubyanka. His eyes were dilated from doses of atropine which he took to feign an eye complaint and thus avoid conscription. Boris attempted to rally his morale and reconcile him with his wife. This episode was reflected in some prose fiction of the early 1920s. See below, p.284.

course, 'Marburg' became one of his best known and most anthologised poems. One of its stanzas likening the poet to a provincial tragedian rehearsing his beloved like some Shakespearian drama was a special favourite of Mayakovsky's.[41]

What was it in all this that convinced Pasternak of his poetic destiny? In *Safe Conduct* he presented the incident as a form of epiphany or conversion. Yet, as we know, this was not his first taste of the inspiring agony of frustrated love, nor by 1912 was the habit of writing poetry a novelty. Retrospectively Pasternak perhaps poeticised what were really two separate events, which vividly coincided in Marburg in late June and which he never saw fit to disentangle. The emotional upheaval of Vysotskaya's refusal merely precipitated a decision which was already overdue: whatever his scholarly enthusiasm and intellectual endowment, Pasternak was temperamentally unsuited to the academic pursuit of philosophy, and the urge and ability to write were too assertive to be ignored. As he half-gleefully admitted to Shura Shtikh, on the very day of his second seminar paper for Hermann Cohen he had written five poems, and although the time in Marburg had been valuable, he had now 'abandoned everything for art and nothing else'.[42]

Following Ida's refusal, yet another incident compounded Pasternak's distress, perhaps throwing fresh light on the nature of his new decision. After returning from Berlin, in the last week of June he gave his paper on Leibnitz for Hartmann. Then, with a dustpan and brush borrowed from Frau Ort, he tidied his room and cleared away the books that snaked across the floor in an enquiry which would never now be completed.[43] On Thursday 27 June came an unexpected letter from Olya Freidenberg. She was travelling alone in Europe, still partly convalescing after a tubercular ailment the previous year, and she had stopped off at Frankfurt's Hotel Deutscher Kaiser und Kaiserhof, as she herself admitted, 'with a certain sly purpose'. Although half-afraid of stirring up old feelings, she wanted to see Boris and wrote suggesting a meeting. He wrote back immediately and turned up at her hotel at lunchtime next day. As he entered the dining-room he was sloppily dressed and seemed disorientated. Olya was disappointed by the sight, and by the rest of their meeting. They spent the whole day in the open air and Boris once again talked endlessly but without mention of his recently shattered feelings. Then, in prosaic contrast to the luxury she was otherwise enjoying, he treated her to a supper of Frankfurters before seeing her to the station for a train that would take her on to Glion, near Montreux. He himself then took a train back to Marburg. Immediately on parting,

Olya wrote Boris a letter of some length, telling him with affectionate pertness that she had 'expected more' of him and pointing out how she had changed and developed in the last two years whereas he had 'not grown as much as I expected'. Amid her detailed discussion of their respective characters there were further remarks, correctly observed but not calculated to cheer her cousin – notably that his enthusiasm for belittling himself was really a piece of 'vainglorious modesty'. Boris' reply, written on Sunday 30 June, two days before his first vital seminar paper for Cohen, expressed regret and irritation at the two years' delay of Olya's letter! After her indifference to him in 1910 he had deliberately sublimated his feelings: 'I acquired other aims, and people who were also – like Petersburg – more classical, complete and definite than I was ... And then I simply went and denied the whole of that cup that was fermenting within me and demanding expression.'[44]

Now, however, the cup was on the point of spilling over. Pasternak had recognised his true artistic nature and was about to shed the self-constraints of the last few years. This was spelt out to Olya in another slightly more affectionate and relaxed message:

Your letter was frightfully fair and exceedingly important, almost salutary in its significance ... In it you talked about your own rapid development. I can only wonder at the perspicacity with which you detected something alien, common-place and decadent that had altered me. You have no idea how I have wandered from my *own* way. But you are mistaken: this happened consciously and deliberately: I thought that 'my own' had no right to exist [...] I had left even myself behind in my philosophy, mathematics and law. Maybe it's possible to return [...] I am going through difficult and serious times.[45]

Thus, not for the first time on the threshold of a perhaps distinguished career Pasternak was preparing for a new act of renunciation. As he told Shura Shtikh, 'I know I would have got on in philosophy – all that I have sometimes mapped out in the drawing-room or in a snowstorm *hat sein gutes Recht*. But this year, in Moscow, I shall break myself for the last time.'[46]

For the remainder of the semester Pasternak took stock of his new decision and its implications while academically free-wheeling through two seminar papers for Cohen and preparations for the July examinations. During his final month in Marburg there were several further distractions, not least a scorching summer that made outdoor activity preferable to study. The rest of his family had meanwhile arrived in Germany and after a stopover with the Rosenfelds in Berlin, they had moved to Bad Kissingen in Bavaria where Rozaliya Pasternak's heart

18 Ida Vysotskaya, Josephine Pasternak, actor Aleksandr Vishnevsky,
Rozaliya Pasternak (Bad Kissingen, July 1912

condition could benefit from the curative spa. At that time the town was popular with Russians. The Pasternaks stayed at the Villa Ölmühle in Rosenstrasse, and despite Leonid's dislike of the many *nouveaux riches* Jewish visitors, they found kindred spirits there, including the Vysotskys, actor Aleksandr Vishnevsky, the eminent pianist Josef Hofmann, and tenor Leonid Sobinov, all of whom appeared in photographs and several of Leonid Pasternak's pictures.[47]

Boris' brother travelled up from Kissingen on 4 July and spent two and a half weeks with him in Marburg. While Boris made nominal efforts to work on his seminar papers, Aleksandr was sent on boat trips and cycle rides and also teamed up as a billiards partner with the friendly head-waiter of the Café Vetter.[48] In the last week of July, Pasternak's father also visited him and was presented to Cohen. Leonid Pasternak found him disappointing and the promised portrait was not produced. Later, however, he made an excellent charcoal reconstruction of Cohen walking through Marburg in his topcoat and broad-brimmed hat, accompanied by a group of students including Boris. Leonid Pasternak also took his son on a trip to Kassel to view the art gallery and its impressive collection of Rembrandts.[49]

Despite the emotional setback of three weeks earlier, on Sunday 14 July Pasternak went to see his family and friends at Bad Kissingen, and to attend the birthday party of Ida Vysotskaya. At Kissingen he discovered her 'dignified and with a beauty I simply found tragic, in every single step she took, in every interruption by the wind, in every proximity to trees'. One of her remarks, which he found simply offensive, in fact served to emphasise their incompatibility: 'Just try to live normally,' she had said. 'You've been led astray by your way of life. Anyone who hasn't lunched and is short of sleep discovers lots of wild and incredible ideas in himself...' Meanwhile his most sympathetic confidante, who had probably also heard Ida's version of events, was his twelve-year-old sister Josephine. In the evening he had discovered her in tears and lamenting 'Poor Boris, you've got tangled up in the past and the present, and now it's hard for you. Everything is bound to sort itself out inside you.' The journey back to Marburg took Pasternak eleven hours, and as he told Shura Shtikh, he returned there 'shattered', both physically and emotionally.[50]

Despite the June incident in Marburg and its aftermath in Kissingen Pasternak continued to associate with Vysotskaya, although what he hoped to achieve from their friendship is uncertain. Apart from his family and Shura Shtikh, he seemingly kept all his Serdarda and

University friends in the dark about their relations, although Loks and others knew he had some romantic attachment. Ida herself was evidently happy to enjoy Pasternak's company without emotional commitment, and probably Pasternak himself soon cooled down or looked elsewhere. Ida Vysotskaya was in fact aware that he had other female acquaintances down by Moscow's Brest Station – possibly through his uncle Aleksandr Margulius' connection with the freight office – and these may have included more casual and carnal relationships. Curiosity about this subject will doubtless continue, but there is no reliable information other than what one could surmise from an unpublished extract of student fiction, or from the later prose *Story*. Whatever occurred in this area of experience did so away from family and friends. Meanwhile, Vysotskaya and Pasternak remained on friendly terms for several years and visited one another's homes. Konstantin Loks once escorted her home from the Volkhonka and had the impression that she slightly regretted the negative outcome of her liaison with Boris (a judgement which her own testimony contradicted). Loks also visited her home next day and one glance at the décor of her room and collection of Parisian perfumes was enough for him silently to congratulate Pasternak on his failure! In February of 1917 Ida finally made an appropriate marriage to a Kievan banker, Emmanuel Feldzer, with whom she left Russia the following year via Siberia. A distant though friendly relationship continued with Pasternak after she and her husband settled in Western Europe, and they met again briefly in Berlin in 1922 and in Paris in 1935.[51]

Even before his trip to Kissingen Pasternak was aware of doing little but serve out his time in Marburg. On the 15 July he wrote to his friend Konstantin Loks half-ruefully and half-complacently: 'I cannot work. But never mind. I have no fears.' And on 19 July, the day of his brother's departure, he admitted (slightly exaggerating) to Shtikh: 'I have done nothing and been to no seminars for a month now. I have never led such an empty existence. But I don't want to disguise the naked truth that I am now only waiting, sitting out the time.'[52] Symptomatic of this indifference to his philosophical future was the fact that after receiving Cohen's invitation to lunch he had preferred to go to Kissingen instead.[53] Having ignored this invitation (much to Frau Ort's consternation), Pasternak was a few days later involved in an embarrassed confrontation with Cohen outside the barber's, where he attempted to apologise and explain himself. Cohen suggested that he should stay on and do his doctorate in Germany.[54] Had Pasternak wished to continue his studies, the offer might have been a tempting one, for as a Jew he was unlikely to be accepted for postgraduate work at Moscow University. In the event he thanked Cohen but explained that he intended returning home, pointing out that his father's limited means prevented his further study abroad. Tactfully, he spared Cohen the details of his artistic ambitions. Even so, Cohen was unimpressed. According to *Safe Conduct* and Mallac's deduction, Pasternak and he had one further awkward encounter in Marburg's Heugässchen which clearly added nothing to their relations. Possibly too they met again in May of 1914, when Cohen visited Moscow on a lecture tour in support of Judaeic culture, but if they did so neither of them left any record of the fact.[55]

As July wore on, Pasternak's main sensation seems to have been one of relief at his recent decision. Writing to Shtikh on the 22nd, he found it hard to convey properly 'why I have made such an epileptic recoil from the path [...] down which till recently I was marching quite enthusiastically [...] just at the moment when I achieved my first unmistakable success... Lord, my head is spinning with happiness! I am going back home – and this home is Russia, this home is the autumn.' Return to Moscow also meant facing the challenge of a newly chosen career, and Pasternak was aware of its seriousness. But 'the punishing hand of an art that does not require me is infinitely dearer to me than the handshake of the octopus' (i.e. academic philosophy)![56]

Inevitably, at this stage Pasternak had no clear view of his future after graduating, but his concern to avoid being a burden to his father led him in late July 1912 to start laying in some literary capital. He began translating some prose by the nineteenth-century Swiss writer Gottfried Keller, no easy task despite Pasternak's now fluent German. But Keller, he found, along with Jacobsen, Flaubert and Maupassant, lent himself to translation: 'All this literature is borne along majestically on its own words – as though upon a raft.' Amidst other distractions, however, he never finished the work and the manuscript was later lost.[57]

In the remaining few weeks in Marburg Pasternak also read some poetry that Sergei Bobrov had sent from Moscow, and to arm himself for his new poetic career, he set out to make a systematic study of recent Russian verse. To this end, on 26 July he hastily ordered from Shura Shtikh a consignment of books by Bryusov, Blok, Sologub, Bely and Vyacheslav Ivanov.[58] However, his main activity of importance was to write original poetry on a scale and with an intensity for him unprecedented:

Night and day and whenever chance offered, I wrote about the sea, about dawn, about rain in the south, and coal in the Harz.

On one occasion I was particularly carried away. It was one of those nights that found it hard to reach the nearby fence and hung above the earth, dazed with exhaustion and with all its strength spent. There was not a breath of wind. The only sign of life was a black profile of the sky leaning feebly on the wattle fencing. And there was one other sign: the strong aroma of gilly-flowers and of tobacco in bloom, which was the earth's response to this enfeeblement. And what is beyond comparison with the sky on such a night? Large stars were like an evening party. The Milky Way – a great company. But the chalky streaks of those diagonal expanses were even more like a flowerbed at night. There were heliotropes and night-scented stocks. They were watered in the evening and bent sideways. And flowers and stars were brought so close that it seemed as if the sky had come under the watering can, and now there was no way to disentangle stars from the white-flecked grass.   (II, 244; *VP*, 232)

At the beginning of August 1912 Rozaliya Pasternak had completed her spa cure (a plan to return to Bad Kissingen in two years' time was frustrated by the First World War), and doctors now recommended further rest with fresh sea air. The family therefore moved down to Italy and established themselves in a Russian-owned guest-house at the small Tuscan resort of Marina di Pisa. Aleksandr Blok had visited the place three years earlier and found it unremittingly boring, but the Pasternaks relished the seaside, sunshine, aromas of pine-trees, and the local colour, and Lydia and Josephine had their first taste of bicycling. The resort was also conveniently sited for Leonid Pasternak to make a number of excursions to see the art treasures of Pisa, Florence, Perugia, Assisi and Siena. His impressions of this visit imparted a distinctly Italian Renais-sance quality to some of his original pictures in the next few years, during which he moved away from smaller-scale genre works towards what he described as 'the grand forms of large and decorative oil portraits' (the best example of which was a family portrait done in 1914 on the occasion of his silver wedding).[59]

Although Pasternak had largely exhausted the academic benefits of Marburg, for his parents' sake he stayed out his time and on 3 August collected his official attendance certificate for the semester. His incli-nation was to return directly to Russia, but his parents insisted that he first spend a fortnight with them in Italy. Funds were running low, but his Russian student friend Mitrofan Gorbunkov, who was an expert on low budget survival in Europe, urged him to go. Pasternak acceded and did not regret the decision. A last letter to Loks on 3 August announced that he would be leaving six days' later and suggested that a reply should be sent to him *poste restante* in Venice.[60]

A final conference was held at the Café Vetter with a couple of French and German students and a reckoning of finances with Gorbunkov and the friendly waiter, who produced a train timetable. Then Pasternak returned quickly to his lodgings, collected his belongings, bade farewell to Frau Ort and set off by rail in the early hours.[61] The journey took him through Basel, which like Marburg was baking in a heatwave; and 'the same kiln fire that blazed in the wild grapevines on private houses burned in the ceramic gold of the Primitives in the clean and cool museum' (II, 253; *VP*, 241).

He dozed and slept through the magnificence of the St Gothard approach, although an enforced change of trains high up in the Italian Alpine morning left a brief mountain impression of jingling cowbells, rushing streams and the aroma of camomile. (One of his loveliest student poems captured a memory of the St Gothard's echoes and flowing water.)[62] These impressions also largely eclipsed the recollection of another half day spent in Milan, apart from the unforgettable changing aspect of its cathedral which 'like a melting glacier repeatedly towered up against a blue declivity of August heat'. Then there was Venice, 'brick-rose and aquamarine-green, like the translucent pebbles thrown up by the sea onto the beach'; later on in his stay he would also see Florence, 'dark, dense, and graceful – a living extract from the terzinas of Dante' (II, 254, 29; *VP*, 242, 444).

In effect Pasternak was repeating for himself the discovery of Italy made by his father in 1904. And, in particular, it was Venice's 'fairytale reality, unlike anything seen before' which Leonid had described that now made the most indelible impression on his son. From the station Boris walked to the steamboat jetty and took a spluttering *vaporetto* to the area of the Academia – the best neighbourhood to seek accommodation, according to Gorbunkov. After inquiries in an Italian based on his attempts to read Dante, he was led on a circuitous nocturnal trek with his suitcase before discovering a run-down hotel near the Campo Morosini. And with this as his base he set out to discover the city.[63] The pages he later devoted to it in *Safe Conduct* remain as one of the most arresting modern descriptions of Venice: 'There are words like khalva and Chaldea, Magi and magnesium, India and indigo, and in the same company belong the nocturnal colouring of Venice and its watery reflections.' Pasternak's first gondola 'had a feminine hugeness, just as everything is huge which is perfect in form and incommensurate with the space it occupies. Its bright crested halberd flew airily across the sky, borne high on the round nape of the wave, and the black silhouette of the gondolier ran with the same ease among the stars.' Up in the sky 'the down of a shedding dandelion seemed scattered along the entire Milky Way, and just in order to let through a column or two of this shifting light the alleys occasionally moved apart to form squares and crossroads [...] People crowded on the arriving and departing *vaporetti*, and the oily black water erupted in a spray of snow like shattered marble, broken to pieces in the mortars of those engines which pounded hotly or abruptly died.' Equally memorable were the buildings of Venice where 'the architect's speech pronounced in stone is so sublime that no rhetoric can reach such height'. As for Venetian painting, Pasternak had been 'familiar since childhood with the taste of its hot well-springs from reproductions and the exported overflow from museums. But one had to go to the geological source in order to see not separate pictures but painting itself like a golden marshland, a primordial pool of creativity.' Having just begun to tap a similar reservoir of inspiration himself, Pasternak enjoyed an enhanced awareness of the meaning of this exposure to Venetian art, and its example confirmed the discovery he had made in the case of himself: 'how little a genius needs in order to explode' (II, 255–62; *VP*, 243–50).

Unlike Blok, Khodasevich, and later Mandelstam, with Pasternak it was in his prose, in *Safe Conduct*, that the discovery of Italy and its culture found fullest reflection. Even Venice figured only briefly in his verse – in an early evocation, of 'Piazza San Marco', and a lyrical impression from his last evening in the town, when an arpeggio struck on someone's guitar sent him scurrying to the window to gaze in search of some new constellation rising in the sky.[64]

After visiting Florence on about 11 August, Pasternak spent almost two weeks with his family at Marina di Pisa. During that time they were also visited by Olya Freidenberg from Switzerland. Despite her warm welcome from the rest of the family, Boris kept aloof and evidently had nothing to say to his cousin. The two of them apparently went together to visit Pisa. While Olya was happy with a superficial impression, Boris wanted to inspect everything in detail with the guidebook; after an ensuing quarrel no further words were exchanged between them for the rest of her stay. Eventually the situation proved too much for Olya. When a telegram from a friend in Switzerland was opened in error by Rozaliya Pasternak, she used her already well-developed talent for taking umbrage and departed.[65] Following this new series of embarrassed meetings and exchanges, several years again passed during which (so far as surviving correspondence tells us) there was virtually no contact between Pasternak and his cousin. It was not until the early 1920s that a new resumption of relations took place.

The only other memories which anyone seems to have preserved from that family holiday are musical ones. In the evenings Boris took to improvising again, and Olya Freidenberg recalled the warm Italian nights filled with his inspired but technically inept outpourings, while his mother sat and trembled by the darkened window. Rozaliya, on another occasion, brought delight to assembled visitors and the guest-house owner with an impromptu piano recital.[66] For Boris, though, music was effectively a thing of the past. He was pursuing his retreat from philosophy and from the two principal amours of his early manhood, and he was pondering the consequences of a 'return to himself' – a flight from the rigours of Academe to the wayward inspirations of poetic creativity.

7

A literary launch

Black spring! Pick up your pen, and weeping,
Of February, in sobs and ink,
Write poems, while slush in thunder
Is burning in the black of spring.

Through clanking wheels, through church bells ringing
A hired cab will take you where
The town has ended, where the showers
Are louder still than ink and tears.

Where rooks, like charred pears, from the branches
In thousands break away, and sweep
Into the melting snow, instilling
Dry sadness into eyes that weep.

Beneath – the earth is black in puddles,
The wind with croaking screeches throbs,
And – the more randomly, the surer
Poems are forming out of sobs.
Translated by Lydia Pasternak-Slater

ஓஜஜஜ

The exact date of Pasternak's return to Moscow via Ferrara and Innsbruck in late August 1912 is not recorded. Only a few impressions of the journey emerged much later in his correspondence:

In Vienna I realised what a penance it is to leave Italy and end up in another country. I regretted that those who travel north were not first chloroformed at Mestre. The operation of crossing the frontier should be carried out under anaesthetic in a state of unconsciousness. It was then that I registered how *artistic* the Italian street is, how talented and genius-like are its sound and its air, and how ungifted the vegetating of folk seems after its slightly roguish optimism.[1]

Rather more sinister were Pasternak's memories of re-entering Russia, recorded in *Safe Conduct*. His return coincided with centenary celebrations of the country's defence against Napoleon. The Brest Railway was renamed after Emperor Alexander I, stations were whitewashed, workmen at the crossings were dressed in clean shirts, and Kubinka station was festooned with flags and manned with extra guards in honour of an imperial inspection.

At the time all this ceremonial perhaps disguised an indifference to the country's history which in retrospect seemed to characterise Nicholas II's reign. Perhaps Pasternak then ascribed only picturesque significance to his recent memories of the Marburg parade ground where soldiers had constantly trained and drilled. With hindsight, though, according to Aleksandr Pasternak, the possibility of war was apparent from about 1912 onwards,[2] and Boris too eventually realised that the centenary celebrations 'heralded a drama of high seriousness and were not at all the innocent vaudeville my frivolous a-politicism saw in them' (II, 267–8; *VP*, 258–9).

Back home Pasternak enjoyed the familiar distractions of contemporary art, music and literature as he continued his philosophy course. But the decision of summer 1912 remained in force, and his final year of studies and graduation became an irksome formality. Together with Konstantin Loks he often worked in the University library, or else the two of them held joint work sessions at home on the Volkhonka and afterwards Loks would spend the night curled on the Karelian birch couch in the Pasternaks' drawing room. Half-way through the academic year Pasternak wrote Sergei Bobrov a humorous account of the effects of all this concentration:

I have to finish university, you understand. I sit for days on end in the library working on my degree exams. With only three weeks left I haven't even started. I walk around incognito in a frock-coat, I don't greet any of my acquaintances, I leave home and repair to my writing-desk, I've changed my voice, I blow my nose holding my handkerchief between both index fingers, my heart is bursting, and my soul is crrrracking – a thousand changes have taken place.[3]

In more serious mood, Pasternak turned to his graduate friend Mansurov, who assisted by lending him textbooks and other aids which he himself had used. Pasternak had to hire a cab to transport all his borrowed materials back home.

To be considered for first-class honours, students were required to write a 'graduate essay' (*kandidatskoye sochinenie*). Pasternak submitted a hastily written treatise on the philosophy of Leibnitz, and although Chelpanov evidently failed to understand the work, it was adjudged 'highly satisfactory'. So too was Pasternak's performance in the remaining exams held in April and May of 1913, and the following month he was awarded a first-class honours degree. Together with his friends he celebrated the end of his university career in their traditional meeting place at the Café Grec.[4]

At eight p.m. on Sunday, 10 February 1913, there was a meeting of the Musaget 'academy', when members gathered in Krakht's studio on Bolshaya Presnya to hear a paper by Pasternak on 'Symbolism and Immortality'. Space was limited and admission was by invitation only. The only direct record of the talk was in a hand-out synopsis, which was kept by Loks, Bobrov and the composer Glière.[5] It was Pasternak's first formal statement on the philosophy of art, pre-dating any publications, and it drew together ideas adumbrated already in his correspondence, verse and prose sketches, and incorporated several perceptions of an academic philosopher. In particular it provided clues to an understanding of Pasternak's poetic metaphor, it helped determine his stance vis-à-vis the Symbolists, and it also threw light on some of his religious views. As the *Autobiographical Essay* recalled:

The paper was based on a consideration of the subjectivity of our perceptions, on the idea that the sounds and colours we perceive in nature and the corresponding vibrations of sound and lightwaves are different. In the paper I developed the idea that this subjectivity is not a quality of individual man, but is a generic, suprapersonal quality, and that it is the subjectivity of the world of man, of the human race. In my paper I pointed out that in dying every human personality leaves behind a share of this undying generic subjectivity, which was contained within that person during his life, and which enabled him to participate in the history of humanity. The main aim of the paper was to suggest that perhaps it is this extremely subjective and universal corner or segment of the soul that has forever been the realm where art operates and the main content of art. And in addition, although the artist is of course mortal like everyone else, the joy of existence which he has experienced is immortal, and centuries later, through his works, it can be experienced by others in a form approximating to that of his original intimate and personal sensations.

The paper was called 'Symbolism and Immortality' because it maintained that all art in essence contains a certain formal symbolism in the very broadest sense, just as one can talk about the symbolism of algebra.   (II, 25–6; *VP*, 438–9)

Death – the death of the artist, or death arising *through* art – were problems that had already exercised Pasternak's attention. His father's friends Tolstoy and Serov had died in 1910 and 1911 respectively, and to Leonid Pasternak these men's lives carried intimations of immortality:

'If our works contain even a grain of real art they will live forever,' Tolstoy had told him. Boris Pasternak himself later erroneously dated his paper on 'Symbolism and Immortality' to the time of Tolstoy's death in 1910. In that year the philosophical journal *Logos* had also carried a translation of Simmel's 'Apropos the Metaphysics of Death' which no doubt caught his attention.[6] Moreover, among his own unpublished writings of that period were a prose sketch on 'The Death of Reliquimini', a philosophical poem which spoke of the soul's 'threat of a fourth dimension / And prophecy of death's perdition', and various notes of the summer of 1911, including a consideration of Kleist's suicide and its motivation.[7] The same motif figured in the first of Pasternak's published poems in the *Lirika* almanac of 1913:

> In obscure thought of my own self
> I lie as in a plaster cast
> And this is death: congealed in fate,
> In destiny, the plasterer's gauze.   (III, 123; *SP*, 491)

In an episode of Pasternak's novel set in the same period, the fate of an introverted, and thus doomed and uncreative consciousness also provides the theme of an impromptu lecture delivered by the hero to Anna Gromeko:

Consciousness is a poison to anyone who applies it to himself. Consciousness is a ray of light beaming outward. Consciousness lights up the way ahead of us so that we don't trip up [...] the lamps in a railway engine... However far back you delve in your memory, you have always discovered yourself in some external, active manifestation of yourself, in the work of your hands, in your family, in others [...] The soul of man is man's presence in other people. This is what you are, this is what your consciousness has breathed and fed on and enjoyed throughout your life. Your soul, your immortality, your life in others.

(*DZh*, 68)

A view of immortality as something immanent, accessible, and independent of the heavenly afterworld envisaged by various religions, was further elaborated in one of Pasternak's student jottings. Referring to the ancient Greek philosophers, he noted Socrates' rejection of immortality as a promised life of the individual beyond the grave 'because the eternity of significance and meaning, the timelessness of ideas has nothing to do with the living soul of man [...] One cannot bowl immortality along in front of one. That is a dangerous *perpetuum*. It leads us away into an infinity of the absurd.' Nor, Pasternak wrote, could immortality be accepted as something given and inevitable; it could arise only from the active ability to conceive it as necessary: 'Immortality is created by those who want it [...] Immortality ceases to exist for us only when it is not there as a problem, nor even as a requirement.'

Examining the theses of Pasternak's paper on 'Symbolism and Immortality', Lazar Fleishman suggests the foundation of his ideas as unambiguously Husserlian. Evidence for this is hinted in several statements in the surviving synopsis:

A sense of immortality accompanies experience when we learn to see in subjectivity not an attribute of personality, but a feature belonging to quality in general [...] Qualities are embraced by consciousness, and the latter liberates qualities from any connection with personal life and returns to them their primordial subjectivity, and it itself becomes imbued with this directive. Immortality takes control of the contents of the soul [...] Vital contents are attributed not to time but are reduced to a unity of meaning.

The poet devotes the visual riches of his life to a non-temporal meaning. The living soul divorced from personality in favour of free subjectivity is immortality. Thus immortality is the Poet; and a poet is never an entity, but a condition for quality [...]

Poetry is madness without a madman. Madness is natural immortality. Poetry is immortality permitted by culture [...]

Reality accessible to the personality is penetrated by the search for free subjectivity belonging to quality. The features of this search derived from reality itself and concentrated in it are perceived by the poet as features of reality itself. The poet submits to the direction of this search, takes it over, and behaves like the objects round him. This is called observation and drawing from nature.[8]

In his paper of 1913 Pasternak thus announced the philosophical basis of almost all his subsequent creative work, preempting the insights contained in later articles and essays, as well as in *Safe Conduct* and *Doctor Zhivago*. By 1913 he was also sufficiently exposed to Symbolist literature and debate to be familiar with both its thought and phraseology. There was much common ground between his 'Musaget' lecture and the general fund of Symbolist theory. Something akin to 'generic subjectivity' had been described by Andrei Bely in his concept of subject and object as functions of one another, when the 'I' ceased to be the subject of individual perceptions and became an all-embracing poetic extension of the Kantian 'transcendental subject'. Contemporary religious philosophers Berdyaev and Frank also wrote of creativity as involving some supra-individual form of consciousness.[9] Pasternak's view of art as 'madness without a madman', is relatable to the Dionysian ecstasy identified by Vyacheslav Ivanov as an organic principle of art, springing from '*taedium sui*, tiredness, of one's particular individuality, freedom from the constraint of individual consciousness'.[10] Another passage in Pasternak's student notes suggested that the Dionysian orgy was no longer that sensuality by which man lives', but 'the sensuality by which he is immortal' – an idea with strongly Scriabinesque associations.

Krakht's studio was an inner sanctum of Symbolist culture. Ellis, who was one of the most naively dogmatic Symbolist theorists, had been the founder and director of this particular discussion circle and the gathering was clearly no forum for a general critique of the movement. Pasternak was still several months away from open dissent with the tenets of mystical Symbolism, and there was little hint of scepticism when he moved on to discuss the controversial question of Symbolism's status as either an art form or instrument of mystical inquiry. On the other hand he laid no special stress on the transcendental *realiora* whose revelation was for Ivanov the main aim of art:

Symbolism reflects fully on this direction of experience and constructs its own system according to it. Therefore, only as a system is Symbolism completely realistic. However, the actual analysis of the directions concealed in reality imparts a religious character to this system. Symbolism achieves realism in religion. Does Symbolism remain an art?[11]

Pasternak's view of the Symbolist claim to have access to transcendental mysteries was shortly to become more critical. In 1913, though, his 'joy in existence' remained greater than any desire to polemicise. Its Husserlian expression emerged in a letter of that summer to Shura Shtikh in which stress seems to be laid not on mystic abstraction but on the empirical world and an objective readership as reflecting mirrors for the poet's ecstatic consciousness:

To become a source of pleasure, and of such pleasure that, when addressed to someone, it has a nature and dimensions that presuppose not that individual at all but 'all the four compass points' whence pleasure comes – to send a wave of such pleasure and, thanks to its special quality, to experience it for oneself in someone else – to give in order to receive back again through one's neighbour – in this lies the entire closed circle of creativity that rebounds upon itself.[12]

Artistic creativity, as Pasternak envisaged it in early 1913, thus emerged as an activity which relied neither on self-dramatisation, egocentricity, nor fanciful romantic invention. Sensitivity to the object of contemplation rather than to self, and an ability to infect others with this made his art essentially 'interpretative' or *re*-creative – akin perhaps to painting from life or musical performance.

చచచచ

'Symbolism and Immortality' gave its title to a book of articles Pasternak was compiling in 1913 which would have included the main substance of his paper. The book was announced as 'in preparation' in the first two issues of the Musaget sponsored journal *Trudy i dni* (Works and Days) for that year, but it never materialised and was one of several works lost in the early days Pasternak's career.

In the winter of 1912–13, however, a new publishing enterprise came into being which enjoyed Musaget support and stored its editions at their offices at 31 Sivtsev Vrazhek. The new concern had the title 'Lirika', and its members were the Anisimovs, Nikolai Aseyev, Sergei Bobrov, Sergei Durylin, Konstantin Loks, Boris Pasternak, Semyon Rubanovich and Aleksei Sidorov. This was in effect the Serdarda 'publishing division' and it operated on the pooled resources of its members, each of whom gave 10–15 roubles, with the Anisimovs as main guarantors. Lirika was a very mixed company. The most active and business-like member was Bobrov. He had had valuable professional experience while working for the historical monthly *Russky arkhiv* (Russian Archive), where Aseyev also for a time worked as secretary.[13] According to Loks, Sidorov was mainly interested in the history of art and resembled some mystic out of Leonid Andreyev's *Life of Man*, while Rubanovich was just 'a young society gent who wrote verse and mainly chased after the ladies'. Initially Pasternak enjoyed collaborating and he happily recalled the editorial evening at Bobrov's on Prechistenka on 29 January 1913, and other gatherings *à quatre* (with Loks, Bobrov and Aseyev) to read and discuss their poetry. But there was no proper cohesion in the Lirika group as a whole and it only lasted for little more than a year. For some members poetry was a very secondary activity, finances were not strong, and Loks quickly took against Bobrov, whom he described in his memoirs as a 'bundle of nerves and an assemblage of moral garbage'.[14]

Nevertheless, in its short life Lirika was active and important. In late April of 1913 appeared a collective poetic miscellany, and further productions included Anisimov's renderings of Rilke, Sidorov's version of Goethe's *Mysteries* (*Die Geheimnisse*) (which Pasternak also translated a few years later), and three solo poetic debuts: Bobrov's *Gardeners over the Vines* (*Vertogradari nad lozami*) in the summer of 1913, and Aseyev's *Nocturnal Flute* (*Nochnaya fleita*) and Pasternak's *Twin in the Stormclouds* (*Bliznets v tuchakh*) published late in December.

In the miscellany entitled *Lirika*, the eight poet-members (i.e.

153

excluding Loks) each contributed five items. The book's provenance was advertised by an epigraph quotation from Vyacheslav Ivanov and by Bobrov's poetic 'Testament' ('Zavet') acknowledging the revelations of 'Blessed Symbolism'.[15] Bobrov's pieces showed virtuosity and formal precision, and along with Pasternak's lyrics they were the outstanding items in an otherwise superannuated display of Symbolistic autumnal languor and melancholia.[16] There was little public comment about the collection as a whole. A few readers, however, disliked Pasternak's evidently peculiar contributions with their 'dialect of chemists' and hospitals'. The composer Medtner was unappreciative, and Durylin lost his earlier enthusiasm for Pasternak's work. (He was about to disappear from literature for several years; his mother died in 1914 after which he went into religious retreat at Optyna Pustyn monastery.)

Pasternak was later dismissive about his publishing debut. His poems in the *Lirika* miscellany were culled from his student verses and varied greatly in style and content. 'Trifles' he called them in a letter of late 1913 to his uncle Mikhail Freidenberg. 'It is so irritating to encounter these belated realisations of what was ready years ago and cut short through my own frivolity instead of developing,' he wrote, hinting at his recent philosophical aberrations.[17] Certainly his contributions contained elements which in literary-historical terms were already obsolete. For instance, one covertly erotic sunset piece developed similes of rose-blossom and mediaeval chivalry and used tonic *vers libre* of a type adopted from the French *symbolistes* by Bryusov and Blok.[18] But despite some lusty apostrophising and mystic cliché depicting the night as a Gnostic revelation,[19] three other poems contained enough mature virtues for Pasternak to revise and publish them in 1929 in only slightly modified form. Some authentic modern traits were the concretisation of abstracts, anthropomorphism of nature, semantic bridges based on acoustic similarity, and a tendency to combine expressions from the colloquial and formal registers. The three poems in question also showed a firmly grasped technique of 'realist impressionism'. Recognisably objective settings of garden, rural, or urban landscape were used as receptacles for dark emotion as the poet escaped from personality and self-expression and allowed his gaze gradually to disappear into the depths of an observed perspective. One of the poems in particular (printed in translation at the head of this chapter) was a masterly seasonal mood picture and was later much anthologised. Dedicated to Loks, it was probably a composition that caused him to remark on Pasternak's kinship with Annensky, although its particular configuration of images is also linked in *Safe Conduct* with the episode of the poet's infatuation with Ida Vysotskaya.[20] In Pasternak's other *Lirika* pieces, the surrounding scene itself undertakes to 'fulfil' the poet's sorrow; his sadness is heard all day on the city's lips; and the earth is a gangway leading to a voyage into self-forgetfulness and to the rediscovery of emotion absorbed by the objective world.[21]

In 1913 and for the three summers following, the Pasternaks rented a dacha on the Borodin family's estate of Molodi, a short horse or carriage ride from Stolbovaya station and some fifty kilometres due south of Moscow along the Kursk Railway. With no immediate employment in prospect, Pasternak went out there in advance of the rest of his family on 8 June. Free of university, he now confronted the problem of making his way in literature. There was no hope of full-time professional literary work, and the future promised only a continuation of his earlier casual employments. 'I am faced by the search for work,' he said in a letter to Shura Shtikh at Spasskoye, 'probably secretarial work in some commercial enterprise.' Another letter, to Loks, who was back at home in Surazh, envisaged a 'mélange of private tutoring, secretarial or correspondence work and literary handiwork'. The possibility of working in a bank was considered (Pavel Ettinger and cousin Fedya could have furnished suitable contacts), and at one point in August there was even promise of an opening in some private cinematographic firm, which prompted Pasternak to set down some interesting ideas in a letter to Bobrov about the nature of cinema as the 'tenth muse'.[22] None of these possibilities seem to have been seriously pursued, however; in the autumn of 1913 Pasternak moved into a single-room lodging at 1 Lebyazhii Lane, apartment 7, and continued to finance himself by private tutoring.

Prior to this, however, thoughts of employment were overshadowed by creative inspiration. At Molodi the Pasternaks lived in a magnificent two-storey house built in the time of Catherine the Great. The rooms and windows were tall, and in the room Pasternak shared with his brother their kerosene lamp threw huge shadows on the ceiling and claret-coloured walls. The grounds of the house contained a linden avenue and the overgrown graves of Cossack snipers who a century before had fallen in their attempts to repel the Napoleonic army. At the end of the park was a meandering stream, and in the branches of an overhanging birch tree, unknown to his family, Pasternak regularly perched and 'for the first time in life wrote verses, not as a rare exception but often and constantly, as people paint or compose music' (II, 31; *VP*, 445).

Pasternak's professional start was anything but confident and he was filled with self-doubt whenever inspiration faltered. 'I am still not free of the feelings I wrote to you about,' he told Bobrov. 'If I were to look for a name for my basic mood over all this period I would call it one of resentment and assiduous idleness [...] All the same, I have started on one or two things, both theoretical and non-theoretical, but whether written or only planned, none of this pleases me at all.'[23]

Nevertheless, as the summer continued ideas flowed and Pasternak's later memory of this period was a happy one. The harvest of verse written at Molodi provided material for his first complete poetic collection. 'To write these verses, alter them, and then restore the original lines fulfilled a deep need and was the source of an incomparable joy that brought tears to my eyes,' he recalled. Even the pauses between onrushes of inspiration became painfully pleasurable. 'How useful a decline in creativity is!' he wrote to Shura Shtikh on 6 August. 'Like the imagination of the hungry servants, this conditon can with one short line enclose and express the whole essence of the absent master.' Then, after contemplating other tempting but less satisfying pleasures, 'the considered possibilities multiply and follow one another, and they are all just as insubstantial as the first two, until you arrive at that strange and unusual illumination which is so unforeseen and simple, and you start to name it with your own complex words!' Thus, verses would again begin to flow.[24]

In the *Autobiographical Essay* Pasternak recalled a constant concern with content in his verse of 1913, a constant ambition 'that the poem should actually contain something, contain a new thought or a new image'. Thus in the poem 'Venice' ('Venetsiya'): 'the town on the water stood before me, and the circles and figure-eight loops of its reflections drifted and multiplied, swelling like a rusk soaked in tea!' Similarly in 'The Station' ('Vokzal'): 'In the distance, where the tracks and platforms ended in clouds of smoke, a horizon of departure arose beyond which trains vanished and the whole history of relations, meetings, farewells and events before and since came to an end' (II, 32; *VP*, 446). A recognisable autobiographical basis underlay several other poems. One of them, later entitled 'Winter Night' ('Zimnyaya noch''), which bore the initials 'I.V.', evoked a nocturnal snowbound reminiscence of the affair with Vysotskaya. 'By no means the person you once knew', the poet in 'hibernacles' numbing visor' was oppressed by memories and, recalling his boyhood, vainly endeavoured to lull his former self to sleep.[25] Several verses of the summer of 1913 rehearsed the poet's melancholy and unrequited love in various urban and suburban settings. Another item with an epigraph from Sappho ('Virginity, virginity, wherefore hast thou forsaken me?') suggested some form of erotic initiation for 'those who yesterday as children went to sleep', and who today arose at crack of dawn in a Muscovite setting with shouts of Tatar tradesmen and a 'horizon of theatres, ambrasures and post offices'.[26]

By 1913, the 'ville tentaculaire' was a poetic commonplace throughly explored by the Symbolists. The phantasmagoric visions of Pasternak's new verses perhaps owed something to their example, but they were juxtaposed with features of modern life and technology in a 'metalworks horizon', 'observatories' and 'telephonic celluloid'. Pasternak's poetic city was in fact derived less from literary sources than from a dramatic urban awareness that eluded common language and which he described in a letter to Bobrov from Molodi:

You will understand me if I call reality – and preferably urban reality – a lyrical stage in exactly the sense I have been talking about. Namely, the city as a stage competes, and enters into tragic correlation, with the auditorium of the Word, or Language, that engulfs us.[27]

The city for Pasternak thus becomes synonymous with the 'poet's predicament' – that of a sensitive and passionate observer seeking to give voice to all-pervading ineffable nostalgia. And repeatedly, in Pasternak's already characteristic manner, urban reality itself speaks out and 'interprets' the poet, as it were, to himself:

> I am the converse of lips unknown,
> Seized on by the towns like rumour.   (I, 363; *SP*, 493)

> Arising from the thunderous rhombus
> Of city squares before the dawn,
> By unrelenting showers my song is
> Sealed with seals of leaden rain
> [...]
> Oh, then the poem encircles all
> [...]
> Oh, everything's a likeness then
> Of my own murmuring lips.   (I, 384; *SP*, 583)

Other metaphors describing a divorce of emotion from its personal source seem to evoke a roving 'free subjectivity'. In 'Venice', for example, where the poet 'fathomed the rootless mystery of existence' at daybreak,

> My eyes and dreams had more space then
> To scurry through the mists without me.   (I, 382; *SP*, 58)

A letter Pasternak wrote to Nina Zavadskaya, Loks' first wife, on the eve of his first book's appearance described that 'strange occupation when metaphors chase reality aside and force it to flow past, as though actuality [*yav'*] is a world in which someone's gaze forever wanders, and it mixes and thickens the colours to the ultimate limit, producing a colourless black, real event [*byl'*] that is saturated with every shade of colour and acute simplicity'. The metaphoric idiom of this first book was probably its most striking feature. Yet, as Pasternak realised, this device was not always under tight control; in 'My Sadness' ('Grust' moya'), for instance, his obstinate 'martyrology' of similes becomes monotonous. Elsewhere metaphor was diluted by conventional bombast. Whilst working on the poems Pasternak also told Bobrov of his fear of lapsing into rhetoric as an invariable result of striving for powerful effect. As Loks later commented, 'Symbolism taught almost everyone bad habits. It taught false pathos in regard to simple things.' Conversely Pasternak also regretted the semantic obscurities of 'Lyric Space' ('Liricheskii prostor'), a poem dedicated to Bobrov which used the image of the town tethered to its mooring like a ship, and straining to leave on a voyage into the autumn.[28]

Hints in several poems of mystery and 'higher spheres' perhaps stemmed from Pasternak's rereading of Tyutchev at Molodi in summer of 1913. But they also suggested Symbolist liturgical phraseology still resounding in the 'auditorium of the Word'. The Gnostic idea of man's dual nature with a heavenly *alter ego* was implicit in the zodiacal images and classical myths of Castor and Pollux, the Gemini, and Ganymede which some poems exploited. But realistic landscapes also acquired mystic accretions. In 'The Station' the departing express was redolent of some angel and the *beau monde* was 'somehow not of this earth'. In a later revision of 1928 Pasternak trimmed away many of these fanciful derivative excrescences, leaving several objective landscape poems which he was willing to reissue.[29]

By 1913, however, Symbolism was becoming obsolete both in literary-historical terms and in Pasternak's own development, and it was not long before he, Bobrov and Aseyev adopted a negative attitude towards Musaget. Bobrov's defence of the 'Lyric Theme' in *Trudy i dni* in 1913 initiated a revolt against those of the Vyacheslav Ivanov school who maintained that, far from being mere literature, Symbolism was a theurgic pursuit. By summer of 1914 Pasternak was giving advice to Shura Shtikh about writing verse and stating that the only 'real symbolism' he could advocate was his own brand of 'realistic impressionism, far removed from any allegory'. Of Ivanov he wrote that 'he has no feeling for some elementary things in poetry – even its most piquant root, which is metaphor. Metaphor, in his words [...] must be a "symbol", i.e. a realistic revelation of an object (not in an artistic, but in a "mystical" sense). How about that? There are your Symbolists for you! They are quite simply anti-poets.'[30] Later, in February 1917, by way of response to Bobrov's continuing fulminations against Bely's mysticism, Pasternak wrote:

It is remarkable that the Symbolists had the feeblest understanding of the spirit of maturity. What if they did prepare their cosmogonies – their words about the cosmos have a certain air of cosmic provincialism about them. That is how people in the distant outback talk about capital cities when they have never been there themselves.[31]

Pasternak never substantially revised this judgement, nor his view of some form of realism as a foundation of his own artistic method.

Stylistically, Pasternak's verse of the summer of 1913 pointed beyond traditional mellifluous alliteration and assonance. Viscous orchestration and some thick consonantal crunches anticipated further developments in his own writing and showed a 'modern' approach to dissonance that was more fully exploited by the Futurist poets – a counterpart to some features of Prokofiev's and Stravinsky's music. Admittedly, some of Pasternak's 'modernity' was fairly superficial: a relish for Gallic barbarism, especially in novel rhyme effects, was observable already in certain Petersburg Ego-Futurist poetry. It was cultivated by Pasternak, however, only in his poems of 1913 and was a passing fancy; it also helped confirm Loks' view that Lirika as a whole valued 'originality' rather than 'essence'.[32]

In the late summer of 1913 Pasternak took Loks to spend a few days at Molodi, where they discussed what to do with all the poems he had now accumulated. From the summer's garnerings a first volume of verse was assembled for publication. Pasternak's original title was 'Twin Behind the Stormclouds' ('Bliznets za tuchami') which Bobrov amended to its published version. This heading picked up the zodiacal motif from some of the poems and, as Pasternak later confessed, it was a pretentious imitation of the 'cosmological obscurities that distinguished Symbolist book titles and the names of their publishing houses' (II, 31; *VP*, 445–6). According to Loks, it was partly Bobrov's choice of items which dictated the book's final appearance as a 'new form of Symbolism'.[33]

But changes were in the air and in the minds of some members of Lirika. If Pasternak was amenable to modernist experiment, Bobrov by the autumn of 1913 was exceedingly impatient with Lirika's reactionary mysticism. His natural leanings were towards the *esprit* of Gallic tradition, and for all his nominal Symbolist stance he had little sympathy with the foggy Germanic romanticism of the Musaget coterie. He was positively hostile when the Anisimovs returned from Europe in September 1913 and, under the influence of Bely, Ellis and their readings of Rudolf Steiner, turned editorial meetings into something resembling an anthroposophical sectarian gathering. This, aggravated by Bobrov's ambition and desire for personal authority, led to acrimonious disputes in the autumn and put an end to plans for a second Lirika miscellany and a journal.[34]

This wrangling was a modest overture to what followed in 1914. Bobrov was meanwhile in effective charge of Lirika publishing and he used the prefaces in Aseyev's and Pasternak's books to measure swords with other colleagues. His introduction to Aseyev's *Nocturnal Flute* drew a sharp distinction between the symbolic function of all art and the 'symbolism of yesterday', and it called for a return to the cult of 'pure lyricism' and Pushkinian models. To introduce Pasternak's book Bobrov hoped for some prefatory polemical lunge from the author himself. Pasternak showed no interest in this, nor in Bobrov's plans for an ornamental cover. Aseyev was therefore charged to produce a preface, which he did apparently without ever reading Pasternak's manuscript! His remarks referred to the 'weighty armada of "Senior Russian Symbolists"' that was now superseded by 'the poet himself coming into battle with his steel plating. Enough of dull muttering! The words he speaks are clear!' Pasternak was proclaimed as legitimate successor of the now *passé* Symbolist movement: 'These verses will ring sonorously in the numb silence of Russian Symbolism, for they are its legacy by birthright, and to them belongs the blazing sword of the chevalier.'[35] Pasternak found the tone of all this quite inappropriate, but not wishing to hurt Aseyev's feelings he allowed the preface to appear.

A modern commentator has observed that 'talent and originality of the first rank are visible in practically every poem' of Pasternak's book, yet *Twin in the Stormclouds* received little attention from the critics at the time and its reception was at best lukewarm.[36] Evidently Pasternak was warned by the wife of the poet Baltrušaitis that he might regret publishing an immature book. But youthful ambition proved stronger than discretion.[37]

In early 1914 dissension between Bobrov and the anthroposophising Anisimovs came to a head. After a particularly stormy meeting on Saturday, 18 January 1914, Bobrov took with him the Lirika 'progress-ives', Aseyev and Pasternak, and with himself as leader set up a new group and publishing enterprise called 'Tsentrifuga' (Centrifuge). Bobrov set down his own record of events about half a century later:

So the fatal evening came when our precious Tsentrifuga was created. The three of us met in my small room in Gagarinsky Lane, and I had already prepared some sheets of writing paper with a stamp in the top left corner: 'Provisional Extraordinary Committee of TSENTRIFUGA concerning the Affairs of the "Lirika" Publishing House'. On these pompous sheets was written a similar haughtily Hoffmannesque text, roughly as follows: 'We the undersigned, having gathered together to discuss the position of the "Lirika" publishing concern, in view of the general degeneration and manifestations of anti-artistic passéistic tendencies, have deemed it necessary to elect from our midst a prov[isional] extra[ordinary] com[mittee] of Ts[entri]F[u]G[a], formed by A[seyev], B[obrov] and P[asternak], which has decreed that the "Lirika" pub[lishing enterprise] shall be closed down and abolished, of which fact you are hereby informed.' This document (each copy) was signed by the three of us and sent by post to the Anisimovs, Durylin, Rubanovich, Sidorov and Loks.[38]

The letter in question was sent out on Wednesday, 22 January 1914.

Pasternak was not pleased by the wedge driven between him and friends whom he genuinely liked. With Loks he remained on good terms and on 28 January sent him a letter à propos the recent 'insult' offered to Yulian. Prior to that, on the 24th, the other five members had convoked their own 'general meeting of Lirika publishers' and confirmed the expulsion of the three dissidents. (They also eventually planned a new publishing enterprise entitled 'Strelets' [Sagittarius], but this project quickly foundered.) During the next few days, after taking offence at some remark by Anisimov, Pasternak allegedly lost his own head and challenged him to a duel, which was only avoided thanks to the mediation of Aseyev and Loks. In the aftermath, however, and perhaps with good reason, he blamed Bobrov for precipitating this temporary rift with Anisimov. Realising he was being manipulated, Pasternak was keen to preserve good relations with Musaget associates, several of

161

whom received signed copies of *Twin in the Stormclouds*. Bobrov, though, had none of the qualities of peacemaker. He was excessively tenacious in all disputes and continued shielding his selected protégés from 'harmful influences'.[39]

The official date of Tsentrifuga's foundation was 1 March 1914, and its creation was accompanied by endless scandals.'The whole winter I was aware only of playing at group discipline, and all I did was sacrifice to it both taste and conscience', *Safe Conduct* recorded (II, 269; *VP*, 260). Not a rebel by nature, Pasternak was unwilling and unable to throw overboard all his recent allegiances and artistic values, and amid the wrangling only through native talent was he able to salvage some experiences and a definition of ideas that were of value to him.

Despite Bobrov's embarrassing abrasiveness, for the time being he and Pasternak maintained a bond based on common interests. Eventually, though, Pasternak's friendship with the third member of their trio, Aseyev, proved longer lasting. Aseyev came from the town of Lgov in the Kursk area and had arrived in Moscow in 1909 to study at the Commercial Institute. Following his artistic interest, he had also registered as an extramural student at the Moscow University Philological Faculty. In January 1913, while staying with Bobrov, he was introduced to the Anisimovs' circle. Aseyev and Pasternak quickly became friends. 'Pasternak conquered me with everything: his appearance, his verses, and his music,' Aseyev later wrote. Aseyev had known Bobrov even before arriving in Moscow, since both of them were friends of the Sinyakov sisters in Kharkov. One of them, Kseniya (or 'Oksana'), in 1914 became Aseyev's wife, and she later suggested that the foundations of Lirika and Tsentrifuga were laid at their apartment in Kharkov.[40] But the actual founding triumvirate of Tsentrifuga was the result of Bobrov's talent-spotting in Moscow. Aseyev and Pasternak were the only former Lirika members who went on to make a prominent name as poets. Aseyev's *Nocturnal Flute*, written before he pursued more avant-garde experimentation, displayed a natural clarity and classicality that led Pasternak to single him out among the poetic youth of their generation.[41]

Originally it was Bobrov's plan to adopt an anti-Symbolist stance in Tsentrifuga. However this was forestalled by a series of events which had a deep impact on all of them and permanently influenced Pasternak's career. Instead of the *vieux jeu* Symbolist debate, Tsentrifuga found itself plunged into the scandal and skirmish of Futurist polemics. In the ensuing verbal violence Bobrov at least was thoroughly in his element.

In 1911 an innovatory poetic group of so-called Ego-Futurists was set up in St Petersburg. Their founder and most talented representative was Igor Severyanin, who specialised in slick presentation of traditional poetic themes spiced with a snobbish eccentricity and with an abundance of novel rhyme and foreign lexicon, as well as neologism supposedly reflecting sophisticated modern culture. A brilliant reciter, Severyanin enjoyed wide popularity and Pasternak described him as having created 'a particular curious genre' in its own right (II, 42; *VP*, 455). In November 1912 Severyanin went independent, but while still in Lirika, Bobrov had established contact with his former followers and contributed to some of their publications, and in the spring of 1914 he invited their collaboration in Tsentrifuga.[42]

Meanwhile Moscow had become the centre of a more radical, flamboyant modernist movement of Cubo-Futurists, the Russian precursors of Dadaism. Its members brought out a series of artistic albums whose bizarre and challenging contents were indicated by titles such as *Judges' Hatchery* (*Sadok sudei*, 1909 and 1913), *Cadaverous Moon* (*Dokhlaya luna*, 1913), and *Roaring Parnassus* (*Rykayushchii Parnas*, 1914). A sensational *Slap in the Face of Public Taste* (*Poshchechina obshchestvennomu vkusu*) delivered in February 1913 had contained the Cubo-Futurist artistic manifesto, and its signatories, David Burlyuk, Aleksei Kruchenykh, Vladimir Mayakovsky and Velimir Khlebnikov became the dominant quartet in the movement. Viewing the world 'from the height of skyscrapers', they proclaimed the rejection of accepted civilised taste and standards, and of the entire traditional heritage of culture. Pushkin, Dostoevsky and others, they claimed, should be 'thrown overboard from the steamship of modernity'. Special targets for abuse, inevitably, were their Symbolist predecessors. The Cubo-Futurists maintained an 'inconquerable hatred for the language existing before them' and declared their right to 'enlarge vocabulary in its scope with arbitrary and derived words'. Their renovations of poetic language involved Kruchenykh's compositions in an invented, or 'transmental' language (*zaum'*), Khlebnikov's neologising use of existing Slavonic roots, and Mayakovsky's word creations based on colloquial etymologies. This innovation was accompanied by bold experiment in the field of rhyme, metre and typographical layout; style ranged from the technically contrived to the cultivated primitive. The Cubo-Futurists immensely broadened the traditional range of poetic themes and imagery, exploiting modern technology and urban civilisation as well as challenging traditional taste by introduction of indelicate, faecal and erotic imagery. Scandal and assaults upon the senses were the stock-in-trade of their communication, and publishing activities were supplemented by public 'happenings' with outlandish behaviour and dress before a deliciously outraged bourgeois audience.[43]

Pasternak was not unfamiliar with these stirrings, although they emanated from a bohemia far removed from the circles he and his family frequented. The Cubo-Futurist poets were closely associated with the artistic avant-garde, and several of them, including Burlyuk, Kruche-nykh and Mayakovsky, were themselves painters. Perhaps it was through his father that Pasternak first learned of the 'Jack of Diamonds' and 'Donkey's Tale' exhibitions in 1910 and 1912, and of primitivist pictures by Larionov and Goncharova which were later mentioned in his *Auto-biographical Essay*. He must also have heard from his father about avant-garde elements within the Moscow School of Painting. Although no reactionary. Leonid Pasternak was unsympathetic to students' indis-criminate pursuit of 'isms' and post-Impressionist trends from Western Europe. Opposed to the cult of what he saw as artistic illiteracy, he had in 1906 already dismissed even Kandinsky as 'rubbish'.[44] Mayakovsky, who had been in Aleksandr Pasternak's class at school, enrolled in the School of Painting in September 1911 and there befriended David Burlyuk, who was already known as a Cubist and therefore a misfit among the main body of students. The *enfants terribles* had a rough passage, however. Larionov was expelled for refusing to remove a nonconformist picture from an exhibition of pupils' work, and finally on 21 February 1914 Burlyuk and Mayakovsky were dismissed for having engaged in public disputes contrary to the School council's instructions. By this time both of them were achieving notoriety by their Futurist activities and Mayakovsky had published his first avant-garde poems.[45]

If Boris Pasternak did not wholly accept conservative attitudes, he could not sympathise with the modernist destructive fervour. Some contemporaries saw the established arts as little more than a cultural museum display, but for Pasternak they had always been the object of an unforced filial veneration, and his whole education and experience had reinforced a sense of the continuity of world culture. The mentality of the image-breaker was alien to him, as indeed it was to Aseyev and Bobrov, despite their quarrel with the Symbolist mystagogues. As Pasternak wrote in *Safe Conduct*, 'the limit of culture is achieved by the man who conceals within himself a tamed Savonarola. The untamed Savonarola destroys it' (II, 264; *VP*, 253). But certain innovations and formal experiment elicited Pasternak's favourable response and figured in his verses of 1913. The Symbolist poet Valerii Bryusov mentioned Pasternak's first published verse in a survey in the June 1914 issue of *Russkaya mysl'* (*Russian Thought*). He described it as an example of 'straddling the frontier' (*porubezhnichestvo*), and when the first Tsentrifuga miscellanies appeared, the same critic pointed out their ties with the work of preceding generations, which Burlyuk and company would happily have jettisoned. Pasternak himself regretted only the lateness of his exit from the Symbolist fold. As he wrote on 1 July 1914 to Shura Shtikh, Bryusov's comment simply 'reflected the tragedy of my ignorance, which forced me in 1911 to be in Anisimov's clique when the Futurism of the Hylaeans* already existed.'[46] Pasternak's apparent Futurist fervour only arose, however, as the result of events in the spring of 1914.

Winter 1913–14 was the high season of Cubo-Futurist scandals. In January amid uproar they had rebuffed Marinetti, leader of Italian Futurismo, who had come on a tour of Russia intent on 'claiming his own'. Throughout the winter Cubo-Futurist leaders also toured Russia's major cities, and their progress through Kharkov, Simferopol, Petersburg, Sevastopol, Kerch, Odessa, Kishinyov, Nikolaev, Kiev, Minsk, Kazan, Penza, Tiflis, Baku, Kaluga, Rostov-on-Don and Saratov was attended by predictable outrage. Performances were frequently interrupted and sometimes curtailed by police on the lookout for indecency, blasphemy or treason. Though not a political group as such, the Futurists held social attitudes in keeping with their aesthetics; they were anti-bourgeois, anti-establishment, and therefore suspect. Mayakovsky, in particular, had even as a schoolboy served a short term in prison for his involvement with the Bolsheviks.[47]

In March 1914 the Cubo-Futurists brought out their *First Journal of Russian Futurists* (*Pervyi zhurnal russkikh futuristov*) which for the first time united mainstream Cubo-Futurism with Severyanin and the 'Mezzanine of Poetry' (an independent Moscow group of Ego-Futurist orientation founded by Vadim Shershenevich in late 1913). Since the major figures of the movement were away on tour, production of the *First Journal* was left to Shershenevich, and the result was a naïve, third-rate display of affectation and abuse that fairly reflected the acting editor's abilities. Shershenevich gave prominence to his own cheap

---

* Hylaea (*Gileya* in Russian) was the ancient Greek name for the area near Kherson where the Burlyuk family hailed from, and the title *Gileitsy* was used by the three Burlyuk brothers for a couple of years before they called themselves Futurists.

imitations of Mayakovsky, while the review section (much of it written pseudonymously by Shershenevich) also eulogised his works. Bobrov had earlier seen through Shershenevich's posturing superficiality and had rejected his attempts to join Lirika. Angered, Shershenevich now exacted revenge in the review section of the *First Journal* by singling out the Ego-Futurists and Lirika (including the work of Bobrov and Pasternak) for special vituperation.[48]

Thirsting for vengeance, Bobrov set aside all his earlier plans for battle with the mystics. Tsentrifuga's counterblast came a few weeks later in a miscellany with the neologistic title *Rukonog* ('Brachiopod', in Markov's suggested translation). Though still critical of Ellis, the review section defended Lirika and launched a blistering attack on Shershenevich, alerting the Moscow City Corporation to the putrid malodour coming from the Cubo-Futurist sewers. Bobrov's ambition was to secure the status of Tsentrifuga as an innovatory group and to question his opponents' claim to the Futurist title. In 1913 already he had pointed out the derivative nature of some of the Hylaeans' work, and the question of Cubo-Futurist legitimacy acquired a new pungency after Marinetti's visit. In *Rukonog* an obituary of the young poet Ivan Ignatyev (who had died by his own hand on 20 January) proclaimed him as the 'First Russian Futurist', and verses by his Petersburg Ego-Futurist colleagues were featured.[49] A poem called 'Turbopaean' (probably Bobrov's work) sounded a welcome to Tsentrifuga and mimicked Hylaean hyperbole in its proclamation that 'Aseyev, Bobrov and Pasternak / Make their nests high above the world'. Also identifiably 'Futuristic' was Bobrov's poetic 'Oratorio', stuffed with geometric and technological imagery. Aseyev's incantatory, songlike poems revived obsolete vocabulary in a manner redolent of Khlebnikov's lexical discoveries, while Bozhidar (Bogdan Gordeyev) contributed a poem of conventional context but printed in a mixture of Latin and Cyrillic, thus Futuristically underscoring the typographic 'texture of the word'.[50]

Pasternak's contribution to *Rukonog* was a threefold one. His polemical article *The Wassermann Test* (*Vassermanova reaktsiya*) was a typically oblique Pasternakian response to a commission from Bobrov which at the same time pursued issues bound up with his own creativity. The set task in this case was to destroy Shershenevich's credibility as a poet and undermine the Hylaeans' claim to be authentic Futurists. While doing this, however, Pasternak provided a first printed statement of his own approach to poetic metaphor, whose success allegedly stemmed from its a-rational, unfathomable quality, in which the mingling of attributes from contiguous objects reflected a 'Husserlian' view of perception. Briefly identifying the authentic Futurists, he wrote: 'We can name Khlebnikov, with some qualifications – Mayakovsky, only partly Bolshakov and poets of the "Petersburg Towncryer" group.'* Named after the medical test for syphilis, Pasternak's article accurately diagnosed the artistic debility of Shershenevich. A product of poetry's democratisation, which now admitted even spiritual plebs to the sanctum, Shershenevich's work allegedly lacked a vital 'quantité imaginaire' and was characterised by its prosaic, 'scientifically descriptive' way of thought. His verse could therefore be deciphered by any reader without any effort of the imagination. By contrast, Pasternak likened true poetic metaphor to an 'ornate lock' whose key should never be in the hands of 'amateurs from the crowd':

The fact of similarity – or, more rarely, an associative link based on similarity and never on contiguity – there is the origin of Shershenevich's metaphors. Yet only phenomena of contiguity possess that element of compulsion and spiritual dramatism which can be justified metaphorically [...] A word with impervious colouration cannot borrow colour from its object with which it is being compared. Only the painful need for some association, a melting of boundaries such as obtains in the lyrically supercharged consciousness can impart colour to an idea.[51]

The three poems Pasternak contributed to *Rukonog* in illustration of this article were his farthest and most fascinating venture down the avenue of obscurity, and they presented metaphoric 'locks' which were virtually unpickable. Their contrast with his other poems of the period suggests they were not altogether spontaneous outpourings, but were probably specially ordered by Bobrov to demonstrate Tsentrifuga's avant-garde prowess. (As with all his other specially commissioned poems, Pasternak never himself republished them.) Loks' memoirs recalled conversations with Pasternak which established that for him 'the word was not a semantic or logical category but, if one can put it thus, a polyphonic one. It was capable of captivating him by its musical accent or some secondary meaning concealed deep within it.' The *Rukonog* poems are in fact musically based compositions. The dominant influence, if any, is that of Khlebnikov. In common with him Pasternak uses old Slavonic and dialect forms, exploiting the musical effect of words in close proximity and achieving both an acoustic and semantic 'melting of boundaries', while beneath all this a residual thematic substratum is just

---

* 'Peterburgsky glashatai' – title of the Petersburg Ego-Futurist publishing enterprise.

discernible. 'The Gypsies' ('Tsygane') contains hints of Pushkin's epic, with scattered images of Moldavian summer heat and burning passion. Two other poems, 'Cupro-Nickel' ('Mel'khior') and 'On Ivan the Great' ('Ob Ivane Velikom'), are evocations of old Moscow with its Kremlin belfries and pealing bells, which offer a biographic pointer to Pasternak's life at the time. His rented room in Lebyazhii Lane where he moved in the autumn of 1913 and lived throughout 1914 commanded a view of the Kremlin and the opposite, Sofiiskaya, embankment. In these quarters he was often visited by Nikolai Aseyev, who at about the same time showed an interest in bell sounds in his poem called 'Greml'' – a Khlebnikovian pun on the words *kreml'* (kremlin) and *gremet'* (to peal or ring).

The first verse of 'Cupro-Nickel' emerges as a bell-ringing, musical fantasy on the Russian word forming its title. A phonetic rendering demonstrates its dense alliterative patterning derived from the 'key-word':

> Khramovói v malakhíte li khólen,
> Vozleléyan v srebré l' kosogór –
> Mnogodólnuyu gól' kolokólen
> Melkovódnyi nesyót mel'khiór

And translation confirms the semantic clouding: 'Be temple's cupro-nickel cossetted in malachite,/Or hillside nurtured in silver – /Still the many-segmented naked poor of the belfries/Are borne by shallow cupro-nickel.'[52]

Pasternak's signature also appeared in *Rukonog* together with those of Aseyev, Bobrov and Ilya Zdanevich (an artist friend and purely 'make-weight' signatory) at the foot of a Centrifugist 'Charter'. This document, a frenzied polemic clearly written by Bobrov, branded the Cubo-Futurists as an insolent, high-handed gang of usurpers and – with the exception of Khlebnikov and Mayakovsky – as a 'corporation of Russian mediocrities'. The rest of these traitors, renegades, slanderers, cowards and 'passéists' were challenged to come into the open for a personal showdown and to defend their untenable position.[53]

The response was rapid. On Friday, 2 May, a letter was sent from the Futurist publishing office on Krestovozdvizhensky Lane, signed by Mayakovsky, Shershenevich and Bolshakov and demanding a confrontation on neutral territory within the next four days. The time and place and choice of its representatives were left to Tsentrifuga, with the proviso that Boris Pasternak and the author of a review note about the *First Journal* were included. Failing a response, the writers of the letter reserved the option to 'resolve the misunderstanding by any of the methods normally applied to cowards'.[54]

Bobrov was anxious to limit dealings with the enemy to written exchanges, and it was evidently Pasternak who insisted on accepting the challenge of a personal encounter. Maybe Bobrov was afraid of what actually happened: a breach in Centrifugist loyalty and unity. Through the Sinyakov sisters, Aseyev had apparently already met and was on suspiciously friendly terms with Mayakovsky. From spring 1914, his work showed unmistakable Mayakovskian traits and later that summer, without actually leaving Tsentrifuga, he set up a new publishing venture with Bogdan Gordeyev and Grigorii Petnikov down in Kharkov. The Hylaean insistence on Pasternak's attendance was likewise based on Shershenevich's hope of weaning him away from Bobrov. ('Dima' Shershenevich was an acquaintance of the Shtikhs and of Elena Vinograd's family and had already met Pasternak in slightly friendlier circumstances in their company.) As a result of the winter's squabbling Pasternak was already somewhat cooler in his friendship with Bobrov, and although the Cubo-Futurists failed to 'kidnap' him, he too came away from the meeting with his views and attitudes transformed.[55]

Pasternak perhaps had his own apprehensions before the confrontation which took place in one of the Arbat coffee-houses. The figure of Mayakovsky and his writings were not unfamiliar. Anisimov had shown Pasternak some of his verse in the *Judges' Hatchery* at a time when Mayakovsky could be freely admired as a 'phenomenon of promising proximity and a giant' (II, 269; *VP*, 260), and Pasternak had liked some further examples of his produced by Aseyev in spring of 1914. Pasternak's brother had also known Mayakovsky at school (where his nickname was 'one-eyed Polyphemus') and recalled him as a guarded and sensitive youth wearing a frequent expression of 'kindly gloom'. Mayakovsky had left school in 1908, but Aleksandr Pasternak and he renewed a friendly, though no more than jesting, acquaintance in the autumn of 1913 when, after a false start in mathematics and physics at the University, Aleksandr entered the Moscow School of Painting to study architecture. Boris too recognised Mayakovsky from the corridors of the Fifth High School and from the audience at symphony concerts. But it required the proximity of Mayakovsky's poetic presence to light the touchpaper of an irresistible fresh enthusiasm.[56]

Many accounts confirm that the adult Mayakovsky had a dominating presence which was skilfully exploited in the rhetoric of public recitation. His hold on Pasternak's attention that day in the coffee-house was therefore no surprise. The Tsentrifuga team consisting of Pasternak, Bobrov, and the poet and publicist Boris Kushner, were dressed in careless manner and were already installed when the unexpectedly elegant opposition arrived. Shershenevich, Bolshakov and Mayakovsky entered noisily from the street, handed their hats to the porter and made a dignified approach. Once they were seated the main hostilities were exchanged, predictably, between Bobrov and Shershenevich. Meanwhile Pasternak's gaze was riveted on Mayakovsky who happened to sit opposite him. There was evidently mutual understanding from their very first words.[57] Pasternak recalled:

Before me sat a handsome, sombre youth with the bass voice of an Orthodox precentor and the fist of a boxer, inexhaustibly and murderously witty [...]

One immediately guessed that [...] the main thing about him was his iron control of himself, certain principles of nobility and a sense of duty which forbade him to be different, less handsome, less witty, less talented.

And his resolute manner and tangled mane of hair which he ruffled with all five fingers immediately reminded me of some terrorist underground figure out of Dostoevsky.   (II, 39–40; *VP*, 453)

Pasternak did not recount the substance of his conversation with Mayakovsky. Bobrov, however, recalled some details overheard amidst his own altercation with Shershenevich:

I noticed that Mayak's* nervously mocking and angry face, full of ferocious haughtiness [...] suddenly began to show strange signs of thoughtfulness, and attention [...] there was even a flash of something akin to proud embarrassment [...] but only for an instant [...] then Mayak's face relaxed completely. He propped himself on one arm and began to listen to Borya with attention and interest. I don't remember very well what they were saying. I hadn't time for that, for Kushner was seething and that gave Shershenevich immense pleasure – but I do remember two or three of Borya's phrases, which he spoke in a calm and rather sad voice: 'And what have we to talk about? Poetry? Certainly, I'm quite happy to talk about poetry. That's a worthy subject and I believe it's a familiar one to you...' Mayakovsky glanced at him with mocking distrust: 'Why do you think that?' Borya shrugged and quoted Lermontov [...] After that the two of them took no further part in our inter-journal argument [...] They talked about other things.

Another remark by Pasternak which Bobrov recalled was:

'But after all there are limits beyond which a literary discussion ends, and simple shouting and banging of fists starts up [...] but you can't call that art...' Borya's face showed fatigue and alarm, while Mayak's had slightly softened...

* *Mayak* – Russian for 'lighthouse', a frequently used abbreviation of Mayakovsky's surname.

And a further recollected exchange:

'So you're a philosopher?' – 'Every poet has something of that sort within his soul,' Borya answered. 'You surely wouldn't quarrel with that?'[58]

Predictably, the disputations led nowhere. Pasternak's only comment in *Safe Conduct* was that their opponents had departed unbeaten and that for Tsentrifuga 'the peace terms arrived at were humiliating' (II, 271; *VP*, 263). Bobrov recalled that they all left the meeting depressed, and some notes which he made indicate that Tsentrifuga was forced to admit its unconscientiousness and breach of literary etiquette.[59] Bobrov's apology to the Hylaeans was published in the newspaper *Nov'* (Virgin Soil) no. 109, and the only other public reaction to the incident was on 9 May in the newspaper *Den'* (The Day) in V. M. Friche's contemptuous article 'War of the Mice and Frogs'. For Pasternak, however, all this was overshadowed by his new enthralment with Mayakovsky.

By coincidence, the impressions of that first encounter were enriched the very next day when Loks and Pasternak met Mayakovsky at the Café Grec on Tverskoi Boulevard. The latter had just finished a game of 'heads or tails' with the poet Vladislav Khodasevich, who paid his debts and rose to leave as they arrived. Pasternak and Loks joined Mayakovsky, got into conversation, and were presently regaled with a recitation. It was an extract from the dramatic tragedy *Vladimir Mayakovsky* with a title role conceived for and played by the poet himself. Pasternak listened with bated breath to that 'sultry, mysterious, summery text' the like of which he had never heard before. 'The title concealed a discovery that had the simplicity of genius: the poet was not the author but the subject of the lyric, which addressed the world in the first person singular. The title was not the name of the author, but the surname of the contents' (II, 272–3; *VP*, 263–4).

'I carried him away with me from the boulevard and into my life', (II, 273; *VP*, 264), wrote Pasternak as he entered a period of fascination with Mayakovsky which for some time obscured all awareness of his own worth and originality. As he observed in *Safe Conduct*: 'Had I been younger, I might have abandoned literature' (II, 281; *VP*, 272). Like Scriabin, Mayakovsky's attraction lay partly in his very contrast with Pasternak: the spectacular fascinated precisely because of its alien impressiveness. Here was a poet who did not metaphorically 'surrender' to surrounding reality but imprinted his own personality on every feature of the landscape, playing Byron to Pasternak's Keats. Mayakovsky conceived even his lyric poetry as an essentially dramatic event, casting the poet in the central role of hero and martyr. In the *Auto-biographical Essay*, Pasternak tells of his fondness for Mayakovsky's early lyrics:

Against the background of contemporary clowning, their seriousness, weighty, menacing and complaining, was unusual. This was poetry sculpted in masterly fashion, proud, demonic and at the same time infinitely doomed, perishing and almost appealing for help.

> O Time, I pray you:
> Though you are a sightless icon-dauber,
> Still paint my likeness
> In the icon-frame of our hideous age!
> I am lonely as the last eye left
> To a man who goes to the blind;   (II, 40; *VP*, 454)

But Mayakovsky's attractiveness to Pasternak was not founded only on their contrast. Both were poets of the town. Pasternak's lyrics usually depicted it in collusion with natural elements and seasons. Yet, as his autobiographies and early fiction demonstrated, he was not blind to the tragic human aspects of modern urban awareness. And the home of Mayakovsky's poetry, as Pasternak perceived, was 'the labyrinth of the modern city where the lonely soul of modern man has got lost and become morally confused, and he [Mayakovsky] depicts its dramatic, passionate and inhuman situations'. Pasternak also detected that ulti-mately, unlike some of his second-rate imitators, Mayakovsky's hyper-bolic self-projection in his works was not a sign of megalomania. 'The mainspring of his brazen boldness was a farouche timidity, and beneath his feigned willpower there lay hidden a phenomenally hypersensitive lack of will' (II, 271; *VP*, 262). These latent traits of character in Mayakovsky were prominent in the personality of his new admirer, and although Pasternak had with age acquired some sophistication and self-assurance, he nevertheless detected their kindred qualities. As he told Shura Shtikh in a letter that summer, 'All retreat is cut off for me because Mayakovsky is me as I was in my youth, perhaps even before Spasskoye' (i.e. before the summer of 1909).[60]

Bobrov was displeased at signs of disaffection within Tsentrifuga, but he was careful not to exacerbate relations and provoke a breach with Aseyev or Pasternak. In June 1914 he began assembling material for the next Tsentrifuga album. Pasternak meanwhile left Moscow for the summer and during his absence exchanged several letters with Bobrov discussing, *inter alia*, the events of the last few months. The very first of

Pasternak's messages made clear his desire for change and for greater freedom to pursue his own artistic path:

Sergei, hear me out to the end. I have written nothing, and I am not deceiving you when I say that. However, I haven't told you anything about the reason for such a lamentable fact. I want to write again in the way I once began. I am now talking not about the form, but the spirit of these enterprises. Your advice has been an indispensable school for me, and I shall never forget what you have done for me. But if I again achieved the manner that I have lost – and that is the only way I am content to continue – then I would leave you and Nikolai [Aseyev].[61]

But the impact of Mayakovsky ensured there could be no return to the past. Although Pasternak did not become a blind imitator, the discovery of Mayakovsky caused a major poetic disorientation; to recover the natural authenticity manifest in early masterpieces like 'Black Spring' would be no straightforward task.

In his summer correspondence Pasternak made no secret of his misgivings about Tsentrifuga activities. One product of the latter was the eight-page draft of an abusive tract which Bobrov planned as his next salvo against Hylaea and which he sent for Boris' approval. But, as Pasternak had told Mayakovsky and now reiterated to Bobrov, polemical skirmishing had little to do with art: 'To this day it is a puzzle to me why this form of condiment is a need and requirement of Futurism.' And à propos the claim made in *Rukonog*'s 'Turbopaean': 'It was quite pointless for us to make our nests high in the sky – I not only never wanted that, but resisted it with all my being. It's hardly surprising that I have eventually fallen out of the nest.'[62] Bobrov's perspicuity, alertness and infallible instinct, the transparent clarity of his lyrics, and the happy combination of qualities essential in editorial and administrative work made him indispensable – this much Pasternak recognised. 'But I have been not a little amazed at your recent concessions to bad taste,' he told Bobrov. 'Tsentrifuga [...] could and should become a leading, trend-setting publication. Certainly, you are on the verge of achieving that – but only that, although it strikes me as easy to achieve such a position. But if you feel like the heir to the throne in the kingdom of poetry, then at least speak with the tone of an aristocrat. Yet instead of that you prepare eight pages of abusive attack! The same old thing over again!'[63]

Exactly how effective Pasternak's exhortations to Bobrov might have been is hard to tell. In the summer of 1914 money was in short supply and Tsentrifuga activities were suspended. Before their next edition was ready, the country had been overtaken by war.

8

Wartime in the Urals and Over the Barriers

'First Glimpse of the Urals'

Without any midwife, in darkness, unconscious,
Prodding the night with its hands and falling
In faint, the fortress of Urals crashed howling, and
Blinded by torment gave birth to the morning.

And thundering, randomly riven, upturned
Were obscure mountain masses and bronzes.
The train and its passengers panted, causing
The fir trees' shivering spectres to topple.

And the vapouring dawn was a sleeping-draught, given
By a woodland stove-stoker, an evil-tongued dragon,
Furtively slipped to the mountains and mills
As a thief gives a drug to his journey's companion.

In fire they came to. From a crimson horizon
On skis to the forests the Asiats rode
And licking their soles offered crowns to the pines
And sounded a summons to rise up and rule.

On a snow-crusted veil draped with velveted orange
And fashioned from damask and threaded with gold,
Like maned monarchs mounting, the pine trees arose
And in order of precedence regally strode.

Terrible times are drawing nigh.
Soon men will lie in fresh-dug tomb.
Await now earthquake, famine, plague,
Eclipse of stars and sun and moon![1]

This was the macabre prophecy of a one-legged cripple in the poem 'July
1914' which Anna Akhmatova wrote at her mother-in-law's country
estate near Bezhetsk in the province of Tver. That same summer

174

Pasternak was residing on a similar estate further east, and there he witnessed the solar eclipse on 8 (21) August, when at noonday 'knives and plates on the terrace took on a green hue, twilight fell on the flowerbed and the birds were silent' (II, 276; *VP*, 267). Before he left Moscow he also recalled how the city had 'blazed with enamel and tinfoil as in *The Golden Cockerel*. The lacquered green of the poplars glistened, and for the last time colours had that poisonous, grassy lushness that shortly they would part with forever' (II, 272; *VP*, 263). Pasternak's later prose story extended that farewell feeling to human relations and was set in 'the last summer when life still appeared to heed individuals, and when to love anything in the world was easier and more natural than to hate' (II, 200; *VP*, 188).

Before the outbreak of war and the appearance of that dark omen, however, there were a few days in which to enjoy a life style now under sentence. Pasternak's summer hosts and their neighbours and guests were mostly people with Symbolist affiliations. He had known the poet Jurgis Baltrušaitis for some time already. Baltrušaitis was Lithuanian born but lived most of his life in Russia, married a Russian wife and wrote mainly in Russian. He was an established Moscow Symbolist elder and since 1908 had been a friend of Scriabin's. Although taciturn ('sullen as a cliff face' was Bely's description) he had a quiet charm, and despite his Symbolist status he was tolerant and interested in new artistic trends. Pasternak was a regular guest at his spacious apartment on Petrovka Street and had read his own verse there.[2] Baltrušaitis had also tried – unsuccessfully so far – to arrange publication of Pasternak's prose *Tale of the Carp* in the journal *Zavety* (Testaments). The Baltrušaitises had an 11-year-old son, also called Jurgis and known to family and friends as 'Zhorzhik'. Pasternak found him 'spoilt, very capable, maybe even talented, but unpleasant'. Nevertheless, for the summer months of 1914 he agreed to come as a house guest and act as the boy's tutor.

In late May Pasternak therefore travelled with the Baltrušaitises to a summer dacha on the Ber family estate by the river Oka. It was located close to the town of Aleksin, some 150 kilometres south of Moscow, and was reached from Srednyaya station on the Syzran–Vyazma Railway. As Pasternak recalled, it was a hot and opulent summer with a profusion of lilac at the entrance to the estate, and to Shura Shtikh he described the local atmosphere as 'unusual and intoxicating'. At the dacha there were frequent readings and discussions, outdoor literary teas, and bathing in the river, and the only unwelcome guests were a profusion of vipers on the estate. The stimulating company included artist Nikolai Ulyanov and

Evgeniya Muratova, who was married to author and art historian Pavel Muratov and recently had been mistress and muse of Khodasevich. Not far away, at Ladyzhino, Balmont had his summer residence and kept appearing as a visitor. Another regular guest was Vyacheslav Ivanov, whose arrival on 10 July was celebrated with a literary tea-party.[3]

Evidently Pasternak called almost daily on the Ivanovs and was on friendliest terms with the poet. Their relations were shortly to be soured by Bobrov who publicly mocked an inscription by Ivanov to Pasternak and so implicated the innocent dedicatee that Ivanov cut him dead at their next meeting. At Aleksin, however, cordiality and even pranks were still in order. On one occasion Pasternak, Baltrušaitis and Zhorzhik concealed themselves beneath Ivanov's window and proceeded to hoot like owls. Asked later whether he had heard the birds, the Symbolist *mage* announced that, indeed, 'that's how they always call when there's going to be a war!' Despite its black humour, Pasternak subsequently recounted the incident with much glee.[4]

Baltrušaitis evidently thought enough of Pasternak's talent to suggest in the train en route for Aleksin that they cooperate in writing a play concerned with King Arthur. Nothing came of this, but Boris' main project for the summer was also a commission from Baltrušaitis. His task was to translate Kleist's comedy *The Broken Pitcher* (*Der zerbrochene Krug*) for the Moscow Chamber Theatre (Kamerny Teatr), which Tairov had set up earlier in the year in reaction against Stanislavsky's 'realistic' theatre. The Chamber Theatre's repertory board included Gorodetsky, Bryusov and Balmont, and it was headed by Baltrušaitis, who ordered the translation. There was widespread interest in Kleist at that time and a place had even been found for him in Symbolist prehistory. That same year Sologub and his wife had translated his *Penthesilea*, and in an article the scholar Zhirmunsky had drawn attention to Kleist's 'psychological idealism' and exploration of the *Nachtseite* of the human soul, describing him as an 'important representative of symbolic drama'. Although Baltrušaitis was pleased with his efforts, Pasternak made heavy weather of *The Broken Pitcher*. At the outset he described his task to his parents as 'devilishly difficult' – and the play itself as 'slightly monotonous' and 'devoid of artistic splendour'. By 1 June, however, he reported to Shura Shtikh that he had 1,500 lines ready and he was anxious to complete it by the 15th to show to producer Arkadii Zonov. 'In the meantime,' he added wrily, 'I shall probably forget how to write poetry.'[5]

Pasternak's later memory of that summer was closely bound up with his recent literary discovery. 'Whenever asked to say something about myself, I talked of Mayakovsky [who] . . . was my god' (II, 275; *VP*, 266) he recalled, and he was delighted to discover that Baltrušaitis too considered Mayakovsky 'a genuine talent.' Although he had little time for original work, Pasternak's letters from the Oka suggest that he was at least taking stock of his new situation. 'This last year I have become known in literary terms in Moscow's young circles, i.e. not simply by acquaintance but in such a way that I am known and talked about by people I don't know and who, fortunately, remain unknown to me,' he reported to his parents.[6] As for his own poetic style, he admitted the critics were right about the mixture of registers in his *Twin in the Stormclouds* (in fact a modernistic feature which several readers had failed to appreciate). However, he had plans for a change of idiom:

The fresh inspiration and perpetual unusualness and novelty of nature which begins anew each year inspires me with hope that I might manage to shake off all this official bombast that derives from the classics, who created and upheld it, and which was a living artistic truth only in this derivation [. . .]

My new book of verse must be fresh as the summer rain, every page should threaten the reader with a chill – that's how it should be. And if not, then better that it shouldn't exist.[7]

In fact, although Pasternak complained about his present únproductiveness in letters to Bobrov, the latter wrote back predicting he would shortly experience a new 'poetic explosion'.

Apart from discussing his own plans and Tsentrifuga affairs with Bobrov, Pasternak had a regular correspondence with Shura Shtikh concerned largely with his friend's own poetry, searches for a pseudonym and for someone to write him a preface. Pasternak had made some detailed comments on his verse and offered his own 'Reliquimini' as a *nom de plume*, but declined any assistance with a foreword. Perhaps he wished to avoid hypocrisy or offence: he mentioned Shtikh's poetry in a letter to his parents and described it as 'lyrical, warm and sincere, but pale just at the points when he becomes more daring.'[8]

Literary pursuits were soon upstaged, however, by more tragic issues. It required no special powers of divination to sense the imminence of war, and when the eclipse occurred someone in the company was ready with a reference to the old epic *Tale of Igor's Host* (*Slovo o polku Igoreve*) in which a similar event foretold the defeat and downfall of Kievan Russia; the memory of it later featured in Pasternak's *Three Chapters from a Tale*.[9] In May 1914 Pasternak had already been vetted for military service and was discharged as unsuitable because of his shortened right leg after the

19 Family dacha at Molodi (1915): Leonid, Rozaliya, Josephine, Lydia,
Berta Kofman, Aleksandr

riding accident of 1903. In July, when Russia mobilised, he was recalled
to the Moscow recruitment office but again rejected. Returning to the
Baltrušaitises, he was acutely aware of his enforced inactivity as others
mustered and volunteered. One evening through the mist on the river
the sound of military music was heard, and guests at the dacha watched
from the terrace as a tugboat with three barges carrying newly conscripted grenadiers hove into sight and tied up for the night. The soldiers
camped and made bonfires on the river bank while the officers were
invited up to the dacha to dine and sleep. The following morning they
left.[10]

For a second year Pasternak's parents, brother and sisters were
meanwhile spending their summer holiday at Molodi (just one station
up the line from Grivno where Scriabin was staying). To them Pasternak
registered his first stunned reaction to the outbreak of war: he was
alarmed, horrified and amazed that he and others had been to Germany
supposedly to learn the basics of culture. 'History has known nothing
like it,' he wrote, 'and even Napoleon's usurpations seem like a genius'
forgivable caprices in comparison with this inhuman act of banditry by
Germany.'[11] While picking up a book parcel from Srednyaya station

Pasternak also witnessed scenes which he described to his parents and later incorporated in *Safe Conduct*: local men travelling up by train to the recruitment centres were escorted to the station by their families, and the ritual wailing at their departure became a regular feature of the first months of the war. Similar sights were seen at Molodi: the day war was declared, the Pasternaks all watched as peasant carts came past one by one on their way to the mustering point.[12] In a letter of 21 August Pasternak posed the question whether he should not himself try to volunteer, and he promised to visit Molodi and talk it over with his parents on Sunday, 24 August. Details of their discussion are not on record, but it seems that Leonid Pasternak was not unsympathetic to his son's ambition. After a brief return to Aleksin, Pasternak made his way back to Moscow. His parents' return was delayed, however: Josephine was taken ill with scarlet fever, and was eventually brought home by motor car with Dr Levin in attendance.

Unlike the Russo-Japanese war of ten years earlier, this was a war in Europe, close at hand and acutely felt. And characteristically for Pasternak, nature seemed to share in the nation's misery. When war was declared the weather turned, he recorded, and the rains began. The universal lamentations were framed in a pewter icon-case of foul weather:

September was ending. A hazel grove blazed garbage-golden in the hollows like a mud-quenched fire. It was bent and broken by winds and by climbers after nuts, a chaotic image of ruination, all its joints twisted in a stubborn resistance to disaster. (II, 276; *VP*, 267)

Despite his urge to enlist, Pasternak's artistic reaction to events was neither prompt nor prolific. Mayakovsky, by contrast, reacted with vehement rapidity. On 21 July, three days after the outbreak of war, he had read a poem called 'War is Declared' at an open-air meeting in Moscow; in August he went to Petersburg and returned the next month bringing more war poetry. In the autumn, he printed several militant Futurist sabre-rattling publicist articles in the Moscow newspaper *Nov'*, calling on the arts to assist Russia's armies and produce a 'poetry that streams like a spirited march and is as necessary to the soldier as his boots.' 'We want the word of speech now to explode like a mine, now to ache like the pain of a wound, and now to rumble joyously like a triumphal "hurrah".'[13] Such poetry was intended to contrast with recent examples of traditional patriotic verse by several poetic contemporaries. Some examples of what Mayakovsky had in mind appeared on a special literary page in *Nov'* on Thursday, 20 November. Entitled 'Funereal

Hurrah', the page included a short fiction by D. Mikhnevich (David Burlyuk), Mayakovsky's own 'Mama and an Evening Killed by the Germans', and verse by Aseyev, Bolshakov and Pasternak, all incorporating a strong element of 'Mayakovskian' martial hyperbole.[14]

With its quirkily scholastic touch, when a foundering night attempts to conjugate the Greek verb Ζάω (I live), Pasternak's poem seems to reflect a move in the direction of Mayakovskian poetics. By contrast with Pasternak's earlier verse, his lyric hero now appears in sharp relief. Manning his battle post like a 'gunner at the helm', he senses the whole universe swing round like a ship which he himself steers. God is there as captain on the bridge, but His words are inaudible above the roar of battle. Personified nature is meanwhile engulfed in violence:

> Not fearing to land in the guard-house,
> The clouds pray for disarmament,
> And the universe moans with vertigo,
> Quartered hastily in smashed skulls.   (*SP*, 504)

The animation of nature was familiar in Pasternak's earlier verse, but grotesque theomachy, realistic hyperbole, a clearly delineated 'hero', and the collapse of a regular stanzaic and metrical scheme were all new, and contrasted starkly with the mesmeric incantation of the *Rukonog* poems earlier that year.

Pasternak's poem and the other contributions to 'Funereal Hurrah' were so out of line with Mayakovsky's prefatory swashbuckling articles and with official patriotic attitudes that a minor journalistic uproar ensued. The literary page was attacked in *Nov'*'s own next issues and the poet Georgii Ivanov criticised its unpleasant defeatist tone in the Petrograd journal *Apollon*. Pasternak's poem continued to attract official disapproval two years later, when its inclusion in *Over the Barriers* was allowed only after excision of the final six lines (including those quoted above).[15] It would be wrong to accuse the authors of 'Funereal Hurrah' of squeamishness, but when the creative artist in them spoke, the voice that sounded was not that of patriotic sentiment but of human compassion and outrage.

There was another aspect of Pasternak's poem, however, which censor and critics failed (or did not dare) to observe: despite a decoy reference to 'Japanese cannon' (i.e. suggesting the Russo-Japanese war), the poem hints at a satirical picture of the Tsar himself and his predicament:

> The artilleryman is a volunteer, modest and simple,
> He sees no dangerous landspurs,

He hears no words from the captain's bridge
Although he believes in God this night.   (*SP*, 503)

Pasternak had seen Nicholas II just once in his adult life. On 24 May 1913 he had stood on Strastnaya Square with Konstantin Loks and observed part of an imperial visit to Moscow to celebrate the tercentenary of the Romanov dynasty. Both Loks and he were struck then by the apparent lack of identity between the ruler and his people. The impression of power vested in a naïve, unperceiving and feeble personality was conveyed in Pasternak's poem.[16] Later it also emerged in the novel, where after a brief sighting of the Emperor Zhivago finds it 'awful to think that such apprehensive restraint and shyness were the essential traits of an oppressor, that such weakness could be used to execute or pardon, bind or loose' (*DZh*, 123).

(In view of what the authorities saw as Pasternak's faint-hearted reaction to the war, his father's similar response is of some interest. In summer 1914, while still out at Molodi, he received a commission for a war charities poster from the Moscow City Duma, and a soldier in full battledress came out to pose for him. The resulting poster showed a wounded warrior leaning on a wall for support and was a public success, but the artist heard later that his vision of the pathos of war caused official displeasure: Nicholas II's comment reported by a court adjutant was that '*My* soldier holds himself up gallantly – not like *that!*')[17]

Another poem by Pasternak on the First World War was called 'Bad Dream' ('Durnoi son'). Though probably written in 1914, its publication was delayed until his second verse collection in 1917. It was more obviously Pasternakian – in triple metre with repeating incantation and macabre imagery in which a devastated landscape was likened to a mouth with blackened, toothless gums, while the whole war was presented as nothing but a nasty nightmare of the Almighty, referred to as the 'Celestial Abstainer'. Another lyric was probably even more explicit, for its last five quatrains were replaced with dots by the wartime censors and only four lugubrious lines about autumnal 'blind rains' and overcrowded trains later found their way into print in *Over the Barriers* (1917).[18]

While Russian soldiers fought and died, Pasternak's Moscow showed only a distant awareness of the war. Social and cultural effervescence seemed unaffected by operations at the front. What Pasternak and others did notice was the spread of speculation, the appearance of a new public vocabulary, and the arrival of wounded men in ambulance trains while others departed for the front. Pasternak's mother started giving charity concerts and many women signed on as nurses – including cousin Olya

Freidenberg in Petersburg (now patriotically renamed Petrograd). But the security of Moscow was part of a deception. Pasternak was aware of it and felt uneasy:

The place for true situations was up at the front, and the rear would be in a false position even if it had not excelled in deliberate deception. The city hid behind phrases like a thief caught in the act, although at the time no one was yet trying to catch it. Like all hypocrites, Moscow lived a life of unusual external brilliance and was bright with the unnatural brightness of a flowershop window in winter.

(II, 279; *VP*, 270)

Early in the war Pasternak did attempt to enlist. So did several of his friends: it was not long before he ran into Bolshakov and Mayakovsky at police headquarters in November of 1914, where they had each gone independently to register as part of the procedures. Mayakovsky was turned down on political grounds and was finally called up only in September of 1915. Bolshakov entered the Tver Cavalry School. Aseyev was conscripted later in the fall of 1916. Meanwhile, Bobrov, Loks and Pasternak all received the medical 'white ticket'. Loks stayed initially in Moscow then went to his home town of Surazh for most of 1915. Bobrov stayed in Moscow pursuing journalistic work and contributing to the inter-party socialist journal *Sovremennik* (The Contemporary), where both he and Pasternak were invited to send their writings by the writer, journalist and critic Evgenii Lundberg who was editorial secretary.[19]

Pasternak's initial enthusiasm to take up arms gradually evaporated. A friend of his was Sergei Listopad, the musically talented natural son of the philosopher and critic Lev Shestov. Pasternak first met him at the house of Elena Vinograd, to whom Listopad eventually became engaged, and with the Shtikhs and pianist Samuil Feinberg they belonged to the same coterie of young people. Listopad had seen Pasternak in the summer of 1914 at Aleksin, but then he had volunteered and was on active service from the very start of the war. Later, while on leave, Listopad attempted to dissuade Pasternak from enlisting: 'With sober seriousness he told me about the front and warned me that I would find the exact opposite of what I expected to find there' (II, 280; *VP*, 270). After their conversations Pasternak's martial ambitions subsided and he eventually took measures to avoid conscription. After being twice wounded and decorated, Listopad was killed in 1916; his Ukrainian peasant mother came to Moscow to collect his belongings; Lev Shestov's life and attitudes were permanently overshadowed by the tragedy.[20]

ৡৢৡৢ

Leonid Pasternak had viewed Boris' first literary exploits with reserve, but the news of his new association with Mayakovsky and the Futurists caused him genuine distress. Leonid and his colleagues had a totally negative view of them since their trouble-making at the School of Painting, and he regarded Boris' admiration of Mayakovsky's poetic work as final proof of his son's misguidedness. (Aleksandr Pasternak disclosed in an interview in 1980 that his parents' belief that Boris was 'on the wrong road' and would come to a sorry end was finally dispelled only after reading his post-Revolutionary verse and the story *Zhenya Luvers' Childhood*.) Not surprisingly, the new bohemian friends were never introduced at the Pasternaks' home and Leonid Pasternak branded their whole company as a 'cesspool' (*kloaka*). Aleksandr and Josephine Pasternak met them, though, and Mayakovsky was taken one evening in autumn of 1914 to Ida Vysotskaya's, where he recited to a company gathered in her father's upper-floor art gallery.[21]

Through Mayakovsky and Aseyev, Pasternak got to know the five Sinyakov sisters. They were the daughters of a land-owning family from the Kharkov area. According to Lili Brik, their father was a member of the chauvinist, arch-conservative league of Black Hundreds, while their mother was an atheist progressive. By early 1914 all the daughters had made their way to Moscow. The eldest, Zinaida, was an opera singer with the married name of Mamonova, and she frequently entertained the artistic community at her elegant apartment on the top floor of Korovin's house at 9 Tverskoi Boulevard.

Of the remaining Sinyakov sisters, Maria, the second, and Kseniya, the youngest, had come to Moscow to study painting and music respectively. Maria was friendly with David Burlyuk and under the surname of her artist-husband, Arsenii Urechin, she herself subsequently became a well-known artist. Kseniya married Aseyev. Vera, the fourth sister, was friendly with and eventually married Petnikov, a Kharkov music student and poet who had come to study at Moscow University in 1914; her second marriage was to writer Semyon Gekht (Hecht).

It was the middle sister, Nadezhda Sinyakova, who was the main object of Pasternak's interest. She was never even mentioned in his autobiographies, but there is evidence that between 1914 and 1916 he and she were romantically involved. Nadezhda was a piano student and already married, although her advocate husband surnamed Picheta seems not to have figured on the scene. She was evidently of short stature, had dark hair and, according to Maria Gonta, she was the least attractive of the sisters and a very mediocre musician. Nadezhda, Maria and Kseniya had lodgings together on Malaya Polyanka in Moscow's Zamoskvorechye region, the former Tatar quarter south of the river.[22] In 1980 Aleksandr Pasternak gave me a humorous account of his one visit to Malaya Polyanka, where the guests included Mayakovsky and Aseyev. Apparently Aleksandr felt out of his element and Boris regretted introducing him to the company:

Altogether they were a bohemian set who had decided it was necessary to *épater le bourgeois*... All the Sinyakovs were like that... They were all drinking vodka and eating dried herring, and in order to show that this wasn't the usual sort of party held in decent society where you ate from a plate using cutlery, it was served on newspaper. Vodka was drunk straight from the bottle or from cups that had lost their handles. I had the impression they wanted to get me drunk and have a laugh at my expense. But I steeled myself and withstood the test, although afterwards Borya told me he would never take me there again... They were a bohemian and provocative set of folk – all very pleasant – I can't say anything against them – and all very interesting maybe. But that typical trait of readiness for a quarrel that was very much part of Mayakovsky was shared by them all. And the three Sinyakov sisters [i.e. Nadezhda, Maria and Kseniya] were notable for butting into your conversation and terrorising you with their rapier thrusts. That was how they operated.

Among the Sinyakovs' regular guests were Sergei Bobrov, although for 'ideological' reasons he disliked coinciding with visits by other Cubo-Futurists. On one occasion he left after Mayakovsky rang to say he was about to arrive with Vasilii Kamensky.[23] On several occasions Pasternak met Nadezhda and her sisters at the house of Zinaida Mamonova, to whose circle he also introduced Loks and Dobrovein. *Safe Conduct* later recorded one particular party at the Mamonovs on Christmas Eve of 1914. A novelty of the occasion was a primus stove on which the cooking was done – Pasternak's first glimpse of this new invention.[24]

Little is known of Pasternak's involvement with Nadezhda Sinyakova; there is only some circumstantial poetic and epistolary evidence. 'The Blizzard' ('Metel'') records impressions of a winter-time visit to Zamoskvorechye; 'What hot blood has the twilight...' ('Kakaya goryachaya krov' u sumerek...') is clearly related to a visit to Zinaida's at Korovin's house; another poem talks about love in terms reminiscent of an act of arrest in which the two partners are manacled and cast into prison ('Following my lead all call you miss...' ['Vsled za mnoi vse zovut vas baryshnei...']). Although the fact was not recorded in print, later Pasternak privately dedicated his collection *Over the Barriers* (1917) to Nadezhda.[25]

In April 1915 Nadezhda Sinyakova apparently fell ill and went back home to her parents' home in Kharkov. Probably Pasternak went with her by train as far as Tula, and some impressions of an agonised parting may have later provided material for the story *Letters from Tula* (1918). Their correspondence continued during the spring and summer months of 1915 and some fragments of her letters survived in the Pasternak family. Her messages to Boris were affectionate (couched in polite *vy* terms) rather than amorous: perhaps it was another case of his unilateral infatuation. She did not keep his letters, and after his death her letters to him were handed back to her; Nadezhda Sinyakova has herself since died.

For several years Boris Pasternak's staple income had come from private tutoring. During the First World War one particular long-term appointment had an effect on his life and literary work. For two lengthy spells in 1915 he lived at the home of Moritz Philipp, a well-known German haberdashery manufacturer, and acted as tutor to his son Walter. He first moved to their home at 10 Prechistenka (now Kropotkin Street) in March 1915. At the start of the war the Russian government had declared the inviolability of property owned by German nationals, and the latter were allowed to retain their peacetime jobs under protection of the law. One of Pasternak's own relatives benefited from this: his father's cousin Karl Pasternak and his wife had been cut off in Austria at the start of the war (in May of 1915 both of them died suddenly in Vienna within twenty-four hours of one another), but their son Fyodor (Fedya), an Austrian subject, still continued working for Ryabushinsky's bank in Moscow. Only in May of 1915 was he politely ushered into internal exile (without an escort) along with other enemy aliens. Until 1917 he spent the time idly but pleasantly quartered in the Bashkirian town of Ufa. The Pasternaks' own horror at the war had not affected their many friendly contacts with Germans in Moscow and Boris frequently took Walter to visit his family (Leonid Pasternak made a pleasant pastel showing Walter colouring Easter eggs in 1916 with Josephine and Lydia). Apart from tutoring him, Pasternak also took his young charge on walks and outings and they read Kleist together. Walter later recalled Boris' special interest in *Faust*, but his recollections in general were disappointingly scanty and he was evidently too young to appreciate properly Pasternak's literary interests.[26] (After Pasternak gave up his duties as tutor Walter had very little contact with him. Moritz Philipp died in 1919 and his widow and son left Russia for Germany in 1921; Walter's sister remained in Moscow. Contacts between the families were resumed in Berlin in the 1920s, and Walter also met Aleksandr Pasternak there in 1924, but there was no meeting with Boris. Latterly Walter Philipp worked in Berlin in the Archiv für Energiewissenschaft and died in 1983.)

As the war continued, initially liberal official attitudes changed, rules were altered and measures taken to limit the rights of enemy aliens. There was also official connivance at acts of violence against German property, and on 28 May 1915 anti-German demonstrations and riots took place in Moscow. Special targets of attack were the prominent or wealthy, and they included von Einem the confectioner and Ferrein the pharmacological manufacturer, in whose home Shura Shtikh was tutoring. Moritz Philipp's house and offices also suffered damage. Only German property was meant to suffer, but in the ensuing *mêlée* most of Boris' books and papers were lost, a mishap for which the rescue of his clothes and other belongings proved little consolation. The Philipps were forced to abandon their half-ruined and burnt-out house and the relics of what had been a fine collection of porcelain and Dutch masters.[27] Boris took Walter immediately to stay with his own parents at Molodi. Then, after a short spell at their Volkhonka home, he went in mid-June for a brief stay at the Philipps' temporary refuge with their married eldest daughter Irina Kotlyarevskaya at 1 Krestovozdvizhensky Lane. Following this he moved with them to their estate and dacha at Osipovka near Khlebnikovo on the Savyolovsky Railway (this episode was later reflected in the prose *Story*). Then, after another short stay at Molodi, Pasternak went off in July for a three-week visit to Nadezhda Sinyakova who was at her parents' home in Krasnaya Polyana near Kharkov. At various times several other poet admirers of the sisters had made this trip, including Aseyev, Khlebnikov, Bobrov, and Dmitrii Petrovsky. Pasternak's poem 'Windmills' ('Mel'nitsy') contained a reminiscence of his journey, and 'Parting' ('Proshchan'e') probably related to his departure for Moscow in August. The poetic evidence here suggests that he and Nadezhda met again in Moscow one month later.[28]

Upon returning to Moscow, Pasternak moved in with the Philipps again. They now lived in furnished luxury quarters at 3 Sheremetevsky Lane (now Granovsky Street), apartment 90, in one of several houses now occupied by important Soviet officials.

It was after moving into these new quarters that Pasternak recalled first reading Anna Akhmatova's poetry – probably her earliest verses from *Evening* (*Vecher*) (1912) that were reprinted in *The Rosary* (*Chetki*) (1914). Pasternak envied her ability to 'capture particles of reality by such simple means'.[29] His own modernist tastes, however, were far removed from her restrained classicism and their aesthetic views and biographies began converging only in the 1920s. Another aspect of Pasternak's stay with the Philipps which had literary consequences was his friendship (of what sort or intensity remains unclear) with their English governess. She had earlier worked in the Vysotsky household and now evidently helped Boris with his English. In transposed form she and the Philipps became Anna Arild and the Fresteln family in Pasternak's prose *Story*, which contained several incidents and impressions from his life at this time.

When Pasternak left the Philipps at the end of 1915, his place was taken by Aleksei Losev (subsequently a celebrated classical scholar), and there was later talk (but no more than that) of Aleksandr Pasternak taking over as Walter's tutor in the spring of 1916. Perhaps Boris' own comment on the household discouraged his brother: 'It's a nice place and the people are pleasant too. Of course, there's a lot of conventional, formal and class-ridden dissemblance and nastiness, but one can close one's eyes to that, although it is a bore.'[30]

In February 1915 a note to Shura Shtikh announced that he should come bringing a bottle of port and cognac, since Boris was 'about to become solvent'.[31] The beginnings of an income from literary work now seemed likely. Thanks to Evgenii Lundberg, Pasternak's translation of *The Broken Pitcher* as well as an article on Kleist were accepted by the journal *Sovremennik*. In fact, only the translation actually appeared – in the fifth issue for May 1915. By this time the journal was in difficulties and it folded in October 1915,[32] not before Pasternak had sent the editors at least a dozen increasingly impatient letters (between March and August) inquiring about the fate of his work, the state of the manuscript, offprints, honorarium etc. The climax had come on 7 May when, at Bobrov's instigation, he wrote to Gorky himself (director of the journal) objecting to 'distortions of the text, in which the proofs abound, shortenings, prosaic insertions, and excisions of the comedy's most colourful points'. The corrections, all of which Pasternak later acknowledged as justified, eventually turned out to be Gorky's own interventions – later, in 1921, Pasternak sent him an embarrassed letter of apology for the misunderstanding![33]

More important than this publication and the ensuing contretemps were Pasternak's other writings of the war years. Our picture of his development after meeting Mayakovsky and announcing new poetic intentions in the summer of 1914 remains incomplete. The 'Artilleryman' poem of December 1914 was already a sign of new developments in his verse and it formed part of his eventual collection *Over the Barriers* (1917). But in the *Autobiographical Essay* Pasternak talked about the loss of another book of verse 'midway between *Over the Barriers* and *My Sister Life*'.[34] We know more of this book only from later verbal reports by Loks and the scholar Vyacheslav Vsevolodovich Ivanov. By the spring of 1914 Pasternak was an enthusiast of the French Decadents and Baudelaire. At about that time he visited the young poet Dmitrii Petrovsky in this attic flat in Zachatyevsky Lane and apparently regaled him with recitations of Verlaine and Baudelaire. By the following year he had apparently written a complete new book of original verse – Loks recalled its use of irregular metres, and Pasternak later described it to Ivanov as being in the spirit of Pierre Laforgue. (This in no way negated any influence by Mayakovsky – in an appreciative review of the latter's work in 1917 Pasternak asked rhetorically: 'How can one admire Pushkin who is so unlike Laforgue and Rimbaud?'[35] Indeed, Laforgue and Mayakovsky shared a common avoidance of regular strophic and metrical patterns, a rejection of traditional notions of harmony and balance, an interest in contemporaneity, and a tendency to use self-defensive irony and comedy.) Pasternak gave Loks the book to read and retain. He himself was dissatisfied with it, though, and later took it back and either destroyed it, or else it was lost in the ransacking of the Philipps' home in May 1915. Possibly some individual items did survive and were printed separately during the war years, e.g. the poems 'Arctic Seamstress' ('Polyarnaya shveya') or 'Anguish' ('Toska'), but we can do no more than speculate about this.

Most of our information about Pasternak's verse of 1915–16 therefore derives from a handful of lyrics in various miscellanies and the book *Over the Barriers*, an obviously incomplete and chronologically disorganised compendium. What is apparent, though, is that despite the impact of Mayakovsky and an initial impulse to give up literature on first encountering him, at no point did Pasternak become Mayakovsky's mere imitator. (This is not clear from the over-grateful obituary remarks in *Safe Conduct*, which have encouraged distorted readings of Pasternak's achievement in the First World War period.)[36] His discovery of Mayakovsky as an avatar of his own youth and his realisation in 1915 that they shared a multitude of devices in common was a blow to Pasternak's pride. But their shared qualities were not the result of imitation. 'The times and a community of influences made me similar to Mayakovsky,' Pasternak recalled (II, 281; *VP*, 272). *Safe Conduct* mentions several Futurist poets comprising that 'community of influences', which included original artists like Khlebnikov, Kamensky and Bolshakov, with whom Pasternak shared his acoustic etymologies, 'modern' dissonant orchestration and grotesque imagery. But Pasternak doubtless had in mind lesser poets like David Burlyuk or Shershenevich, when he wrote that he could not fathom how, as 'a man with an almost animal craving for the truth', Mayakovsky 'surrounded himself with petty, pernickety people with fictitious reputations and false, unjustifiable pretensions' (II, 278; *VP*, 269). The only poet, seemingly, who could stand comparison with him was Bolshakov, for whom Pasternak had a considerable liking and who shared Mayakovsky's impressive physique and genial manner. 'He is a lyricist beyond doubt and as such bound to be original *a priori*,' Pasternak told Bobrov in a letter of 1916. A handful of Pasternak's poems showed hints of a specifically Bolshakovian device in the incantatory 'Improvisation', or 'The Blizzard'. These were printed in May 1915 in the miscellany *Muses' Vernal Forwarding Agency (Vesennee kontragentstvo muz)*, where their stuttering repetitions successfully evoked spontaneous poetic composition and a bewildered retracing of steps and thoughts through the Zamoskvorechye snowstorm.[37]

The missing book of verse and the extreme rarity of Pasternak's wartime appearances in print thus make it difficult to identify direct poetic debts to Mayakovsky. The only exception is the poem by Pasternak that eventually appeared in 1916 in Mayakovsky's *Taken! The Futurists' Drum (Vzyal! Baraban futuristov)*. This extended lyric or *poema** featured the poet-hero as 'treasurer of the last of planets' or 'treasurer of mankind', condemned to pay with his soul for the 'maintenance of love, of men, of spring' and of 'tragedies, kingdoms and chimeras' (III, 126–8; *SP*, 504–6). The poet's martyrdom to love was celebrated in seventy-odd lines, with breaks, subsections, metrical variations and episodes in tonic metre, and was cast in a hyperbolic idiom strongly recalling Mayakovsky. Indeed, there were even a few near-echoes of *The Backbone Flute (Fleita-pozvonochnik)* on which Mayakovsky was working in late 1915.[38] It was at that time, during a brief visit to Petrograd, that Pasternak had taken him the 'Treasurer' poem.

During the First World War, several Moscow writers and artists,

---

* *Poema* in Russian designates a 'long poem', as distinct from a short lyric (*stikhotvorenie*).

including Urechin, Kushner, Kamensky and Mayakovsky, had moved to Petrograd, apparently because of the better conditions and opportunities for work. Mayakovsky had gone there in January 1915 and spent most of the year writing and publishing in *Novy Satirikon* and other journals. At their December meeting Mayakovsky told Pasternak of his own recent meeting with Gorky and introduced him to his new friends, the critic Osip Brik and his wife Lili at their Zhukovsky Street apartment. By now Mayakovsky himself had been conscripted and was posted with the same motorised unit as Brik.

To Pasternak, in Petrograd the war seemed much less in evidence than in Moscow:

As always the lively movement of the capital was moderated by its generous dreaming spaces which life's necessities could not exhaust. The avenues themselves were the colour of winter and twilight, and in order to send them sweeping and tinkling into the distance their silvery urgency required little in the way of extra snow or lamplight. (II, 280; *VP*, 271)

Pasternak and Mayakovsky strolled together around the snowbound capital. Delighted with his friend's new verses, Mayakovsky recited to him from his own latest major compositions, *The Backbone Flute* and *War and the Universe* (*Voina i mir*).[39] He also explained how 'the social theme was entering increasingly into his literary projects, enabling him to work in a new way, at definite hours and in measured portions' (II, 280; *VP*, 271). By contrast, Pasternak's creative method remained wayward and elemental. Despite his pathos-laden poem in 'Funereal Hurrah' and a few other topical verses (above pp. 180–1), for Pasternak the notion of historical or social 'commitment' struck no common chord, as the contents of the next Tsentrifuga almanac were to show.

Only a few verses of winter 1915–16 bearing a certain romantic imprint belatedly reached Pasternak's readers in 1917. One poem, 'Petersburg', probably stemmed directly from his visit to the capital and was partly concerned with Peter the Great, the city's founder:

> There was no misfiring as Peter unleashed
> This volley of streets and embankments.
>
> Oh, how great he was! What a web of convulsions
> Invaded those iron-clad cheeks.
> What tears to his eyes bring those sedge-covered gulfs
> As the Emperor beholds them and sees!
>
> [...]

Clouds stood on end like the hairs of his head
Over the smoky, pallid Neva. So
Who then are you? Who are you? Whoever you are,
This town is your own invention.   (I, 192, 195; *SP*, 79, 81)

(The close identity between Peter's colossal stature and his city was later strikingly echoed in *Safe Conduct*'s observation that Moscow by night 'looked the very image of Mayakovsky's voice. What went on there and what was piled up and broken down by that voice were like two drops of water. But this was not the similarity that naturalism dreams of, but the connection that links together the anode and the cathode, the artist and life, the poet and his time' (II, 279; *VP*, 270).)

Other romantic poems of 1915–16 later found in *Over the Barriers* showed the 'Materia Prima' of an anthropomorphic universe as being the poet's own blood, while the spring thaw was a ceremony in which he himself was dismembered and dissolved. Even in an otherwise Pasternakian candle-lit nocturnal setting, the advent of inspiration was a call to martyrdom: 'This is the hour of murder! Somewhere out there I'm awaited!' (*SP*, 515). The alternatives to being done to death in love or creativity were either a lapse into irony at the expense of romantic feeling (as in the 'Arctic Seamstress', whose clustered images recall the description of Levitskaya's dressmaking atelier in chapter 2 of *Doctor Zhivago*), or else an escape into comic protective disguises. An instance of the latter occurred in 'Anguish', a poem printed like 'Seamstress' in the *Second Tsentrifuga Miscellany* (*Vtoroi sbornik Tsentrifugi*) of 1916. Here the poet's emotional torment is detached and objictified as a pine-marten, which goes on a wild rampage through the nightbound landscape, ending up tragically with a splinter in its paw.[40] Similar examples of soulful and suffering fauna were not uncommon in Mayakovsky.

Perhaps under Mayakovskian or general Futurist influence, Pasternak's earlier kaleidoscopic impressionism temporarily gave way to more extended metaphors that spanned long episodes or whole poems (as in 'Anguish'). This might explain the greater length of several wartime poems, as distinct from the four to six stanzas found in earlier (and subsequent) compositions. Metrical and rhyme schemes, and lay-out too, became freer, often dictated by the colloquial or rhetorical spoken phrase. Most of these features of Pasternak's verse of 1915–16 could be aligned with similar examples by the Hylaean modernists.

In the *Autobiographical Essay* Pasternak writes of his stylistic coincidences with Mayakovsky as follows:

When I got to know Mayakovsky more closely, some unforeseen technical similarities emerged between us, a similar construction of images, similar rhyming [...] In order not to repeat him and not to seem to be imitating him, I began to suppress in myself those tendencies that echoed his – the heroic tone, which in my case could have been false, and the striving for effects. This confined my style and purified it.   (II, 41; *VP*, 455)

The heroic tone was one aspect of what *Safe Conduct* described as the 'romantic manner', and which Pasternak traced to the Symbolists' concept of the poet's quasi-sacerdotal role, and to nineteenth-century Romanticism. According to the romantic heroic programme, the artist's whole life is regarded as a spectacle. The poet is 'inconceivable without the non-poets who throw him into relief, for this poet is [...] a visual and biographical emblem requiring a background to show up its outline [...] This drama needs the evil of mediocrity in order to be seen, just as romanticism always has need of philistinism' (II, 281–2; *VP*, 272–3). Exactly when Pasternak realised all this is not stated in his autobiographies. He must have seen from the outset, however, that Mayakovsky and he had quite different views of poetic 'voice production' and of the poet's relation to his public. Theirs was an attraction of opposites. Pasternak's approach to Mayakovsky was like a comet around the sun. He came from the depths of 'lyrical space' and even at perihelion his course and speed of approach were bound to fling him quickly away again. In late 1915, just when he and Mayakovsky seemed to have so much in common, he was most profoundly ill at ease. This emerged in his letter of 16 December 1915 to Dmitrii Gordeyev in Kharkov. The latter's poet brother Bogdan, or 'Bozhidar', had committed suicide on 7 September 1914 aged only nineteen, and Dmitrii had requested Pasternak's help with producing a memorial volume. Pasternak declined, hinting at Bogdan's lack of distinction, allegedly shared with all those around him:

You are probably not aware what a low opinion I have of everything that has been going on in Russian literature and poetry of the last decades and is still going on today.

Without detailing his own romantic aberrations, Pasternak explained that for the last couple of years 'other matters' had prevented his engagement in serious writing, and 'such a half-serious attitude enabled me to reconcile myself with a lot of things in me and those around me which cannot exist in the closed system of an artistically true and living organism.'[41]

ತಿಕ್ಕೊ

Pasternak's published output in the earlier 1910s may seem to reflect the Symbolist and Futurist bias towards poetic genres; his debut as the author of belletristic, non-polemical prose took place only in 1918. During the First World War, however, he worked on various items of fiction. Several of these manuscripts and sketches were subsequently lost or destroyed, but we know something of them from secondary sources and from people who read or heard about them.

The example of the German Romantic E. T. A. Hoffmann was cited by both Lydia and Aleksandr Pasternak in recollections of their brother's lost fairy story entitled *Tale of the Carp and Naphtalain* (*Povest o Karpe i Naftalene*). Written in late 1913 or early 1914, the work consisted of a prose text interlaced with poetic interludes. Lydia Pasternak later recalled: 'It had a juxtaposition of round, heated vulgarity and savageness, embodied in the Carp, alias the sun, alias the summer on the one hand, and the pale blue, cool silkiness, moonlit princeliness of Naphtalain on the other. I think the Carp finally stole the Prince's regalia and killed him.' Pasternak's sister also suggests that the tale may have arisen from associations with spring-cleaning and the storing of winter things in naphthalene ('a kind of present-day symbolic burial-rite'). All that survives of the actual text is a few lines quoted in a letter from the author and Lydia Pasternak-Slater's recollection of some hauntingly beautiful verses on Naphtalain's funeral.[42] Pasternak was well pleased with his *Tale of the Carp*. After Baltrušaitis' failure to print it in 1914, he later, in December 1916, offered the typescript to Sergei Bobrov for publication along with *The Apelles Mark* (*Apellesova cherta*), describing it as 'colourful, condensed and technical'.[43] Sadly, Bobrov did not take up the suggestion. The work was never published and its manuscript disappeared. Also written but subsequently lost during the First World War were the article on Kleist submitted to *Sovremennik*, and a tercentenary appreciation of Shakespeare. About the contents of these we can only guess.

In early 1915 Pasternak had been to see Evgenii Lundberg, the editorial secretary of *Sovremennik*. Lundberg was a man of strongly anti-Futurist tastes (which emerged in his article 'About Futurism' in March 1914 issue of *Russkaya mysl'*), and he perhaps cherished hopes of rescuing the 'moderate' Centrifugists. In 1914 he had solicited contributions from Pasternak and Bobrov, and Pasternak reported to Shtikh on 6 February 1915 that he had delivered to Lundberg 'a novella, Italianate, passionate and bubbling', and that there was promise of its appearance both in *Sovremennik* and as a separate book. 'He wants to publish me,' wrote Pasternak. 'He asks me to write freely in my own style. He thinks I ought to try a novel, a drama, etc. That's quite sufficient. But, as before, I've not been paid a sou.' In fact it was another three years before the story concerned was printed, and it was meanwhile successively rejected by *Sovremennik*, by Gorky's *Letopis'* (The Chronicle) and by *Russkaya mysl'*. And when it finally appeared in 1918 it was scarcely noticed, upstaged by Pasternak's emergence as a full-fledged poet.

The 'Italianate' novella was Pasternak's first major completed prose fiction. Its title was *The Apelles Mark* (*Apellesova cherta*). (An edition of 1925 acquired an Italian heading: *Il tratto di Apelle*.) The setting was based partly on Italian reminiscences of 1912, with spectacular evocations of an August sunset in Pisa, the hot Tuscan night, a train journey across the Apennines, and impressions of Ferrara. But Pasternak's sources were also partly literary: a character named Relinquimini from his early prose sketches reappeared (although now no longer as an authorial self-projection) and a prose epigraph retailed a Greek classical story on which the narrative was based:

It is said that on finding his rival Zeuxis out one day, the Greek artist Apelles drew a mark on the wall by which Zeuxis could guess who had called in his absence. But Zeuxis did not remain in debt for long. He chose a time when he knew that Apelles was away from home, and he too left behind a mark which has since become a byword for artistry.　　　　　　　　　　(II, 53; *VP*, 19)

The story also had two German Romantic sources. Robert Payne has pointed out that Kleist's 'The Marquess of O.' ('Die Marquise von O.') seems to have prompted not only the motif of newspaper intrigue, but also some of the playful atmosphere of irony, scandal and mystification.[44] Meanwhile Elliott Mossman suggests Heinrich Heine's 'Florentine Nights' ('Florentinische Nächte') as a second partial source. In Heine's narrative the main character regales his consumptive beloved with stories, including one of a performance by Paganini when the experience was both auditory and visual – a series of 'signatures' which enabled a deaf painter to portray Paganini so accurately that his picture evoked both laughter and tears.[45]

Pasternak's story concerns a poet in search of a personal 'signature' that will establish his own authenticity in the face of a powerful popular rival. 'Apelles' is the fictional romantic Ferraran poet Emilio Relinquimini, author of the celebrated poem 'Il Sangue'. 'Zeuxis' is the Westphalian poet Heinrich Heine – a 'resurrected' Heine, but still the real one, now making a second *Journey to Italy* (*Reise nach Italien*) (cf. Mozart, Salieri and other historical figures in Pasternak's earlier sketches).[46] Relinquimini has first written Heine an anonymous letter challenging him to write of love 'in such a way that is as succinct as Apelles' mark. Remember the only thing that Zeuxis is curious about is your membership of the aristocracy of the blood and spirit (inseparable concepts).' (II, 54; *VP*, 20–1). Later, Relinquimini leaves a blood-spotted card at Heine's hotel in Pisa announcing he will be there next day to inspect the 'signature of Apelles'. Heine departs, leaving with the hotel porter a parcel for Relinquimini which contains a scrap of manuscript: 'but discarding their former names, Rondolfina and Enrico managed to exchange them for hitherto imaginary ones: "Rondolfina!" he shouted wildly. "Enrico!" came her responding cry' (II, 55; *VP*, 21). On reading the message Heine goes to Ferrara and books in at the Hotel Torquato Tasso. He is just in time to insert in that day's issue of *Il Voce* a notice of the discovery of a manuscript by Relinquimini, requesting the claimant to apply to room 8 of his hotel. In Relinquimini's absence his mistress Camilla Ardenze turns up. She is amused and fascinated by Heine. He is a captivating host, providing conversation, flowers and entertainment for her delight, and he finally seduces her and in that same instant genuinely falls in love with her. Thus, indelibly and in real life, Zeuxis-Heine makes his mark before Relinquimini has time to return.

Pasternak's story of revenge on a boastful rival is in fact a parabolic statement on the nature of art and a form of reckoning with the romantic manner. The very name Relinquimini suggests one who is both physically and artistically doomed to abandonment. His beloved Camilla lives next to the theatre, and his own theatrical posturing, emphasis on the poet's 'aristocracy' and hints of the artist's martyrdom and blood sacrifice are identifiable as elements of Mayakovsky's poetics (and of Pasternak's in his romantic phase). It is also no coincidence that Heine is the name of that German ironist who specialised in exposing the naïveté of Romantic statement. His exploits in Ferrara are a probing of the frontier between fanciful literary invention and reality, and he punctures Relinquimini's ponderous make-believe by transferring the contest from the realm of fantasy to real life. The conversation between Heine and Camilla Ardenze is also highly revealing: it identifies Relinquimini's rival as a true poet, and one after Pasternak's own manner. A Pasternakian effacement of the artist's personality is suggested by the very title of Heine's book, *Verses Unpublished in the Poet's Lifetime*; and just prior to their first embrace Heine reminds Camilla that there are moments in life

195

when 'eternities come bursting forth [...] and then – away with words!'
Camilla rebukes Heine for acting as though he were on the stage, but his
retort is: 'You are wrong, Signora. All our life we are on a stage, and by
no means anyone is capable of that naturalness which is imposed like a
role on everybody from their birth.' Nevertheless – or precisely because
of all this – Camilla successfully identifies Heine as an authentic poet:
'You are a sort of unusual child. No, that is not the word – you are a poet
[...] an idler chosen by God and spoilt by fate' (II, 60–73; *VP*,
26–30).[47]

Heine's final achievement of a form of expression that substitutes
wordless passion for naïve romantic statement is inseparably bound up
with what Pasternak wrote to Shura Shtikh in his letter of 6 February
1915, recalling his amorous misadventure with Ida Vysotskaya three
years earlier: 'If at that time I wrote about femininity, then only because
I was badly deluded: I did not realise that an access of passion is nobler
than any unrecognisably ornate phrases about it.' Evidently, therefore,
the 'Marburg incident' opened the way to Pasternak's discovery of an
oblique form of emotional yet non-romantic impressionistic 'signature'.
And *The Apelles Mark* (about which Pasternak told Shtikh in the same
letter) adumbrated an artistic approach whereby Pasternak could redis-
cover his natural poetic voice and escape the forced accents of the
romantic one. Significantly, the theme of the story was also rehearsed at
about the same time in a poem called 'Paganini's Violin' ('Skripka
Paganini') that was later included in *Over the Barriers* (1917). Not only
does it point to the connection with Heine's 'Florentine Nights' but the
second part of the poem, a dialogue between Paganini and his instrument, contains a virtual restatement of Zeuxis-Heine-Pasternak's
message. In the violinist's final pronouncement, for the sake of musical
eloquence, he renounces other methods of declaring his feelings.

> I love just as I breathe. And I know
> That my body contains two souls.
> And love is that other soul.
> It's unbearably cramped for them both.
>
> From you [i.e. the violin] comes my thirst for assistance,
> Without you, abandoned, I'm lost.
> I would joyfully hand over both
> But you need only shelter just one.
>
> Laugh not, you know which I mean –
> Laugh not, the reason you know –

20 Boris at Vsevolodo-Vilva (1916)

I risk the loss of the old one
If I don't gag the mouth of the new.   (*SP*, 518)

Whether or not this poem preceded or followed the Mayakovskian 'Treasurer' poem, or *The Apelles Mark*, one thing is certain: 1915 was the year when Pasternak identified an alien romantic element in his work and began the rediscovery of his own personality and style.

Shortly after his visit to Petrograd in late 1915, Pasternak left Moscow and spent the first half of 1916 in the Urals. The literary life of his immediate surroundings was at a low ebb and he was unsettled and dissatisfied with his own recent achievements. He had not yet been called for military service but, according to Loks, mistakenly assumed that he soon would be. Engagement in civilian work connected with the war effort could possibly delay or prevent his conscription, and his retreat to the Urals would offer an escape from immediate availability. The idea probably came from Evgenii Lundberg, who viewed this scheme as a chance for Pasternak to concentrate on writing without the distractions of Moscow life. It would also remove him from contact with the Futurists (a factor greatly welcomed by his parents) and enable him to take stock of his artistic situation and purify his style away from 'influences'.

In early January of 1916 Pasternak arrived by rail at the town of Vsevolodo-Vilva in the north of the province of Perm. The area had once been visited by Chekhov and though still in Europe it was well off the beaten track. One of Pasternak's first letters, to his mother, commented on the quaint telephone, lighting and bathing facilities, and on the strange 'un-Russian beauties of the area, wildness of the climate, distance and desolation'. He enjoyed his first weeks out there. Literary evidence and letters and photographs taken by Pasternak and Yakov Zbarsky record activities such as skiing, horse-riding, and excursions with friends to set lynx traps, and so on. A piano was also available and there was even mention (in a letter to his father) of Boris' possibly acting with the Vsevolodo-Vilva troupe, or in Solikamsk, the nearest major centre.[48]

The chemical works in Vsevolodo-Vilva belonged to Zinaida Rezvaya, the widow of millionaire magnate Savva Morozov, who had entertained Chekhov there in 1902. (In the spring of 1916 she gave up ownership and sold the enterprise to the Ushkov company.) The plant manufactured acetic acid, acetone, chloroform and other chemicals, and in the factory offices a job was found for Pasternak. His duties there were purely clerical and involved no technical knowledge. He had a room in the wooden house occupied by the family of the biochemist Boris Zbarsky. This contact was arranged via Lundberg, who knew Zbarsky as a fellow member of the Socialist Revolutionary Party. Pasternak's job was set up by Zbarsky and the two of them quickly became close friends. Zbarsky was five years Pasternak's senior and held an important post as chemical engineer at the plant. He made regular business trips to Moscow and in March of 1916 visited the rest of the Pasternak family there. One of his trips in the Urals, on which Pasternak accompanied him, was to Tikhie gory (Quiet Hills) on the river Kama, to discuss his patent method of chloroform production with the Ushkov management. With Zbarsky's wife Fanni, Pasternak also made a boat journey to Perm in mid-May 1916, one product of which was the poem 'On Board

21 Vsevolodo-Vilva: Evgenii Lundberg, Boris Zbarsky, Fanni Zbarskaya, Boris Pasternak (1916)

Steamer' ('Na parokhode') (the first of his poems, apparently, which his father liked). Pasternak's friendship with all the Zbarsky family (which included a two-and-a-half-year-old son Eli, and Boris' brother Yakov) was such that by March 1916 there was even talk of his spending the next year with them and travelling in summer of 1917 to Japan.[49]

Meanwhile, in Vsevolodo-Vilva, the war seemed both mentally and geographically remote. Pasternak's letters to family and friends made virtually no mention of it, apart from incidental references to the terrible price rises in Moscow in April and the relative cheapness of Perm. Thanks to this, he was able to help his family by dispatching a hamper and crate of provisions to them in June of 1916.[50]

So far as Pasternak's conscription was concerned, his correspondence mentioned the chance of signing on for service in Solikamsk instead of Moscow. On 16 March 1916, however, he was able to inform his family that 'a few days ago the Ministry ordered call-up to be deferred until October of this year. Yes, yes, my call-up is postponed till October!! I congratulate you.' For the time being, therefore, he was free to concentrate on other interests.

Lundberg himself arrived in Vsevolodo-Vilva in late January 1916 and stayed till the end of April. But he was dismayed to find that instead of writing, Pasternak was spending his time at the piano. Indeed he appears to have had a sudden new craving to resume his music and

199

systematic practising. On 3 February 1916 he wrote to his parents asking them to send him Czerny's piano studies plus musical manuscript paper and scores of Mozart, Beethoven, Schubert and Wagner. After one month his progress was only slight.[51] Pasternak persisted, however, and asked his parents to ensure there was a piano for him at Molodi during the summer. He talked also of hiring a piano during a planned four-week trip to Tashkent, where he hoped to see Nadezhda Sinyakova who was visiting her sister Zinaida, now resident in the Uzbek capital. An earlier idea of living with the Philipps during the summer in Moscow was rejected, because 'to work on music as I wish to is only possible in total solitude or at the house of absolutely devoted friends (as it was here during the blessed months of February and March)'.[52] After April 1916, however, there was no further mention of music in Pasternak's letters home. Hopes of resuming a musical career probably collapsed amid renewed literary impetus, and although he continued improvising, after years of neglect his piano technique was beyond further improvement. (The following winter of 1916–17, he had no access to a piano, and his only mention of music in the correspondence of that period was one agonised burst of nostalgia at the loss of his 'composer's biography' in a letter to Konstantin Loks.)[53]

Under Lundberg's influence Pasternak sat down to write and in mid-March announced plans for a book of novellas. Lundberg also insisted that after failure with *Sovremennik* he should submit *The Apelles Mark* to the journal *Russkaya mysl'*. Meanwhile work on a second story began, although a letter to Pasternak's parents on 19 March reported that it had turned out poorly and Lundberg had accused him of laziness. *Russkaya mysl'* had also reserved space for an article which Pasternak promised for the Shakespeare tercentenary in April, and for this purpose books were urgently ordered from his parents in Moscow.[54] The essay was completed and submitted, although Boris' comment in one letter home was: 'I'm afraid, father, my sketches on Shakespeare won't delight you any more than Tsentrifuga. Write and tell me.'[55] The article was never printed, however, and it joined the list of Pasternak's lost manuscripts. Further projects to write something on Scriabin and on Cervantes also seem to have come to nothing. Unknown to us too is the fate of plans for other Shakespeare articles for *Russkie vedomosti* (Russian News) and *Birzhevye vedomosti* (Stock Exchange News) which were actually commissioned (Lundberg worked for *Birzhevye vedomosti*), and of further contributions projected for *Russkaya mysl'* and *Letopis'*.[56]

ಕ್ಷಿಕ್ಷಿ

While some of Pasternak's initiatives at Vsevolodo-Vilva ran into the ground, back in Moscow Bobrov was active again and there was a new cordiality in his exchange of letters with Pasternak. The 'Centrifuge' was turning once more and financial affairs looked healthy. In 1915 an injection of capital came from Fyodor Platov, a conceited and inept but wealthy poetaster who in 1916 published a poetry book with Tsentrifuga and secured Bobrov's contribution to his own almanac *Peta*. Bobrov was thus able to press on with the *Second Tsentrifuga Miscellany* (*Vtoroi sbornik Tsentrifugi*) which came out in early April. Prior to that, in January, ranks had also been swelled by the arrival of Ivan Aksyonov, who came to play an important part in Tsentrifuga affairs. (He largely replaced Aseyev who returned to Bobrov's fold only in mid-1916.) A former Cubo-Futurist and brilliant avant-gardist of European mould, Aksyonov was an art expert, poet, translator and dramatist. He was also a qualified engineer, and his collaboration was conducted mainly from a distance while serving in the engineering section of Third Army Headquarters. Furthermore, Aksyonov brought financial assistance and initiative: one of his suggestions was for a fortnightly journal as soon as the war ended, which would win over its readership both from the Petersburg Acmeist poets and from Burlyuk's Cubo-Futurists.[57]

The *Second Tsentrifuga Miscellany* contained a mixture of new materials and items Bobrov had had in his drawer since 1914. Recently received contributions included pretentious poetic trivialities from Platov and Evgenii Shilling, some impressive work by Ivnev, Bolshakov and Khlebnikov, and Pasternak's own eccentric 'Anguish' and 'Arctic Seamstress'. Of somewhat earlier vintage were verses by Aleksandr Shtikh, under the pseudonym 'G. Rostovsky'. The critical section, for which Bobrov was largely responsible, was a predictable compound of his bile and supercharged erudition. Critical attack was directed mainly at the Symbolists, with no modernist target other than Shershenevich, who was taken to task by Bolshakov (in phraseology based on Pasternak's earlier 'Wassermann Test') for vulgarising Mayakovsky's and his own poetic discoveries. From an earlier harvest came Bozhidar's complimentary review of Bobrov's *Gardeners over the Vines*, and an article called 'Belinsky and Aikhenvald' by Boris Sadovskoi (under the *nom de plume* of 'PTYX'). The latter item was a contribution to a literary dispute that had been in progress for three years. Its author came out in support of critic Yurii Aikhenvald's earlier attack on Belinsky, the nineteenth-century founder of the democratic critical tradition who had started the allegedly pernicious habit of evaluating literature by its content rather than its artistry. Yet, despite its antiquity, Sadovskoi's article came as a well-timed counterblast to Mayakovsky, who in *Taken!* had inveighed against the tedious debates of 'Aikhenvald-like men' and proclaimed the vitality of Futurism on the new broad footing of a 'Futurist populace' (*narod-futurist*). Sadovskoi's article also meshed easily with Pasternak's new polemical essay called *The Black Goblet* (*Chernyi bokal*).[58]

The title of Pasternak's article referred to the symbol painted on packing cases containing fragile objects – in this case Lyricism itself (picking up a topic of common concern and the particular interests of Bobrov in the days of Lirika). Like Bobrov's work in the genre, the essay was a self-consciously clever piece of writing in which enigmatic allusions almost blunted the polemical cutting-edge. The main aim was to clear away misconceptions infecting the pure ideal of Futurist lyricism. But at the same time Pasternak managed (as in *Rukonog*) to state his arguments in a way that illuminated his own current ideas.

Section one of the article describes the 'impressionists' as specialists in the ultra-rapid 'packaging' of perceptions and impressions. Exactly which impressionists are meant is left perhaps intentionally vague. (Artistic impressionism might include even some works by Leonid Pasternak; the founders of Russian Futurism had also used the title 'impressionists'; and some early Symbolist poets like Balmont and Bryusov had used impressionist 'hinting' rather than 'naming', as also had Annensky, Fet, Aleksandr Dobrolyubov and Lokhvitskaya.) Pasternak's main intention here is to present modern Russian Futurism as a form of 'post-Impressionism' which has, however, been schooled technically by Symbolist teachers (impressionism being seen as an aspect of Symbolism).[59] The second and third sections of the article are qualifications allegedly demanded by the 'demon of accuracy' and concern the nature of that impressionistic rapidity inherent in Futurist art.

Pasternak maintains that the illusion of speed and fleeting sensation in impressionist lyric has nothing to do with the speed of the Mercedes or of modern technology (as cultivated by simplistic Marinettian Futurists like Shershenevich) but with rapidity of perception and its successful recording in Futurist metaphor, creating an 'impressionism of the eternal'. In a passage faintly recalling his earlier ideas in 'Symbolism and Immortality', Pasternak also states that 'the subjective originality of the Futurist is not at all the subjectivity of the individual. His subjectivity must be understood as a category of Lyricism' (III, 149).

A second qualification concerns the question of Futurism and its recent historical – i.e. socio-political – involvement. Pasternak questions the fashionable Futurist claim to be the 'inhabitants of the future' and he blames the Symbolists for having initiated the modern literary habit of pronouncing on all manner of subjects lying outside the competence of Lyricism. But, Pasternak maintains, 'No forces will compel us [...] to set about the preparation of history for the morrow [...] In art we see a peculiar form of *extemporale* whose task consists solely in that it be executed brilliantly [...] Reality is disintegrating. As it does so it gathers about two opposite polarities: Lyricism and History. Both are equally *a priori* and absolute.' No offenders against lyrical purity are actually named. Clearly, all social and topical writers and poets are potential culprits, and they would include Mayakovsky in his newly adopted wartime role of poetic satirist and commentator. For those able to catch it, there was a more specific allusion to the authors of 'Funereal Hurrah' in Pasternak's statement that as years went by 'at the end of one of them, the 1914th, you brazen ones, you and none other, awoke them with an unprecedented shriek' (III, 147–51).[60]

Pasternak's divergence from Mayakovskian poetics thus acquired a dual foundation: an opposition not just to the 'romantic manner' but also to any extra-literary, 'historical' commitments. And while implicitly clearing accounts with Mayakovsky, *The Black Goblet* still fitted the stance adopted by Bobrov and other Centrifugists who aimed, as before, at defining a 'purified' form of Futurism.

Pasternak received his copy of the *Second Tsentrifuga Miscellany* from Bobrov at the end of April 1916, while still out in the Urals. He was evidently pleased with it and on 2 May wrote to say so. 'Its exterior is splendid, I say this quite sincerely, uncoerced and frankly [...] the type is splendid, and the proportions could not be bettered.' He went on to praise Bobrov's critical acumen but was baffled, as any reader must have been, by the allusive complexity of his article titled 'The Philosophical Stone of a Fantast' which seemingly made a virtue out of a 'fundamental confusion': 'Who will understand you, Sergei? Eh? I ask you this quite seriously.' Though complimenting the verses by Bobrov, Bolshakov and Khlebnikov, Pasternak had strong reservations about Ivnev and Kushner as poets. About his own contributions he remained critical too, and, inevitably, he was utterly contemptuous of Fyodor Platov. (Other verses in Bolshakov's *Sun's Last Trajectory* [*Solntse na izlete*] and *Poem of Events* [*Poema sobytii*] had left Pasternak less than delighted, mainly because of their apparent closeness to Mayakovsky and lack of originality; in October 1916, when Bolshakov was at the front, however, Pasternak sent him a more enthusiastic congratulatory letter.)

Pasternak's enthusiasm for the *Second Miscellany* did not signal a wholehearted willingness to engage in group activities again. As he told Bobrov quite frankly, 'I found it difficult to match my own chilliness to the warmth that your letters and the almanac have awakened in me.' Whatever his pleasure too at Khlebnikov's and Bolshakov's new 'alliance' with Bobrov (a Centrifugist dream of spring 1914 now realised) he had now put polemical diversions behind him. 'I have had my fun at the expense of Shershenevich and in getting close to Mayakovsky and the Obelisk* and a good deal more besides. But now it doesn't amuse me any more.' Pasternak kept to himself the still unclarified plans for new works of his own. 'I don't have anything for print,' he told Bobrov. 'When I have, I'll tell you [...] Nobody can help me to write, and when I've written something, then we can talk about it.'[61]

Pasternak's letters from Vsevolodo-Vilva to his family described both local impressions and also journeys which became possible as the winter snow cleared. After a visit on 27 May to some local coal mines he told his parents: 'I shall remember it all my life. That is a real hell!' There were mentions too of Austrian prisoners of war and of a local Chinese population, including workers and policemen armed with lashes. Memories of another ore-mining location were incorporated in a poem called 'The Mine' ('Rudnik').[62] In the second half of June Pasternak was sent on business for two days to the Belgian owned firm of Solve at Ivaka, and nature impressions from the journey figured both in his letter home on Monday, 19 June and in a lovely rain-spangled poem in *Over the Barriers*.[63] Another trip, to Usolye, was described in a letter to Bobrov: 'Before my window is the Kama river – to one side is a little industr[ial] Belgium – elevators, chimneys, concr[ete] frameworks, approach roads, gigantic tanker trucks of the Mazout Company and so on ...'[64] Local observations and business trips provided a multitude of landscapes and various *realia* that appeared in further verses of the time, as well as in subsequent narrative works such as *Zhenya Luvers' Childhood*, *Spektorsky*, *The Story* and prose fragments of the 1930s.

Finally, at the end of June, although the new owners of the Ushkov chemical works wanted him to stay on, Pasternak determined to return home. Zbarsky had evidently had disagreements with the new manage-

* 'Obelisk' – an almanac planned by Aleksandr Shtikh in the summer of 1914; the project was never realised.

22 Family dacha at Molodi: Josephine, Aleksandr, Lydia, Boris, Rozaliya
and Leonid Pasternak (1916)

ment and he too was planning to leave and take up another post at Tikhie
gory. There was talk of Boris perhaps joining them there later in the
year.[65] Meanwhile, having abandoned his planned trip to Tashkent,
Pasternak paid a brief visit to Perm, then moved on to Ekaterinburg
where he stayed just six hours (long enough for a description of the place
to his parents in early July; his later heroine Zhenya Luvers was to echo
his impressions). Thereafter he moved on to Ufa where he visited his
exiled Austrian cousin Fedya. His two and a half day visit was evidently
not a total success. He was unable to stay at Fedya's and, as he reported
in a letter to his family from Samara, boats along the Volga were
uncomfortable, crowded and expensive.[66]

Pasternak probably spent most of the summer months with his family
at Molodi, where he assembled the poems for his next book of verse. On
various trips into Moscow he met up with Sergei Bobrov, and in the
autumn he saw other old friends, including Elena Vinograd (whose
fiancé had recently been killed in battle). Konstantin Loks was also back
in town after nearly a year in Surazh. Pasternak described him to Bobrov

23 Elena Vinograd (c. 1917)

as a terrible 'stick in the mud' (*tyazhel na pod"em*), but Loks was himself now enthusiastic about joining Tsentrifuga and had a theoretical philosophical book in preparation. Unfortunately it never appeared, although Pasternak regarded this 'Catechism of the Not Indiscriminate in Art' as a potentially valuable addition to the Tsentrifuga publications list.[67]

Bobrov was again in the middle of a busy bout of publishing activity. In September he left Moscow for a Caucasian cure at Mineralnye Vody and later Zheleznovodsk, but Pasternak and Loks maintained contact with his wife at their Pogodinskaya Street address, and outstanding business during the autumn and winter was dealt with by post.

Bobrov had further strengthened Tsentrifuga during 1916 by recruiting Samuil Vermel, another poet and critic with means of his own. The *Muses' Vernal Forwarding Agency* of 1915 was one of his productions, and his cooption to Tsentrifuga had a fairly cynical economic motivation. (Earlier on Bobrov had roguishly suggested that they should rally round and marry Boris off to Ida Vysotskaya as a means of securing their finances!)[68] Vermel was also a leading actor at the Chamber Theatre and Pasternak saw him in Shakespeare's *The Merry Wives of Windsor* during the summer. But neither Bobrov nor Aksyonov was keen to have Vermel's artistic (as distinct from his financial) participation in Tsentrifuga. As Aksyonov put it in a letter to Bobrov on 3 August 1916, he himself would handle the fine arts section of the next almanac, Bobrov, the literature, while Vermel could be entrusted with 'theatre, music, circus, racing, fires, floods, murders and other social diversions and theories about them'![69] Not surprisingly there were frictions, which eventually led to Vermel's break-away in mid-February of 1917 – but that was a chapter which Pasternak missed owing to his absence from Moscow. In the short term, though, Vermel's involvement led to a flurry of publications, including editions of *Death's Gold* (*Zoloto smerti*) by Ryurik Ivnev and Aseyev's *Oksana* in September and November of 1916, Pasternak's *Over the Barriers* which was datelined 1917 but actually produced in the last few days of December 1916, and Bobrov's *Diamond Forests* (*Almaznye lesa*) and *Lyre of Lyres* (*Lira lir*) in January and April of 1917.

The success of Tsentrifuga and relaxation of earlier animosities pleased Pasternak. In September 1916 he wrote to Bobrov in Zhelezno-vodsk saying 'The whistle of Tsentrifuga is certainly deafening. More than anything I am glad that TsFG is now a serious, solid, first-rank, progressive publishing enterprise, and that it promises ever increasing success in this respect. I am also glad that we are all together again.'[70] The two of them kept up a regular correspondence throughout the winter and Pasternak received commissions for various review articles. Like *Over the Barriers*, Aseyev's *Oksana* was a compilation of verse written over several years. Pasternak welcomed it enthusiastically both in their correspondence and in a review for the projected *Third Tsentrifuga Miscellany*. In line with his statement in *The Black Goblet* that poetry's sole requirement was to be executed brilliantly, he concentrated on Aseyev's virtuoso metaphor and imagery, qualities that characterised his own latest creations.[71] In a letter of 11 October 1916 he also praised Bolshakov's 'metaphoric materiality of content',[72] and the same feature of 'metaphoric batteries' and 'epidemics of imagery' was at the centre of his attention in reviewing Mayakovsky's recent verse collection *Simple as Mooing* (*Prostoe kak mychanie*). While he shared Bobrov's critical attitude to prosaic interludes between Mayakovsky's metaphoric salvoes (a modernist anti-aesthetic feature present in some of Pasternak's verse) he held out against Bobrov's insistence that Mayakovsky be taken to task for lapses into 'cab-drivers' language'. In his letter of 26 November 1916, Pasternak objected that first of all such criticism was pointless because this was part of Mayakovsky's 'deliberate search and discovery of his own style' and he himself entirely sympathised with such explorations. Secondly: 'In my view Mayakovsky is the only one among those of us writing who is a poet [...] This being the case, I will not undertake to speak of any cleaning-up of his phraseology [...] for the sole reason that this would revolt me and offend the sense of delight in Mayakovsky which, as you well know, is a basic ineradicable weakness with me.'[73] Nevertheless, Pasternak's attitude to Mayakovsky was by now in some respects more objective and sober. He could now afford to be delighted without losing his own personality, and the best items in *Over the Barriers* demonstrated this.

Before leaving Moscow again in early October, Pasternak had been to see Vermel on 16 September and handed him the ready manuscript of his new book. After his recent changes of direction and sympathy, he was not confident about this fairly arbitrary selection from two years' worth of verse. The heterogeneous contents even led to difficulties over the title. 'I hesitate,' he told Bobrov, 'because I cannot see independent value in any individual poem. The old concept of technique is not observed in the book, and if I emphasise this through the title one can easily anticipate the misunderstanding it will cause.' Various titles mooted were: 'Gradus ad Parnassum', 'Deposits' ('Nalety'). and 'The Unshackled Voice' ('Raskovannyi golos' – the title of one of the poems).[74] All of these, like the finally selected *Over the Barriers* (a quote from the poem 'Petersburg'), suggested some idea of 'progress', laying of new strata, or self-overcoming and liberation. Pasternak was also aware of the book's uneven quality: 'There are about ten pieces in the book which have a totally innocent quality à la Zhadovskaya,* if not worse. They will go into anthologies.'[75]

In view of the social upheavals in early 1917, it is not surprising that the book's appearance was scarcely noticed. Aksyonov, a stern critic, nevertheless regarded it as the best of Tsentrifuga's productions over the last year. His comments in a letter to Bobrov on 18 February 1917 would not all have pleased the author, though. He regretted the omission of poems from *Rukonog* and the *Second Miscellany* and claimed that Pasternak 'still has a lot – oh, a lot – of work in front of him, and his iambs [...] are a bit monotonous.'[76] The outward presentation of the book was also not a spectacular success. Some poems were mutilated by the censor and there were misprints in abundance. Nevertheless it was an auspicious publication – one which, in Vladimir Markov's words 'can

* Zhadovskaya was a nineteenth-century poetess specialising in bland love and landscape lyrics.

hardly be dismissed as an immature product of Pasternak's early days', and it was 'the beginning of the Pasternak we know'.[77] To the author it was also memorable as his first book for which he received a fee – a handsome 150 roubles.

The forty-nine poems of *Over the Barriers* included a number of items printed separately in 1915–16, but most of them were first publications. The poems were presented in no obvious chronological or stylistic order, but there were hints at an overall seasonal thematic cycle, and the appearance of 'Marburg' as the final item may have pointed to its special significance for the author. (The earliest known manuscript of this poem was dated 10 May 1916, dedicated to Fanni Zbarskaya and titled 'From Marburg Reminiscences' ['Iz marburgskikh vospominanii'].) The fact that thirty-one of the items in the book were later reprinted in a revised 1929 edition suggests that there was plenty of material here which Pasternak would recognise as typifying his mature manner. But the collection contained several immature pieces, some bearing signs of Cubo-Futurist aesthetic habits. Metaphoric dislocations were more vehement and extreme than anything in *Twin in the Stormclouds*. Sudden concretisations or 'evaporations', animations of dead matter, incongruous juxtapositions, or absurd escapades and incidents took the reader into a world that barely corresponded with the empirical one, nor even impressionistically suggested it. Only occasionally was it stated or suggested how metaphor was generated (as in 'Marburg' where high passion casts prancing linoleum squares underfoot)[78] and the origin of some tropes was highly arbitrary. In much of this metaphor there were remnants of Futurist *épatage*: 'hoar-frost was rotten'; 'the hawking thaw plucked the streetlamp as a cook plucks a partridge'; the poet carried dawn loaded on his back 'like a basket of dirty linen'; and October's frozen ulcer was 'poked open by the heavens' senile finger-nail'. In the book's more mature items, however, the imagery did appear to have an objective source, and Pasternak later talked of 'objective thematism and a momentary pictorial quality depicting movement' as typical of the book as a whole.[79] Many of these objective or historical themes, though, were baleful or cataclysmic: the War, the massacre of St Bartholomew's Night, and the last day of Pompeii were among them. Konstantin Loks in his memoirs described *Over the Barriers* (1917) as a 'book of doom' reflecting the contemporary atmosphere of war.

Some darker notes and *Sturm and Drang* emotions in the book were perhaps parts of the Laforgue legacy, reinforced by Mayakovskian example. But by the time the book appeared in print these features belonged already to Pasternak's past. Items such as 'Apassionata' were thus not a true indication of the state of Pasternak's art in the winter of 1916–17. But few could have realised this at the time, and it is typical that Bobrov's article on Pasternak, written for the *Third Miscellany*, took as its title the obsolete heroic epithet 'Treasurer of the Last of Planets'.[80] Later on, in 1917, Pasternak spelt out to Shura Shtikh in a letter that 'you and I will probably disagree about the concept of nobility and courage, in which I always disagree with folk who mix them up with romanticism. The latter is the start of human weakness and of fog. I do not like either of these.'[81]

But there were other positive qualities in *Over the Barriers*, as Pasternak pointed out to Tsvetaeva in the mid-1920s, although his general verdict of the book was negative:

Don't despair. From about page 58 onwards slightly more heartening things occur. The middle of the book is worst of all. It starts with greyness, the north, the city, prose, forebodings of revolution (dully rebellious predestination outraged at every movement of labour, unconsciously revolting at work like in some pantomime) – the start, as I say, is maybe still tolerable. The treatment of the language is inadmissible. If shifts of stress are needed for the rhyme, this liberty is served by regional variants or foreign words taken back to their sources. *Fiacres* instead of cabs, and Ukrainian *zhmeni*,* because Nadya Sinyakova to whom this is dedicated is from Kharkov and speaks like that. A heap of every imaginable rubbish, and awful technical clumsiness, yet with an inner tension that is possibly greater than in later books.[82]

The 'slightly more heartening things' in the book are identifiable with that rapture so characteristic of the mature Pasternak. Pages 58–9 contained 'The Last Day of Pompeii' ('Poslednii den' Pompei'), the last of a whole group of brooding, disaster-ridden items, after which came a springtime sequence. These later more exultant poems struck Loks by their novelty, and in late January of 1917 Pasternak wrote in response to his friend's first impressions of the book:

You very correctly single out in *Barriers* the book's most essential principle: a dithyrambic quality [...] There is no marvel upon earth that can nonplus the marvel of human perception. This marvel needs only to be on this earth. I.e. it needs only to indicate by its form the origin of its vitality and the adjustment of its symbiosis with all the rest of life. And your words about the 'comprehensive voices of tragedy' strike at my sorest point.[83]

Dithyrambic exuberance, distinguished by Loks and recognised by Pasternak, was present in poems such as 'Ivaka', 'On Board Steamer',

* *zhmenya* – Ukrainian for 'handful'.

'First Glimpse of the Urals' ('Ural vpervye') (above p. 174) and several more. It was a newly discovered quality whose influence was to spread to Pasternak's next two books of verse.

Another feature of *Over the Barriers*' best and recent items was their discovery (after earlier romantic heroics) of a natural voice that seemed to emanate not from the poet himself but from the imagery speaking 'on his behalf'. This was captured in the epigraph to the whole book. Taken from 'Studies in Song' by Swinburne, whom Pasternak began reading and translating in 1916, this couplet attributed the entire collection

> To the soul in my soul that rejoices
> For the song that is over my song.[84]

And the same thought was caught in 'The Poetry of Spring' ('Poeziya vesny'), which was likened to a Greek sponge with suckers left out amid greenery on the garden bench to 'grow sumptuous frills and farthingales and absorb clouds and ravines' – all this in anticipation of night-time when the poet would wring out the sponge and give the order to 'put blotches and weep onto paper'[85] in a creative act that seemingly took place without human intervention.

Pasternak's first glimpse of the Urals thus coincided closely with his first glimpse of a way ahead to the poetics of 1917.

9

Quiet Hills and revolution

'Spring Rain'

With a sob and wry grain to the bird-cherry, it wetted
The carriages' lacquer and tremble of trees.
'Neath the bulge of the moon the fiddlers filed
To the theatre. Citizens, please join the queues!

The rainwater pools on the stone. And flooded
With tears, the roses' deep gullets show a flash
And dampness of diamond. Upon them and on clouds
And eye-lashes the stipple of gladness is splashed.

For the first time an epic in plaster is carved
By the moonlight from murmuring crowds and frocks' flutter,
And from power possessed by rapturous lips
Is fashioned a bust that no hand has sculpted.

Whose is that heart? Whose the blood that now surges
Away from his cheeks and floods towards glory?
Here's where it beats: the minister's fingers
Have clutched in a bunch all our mouths and aortas.

This is not night, it's not rain, nor is it
A roaring chorus of 'Hurrah for Kerensky!'
This is a blinding debouch in the forum
From catacombs dim, hitherto without exit.

These are not roses, not mouths, nor the murmurs
Of crowds. By this theatre – here is the sight:
Proudly it foams and pounds on our asphalt –
The surf of Europe's wavering night.

ૐૐૐ

For Pasternak the winter of 1916–17 was another period of retreat from
Moscow. In the spring of 1916 he had visited the Elabuga district in the

province of Vyatka, and by the autumn of that year Boris Zbarsky was working there in the P.K. Ushkov chemical plant at Tikhie gory and had undertaken to arrange a job for him. In early October 1916, therefore, Pasternak set out on the rail and road journey to this remote provincial area by the river Kama, near the western approach to the Urals.[1]

Despite its distant location there were still plenty of reminders of the war in Europe. Industrial plants evacuated from the Baltic lay rusting by railtracks; refugees and Austrian prisoners of war were employed in local industry, and Pasternak and the Zbarskys found themselves among a large influx of civilians and military personnel from the cities. By late 1916 rationing had been introduced and supplies were increasingly irregular; prices had inflated over 300 per cent since 1914. But the eastern provinces were spared some of the hardship in Moscow and elsewhere, and Pasternak sent several food parcels to his family, including a whole side of bacon in January 1917.

Pasternak's work was bound up with the war effort. Conscriptions had more than doubled the size of the Russian army since 1914, and it was his job to run the Ushkov works 'military desk' and arrange cancellation or postponement of army service for local peasants and labourers involved in essential civilian work. His duties involved dealing with some two thousand employees, hundreds of village workers and various organisations, all of which had to be shielded from a district military authority which might otherwise send them to the front or to compulsory labouring jobs at the Izhevsk ordnance works. In slightly over four months Pasternak managed to secure exemption for the male population of several rural districts.[2]

So far as his own liability for service was concerned, rumours continued that even 'white ticket' holders would eventually be called up. But in mid-December 1916 he attended a further medical examination at Elabuga and afterwards reported that he had been 'acknowledged by the commission as totally unsuited and *permanently released*' On a later visit to Elabuga he learned that a young army doctor called Morev had recognised the name Pasternak and knew his father's work, which may well have helped secure his exemption.[3]

In some fragments of a novel Pasternak drafted in the 1930s, the hero was described during the First World War as 'possessed by a set of thoughts which were common to everybody in those years and which differed only in their amount, personal quality and features of the period when they occurred: alarmed in 1914, even more disturbed in 1915, and totally bleak in the year 1916' (*VP*, 296). This traced a general sinking of morale after the collapse of the Russian southern front in 1915 and the renewed heavy losses of September 1916. After the seemingly happy insularity of Vsevolodo-Vilva, Pasternak's correspondence from the Kama betrayed a new graveness and concern. 'To a certain extent we are informed here about everything going on in Roumania', he told his parents in October 1916. And a few weeks later, in December, he reported that although work had perhaps provided some distraction hitherto,

now there is certainly reason to get alarmed – the times are such [. . .] The papers reach here after incredible delays. Moreover, they are half-filled with what the Romans called a *tabula rasa*.

Nevertheless, a number of letters home betrayed Pasternak's sense that some relief and release must now soon come. To him it seemed 'perfectly obvious that people will soon be living a quite different life',[4] and on 9 December 1916 he spelt out in detail a feeling that some transforming event would shortly end their present despair:

Dear Papa and Mama,
    Don't expect frequent, detailed letters from me for now [. . .]
    Glancing through the newspapers, I often shudder at the thought of the contrast, the abyss which is opening up between the cheap politics of the day and what is just round the corner. The former is associated with the habits of living in a time of war and coming to terms with it. The latter, not billeted in the human brain, now belongs to the new era that I think will soon arrive. God grant it be so. One can already feel its spirit. It is absurd to expect an end to absurdity. Otherwise absurdity would be consequential and finite and would no longer be absurdity.
    Absurdity has no end. It will just break off at one of its absurd links when no one expects it to. And it won't break off because the absurdity has come to an end, but because the meaningful has a beginning, and that beginning excludes and annuls the absurd.
    That is how I understand things. So I am expecting what you too probably expect. In other words, I am not seeking a gleam of light in the prevailing darkness, inasmuch as darkness is incapable of sharing light. There will be no gleam of light because *there will immediately be light*. There is no point trying to seek it out now in what we know: it is seeking *us* out and tomorrow or the next day it will flood us with light.[5]

Meanwhile, however, winter life at Tikhie gory was desperately monotonous. Newspapers and post from Moscow took at least a week to arrive, and there were depressing gaps in correspondence with the outside world. The rest of life was similarly slow, and laundry took so long that in October Pasternak had to write to his mother and have extra sets of underwear and towels sent out. Local society was composed largely of grey mediocrities. Particularly irritating were some of the armchair politics and discussions of 'the situation such as it is' (soz-davsheesya polozhenie) that went out there.[6] The apparent inability of such earnest folk (including Zbarsky) to appreciate distant situations or adopt sensible priorities in life was later reflected in the prose fragment *Lovelessness* (*Bezlyub'e*), and another grotesque sample of locally heard conversation was allotted to Galuzina in chapter 10 of *Doctor Zhivago*. Even polite social events out at Tikhie gory were so few that Boris wondered in a home letter of November why he had bothered bringing so many cuffs and collars. Even the 1917 New Year celebrations, which consisted of a champagne supper party for eighty people and ended at 8.00 a.m., Pasternak described to Konstantin Loks as 'tolerable but boring'. Pasternak's original plan to return to Moscow for the New Year was abandoned, and owing to lack of a replacement he was persuaded to stay on at his job.

Compared with the Urals and life last year, my present place of residence is more boring than the tomb. Bare hills, about one and a half dozen factory chimneys, people who have spent their life in a gas cloud, woodless Tatar villages. In a word, everything disposes one towards work.

Such was Pasternak's report to Shura Shtikh in February 1917, as his stay on the Kama drew to a close.[7]

In fact, however, a small handful of interesting and cultivated folk did help relieve the dead monotony. After his daily five-hour office stint, Pasternak in October started giving tuition to Vladimir, the schoolboy son of chemist Lev Yakovlevich Karpov. Although not as close to him as the Zbarskys, the Karpovs proved congenial friends, and when they went to Moscow in January 1917 Pasternak arranged for them to meet his parents. Later Leonid Pasternak made a portrait of Lev Karpov, who became a celebrated Soviet academician.[8]

At Tikhie gory friendship with the Zbarskys continued and deepened. Pasternak found Zbarsky similar to Dobrovein, a highly interesting personality and 'in human essentials terribly close to me'.[9] A feature they both shared was their depression and dissatisfaction with the course of their lives: just as Pasternak was a frustrated musician, so Zbarsky was a still unfulfilled scientist, and the discovery of a new process for producing chloroform and his senior position at the Ushkov plant did nothing to raise Zbarsky's morale. Evidently this also upset relations with his wife. 'He manages to convey she is to blame for this. Not as a woman, not in the category of feelings [. . .] but as a human being. It's an obscure problem. Perhaps he is prejudiced. She is affectionate, an ideal wife and friend and a fine person,' Pasternak told his parents.[10] Perhaps Pasternak and Fanni Zbarskaya were not indifferent to one another: an allusion to some heart-to-heart talk between the two Borises – presumably on the subject of Fanni – appears in Pasternak's poetic 'Sketches for a Fantasy "Poem of a Kinsman"' ('Nabroski k fantazii "Poema o blizhnem"') of early 1917;[11] memories of Fanni also possibly provided material for chapter 2 of the verse novel *Spektorsky* and the character of Olga Bukhteyeva. However, there can be no certainty of this, and Zbarsky's marriage and friendship with Pasternak certainly survived the episode. For many years Fanni Zbarskaya preserved manuscripts of several lyrics by Pasternak, most of them short circumstantial pieces of no great interest or merit.[12]

Among correspondence from Moscow came heartening news at the end of December 1916 that Leonid Pasternak had read and liked *Over the Barriers*. After his father's misgivings about his earlier verse, Boris expected a new shower of disapproval and had already warned that if Leonid disliked the book he should refrain from saying so.[13] His relief on 3 January 1917 elicited the following comment to his father: 'I always suffered so from the fact that you never saw your own features in me; that you measured me with the yardstick of mediocrity, and when you failed to find them in me you complained at my lack of contact with you, blaming me for this; and that you described what produced *Barriers* as a cesspit.'

The edition of *Over the Barriers* was unfortunately riddled with misprints, despite an express order that Vermel should not go to press without Pasternak's having read the proofs.[14] In fact, in December 1916 the censor had been all set to halt publication of the book altogether because of its pacifist and revolutionary motifs, but Bobrov's arguments and a bottle of cognac had persuaded him merely to excise the offending passages.[15] But the time lost over this prevented the issue of printer's proofs. Although pleased at the book's publication, Pasternak was annoyed at the blemishes. His suggestion to Bobrov that an errata slip be distributed to bookshops was not carried out.[16] Eventually, on returning to Moscow in spring 1917, he himself corrected several of the unsold copies by hand. Nevertheless, *Over the Barriers* was an important achievement for Pasternak quite apart from its artistic merits and the fee it earned. It was, as he pointed out to his sister Lydia, 'my first *book*, however flimsy. This is what I am now working on. I am learning to write not novellas, but a *book* of novellas, a *book* of verse, etc.'[17]

The next collective publishing project, the *Third Tsentrifuga Miscellany*, held out further attractive prospects. It was planned to contain Pasternak's reviews of Aseyev's *Oksana* and Mayakovsky's *Simple as Mooing*, various poems by him, and the *Tale of the Carp* – this manuscript had been looked out by Aleksandr Pasternak from various papers Boris had left behind at the Volkhonka apartment and had been forwarded to Bobrov.[18]

So far as other literary activities were concerned, Pasternak's letter to his father in January 1917 outlined the main tasks ahead: translation of two dramas by Swinburne, a new edition of his Kleist translation with an introduction (for publishing 'after the war'), a book of prose fiction to include three items: *Tale of the Carp*, *The Apelles Mark*, and something new which had been started but interrupted, and which can be identified as the *Suboctave Story (Istoriya odnoi kontroktavy)*.[19]

Pasternak's most time-consuming project in the autumn of 1916 was a translation. Mulling over ideas for the *Third Miscellany* at the end of September, he wrote to Bobrov mentioning Swinburne's splendid lyrics and dramas, such as *Atalanta in Calydon* and the Mary Queen of Scots trilogy, as well as Balmont's earlier unsuccessful attempt to translate Swinburne. Nothing daunted, Pasternak translated the sonnet to John Ford in October and then set to work on *Chastelard* from the drama trilogy.[20] Its theme of suffering womanhood probably made a natural appeal to him; he later translated the tragedies of Mary Stuart by both Schiller and Słowacki. But eventually, and despite its 'lyrical effect upon the reader', he found the drama 'poor in action and scenically monotonous'. He completed the work partly, as he told his parents, as an act of self-discipline, partly because it was a potential source of income, and partly because of its worth as a literary 'feat' in its own right. Not having a copy of part 2 he then started on the third part of the trilogy. He described it to Loks as similarly boring and inflated[21] and he eventually abandoned the work on returning to Moscow. Part 1 was submitted to a publisher, but in the confusion of the following years the manuscript disappeared and was never retraced or printed.

During the final two months of his stay at Tikhie gory, Pasternak experienced a new rush of poetic energy and penned two verse 'Dedi-

cations' ('Posvyashcheniya'). These were intended for the next Tsentrifuga miscellany but were later replaced by the 'Sketches for a Fantasy'
written in early February of 1917. A letter of the 12th of that month to
his father also mentioned another project:

At the moment I am writing various things and rushing from one to another. I
am writing a book of prose. Nor must I forget my verse [...] Apart from the
prose I am also thinking of writing an ideological book. You know, like some of
the things I keep talking about – about art, about man writ large [*o bol'shom
cheloveke*), about the fact, for instance, that vital feelings which tangibly penetrate
our social environment like summer vapours in the garden greenery and lawns at
midday after a thunderstorm – that such feelings which everybody has carried
within himself and lives out in his life are sustained by mankind in general.

The last idea sounds like an echo of 'Symbolism and Immortality', but
the attempt at a book of articles was also abandoned. Pasternak worked
at it sporadically for another two years and wrote some items on
Tyutchev, Kleist, Swinburne and Shakespeare, but the manuscripts were
eventually lost.[22]

Pasternak's best achievements in winter 1916–17 were left
unpublished, partly owing to cancellation of the *Third Miscellany*.
Nevertheless, they marked important stages in his artistic growth. In a
letter of 11 February 1917 to Bobrov, he wrote enthusiastically of
'Poem of a Kinsman' and sent a telegram withdrawing his other verse in
favour of this work, even though it existed only as a series of sketches. 'I
recognise myself in it,' he told Bobrov. 'I have written (and continue
writing) this piece with great urgency. Now I am suffering from such a
headache and such anguish that I don't know where to turn. I feel like
sleeping and renewing my strength and starting work again. I'm just like
a madman.'[23]

Unlike *Over the Barriers*, these sketches conveyed a clear picture of
Pasternak's 'post-Futurist' identity. Together with a few other *poema*
drafts of 1916, they were Mayakovsky's last legacy to him in the form of
an interest in expanded lyrical statement (cf. Mayakovsky's *Cloud in
Trousers* and *Backbone Flute*). Pasternak published several of these drafts
in the 1920s, but the fact that none had been completed suggests his
reservations about them. Pasternak set himself an almost impossible task
by attempting to write in extended impressionist forms. Effective in
short pieces like 'The Muse of 1909' or 'Black Spring', his medium was
normally too fine-grained for use on a broad canvas (as in 'The City'
['Gorod'] of 1916), and loss of focus and concentration were inevitable.[24] The scope for narration or argument was also reduced by the

poetic speaker's absence or his disappearance. As Akhmatova commented on 'Ballade' ('Ballada') in *Over the Barriers*, there was only the 'tantalising hint of some theme', even though the poet was clearly writing of some real event, a visit to Tolstoy.[25] The 'Sketches for a Fantasy' were Pasternak's most successful 'impressionist epic', partly because their obscurities were clarified by textual overlaps with 'Marburg', with another *poema* extract, and with some verses from Shtikh's archive concerning the Vysotskaya story of 1912.[26] Yet despite this successful evocation of a life which had 'painfully salted the body of my poems' (*SP*, 524), Pasternak was evidently persuaded that his talent and technique in 1917 were at present best suited to the short lyric poem. When next he attempted extended verse compositions, in the 1920s, his approach would be different.

Pasternak's most substantial original work in winter 1916–17 was in prose. *Suboctave Story* was written in the white heat of inspiration over the Christmas holiday of 1916. 'I jumped, up at night, able to *see* this thing in its entirety from beginning to end, and as I was unable to doze off again I got up and began writing,' he told his parents. And a day later on 12 January 1917 he wrote to Loks saying 'Let me tell you seriously: I believe in this year [. . .] It began quite unmistakably well for me [. . .] For three days I was possessed. I sketched a whole lot down, and I wrote and then rewrote one piece (something like a novella, but a bit better than that).' The resulting story was intended for inclusion in the book of fiction projected for completion in the April of 1917.

Pasternak's letter of 11 January to his parents described the new story as 'in the style of "The Apelles Mark" but much more brilliant and serious [. . .] more original in both subject and style, and more powerful, through the temperament that has gone into it.'[27] (His assessment of *Apelles* was by now fairly critical: 'You'll find a lot of rubbish in it,' he told Bobrov as he sent him a typescript in late 1916. 'Perhaps through my lack of skill its particular technical quality excludes narrative animation, using too much energy on vertical saturation and leaving none for the horizontal impetus.')[28] Like *The Apelles Mark*, *Suboctave Story* was also concerned with the artist and his predicament, but it had none of the earlier novella's skittish mannerism. The setting was a German one based on impressions of Berlin and Marburg in 1906 and 1912. Some fertilisation also came from German literary sources, in particular Kleist's story *Saint Cecilia, or the Force of Music* (*Die heilige Cäcilie oder die Gewalt der Musik*), and various tales by Hoffmann exemplifying music's supposedly fatal destructive power. In the background, probably, were further works such as Tolstoy's *Kreutzer Sonata* and Thomas Mann's *Tonio Kröger* – both on the theme of the artist as a moral outcast, stigmatised and rejected by society because of his devotion to art and the tragic consequence of this.

The story is set in the nineteenth century, in the small fictional town of Ansbach in Hesse. The central character, Knauer, is organist of the town church. During his improvisations he is described surrendering totally to the controlling forces of inspiration, and during one such fantasia he fails to notice that his young son Gottlieb has clambered inside the organ chamber; as his father plays, the boy is crushed to death in the suboctave coupler mechanism. The solid local bourgeois citizens see the tragedy as Providence's vengeance on the musician for his godless cult of art. Later, as he sits by the corpse of his son, the awful power of music dawns on Knauer too when he observes that his fingers are moving in octaves over the boy's body. Struck by this dread realisation, he leaves home and disappears. The story's conclusion is set ten years later. Knauer reappears in town, secretly tries out the organ, and applies to be reinstated. He is turned down. His application is a shameless act, the town council tells him, and his presence cannot be tolerated after he has again tampered with an instrument which he should never have dared to touch. Thereupon Knauer makes a second and final ignominious departure.

In Tikhie gory Pasternak had no access to a piano,[29] but while there he was evidently again tormented by nostalgia for his abandoned musical career. Music's 'elemental claim' which he described in a letter to Loks in late January was also felt in the story by Knauer, who 'shuddered at the identity which existed in that instant between him and the cantilena and at the fact that it knew him just as well as he knew it'.[30] But one can read this last phrase as more than an expression of music's unrelenting demands; it is one of several descriptions in the story of the interpenetrating worlds of object and emotion; it is a metaphor exemplifying Pasternak's whole artistic vision. Moreover what at first seems like a pastiche Romantic narration thus emerges as something idiomatically personal and 'modern': events in the story are viewed through angles and prisms that suggest not one but several streams of shifting consciousness – sometimes the author's, sometimes another character's, and sometimes also a hypothetical consciousness attributed to objective surroundings.

Before *Suboctave Story* was complete, a further rush of inspiration in early February 1917 produced yet another Hoffmannesque novella whose title Pasternak mentioned to his sister Lydia: *The Duchess' Coach* (*Kareta gertsogini*).[31] In 1921 during a summer evening stroll at

Pushkino, Pasternak told the translator Rita Rait-Kovalyova about the story, and she later recalled some of its details:

The duchess herself and her retinue had galloped away on the horses that they had unharnessed from the coach in order to escape some danger, and the coach was left in the forest. But inside the coach – this was the main point – lay some orchestral trumpets abandoned by the musicians. Years went by and the coach became overgrown with ivy and convolvulus. From the proximity of brass trumpets the convolvulus blossoms grew huge and rang like bells, while the trumpets acquired a fragrant aroma [...] 'and you could smell them, honestly [...] you could smell them, slightly like almonds, or just like when you pluck convolvulus, a kind of bitter, burnt smell'.[32]

Nothing more is known of the story. Before its completion it was laid aside in favour of the poetic fantasy and a further bout of translating Swinburne. A letter of 13 February 1917, in fact, told Sergei Bobrov that as of that date Pasternak was resuming work on his prose. But the volume of stories was never finished and the manuscript of *The Duchess' Coach* was lost. If *Suboctave Story* was ever polished up for printing, this version too has disappeared. Pasternak kept the manuscript till the end of the Second World War, when he handed it to his son Evgenii as stove fuel. The latter's prompt action saved it from the flames; the full but still unpolished text appeared in an academic edition only in 1977.[33]

The First World War years and Pasternak's two retreats from the Moscow literary scene brought him immense artistic benefits. In that time he found and purified his voice in poetry and prose and freed himself from distorting influences. The escape from social and other quasi-literary distractions of the city also taught him self-reliance, asceticism, and industry. As he told his mother in mid-February of 1917: 'Here I have acquired a few working habits (not in technique, but in treating myself as one would an idle slave)'.[34] Pasternak was now aged twenty-seven, his apprenticeship was over, and his subsequent work had all the marks of a mature master.

With national morale collapsing and Petrograd gripped by civil disorders, the tsarist autocracy effectively came to an end on 27 February 1917.[35] The State Duma was dissolved by ukase, but remained in session as a provisional government to hold office till the election of a Constituent Assembly. Meanwhile the war raged on and Russia's civil and military disintegration continued.

News of the February Revolution reached Pasternak on the Kama a few days later, confirming presentiments voiced in his earlier letters and throwing all his personal and literary plans into the melting pot. His letters of mid-February to Loks,[36] his mother and sister Josephine had announced an intention to return to Moscow only in May. To his mother he had also outlined his literary plans:

I have already started thinking about the summer. I keep dreaming more and more often and with increasing faith in the realisation of this dream about writing a drama (of a classical type but in the modern spirit – i.e. as I understand modern times) [...] I fear to say who it will be about. For that I shall have to do a lot of work in he Rumyantsev Library.[37]

Pasternak's letter to Loks on 13 February also held out the alluring prospect of a Tsentrifuga meeting at Bobrov's, lubricated by liquor which was still obtainable on the Kama – Curaçao de Chipre or any other brand Loks dared to name (public sale of wine and spirits was prohibited during the First World War). If that meeting ever did take place, nothing memorable emerged from it. Tsentrifuga plans were in disarray. The advent of new uncertainties and the disappearance of Vermel's backing meant cancellation of schemes for an artistic salon organised by Aksyonov, a bi-monthly journal, and a collective volume of articles entitled *The Prosodist* (Stikhoved). And though it continued to be announced until Tsentrifuga's final demise in 1922, the group's *Third Miscellany* never appeared; some of its materials lay in Bobrov's archive for almost half a century before appearing in print.[38]

In early March Pasternak set off back to Moscow. It was a scenically memorable trip along the winter mail route from Tikhie gory. The first lap to the nearest rail station at Kazan was made in a *kibitka*, a covered waggon mounted on sledge runners. Throughout the night and part of the next day Pasternak was 'swaddled in three sheepskins, smothered in hay, and with no freedom to move, rolled around on the floor of the sleigh like a heavy sack' (II, 25; *VP*, 449). For most of the journey he dozed and slept fitfully. The track was humped with snowdrifts, overhanging pines scraped the roof, and starlight was reflected in a shroud of white snow. At one point they halted at a coaching station which resembled a robbers' camp in some fairytale. Then, from Kazan on the frozen Volga it was another 700 kilometres by rail to Moscow.

The impressions of that journey were significant enough to figure both in a piece of fiction written in 1918 and in the *Autobiographical Essay*. The sleigh ride to Kazan passed through the town of Izhevsk, and there they picked up Boris Zbarsky who continued the journey with him.[39] Like his colleague Lev Karpov, Zbarsky had ever since 1905 maintained links with the Socialist Revolutionary Party, which embodied the Russian tradition of populist radicalism. (In Moscow in August of 1917, Zbarsky arranged for Leonid Pasternak to attend a luncheon of old Socialist Revolutionaries including the so-called 'grand-mother of the Russian Revolution' Breshko-Breshkovskaya, Prince Kropotkin, Morozov, Burtsev and Chaikovsky; this event was recorded in a pastel, and later Kropotkin came to the Volkhonka apartment and sat for his portrait.)[40] During the sleigh ride from Izhevsk to Kazan, Zbarsky evidently talked animatedly of Russian political developments, which totally absorbed him, and confirmed Pasternak's impression that he both lacked self-awareness and failed to realise how he stood out from the grey mass of armchair politicians at Tikhie gory. For his part, Pasternak was elated and shared the general sense of relief at the fall of the autocracy and the promise of a new liberation, but as an artist he was uninterested in the minutiae of political disputation and party pro-grammes. In November of 1918 he wrote a 'chapter from a tale' entitled *Lovelessness*, which was published in the Socialist Revolutionary news-paper *Volya truda* (Liberty of Labour). In it he himself and Zbarsky were recognisable as prototypes for the contrasting characters of Konstantin Goltsev and Yurii Kovalevsky. Like their real-life models, the two characters are travelling by sleigh through the Urals on the first lap of a journey to Moscow. Goltsev has been on the Kama and during their journey he is absorbed by casual memories of a theatre visit with a girl who evidently (like Istomina and Larisa Guichard in Pasternak's later prose fragments and novel) intends signing on as a nurse. Goltsev seems to his fellow-traveller to be asleep, but he is, so we are told, fully alert to the most important aspects of existence. The real dreamer is Kovalevsky, who incarnates the lovelessness of the work's title. He is

thinking about the aim of their sudden departure [...] about the reception awaiting him, and about what should be done first of all [...] He did not suspect that Goltsev was wide awake and that he himself was asleep, plunging from dream to dream and pothole to pothole, together with his thoughts about revolution, which again, as once before, were dearer to him than his furcoat and other belongings, dearer than his wife and child, dearer than his own life and that of other people. (II, 324; *VP*, 51)

Later the two travellers call on a Socialist Revolutionary factory manager; there is conversation concerning Breshko-Breshkovskaya and the disposal of Kovalevsky's illegal political literature, which the imprac-tical Goltsev has forgotten to remind him about. The extract ends with

Goltsev and the manager enjoying coffee and a snack as Kovalevsky pens instructions for the papers to be forwarded.

As a work of art, *Lovelessness* is incomplete and insignificant. But it is of interest, firstly, because it foreshadows the contrasting characters of Zhivago and Antipov in Pasternak's novel four decades later (a connection underlined by the setting and some identical Tatar names). Secondly, it serves as a prominent example of the close link in Pasternak between belles-lettres and real-life experience.[41]

Despite the apparent evidence of *Lovelessness* and of *The Black Goblet* with its strict demarcation between Lyricism and History, Pasternak was neither insensitive to the events of his time nor intent upon avoiding their impact. *The Black Goblet* and *Lovelessness* were *not* offering a rounded picture of his personality or views on history, war and revolution; they were concerned only to describe a stance that would protect the integrity of art and the artist. This integrity was often defended by his seeming obtuseness or naïveté, a means of avoiding the self-compromise that any commitment to political schemes and utilitarian philosophies would entail. As a lyricist, Pasternak was given more to expressions of feeling and mood than to analytical comment (which, as a professional philosopher with a sound historical training he was perfectly equipped to offer). But since he followed newspaper reports and took a keen interest in the events of the war, there was perhaps more than naïve optimism in the letters he sent to his parents from the Kama; there had also been a certain ironic foresight in a doggerel quatrain that he wrote for his family's amusement during the war years, hinting at the high Jewish membership of the Marxist Social Democrat Party:

> Whether Moscow and we all go Jew-wards,
> Or the Jews all in Moscow arrive,
> It will all doubtless happen much sooner
> Than the house of Romanov desires.[42]

If his first appreciation of the February Revolution lacked political focus, it was no different from general public reaction in Moscow and elsewhere. Overflowing enthusiasm was a widespread response to the fall of an enfeebled and corrupt tsarist rule and the promise of social liberation. In March 1917 Pasternak reached Moscow and shared in the euphoria. 'Day followed day,' Konstantin Loks recalled, 'and on one of those days came Boris Pasternak. He was happy. He was contented. "Just imagine," he told me at our first meeting, "when an ocean of blood and filth begins to give out light . . ." And an eloquent gesture completed the expression of his rapture. He immediately set down to work and planned a novel set in the times of the French Revolution.'[43]

Almost all that we know about this novel is contained in Loks' memoirs. He recollected seeing rows of books about the French Revolution on Pasternak's desk, borrowed either from the University or the Rumyantsev Library, and Pasternak read out to him part of a chapter opening with a scene in which a man sits reading his Bible.[44] Probably such a project was only a passing fancy – the times were hardly conducive to the prolonged patient labour needed for a novel, and what became of Pasternak's sketches is not known. However, the French Revolution as an obvious, conscious echo of the Russian situation was used in some dramatic fragments written in 1917 in part fulfilment of his earlier plan for a drama 'in the modern spirit'. The planned 'ideological book' of articles was discarded, and almost all Pasternak's writings of 1917 seem unconnected with what he had projected earlier. Their genre and tonality were dictated not by literary trends, personalities, or commissions, but by ideas and impressions thrown up by personally observing the Russian scene. It was largely for this reason (rather than the self-dismissive one advanced in the *Autobiographical Essay*) that Pasternak failed in July 1917 to respond to Ehrenburg's attempts to interest him in Tsvetaeva's poetry.[45] And his independence of all 'literature' was probably apparent in his meeting with Mayakovsky in the spring of that year.

At the end of March, Mayakovsky came from the capital to report at the council of Moscow artists' organisations on the newly founded Union of Artists in Petrograd, and to give a reading on 26 March at the 'First Republican Evening of the Arts' organised by Kamensky in the Hermitage Theatre. During his stay Pasternak visited him early one morning at his hotel in Stoleshnikov Lane, and as Mayakovsky washed and dressed he regaled Pasternak with recitations from his latest long poem *War and the Universe*, which revived the arresting impressions of earlier days. The conversation turned to Futurism. Conscious of his own newly found independence, Pasternak evidently suggested to Mayakovsky 'how splendid it would be if he now publicly sent all this to hell'. Apparently Mayakovsky laughed and half-agreed.[46] He kept his colours nailed to the Futurist mast for nearly another decade, yet his response to Pasternak pointed to a certain falsehood in his position and in the actual phenomenon of Futurism. An unpublished part of Pasternak's *Safe Conduct* continued the account of their March meeting.

'That's Futurism for you. Look,' he said suddenly, pausing at the window of a music shop on Petrovka. On the cover of some music was a picture of an irredeemably unreal but pretty girl. Yet the example was a good one because this sample of innovation was a piece of anonymous pre-Itinerant vulgarity which maintained a certain faith to some of that age's legacy and did not totally betray it – even if only in order to rank along with the Itinerants. He agreed with me but did not accept a suggestion that he speak out against the exoticism of that period. We walked along as far as the Lubyanka then went our separate ways.[47]

The apparently bloodless handover of power in Moscow brought unexpected delight to many liberals including all of Pasternak's family. Some verses by Lydia to her father on his birthday in 1917 recalled the tensions of 28 February, when the family had stored water, tramcars came to a standstill, and a grim confrontation of students and populace with grey-coated, bayonet-bearing soldiery suddenly ended in fraternisation, dissolving fears of a repeat of the 1905 bloodletting.[48] Unlike his children, Leonid Pasternak remained cautiously sceptical about a happy final outcome – as it turned out, with good reason. But Boris' own idealism of 1905 was now vividly conjured up again. Having avoided war service, he had had no close encounters with history to blunt that fervour in the interim. The mood in which he greeted the February Revolution was probably attributed to some characters in his later prose *Story*:

They believed in the depths of their hearts that there would be another revolution. By a self-deception forgivable in our day too, they imagined that the revolution would go on again, like a drama temporarily cancelled then later revived, with a fixed cast – that is with all of them playing their old roles. This delusion was all the more natural since, believing deeply in the popular universality of their ideals, they still thought it necessary to test this conviction of theirs on the living people. (II, 159; *VP*, 144)

Perhaps as the year advanced it became clear that this was a delusion. The challenge to Pasternak's bright-eyed laissez-faire liberalism by a harsher revolutionary fanaticism was later represented fictionally by two circles or skeins of thought that were attributed to Yurii Zhivago in the period between February and October of 1917. In one circle were the thoughts concerned with his settled life, home and poetry:

Also in this circle were his loyalty to the revolution and admiration for it. This was the revolution in the sense in which it was accepted by the middle classes, and as it was understood by the young students of 1905, the worshippers of Blok.

This close and familiar circle also contained the sign of new things, promises and omens that appeared on the horizon before the war, between 1912 and 1914, in Russian thought and art, and in a fate shared by the whole of Russia that was also his own. After the war he wanted to return to these trends, to renew and continue them, just like some desire to go back home.

New things were also the subject of the other circle of his thoughts. But how different, how utterly new! These were not familiar and dear things prepared for by the old, but things unchosen and relentless, prescribed by reality and sudden as an earthquake. Among them was the war, its blood and horrors, its homelessness and savagery [...] Such also was the revolution, not the one idealised in student fashion around 1905, but this modern one, born of the war, bloody, a ruthless soldiers' revolution, directed by the expert operators in this element, the Bolsheviks. (*DZh*, 162–3)

But if Pasternak sensed how the fabric of Russian political and social life was collapsing in the spring and summer of 1917, the feeling was drowned in a rapturous shared experience of liberty. His novel later recalled how the Revolution was 'God come down to earth, the God of that summer, and everyone went mad in his own way, and the life of each one existed in its own right and not as an illustration to confirm and explain the correctness of high-level politics' (*DZh*, 466).

The universal public animation of those months was recorded by innumerable eye-witnesses. John Reed's account in *Ten Days that Shook the World* vividly recalls the 'talk, beside which Carlyle's "flood of French speech" was a mere trickle'.[49] Pasternak's own memoirs describe 'crowds that by day and night took council together on the summer squares beneath the open sky as at an ancient *veche** [...] The multitudes of aroused and alerted souls stopped one another, flowed together and, as they would have said in days of yore, thought aloud "with one accord". Men from the common people unburdened themselves and chatted about the most important thing of all: how life should be lived and for what purpose, and how one could establish the sole conceivable and worthy form of existence' (*VP*, 491).

Poetic metaphor now seemed to come true in a general fusion of nature and human activity:

In that celebrated summer of 1917, in the interval between two revolutionary periods, it seemed as if together with the people the roadways, trees and stars held meetings and delivered speeches. From end to end the air was gripped in a blazing, thousand-league inspiration, and it appeared as a personality with a name, seemed clairvoyant and animated.[50] (*VP*, 491)

* *Veche* – a popular assembly in some mediaeval Russian cities.

227

In his original version of *Safe Conduct* Pasternak described how pressures leading to a national explosion built up precisely through the autocracy's resistance to change and lack of dynamism. And as in the nation at large, so in the moral sphere in 1917 there was a burst of energy that followed years of enforced atrophy. This was described in an autobiographical note of the mid-1950s:

Throughout long ages of calm, beneath the everyday superficial and deceptive tranquillity full of compromises with conscience and subservience to falsehood, mankind secretes large funds of lofty moral requirements, cherishes a dream of a different, more courageous and pure life and is unaware of and does not suspect its own secret idea.

But the stability of society needs only to be shaken. It is sufficient for some elemental catastrophe or military defeat to shake life's firm routine which seemed immutable and eternal, and the bright columns of those latent deposits of morality miraculously break forth from beneath the earth.

People grow taller by a head and are amazed and fail to recognise themselves. They emerge as heroes. People encountered on the street seem not just anonymous passers-by but appear as if to demonstrate and express the entire human race as a whole. This sensation of everyday reality observed at every step yet at the same time becoming history, this feeling of eternity come down to earth and everywhere apparent, this fairytale mood I attempted to convey in the book of lyrics *My Sister Life* which I then wrote on a personal prompting.

(*VP*, 491–2)

My Sister Life, published in 1922, bore the subtitle 'Summer of the Year 1917', which indicated when most of its poems were composed. Despite the important public events of that year, it is not a book overtly about revolution. (The adjective 'revolutionary', in fact, occurs only once, and it describes a haystack.) As Pasternak recalled in an afterword to *Safe Conduct*, 'I saw one summer on the earth as though it had just recognised itself, natural and prehistoric, as in the Revelation. I have left a book about it. In it I expressed everything one could find out about the revolution that was most unprecedented and elusive' (II, 345; *VP*, 481).

Much less elusive was the element of amorous passion in this verse. The personal prompting that gave rise to it was Pasternak's deepening friendship with Elena Vinograd. They had met infrequently during the war years, but had seen one another the previous autumn shortly after her fiancé, Sergei Listopad, was killed in action, and when Pasternak was completing *Over the Barriers*. The following year Elena asked him to give her a copy of the book, but as he later told Zoya Maslennikova, 'I felt that I could not – at that time I was caught up with Cubism, but she was a fresh and unspoilt girl. So on top of that book I began writing another one for her. Thus *My Sister Life* was born.'[51]

Pasternak did not write to Elena during the winter of 1916–17 – so he told Shura Shtikh in a letter of 7 February 1917. But after his springtime return to Moscow their meetings became more frequent. Elena lived in Khlebny (Bread) Lane near the Arbat, but she often visited Boris in his box-like room in Lebyazhii Lane where he had moved in again – 'from superstition', as one of the poems of *My Sister Life* recorded, and where he lodged until August 1917 (apart from a short period in June when he took over the empty quarters at 6 Nashchokinsky Lane, apartment 16, belonging to Fanni Zbarskaya's sister, Dr T. N. Leibovich). In 1986 Elena Vinograd still clearly recalled the circumstances recounted in that poem, which concluded with Pasternak's confession:

> It would be a sin to think you're no vestal:
>   You came in carrying chair,
> You took my life as though from a shelf
>   And blew the dust away.   (I, 12; *SP*, 118)

Elena had meanwhile enrolled as a student on the Higher Women's Courses and was, like Pasternak, infected with the general revolutionary euphoria. In addition to outings to Moscow's Sparrow (now Lenin) Hills and the Neskuchny Garden, they followed the events of March and the strikes of janitors and house-staff (recorded in the poem 'Militiamen's Whistles' ['Svistki militsionerov']); the two of them were both present at the Bolshoi Theatre for Kerensky's visit in late May, when he was showered with rose petals (see 'Spring Rain' ['Vesennii dozhd'] at the head of this chapter);[52] Elena also persuaded Pasternak to join her at various other public meetings, and in this way amorous and revolutionary elements were biographically intertwined.

During the summer holidays Elena followed an urge to be involved in the age's exciting new issues. In June she went off to do social work in country areas, or to work in local government, and she ended up at the small town of Romanovka in Saratov Province on the Volga. While she was out there Pasternak came to visit her for a few days. (Impressions of that journey figured later in 'Blank Verses' ['Belye stikhi'], in a group of poems titled 'Romanovka' in *My Sister Life*, and also in the Melyuzeyevo episode of *Doctor Zhivago*.) In July Pasternak was back in Moscow – in 'an attempt to part the soul from you' (I, 38; *SP*, 140), and with only a photographic 'Replacement' ('Zamestitel'nitsa') for Elena. In the meantime the two of them corresponded in a tender but formal '*vy*' mode. Not all their exchanges were happy, and Elena was at one point distraught and ready to break off relations after Boris' angry attempt to persuade her to do in life what her feelings dictated and not follow the dictates of other folk, her mother in particular. (Most of Elena's letters were not kept by Pasternak and all his letters to her were lost through bombing in the Second World War.) In late July Pasternak also corresponded with Elena's brother Valeryan, who had gone to the provinces to assist with *zemstvo* welfare work and with preparing electoral lists for the forthcoming Constituent Assembly elections. As a student of Moscow University, Valeryan sought Pasternak's advice and help in arranging to intermit a year's social work between his courses.[53]

In August Pasternak paid Elena Vinograd another visit, this time to Balashov in Saratov province where she had now transferred, and there the two of them spent a further few days together. During this period Pasternak's affection for Elena developed into an intense infatuation. He wrote nothing of it, or of her, in his autobiographies and the poems of *My Sister Life* are the only public evidence. Evidently it was another affair akin to the ones with Cousin Olya and Vysotskaya. The relationship remained platonic, unphysical and emotionally one-sided. Elena latterly recollected that their 'meetings were rather monologues on his part', while she merely basked in the rays of his charm without sensing that there was ever a meeting of hearts and souls. About the reality of Pasternak's unexpressed passions there can be no doubt, however, and the torment of this muted adoration doubtless injected power into the resulting poetry. It also helped reinforce his sense of inadequacy in dealing with women. Elena saw herself there as tinder which set off an eruption of poetic forces, but no more than that. As she told him in a letter of 1 September: 'I am unfair to you, it's true. My pain seems to me more painful than yours – that is unfair, but I feel I am right. You are immeasurably higher than me. When you suffer, nature suffers as well; you aren't abandoned by it any more than you are by life, and meaning and God.' Pasternak's confessions and almost daily letters were therefore to Elena only symptoms of an 'artistic personality'; in the actual verse of *My Sister Life* she failed to discover any of her personal characteristics.[54]

The seasonal cycle of winter, spring and an emotional climax in a sultry summer was followed both in the calendar and the poetic sequence by a cooler autumn. The poetic evidence suggests that after Pasternak's sleepy and dejected train journey back to Moscow, passions had burnt low, leaving a mood of sadness and regret in which the poet concluded that 'with the anguish of so many words / One grows tired of being friends!' (I, 54; *SP*, 155). Elena herself returned to Moscow in October. There was no resumption of earlier relations, but there was still plenty of creative mileage in Pasternak's frustrated infatuation. The impetus with which verse poured from him that summer and autumn largely dictated the style and structure of *My Sister Life*. For the first time, unlike his earlier books, this was a genuine sequence which preserved the outlines of a story; structurally the book retained some attributes of a work in prose fiction. Lev Ozerov, the poet and editor of Pasternak's collected verse, described it as 'an original sort of novel consisting of separate poems and poems combined in cycles'.[55] The final shape and contents of *My Sister Life* took some time to crystallise, but the novelistic conception, with chapters, and subsections entitled 'Diversions of the Beloved', 'Studies in Philosophy', 'Songs in Letters to Entertain Her', etc., doubtless arose along with the initial inspiration. Another feature of intertextual interest is the love story's emergence from among various experiences in Pasternak's earlier life. Part of 'The Replacement', for instance, has links through its imagery with the early prose sketches and with the young Pasternak's social rounds, as well as with the Sventitskys' Christmas party episode of *Doctor Zhivago*.[56]

Within *My Sister Life*, continuity is assisted by a web of cross reference and quotation between items. A poem called 'Sultry Night' ('Dushnaya noch') is followed by a 'Yet More Sultry Dawn' ('Eshche bolee dushnyi rassvet'), and some snatches of prose fill in details of a skeleton 'plot'. All this is further evidence of the permeable membrane between Pasternak's verse and prose. Yet despite the hints of narrative, the book was essentially an impressionistic sequence, applying structurally the technique at work in individual poems (like the 'hundred blinding photographs' taken at one point by a thunderstorm). It was left to the reader to supply mental links between episodes and to relate to them a series of interlude excursions into metaphysics and aesthetics.

In one of the opening poems 'About these Verses' ('Pro eti stikhi') the author describes his domestic winter refuge where, while blizzards blow, he communes with Byron, Lermontov and Poe.

> Shielding my mufflered face with a hand,
> Through the window I'll call to the children:
> 'What millenium is it outside, my dears?
> What age are we in? Do, please, tell me.'   (I, 4; *SP*, 111)

This quatrain was later often cited by Marxist critics as illustrating Pasternak's cosy, bourgeois, housebound indifference to the outside world. It is true that history and the revolution are not given explicit foreground prominence. Two overtly topical items, 'Spring Rain' and 'Militiamen's Whistles' are set half-dismissively amidst 'The Beloved's Diversions', and elements of current events appear only as the second term in a simile or other trope. Clouds drift by 'like recruits passing a farm at dawn', or 'like Austrian prisoners of war'.

> And the air of the steppe is startled:
>
> It senses and imbibes the soul
> Of soldiers' mutinies and summer lightnings.
>
> (I, 29–30; *SP*, 134)

But even in a year like 1917, Pasternak's chief priorities lay in a different quarter:

> The life of all was scoured and parched,
> And conflicts turned men sour,
> And no one was concerned: the miracle
> Of life lasts but an hour.   (I, 15; *SP*, 121)

The wonder of life and unquestioning involvement with all its facets which gave the book its title was spelt out in one of the opening poems: 'My sister life has today overflowed, / And everyone's showered with torrents of spring' (I, 5; *SP*, 112). For one in such a state of exuberance even the rail time-table of the Kamyshin branch-line acquired the aura of holy writ!

One of the programmatic statements in the section on 'The Study of Philosophy' was a 'Definition of Poetry' ('Opredelen'e poezii') which offered two stanzas of kaleidoscopic metonymies for poetry:

> It's a whistle teeming steep,
> It is crushed icefloes jarring,
> It is night-time's gelid leaf,
> Two nightingales sparring.   (I, 22; *SP*, 121)

The book contains little explicit mention of the poet himself. Yet, though absent as an 'ego' or directing agent, the author's personality is immanent in all the vibrant love and nature lyrics, in the elemental force of the imagery. A 'Downpour of Light' was how Marina Tsvetaeva characterised the book, and Mandelstam talked of a 'floodtide of images springing up in Pasternak's poetry with unprecedented force'.[57] In fact, vocal initiative is ceded to the objective world. The poet will 'give damp corners chance to sing' and 'the garret will begin declaiming' (I, 4;

SP, 111). And in a 'Definition of Creativity', 'gardens and ponds and enclosures / And the cosmos' seething lament' are identified as 'discharges of passion / Stored up in the human heart' (I, 24; *SP*, 128). If the poet is present, he is most often an object of the action, a theme of disputation ''twixt pale wind and wet twigs'. And 'Afterword' ('Posleslov'e') lists reasons for the beloved's grief that are none of the author's making; responsibility is discharged in an impressionist subversion of routine logic:

> No, it was not I caused you grief [...]
> It was the sun ablaze in inkdrops [...]
> It was dust-formed evening that panted and
> Kissed you with pollen while choking in ochre.
> It was shadows feeling your pulse.   (I, 52–3; *SP*, 153–4)

One of the lyrics encourages identification of the poet with his own 'Weeping Garden' ('Plachushchii sad'). These tears together with other ubiquitous torrents of water, rainfall and dew readily suggest emotions and inspirations flowing in full spate. Just as wind and blizzard were germane to Blok, so various forms of liquidness became a resonant Pasternakian image, almost a personal symbol.[58] And taking all the imagery together, as Sinyavsky has maintained, 'In writing of springs and winters, rains and dawns, Pasternak is telling about the nature of life itself, about the essence of the universe. He is confessing his faith in life which seems to dominate his poetry and makes up its moral foundation.'[59]

The poet's self-effacement extends also to his love poetry. (Does this perhaps reflect his early record of failures as a suitor?) 'She's with me now,' Pasternak tells the rain and leaves the latter to express his passion:

> She's with me now. Strike up and laugh.
> Teem torrents, rip the dusk,
> Come flood and pour an epigraph
> To love, for you are such!   (I, 9; *SP*, 116)

When the lovers lie in a rowing boat 'With Oars at Rest' ('Slozha vesla') it is the willows, not the poet's lips, that bend low to kiss her collarbones, elbows and the rowlocks. Mayakovskian hyperbole still remains in the poet's armoury (the lovers' embrace is likened to 'clasping of hands round immense Hercules') but Pasternak's main metaphor springs from a 'melting of boundaries': moving beyond pathetic fallacy or self-dramatisation through nature, is the discovery of a mutual interaction of all elements in the landscape on the poet's behalf; in it subjects, objects and qualities are realigned through acoustics and contiguity – as in some Cubist or Expressionist painting which yet still retains the subtleties of impressionist or pointillist technique.

In view of the poet's evanescent personality, it seems strange to find *My Sister Life* dedicated to Lermontov, a poet of Byronic mould. The whole cycle begins with 'To the Demon's Memory' ('Pamyati Demona'), recalling the hero of Lermontov's epic and supposedly evoking a creative force that gave rise to Pasternak's book. While avoiding any melodramatic soul-baring, Pasternak shares with the Romantics an exclusive degree of passion that animates poetic statement. Heroics are banished, yet avalanches, floods, storms and other 'elemental' images seem the only adequate correlatives of emotion, just as they were with Lermontov. Recalling the book's dedication many years later, Pasternak wrote:

When in 1917 I hastily and without long consideration wrote on the title page of 'My Sister Life' not 'To the Memory of Lermontov' or something similar, but 'Dedicated to Lermontov', just as though he were still there, not just alive but among the chance passers-by [...] as though he could still be met somewhere that summer, I not only intended to express that feeling [...] of the undried traces of night rain or still sounding echoes of a sound that had just pealed out [...] All my life I flattered myself with the hope of revealing in an article in prose that mysterious potency [*mogushchestvo*] of Lermontov's essence, that drama of freshness, as it were, and its secret and riddle.[60]

Composing *My Sister Life* was the author's first complete experience of the 'miracle of a book's formation', as he later described to Nadezhda Mandelstam. He was himself astonished at the verses that poured from him; the creative force that gave rise to the book was 'immensely greater than me myself or the portic conceptions surrounding me' (II, 282; *VP*, 273). And the yield was so rich that Pasternak later had to trim and reduce *My Sister Life* in order to 'keep it light', as he once told Sinyavsky. Symptomatic, too, of the impetus with which all this new verse appeared was a change that Pasternak consciously made in his style of hand-writing. His hitherto somewhat routine letter formation (see Figure 17) was exchanged for the sweeping 'winged' script that he cultivated henceforth throughout his life.[61]

Only one poem from the book was actually printed in 1917 – 'Spring Rain', in the October miscellany *Put' osvobozhdeniya* (Way of Liberation). And only a handful of its poems appeared in print during the next few years. With public affairs and paper supplies in disarray, there was no chance of bringing out the complete book until 1922. Pasternak also had personal reasons for reticence in publishing this verse, and as a result of its non-appearance there was misunderstanding in literary circles about the state of his art. Some poems in *Over the Barriers* had in fact advertised a by now quite outdated commitment to Futurism. Maybe this explained a contretemps with Mayakovsky reported in *Safe Conduct*. Assuming his interest in public recitation together with other Cubo-Futurists, Mayakovsky had in 1917 placed Pasternak's name on a programme to appear alongside Bolshakov, Konstantin Lipskerov and himself, and Pasternak was angered by this bland assumption that nothing in him had changed since they met in late 1915. The precise dating of their disagreement poses problems. It may have occurred soon after their meeting in March 1917, when allegedly Pasternak had made his position clear with regard to any Futurist ventures, although he later dated their telephone argument to some time in August. Mayakovsky's only other appearances in Moscow that year were in the autumn on 24 September and later in a series of nightly entertainments at the so-called 'Poets' Cafe'. At some point in the winter of 1917–18 Pasternak must certainly have visited these premises on the corner of Nastasinsky Lane and Tverskaya (now Gorky) Street, and there he was doubtless even more firmly persuaded of the incongruity of *My Sister Life* amid such aesthetic anarchy and bohemianism.[62]

In addition to his travels to Saratov Province and the writing of lyric verse in June and July of 1917 Pasternak also worked on the drama he had announced to his mother in February. What emerged were no more than three incomplete fragments, published in that form the following year. Two of them had a French Revolutionary setting, like the sketches for a novel. Carlyle's *The French Revolution* was already favourite reading of Pasternak's; the analogy between February's events in Russia and those in eighteenth-century France was explored in several authors' belletristic and publicist writings in 1917; and the response to the happenings of that year by some Russian poets – Bely, Blok, Esenin, Mayakovsky – was certainly comparable with the French Revolution's reverberation in the Romantic imagination. 'Bliss was it in the dawn to be alive, / But to be young was very heaven!' – Wordsworth's feelings accurately summed up Pasternak's own.[63]

According to various surviving relatives, Pasternak was never gripped by the theatre as an art form, despite his admiration of certain artists like Kommissarzhevskaya or Meyerhold. His family were not habitual theatregoers, and for him the actor was a 'performer' rather than a genuinely creative artist. (This did not prevent his frequent use of the *image* of an actor as metaphor for the poet's role as a *medium* for inspiration – but this function Pasternak viewed as the antithesis of any contrived theatrical spectacle.)[64] Unused as he was to speaking in any voice other than his own lyrical one, he used the dramatic genre not as a spontaneously chosen mode of expression, but usually in response to some external *literary* influence. In this instance it was probably his translation work on Swinburne's trilogy that implanted the idea. Another relevant source was the drama of *Danton's Death* (*Dantons Tod*) by the German Georg Büchner: according to Aleksandr Pasternak the title of his brother's drama was to have been *Robespierre's Death* (*Smert' Robesp'era*). But beyond this we have no information except what can be inferred from the published fragments. Was this drama of Robespierre's death and downfall a fearful prophecy about Russian history? Probably not. After the bloodless February Revolution everything must have suggested a *contrast* with the French Revolutionary terror. Rather than offering a dramatised chronicle of French historical fact, Pasternak is evidently making a statement of his own view of revolution in general. At first sight the main protagonists are not at all typical Pasternakians; they are not inspired observers, but the active agents of revolution, living romantics who bring about their own deaths.

In the first *Dramatic Fragment*, Saint-Just gives an existential account of the human condition, in which man is required to justify himself creatively. Mere birth is no warranty for living:

> Man is nothing
> Save the Creator's Sword of Damocles.
> Man's soul has no abode but in the world
> That he himself has snared and recreated. (*SP*, 529)

Saint-Just views revolution as a form of creativity and a sublimation of his love for Henriette. He speaks of his labours as an 'instant of ecstasy transformed into years'. But his medium is not art but history: he is accustomed to 'leave on men the brandmark of self-immolations'. But creativity is achieved only at the price of total surrender to the powers he invokes, renouncing any control over his own fate and risking genuine immolation by the revolutionary forces. Yet this is a triumph in its own terms. Saint-Just sees himself as one of those who

> overcame the infernal
> And brazen uproar, smiled and laid their heads
> Triumphantly beneath the guillotine.

And those brief days preceding their demise
Compose the history of our republic. (*SP*, 536)

The second *Dramatic Fragment* is a dialogue between Saint-Just and Robespierre on the eve of their surrender, on the night of 9–10 Thermidor. Neither is capable now of steering events, and both men await their destruction by the revolutionary process they once commanded. But while Saint-Just enjoys an ecstasy of sacrificial self-fulfilment, Robespierre tries bringing reason and intellect to bear and is in a fury of frustration at the 'traitorous confusion' of his mind. Unlike the artistic and emotional Saint-Just, Robespierre – the 'incorruptible' and cerebral ascetic – curses his inability to maintain control and vainly seeks refuge behind 'barricades of concepts' and 'fortresses of reason'.

Although Pasternak's portrayal reflected historical reports of Robespierre's behaviour, the accuracy of the portraiture was less important than the characteristics it acquired in this presentation. As professional revolutionaries, neither he nor Saint-Just were kindred personalities for Pasternak. Yet the obvious contrast between the two revolutionaries seems to hint at the theme of the prose fragment *Lovelessness* based on a character contrast of the professional revolutionary and the inspired passive witness, a theme also later developed in the confrontation of Antipov-Strelnikov and Yurii Zhivago in Pasternak's novel. While Robespierre has denied his own humanity for the sake of a ruthless idea, Saint-Just inhabits the 'first circle' of Zhivago's thoughts on revolution, more congenial to the artistic mentality, and at the final hour he confronts his existence and sees it justified as an act of creativity, an instant of political ecstasy 'transformed into years':

> This broad day
> Which lights the world around like dungeon steps
> That form the threshold of my soul, will not
> Forever be a stormy lantern flame
> That shivers worlds into a fevered order.
> This age will pass. The scorching beam will cool,
> Turn charcoal-black, and curiosity
> One day will pore by candlelight in archives
> For works which thrill and dazzle men today.
> [...]
> But who has fame as guest within his soul,
> Fate guides his eye: he draws the shroud across
> His days, himself to write his age's book and
> Inscribe therein his own renown and glory. (*SP*, 528–9)

237

In the *Dramatic Fragments* the polarities of Lyricism and History have thus dramatically converged. Saint-Just's 'instant of ecstasy transformed into years' has its analogue in the 'limiting moment' of artistic illumination which gives rise to Pasternak's 'impressionism of the eternal' (III, 149) described in *The Black Goblet* in 1916.[65]

After February's 'blinding debouch into the forum' came the Bolshevik *coup d'état* in October. Offering a common intelligentsia view of the time, theatrical producer Tairov recalled how 'we accepted the revolution without any qualification. But to accept the revolution was not the same as understanding its motive forces, its laws, the law of class struggle. We accepted the revolution, if you like idealistically and welcomed its destructive tendencies.'[66] Pasternak's own similar recollection was included in some autobiographical notes of the 1950s:

In those cases where they sympathised with the revolution abstract observers, coming mainly from the intelligentsia and ignorant of the sufferings that afflicted the people, viewed it through the prism of a patriotic philosophy that ruled in those years and which was inherited from the Slavophiles and now revived.

They did not contrast October and February as two opposites, and in their conception both uprisings blended in the single indivisible whole of the Great Russian Revolution which had immortalised Russia among the nations and which in their eyes flowed naturally out of Russia's entire formidable and sacred spiritual past. (*VP*, 491)

The partly autobiographical *Doctor Zhivago* also showed the hero's view of October as a continuation of February's revolutionary impetus. Zhivago anticipates this in the summer of 1917 in an impromptu exposé to his family:

The sea of blood will rise until it reaches everyone and engulfs those who have dug in and are trying to sit it out. The revolution is this flood.

At such a time it will seem to you, as it did to us who were fighting the war, that everything has come to an end, and that nothing else is going on in the world but killing and dying. And if we survive to the days when records and memories of this time are written and we read these recollections, we shall realise that in these five or ten years we have lived through more than other people do in a whole century. (*DZh*, 185)

When news of the October Revolution reaches Moscow, Yurii Zhivago stands out in the blizzard, attempting to read a fresh newspaper announcement of the new decrees, and he is 'shaken and overwhelmed by the greatness of the moment and the thought of its significance for centuries to come.' Shortly afterwards he reflects:

What splendid surgery! You take a knife and all at once skilfully cut away all the old stinking ulcers! [...] There is an old and familiar national look to the way in which this has so fearlessly been carried through. Something of Pushkin's uncompromising clarity, and of Tolstoy's unwavering attachment to the facts [...]

And now, if you please, here is this unprecedented marvel of history, this revelation suddenly hurled into the midst of our daily routine without any concern for its course [...] That is the greatest act of genius. Only the greatest things can be so misplaced and so untimely.   (*DZh*, 198–9)

A consideration of Zhivago's and Pasternak's whole education, which led to their veneration for centuries' worth of inherited European cultural tradition and civilisation, makes one sceptical of reading this passage as an endorsement of what had already been identified as a 'ruthless soldiers' revolution'. Here indeed was an 'untamed Savanarola' at work, not in art but in morality and history. And although Pasternak could wax eloquent about the splendid spectacle and the decisiveness of Bolshevik proclamations announcing measures that people had waited for in vain from the Provisional Government, he was no more capable of participating than he had been in the Cubo-Futurist aesthetic revolt. Nevertheless, the mentality that perceived behind the October action a form of uncompromising 'genius' was something Pasternak identified as a permanent Russian national trait. In some later reflections on the Second World War he also referred to 'the element of genius which prepared our revolution as a phenomenon of national morality'. This genius he defined as

a deeply felt right to measure everything in the world by one's own yardstick, a sense of being at one with the universe, the enjoyment of one's own close blood tie with history, a feeling of access to all things living. Genius is a quality that is primary yet unobtrusive. These same traits of novelty and originality were responsible for our revolution.   (*VP*, 376)

At about the time of the Bolshevik seizure of power, Pasternak was writing in the same intoxicated, supra-political vein in the third of his *Dramatic Fragments*. This was a prose *scena* entitled 'Dialogue', which was published on 17 May 1918 in *Znamya truda*. Set in early twentieth-century France, it also had a distinct Swiftian colouration. The action introduces an absent-minded, eccentric Russian intellectual who has been arrested for the theft of a melon and for preaching dangerous but unspecified doctrines in a public place. The dialogue consists of his interrogation by a police official and his attempts to justify his behaviour. This he does by describing his mysterious national Utopian philosophy and inspired, ecstatic involvement with all life's activities. Hence his unconcern for material surroundings or for private property, his own or other people's. His philosophy contrasts with the inert rationality and dullness of life in France and implicitly suggests that Russia has succeeded where a once revolutionary France has failed. In Russia,

man lives as it were a game [...] Wherever his inflammable nature finds a spark. Nobody pays him anything. That would be absurd. It's an absurdity that fixes you to a particular place. Your man, here is a mere point in space. With us humanity is a state, a degree, a boiling-point [...] Every day you wake up burning, full of reserves of heat [...] I love my country, madly sometimes [...] Everyone is a genius, because everyone gives himself up to it, like a flax, gives up the last fibre of himself to make its web.[67]

The concept of a new individualism born from revolutionary socialism, as elaborated in the 'Dialogue', was attributed also to Zhivago:

One might say that everybody has undergone two revolutions, his own personal one, and another general one. Socialism seems to me like a sea, in which all these personal, individual revolutions must flow like streams running into the ocean of life.   (*DZh*, 148)

Pasternak outlined the same idea again in 1922 when questioned by Trotsky on the reasons why his work seemed to avoid social issues. His explanation 'amounted to a defence of true individualism like a new social cell in a new social organism'. Their conversation led him to reflect also that 'the stage of revolution closest to my heart and to poetry is the revolution's *morning* and its intial outburst, when it returns man to his own *nature* and regards the state through the eyes of *natural* law (the American and French declaration of rights)'.[68] Pasternak's interest in natural law could have stemmed from various sources. In winter 1916–17 he was well informed of Loks' plans to write a book *On Natural Man* (*O estestvennom cheloveke*). But his awareness of the contrast between Russian and Western society, with their differently based legal norms, may also have owed something to his student reading and philosophy studies. This difference had been explored in Kistya-kovsky's contribution to the *Vekhi* collection of 1909 and it was implicit in Professor Evgenii Trubetskoi's teaching and his *Lectures on the*

240

Encyclopaedia of Law (*Lektsii po entsiklopedii prava*) (Moscow, 1917). Pasternak was doubtless familiar too with the writings of Proudhon, who in the nineteenth century had proclaimed that 'property is theft', envisaging a form of libertarian socialism different from both Marxist and traditional concepts of the state.[69]

Following the Bolshevik seizure of Petrograd on 25 October, there was a pitched battle for control in Moscow, as in various other Russian cities. Cossacks and loyal troops managed to clear the Kremlin of a Soviet occupying force and held the centre of the city while Bolshevik forces dug in in various areas of the periphery. After a short lull, key buildings and the city centre and Kremlin were bombarded for six days by Bolshevik artillery. The Whites finally surrendered on 2 November, and Bolshevik rule was established. During most of that period there was no electricity or telephone communication. And since machine-gun and rifle fire had no identifiable focus, most citizens uninvolved in the fighting stayed off the streets and sheltered indoors.

From their home situated fairly close to the centre and commanding a view across the Moskva River, the Pasternaks saw probably more than most residents. They could observe, for instance, as government troops and Cossacks moved into the Zamoskvorechye area on the south embankment. One fine afternoon, cousin Fedya, who had now returned from exile, called by and suggested a walk with Lydia and Josephine. Within a few minutes of their departure, vehicles with armed and battle-ready soldiers began rolling past and the streets cleared. The girls and Fedya took shelter in his apartment on Prechistenka and rang up to warn their parents that they had been cut off. Boris too was forced to stay on at the Volkhonka apartment although since September he had been renting a room at 12 Sivtsev Vrazhek near the Arbat.

For the next six days the inhabitants of both houses on Prechistenka and Volkhonka were uncomfortably close to the fighting. The troops made trenches and barricades by digging up the street cobbles. Shooting on the Volkhonka made it dangerous to look through the windows, and Boris and Aleksandr and their parents eventually moved into the rear of the house, then down into the ground-floor apartment of the Ustinov family. Throughout the fighting, water ran only intermittently, and both telephone and lights failed ... Then suddenly, it was all over and there was silence. Boris was apparently persuaded by his brother not to start playing the piano immediately for fear of attracting hostile attention. A tank came rattling past and cleared the street once and for all. The telephone rang again announcing that Lydia and Josephine were safe and apparently in a happy mood, unlike their brothers and parents. One week after setting out for their afternoon walk the girls returned home, picking their way across the battlefield. Soviet power was established in Moscow and a new age had begun.[70]

10

Civil war activities

Stars were rushing. Waves were washing headlands.
Salt went blind, and tears were drying gently.
Darkened were the bedrooms. Thoughts were rushing
And the Sphynx was listening to the desert.

Candles swam. It seemed that the Colossus'
Blood grew cold. Upon his lips was spreading
The blue shadow smile of the Sahara.
With the turning tide the night was waning.

Sea-breeze from Morocco touched the water.
Simooms blew. In snowdrifts snored Archangel.
Candles swam. The rough draft of 'The Prophet'
Slowly dried, and dawn broke on the Ganges.

❦❦❦❦

In early March 1918 the Russian capital was moved back to Moscow, and the same month saw ratification of the Brest-Litovsk peace treaty with Germany. These changes did little, however, to avert trials and hardships for the population. By early summer the country was in the grip of a civil conflict which added to the ruin of the war. Meanwhile, workers' control of factories led to disorder and dwindling production, and Bolshevik policy in the villages and destruction of the food distribution apparatus caused breakdowns in the supply of basic provisions and virtual starvation in the towns. As Pasternak later observed in his novel, 'In the days of the triumph of materialism matter had become an abstract concept. Food and firewood were replaced by the problem of food and fuel supplies' (*DZh*, 186–7).

The worst periods were the winters. 'There were three of them, such fearful winters [...] which followed one another, merged into one and were difficult to tell apart.' (*DZh*, 199) The experience was similar in many parts of Russia. One of Zamyatin's stories likened the Petrograd apartment to a cave dwelling in a city that had become a prehistoric settlement inhabited by primitive men and mammoths. And in Moscow, Pasternak's Yurii Zhivago observed how 'in the black distance, on the black snow, there were no longer streets in the usual sense but more like forest cuttings amid a dense taiga of stone buildings, like in the impenetrable forests of the Urals or Siberia' (*DZh*, 209).

At the Pasternaks' Volkhonka home the Tatar janitor Galliulin (his name and function later went directly into *Zhivago*) came twice a day to stoke the Dutch stove once the frosts set in. Later Boris took over this job and apparently became skilled in stacking birch logs so that they burned entirely away, leaving no embers. When fuel supplies gave out, like many town-dwellers, the two brothers went on sorties to steal fencing and other removable items. Aleksandr Pasternak recalled how they also climbed up into the loft at night and together sawed billets of wood from the ends of the roof joists. Fortunately the roofing at number 14 held; other woodcutters were not always so lucky. Further fuel economy was achieved part of the time by not using the stove. The Pasternaks had a succession of short-term daily helps and cooks after October 1917. After that, Motya, the cleaner from the two adjoining flats that were taken over by the Timiryazev Museum, began doing most of the family's cooking. Eventually the only solution to the fuel problem was to close off several rooms during the winter months. The drawing room with its black Bechstein was locked and allowed to freeze up, and the family lived effectively in only two rooms. Rozaliya Pasternak's music making, reduced since 1916 owing to ill-health, therefore came to a halt during the winters of the Civil War. Leonid Pasternak still managed to work with mittened hands and with paints that were barely workable through the low temperature, but when conditions were too severe he wrote instead, and between 1918 and 1920 produced a short volume on Rembrandt and Jewish elements in his work which was published in Berlin in 1923. Boris Pasternak also did most of his writing in the Volkhonka apartment seated by the samovar and drinking endless glasses of strong tea. His usual indoor winter dress was a thick *fufaika* jersey, a quilted jacket, and felt boots.[1]

During the warmer months life became marginally easier, although shortages and hunger still continued. In the summer of 1918 dried carp (*vobla*) was for long spells the only fish obtainable in Moscow, and the only fat came from vegetables or in the form of caster and cod-liver oil. Pasternak's friend and promoter Evgenii Lundberg described a feast put on in one house at which the main course was the meat of a horse's leg cooked in hempseed oil with pies made from potato peelings, carrot and beetroot. Other basic fare included 'boiled millet and fish soup made with herring heads. The fresh body of the herring came as the main course. People also fed on unground rye and grains of wheat' (*DZh*, 201). Although in summer unwanted luxuries like flowers were sold on the streets of Moscow, the more usual items of trade were essentials like bread (sometimes in the form of rusks), sugar, or cigarettes, which starving townsfolk offered for sale along with the pathetic bric-a-brac of a former lifestyle. During the hungry years the Pasternaks sold off many prized possessions. Tsvetaeva recalled meeting Boris in 1919 on his way to sell a complete edition of Solovyov's history in order to purchase bread. Hunger was still a constant condition, along with disease and despair, and many – especially the very young and the very old – did not survive it.[2]

During the summers of 1918 and 1919 the Pasternaks managed to go for their customary dacha holiday. A few kilometres to the southwest of Moscow lay Karzinkino (by the Ochakovo rail halt) where they were invited by Leonid Pasternak's publisher friend Aleksandr Stybel. There they could enjoy some of their traditional recreations, except that for part of the time they now worked in Stybel's vegetable garden where they grew some produce for their own use. Some impressions of this holiday in 1918 with memories of a storm and sunset and of first love were recorded in verses by Lydia Pasternak. Boris himself stayed on in town for much of the summer, only occasionally joining his family for a few days. At Karzinkino in 1918 he drafted his spectacular poetic 'Theme and Variations' which eventually gave their title to a whole book published in 1923. Apart from Stybel and his wife, other guests at Karzinkino in 1918 included the Jewish writer and critic, David Frishman, and S. A. Ansky, the playwright and author of *The Dybbuk*.[3]

The Pasternaks probably endured the hardships of the Civil War little better or worse than other artistic intelligentsia who had no privileged links with the authorities and thus no guaranteed food supply. Until October 1917 their apartment had belonged to the Society of Moscow Artists. Under Bolshevik rule it was taken over by the Moscow City Council and thereafter they became ordinary rent and rate payers. In 1919 came official instructions to concentrate the use of living space and rooms were allocated according to the size of households. In consequence the Pasternaks' accommodation was reduced, and additional residents moved into some rooms of their apartment. Fortunately, these new neighbours were all pleasant and compatible. Vasilii Ustinov and his wife had originally lived on the ground-floor and had got to know the Pasternaks when the latter sheltered with them during the October 1917 shoot-out; they were now allocated one and a half rooms upstairs in the Pasternaks' apartment. Praskovya Petrovna ('Pasha', or 'Pashetta'), the Ustinovs' cook, also took over most of the Pasternak family's cooking. (After his wife died in 1925, Ustinov married her, although she still continued to make meals for Boris' family.) At one point in the early 1920s a further temporary resident had to be accommodated in the communal bathroom.

Boris Pasternak's own living arrangements were affected by these upheavals. In September 1917 he began sharing quarters at 12 Sivtsev Vrazhek, apartment 11. His companion there was Dmitrii Rozlovsky, a 'bearded newspaperman of extreme absent-mindedness and geniality', whom he had probably met through Evgenii Lundberg. Rozlovsky led a slovenly bachelor-style life, although he had a family somewhere in Orenburg Province.[4] During the next few years Pasternak also maintained other occasional residences, but it is difficult to reconstruct all his movements; his brother mentions lodgings in Granatny and Gagarinsky Lanes, but there is no record of dates. What is certain is that he moved back to his parents' in 1919 in order to help reinforce the family claim to living space in the Volkhonka apartment.[5] But he was not happy there. In 1920 he asked for Shura Shtikh's help in seeking a room,[6] and in the summer of 1921 he is known to have lodged with the advocate Semyon Nikolaevich Puritz and his violinist wife at the corner of Georgievsky Lane: he nevertheless retained an official *pied à terre* at 14 Volkhonka and moved in there permanently in the summer of 1921.

By 1918 both Pasternak daughters had left school. For a short time Josephine had a secretarial job in the offices of Glavkozh (Directorate of the Leather and Tanning Industry), while Lydia remained at home to help run the household. At the same time they began attending university courses in natural sciences. Lydia was also showing literary talent and writing her own verse. More restrained than Boris' early virtuosic style, some of her polished lyrics containing impressions of these years were eventually published in Western Europe.[7] Eventually in the 1930s, Josephine too was to emerge as an accomplished publishing poet.

Josephine developed a closer intellectual and spiritual affinity with Boris, Lydia meanwhile shared his robust physical energy and together with him often performed such tasks as collecting wood, humping sacks of potatoes, and so on. When Josephine was drafted along with other students into public service and set to clear snow, it was Lydia, in fact, who took her place. Her memory of accompanying Boris and a team of hungry and weary intellectuals conscripted to clear snowbound rail-tracks in the early hours she eventually found reflected in chapter 7 of her brother's novel.[8]

Like most of the population, the Pasternaks suffered poor health during the years of privation after 1917. A whole section in Pasternak's verse collection *Themes and Variations* is entitled 'Sickness' ('Bolezn''). Written in 1918 and 1919, these poems were a record of some of the sufferings of those years. Rozaliya's heart condition continued to cause worry. Aleksandr spent a spell in hospital in 1918. Boris succumbed to the flu epidemic of 1918 and spent several days in a semi-delirious state; later, in 1920, he suffered from furunculosis, a common deficiency disease at that time. A sketch by his father dated 18 December 1918 shows Boris lying in his sick-bed; and of the poems in his 'Sickness' cycle one imaginatively reconstructs the sensations of 'The Patient's Jersey' ('Fufaika bol'nogo'), in which 'the house is inflamed' and 'chandeliers have pleurisy', while in another poem the ailing patient watches while out of doors for six days on end 'frenzied blizzards rave relentlessly' (I, 70, 73–4; *SP*, 167, 170). However, the worst sights in Moscow, apart from the starvation, were the columns of sleighs delivering those sick with typhus to the hospitals. It was this disease which in the early 1920s carried off Boris' university friend Dmitrii Samarin. Even by late 1918 the outbreak had reached epidemic proportions and a public campaign was launched to control it. Lydia Pasternak caused the family much anxiety when she suddenly resolved to emulate Uncle Osip Kofman by studying medicine and volunteering to assist in the campaign. It was only the family's horror lest the contagion be spread to all of them which finally persuaded her to abandon the idea and continue her science studies.[9]

The seven poems in the 'Sickness' cycle of 1918–19 allude also to another malady – of the heart. Pasternak's inconclusive involvement with Elena Vinograd dragged on into 1918. She herself avoided any commitments despite the competition for her affections. Shura Shtikh was not indifferent to his cousin, and Pasternak and he briefly fell out because of her in December 1917. 'You evidently love Elena,' Pasternak wrote him on 21 December. 'And the very fact of your having been warned not to talk to me about her is ambiguous enough for us to give up meeting for a good long time. It is unpleasant and awkward, but there is nothing for it.'

Pasternak's chances of a romantic conquest were extremely slim. After trying and failing in 1912 to negotiate an emotional barrier, he probably never attempted it with Elena, despite his inner torments. This and the fact that their relations trailed on inconclusively maybe explains why in early 1918 she came to visit him in his Sivtsev Vrazhek lodgings to announce that she had resolved to marry. It was apparently a decision of the head rather than the heart. Her family, in her words, were 'outwardly intelligentsia, but inwardly bourgeois'. Her mother had always been against Boris, and Elena now acceded to her wishes to marry her off to some man of wealth. Elena's intended was Aleksandr Nikolaevich Dorodnov, who was heir to an estate and textile mills at Yakovlevskoye near Kostroma, a few hundred kilometres north-east of Moscow. The marriage took place in spring of 1918. Although at the time materially secure, the couple found within three months that their wealth had disappeared. Dorodnov was kept on for a time as overseer, but he no longer owned the mills and all his property and investments were confiscated by the new régime. He was later to perish in the labour camps in 1942.

The agony that Elena's seemingly arbitrary decision caused Pasternak was registered in several lyrics of 1917–18. One of the poems in *My Sister Life*, for instance, observed how 'weddings are being celebrated all around' (Ida Vysotskaya had also married in late 1917), and it went on to imply that society had avenged itself on the poet for 'lifting your sister from the earth like a Bacchante from an amphora and using her'. The poem also jibed against the bourgeois mores and 'smirking comfort' that had conspired to frustrate the poet's amour (I, 48; *SP*, 149). Several other poems of late 1917 and 1918 expressed a bitter nostalgia out of keeping with the predominant rapture of *My Sister Life*, and they eventually found their way into *Themes and Variations* instead. 'Spass-koye', for instance, contained a hallucinatory view of the estate where Pasternak had first met Elena in 1909. 'You're still to me a schoolgirl in the twilight...' ('Mne v sumerki ty vse pansionerkoyu...') recalled incidents in their past friendship from the poet's present wintry sleep-lessness:

> How to replace you? Aliphatics? Bromine?
> Sweating, asquint like a horse's eye, I breathe
> From the pillows, fearful of sleepless immensity.

> (I, 76–7; *SP*, 172–3)

Just as the passion of summer 1917 had never properly been articulated or requited, so the cooling-off process was protracted through Pasternak's failure to act and precipitate a final break. Elena seems to have been happy to string the anguished poet along even after her betrothal. Between visits to Kostroma she stayed in Moscow and met him, and some of his agonies on seeing her off to the train may have been reflected in *Letters from Tula* written in April 1918.[10]

Pasternak's mental suffering was poured out in a group of frenzied lyrics which formed one of the central cycles of *Themes and Variations* and were first entitled 'A Fit' ('Pristup', i.e. a fit of anguish).[11] Later they were entitled 'The Break' ('Razryv'). Following immediately on the 'Sickness' sequence, the poems were a compelling and breathless act of poetic indictment, differing in style from almost all Pasternak's earlier work. Here, for extended periods, the language of metaphoric imagery faltered and was replaced by plainer rhetoric:

> O lying angel, immediately I could, I would,
> I'd poison you with purest sadness!
> I dare not, though, like that – not tooth for tooth!
> O sorrow, lie-infected at the outset,
> O grief, o grief beset by mischief! (I, 78; *SP*, 173)

The emotional impetus in these verses played havoc with their structure and metrical scheme. It was particularly this cycle which led Aseyev in 1923 to describe Pasternak's poetic 'Organisation of Speech' as based not on melody but on 'intonation', that is, on the inflections of speech in intense rhetorical or conversational mode.[12] In this cycle the poet gave vent to the entire cacophony of his feelings: 'shame that is a burden', an 'access of sorrow that fulminates today like mercury in Toricelli's vacuum', a hatred that 'has no use for suicide' (a 'tortoise-like step'!). The seventh poem contains a half-mocking address to himself: 'My friend, it will heal before the wedding. Be calm don't weep.' And the final lyric in the sequence releases the beloved:

> I won't detain you. Go, perform good works.
> Get you to others. 'Werther' has been penned.
> And nowadays the very air breathes death:
> Why, opening windows is like slitting veins. (I, 82; *SP*, 177)

Many such bitter reflections eventually found their way into the poems of Pasternak's fourth collection. But while Elena continued as occasional addressee and dedicatee of verses (e.g., 'Two Letters' ['Dva pis'ma'] of 1921 included in *Themes and Variations*), textual evidence suggests that Pasternak was recovering from the affair by the end of 1918. The poem 'January 1919' ('Yanvar' 1919 goda') opens:

That year! How often at the window
'Throw yourself out' that year would say.
But this one, with its 'Christmas Carol'
Has driven all such thoughts away.

It whispers 'Forget it! Shake yourself!'
Its quicksilver stretches at the sunlight smile,
Where last year poured a dose of strychnine
Subsiding in the cyanide phial.

And the poem concludes:

There's not a sorrow in this world
That isn't cured and healed by snow.   (I, 75–6; *SP*, 171–2)

By the time that 'The Break' and other poems revealing the traumas of
Pasternak's love for Elena were published after the Civil War, the whole
experience was history, and Pasternak himself had married in early 1922.

The motifs of death and suicide in Pasternak's evocation of frustrated
love were a partly objective reflection of current realities. These included
not just the afflictions of cold, hunger and disease, but also those of
political terror and coercion. The dramatic 'Dialogue' and other drama
fragments gave a deceptive picture of Pasternak's mood by the time they
were published in the early summer of 1918. By then the memories of an
earlier revolutionary euphoria and of the alleged ideals of the October
revolution were difficult to square with the new regime's programme of
suppression. Yurii Zhivago discerns two circles of thought that contrast
the 'familiar and dear' aspects of a revolution with the 'bloody and
ruthless soldiers' one', and a few informal poems that Pasternak apparently wrote in winter 1917–18 emphasised a similar contrast. In one of
them, the violence of the October aftermath was compared with the
February revolution in which 'Christ's socialism' triumphed without
spilling blood and worked in harmony with the natural order. Another
poem was in horrified response to the events of the night of 7 January
1918 when two former Kadet ministers, Kokoshkin and Shingaryov,
were murdered by Bolshevik sailors and soldiers as they lay in Petrograd's Mariinskaya Hospital.

During the winter of 1917–18 random pot-shotting by Bolshevik
sentries was a regular accompaniment to life in Pasternak's Sivtsev
Vrazhek lodgings.[13] In December 1917 the new régime's political
police, or Cheka, was set up, and the ensuing arrests and executions left a
permanent trace on the Soviet system, introducing terror as a routine

administrative technique for preserving order. The Cheka's main targets were elements of the former bourgeoisie and social élite, liberal and right-wing politicians, and anyone deemed capable of counter-revolutionary 'insurgency'. In July of 1918 Cheka activities were stepped up after the left-wing of the Socialist Revolutionary Party staged an abortive rebellion. The Imperial family were executed, and the Civil War increased in fury.

None of Pasternak's immediate friends or relations was arrested or executed, but reports of continuing oppressions reinforced a general mood of inert embitterment. His father's friend, the former Vekhi contributor Mikhail Gershenzon, merely grumbled; the philosopher Lev Shestov was outraged at the regime's violent methods; and by June 1918 Evgenii Lundberg was convinced of the intelligentsia's doomed 'right to impotence'. 'There is less and less revolutionary intoxication,' he observed, 'but so much severity that people seem to age from week to week'.[14]

The spirit of their remarks was overlaid with a fatalistic irony at the intelligentsia's expense in Pasternak's poem *Malady Sublime* (*Vysokaya bolezn'*). Though written in 1923–4, the work centred on the experiences and moods of the Civil War period, describing *inter alia* how

> Back there amid the glow of legend,
> Hero, idiot, *intelligent**
> 'Mid blazing adverts and decrees
> Burned up to glorify dark force ...
> [...]
> We were the music in the ice.
> I speak about the whole milieu
> With which I had in mind to exit
> From the stage, and so I will.
>
> Here there is no place for shame.   (I, 393–5; *SP*, 239–40)

Pasternak's mood of despair was echoed in several other writings, including a poem evoking 'The Kremlin in a Blizzard at the End of 1918' ('Kreml' v buran kontsa 1918 goda'). In it, the Kremlin, a recognisable metonymy for the Bolshevik state, was depicted as a ship torn from its anchor and driven onward into the new year of 1919. And as the Kremlin dinned at the window with the brass of its belfries, the poet concluded:

* pronounced with a hard *g*, the Russian word denotes a member of the intelligentsia. There is a distant sub-textual echo here of the nineteenth-century poet Nekrasov's lines on the 'Liberal Idealist' in *The Bear Hunt* (*Medvezh'ya okhota*) (1867).[15]

Beyond the sea of this ill-weather
I foresee how, shattered as I am,
This not yet started year will take me
And re-educate me once again.   (I, 75; *SP*, 171)

The poet's seeming openness to re-education might appear at first as mere naïve acceptance; but the poem's whole atmosphere is storm-swept and joyless. On the barometer of poetic attitudes to Bolshevism, it probably stands somewhere midway between Mandelstam's vituperative appraisal of the new regime in November of 1917 and his later, more equivocal works such as his 'Freedom's Twilight' ('Sumerki svobody'), or Blok's *The Twelve*.

If the events of 1918 attracted bitter private analysis, not every aspect of life under the new order was fraught with misery. Pasternak's dealings with Lunacharsky in charge of the new Commissariat of Education (acronymously known as 'Narkompros') and with several of the latter's colleagues were cordial. For instance, he later recalled visiting a revolutionary naval barracks in Moscow where he had an enjoyable meeting with the Bolshevik female activist Larisa Reisner, whose article on Rilke he had read in 1917. As sailors came and went 'the din of the Revolution penetrated from the streets to the room where we were sitting, but we sat there and recited Rilke's verses by heart to one another. It was a special moment, an unforgettable moment.'[16]

Despite occasional moments of communion with the country's rulers, Pasternak later took a jaundiced view of the Civil War régime, its propaganda, falsehood and suppression of liberty:

Space, once the homeland of material, had grown sick with the gangrene of rearguard fiction and was consumed by the fading scraps of abstract non-existence [...] we were melted in a liquid tundra and our souls were beset by a lingering, tinkling state-owned drizzle [...] having tasted independence, we were forced to part with it and relapse long before old age into a new infancy at the imperious prompting of things.   (*VP*, 238–9)

Active collaboration with the new administration for Pasternak involved an ill-defined but tainting moral compromise, a 'dampening' of conscience. His Marburg university friend Gorbunkov turned up as a near neighbour in the winter of 1918–19. Narkompros, for which he was working, had been transferred to Moscow, and the Gorbunkovs were accommodated across the yard in the former Hotel Knyazhii Dvor, now converted as a commissariat staff hostel. Pasternak 'ran to see him [...] in order to glimpse the colour of my inescapable plight [...] to look at just that living absence of escape an awareness of which would have amounted to escape. But there was nothing to look at. This man could not help me. He was harmed by the rising damp even more than myself' (*VP*, 238–9). A similar image of dampened national conscience, affecting even artistic integrity, was developed in the story *Letters from Tula* (1918).

Quite apart from its oppressiveness, the new régime's paralytic dogmatism contrasted ironically with the spontaneous vitality which initially brought it to power. Pasternak's changing view of it was probably accurately reflected in his novel by Aleksandr Gromeko:

Do you remember [...] the first government decrees? Do you remember how utterly unconditional and absolute they were? It was that single-mindedness that won us over. But such things retain their original purity only in the minds of those who conceived them, and then then only on the day of their first proclamation. But on the next day they are turned inside out by political casuistry. (*DZh*, 246–7)

Pasternak was several times to point out this contradiction between doctrinaire 'revolutionary conservatism' and the 'spirit of revolution' to which nominal lip-service was still paid. All too obvious was the rift between Bolshevik romantic ritual language and the dispiriting dogma and grim realities of everyday life. Pasternak's dejection at this was apparent in a letter sent on 6 April 1920 to Dmitrii Petrovsky in Chernigov Province:

Here Soviet rule has gradually degenerated into a sort of philistine, atheistic almshouse with pensions, rations and subsidies. All that is missing is for the intelligentsia to wear cloaks and get taken out for air in pairs. Otherwise, though, it is a perfect asylum for orphans. They keep people starving and make them profess their lack of faith as they prey for salvation from lice. They make them remove their hats when the Internationale is played and so forth. Portraits of the All-Russian Central Executive Committee, couriers, office working days and non-working days. There it is. Was this worth all the fuss and bother?[17]

Despite all the privations and insecurity of the first years of Bolshevik rule, cultural life still continued. Pasternak attended meetings of the Moscow Linguistic Circle, whose membership overlapped partly with the ranks of Futurism. In 1918–19 the speakers included Osip Brik, Roman Jakobson and Sergei Bobrov, and other occasional Centrifugist visitors were Aseyev, Kushner and Shilling. The foundations of Formalist literary analysis that were laid in these meetings had little interest for

Pasternak, just as he had earlier boycotted Bely's Musaget 'rhythmic circle'. However, during the Civil War the same group of people often met for more creative or light-hearted activities at Mayakovsky's and the Briks' lodgings in Poluektov (now Sechenovsky) Lane where they had moved from Petrograd in March 1919. Some fruits of an evening's poetic improvisations on a set of given rhyme endings by Jakobson, Khlebnikov, Mayakovsky and Pasternak were recently published by Vasilii Katanyan.[18]

In some respects material hardships lent an added intensity and significance to artistic life and achievements. 'How many splendid poems were written in the years of war communism,' Ilya Ehrenburg commented. 'People had never lived so badly, and never had such creative fires blazed within them.'[19] Pasternak witnessed one event where these fires burned with particular brilliance. Since the early 1910s he had been acquainted with Mikhail Osipovich Tsetlin who held shares in Vysotsky's tea-importing concern and was a first cousin of Ida Vysotskaya; he was immensely wealthy and according to Ehrenburg, 'a frail cripple, exhausted by constant requests for money'.[20] Like others in his family, Tsetlin had Socialist Revolutionary sympathies, which he vented partly in amateurish revolutionary verse circulated under his pen-name of 'Amari'. The Tsetlins eventually lost their house in Trubnikovsky Lane when it was seized by anarchist squatters in March 1918, and in the summer after confiscation of most of their investments they emigrated to Paris. But the previous winter, while their wealth was still intact, they played munificent hosts, offering veal, ham, fish in glittering aspic and other delights to an otherwise malnourished set of littérateurs. Their most famous soirée was a poetic 'meeting of two generations' in late January 1918, which brought together Symbolist elders and Futurist 'youth' including Balmont, Bely, Vyacheslav Ivanov, Baltrušaitis, Khodasevich, Ehrenburg, Antokolsky, Tsvetaeva, Vera Inber, David Burlyuk, Kamensky, Mayakovsky and Pasternak. After various speeches celebrating this historic encounter of once antagonistic forces, there were poetic recitations by the guests, the most impressive performance being given by Mayakovsky, who declaimed his newly complete 'Man' ('Chelovek').[21]

Pasternak had special reason to remember that recitation. Mayakovsky still retained the power to spellbind him, but that evening he exercised it for the last time before its forfeiture and the commitment of his art to political ideology. At the Tsetlins' soirée Mayakovsky stood 'like a bas-relief against the background of his age' and recited 'a piece of extraordinary depth and elevated inspiration'. Hardly had he finished when Andrei Bely sprang up and greeted the work as an unparalleled masterpiece. In Pasternak's presence it was an encounter of 'two geniuses who justified two literary movements that had successively exhausted themselves' (II, 284–5; *VP*, 275–6).

Another of the Tsetlins' guests was to be closely involved with Pasternak in the years to come. The poetess Marina Tsvetaeva was still almost unknown to him and on that evening they met and did little more than exchange polite remarks. Their kinship was detectable by Pasternak only in her 'readiness to part at any moment with all convention and privilege if something lofty inflamed her and excited her rapture' (II, 284; *VP*, 275).

Poetic gatherings and readings, private and public, became increasingly important in the first years after the Revolution. This was due partly to an acute shortage of paper, printing facilities and finance. But the drama of the revolutionary moment was also ideally captured in the poet-orator's dramatic confrontation with his audience. Poetry as a form of public 'happening' was already an established Cubo-Futurist ritual, and the early days of Bolshevism, in fact, marked the heyday of this movement. On 1 May 1918, central Moscow was decked out with Futurist decorations, and thanks especially to Mayakovsky's good socialist standing and collaboration with the new order (after initial doubts), Futurist art and literature enjoyed a lease of life that lasted into the late 1920s.

Thus began the so-called 'café period' of Soviet literature. The lean years saw the mushrooming of many ephemeral and often bohemian artistic cafés. One of the earliest and most spectacular was Mayakovsky's 'Poets' Café' on the corner of Tverskaya Street and Nastasinsky Lane. Set in a former laundry, with sawdust on the floor, infantilist murals by David Burlyuk and Kamensky's dusty black trousers exhibited in one corner, it offered programmes that had more in common with the circus than a literary gathering. One of the star turns was Vladimir Goltsshmidt who was part-owner and official 'bouncer'. Performing as the 'Futurist of Life' and wearing a red silk tunic and gold head-band, his speciality was breaking wooden planks across his forehead. Futurist poets Mayakovsky, Kamensky, Burlyuk and Khlebnikov regularly recited at the Café, and other entertainment was provided by actors, singers and musicians. The clientele was a mixed company of sailors, soldiers, anarchists, profiteers, and inquisitive middle-class folk who were not put off by Mayakovsky's much-touted doggerel about the imminent doom of the pineapple- and grouse-gobbling bourgeoisie.

Apart from the Poets' Café, which lasted from autumn 1917 to mid-April 1918, the other best-known cafés were the 'Red Cockerel' (previously named the 'Pittoresque') on Kuznetsky Most, and the 'Bim-Bom' (later known as 'Pegasus' Stall') and the 'Domino', both on Tverskaya. The poets and other entertainers usually received a free meal and sometimes a fee of up to fifty roubles in return for their services. If audiences were untutored and inattentive, poets were at least able to reach a certain public and to hear colleagues' reactions to their work. Indeed, apart from providing a 'floor show', the cafés became centres of literary social life, partly replacing earlier salons and societies. The Café Domino actually enjoyed official status since it was adopted as an official venue for the Union of Poets (Soyuz poetov, or SOPO) under the auspices of the All-Russian Union of Poets set up in November 1918. It served as a presidium meeting room and auditorium along with the larger Polytechnical Museum, Narkompros headquarters in Ostozhenka, and later the Narkompros Literary Section on Nikitskaya Street.[22]

It is not hard to appreciate Pasternak's minimal contribution to the literary menu of these cafés. His passive lyrical persona in *My Sister Life* reflected a general desire to avoid posturing or making a spectacle of his poetic personality. If this was misunderstood (as it had been by Mayakovsky in 1917) it was mainly because Pasternak kept most of these verses concealed until 1919 (*My Sister Life* was only printed complete in 1922). Apart from the occasional publication of individual items, his reputation increased among Moscow cognoscenti mainly thanks to handwritten manuscript and oral transmission. But while poets everywhere, as Nadezhda Mandelstam recalled, were 'mastering their new profession of stage performers',[23] Pasternak in December 1918 drafted a set of 'propositions' (part of *Quinta Essentia*, his projected book of articles on man) in which he spelt out his opposition to this trend:

Some modern movements have imagined that art is like a fountain whereas in fact it is a sponge. They have decided that art ought to spout and gush, whereas it should absorb and saturate itself. They consider it can be resolved into means of representation, whereas it is composed of organs of perception. It should always be one of the audience and have the clearest, most perceptive view of all. But in our day it has seen make-up powder and the dressing-room, and it is exhibited on stage [...] It is put on show, whereas it should be hiding up in the gallery, unrecognised, hardly aware that it cannot fail to give itself away, and that when it hides in a corner it is stricken with translucency and phosphorescence as though with some disease.[24]   (III, 152; *VP*, 110)

In his reply to a questionnaire from the Poets' Section of the Moscow Professional Union of Writers in March 1919, Pasternak stated his unwillingness to recite publicly in Moscow or the provinces because of 'the ugliness of the conditions in which recitals take place at present'. He did, however, agree to give readings 'gladly in the society of writers and poets enjoying my respect'.[25] The following year, in fact, he made a major official appearance along with other poets at the Polytechnical Museum. Tsvetaeva heard him there and was unimpressed by his dull reading voice, poor memory, 'estranged manner' reminiscent of Blok, and by his impression of 'tormented concentration'. She was evidently not alone in her reaction.[26]

Nikolai Vilyam (or Vilmont), the literary scholar whose sister Irina later married Aleksandr Pasternak,* recalled another occasion in spring of 1920 when Pasternak gave a reading at a literary café. The event was typical of the period. The master of ceremonies was the poet Sergei Budantsev, and an incongruous overture was provided by altercations between a peasant and the former wealthy merchant Ivan Rukavishnikov. Pasternak's contribution was not poetry, but a discourse on the subject, evidently based on his 'propositions' mentioned above. Probably few of the audience appreciated the irony of this dismissal of precisely the type of performance they were witnessing. Public reaction to Pasternak's speech was evidently limited to some half-baked inanities from an ambulance-train guard who was enjoying a night on the town.[27]

Although Pasternak shunned the stage, Tsvetaeva's report of his performance conflicts with other accounts of his recitations in more congenial surroundings. His talent cannot be assessed from the dreamily sing-song recordings of his latter years,[28] and had he really been a poor performer it seems unlikely that Mayakovsky would have wanted him in his programmes in 1917. Rita Rait-Kovalyova recalled one occasion in the Café Domino when Pasternak appeared before a small audience that included Mayakovsky and recited 'as never before'.[29] Nikolai Vilmont also remembered his vivid rendering of poems from *Themes and Variations* in the early 1920s. The 'Sickness' cycle he delivered 'with impetuous passion, striking the ear with a furiously roaring stream of language'; 'The Break' in his rendering sounded like 'the menacing roar of a waterfall'; and 'Kremlin in a Blizzard' he always read 'with special élan'.[30] It seems likely, therefore, that in many public performances

* Vilyam-Vilmont was used by Nikolai Vilyam as his pen-name; the second element in this surname was evidently adopted from the family's Anglo-Scottish forebears named Wilmont.

Pasternak consciously 'under-performed' as a gesture of dissent with modern 'theatrical poetics'. (Moreover, by no means all Pasternak's earlier verses could be properly apprehended from their first aural impact; Aseyev rightly described his work as 'literature for study' rather than for reading.)[31]

All this notwithstanding, Pasternak still admired the theatrical manner as embodied by Mayakovsky or Bolshakov, and rejected it as unnatural only to *himself*. Hence his desire to rescue Mayakovsky from the embarrassment of second-rate imitation. There was no shortage of the latter – it had begun with Shershenevich in 1914, and Pasternak found the vaunting of such mediocrity repugnant. His story of April 1918, *Letters from Tula* included description of actors in a restaurant, 'the worst form of bohemia', who were seen 'playing the genius, holding forth, hurling phrases at one another, and theatrically flinging their serviettes on the table' (II, 77; *VP*, 42). All this was drawn from observations of contemporary café culture.

Despite its serious literary standing, the Café Domino was also capable of providing 'ugly conditions' of the type Pasternak objected to. At one point during the Civil War, Ryurik Ivnev observed the rowdy inebriated Esenin dismiss Pasternak as 'tongue-tied' and incomprehensible. Pasternak on that occasion replied with venomous courtesy,[32] but there were other times recalled in his memoirs when Esenin and he 'either swore devotion amid floods of tears or else fought and had to be dragged apart' (II, 43; *VP*, 457). Esenin's alcohol intake doubtless affected such issues, but the crux of their disagreements, described in the original manuscript of *Safe Conduct*, was the issue of the poet's relation to his public:

Of my contemporaries only Mayakovsky knew that I was not inventing when I said I was totally uninterested in rapid recognition. It was precisely on this point that Esenin would not believe me. He rejected me altogether and there were several inborn reasons for his antipathy. I always recognised and even respected their natural force [...] but I am talking about the fact that when in conversation I said what I thought, Esenin believed this was coquettishness on my part. And I was incensed only by the aplomb and total assurance with which he reasoned at times when he gave me clearest proof of his ignorance.[33]

Their opposing temperaments fuelled an on-going feud between Pasternak and Esenin which was only brought to an end by the latter's suicide in 1925.

If Pasternak's lyric persona was retiring, and if he himself was averse to theatricals and was sometimes 'other-wordly', he was far from being a hermit. Ehrenburg described him at that time as 'a willing socialiser' who was happy in company.[34] During the high season of literary café life he and his circle of friends were often seen at the Domino and he owed his first serious renown to the colleagues who attended such establishments, even though no one yet knew of his two major poetic collections that were crystallising privately.

Although publishing as a whole declined, short-lived journals and almanacs continued appearing sporadically during the Civil War. Several such literary ventures had the nominal backing of political groups and parties, and Pasternak's own few appearances in these provided an interesting hint of his temperament without necessarily implying a political stance. Futurist platforms were obviously unacceptable to him, and his apparent apoliticism and stylistic complexity made him ill-suited to Bolshevik or 'proletarian' media. But the revolutionary élan evinced in some lyrics and in the dramatic 'Dialogue' suggested a view of revolution which enjoyed currency among the intelligentsia with Socialist Revolutionary sympathies. Largely owing to a traditional intellectual link with populism, the Socialist Revolutionaries (SRs) representing the peasantry in 1917–18 attracted a heterogeneous company of writers, poets and publicists towards publications enjoying their party sponsorship. Pasternak's one poetic publication in 1917 (apart from *Over the Barriers*) was the poem 'Spring Rain'. Its phrase 'Hurrah for Kerensky!' did not express authorial sentiment and was a montage quotation, yet it clearly facilitated the poem's appearance in an October issue of *Put' osvobozhdeniya* (Path of Liberation), a fortnightly journal issued by the Culture and Education Section of the Moscow Soviet of Soldiers' Deputies and marked by obvious Socialist Revolutionary sympathies.[35]

Pasternak's main channel into print during the early post-revolutionary period was via his old supporter Evgenii Lundberg. Lundberg was an important member of the so-called Scythian group of writers which was set up near St Petersburg (Petrograd) in 1916, and which in 1917 issued two miscellanies entitled *Skify*. The Scythians (who included Bely, Esenin, Klyuev, Remizov, Oreshin, Ganin, Erberg and Ivanov-Razumnik) used the idea of revolution in a loose sense, devoid of precise socio-historical meaning. They cultivated the idea of elemental, cosmic revolt against any manifestations of philistinism or moderation, and their nebulous pronouncements had a strongly Russian messianic colouration. Pasternak was not one of their number but in 1917 he was obviously in tune with the spirit of their ideas. There were Scythian intonations in the dramatic 'Dialogue' and also in Yurii Zhivago's first reaction to the October uprising. Although the Scythians emphasised their political independence and primary concern with aesthetic and moral questions, they began publishing in the Petrograd paper *Znamya truda* (Banner of Labour) which after November 1917 became the official organ of the left SRs. It was on its pages that Pasternak's *Dramatic Fragments* appeared in May and June of 1918, and other literary items published there that summer included Blok's *Scythians* and *The Twelve* and Bely's religioso-revolutionary paean, 'Christ is Risen'. Other contributions came from Pasternak's old associates Anisimov, Stanevich, Kushner and Lundberg, among items by regular group members and topical extracts from Herzen, Bakunin, Lavrov, Marx, Victor Hugo and Richard Wagner.[36]

Apart from inviting ex-Lirika and Tsentrifuga members into *Znamya truda*, Lundberg also arranged belated publication of Pasternak's story *The Apelles Mark* in the newspaper's supplement. Its appearance attracted no critical attention. In early July 1918 *Znamya truda* was closed down after the left SRs broke with the Soviet government over treatment of the peasantry and ratification of peace with Germany, and staged an abortive uprising in Moscow. Pasternak and other non-aligned writers continued to use page space in SR publications however. Such activity was not unusual or compromising at a time when the Bolsheviks still allowed some political pluralism and refrained from intervention in cultural affairs. November 1918 saw publication of Pasternak's *Lovelessness* in *Volya truda* (Liberty of Labour), an ephemeral paper put out by former SR Georgii Ustinov. In spring of 1919 he was invited to contribute to the literature section of the SR paper *Delo naroda* (People's Cause) although he seems not to have responded. The same year in Kharkov (a centre of Socialist Revolutionary and Menshevik opposition) a *New Art Miscellany* (*Sbornik novogo iskusstva*), which printed work by proletarian poets, Futurists and others, tried to make some editorial capital by pointing out that 'Pasternak, one of the most distinguished representatives of the extreme left tendency in art, is publishing his works with the left Socialist Revolutionaries'. He was also identified among artists who had 'linked their creativity with that of the proletariat as a special form of weapon in the struggle for mankind's liberation'.[37] The jargon, however, was not Pasternak's; it betrayed little understanding of his art and mistook temperament for political assent.

Publications with a political hue were thus a *pis-aller* outlet for Pasternak's verse and prose in the first couple of years of war communism. But with most presses at a standstill and paper in short supply, priority was given increasingly to Bolshevik-sponsored publications. State monopolies and black market conditions forced private presses and publishers to charge ever higher prices, and the usual outcome was their collapse and bankruptcy. The number of Pasternak's publications fell off sharply during the Civil War, and the nadir was reached in 1920. His creativity also dwindled. Although not directly dependent upon printed page space, it required both time and opportunity to write. In the struggle to keep body and soul together, such opportunities almost disappeared and actual creativity became an indirect victim of economic collapse.

Nominally Pasternak remained a member of Tsentrifuga which at first had hopes of renewing activity in 1918. The poet Ryurik Ivnev was secretary to Lunacharsky, and there was verbal encouragement for a collective application for aid by Bobrov, Bolshakov, Aksyonov and Pasternak (the latter's 'Propositions' were originally dedicated to Ivnev). Some money did appear eventually but not enough to finance publication. 'We have been given money for Tsentrifuga,' Bobrov told Boris Sadovskoi in February 1920. 'We shall be publishing, but things are going badly at the moment since all Moscow presses are at a standstill.' A further announcement of Tsentrifuga's revival in 1921 was similarly unfruitful. In theory the group continued to exist until 1922, when Bobrov brought out his own novel *Revolt of the Misanthropes* (*Vosstanie misantropov*) under a Tsentrifuga imprint.[38] By that time, however, Pasternak was pursuing other more promising opportunities to publish: *Poets' Spring Salon* (*Vesennii salon poetov*) (1918) was the printed outcome of Tsetlin's gathering and partly financed by him; it carried two reprints from *Over the Barriers* and a couple of lyrics from *My Sister Life*. 1919 saw further 'Sister' poems printed in the Kharkov journal *Puti tvorchestva* (Paths of Creativity) and the *New Art Miscellany*, while *Reality* (*Yav'*), a Moscow miscellany, included 'Street Scene' (Ulichnaya) with its impressions of a 1917 strike and demonstration. Another poem from *My Sister Life* plus an impressionistic fragment of 1916 appeared in the *Liren'* collection in Moscow in 1920. Two Faustian poems appeared in *Bulan'* (Moscow, 1920), and two more 'Sister' lyrics in *We* (*My*) (Moscow, 1920), promoted by the All-Russian Union of Poets.[39] Material from *My Sister Life* also came out in the 1920 and 1921 issues of *Khudozhestvennoe slovo* (Artistic Word), an ambitious but short-lived journal edited by Bryusov and published by Lito. The first of these issues (October, 1920) also announced the first volume of a forthcoming edition of Pasternak's works, and that spring he had received a first instalment of 2,500 roubles. But like so many projects of that period, nothing came of it. Aksyonov had published a positive review of the manuscript in *Khudozhestvennoe slovo*, no. 1, 1920, but Bryusov's carping reader's report of 8 June disputed Pasternak's mastery of metre and orchestration and recommended a radical reduction of the text, thereby probably promoting cancellation of the edition.[40] Fortunately, the year 1921 saw the end of the Civil War and a revival of literary life and publishing. It was then that Pasternak made a significant debut in Voronsky's newly founded 'thick journal', *Krasnaya nov'* (Red Virgin Soil), a publication launched with Lenin and Gorky's personal backing and to which during the next ten years he was to make important contributions.

The trickle of publications during the Civil War years was no proper indication of Pasternak's actual creativity, however. Despite the hold-up of printing, his rush of inspiration continued uninterrupted from the summer of 1917 till the middle of 1918. By the winter of 1917–18, *My Sister Life* was taking shape as a complete cycle. Pasternak was keen to preserve its structure intact. 'On account of the book's character I can separate the poems out only if I have to. I would prefer to publish books of verse in separate form,' he told the Moscow Poets' Section in mid-March of 1919.[41] The scattered appearance of individual items between 1917 and 1922, in fact, revealed very little of the core and total impact of the book, whose existence remained for a long time concealed. It was probably only in early March of 1919, after arriving from Petrograd, that Mayakovsky had the privilege of a first insight into the book's wonders, and Pasternak heard in response to it 'ten times more than I ever expected to hear from anyone' (II, 285; *VP*, 276). He handed the manuscript of the book to Mayakovsky and Brik and it was announced in May 1919 in the publication programme for a new officially sanctioned venture called 'Art of the Young' (Iskusstvo molodykh – IMO). In this version the work acquired a cluster of epigraphs – from Edgar Allen Poe, Aseyev, and Mayakovsky's own lines:

> How can one slip a quiet word
> Into their bloated ears?[42]

Pasternak also received a royalty for the work, but unfortunately this was only by way of settling accounts when IMO was wound up in July after losing Lunacharsky's sponsorship and fusing with Gosizdat (State

Publishers). Nothing came of the planned edition, and in the autumn of 1919 Pasternak presented the manuscript to Lili Brik.

The following year Ehrenburg was also privileged with a preview of the book. Pasternak turned up to see him on 28 December 1920 wrapped in a thick scarf, and Ehrenburg was 'struck by his shy and challenging manner, by the touchiness of his outward pride, and by the infinite bashfulness of all his inner gestures. After long and painful introductions he began to recite a poem about the scorched wings of the Demon...'[43] Shortly before this, on 14 October 1920, Pasternak had signed a contract for publication of *My Sister Life* with 'Giz' (State Publishers). But nothing came of this initiative either. The manuscript (which since 1919 had acquired another six poems) was eventually retained by the Marxist critic and literary scholar Pyotr Kogan and it was 1922 before the work appeared with Grzhebin's press in Moscow.

Although attempts at publication were frustrated by administrative and economic problems, Pasternak's initial diffidence about publicly revealing *My Sister Life* stemmed partly from the personalities and the nature of the relationship it celebrated. (Five years had elapsed before the poem 'Marburg' revealed details of the misadventure with Vysotskaya in 1912, and Vysotskaya, who had left Russia in 1918, was the only one of Pasternak's early loves who received any coverage in his autobiographies; those who stayed were left unmentioned.) In the period before *My Sister Life* appeared, the book underwent several alterations, partly for artistic reasons but also because of still sensitive feelings and painful memories. In his reply to the Moscow Poets' Section questionnaire of March 1919 Pasternak referred to his third book of verse as 'Neskuchny Garden' and talked of it as a work of a hundred or more pages. The title, *My Sister Life*, was settled on only in mid-1919 for the projected IMO edition which was planned to contain only forty-three poems. Seven items, all concerned with the bitter cooling of relations with Elena were omitted from that manuscript; two poems headed 'Neskuchny Garden', and another five making up a section called 'Autumn', eventually found their way into another book, *Themes and Variations*. In these poems the enamoured poet likens himself to the 'shade of a guitar' from whom the strings have been ripped for amusement, and he hears only her mocking reproaches: 'Leave off! You're worse than a little boy!' (I, 87–8; *SP*, 181). Similar embittered reflections filled the other transferred verses, and the poems 'Summer' ('Leto') and 'Afterword' ('Posleslov'e') first appeared only in the manuscript of 1922.

Thus during its evolution *My Sister Life* gradually shed its more anguished statements relating to the autumn of Pasternak's love for Elena Vinograd. The jaundiced passages that survived (e.g. a jibe at the life of comfort Elena opted for by marrying her opulent spouse) were few in number. By contrast, the book *Themes and Variations* served partly as a receptacle for materials excluded from *My Sister Life*. It was, as it were, the 'other side of the coin', and Pasternak at one time considered this phrase ('obratnaya storona medali') as its title.[44] Later on, the close link between *My Sister Life* and *Themes and Variations* led to their being published in 1929 and 1930 under the same cover and under the paradoxical heading *Two books* (*Dve knigi*). (An earlier title considered for this double collection had been 'Thirst into Fever' ['Zhazhda v zhar']).

Themes and Variations contained work written during the whole period 1916–22, but most of it overlapped in date of composition with *My Sister Life*. The book appeared only in January 1923 and even items published separately appeared no earlier than 1922, by which time bitter memories were effaced by Pasternak's own marriage that year. A couple of poems entitled 'Two Letters' ('Dva pis'ma'), addressed to Elena in 1921, suggest that by that time already Pasternak could write of the past with a certain equanimity.

Since it contained poems written over six years, the evolution of Pasternak's fourth book was a long one. Some items were inserted only at the last moment before publication in 1923, and the book lacked the unity and thematic impetus of its predecessor. But it is far from being a random assemblage of 'rejects', and some sections have a unique power and individuality. Aseyev and Tsvetaeva, two demanding readers, saw it as no less original than *My Sister Life*. Parts of it indeed, especially 'Sickness' and 'The Break', are emotionally more searing than the earlier work. In *Themes and Variations*, sixty-two poems are divided into six chapters or sections. The second of these is itself a 'Theme with Variations'; the last and longest chapter, 'Neskuchny Garden', contains twenty-nine poems subdivided into twelve sections, four of which are miniature 'seasonal' cycles of five poems each. As migrants from *My Sister Life*, many poems of the final chapter deal with related themes of nature and disappointed love, and have a similar texture and phraseology. Splendidly executed though they are, they are less striking than the new departures in *Themes and Variations*. The book's title suggests a preoccupation with matters of structure and technique; the theme of artistic creativity is indeed a central axis of the work, and several episodes display a virtuosity that was held in tighter check in *My Sister Life*.

Chapter 1, entitled 'Five Tales', opens with 'Inspiration' ('Vdokhnoven'e'), and there is a distantly romantic hint (picked up in other poems) of bitterness and of a penalty paid by the artist: the city is desolate at dawn because 'the least of mortals sits in his carriage beset by verse and watched by a sentry' (I, 57; *SP*, 156). In 'Meeting' ('Vstrecha'), a complex Cubist poem perceptively discussed in Henry Gifford's book, the author and the March night appear as fellow wayfarers.[45] In 'Shakespeare' ('Shekspir') the bard's sonnet has a life of its own, 'written at night, unsmudged, and with fire' (I, 61; *SP*, 160). Another two 'tales' are examples of several poems of 1919 written on a Faustian theme. The first of them, 'Margarita', contains a thrilling evocation of the nightingale's song, an exultant study in the manner of Gerard Manley Hopkins.

The second chapter is itself entitled 'Theme with Variations'. It is an ambitious composition, reminiscent of Pasternak's extended impressionist fantasies of 1916–17. The problem of thematic cohesion is here cleverly solved by the variation form. In the manuscript the sections are headed 'Original', 'Imitative', 'Sacrocosmic' (a misprint for 'Macrocosmic'), 'Dramatic', 'Pathetic' and 'Pastoral'.[46] Some of these titles characterise the flamboyant elemental imagery that frequently disrupts the normal quatrains or other stanzaic units. Where the quatrain does assert itself, it further concentrates metaphoric energy – as in the 'Macrocosmic' epigraph to the present chapter (p. 243): an evocation of the creative force that produced Pushkin's poem 'The Prophet'. Pushkin is in Russia the primordial archetype of the poet and his name is a byword for transparent clarity, simplicity and a 'childlike Russian quality' (*DZh*, 294). Even Pasternak's Pushkin of 1918 possesses this quality beneath his metaphoric exuberance:

> Hidden from all indiscreet
> Eyes – most strange and most mild,
> Childish laughter that since Psymmetichus
> Has played on the desert's cheeks . . . (I, 64; *SP*, 162)

In the opening 'theme', other images with Pushkinian associations appear in an apparently improvised deluge: his 'flat-lipped Hammite' grandparentage, cliffs and surf that hint at Aivazovsky's seascapes, Repin's picture of Pushkin, and at motifs from *The Bronze Horseman* and *The Gypsies*.[47] It is no coincidence that Yurii Zhivago's enthusiasm for

Pushkin was dated to this Civil War period, and Nikolai Vilmont has recalled Pasternak's pleasure in reciting Pushkin's *poemy* to his friends in the 1920s.[48] Clearly, the figure of Pushkin serves additionally as an emblem for Pasternak's own artistry. The 'Imitative' variation opens with a direct quotation from *The Bronze Horseman*. But it is not Peter the Great standing 'on the coast of the desolate billows. Filled with deep thought', but Pasternak-Pushkin who contemplates not the site of his capital but the still misty pages of his dream – a literary novel.[49]

The third and fourth chapters, entitled 'Sickness' and 'The Break', have been discussed already, as also have several poems in the final chapter relating to the affair with Elena Vinograd. Chapter 5, 'Could I Forget Them', introduces five lyrics with somewhat broader perspectives. In the first, childhood is apostrophised as a 'scoop of the soul's profundity', 'aboriginal of all forests', and as 'my inspirer and choirmaster' (I, 83; *SP*, 177). Another poem (above, p. 1) elaborates on the origins of a 'life by verses', and its 'quarrels with the sun' may allude to Mayakovsky's poetic 'Unusual Adventure' of 1920.[50] But it is an adult poet in a revolutionary age who addresses himself 'To Slanderers' ('Klevetnikam'), with an echo in its title of Mayakovsky's satirical wartime hymns (for example, 'To a Judge', 'To a Scholar', 'To a Critic'). Here, however, there is a note of self-sentence.

> O life, our name's degeneration,
> Counter to you and all good sense.   (I, 84; *SP*, 178)

Yet another item, written in 1921, begins:

> We are few. We are maybe but three,*
> Blazing and hellish from mines of Donetsk,
> Who live beneath grey, shifting crusts
> Of showers and clouds,
> And of military councils, poetics,
> Discussions of transport and art.
>
> Once people, now we are epochs...   (I, 86; *SP*, 179)

Pasternak did not name his two partners, but presumably the other members of the trio were Aseyev and Mayakovsky. Later on he used the second line of the poem as an epithet for Tsevetaeva, to whom he inscribed a copy of his *Themes and Variations*. (In 1961 Akhmatova wrote a poem titled 'Four of Us' ['Nas chetvero'] picking up Pasternak's

---

* 'Nas malo. Nas mozhet byt troe...' Cf. 'Nas malo izbrannykh...' in Pushkin's *Mozart and Salieri*.

lead and implying admission of herself and Mandelstam to the elect group. Three years later Andrei Voznesensky impudently travestied the line and included himself and poetess Bella Akhmadulina in the statement: 'We are many. We are perhaps four'.)[51]

In *My Sister Life's* 'Definition of Poetry', verse could be constructed of nothing but lush nature – crushed ice-floes, frozen leaves, nightingale's song, and so on. However, the final chapter of this new book provided definitions of verse suggesting a rawly prosaic encounter with real life, hinting at more hazardous aspects of the poet's calling. 'On the Creator's nib I hang / In a large drop of lilac lustre', is how one poem opens, but its central stanzas take us through a city-scape of gutters, stations breathing vodka, coke, serge cloth and sludge, with echoes of nail-factory gates. And instead of repeating the opening couplet, the poem ends in a lustreless de-romanticised variation:

> To the Creator's nib I cling,
> A bitter droplet of dense lead.   (I, 99–100; *SP*, 192)[52]

Another poem of the same year, entitled 'Poetry' ('Poeziya'), redefines the art:

> Poetry, I'll swear by you
> And end up growing hoarse:
> You've not the stance of some sweet bard,
> You are a summer, travelling third,
> You're a suburb, not a chorus.
>
> You're the stuffy Yamskaya in May,
> Shevardin's night redoubt...*   (I, 101; *SP*, 193)

Yet another poem points to a new and potentially tragic view of the age. Pasternak's poetry is not yet so bleak and death-infected as Mandelstam's, but some urban *realia* akin to those of 'We'll meet again in Petersburg [...] in the black velvet of a Soviet night' are registered with the same aura of menace.[53] One of Pasternak's images, for instance, is the noise of the revving motorcycle which was frequently used to mask the sound of Cheka execution squads at work:

> Age struck with madness, when can I bring reason
> To the fathomless past's darkened pace?
> Samsonov's slumbering bugler's boots
> Are still worn in depths of Mazurian lakes.†

---

* One of the features of the Borodino battlefield of 1812.
† An allusion to the rout of General Samsonov's divisions in August 1914.

Later, a Muscovite motorbike's rattling staccato
Stuttered loud to the stars – Second Coming!
It was the plague, a stayed execution
Of Last Judgements by courts yet unsummoned.

(I, 100; *SP*, 192–3)

One of the poems of *Themes and Variations* written in 1917 contained a
couplet which had both short- and long-term significance for Pasternak:

I shall say farewell to you verses, my mania.
I've appointed your meeting with me in a novel.

(I, 104; *SP*, 196)

During the Civil War, while two poetry books were still taking shape,
Pasternak's main activity was the writing of prose.[54] In April of 1918 he
completed a new short story called *Letters from Tula*. The work reflected
incidents both from Pasternak's involvement with Elena Vinograd and
his earlier affair and from travels with Nadezhda Sinyakova; it was also
linked with his artistic biography and attempt to rid himself of romantic
self-dramatisation. In part 1 of the story, a young poet wanders at night
around the rail station of Tula after saying farewell to his beloved, and as
he waits for the train back to Moscow he ruminates and writes impassioned letters to her. The letters are full of purple rhetoric and
hyperbole, abounding in such words as 'genius, poet, ennui, ungifted,
philistinism, tragedy'. But various circumstances bring the young hero
to earth. First is the depressing sight of amateurish attempts by a bunch
of film actors to re-enact the 'Time of Troubles'* and then pack up this
record of 'history' in their suitcases in order to flash it later on the screen
of the 'Magic' cinema house. Through all this one detects the author's
own contempt for the cinema, in marked contrast to his earlier view of
the possibility of this art form in 1913.[55] Probably this resulted from a
scornful recent observation of attempts at film production in Moscow's
'Neptune' cinema studios: in March 1918 Mayakovsky had produced
and acted in a film version of Jack London's *Martin Eden*, and two
similar productions followed in April and May.[56] In Pasternak's story
the poet-hero is also appalled at the behaviour of the film actors in a
restaurant and he sees himself involuntarily associated with their playing
the genius and their declamatory gestures and phraseology. All this
prompts the awakening of his own sense of integrity, and a further
realisation:

* i.e. the late sixteenth and early seventeenth centuries, when dynastic uncertainties in
Russia led to foreign intervention, the appearance of several false claimants to the throne
and a peasant uprising.

This night is a night in Tula. Night in a place bound up with the life of Tolstoy. Is it any wonder that compass needles start dancing here? Such events are in the very nature of this place. This is an occurrence on the *territory of conscience*, in its gravitational, ore-bearing sector. (II, 78; *VP*, 43–4)

Thus, the poet-narrator acquires a Tolstoyan awareness of art's moral and communicative function. To obey its command must automatically eliminate all posturing and superficiality.[57]

The second part of the story illustrates the same point. It introduces an old provincial actor who is described in terms reminiscent of the elderly Knauer in the later part of *Suboctave Story*. He too is depressed after watching the filming. Returning home to his quarters, he roots around in his memories, and as he begins playing through to himself one of his old roles, he is transformed. Even away from an audience, he discovers both the personality he impersonates and, in the process, his own self as he becomes a medium through whom something outside himself can speak. This is for Pasternak the realisation of art's aim, and here for the first time he links creativity with the Tolstoyan element in which his childhood was immersed.

Pasternak's main achievement in prose in 1918 was the draft of a novel estimated to fill some fifteen printer's signatures (240 pages). Its projected title, described to Sergei Bobrov and others, was 'Three Names' ('Tri imeni').[58] The first draft must have been completed rapidly, with the same impetus that produced the lyrics of 1917–18 and *Letters from Tula*.

In January 1918 at the Tsetlins' Pasternak had told Tsvetaeva of an ambition to write a novel 'with a love intrigue and a heroine in it – like Balzac', and by summer he was showing the first part of it to friends and colleagues.[59] Lundberg, who probably expected something in the style of *The Apelles Mark*, found the new work 'dreamy, boring, and tendentiously virtuous in its outward tone and aspect'. This was what Pasternak reported when he sent the manuscript to Bobrov on 16 July 1918. Bobrov was asked for a quick reading and an opinion. His reaction is not recorded, but in the conditions of the time he was in any case unable to assist with publication. Probably this persuaded Pasternak to abandon efforts to have the work printed, despite the fact that 'it set those who were unprepared for it all atremble'. With Bobrov the matter and the manuscript rested for nearly three years. In the spring of 1921 he brought the work back to Pasternak, who had meanwhile come to regard it as no more than a mere useful trial of the pen.[60] Once again, though, Pasternak passed the manuscript around and showed it to Boris Zaitsev, who until his emigration in 1922 was on the board of the All-Russian Union of Writers. Though a far cry from Zaitsev's prose aquarelle style, it greatly impressed him, and many decades later he recalled 'the impression of something fresh and authentic yet unaffected. If Chekhov's prose was fine-grained, this man's had a coarse grain'.[61] Possibly Pasternak also showed the work to Gorky during the latter's Moscow visit between 20 January and the end of February 1921. Whenever it was that he read Pasternak's story, Gorky was enthusiastic; later in the 1920s he tried to arrange an American translated edition for which he himself wrote an introduction.[62] In the summer of 1921 Pasternak made an overture with his manuscript to another authority, Vyacheslav Polonsky, chief editor of the journal *Pechat' i revolyutsiya* (The Press and Revolution). Polonsky had already written a strong, though unsuccessful recommendation for publication of *Themes and Variations* by Gosizdat and his opinion was a weighty one.[63] Perhaps his impressions were helpful in finally placing the work in the first issue of Veresayev and Voronsky's journal *Nashi dni* (Our Days). There it appeared under the title *Zhenya Luvers' Childhood* (*Detstvo Lyuvers*) in mid-May 1922. Unfortunately, the rest of the drafted novel was not polished up for publication, and although Pasternak's wife later recalled hearing him read out episodes in the early 1920s, in 1932 he destroyed the manuscript.[64]

To Polonsky Pasternak described his new prose fiction as part of a conscious attempt to escape the mannered 'neo-aesthetism' of his earlier work. Prior to 1917, he maintained, a widely shared

fatal originality had driven me into an impasse. And I became painfully aware earlier than the rest [...] of the dead end to which our age of *originality in inverted commas* was leading [...] I decided to make a sharp turn. I decided I would write as people write letters, and not in the current manner, revealing to the reader all that I think and intend to tell him, refraining from technical effects fabricated outside his field of vision and served up to him in ready form, hypnotically [...] I decided to dematerialise my prose, and in order to impose on myself the required conditions of objectivity, I began to write about a heroine, a woman, with her psychological genesis and a scrupulous account of her childhood.[65]

Although recognisably fragments of a larger whole, the two parts of *Zhenya Luvers' Childhood*, entitled 'Long Days' and 'The Stranger', stand together as an independent work, one of Pasternak's major achievements. There is here little of his earlier patterning and of the ornamentalism common in other contemporary Russian prose. The 'dematerialised' style was still often brilliantly metaphoric, but totally adapted to reflect and express the psyche of a growing child. This was no routine fictional biography, or *Bildungsroman*, although it opened with certain formalities: 'Zhenya Luvers was born and brought up in Perm [...] Her father managed the affairs of the Lunyev mines...' But these announcements were submerged in the wandering, associative thought stream of the child: 'Just as once her little boats and dolls, so later on her memories sank deep into the shaggy bearskins of which there were many in their house [...] The bearskins were gifts, deep brown and sumptuous. The white she-bear in her nursery was like an enormous chrysanthemum shedding petals', and so forth (II, 83; *VP*, 56).

Set in Perm and Ekaterinburg, which Pasternak recalled from his own visits there in 1916, the two parts of the story are concerned respectively with Zhenya's infantile perceptions and attempts to find names for them, and with her burgeoning moral awareness. The young heroine is gifted with a wondering sensitivity to her surroundings reminiscent of the author himself. As Pasternak later told Tsvetaeva: 'I have a mass of feminine features in me. I know far too many sides of what is called a "suffering condition". For me it is not just one word denoting merely one failing [...] The whole real world [...] is reduced by me to this suffering condition, and in my novel I have a heroine, not a hero – which is no coincidence'.[66] Both Pasternak and his heroine thus emerge as enraptured passive observers, rather than as demonstrative masculine 'doers', and Zhenya Luvers is seen in contrast not just with the adult world, but also with her boisterous brother Seryozha, who fails to see, or ignores, the rich experiences to which she is attuned.

The year after Pasternak wrote his story, the Formalist critic Viktor Shklovsky (whom he knew through the Moscow Linguistic Circle) published an essay describing *ostranenie* (or 'making strange') as a literary device used already by Tolstoy and others.[67] Among Russian prose writers of the 1920s there was to be a cult of such novel vision, which represented the world as if viewed with an 'innocent eye'. *Zhenya Luvers' Childhood* was one of the most startling examples of this manner which later explored by Yurii Olesha, Vladimir Nabokov, and also implicit in some of Voronsky's critical writing in *Krasnaya nov'*.[68] The non-congruence of acquired language and immediate experience had long been familiar to Pasternak; and he had no doubt also read reflections on the subject by such as Humboldt, the philologian Potebnya, and Andrei Bely.[69] At about the time when Pasternak began work on *Zhenya Luvers' Childhood*, Bely's own account of a childhood, *Kotik*

Letaev, was serialised in the Scythian journal *Skify* (no.1, 1917 and no.2, 1918). Both works depict a child-hero's dawning perception and use of language to cognise and 'tame' inchoate impressions. A vivid example occurs in the opening of Pasternak's story when Zhenya is aroused and sees the scaring illuminations of Motovilikha iron foundry:

That had no name, and no precise colour or definite outline [...] Zhenya burst into tears. Father's explanation was brief: 'That is Motovilikha. For shame! A big girl like you! Go to sleep!

The little girl understood nothing and contentedly swallowed a rolling tear. In fact that was all she needed to know: what the mysterious thing was called – Motovilikha. (II, 83–4; *VP*, 57)

Zhenya's rise to moral awareness is characterised by the same elements as her sensory development, bypassing the prescriptions of a copybook adult moral system. The 'Stranger' in the title of part 2 is Tsvetkov, a crippled friend of Zhenya's tutor. She encounters him several times by chance. One night he is trampled and killed outside the theatre by the Luvers' rearing carriage horse. Zhenya hears the name of the victim only a fortnight later, on a day when she erroneously believes she has seen Tsvetkov again. The news fills her with horror. The significance of the experience 'consisted in the fact that this was the first time *another* human being had entered her life – a third person, totally different, with no name, or only a fortuitous one, neither arousing hatred nor inspiring love, but *the person the Commandments have in mind*, addressing men with names and consciousness, when they say: "Thou shalt not kill", "Thou shalt not Steal", et cetera' (II, 135–6; *VP*, 107–8). The message of the story is Tolstoyan – perhaps, as Angela Livingstone suggests, even Christian. And like sensory perception, a moral epiphany is made all the more compulsive by the accidental manner of its occurrence.[70]

Most readers of Pasternak's story doubtless viewed it as a tender evocation of childhood, pleasingly divorced from the raw reality of modern Russia. But typically of Pasternak, one of its main themes was only suggested by metonymy, and Evgenii Lundberg for one picked up, and disliked, its 'tendentiously virtuous' tone. The story was composed at a time when arrest, execution, destruction of families, and the swallowing up of the individual by mass movements and statistics were part of everyday life, and it was written in opposition to all this. Behind alienating official titles and names Zhenya discovers vividly individual experiences and personalities; and in part 2, through family involvement and chance circumstances she shares in the tragedy and death of someone who was a victim of her earlier indifference and now becomes, in a

Biblical sense, her neighbour. Pasternak thus makes a powerful, if oblique, statement on the sanctity of the individual and of human life at a time when these were unrecognised by the agents of the new order. His next complete prose story, *Aerial Ways* (*Vozdushnye puti*) was to state this point more overtly.

In mid-1918 Pasternak's productivity was interrupted. He and his family were underfed and in poor health, and his prospects of professional earnings were depressing. He had survived creatively longer than some, but he now needed to find employment to help maintain the family. A short biographical note written in 1923 reported that 'serious creative work came to an end in the second half of 1918', and there followed 'a four-year interval whose greater part was taken up with verse translation work on commissions from TEO and World Literature publishers.'[71]

TEO was an acronym for the Theatrical Section (Teatralny otdel) of Narkompros. It was run from offices on Znamenka Street by a succession of personalities including Trotsky's sister Olga (married to the prominent Bolshevik, Lev Kamenev), Lunacharsky, Vera Menzhinskaya and Meyerhold. The TEO repertory department was chaired for a time by Baltrušaitis, and during the Civil War it commissioned several writers including Balmont, Bryusov, Vyacheslav Ivanov, Khodasevich and Pasternak to make Russian translations of foreign theatrical works. 'World Literature' ('Vsemirnaya literatura') was another Narkompros venture set up, like TEO, in August-September of 1918. Gorky's initiative was designed to bring treasures of world literature to the masses in high-quality new translations; probably Pasternak's collaboration was arranged during Gorky's visit to Moscow in June of 1918. Like many Narkompros projects, it did not solve the problem of publishing original work, but in the short term it brought welcome earnings to the starving littérateurs of Moscow and Petrograd.

The second half of 1918, therefore, found Pasternak at work on Kleist's *Prince Friedrich of Homburg* (*Prinz Friedrich von Homburg*), published eventually in 1923, and TEO commissioned from him versions of the same author's *Robert Giskard* and *The Schroffenstein Family* (*Die Familie Schroffenstein*). By mid-1920 his translation of Goethe's *Mysteries* (*Die Geheimnisse*) was ready and, despite an unenthusiastic reader's report by Aleksandr Blok, it was brought out by 'Sovremennik' in 1922. In November of 1919, Gosizdat was set up under Vorovsky, and the following year Pasternak signed a contract with them for translations of Shrovetide plays by the German Meistersinger Hans Sachs, and between 1920 and 1922 he was also at work on Ben Jonson's *The Alchemist*, which was initially scheduled for performance in his version of 1923.[72]

It was during this translation work, in December 1918, that Pasternak drafted his 'propositions' on art. Originally planned for inclusion in an unfinished book of articles, this document appeared eventually as *Some Propositions* (*Neskol'ko polozhenii*) in *Sovremennik* in 1922.[73] In one of its sections Pasternak recalled his earlier translation of *Chastelard* and spoke of the 'law of the miraculous' that bound together the heroine of the play, the author Swinburne, the translator, and 'many others (eye-witnesses and spectators of three epochs, characters, biographies, readers)' (III, 154; *VP*, 112). Nevertheless, Pasternak was unhappy with this enforced substitute for original work. Though in some sense 'creative', it was a secondary activity. An indication of his attitude to it was provided by his answers to the Poets' Section questionnaire of March 1919. Pasternak confirmed that his sole income was now from authorship, for he had 'resolutely turned down any subsidiary income possible at the present time, i.e. in state service.' But, Pasternak maintained, 'I am unable to regard my constant work on *translations* as direct earnings (although, as income, I cannot object to it). As direct income I would regard payment for original artistic work with the possibility of publication. However, I have renounced the form which this has taken among the "young"* for reasons of principle.'[74]

In addition to translation work, Pasternak was forced at various points during this period of 'war communism' to undertake other forms of humdrum employment. The first such occasion was in March–November 1918, when he held a minor clerical post in the Narkompros library. His job was to write out official preservation orders for book collections still in private hands; this was under the auspices of the Narkompros Committee for Preservation of Cultural Values, chaired by Bryusov. The job was largely a sinecure of the sort assigned to many intellectuals at the time. Tsvetaeva, for instance, who was destitute by November 1918, took on a soul-destroying job for six months as filing clerk in the Commissariat of Nationalities.[75]

During the Civil War, most writers' earnings continued to dwindle, and even greater exertions were needed to survive. An attempt by several

* An allusion to Mayakovsky's group and to IMO (See above p. 262).

writers and poets including Pasternak to lobby Lunacharsky in his 'White Corridor' in the Kremlin was described by the poet Khodasevich. In their presence Lunacharsky mooted the idea for 'Lito', a special Literary Department (Literaturnyi otdel) within Narkompros.[76] This body was indeed set up in late 1919 and was functional by February of 1920. But hopes and promises were no cure for hunger. In early April of 1920 Pasternak wrote requesting assistance from Dmitrii Petrovsky, who had gone back to his native Chernigov Province. 'Poverty is the only real thing in Moscow,' he told him, and sent three thousand roubles with a request for regular supplies of rusks, honey, groats and fat. Petrovsky evidently obliged with several parcels; in the countryside produce was cheaper and more readily obtainable than in large towns, and through his army connections Petrovsky was able to send almost any food parcels, whereas ordinary citizens were limited in what they could mail. Nine months later, as Pasternak admitted in a further letter, he owed Petrovsky a veritable fortune for apples, rusks and other items, but was still incapable of paying.[77]

As a further aid to survival, on 14 June 1920 Pasternak indented for an official food ration for himself and his father with Lito. His somewhat sarcastically phrased application pointed out that he was not in government service, and he appended a list of completed works including twelve thousand lines of translated verse. The latter, in particular, represented an 'intensity and a form and condition of involuntary labour whereby its vehicle and agent, first launched on this path by the attraction of a calling, gradually abandons the province of art, then of independent craft as well.' Pasternak saw himself 'subjected to an impossible professional servitude that goes on and on, becomes more and more burdensome and, given the inevitable social inertia, cannot be relieved'.[78] During the Civil War, more and more of the literary intelligentsia became dependent on ration allocations from various sources – artistic, educational, even the military authorities. As Ehrenburg recalled, 'Money was so devalued that hardly anyone thought about it. We lived on rations and hopes.' Deputy chairman of Lito was Bryusov, and in view of Boris' earlier friendly relations with him, the Pasternaks hoped for allocation of a first-grade academic supply ration. (On somewhat spurious grounds Bryusov appointed Mandelstam only to second grade and delayed Khodasevich's grant because of a negative political evaluation.)[79] But although the Pasternaks were entered on the list, no rations had come through by January 1921, and when they did both Boris and Leonid Pasternak disliked this enforced parasitism in lieu of fruitful paid employment.[80]

In July 1920 Leonid Pasternak and his wife were able to spend a month at a country sanatorium near Moscow. Meanwhile Lydia, followed later by Boris, went to visit and collect supplies from their mother's brother Osip Kofman, who was still serving as a doctor at Kasimov in Ryazan Province. (To ensure she obtained a seat on the train, Lydia had a travel permit signed by Lunacharsky stating that she was collecting local folklore materials!) 'The journey out to this paradise was a pure Scheherazade,' Boris told Shura Shtikh.[81] He and his sister spent several days in the rural outback with their uncle and aunt. Working as a rural physician, Osip Kofman was frequently paid in kind and here, as in Chernigov Province, local produce was in relatively plentiful supply. The Kofmans were therefore happy to assist their Moscow relatives. Boris wrote enthusiastically about conditions in Kasimov – 'something like a Russian Marburg' – and suggested to his parents that they move out to the provinces.[82] Pasternak, in fact, dreamed for years of just such a rural idyll, with a life untroubled by affairs of state, and where artistic labours and rewarding physical work amid nature could be combined. Perhaps all this was reflected in his earlier interest in 'Natural Law', and all the family had had a taste of this existence at Karzinkino in the summer of 1918. The same theme was to emerge in Pasternak's prose writings of the 1930s, in a wartime play, and in the Varykino episode of *Doctor Zhivago* (whose hero shares the same profession as Osip Kofman). Pasternak's plan was never pursued, however, and the relative rural prosperity was also shortlived. After a trip to Ryazan where he gave a poetry reading (in 1921 he published some verse in *Cinnabar* [*Kinovar'*] a local almanac), Boris and Lydia journeyed back to Moscow by river steamer with new boots and clothing and a large hamper of provisions. Despite severe furunculosis under one arm, Pasternak's morale for the time being was high.

On returning from Kasimov Pasternak was forced once again to seek some routine form of income. For four months he went to work for the railway newspaper *Gudok* (The Whistle), which provided notional employment for several writers and intellectuals. In those offices, as Pasternak later reported to Petrovsky, he 'wrote not a line for the paper, but spent my time correcting other people's verses and received a good Red Army ration for doing so'![83] Only in November came the promise of an official academic ration, and also of publication by Gosizdat of *My Sister Life*. Thus encouraged, Pasternak gave up his post at *Gudok* and for the first time in two and a half years attempted to resume creative writing. It was still several more weeks before distribution of rations began however, and so far as the publication was concerned, it was another false hope. By January 1921 he was once again bereft of money and food.

11

Berlin interlude

'Famine'
O fear me as you would crusaders!
Away from pestilential Mongols!
Overnight my jacket hem
Has brushed against these lines on hunger.

And no carbolic's rinsed my verbs.
Nor did I then remove my clothing.
Nor did I pour away the ink –
The ink with which I wrote of famine.

I should have known it in advance –
Such torments have no designation,
But I sought out their names and bear
The disgrace of endeavouring.

৩৵৵৵

Leonid Pasternak found it increasingly difficult to maintain his family after the Revolution, even with his wife and children's occasional earnings. His salary was supplemented by sporadic allocation of supplies to institutes of learning, and official commissions were paid for with cocoa, stockings, and other items in short supply. But only in 1921 was he assigned a regular academic food ration. Meanwhile, although some of his darkest premonitions had been realised by Bolshevik excesses, the question of rejecting or approving the new order was almost an irrelevance: the family saw their immediate task merely in surviving and finding some useful role for themselves in a historical context they could not alter.

Whatever Leonid Pasternak's misgivings on other scores, the new régime's policy of popularising the arts coincided with his ideals. Throughout the Civil War, he had carried out official commissions and maintained his own graphic record of events. His pictures of the period included sketches and a portrait of the revolutionary poet Demyan

Bedny, an illustration of the Bolshevik leader Sverdlov's funeral procession in March 1919, and several studies of Lenin: a fine impressionistic pastel of him addressing the Seventh All-Russian Congress of Soviets in the Bolshoi Theatre in March 1918; some black chalk sketches from life at the Second Congress of Comintern in 1920 and the Central Executive Committee plenum in 1921; and sketches done in the Kremlin for a planned but never completed portrait. Leonid Pasternak's ability to capture Lenin's reputed qualities of concentration and resolve were later matched poetically in part of Boris Pasternak's *Malady Sublime*.[1]

In fine arts, however, the socialist revolution had also offered an indulgence to the new 'revolutionary aesthetic' and the Moscow School of Painting was dominated by modernist trends, especially after it had been restructured in December 1920 as 'Vkhutemas' (an acronym for *Vysshie khudozhestvennye masterskie* – Higher Art Studios). Life was further unsettled by Narkompros attempts (curtailed only after Lunacharsky's intervention) to evict the Pasternaks from their apartment, which would have deprived Leonid of studio facilities. He and his wife had managed a summer sanatorium holiday in 1920, but Leonid Pasternak had an eye complaint and Rozaliya had that year suffered a severe heart attack; the only adequate treatment to be had was in Western Europe. At the School of Painting Leonid now had only a small group of appreciative like-minded students, and their pleas were unable to dissuade him from applying for a permit to go abroad for a two-year rest cure.[2]

In the summer of 1921 the Pasternak parents and daughters left Russia for Germany. The first to depart was Josephine. She had at one time considered taking monastic vows, and her religiosity (initially fired perhaps by Akulina Gavrilovna) now prompted a desire to study philosophy abroad as part of a 'Christian readjustment' of her life. Her parents never objected, convinced that she would never obtain an exit visa. However, she managed to obtain a signature from the Cheka (with Boris' help via connections which the critic Osip Brik could muster), and two further Kremlin endorsements were secured from Enukidze and Lunacharsky. The latter showed avuncular concern at her being unchaperoned in Berlin but was relieved to hear that her Austrian cousin Fedya would be there to help her (having left for Sweden during the Civil War, he too arrived in Berlin in 1921). Josephine was accordingly granted a one-year exit permit.

Travelling via Riga, where the family of Leonid's sister Ekaterina lived, she went on by sea to Germany. In Berlin she began immediate

24 Moscow, August 1921, after Josephine's departure. Standing: Aleksandr
and Boris; seated: Leonid Pasternak, Berta Kofman, Rozaliya Pasternak,
Lydia

arrangements for her parents to join her. Lunacharsky in Moscow
assisted; despite a critical attitude towards the liberal intelligentsia, he
was, as Fitzpatrick comments, 'completely vulnerable to their individual
appeals for help'. With his support the Pasternak parents and Lydia left
Moscow for Berlin in August 1921.

Foreign travel became altogether easier that year when a New
Economic Policy (NEP) was adopted, and diplomatic links were established with Germany and other nations. As a result members of many
intelligentsia, including several of Boris Pasternak's circle of associates,
found their way abroad – some temporarily, like Bely and Shklovsky;
others forever, including his friend Dobrovein, who left in spring of
1922, indignant at the non-renewal of his Bolshoi Theatre contract.
Links with Germany became especially easy, and thousands of Russians
in Berlin still hesitated between exile and return, profiting from a
situation that demanded no final commitment to ideology or place of
residence. The Pasternaks were in this situation. They retained their
Soviet passports and hoped eventually to return. But cherished hopes for
their old age had crumbled. Their plot of land in the south for which they

had almost paid off the mortgage and where they intended building a retirement home had been nationalised; recent years of hardship had devoured all their savings, and life in Moscow had proved to be insecure, cramped and uncomfortable.[3]

Boris and Aleksandr Pasternak opted for the time being to remain in Moscow. The separation saddened their parents and was aggravated by a further breach with Asya's family. Her husband, Mikhail Freidenberg, had died in August 1920, and when her brother Leonid left the country she could not forgive him for not coming to Petrograd to say goodbye. His suggestion that she and Olya should go and settle in the Volkhonka apartment with Boris and Aleksandr was turned down with bitter pride.[4] Leonid Pasternak therefore installed two other families in the rooms that remained of their Volkhonka residence. Samuil Frishman, originally from Belostok, was a brother of David Frishman whom the Pasternaks had befriended at Karzinkino in 1918. With Samuil and his wife Yulia lived her sister Frederika, together with their own daughter Stella and her husband Abram Adelson, plus a maidservant. These six, who had hitherto lived in cramped quarters in Nashchokinsky Lane, thus came to occupy the original dining-room and two bedrooms vacated by the Pasternak parents and daughters. Boris and Aleksandr meanwhile retained one room each: Boris moved into his father's studio while Aleksandr settled in the former drawing-room.

In Berlin the Pasternaks rented an apartment in Monsstrasse near Nollendorfplatz and later, in 1923, moved to Bayreutherstrasse. The first few years of émigré life were not easy. The middle-class accommodation they could afford had no studio space and was 'cramped, dark and cluttered with bulky furniture we did not need,' Leonid recalled.[5] They were eventually to prosper in Berlin, however. Rozaliya responded to treatment and resumed playing the piano and serving as secretary to her husband. Leonid Pasternak's eye trouble also cleared and he again worked successfully. Portrait commissions flowed in and, as one biographer records, he worked 'eagerly, freely, boldly, not trying to please the public, or the critics, or the press'.[6] The Berlin phase was one of his most brilliant. In 1923 Leonid Pasternak published the monograph on Rembrandt which he wrote during the Civil War. That same year he also made an *hors concours* contribution to the Berlin Sezession exhibition. In 1927 his one-man exhibition was mounted in the Galerie Hartberg and was enthusiastically previewed by Lunacharsky; it was a triumphant demonstration of his Berlin achievements and included the fruits of a journey in 1924 to Egypt and Palestine and a series of boldly impressionistic portraits.[7]

Josephine Pasternak studied philosophy at Berlin University in the early 1920s. In 1924 she married her cousin Fedya, who by then worked for Crédit Lyonnais in Munich. Josephine joined him there, eventually completing her studies and bringing up a family in the Bavarian capital. Lydia lost a year catching up on the German school-leaving qualifications in order to continue her science studies. She then graduated in Berlin as a psychologist and in 1929 also moved to Munich to work at the Psychological Research Institute there.

After the devastation of war, revolution and economic failure, the Soviet government's New Economic Policy proclaimed in May 1921 inaugurated a period of relative relaxation and restored small-scale capitalist enterprise in order to help resuscitate trade and production. Coercion was not completely abandoned however. Concentration camps, first introduced in 1920, continued operating, and shortly in store were show trials of a large number of Socialist Revolutionaries, persecutions of the clergy, and so forth. The wave of repressions affected some people known to Pasternak. The Petrograd poet Gumilyov was executed for conspiracy in mid-1921. Pasternak's friend Sergei Durylin, who had been ordained during the war and served as a priest in Moscow, was arrested in 1922 and exiled first to the Crimea and later to Tomsk. (In the later 1920s he returned to Bolshevo, near Moscow; subsequently he made a name for himself as a literary and theatrical historian.) The autumn of 1922 also saw forcible expatriation of over 200 leading writers, scientists, educators and intellectuals, including philosophers Berdyaev, Frank, Lossky and Stepun, all of whom were articulate opponents of Bolshevism.[8]

Some impressions of the changes in economic conditions are preserved in Pasternak's later fiction:

Bargains were made on the scale of turnover at a rag-and-bone merchant's in the flea market. And the paltry amounts they dealt in encouraged speculation and led to abuse. The bustling of the dealers produced nothing new and brought no substantial improvement to the urban desolation [...]

The owners of several very modest home libraries took down the books from their shelves and assembled them. They notified the City Council of their wish to open up cooperative book trade and requested suitable premises. They were granted use of a shoe warehouse that had stood empty since the first months of the revolution, or a market-gardener's greenhouses closed at the same time, and under these broad vaults they sold off their slim and haphazard book collections. (*DZh*, 485)

After the literary 'café period' came a short but colourful epoch of 'writers' bookshops'. Organised by individuals, clubs and societies like the Union of Poets, the shops were staffed often by writers themselves and apart from second-hand books sold some handwritten manuscript editions by Bely, Shershenevich and others. Pasternak did not rely on this form of poetic propagation. In September 1920 Loks had introduced Rita Rait-Kovalyova to him in order that he give an opinion of her translations of Futurist poets into German, and she became one of their coterie. Pasternak presented her with a copy of *My Sister Life* and later visited her in the summer of 1921, part of which she spent at the Briks' dacha at Pushkino. That period, she recalled, 'passed for me under the sign of Pasternak. I was stuffed to overflowing with his verse. Splinters of his lines flew apart and even became caught in the most ordinary speech'. Rita Rait's experience was shared by several. In a 1922 review of Russian poetry Bryusov pointed out 'Pasternak's verses have had an honour conferred on them that has befallen hardly any poetic works (apart from those forbidden by the censorship) since the time of Pushkin: they have been distributed in manuscript copies! Young poets knew these verses by heart and recited them before they ever appeared in print and imitated them more fully than Mayakovsky.'[9]

The small-scale writers' shops had meanwhile changed nobody's fortunes and they began disappearing in 1922 as larger traders and official organisations monopolised the market. But now, for the first time in years, publication and sale of books became possible on a broad scale; Pasternak's 'printed biography' could resume.

After their earlier existence on ration allocations, writers began to live largely on advances. In some circles Pasternak was even regarded as a master of this survival technique. The poet and editor Pyotr Zaitsev, his friend since Musaget days, wrote on 23 June 1921 to Bely, revealing that 'a certain young poet' (i.e. Pasternak) had 'concluded via Lito and Lunacharsky an agreement with Gosizdat for the sale of not just his finished works but also his planned ones, on the basis of which he is paid 200,000 roubles every month by the State. Formally it is an advance on his fee, but in fact it is a subsidy to the writer by the state.' In 1921, however, Pasternak actually had verse published in five different journals and miscellanies. By 1922 single items or selections from *My Sister Life* and *Themes and Variations* appeared in at least a dozen different editions, including two in Berlin.[10]

Among his new publications, the poem 'Kremlin in a Blizzard' first appeared in *Help* (*Pomoshch'*), no. 1, an almanac put out in Simferopol in 1922 to assist the famine relief campaign following the harvest failure of 1921. Two new poems on the subject of famine were also printed in the government paper *Izvestiya* on 15 March 1922. Just over a month later, on 24 April, Pasternak found himself walking next to Tsvetaeva as they followed the coffin of Scriabin's second wife to the Novodevichy Cemetery. He was embarrassed to learn that she had read them. 'Don't talk about it,' he said. 'They are a disgrace. I intended something quite different. But you know how it is: a host of inspiring angels around your head, and then when you look down there is just a blank sheet of paper. It all floated past and never reached the desk. They were what I wrote down at the last minute when they began agitating and ringing to say that they wouldn't make the issue in time...'[11] Good journeyman products, the poems (one of which appears on p.278 above) were evidence of Pasternak's professionalism and ability to write to order. Yet his remarks to Tsvetaeva suggested that he found it hard to resume regular creativity after more than three years' enforced break. An interesting feature of the poem 'Famine' ('Golod') is its implication that – even after the Futurist emancipation – certain subjects are so cruel that they lie beyond the expressive grasp of poetry.

Like most of his verses that appeared in 1921–3, Pasternak's prose publications were also works of some antiquity. *Letters from Tula*, *Zhenya Luvers' Childhood* and *Some Propositions* were all written back in 1918. Only one new publication was probably a recent effort: *Three Chapters from a Tale*, printed on 12 June 1922 in the short-lived *Moskovsky Ponedel'nik* (Moscow Weekly). The work introduced material that was to occupy Pasternak for another dozen years (the verse novel *Spektorsky* and prose *Story* sprang from the same thematic kernel). Among the characters introduced in the *Chapters* is a rich relative of Russian revolutionaries named Schütz. He is seen first during 1905 and then later on in 1916. The figure of Schütz was based obviously on Sasha Gavronsky. Wealthy parentage, revolutionary connections, cynicism, abandonment of his wife, evasion of military service, faking of an eye defect – all these were traits drawn from memories of Gavronsky's behaviour in 1911. Also recounted in the 'Chapters' is Schütz's meeting with Sergei Spektorsky, another of Pasternak's semi-autobiographical figures. The second chapter portrays Spektorsky during the 1914 mobilisation in a setting reminiscent of the Baltrušaitis family *dacha* of that year. The third and final chapter introduces Sergei's eccentric father, his reaction on hearing his son has been injured in battle, and the homecoming of Sergei, slightly crippled and with a foreshortening of one leg – an injury Pasternak sustained in more peaceful circumstances.[12]

Although they opened up an interesting thematic avenue, the new *Chapters* were overshadowed by the almost simultaneous appearance of *Zhenya Luvers' Childhood* and *My Sister Life* in May of 1922. (A separate volume of Pasternak's collected prose, to be issued by Sovremennik publishers in 1922 failed to materialise.) *My Sister Life's* appearance in an edition of 1,000 copies was an event of cardinal importance. Writing in a Berlin journal, Ehrenburg described Pasternak as 'a mountain ridge of pure lyricism' demonstrating the 'nakedness of lyrical excitement, choking on the very essence of poetry'.[13] In Moscow's *Pechat' i revolyutsiya* the literary editor and reviewer Yakov Chernyak greeted Pasternak's bright maturity after the storm and stress of *Over the Barriers*. Despite his complexity, Pasternak allegedly demonstrated a 'Pushkinian clarity', his book's most striking feature was its 'instantaneousness of depiction' combined with evident signs of careful, disciplined composition. It was, Chernyak claimed, European in its gentle irony and infused with 'modernity'.[14]

'Modernity' or 'contemporaneity' (*sovremennost'*) was evidently a key criterion with all critics. Whether Marxist or not, they expected that modern literature should in some way register the new Russian atmosphere and reality. Reviewing *My Sister Life* in the journal *Korabl'* (The Vessel), the poet Aleksandr Romm emphasised Pasternak's modern quality, achieved without any superficial effort to be merely 'up-to-date'. There was, Romm maintained, a consistency in Pasternak's imagery, semantic play and lexical variety and power to excite which made even Mayakovsky seem 'flatter than a floorboard'.[15] Aseyev welcomed *My Sister Life* from the pages of *Krasnaya nov'* and linked Pasternak's modernity directly with his complexity: 'If a poet is difficult for you and still you are sorry to leave him, if this difficulty exhausts but does not repel, you have before you your contemporary who sings on your behalf.'[16] Another testimonial came from Bryusov. Now a Bolshevik convert and elder literary statesman, he forecast the future of Russian poetry as lying with proletarian verse. But among present-day poets, despite Pasternak's intellectual anaemia and philosophising, Bryusov believed he occupied a unique place: 'Pasternak has no separate poems about the revolution, but his verses, maybe without the poet's own knowledge, are saturated with the spirit of modernity. The psychology of Pasternak is not borrowed from old books, it expresses the essence of the poet himself and could only be formed in the conditions of our life.'[17]

A cold douche was administered by the utilitarian Marxist critic Valerian Pravdukhin. In his review of modern verse, few figures emerged unscathed. Even Mayakovsky, he claimed, was hampered by his bourgeois origins and his latest work was dismissed as 'agitation' rather than literature (a view with which Pasternak might have concurred). Pasternak himself was branded by Pravdukhin as a 'hot-house aristocrat of our society's private residences' and a faded 'philistine'. His only response to the age was a shudder, life for him was a mass of incoherent details, and world culture was reduced to his low level as he 'smoked with Byron and drank with Edgar Allen Poe'. A curio among the responses to *My Sister Life*, Pravdukhin's article nevertheless established a pattern for orthodox critics in the later 1920s and 1930s. Lunacharsky's response, in a letter of thanks for the inscribed copy of *My Sister Life* Pasternak gave him in May 1922, also contained some signposts for future 'establishment' critiques. His message contained no class-conscious jibes but condescended to point out 'faults' and preached the virtue of 'simplicity' to this 'horribly difficult poet', whose splendours he nevertheless savoured and towards whom he emphasised his friendship.[18]

Two great poets of the epoch also reviewed Pasternak's book and, characteristically perhaps, laid stress on the exhilarating physicality of his verse. Tsvetaeva's essay was an ecstatic dithyramb with 'dreaming eddies of interpretation' followed by 'daylight reality, a sober shoal of theses and quotations' which reflected on the central prosaic, photic and liquid sources of Pasternak's imagery.[19] Meanwhile, Mandelstam dwelt on the 'sheer joy of the vernacular, the lay language freed of all extraneous influence' (a true Acmeist's relief after the sacramental tones of Symbolist verse). Rephrasing a line of the nineteenth-century lyricist Fet, he continued:

This burning salt of speech, this whistling, crackling, rustling, flashing, splashing, fullness of sound, fullness of life, high tide of images and feelings have sprung up in Pasternak's poetry with unprecedented force [...] To read the poems of Pasternak is to clear one's throat passage, strengthen one's breathing, renovate one's lungs. Such verse must be a cure for tuberculosis. At present we have no healthier poetry.

For Mandelstam, Pasternak was also 'contemporary' in the sense that 'the major domesticity of Pasternak's poetry [...] is tasteless because it is immortal. It is styleless because it splutters over banalities with the classical ecstasy of the trilling nightingale'.[20]

Both Tsvetaeva's and Mandelstam's appreciation sprang from the same world as Pasternak's *Propositions*, a work with which Mandelstam was clearly familiar. In it, Pasternak left little place for 'modernity', cults of complexity, or any form of 'audience awareness':

A book is a cube-shaped chunk of blazing, smoking conscience – nothing more [...] A book is like a capercaillie sounding its mating call. The book hears nothing and no one, deafened and enraptured by its own music.

And the only contemporary hint in the *Propositions* was an awareness of poetry's capacity to 'disturb us like the sinister turning of ten windmills by the edge of some bare field in a black and hungry year' (III, 152–5; *VP*, 110–13).

Plaudits for *Zhenya Luvers' Childhood* identified Pasternak as a major force in modern prose. A new admirer was the Petrograd poet and author Mikhail Kuzmin who, as Pasternak boasted to Bryusov in August 1922, 'strongly singled out my prose, placing it higher than Bely and Aleksei Tolstoy, not to mention Pilnyak and the Serapions'. By comparison with Pasternak's 'incomparably weaker' poetry, Kuzmin viewed this story as a real 'artistic event', outstanding in its 'huge wave of love, warmth, sincerity' and in the 'chaste openness of the author's emotional perceptions'.[21] Another appreciative Petrograd author was Evgenii Zamyatin who saw the story's novelty 'in a plane where apart from him [Pasternak] hardly anyone operates: [...] his symbolism is acute and all his own. He does not seek for external modernity with gunfire and flags, yet he still of course belongs completely to modern literature'. This same touchstone of modernity was applied in another review by Nikolai Ashukin for the Berlin periodical *Novaya russkaya kniga* (The New Russian Book).[22] Among ideologically committed readers, it was Gorky who was most positive in his praise and promotion of *Zhenya Luvers' Childhood*.[23] But probably neither he, nor the other contemporary reviewers identified any 'modernity' of a thematic type such as led Lundberg to view the work as 'tendentiously virtuous'. The 'contemporary quality' discovered in Pasternak's poetry and prose was thus largely an honorific epithet, denoting a degree of originality in style and structure rather than in content. The only obvious sense in which *My Sister Life* was 'contemporary' was in its conveyance of the élan and euphoria of 1917. It was a point which Pasternak made to Bryusov:

Sister is revolutionary in the best sense of the word [. . .] The stage of revolution closest to my heart and to poetry is the revolution's *morning*, and its initial outburst, when it returns man to his own *nature*.[24]

That same summer of 1922 Yurii Yurkun, a literary protégé of Kuzmin's, heard from Pasternak the following:

Here are these two things of mine which I am sending you. Find anything 'revolutionary' in them in the popular sense! It is simply laughable what fortune *Sister* has had. An apolitical book, to say the least, in which it is possible with a certain effort to fish out one political word – and then it turns out to be 'Kerensky' – this book ought to have attracted the most routine and ordinary attacks, and yet – one can forgive the terminology – it is recognised as being 'most revolutionary'.

Pasternak went on to mention that he had also sent a copy of the book to Akhmatova 'as a person who has unjustly suffered from friendly criticism, which prematurely proclaims someone a master, canonises them according to the measure of its moderate demands and then requires nothing more from them'.[25] In a slightly different sense Pasternak too was a victim of this. His critical accolade, though welcome in one way, was embarrassing as a reaction to works written as much as five years previously. It raised false expectations, particularly uncomfortable at a time when he was having difficulty in resuming his creative writing. As he told Bryusov in 1922, 'In the last few years I have become steeped in an element of pernicious slovenliness, from which I myself alone suffer most of all.'[26] As he returned to serious writing, the question of his whole 'post-Futurist' orientation was opened up. The Pasternak of the 1920s was a very different artist from that of the previous decade.

A major factor in Pasternak's inner development and crisis was the recent transformation of his literary milieu. Mayakovsky's willing engagement in satirical, 'committed' art during the war was eventually followed by the full-time hiring of his poetic and placarding skills to the new regime. Though not widely appreciated by Party and government leaders or the general public, he had the support of Lunacharsky and of modernist sympathisers in Narkompros.[27] For the October anniversary in 1918 he wrote a *Mystery-Bouffe* (*Misteriya-buff*) for the modern age, abounding in Mayakovskian verbal humour and depicting the victory of the 'unclean' workers over all adversaries. In 1919 appeared his *poema 150,000,000*, a travesty of the Russian heroic epic, in which President Wilson is vanquished by 150 million Ivans (Russia's 1919 population). These nakedly propagandistic works had put an end to Pasternak's unbridled enthusiasm for Mayakovsky. When he eventually read *Mystery-Bouffe*, he found 'no appeal in these clumsily rhymed maxims, elaborate vacuity, commonplaces and hackneyed truisms, expounded so artificially, confusedly and unwittily' (II, 43; *VP*, 456–7). *150,000,000* Pasternak first heard in its author's own rendering, probably in January of 1920 in Poluektov Lane. 'While he existed as a creative artist,' Pasternak recalled, 'I tried for four years to get used to him and could not do so. Then I did get used to him inside two and a quarter hours, the time taken to read and discuss his uncreative *150,000,000* [. . .] For the first time I found I had nothing to say to him' (II, 273–4, 285; *VP*, 265, 276).[28]

Artistic differences did not affect the warmth of earlier relations with Mayakovsky, although by the time Pasternak lifted the veil on *My Sister Life*, both men must have realised their degree of divergence. But Pasternak continued to enjoy Futurist cameraderie, and various circumstances helped cement their relations. With Burlyuk's departure in 1920 for Japan and eventual exile in America, and with Khlebnikov's death in 1922, the avant-garde was deprived of two important founder-members. The nucleus of survivors was thus drawn together and was reinforced in late January of 1922, when Aseyev returned from several years' enforced sojourn in the Far East during the Civil War. Their friendship and late-night socialising sessions resumed. After one of them Pasternak set down some poetic 'notes of a habitué / Of quarter to four' on a presentation copy of *My Sister Life* given to Aseyev. These verses enjoyed a certain currency among their group, and Rita Rait later claimed that they encapsulated her impressions of returning from a visit to the circus on Moscow May nights. Another factor favouring Pasternak's close friendship with Mayakovsky's circle was the fact that after the summer of 1921 most of his family had left Moscow and he was now more dependent on his friends; moreover, he could now offer hospitality on the Volkhonka, where previously the avant-garde would have been unwelcome guests.[29]

Despite Pasternak's misgivings about Mayakovsky's new developments, according to Lili Brik Mayakovsky himself wholeheartedly loved his intriguing and slightly enigmatic colleague. He knew Pasternak by heart and for years 'was always reciting *Over the Barriers*, *Themes and Variations*, *My Sister Life*.'[30] Ilya Ehrenburg recalled an occasion at the House of the Press in early March 1921 when Pasternak and the actress Alekseyeva-Meskhieva gave a programme of readings from his recent work; and when someone was bold enough to point out some poetic defects, Mayakovsky stood up and eulogised Pasternak's verse, defending it 'with the fury of love'.[31]

That Pasternak had not totally lost faith in Mayakovsky's talent emerged in his dedication on a copy of *My Sister Life* in 1922. Expressing puzzlement at Mayakovsky's absorption with state finance and the 'tragedy of the Supreme Economic Council', and at his pronouncement of 'maxims about crude oil', Pasternak never doubted his sincerity and he recalled the old Mayakovsky as a poetic 'Flying Dutchman', asking what had reduced him to his present professional 'alms-house': 'What therapist could restore your anger?' (III, 134).

About Aseyev Pasternak had no misgivings as yet and in the summer of 1922 was impressed by Aseyev's *Steel Nightingale* (*Stal' noi solovei*).[32] The only poem in it with a dedication was 'Birdsong', addressed to Pasternak, and along with elements of Khlebnikov and Mayakovsky several other items showed Aseyev's exultant temperament, love of crisp alliteration and the appealing cluck, gush and twitter of his orchestral wordplay. Pasternak also regarded Aseyev as 'a good friend, a talented and intelligent man, who retained his inner freedom and did not blind himself to anything' (II, 44). The assessment was over-flattering and ignored Aseyev's eventual taint by ideological infections. Nevertheless, Pasternak both fraternised with the Futurists and, according to Aseyev, even considered a re-edition of his first two Futurist books.[33] Pasternak also appeared among Mayakovsky's circle on numerous social occasions, including a reception in May 1922 at Narkompros headquarters in the former lycée building at 53 Ostozhenka Street, when the company included Khlebnikov, Kruchenykh, Kamensky, Rita Rait and Kushner. As Aseyev recollected, 'everyone kept attacking Lunacharsky, and all he did was snap back. The argument was on the subject of the Futurists' present work: the contemporary element [*sovremennoe*] in them supposedly obstructed the "eternal". Everyone allegedly 'tweaked Anatolii Vasilyevich Lunacharsky about this "eternal element"'.[34] Pasternak's contribution to the debate is not on record. But the discussion obviously centred around the superficial Futurist view of 'modernity' (*vis à vis* the 'impressionism of the eternal' as understood by Pasternak). Paradoxically, some of Pasternak's sympathy on that occasion must have been with Lunacharsky.

In early May of 1921, just three months before he died, Aleksandr Blok paid a last visit to Moscow. He was scheduled to give three separate readings on the evening of 7 May. At the first of these Pasternak was introduced to him on the steps of the Polytechnical Museum – their one and only actual meeting, although they had a decade previously been in one another's presence.[35] As Pasternak recorded, 'Blok was friendly towards me and said he had heard good things of me. He complained of feeling unwell and asked to postpone a meeting until his health improved' (II, 17; *VP*, 430). Meanwhile, Pasternak heard from Mayakovsky that a reception of whistling and catcalls was to be staged at Blok's next engagement, at the House of the Press on Nikitsky Boulevard. Blok went there by car, and Pasternak and Mayakovsky arriving on foot were too late to prevent the scandal. In the discussions following the reading some of the company, with the critic Aleksandr Struve prominent among them, 'showered Blok with monstrous insults and did not stop short of telling him to his face that he was finished and inwardly dead – all of which Blok calmly agreed with' (II, 17; *VP*, 431). After that, however, Blok got a warm welcome at the Moscow Dante Society and gave a moving recitation of his Italian Verses. As an avant-gardist, Mayakovsky had little in common with Blok, and his obituary note later talked of the graveyard silence and half-empty hall in which Blok 'quietly and sadly recited his old lines about gipsy songs, love and the Beautiful Lady', yet privately (as he admitted to Lev Nikulin the day after the recital), he knew that Blok was capable of an artistic perfection which he himself could never match. Pasternak, understandably, was horrified at the remarks addressed to a poet who inspired his whole generation, especially when this turned out to be within a few months of Blok's actual death. Though not an instigator of the scandalous reception at the House of the Press, one of Blok's literary executioners turned out to be Sergei Bobrov, who shortly before Blok's death pronounced him as artistically defunct in *Pechat' i revolyutsiya*. The coincidence of this with Blok's physical demise helped confirm Bobrov's reputation for literary nastiness. Although Pasternak delivered no *ad hominem* rebuke, Bobrov was morbidly displeased when this episode (among many others that supposedly denigrated him) was later recalled in the *Autobiographical Essay*.[36]

But for Blok's death in August 1921, Pasternak's contact with him might have been more significant: in the early 1920s he made several new friendships among Petrograd writers. There is no reliable information to confirm suggestions that Pasternak went there during the Civil War. His portrait, for which he sat in the Petrograd apartment of artist Yurii

Annenkov and which was used as the frontispiece for the Berlin edition of *My Sister Life*, was probably produced in early 1922.[37]

Pasternak had first read Akhmatova in 1915 and in a later review of her work talked of the 'frankness in her treatment of life [which] she shared with Blok' and which gave her first books an 'original dramatic quality and the narrative freshness of prose'. But his first actual meeting with her took place in Petrograd in January 1922; he probably called on her to express sympathy after seeing how several critics had treated her, and after hearing report of her despair – and even rumour of her suicide – in the months following Gumilyov's execution.[38] Whatever the pretext, it was only now that Pasternak took a personal interest in her and came to appreciate her own and other Acmeists' poetry. The reason for this was partly geographical and partly connected with poetic ideology. Akhmatova, Gumilyov, Mandelstam and their associates were a specifically Petersburgian school, and it was probably Pasternak's Futurist leanings which explained his earlier failure to appreciate them. Indeed, he himself admitted his hearing had been

distorted by the whirligigs and the hacking around of everything familiar [...] Everything normally expressed ricocheted off me. I forgot that words can contain and mean something in themselves without the jingling ornaments with which they are adorned. (II, 45; *VP*, 460)

Even as late as 1920 Pasternak had expressed to Vilmont his contempt for the trivial thematic concerns of Acmeist poets Gumilyov and Mandelstam:

Why, even Kuzmin writes better than they [...] They only harness toy horses up to the cab. They know about harness, about the shaft-bow and the saddle-girth. Mandelstam? I dare say he also knows about the saddle-girth and how to prevent the saddle from slipping off ...[39]

Four years later, however, after reading a recent reprint of Mandelstam's *Stone* (*Kamen'*, first published 1913), Pasternak shamefully admitted his previous ignorance of a book the like of which, he claimed, he could never write.[40]

Such reassessments were part of Pasternak's reorientation in the early 1920s. But they were no doubt influenced by a particular series of events and circumstances. Public eyes were turned towards Petrograd when Blok died there on 7 August 1921 and when a fortnight later Gumilyov was executed for alleged complicity in an anti-Bolshevik plot.[41] That year Akhmatova, Gumilyov's ex-wife, published her poetic collection *Plantain* (*Podorozhnik*), and her *Anno Domini MCMXXI* and Mandelstam's *Tristia* appeared in early 1922. All three books registered the tragic personal losses inflicted by recent history and they far transcended original Acmeist programmatic concerns with craftmanship and *nature morte*. This minor-key 'bourgeois' response to the Revolution unleashed a wave of hostile criticism directed mainly at Akhmatova. The Acmeists were dismissed as masters of the past, deserving no place in the culture of the new worker state. Such criticism came mainly from Marxists such as Chudovsky, Gorbachev and Arvatov, but Blok had also produced a negative assessment in April 1921, and even Kornei Chukovsky's well-intentioned review of Akhmatova and Mayakovsky as equally valuable yet diametrically contrasted contemporaries involuntarily added fuel to the flames.[42]

Pasternak responded to all this on 6 June 1922 in dedicating to Akhmatova a copy of his recently published *My Sister Life*: 'To Anna Akhmatova, poet and comrade in misfortune. To a modest, youthful and less than half-exploited sensitivity, and therefore a special and exclusive victim of criticism that is incapable of feeling and tries to be sympathetic, the victim of unsolicited and ever inopportune summings-up and schemes'[43] Pasternak, in fact, felt an increasing bond with Akhmatova and other poets of his generation whose early flowering had coincided with the recent Russian historical tragedy. On 14 June 1922 he wrote as follows to Yurii Yurkun:

I consider close to me those people whose sensitivity and expressive abilities blossomed at the start of the war. A maxim has been established about them, referring to some 'pre-revolutionary quality', to their having been 'heard out to the end' by their readers, to the fact that they have 'said their last word leaving no remnant of artistry', to their 'Symbolism, Acmeism, bourgeois quality' and so on. And as you well know, in the now established view – a mere hour ago on our clocks – this means they have well nigh prehistoric origins. Yet would these 1917s and 1918s and so on be at all worthwhile – let alone the years of a great revolution – if these years had not been my own or your thirtieth, or somebody's fortieth or fiftieth? Or their sixtieth?[44]

Another new Petrograd ally and friend of Pasternak was Mikhail Kuzmin, who wrote an appreciative review of his recent prose and, as joint editor of the paper *Abraksas*, published part of *Themes and Variations* in 1922. (The next year *Abraksas* was suppressed on grounds of its 'unintelligibility' and 'extremeness'; later in the decade Kuzmin was to be forced out of modern literature and silenced altogether.)[45] Among a younger generation of Petrograd poets was Nikolai Chukovsky, whose verse Pasternak praised (in a letter of 11 July 1922) for its

293

'Mörike-like quality of geniality'. It was an opinion shared apparently by Mandelstam, whom Pasternak now also befriended. Mandelstam came to settle in Moscow in the spring of 1922, repelled by the inhospitable atmosphere and cultural devastation in his beloved native Petersburg.[46] After first lodging with the scholar Nikolai Gudzii, he and his wife found a room for themselves on Tverskoi Boulevard. A certain similarity in his and Pasternak's biographies probably brought them closer: their shared uncertainties in difficult times, recent publication of a significant book of new verse, and their recent marriages – each to an artist.[47] Probably Mandelstam was among the first to receive a copy of *My Sister Life* and his enthusiastic knowledge of it and of Pasternak's *Propositions* figured in his otherwise unenthusiastic review of the Moscow poetic scene in 1923.[48]

Although Mandelstam found Petrograd no longer tolerable, Pasternak's gaze was attracted there by new friends and the quality of the city's literary life. Bely had removed to Petrograd from Moscow in 1921, apparently because of the freer atmosphere and better conditions; the same year a transfer to Petrograd, recommended by no less a figure than Gorky, had a rejuvenating effect on Khodasevich's poetic talent.[49] Despite increasing official interference and a continuing tide of emigration abroad, Petrograd retained a still free and vital literary community largely centred on the so-called House of the Arts (opened in 1919 and closed on Zinovyev's order in the autumn of 1922). In early 1921, the Petrograd literati had clearly grasped Blok's Aesopic message at the Pushkin celebrations on 13 February:

It was not at all the bullet of d'Anthès that killed Pushkin. He was killed by lack of air. It was his culture dying with him. *Peace of mind* and *freedom* [...] are essential to a poet for the release of his harmony. But they take away peace of mind and freedom too. Not external, but creative peace of mind. Not childish liberty, not the freedom to act liberally, but creative liberty – a mysterious freedom. And the poet dies because he no longer has anything to breathe. Life has lost meaning.[50]

Blok's death from spiritual asphyxia in August 1921 was the unofficial diagnosis of several of his friends. Nevertheless, the values Pasternak respected and sought to preserve seemed to survive more intact in Petrograd literary circles, and in 1922 he seriously considered the idea of settling there.

At the Petrograd House of the Arts in early 1922 Pasternak doubtless encountered the writer Evgenii Zamyatin, who lectured there on modern prose technique and who in 1923 gave a positive evaluation of

Zhenya Luvers' Childhood. Pasternak was intrigued by Zamyatin and by his associates in the Serapion Brotherhood group, which was founded in 1921 on the idea of opposing 'coercion and tedium' and on a concern to promote individual authenticity rather than any clear-cut artistic programme. Pasternak's interest in these writers (Fedin, Vsevolod Ivanov, Kaverin, Luntz, Nikitin, Pozner, Slonimsky and others) emerged in his letter of 14 June 1922 to Yurkun. His message (couched in an idiosyncratic paradox) also showed an awareness of the emblematic significance of Pushkin in precisely the sense that Blok's audience had understood the previous year:

Probably there are some talented folk among the 'Serapions'. Probably Zamyatin is very good [...] And probably Pilnyak is not bad. All these are people of the Revolution (with the exception of Zamyatin) [...] And even they, of course, are non-party men. About my own party-mindedness I need say nothing. But do you know how I like to flabbergast people of this ilk?

I tell them seriously and angrily that I am a communist and that I don't hold woolly conversations. And then I snap out irritably that both Peter the Great and Pushkin were communists, that thank God we are living in a Pushkinian age, and that however crazy Petersburg might find it to be in Moscow, it would master this geographical paradox more easily if all these 'men of the revolution' were not personal enemies of the monument on Tverskoi Boulevard* and – *consequently* – counter-revolutionaries. And this is not a mere pose, I can tell you.[51]

One further important discovery turned Pasternak's attention away from the Moscow literary scene: the personality and poetry of Tsvetaeva. Apart from their few chance meetings during the Civil War and at Tatyana Scriabina's funeral, Pasternak had paid her no more than scant attention.[52] Tsvetaeva's husband had fought with the Whites in the south and been swept abroad by the tide of emigration. She herself spent the Civil War period amid awful privations. Her White-Guardist sympathies were known and Bryusov, abetted by his consultant Bobrov, had blocked publication of her work by Lito. In 1921 she began receiving a ration allocation, but at the end of May 1922, having set up publication of two books in Moscow, she left for Berlin on the first lap of a journey to rejoin her husband in Prague.[53] Tsvetaeva was already abroad when Pasternak came across a copy of her *Mileposts* (*Versty*), recently published and on sale in Moscow bookshops. Like his own *My Sister Life* it was a work of some time past – a sort of poetic diary of the year 1916 – yet its impact was fresh and unspoilt. Pasternak was 'immediately won over by the lyrical power of Tsvetaeva's form [...] It was not weak-chested but

* Monument – i.e. the memorial statue of Pushkin in Moscow.

highly compressed and concentrated. It did not get breathless on individual lines, and in the unfolding of its periods it took in whole sequences of stanzas without breaking the rhythm'. (II, 46; *VP*, 461)

On 14 June 1922 Pasternak wrote to Tsvetaeva via Ehrenburg who was also then resident in Germany:

Dear Marina Tsvetaeva,

With a quiver in my voice I have just now been reading to my brother your 'I know I shall die in the skyglow, But which of the two ...' and I was interrupted by a wave of sobbing that filled my throat and finally burst out ...

You are not a child, my dear, golden, incomparable poet, and I hope you realise what it means these days when there is such an abundance of poets and poetesses, not just those known to the Union, such an abundance not just of Imaginists but even of untainted talents like Mayakovsky and Akhmatova [...]

How could it happen that when I was walking behind Tatyana Fyodorovna's coffin along with you, I did not know who I was walking next to?[54]

Pasternak's long message was 'shapely in its confusion, written in one burst, in one ecstatic breath', as Tsvetaeva's daughter Ariadna later recalled. It was not his first such epistle, but it was his first letter to someone capable of responding in kind, with the same emotional vehemence. According to Ariadna Efron, the two of them 'gained one another only when irreparably separated, only in letters and verses, yet as in the firmest of earthly embraces. It was a real friendship, a genuine concord and a true love'.[55] In the here-and-now she was involved with her family (and Pasternak too had married in 1922 and remained for several years happily wed). But Tsvetaeva looked on him as her 'brother in the fifth season of the year, the sixth sense and the fourth dimension'. Their totally unphysical rapport was for her a guarantee against disenchantment, and she claimed that 'only imagined meetings do not bring disappointment'.[56] On the other hand their vicarious relationship was prey to two vivid imaginations. A recurrent feature of Tsvetaeva's emotional life was in some degree shared by Pasternak. As Simon Karlinsky writes: 'The literary creator in her took over and, by embellishing and developing her initial impression of a person, produced a poetic creation, which Tsvetaeva then proceeded to confuse with its model in real life.'[57] Pasternak's own poetically fruitful but emotionally miscalculated relations with Vysotskaya and Vinograd had demonstrated a similar quality. Like Tsvetaeva he could think and write himself into a state of frenzied passion, and in correspondence it was he who was to become the more reckless of the two.

Tsvetaeva's first letter, on 29 June 1922, and sent via Leonid Pasternak, was shiningly responsive and rehearsed the detailed prehistory of their Civil War meetings.[58] She had still not seen *My Sister Life* and know of it only from Ehrenburg. When she received a copy, though, she began an appraisal of its 'Downpour of Light' within a couple of days, and the book remained her constant companion in Berlin.[59] She sent Pasternak copies of her own *Verses to Blok* (*Stikhi k Bloku*) and *Parting* (*Razluka*) and also enquired about his own plans to visit Germany, doubtless thinking they would soon meet. It was not to be: she left Berlin for Prague at the end of July 1922, nearly a month before Pasternak reached Germany. But the circuit of communication was completed, and in the next few years they were to exchange many letters and poetic dedications.

In the summer of 1921 while living with the Puritz family in Vspolny Lane, Pasternak met the 22-year-old artist Evgeniya Vladimirovna Lurye, who early the following year became his wife. She was of Jewish stock, well educated, small and fine-featured. Recalling first impressions of her, Pasternak described how

a smile rounded the chin of the young artist like a small loaf, suffusing her eyes and cheeks with light. And then, as though from the sun, she screwed up her eyes in a brief and cloudy squint, like someone shortsighted or suffering from a weak chest. When the flood of her smile reached her beautiful open forehead, causing her pliant features to shift increasingly between a circle and an oval, one was reminded of the Italian Renaissance. Illuminated by her smile from within, she was highly reminiscent of one of Ghirlandaio's female portraits. At such times one wanted to bathe in her face. And since she always needed this illumination in order to be lovely, she required happiness in order to appeal.

(II, 343–4; *VP*, 480)

Evgeniya Lurye came from a one-time wealthy Jewish merchant family from Mogilev Province. Early in the First World War they had removed to Petrograd, where her parents, brother and married elder sister had settled. After first attending Higher Women's Courses in Moscow, Evgeniya studied painting successively under artists David Shterenberg, Robert Falk, Pyotr Konchalovsky and Ilya Mashkov at Vkhutemas. She eventually graduated from there in 1929. Eager to establish herself professionally, in the early 1920s she gave art lessons to the daughter of an actor at Moscow Arts Theatre and also earned money at home by ruling lines in cash books and ledgers (*sic*). Her meeting with Pasternak occurred through the Shtikhs. They first met at a party to celebrate Misha Shtikh's safe return from the Civil War. While cut off in

25 Evgeniya Pasternak (1922–23)

the Crimea, Shura Shtikh's younger brother had met Evgeniya's girl cousin, and she had asked him to look up Evgeniya when back in Moscow. Owing to Boris' otherwise lonely bachelor life after his parents and sisters' departure, and because of the fairly informal relations in literary and artistic circles, their friendship developed rapidly. She regularly visited Pasternak, who allowed her to take away and use his father's remaining paints. Stella Adelson, who shared the Volkhonka apartment, later recalled seeing Pasternak carry Evgeniya into the communal kitchen on his shoulders in a flush of youthful amorous exuberance. Shortly afterwards, at her Rozhdestvensky Boulevard lodgings, Pasternak met Evgeniya's brother Senya, who was apparently surprised by his sister's intimacy with a somewhat 'otherworldly' young poet. She was summoned home to Petrograd to explain the situation, and a letter from Boris followed. It was perhaps less poetic than earlier missives to his unresponsive *inamorate*, but its sentiments were eloquent enough:

Wednesday, 22.XII.21

Zhenichka, I shall not make a cult of your absence, I believe I am not thinking of you, and this is my first 'calm' day for the last month.

Yet all day today, since yesterday, my heart has been beating irregularly, as if these palpitations were imitating something of yours, something precious and calm – perhaps that goldfish evasiveness with which you start singing 'Ah, the bird is caught . . .'

The weather has been like this too, and so have my encounters. Which means without noise or drama. But both in sound and soul, I am filled with you and ache for you.

Zhenichka, Zhenichka, Zhenichka, Zhenichka! Ah, it were better I never lose this feeling. It is like a conversation with you, murmuring profoundly, dripping mutely, secretly – and true. One walks about, and in one's heart one involuntarily leafs through something a thousand pages long, like a book, but without reading and too lazy to read it. I would never part with this feeling and would never write you, were it not for your precious hairpin. As I tidied up I moved the settee, and it pinged on the floor, and again I heard 'Ah, the bird . . .' Don't be angry with me, my treasure. From a distance this probably sounds like stupid and oily sentiment, but that is because it doesn't lend itself to words. Your voice, left behind in the corners of this silence, is more mine than yours. It is distant and dark, most precious, and more mine. Write and tell me how you arrived. Did you have to change? I sense there was no heating, despite the man who looked at you through blue-tinted spectacles. Do you remember how I shuddered when you rebuked me for my rose-tinted ones? Ah, my dear darling!

This constant firewood! They brought more of it this morning at nine o'clock. By mistake perhaps? It gradually piles up. Someone is sending it because of his distraction – having caught it from me. In the mornings I am transported to some forest, snowed-up, still full of sleep, damp, a mixture of trees, more aspen than birch. And the peasant delivery men in the mornings are right: I am in the woods, really lost in the woods without you. Majestically dark, uniformly enthralling. That is you. But I have to get out of these woods, and by several paths at once. And I shall. Meanwhile you breathe your air of home and family. My joy, just you work, relax, and look how Petersburg shimmers, smokes and works magic round about you, completing what Blok began. And write, write to me if you can. I kiss you, long, long and tenderly.

My dear Zhenyurochka, what am I to do, and what am I to call this magnetism and saturation with the melody of you other than the distraction you compel, and which I would dispel – like one lost in the woods.[60]

Despite the emotional eloquence of this letter, Pasternak evidently (as he recalled in retrospect) tried hard not to repeat the mistakes of his earlier affairs. Perhaps at some effort, he refrained from 'using' Evgeniya merely as a target for his monologues or as a launching-pad for lonely flights of poetic fantasy. Indeed there is a surprising and almost complete absence of verse addressed to Zhenya. Self-restraint, however, seemed to work and their relationship blossomed. Following his letter

Pasternak himself arrived in Petrograd. (A letter to Bryusov of 12 January 1922 announced a forthcoming trip for a week or two without disclosing the reason.) Evgeniya's mother evidently desired a synagogue wedding for her daughter – a proposition to which Pasternak acceded only reluctantly. (An interesting reflection of his attitude to Jewish culture was contained in a letter he wrote in late 1922 to his brother, encouraging his partnership with Irina Nikolaevna Vilyam. The fact that she was a non-Jew, he opined, made their match all the better, for in their hearts if not in their heads Jews liked Russians more than 'their own sort'.[61] Pasternak's distaste for Jewish religious ceremony emerged also in November 1928, when Evgeniya's mother died; as he told cousin Olya, 'For the first time in my life I saw how they bury Jews, and it was awful.')[62]

In a post-Revolutionary situation when traditional social institutions were being questioned or abandoned, many women were enjoying their emancipation and even civil registration of marriage was by no means automatic. Despite his conservatism and 'Tolstoyan' morality, for instance, Aleksandr Pasternak never registered his marriage with Irina Vilyam till the 1960s; Mandelstam's partnership with Nadezhda was never formalised, and such instances were many. Evgeniya Pasternak for her part was anxious to pursue an independent artistic career and was not even keen to take her husband's name. Within a year she admitted to Chernyak's wife a sense of impermanence about their marriage; despite her charm and refinement, her desire for independence sometimes created difficulties and she was also jealous of her husband and his friends (something about which Bobrov and Loks complained). All this notwithstanding, in late February 1922 Boris and Evgeniya were wedded in Petrograd according to civil and Jewish religious rite. After their marriage they visited all her relatives in Petrograd and he took her to see the Marguliuses and eventually also the Freidenbergs. 'She liked us and we liked her,' cousin Olya recorded. 'Borya would come to see us, always seized by a strange tenderness towards me, and together with him there always burst in an atmosphere of great kinship, festivity and inner lyricism [...] he told us about Zhenya and brought her to see us and lavished such tenderness on her that she blushed.'[63]

New family links with Petrograd encouraged a gradual resumption of relations with the Freidenbergs after the antagonism of 1921; these ties also further underpinned Pasternak's links with the literary community of Petrograd throughout the 1920s.

꽃‑꽃‑꽃‑꽃‑

In 1921 and thereafter, Pasternak often invited his literary confrères back to his Volkhonka residence, when there would be recitations, drink, discussion, and sometimes music. A typical occasion in spring of 1922 was recalled by Vilmont: the guests included Shura Shtikh and his wife Tatyana Sergeyevna, Sergei Bobrov, the Anisimovs, Konstantin Loks (who now taught at Bryusov's Literary Institute where Vilmont was studying), and later on Boris' brother and Irina, with Mayakovsky and Bolshakov putting in an appearance right at the end. There was evidently animated discussion of issues that still rankled from the pre-war years. Vilmont wondered at this, but despite its inflammable potential the same group survived many evenings together at one another's houses.[64]

Despite his own limited creative output in early 1922, Pasternak was busy promoting literature both by himself and others. On 2 January he spoke at a Union of Writers' meeting at which Pilnyak's new story *The Snowstorm* (*Myatel'*) was read. (Pilnyak was about to leave for Berlin. Pasternak had already helped bring his work – notably the novel *The Naked Year* [*Golyi god*] – to Gorky's attention, and his friendship with Pilnyak was to become important in the later 1920s.) The editor of *Pechat' i revolyutsiya*, Vyacheslav Polonsky, also prevailed on Pasternak to give various poetry readings. Artist and photographer Lev Gornung recalled Pasternak's appearance in the House of the Press in March. Afterwards, seated on a settee, the poet held court with his new wife and regaled a semi-circle of young admirers with conversation cast in an obscure shower of metaphors, and punctuated with droning and humming and a ready smile.[65] E. F. Kunina, Loks' student from the Bryusov Institute (and later the companion of his old age), was among the audience and persuaded Pasternak to repeat his performance for her student friends on 13 April at the Turgenev Reading Room.

Some of Pasternak's circle were also able to throw light on his first contact with Trotsky, which took place soon after the publication of *My Sister Life* in June of 1922. Shortly before leaving on a visit to his relatives in Berlin, Pasternak and his wife threw a farewell party at the Volkhonka residence, where the guests included the Shtikhs and Anisimovs, Loks, Bobrov, Aleksandr Pasternak and his wife, and her brother Nikolai. Apart from Pasternak's wife, brother and sister-in-law, the company was fairly tipsy. Feeling the worse for his drink, Nikolai Vilmont did not return home to Mashkov Lane but stayed overnight with the Pasternaks and thus witnessed the intriguing events of the next day. In the morning came a telephone call from the Revolutionary Military Council. It was Trotsky ringing to summon Pasternak for an interview at 1 p.m. that day. Pasternak rinsed his mouth with cold black coffee, doused his head with water, and dressed himself up in a white shirt and newly pressed blue jacket before being whisked away by an official motorbike and sidecar. Details of the ensuing interview are known partly from Vilmont's report of what he heard when Pasternak returned about 3 p.m. and partly from Pasternak's account in a letter to Bryusov. The audience lasted about half an hour. *Inter alia*, Trotsky sought to verify Pasternak's philosophical position as that of an idealist pupil of Hermann Cohen and the Marburg school. Part of the conversation turned on *My Sister Life*. Trotsky was at that time engaged in various literary researches for articles in *Pravda*. The following year he brought out a book on *Literature and Revolution* (*Literatura i revolyutsiya*) which significantly made no mention of Pasternak. Trotsky evidently made heavy weather of reading Pasternak's verse. One exchange, which in Vilmont's account ended the conversation, was as follows: 'Trotsky: Yesterday I began struggling through the dense shrubbery of your book. What were you trying to express in it?' – Pasternak: 'That is something to ask the reader. You decide for yourself.' – Trotsky: 'Oh well, in that case I'll carry on struggling. It's been nice to meet you, Boris Leonidovich.'[66] Pasternak's letter to Bryusov, written shortly after the conversation, provided more details:

He chatted with me for more than half an hour about literary subjects. It is a pity that I had to do most of the talking. I wanted more to listen to him. But the need for me to make my pronouncements arose not just from the two or three questions that he put [. . .] The need for such explanations arose directly from my prospects abroad, which were pregnant with possible misinterpretations, distortions of the truth, and disillusions on the part of the person leaving. Referring to *My Sister Life* and one or two other things he knew, he asked me why I 'refrained' from reacting to social themes. Altogether he captivated and quite enraptured me. And it should be said that from his point of view he was perfectly right to ask me the questions he did. My answers and explanations amounted to a defence of true individualism, as a new social cell in a new social organism.

Put more simply, I began with a tentative affirmation that I *was* contemporary [*sovremenen*] and that even the French Symbolists, as contemporaries of the decay of the bourgeoisie, thereby belonged to our time and not to the history of the lower middle class [*meshchanstvo*]: if they had shared its decay with the latter, they would have been reconciled with the literature of Hugo's period and would have silently and contentedly perished without any acute experience or creative self-expression. I limited myself to general propositions and warnings about my future works that had been conceived even more individualistically.[67]

Pasternak afterwards regretted not having pointed out to Trotsky the one obvious sense in which *My Sister Life* was a 'revolutionary' work. (His afterthoughts outlined to Bryusov are quoted above, p.288).

Probably the pretext for Trotsky's summons was Pasternak's imminent departure for Germany and the possibility that he might not be returning. Certainly there is evidence that Pasternak was at this time plagued by doubts and worries concerning his fate as a writer in Moscow. Rita Rait, for instance, recalled his visit to her on 25 June 1922, when he insisted on walking with her for hours through the streets and treating her to a 'troubled confusion of complaints, regret, confession, apocalyptic incomprehensibility and incoherent regrets and grievances'.[68] Pasternak and his wife no doubt considered the prospect of a prolonged absence: they took with them several of Evgeniya's pictures and a large part of their library and other property, which forced them to travel by the cheaper sea route instead of by train. But there were other reasons for desiring an immediate, albeit short-term visit to Berlin: Pasternak wanted to see his family again and introduce his new wife, and he also hoped that the change of scene would offer stimulus and conditions for serious creativity. Despite his flurry of publications, recent output had not been impressive. As he told Yurkun in mid-June, this was now the 'fifth year in which I have done nothing', and he outlined a plan to go abroad for about six months: 'Probably I shall settle somewhere in Marburg or Göttingen [...] I shall of course keep well away from the literary ballyhoo in Berlin, into which I have reluctantly and unwittingly been drawn,' he wrote.[69] To secure the conditions for writing, Pasternak was willing to risk that critical attention to his work might wane. To Bryusov on the eve of embarkation, he wrote:

I am going away to Germany for half a year, or a full year if I can. I am going to work. The same inability to live gives me no opportunity to divide my time between work and non-work in the way that Moscow requires. That is why I am going. I realise that outwardly I shall spoil things for myself, since undoubtedly during my absence they will push me downhill just as they launched me without asking to a perfectly arbitrary altitude, which I neither deserved nor understood.[70]

Pasternak's planned visit to Germany was to serve other useful purposes. Under the restored free market conditions of NEP and the Russo-German trade agreement, a number of publishers had opened offices in both Moscow and Berlin. The security of international copyright was thus possible, and was achieved by publication in both cities under the imprint of such houses as Grzhebin and Helikon. In

Berlin, Pasternak was able to see *My Sister Life* into its second edition with Grzhebin, and to place *Themes and Variations* with Helikon. He also managed to interest Abram Vishnyak, Helikon's director, in Sergei Bobrov's second novel *The Iditol Specification (Spetsifikatsiya iditola)*.[71]

The issue of a visa was probably a routine matter, handled via Lunacharsky and Narkompros. Financially, though, it was a strain, overcome in the manner of the times by raising loans, from Nikolai Vilmont and from Pasternak's old friend Zbarsky, who now held a prestigious scientific post at the Karpov Institute and came to his aid with three million roubles. (Pasternak later wrote his brother from Berlin, telling him to repay this sum – the equivalent of $64 – as soon as fee payments came through from Voronsky, including, probably, remuneration for two poems in the February issue of *Krasnaya nov'*.) Pasternak raised some advances for future contributions to the newly established publishing enterprise 'Krug' (The Circle),[72] and to *Izvestiya*; Polonsky also granted an advance for various freelance articles which Pasternak would send from Berlin. (In fact Pasternak wrote nothing of the sort and in January 1923 returned the money via a Narkompros representative in Berlin.)[73]

Armed with papers and borrowed money, Pasternak and his wife left Moscow by train. With all the formalities of departure (export licences for pictures, military censorship, and customs) there was little time to spare in Petrograd. Not having seen Bryusov before departure, Pasternak wrote to him and sent a dedicated copy of *My Sister Life*. But there was no opportunity for a poetry reading in Petrograd, and little chance to visit friends. The only person Pasternak made a special point of seeing was Kuzmin, to thank him for the flattering review of his prose. They sailed on 17 August. As the ship left the harbour Anna Akhmatova came down to the wharf to wave their party off.[74] Pasternak's short poem recording their exit from port into the Gulf of Finland contained little hint of what proved to be a very stormy voyage. Evgeniya apparently suffered badly and the only good sailors, who spent most of their time standing on deck, turned out to be Pasternak, the artist Margarita Sabashnikova (a guest of the Tsetlins' in January 1918) and the avant-garde composer Artur Lurye (or Lourié). The latter had been head of the Narkompros Music Section (*MUZO*) until dismissed in January 1921, and for a time he had been living with Akhmatova. Both he and Sabashnikova were heading for permanent exile.[75]

Docking at Stettin, the Pasternaks travelled on to Berlin by rail. Accommodation had been arranged in advance and they moved straight into second floor lodgings in the Pension Fansaneneck, at 41 Fasanen-strasse, a street with a several family guesthouses of a type preferred by many of the Russian émigré population.[76]

Berlin was a pleasant haven after the difficulties and hardships of Revolution and Civil War. Pasternak reported to his brother in amazement on 'the absolute, almost transcendental cheapness here', and incredulously reeled off the prices of a suit, and board and lodging, and so on. Lower costs and better conditions, as well as amenities like vacuum cleaners and gas cookers, had made a great difference to Pasternak's parents, who seemed rejuvenated in their new setting.[77] But life was not without its insecurities. By the autumn of 1921 the Pasternaks had no doubt observed what Ehrenburg also noted:

The Germans lived as though at a railroad station. Nobody knew what the morrow would bring. The newspaper vendors were shouting 'Berliner Zeitung! Late final! Communist action in Saxony! Putsch planned in Munich!' People silently read the paper and went to work. Shop owners changed their price tags daily. The mark was falling. Along the Kurfürstendamm wandered droves of foreigners who bought up for a song the remnants of a former luxury. It seemed as if everything must collapse, but factory chimneys still smoked, bank clerks still painstakingly wrote out cheques running into many figures, prostitutes carefully applied their rouge, journalists wrote about famine in Russia or the noble heart of Ludendorff, and schoolboys swotted up the chronicle of Germany's former victories . . .[78]

Germany's economic crisis was deepening and by 1925 unemployment was to drive half the Russian émigrés to other Western lands. But in 1922–3 their numbers in Germany were estimated at half a million; in Berlin the majority were living in the south-west suburbs of Charlotten-burg, Friedenau, Wilmersdorf and Schönenberg. There were innumerable Russian societies, football and tennis teams, publishers, restaurants and the inevitable literary and artistic cafés, where every hue of political opinion was represented. Specially noted as cultural centres were the Café Leon on Nollendorfplatz (just round the corner from the Paster-naks), the Prager Diele on Pragerplatz, and the Café Landgraf, where every Sunday in 1922–3 the Russian Club met as an expatriate branch of Petrograd's House of the Arts.[79]

It is not easy to plot details of Pasternak's life in Russian Berlin, despite the fact that against his wishes and better judgement he was drawn into the 'literary ballyhoo'. His autobiographies shed no light on his activities, and his correspondence is insufficient to reconstruct a coherent picture. Caught up in the fringe of literary society, he kept a fairly low profile and figured only in the margins of some memoirs of that period.[80]

Evidently he visited Ida Vysotskaya two or three times. She and her husband Emmanuel Feldzer were now committed to a life of exile. She recalled telling Pasternak the story of her own departure from Russia via Siberia, and his having appeared to her to be extremely unhappy. Doubtless, all this reflected worries about his status in Berlin and the unknown fate that awaited should he return to Russia.[81] Contrary to some accounts, Pasternak fraternised equally with declared permanent exiles as well as those intending to return.[82] At Zinovii Grzhebin's publishing office on 25 September he attended a meeting with Vengerov, Bely, Otsup and Khodasevich to discuss arrangements for the thirty-year anniversary of Gorky's professional career, and presumably he was present at the actual celebration on 1st October. Nina Berberova recollected seeing Pasternak during September at the Café Landgraf and the Prager Diele. Sometimes he was at Berberova's and Khodasevich's several days in a row and allegedly made a special point of turning up when Bely was present. Together they all went to see *Pierrette's Veil* by Arthur Schnitzler on 26 September. Evidently the Pasternaks saw in the new year of 1923 together with Roman Jakobson, the folklorist Pyotr Bogatyryov and his wife, Grzhebin and Andrei Bely.[83] Aleksandr Bakhrakh (the first reviewer of *Themes and Variations* when it appeared in 1923) paid Pasternak several visits at his Pension and also met him at an evening party at the artist Ivan Puni's. He also observed Pasternak at regular weekly literary gatherings, 'although he himself performed rarely': Even when sitting and exchanging remarks with his neighbours, Pasternak apparently introduced a special seriousness to all meetings.[84]

Pasternak also saw plenty of Ehrenburg. The two held one another in great affection. Ehrenburg described Pasternak as 'my favourite of all brothers in our craft'; Pasternak was fond of Ehrenburg's personal qualities, however, rather than his friend's literary talent. Ehrenburg witnessed some of Pasternak's meetings with Mayakovsky when the latter came to Berlin in autumn of 1922. Mayakovsky's visit was partly social, but officially it was to give performances and readings and arrange the Berlin edition of his works. Despite their continuing friendship, he and Pasternak were known to have been in public disagreement. Ehrenburg noted: 'After one of their tiffs Mayakovsky and Pasternak met in Berlin. And the reconciliation was just as stormy and passionate as the rupture.' Ehrenburg apparently spent the entire day with them: 'We went to a café, then had dinner, then sat in the café again. Boris Leonidovich recited his verses. In the evening Mayakovsky performed at the House of the Arts and recited his *Backbone-Flute* turning to face Pasternak.' Pasternak's own hypnotic recitation of verse from *My Sister Life* on the same occasion has also been vividly recorded by Vadim Andreyev. Andreyev also offers a characteristic portrait of Pasternak in Berlin: invariably clad in a crumpled baggy navy jacket and loosely knotted scarlet tie, Pasternak displayed handsome features, wide bright gaze and a 'black bonfire of hair', and most striking of all was his 'frozen energy (suspended only for a moment), the power of his cheekbones, the sweep of his forehead, the firmness of his strong, stone-carved mouth'.[85]

There are no more detailed records of Mayakovsky and Pasternak's dealings. After a brief trip to Paris, Mayakovsky finally left Berlin for Moscow on 13 December 1922. By that time they had sown the seeds of a new rapprochement, perhaps encouraged by the nostalgia and unnatural pressures of an émigré atmosphere, and when Pasternak returned in the second half of March 1923 he immediately became involved in Mayakovsky's projects for a Futurist revival.

By the time he reached Berlin again after the Revolution, Andrei Bely was in a severely unbalanced state. Deserted by his first wife, disenchanted with Rudolf Steiner's movement, and uncertain whether to remain or stay, he was evidently 'drinking and dancing his way through every Berlin café'. When Pasternak arrived, the two of them spent time together, although Bely's tastes and mental condition were hardly conducive to a close artistic sympathy. After a poetry reading by Pasternak, Nina Berberova recalled how Bely 'complained to Khodasevich that he got to the essence only with difficulty, but when he reached it the essence turned out to be uninteresting [...] "And you end up with nothing!" Bely apparently screamed in the middle of Viktoria-Luise-Platz.'[86]

The verses in question were no doubt from *Themes and Variations*, which came out in book form at the very beginning of January with the Helikon Press. (Prior to this a contract of 25 May 1921 with Gosizdat had been cancelled and in January 1922 Pasternak had got them to renounce their rights in favour of Grzhebin's better equipped private publishing house.) The author's intentions in *Themes and Variations* and the public reaction were sometimes ludicrously at variance, and they indicated the gulf separating even the 'post-Futurist' Pasternak from the mainly Symbolist-Acmeist attunement of émigré readers. 'The book is

307

out,' Pasternak wrote to Bobrov on 9 January 1923, and he apologised for having possibly purloined its title ('Themes and Variations' was chosen at very short notice in Berlin). 'Personally,' Pasternak admitted, 'I do not like the book. It has been run into the ground by striving for comprehensibility.' One week later he wrote to Bobrov again: 'They all like me and single me out, but [. . .] "cannot understand me". I suddenly turn out to be a cubist (?!)'. A footnote explained: 'I quote from Bely, Khodasevich and Gorky – they have 'laboured' over *Themes and Variations* and have retreated in the face of its utter incomprehensibility.'[87]

The émigré public's insensitivity to many of his virtues and the rumour campaign concerning his supposed 'incomprehensibility' became a sore point with Pasternak. (In Khodasevich's case, in particular, rejection of his work was fired by a personal animus at Pasternak's refusal to defend him against a negative critique of his work by Aseyev.)[88] All this probably helped persuade Pasternak that his public, if it existed, was in Moscow rather than in Western Europe. It was a similar lack of a sympathetic émigré readership that blighted Tsvetaeva's career in the later 1920s, and Nabokov in 1927 held Pasternak responsible for her infelicities:

In Russia there is a fairly talented poet called Pasternak. His verse is convex, goitrous and goggle-eyed, as though his muse suffered from Basedow's disease. He is crazy about clumsy imagery, sonorous but literal rhymes and clattering metre. His syntax is really depraved [. . .] It is difficult to enthuse about Pasternak: he has a somewhat poor knowledge of Russian, expresses his thoughts clumsily and the incomprehensibility of much of his verse is not at all explained by the profundity or complexity of the thought itself [. . .] To imitate such a poet is a fearful thing. One fears for Marina Tsvetaeva . . .[89]

The Pasternaks' original visas were for an absence of three months only, but when they ran out in November, they were automatically extended. Although Pasternak had not settled immediately to work, he evidently held out hopes of doing so in Berlin – or in any setting other than a cramped Moscow apartment. In a letter of November 1922 to his brother he wrote that he would return to the Volkhonka to live only if he could find nowhere else. Ideally, he claimed, he would like to go back to Moscow in the spring or summer of 1923 for a month and then come to Berlin again for a year. If that plan failed, then he would probably try settling in Petrograd or even somewhere in the outback, like Kasimov, or in Siberia. The letter continued:

You cannot imagine how difficult it has been for me even mentally to reconstruct that world outside which I am not fated to think or work. Only recently, only in the third month of our life here have I started little by little to recall the outlines of that anarchically enclosed atmosphere. Gradually I am entering into it, since only within it can I derive some stimulus to activity.[90]

Like everyone else in Berlin, Pasternak announced that he had written nothing for the last five years. But at least the idleness of Berlin was beginning more to resemble that of pre-1917, that is, it was different in quality and was perhaps now one of choice and thus held a promise of imminent relief. Meanwhile Evgeniya had started painting and Leonid Pasternak was 'pleased with her', and evidently considered her 'basically more talented than Goldinger'.[91] While in Berlin, she had hoped to go on and study further in Paris, but this scheme was not followed up. As his own industry and inspiration hung fire, however, Boris occupied his time reading Charles Dickens in Russian translation and studying books on Einstein's theory of relativity.

Around the new year of 1923 came some form of creative release. A letter of early January told Bobrov that recently he had settled down to continue work on the prose tale, three chapters of which had been published the previous spring. Once Pasternak had struck the correct 'tone', he planned also to resume polishing the novel whose opening had appeared as *Zhenya Luvers' Childhood*. The stimulus for this was credited partly to Boris Zaitsev, and partly to Polonsky. To the latter he explained in detail what he meant by 'striking the tone', an account reminiscent of the inner 'music' or rhythmic impetus described by Blok and other modern poets as a feature of the state of inspiration. In his reliance on this, Pasternak felt that he differed from colleagues around him:

I look all around me, I keep watch on myself, and I am immediately ready to come to two conclusions. No one alive at present experiences art in its specific demand upon the author with the same acuity as I do. And probably no one is quite so untalented as I am. Everyone is doing something, everyone is writing something, or writing about something, and with two or three exceptions everyone is worthy of his fellow. But I am not in a fit state to share either this work – easy and honourable though it is – or this good fortune. There is a special tone particular to me alone. And how little I valued it while I was being ravaged by it! Until I have entered it I am incapable of using even the impoverished circle of modest sensation accessible to any mediocre contemporary – most often to a philistine. And for as long as this obsession disappears, I seem to switch off completely from the whole of ordinary life. But the other day, after a five-year absence, these flashes seemed to start flickering again in the pupils of my eyes. Until this recent joy I longed to return home more than once. But now I shall wait a little. I started developing one extract, but this experiment has led me into the tone of a large work (a novel) I once abandoned. If I manage to preserve this hypnotic state while I do this small task, then I shall continue on the novel. How dreadful that this internal hiss and rumble is a *sine qua non* for my existence.[92]

Despite this welcome new access of inspiration, Pasternak, in fact, completed no prose writing in Berlin, and the flow of poetry too was sparse and produced only a handful of lyrics. (Dating probably from this period was a short series of poems including 'Butterfly-storm' ['Babochka-burya'] which eventually appeared in *Over the Barriers* [1929].) And, in fact, on returning to Russia, Pasternak's prose and poetry took off in a 'revolutionary' direction which could only have been indirectly connected with what he worked on in Berlin.[93]

Finally, despite his new creative impulse, Pasternak decided to return home rather than stay on in Berlin. Lazar Fleishman's study of Pasternak in the 1920s offers evidence for his supposed 'renunciation of emigration'.[94] But Pasternak could not as yet be aware that he was eventually to be 'deprived of Europe' or that emigration would soon mean permanent exile; in early 1923 he believed simply that the right place for him as an artist was in Russia. His return was not a 'moral' decision, or a bitter commitment to share his country's fate. There were not the binding tragic overtones of Akhmatova's rejection of that inner voice which in 1917 already called on her to 'forsake you distant, sinful land, / Leave Russia now forever.'[95]

None of this is to deny that Pasternak weighed up seriously the question of staying in Germany. With the tide of emigration still continuing and even a favoured figure like Gorky choosing to remain abroad, there were obvious grounds for all manner of doubts. Pasternak never wrote or spoke publicly about the problem at the time; only in 1936 did he hint laconically in a speech that while abroad he was 'confronted with the chance of finding some new biography for myself'.[96] But various people have recalled his reflections and hesitations, including the secretary of Grzhebin, Nadezhda Zalshupina, dedicatee of a little poem called 'Gleisdreieck', dated 30 January 1923.[97]

There were thus several moments in Pasternak's decision to return to Russia: increasing distaste for the literary life in Berlin, awareness of his own eccentricity in its midst, and an appreciation of certain positive prospects in Moscow. Concerning the former, one of Pasternak's letters to Nikolai Vilmont towards the end of his stay provided eloquent evidence:

As the result of a long series of 'civilian' quarrels and fights, without which émigré life seemingly cannot exist, and after being spared and left out of all this through my childishness and insignificance, which everyone silently forgave me,

I have suddenly been noticed, roused and summoned into action. I was barely able to get away from it, and only at the price of retreating into a solitude which is now already complete and, I fear, final. This is going to expedite my return.[98]

The triviality of Berlin literary life was emphasised by Pasternak's new bout of creativity. His restlessness and sense of purpose contrasted with his surroundings and were noticed by Viktor Shklovsky, who within a year followed him back to Moscow:

Pasternak is always straining away somewhere, but not hysterically – he pulls like a powerful mettlesome horse. He walks about but would really like to rush along throwing his feet out in front of him [. . .] It seems to me he senses among us the absence of any drawing power [*tyaga*]. We are refugees – no, we are fugitives who have become sedentary.
For the time being.
Russian Berlin is not going anywhere. It has no destiny.
No drawing power.[99]

Small wonder, therefore, that Pasternak characterised Berlin as 'unnecessary to me, lacking quality, and supernumerary'.[100] If Berlin repelled him from the West, there was a complementary attraction back to Moscow. Sergei Budantsev had written on 30 January 1923, saying:

Come and join us. Such publishing houses have opened up shop here – it's splendid!
First of all there is 'Krug'.* They pay in gold at the Commissariat of Finance rate. Boris Pilnyak is coming from Kolomna with such a store of magisterial goodwill that vapours can be observed in the air from the tears welling up in the eyes of us contributors. He is our chief editor. But joking apart, it is possible to work in Moscow. And your absence from Moscow in my honest opinion is having a harmful effect on your celebrity back home.[101]

Similar pressures to return must also have come earlier from Mayakovsky. The Berlin newspaper *Nakanune* (On the Eve) reported a speech by him on 18 November 1922: 'One can only be a Russian poet, Mayakovsky said, when living in Russia and with Russia. Let those authors who have settled down abroad not think of coming riding into Moscow on the white steed of their works in many volumes.'[102] Mayakovsky's rejection of the Berlin emigration was, of course, more vehemently political than Pasternak's. But part of his argument at least reinforced Pasternak's sense that as a Russian artist he could lead a purposeful existence only inside his native country and language.

* The first two issues of the new 'Krug' (Circle) miscellany for 1923 contained the poems of the 'Theme and Variations' (*Tema s variatsiyami*) cycle.

Whatever the disadvantages of Berlin, life there was doubtless much easier than in the starving province of Hesse. After opting to stay on in Berlin, his plans for any early trip to Marburg fell through when Evgeniya became ill. In September 1922 they spent a refreshing day and a half in Weimar, but it was only in early February of 1923, shortly before they finally left Berlin that the two of them went away for a week, visiting Kassel and the Harz, and spending a couple of days in Marburg. Pasternak later felt guilty at failing to make Evgeniya aware of what the town had meant to him. But Marburg had changed since 1912. Cohen was dead, and the people were cold and hungry; recent history all seemed reflected in the stark, wintry view from the room where he had lodged as a student. Frau Ort and her daughter were still there, sitting and sewing as they had done eleven years before, and as Guy de Mallac's researches reveal, they were deeply touched to receive a large walnut cake which Pasternak had delivered to them by a local confectioner after his departure.[103]

On 12 March Leonid Pasternak made his last live portrait of his eldest son (see Figure 27). Neither of them suspected it was their last meeting. The Pasternak parents regarded their Berlin residence as only temporary, and Boris himself had plans to visit them again within the next year. By this time Evgeniya was three months pregnant, and her own sickness and desire to return to familiar surroundings for the birth were a final decisive factor in favour of a return to Russia. On 18 March they therefore took the train for Moscow.

With a new member of the family expected, the problem of living space in Moscow arose more acutely than before. Anticipating his return, Boris had written to his brother stating that he and his wife and child would require two rooms in the apartment – one in which he himself could work. While welcoming the prospect of Irina Vilyam moving in as Aleksandr's wife, he made an awkward issue of the Frishman-Adelson family's residence in the apartment which, he freely confessed to his brother, raised for him 'a purely anti-semitic theme'.[104] He had earlier suggested that Rita Rait or Shura Shtikh be offered one of the rooms. (Unlike the Frishman-Adelsons, Rait and Shtikh were totally Russified, 'assimilated Jews'.) The problem remained unsolved and caused strain and discontent. The Frishmans had no other home, so Boris' family had to make do with only one room in which to live, sleep and work.

Writing from Berlin, Pasternak had urged his brother to visit them there, and on returning to Moscow his stories of Germany and the life of their parents and sisters caused Aleksandr renewed anguish at their separation. Circumstances favoured Aleksandr's own visit to Germany, however. Successful completion and official approval of his first major architectural project, the Karpov Chemical Institute, led to his being recommended to assist Melnikov and Shchusev with the rapid construction of Lenin's Mausoleum on Red Square in January 1924. (The embalming of the corpse was supervised by Boris Zbarsky.) Aleksandr Pasternak provided a design for the interior of the building and he was rewarded with an exit permit valid for one year. That summer he therefore journeyed to Berlin himself. While in Germany he travelled extensively, visiting Bavaria first with his sister Lydia and later with Irina Vilyam who came out to join him. He found work in Berlin in the offices of the building and planning controller Berwald, and with their easily exportable architectural skills both he and his wife could have stayed there to work permanently. However, they finally returned to Moscow in autumn of 1925, strangely and, as it turned out, correctly persuaded that despite promises of further reunions they had seen his parents for the last time.[105] The journey to Berlin was Aleksandr Pasternak's last trip abroad.

12

Malady sublime *and the air of history*

Day by day I'm more ashamed
That in such an epoch of shades
A malady sublime
Is still called song.

Yet is 'song' the word for sheerest din
Mastered with effort by an earth
That rushed to abandon books
For bayonet and lance?

Hell is paved with good intentions.
But a view has now arisen
That if poetry's paved with them
All sins will be forgiven.

from Malady Sublime

৵৶৶৶

In early January of 1923 Mayakovsky received official sanction for a new journal which was to have a modernist and 'agitational' function, contrasting with the 'pure' aesthetics of Voronsky's *Krasnaya nov'*. Thus, at the end of March appeared the first issue of *LEF* (an acronym for *Levyi front iskusstv* – Left Front of the Arts). Three leading articles by Mayakovsky set out the programme of this new dispensation of Futurism. Its priorities included 'throwing off the clinging past' and forming a united front to 'blow up the old trash and fight to embrace new culture'. 'Working to strengthen the conquests of the October Revolution and reinforcing the new art, Lef will use our art to canvass the masses, obtaining organised authority among them.' The new group's designated opponents were 'those who preach a non-class, non-human art; those who subvert the dialectics of artistic labour with a metaphysics of prophecy and soothsaying [...] those who leave a loophole in art for idealistic outpourings about eternity and the soul.' The signatories below the first article were Aseyev, Brik, Kushner, Mayakovsky, Tretya-

315

kov and Chuzhak (although all three items were the exclusive work of Mayakovsky).[1]

Under this rubric Pasternak must have seemed a target for attack rather than a colleague. Even the role announced for him in the first issue of *LEF* seemed forced: he was described as representing 'the application of dynamic syntax to a revolutionary task', while the achievements of others were advertised as:

Aseyev. Experiment and verbal flight into the future.
Kamensky. Word play in all its soundary [*zvukal' nost'*] [...]
Mayakovsky. Experiment with polyphonic rhythm in the *poema* of broad socio-realistic scope [...][2]

Pasternak's part in such a programme is not readily conceivable, especially in view of his pre-Berlin discovery of more congenial spirits in Akhmatova, Kuzmin, Mandelstam and others. Nevertheless, according to the Lef secretary Neznamov, Pasternak was a regular visitor to their headquarters. Other members of the company (in addition to those already named) were artists Rodchenko, Lavinsky, Palmov and Levin; from the literary world came Rita Rait-Kovalyova, Arvatov, Kamensky, Kruchenykh, Shklovsky and Vinokur; from the cinema, Dziga Vertov and Eisenstein, with occasional callers from Petrograd such as Isaak Babel, or the poet Nikolai Tikhonov.[3]

The Lef headquarters in Vodopyany Lane were housed in an apartment shared by Mayakovsky and the Briks and were within hailing distance of Pasternak's old home in the former School of Painting (now Vkhutemas), in whose hostel the Aseyevs had found accommodation. Recollections of the apartment-cum-office confirm that far from being an editorial bureau (most of the technical work was done at the House of the Press) or a temple of the arts, it was mainly a social centre, with jollity and repartee, drinking and endless card games as its main activities.[4] Maybe it was partly this conviviality which attracted Pasternak. But one need only compare the Lefist programme with Pasternak's own recent *Propositions* on art to foresee differences of opinion: the 'murderous jargon' against which he had inveighed was readily wheeled out in June 1923 by Aseyev to credit him with successful 'organisation of speech' and 'intonation' in a review of *Themes and Variations*.[5] The second of these expressions remained a particular pet hatred of Pasternak.

All Pasternak's retrospective comments on Lef were negative and bound up with his complex-ridden relations with Mayakovsky. During the Civil War he had not understood Mayakovsky's 'propagandistic zeal, desire to force himself and his comrades on public awareness, his campaigning, workshop mentality and submission to the voice of topicality'. And now:

Even less could I comprehend the journal *LEF* which he ran, its panel of contributors, and the system of ideas it defended. The only consistent and honest man in the circle of negators was Sergei Tretyakov, who developed his abnegation to its natural conclusion. Along with Plato, Tretyakov believed that there was no room for art in the young socialist state, or at any rate not at the time of its inception. The mechanical pseudo-art that flourished in LEF – uncreative and spoilt by corrections to fit the times – was certainly not worth the care and efforts spent on it.   (II, 43; *VP*, 456)

Mayakovsky's contribution to the first issue of *LEF*, however, was a surprise. His long lyric *poema, About That* (*Pro eto*), seemed almost as if written in defiance of the official Lef programme. With its love theme and echoes of the old Mayakovsky of the 1910s, it dismayed some Lef diehards but no doubt encouraged Pasternak to believe that he and his friend still shared some common ground. The first number of *LEF* also contained lyric poems by Aseyev, Kamensky, Kruchenykh, Tretyakov and Khlebnikov, and Pasternak's own 'Kremlin in a Blizzard'. With its talk of the poet's re-education, the poem no doubt seemed an acceptable statement of new intent for the revolutionary age. For the second issue, as part of a group of occasional verses on the theme of 'May the First', Pasternak produced what Neznamov described as his 'first piece written with a special aim'. The banality of its climactic message about the unity of mankind and the poet and the worker standing side by side was redeemed by a certain routine professional 'originality'. Pasternak never reprinted it.[6]

It would be wrong, however, to think of Pasternak's artistic and social life as centred solely on Mayakovsky's circle in the early 1920s. He had other projects and commitments. In 1924 a joint scheme was discussed with Pilnyak and Bely for a new journal of *Tri Borisa* (Three Borises) which unfortunately was never realised. His wide circle of friends outside Lef included the poet and author Sergei Budantsev – a successful, opulent and vivacious raconteur and conversationalist according to Mindlin – and his wife, the poetess Vera Ilyina, a former member of Bobrov's 'Young Centrifuge' (Molodaya Tsentrifuga). A varied social picture surrounding Pasternak also emerges from the notes and memoirs left by artist and photographer Lev Gornung, and by Yakov and Elizaveta Chernyak. After reading Chernyak's sympathetic appraisal of

My Sister Life in *Pechat' i revolyutsiya*, Pasternak called in at the editorial offices to meet and thank him. After their return from Berlin in 1923 a family friendship with the Chernyaks blossomed, especially during the next three years. In the summer months of 1923 the Pasternaks had a *dacha* at the village of Kostino, near Bratovshchina, to the north of Moscow. They were visited there by the Chernyaks, and despite Evgeniya's pregnancy they all enjoyed walking together. Chernyak was originally from Vitebsk and was a pupil of the literary scholar Gershenzon. A man of compulsive enthusiasms, he was himself a connoisseur and writer of verse. His wife Elizaveta Borisovna was a former piano pupil of Genrikh Neigauz (Heinrich Neuhaus) in Kiev. She had hopes of introducing Pasternak to her teacher when the latter visited Moscow during the 1922–23 concert season. She correctly imagined the two men as kindred spirits. Their eventual meeting – without her agency – when the Neigauz family settled in Moscow was to have far-reaching consequences for Pasternak.[7]

The Chernyaks and Lev Gornung became frequent visitors to the apartment on the Volkhonka. The now unsalubrious conditions in which the Pasternaks lived began as one approached the house. Everyone, including Pasternak himself, used to cross and then recross the road to escape the distressing howls of experimental dogs kept in cages at a nearby Neurological Institute. And inside the now dilapidated house there were rats. They had plagued the residents since the Civil War and were eliminated only in the late 1920s, partly with the help of Samson, the house cat. In the communal flat the Pasternaks could entertain guests only in the ill-lit area of the former dining-room. The family's own private room contained beds, the black Bechstein grand and several 'Gothic' armchairs; its walls were lined with shelves of books and music and with pictures by Leonid Pasternak and Serov.

In the period up to 1925, two new figures among the Pasternaks' callers were the poet Dmitrii Petrovsky and his actress wife Maria Gonta. They were evidently an extravagant pair. Tall and dynamic, he was full of talk about the Civil War and, according to Elizaveta Chernyak, despite his talent seemed a carelessly flamboyant graphomaniac. Maria Gonta was an unusually striking beauty and also a good tailoress, and she had decked herself and her husband out in some bizarre clothing sewn partly from curtains and tablecloths! One of Petrovsky's poems 'Beethoven' ('Betkhoven') was dedicated to Pasternak, in recollection of his musical improvisations at one of their meetings (it subsequently acquired other dedicatees after the two eventually fell out).[8] Petrovsky and his wife lived in Myortvy Lane and themselves often entertained their close neighbours, the Anisimovs and Loks, as well as the Chernyaks and Pasternaks. Chernyak's diary recalls one such gathering in November 1923, when they heard recitations by their host and Varvara Monina. At another, on 19 December, held in Zbarsky's quarters in the Chemical Institute, those present included Bobrov, Pasternak, Loks, the poetess Ferrari, and Evgenii Lundberg (who struck Chernyak as a 'man of immense, cruel, and [...] dissolute [*razvratnogo*] self-esteem').[9]

In 1923–4 Pasternak is also recalled by Gornung as having formed part of a poetic circle around his former Musaget associate, Pyotr Zaitsev. On 23 November 1923, for instance, the Anisimovs played hosts in their wooden backyard dwelling in Myortvy Lane to a spartan bohemian company including Gornung, Zaitsev, the poet and author Sergei Zayaitsky and Pasternak; Anisimov read his translations of Morgenstern, and after tea Pasternak recited his *Malady Sublime* (*Vysokaya bolezn'*), which evidently sparked off an interesting discussion. A few days later, on 5 December, the same company met in Zaitsev's apartment, where Pasternak introduced Petrovsky. On 12 March the following year, Lev Gornung and his brother Boris together with the poets Aleksandr Romm, Sergei Zayaitsky and Sofia Parnok heard Pasternak read his newly completed story *Aerial Ways* (*Vozdushnye puti*). A few days later, on 21 March, the 'Zaitsev Circle' met again when Maksimilan Voloshin on his first visit to Moscow since 1917 recited some recent unpublished verse. (Normally resident in Koktebel on the Black Sea, he was now on the verge of being eliminated from the Soviet literary scene.)[10]

Pasternak's lyrics of the revolutionary period had been composed in an inspired condition later attributed also to Yurii Zhivago, when 'the main work was performed not by himself but by that which was higher than him and directed him – namely the state of world thought and poetry and that which was destined for it in the near future, the next step in the series which it was due to take in its historical development'. (*DZh*, 448) But in a world of ideological coercion and class struggle, the regainment of this state was either impossible or irrelevant. As in pre-Christian classical antiquity (presented symbolically in *Doctor Zhivago* as a prototype of Soviet reality), people now seemed responsive less to private lyrical expression than to the 'public' genres of myth, the ode and the epic.

Leningradskaya Pravda for 18 January 1925 carried a reflection by

Pasternak on the parlous state of modern lyricism, as part of his reply to a questionnaire:

You say that people have not stopped writing verse, although it is not printed, and people do not read verse when it is published. A valuable observation, although that is not what convinces me of the decline of poetry – we are writing large-scale pieces and are drawn into the epic. Yet this is a particular second-hand genre. Verses, whatever their virtues, no longer infect the air. The propagating medium of their sonority was personality. The old personality has been destroyed, and the new one has not yet formed. Without resonance lyricism is inconceivable. In brief, poetry is in a most lamentable state. In all this there is contained just one very consoling fact. It is simply fortunate that there is one area incapable of simulating maturity or prosperity in a period that is arbitrary to a degree and that develops with a constant view towards the new man [...] who himself is sick and changing, and from a propaganda slogan of the day is becoming the free motive force of the generation [...] Only poetry is not indifferent to whether the new man is constituted in reality or only in some journalistic fiction. That it believes in him is apparent from the fact that it still smoulders and glimmers. Yet from the fact that it is expiring it is clear that it is not content with appearances.

The sickness and demise of lyricism was alluded to by Pasternak several times as the 1920s continued. One of his later reflections to the poet Sergei Spassky outlined an unprecedented set of moral problems facing the lyric poet:

Contemporary life suggests to the lyricist neither a common language nor anything else. It does no more than tolerate him. He is a sort of extraterritorial entity within it.

This is why this aspect of creativity has left the circle of aesthetic concern. The general tone of expression [...] is decided by him himself [i.e. the lyricist] as a question of morality [...] whereas in a healthy age we would consider it *natural* to speak in this way or that, we now each in a different way consider it our *duty*, and one sees it in one thing, another in another. The reasons for all this lie outside ourselves. There is nothing we can do. It is stronger than us and our efforts.

This confrontation of ethical matters, going far beyond mere artistic integrity, was to emerge in all Pasternak's major writings of the 1920s and after. Meanwhile, as he told Spassky, lyricism was 'the rarest of rarities':

It sits within you, it sits there and is sick, because just now it can do no other than be sick. And exactly how this malady finds outward expression through you, as distinct from its symptoms in some other hospital ward – that is a question of utterly secondary significance.[11]

The affliction of lyricism described here was reflected in the very title of the poem *Malady Sublime* which Pasternak began in 1923.

Although Aleksandr Blok offered a somewhat equivocal, 'unheroic' portrayal of rampaging Red Guardsmen in *The Twelve* (1918), it was this poem more than any other work which established the epic genre or *poema* as a medium for capturing the panoramic sweep of a revolutionary age. In the 1920s prowess in the longer poetic forms became a matter of prestige for Russian poets. 'At the moment, to obtain an entire *poema* is itself an event of great importance,' Nikolai Tikhonov told Pasternak in early 1924. 'I am up to the ears in *poemy* and am working on three items simultaneously.'[12] Having already tried his hand at extended composi-tins during the First World War, Pasternak was susceptible to this shift of the generic centre of gravity. Moreover, the urge to expand into longer forms was felt not only by those such as Aseyev, Mayakovsky, Tikhonov and others who desired to portray recent history. Many manifestly lyrical (rather than heroic) *poemy* appeared in the early 1920s: Tsvetaeva's *Tsar-Maiden* (*Tsar'-devitsa*) and *Poem of the Hill* (*Poema gory*), Mandelstam's *Finder of a Horseshoe* (*Nashedshii podkovu*) and *Slate Ode* (*Grifel'naya oda*), as well as Mayakovsky's own *About That*. Maybe Pasternak was persuaded by such example. In a letter of February 1923 Tsvetaeva had told him:

You know, Pasternak, you should write a large piece. This will be your second life, your first and your only life...

Lyric verses [...] are individual moments of a *single* movement [...] Lyricism is a dotted line. From a distance it looks complete and black. But if you look closely, the constant breaks between [...] dots are an airless space: death. And from one verse to another you die...

In a book, though (whether a novel, *poema*, *even* an article!), this is not the case. It has its own laws.[13]

Another person who probably encouraged Pasternak's approach to larger-scale works was Vyacheslav Polonsky, the editor of *Pechat' i revolyutsiya* and later of *Novy mir*.

Pasternak's transfer to a new poetic idiom and mould did not come easily. His new poem, begun in late 1923 and published in the first issue of *LEF* for 1924, showed some of the features of his earlier impressionist poema sketches of 1916–17 – notably a tendency to grow an encrust-ation of imagery around an unnamed and sometimes barely identifiably thematic core. The critic Sinyavsky later described *Malady Sublime* as essentially 'a form of protracted lyrical digression, which starts out from certain elements of the age and tries to embrace it with epic breadth and reveal an image of the time by extra-thematic means – using metaphoric structures and changing vocal emphasis'.[14] Although the work approached epic proportions (379 lines), its opening sounded sceptical about the Homeric prototype and its Bolshevik revival:

> The Achaeans show tenacity.
> The siege continues, days go by,
> Months and years elapse.
> Then one fine day the pickets rush,
> Feet scarcely on the ground,
> And bring the news: the fortress surrenders.
> Belief, yet disbelief. And they light fires,
>
> They blow the vaults, they seek an entry,
> They exit, enter. Days elapse
> And months and years pass by.
> Then one fine day they bring the news:
> The epic has been born.
> Belief, yet disbelief. And they light fires,
> Await, impatient, the parade,
> Grow weak, turn blind, and days elapse,
> And the fortress is laid in ruins by the years.   (I, 391)

The distortion of poetry, or 'song' (*pesn'*), as hitherto understood and its affliction by the malady of the age was brought out unambiguously as the poem continued with the lines printed at the head of this chapter.[15]

Not surprisingly, the Graeco-Trojan reference and the antique parallels were viewed as a bizarre anachronism by other members of Lef. As Fleishman comments, the whole opening of the poem can in fact be read as a form of encoded polemic against the Lef concept of agitational civic verse and its ideology of 'good intentions'. The poet's unease with the modern epic persuaded Pasternak's colleagues that their collaboration was an anomaly. The archaic opening line became a standing joke with them (it was altered in later versions to: 'Before our gaze the shifting rebus flickers...') and Lef even appointed a 'commission' to examine the 'failure of Pasternak's poem, which, according to Chernyak, both incensed and dejected him.[16]

Pasternak's malaise was not simply from unfamiliarity with the genre, but from discomfort in the age it celebrated – an age which commanded:

> Wake up, poet, and show your permit.
> This is not the place for yawning.

At heart, of course, Pasternak's poet remained a lyricist, threatened by the looming epic:

> [...] Ah, epos, fortress,
> Why pose this riddle?
> Rhymes, where is your place?
> Where are you not to be discovered?
> We have our place since not for the first time
> Is the blizzard relieved by sentries
> And pickets have been posted in the epic.
> We have our place since terror in the theatre
> Sings to the stalls the same old song
> That once a tenor sang from score
> About the malady sublime.   (I, 398–9; *SP*, 653–4)[17]

Among the *realia* of the age used to flesh out the theme of the poem was the typhus epidemic of the Civil War period. This lent a further dimension to the poem's title. Also implied, however, was the moral typhus of a 'crumbling self-willed collapse' and a political illness that viewed everyone as either class enemies or allies:

> I was not born to look three times
> Into the eyes of men.
> Even more senseless than song
> Is the dull word 'foe'.
> As guest am I here. Another guest in every world
> Is the malady sublime.   (I, 395; *SP*, 340)

The only momentary positive response to what the poet had recently witnessed was a recollection of the Ninth Congress of Soviets in the Bolshoi Theatre in 1921. And the only heroic figure glimpsed was Maksim Gorky – but he and his 'rectilinear glance' were dismissed in a mere couplet. Longer episodes, though, emerged as a travesty of the epic genre, with a recurrent figure of the 'hero, idiot, *intelligent*'* from Pasternak's own milieu, who foresaw his own exit from the historical stage. An extension of this image contained a cryptic, almost prophetic polemic against Mayakovsky who in 1919 had produced illustrated pithy propaganda doggerels that were mounted in the display windows of the Russian Telegraph Agency (ROSTA):

> Back there, amid the glow of legend,
> The hero, idiot, *intelligent*
> Printed and painted placards
> On the joy of his own sundown.   (I, 267, 398; *SP*, 239)

* See note above, p. 251.

323

Sinyavsky's detection of the work's essentially lyrical (rather than epic) conception confirms, and is confirmed by, the circumstances in which it was written in the winter of 1923–4. As Pasternak told Nikolai Tikhonov in a letter of the time, the main fault of *Malady Sublime* – its structural nebulosity arising from 'extra-thematic' forces of cohesion – emerged as part of a specific design and as a response to a similar intention of Tikhonov's:

You were asking about my *poema*. At the start of the winter I began on a large piece of some account, sober, dry, unyouthful, and I had hovering in my imagination only the tone and meter – least of all could I call it a *poema*. Anyway, I started writing it and was stupid enough to show it to one or two people in the actual week when it was first composed. Now it cannot be put right, and a whole winter has passed and reinforced my stupid error. It would need too long threads to tack this year's worth of detached and discontinued extract on to an extention which gets less and less tolerable or foreseeable [...] A portion of this prolixity will soon appear in *LEF* and you will have chance to delight in it. Yesterday I had the proofs, and I must say that this work achieves utmost perfection in its tedium and stupidity. When Akhmatova said that you were about to break forever [...] with writing 'thematic' verses 'about something', I seized on this phrase of hers and rejoiced for you. And under the impact of this theme ended our nocturnal tea session at the Aseyevs, where all of us had recited, rejoiced for one another, regretted our abandoned youthful ways, cursed our deviations, and were all prepared to meet the next morning having made a decisive change for the better.[18]

On 21 January 1924, Lenin died. His body was laid in state in Moscow's Hall of Columns, and over the next few days thousands came to pay homage, queuing up in the bitter frost. Pasternak stood together with the Mandelstams for hours in a queue that never seemed to move. Many ordinary folk stood there too in patient, gloomy silence. The Mandelstams were reminded of citizens of Old Muscovy assembling to bury their tsar. Osip Mandelstam commented acidly: 'They've come to complain to Lenin about the Bolsheviks – vain hope, useless.' The funeral seemed 'a last splash of popular revolution', and Lenin's popularity appeared 'created not by terror, as the adoration and deification of Stalin later was, but by the hope that simple people placed in him'.[19] Mandelstam had in November 1917 dismissed Lenin as 'October's man of the moment',[20] and he was attending the lying-in-state out of curiosity rather than veneration. Pasternak's attitude was different, but also not exactly one of hero-worship. He had preserved a particular

324

memory of Lenin's appearance at the Ninth Congress of Soviets in July 1921 which was later committed to verse:

> I recall: the manner of his speech
> Pierced the nape of my neck with sparks
> Like the rush of globe lightning.
> Everyone rose, vainly searching
> The far table with their eyes,
> When suddenly he emerged upon the platform,
> Emerged even before entering,
> Sliding imperceptibly
> Through ranks of obstacles and helpers
> Like the compressed sphere of a storm
> Flying smokeless into the room . . .
> [. . .]
> He was like a rapier thrust.
> Chasing after the spoken word
> He pursued his own line with flapping coat
> And jutting uppers of his boots.
> The words might have been of engine oil,
> But the curve of his body
> Breathed with the flight of naked essence
> That tears through a stupid layer of husks.
> And his guttural voice
> Sounded aloud in everything that
> Was traced in the blood of events.
> He was their acoustic countenance.
> Envious with the envy of centuries,
> Jealous with their single jealousy,
> He directed the stream of thought
> And, because of that, the country.   (I, 271–2; *SP*, 243–4)

These lines were actually part of a later extension of *Malady Sublime*, and their appearance in 1928 had a special irony peculiar to that year (see below, p. 402–3).[21] However, unlike his view of the regime itself, Pasternak's assessment of Lenin's qualities did not change over the years. These verses recorded eyewitness impressions of an awesome spectacle, not a moral evaluation of it, and were bound up with Pasternak's memory of 1917 and his view of other revolutionary giants of the past, Peter the Great, Saint-Just, Robespierre. Approval or abomination of their actions was irrelevant. Although easily mistaken for such, this poetic extract was thus not a contribution to the posthumous Bolshevik cult of Lenin. It merely foreshadowed a later suggestion in *Doctor Zhivago* that 'wars and revolutions, tsars and Robespierres are history's organic agents, its fermenting yeast. Revolutions are produced by men of action, one-sided fanatics, narrow-minded geniuses.' (*DZh*, 465–6) A drafted autobiographical extract of the mid-1950s contained a similar assessment:

Lenin was the soul and conscience of such a rare splendour, he was the face and the voice of the great Russian storm, unique and exceptional. With the fervour of genius and unhesitatingly, he took upon himself responsibility for bloodshed and breakage such as the world had never seen. He did not fear to cry out to the people and summon them to realise their most secret cherished hopes. He allowed the ocean to rage, and the hurricane passed over with his blessing.

(*VP*, 490)

But without the later 'Leninist' postlude, the generic peculiarity of *Malady Sublime* probably accounted for the lukewarm reception which the work enjoyed. There was nothing quite like it in Soviet verse of the time. It resembled most closely the extended lyrical compositions that engaged Mandelstam's attention in 1923–4, works such as *Finder of a Horseshoe*, *Slate Ode* and *1st January 1924*. These too expressed a poet's discomfort in his age, and the last one in particular, with its evocation of 'the age's sickly eyelids' and its death, struck a common note with Pasternak.[22]

The story *Aerial Ways* (*Vozdushnye puti*) was Pasternak's first completed prose on returning from Berlin. It was written in the winter of 1923–4 and read to the 'Zaitsev circle' on 13 March 1924. Like *Malady Sublime* it conveyed a stark sense of its author's exposure to history. The story was originally considered for publication in the Berlin journal *Beseda* (Colloquy) edited by Gorky, and probably it appealed to the latter's own hopes for a rescindment of capital punishment in Russia. *Beseda* turned down the work after Khodasevich wrongly informed Gorky that it had already appeared in print.[23] It was finally published along with four recent lyrics in the second (August) issue for 1924 of *Russky sovremennik* (Russian Contemporary), another journal with which Gorky was associated. Unlike *Krasnaya nov'*, *Krug*, and others, this was one of several journals protected by a Sovnarkom decree of 1921 designed to stimulate private publication of specialised literature. Such journals attracted authors ranked as 'bourgeois', or *poputchiki* (fellow travellers) who, though not counter-revolutionary, nevertheless lacked proletarian instinct or background and showed no firm Marxist convictions. Despite the decree, the independent journals were shortlived and were officially harassed out of existence. In 1924, though, *Russky sovremennik* especially was a forum for outstanding unorthodox talent.[24] On its pages Pasternak figured alongside Formalist critics Eikhenbaum, Grossman, Shklovsky, Tynyanov and Vinokur, prosaists Babel, Pilnyak, and the Serapions, and poets such as Akhmatova, Esenin, Khodasevich, Mandelstam and Tsvetaeva.

Unlike Pasternak's other recent prose, *Aerial Ways* was a complete work, not a fragment. Even so, as Pasternak told Khodasevich in a letter, the printed version had lost a third of its length through censorship cuts. The manuscript has not been preserved, and there is no information about the story's original conclusion. Nevertheless, the extant work repeats in a sensitive political setting the motif of infanticide or killing of innocents that occurred in *Suboctave Story* and *Zhenya Luvers' Childhood*. The story was dedicated to Kuzmin – doubtless in gratitude for his earlier approval of Pasternak's prose – but it had less in common with Kuzmin than with other ornamental prose writings of the 1920s. After the 'dematerialised' style of *Luvers*, this was in some ways a reversion to earlier self-conscious complexity. Shifts of narrative standpoint and stylistic eccentricity, although now handled with a ripe assurance, did not earn the critical acclaim accorded to *Zhenya Luvers' Childhood*.

The story followed Pasternak's established narrative pattern and was built on a 'situational rhyme' in each of its two parts, with the discordant 'echo' forming a bitter parabolic comment on the discontinuity of modern Russian history. The 'aerial ways' of the title were the roads of history 'down which there passed each day, like trains, the unswerving thoughts of Liebknecht, Lenin and a few other such high-flying minds. These were the ways set up on a level high enough to cross all frontiers' as they passed through the 'sky of the Third International' (II, 144; *VP*, 130–1). In the story these personified historical forces are the only bearers of volition – along with the narrator, whose account is full of arbitrariness: the objective world and narrative tense swing back and forth between past, present and future 'like sand in an often inverted sandglass'; sometimes the author withholds information or jumps ahead of his own story; points of view shift constantly between impressionist absorption, detached reportage, or 'Tolstoyan' comment and reflection.

The mannequin-like human characters in the story are not free agents, but are snatched up and swept along by circumstance. Their helplessness is that of the halfwit hare-lipped shepherdess in the opening paragraph who compulsively chases a runaway steer through a tangle of garden refuse, nightshade, bricks, twisted wire and mouldering half-darkness...

some of several such baleful images which colour the narrative. Nevertheless, in part 1 of the story, at a private family level good fortune is still possible in a pre-Revolutionary country dacha setting, where a mother and father are able to recover their straying infant Antosha, even when midshipman Polivanov (the child's true father) abandons the search. The sequel occurs after an interval of fifteen years during which Antosha's mother and Polivanov lose contact. They meet again under a new sky dominated by the aerial ways of revolutionary thought. The earthly agent of such thought is Polivanov, now an important Bolshevik official on the Local Provincial Executive Committee. Antosha's mother appears unannounced at his office to intercede for her (and his) son who has been arrested. Unrecognised by Polivanov because of his adopted pseudonym, the youth is due to be executed for counter-revolutionary activity. This time the boy cannot be rescued. Telephone enquiries lead from one conversation to another – 'ever deeper and farther into the city and the night, until at last the abyss of the final correct information yawned before him' (II, 148; *VP*, 134–5). Polivanov looks down to discover Antosha's mother in a swoon, lying on the floor like a broken doll.

The contrast between the lyric and historical modes of thought, and between poetic freedom and historical necessity, had been rehearsed already in *The Black Goblet* and *Lovelessness*, where the moral bias had been in favour of the lyrical dreamer. *Aerial Ways* now reinforced a harsher truth grasped through experience of the Bolshevik age: human fate and feelings cannot sidestep history's unswerving finality. This story is not a document of protest, but a statement of grim fact. As Mossman points out, it foreshadows a basic premise of Pasternak's later novel: man lives not in nature but in history.[25]

In November of 1923, Pasternak, had another brush with the censorship in connection with his own personal library. When he returned from Germany in March, his books lay for several months in store on the cellar of Zinovii Grinberg, the Narkompros agent in Berlin. When they eventually arrived in Moscow, falling apart and spoilt by damp, several were impounded. Pasternak had to go and haggle with an official in order to repossess such items as an old edition of Dickens in Russian translation. Since Pasternak was a noted public figure the censor assured him, he may have his books. And what, Pasternak wondered, would have happened had he been less well known?[26] This incident was only one demonstration of the increasing severity and ideological pressures on the intelligentsia and literary community in 1923. The same year saw the foundation of the militant Moscow Association of Proletarian Writers, the creation of their journal *Na postu* (On Guard), and their alliance with *LEF* against non-committed literature. Attempts to usher bourgeois belles-lettres out of existence were dramatised tragically in late 1923 by some events in which Pasternak had a part to play.

Pasternak had always revered Valerii Bryusov as a doyen of Russian Symbolism, and he had himself benefited from Bryusov's perceptive critical reviews. They were not kindred spirits, however. Bryusov's astringent cerebrality and ambition made him in some ways similar to Sergei Bobrov.[27] As a committed fatalist, he had like Gorodetsky and some others thrown his hand in with the new rulers. November 1923 provided an eloquent example of his supine acceptance of what he deemed to be the inevitable. That month the authorities expelled 200 students from the Bryusov Literary Institute, and Bryusov himself wrote off three quarters of them as 'dead souls'. Protest was raised about the obviously talented student Nikolai Vilmont who had only six months to study before graduating. Bryusov dismissed him as a pernicious 'idealist': he had allegedly participated in a students' opposition group and his verses carried references to icons, prayers and the deity. Having reluctantly defended Nikolai Vilmont at one meeting, Bryusov was unperturbed to see a later one reverse the decision. Pasternak heard news of this from both Loks and Chernyak and wrote a furious letter to the influential critic Pyotr Kogan who was a professor at the Institute. Kogan never replied. Vilmont's studies were interrupted, although later he did manage to graduate.[28]

Pasternak no doubt forgave Bryusov, realising that his hands were tied. Within a few days of the incident the two of them shared the same platform: together with Aksyonov, Aseyev, Esenin, Ivnev, Kamensky, Mandelstam, Mayakovsky, Shershenevich and others, they recited at a fifth anniversary celebration of the All-Russian Union of Writers on 20 November 1923. On that occasion, held at 25 Tverskoi Boulevard, the proceedings were chaired by Bryusov.

Despite this and other official tokens of esteem, however, Bryusov's last years were bitter ones. His relish for authority under the Bolsheviks had alienated former friends, and his bourgeois past prevented his acceptance by the avant-garde and 'proletarians' who were bent on forging the new literature. Bryusov's jubilee celebrations in December 1923, marked by ceremonies in the Academy of Arts, the Higher Institute of Literature and Art, and at the Bolshoi Theatre, only highlighted his plight. The speeches and newspaper articles summed up his achievements as part of a literary past, and the ceremonial was a form of premature burial rite.[29]

Pasternak's reverence for the cultural legacy of the past in a generation of icon-breakers perhaps partly explained his continuing affection for Bryusov. This merged in a number of letters to him in the early 1920s, and his jubilee address in the Bolshoi Theatre on 15 December maybe partly compensated for the bitterness of other assessments. Pasternak gave an honest evaluation of Bryusov's achievement vis-à-vis Blok, for example, and referred especially to the 'urban theme' that still played a vital role in his own verse.[30] In addition to this Pasternak addressed a poem to Bryusov. It opened with congratulations but also contained a compassionate allusion to the recent 'proletarian' critical campaign that had quashed Bryusov's candidature for a state award. Then followed a reflection on Bryusov's status – and implicitly on the predicament of any artist under the new order. Here, not for the last time, Pasternak invoked the image of Hamlet to convey a tragic confrontation with the age:

> What can I say? That Bryusov's
> Widely broadcast fate is bitter?
> That minds grow stale in fooldom?
> That it's no small thing to smile and suffer?
>
> That you first opened wide
> The gates to sleeping civic verses?
> That wind's dehusked citizenhood?
> We've torn our wings up into feathers?
>
> [...]
>
> Shall I break down the door of vulgar axiom
> Where words tell lies and rhetoric limps?
> Oh, maybe Shakespeare's all contained
> In Hamlet's chatter with a shade.   (I, 236–7; *SP*, 211–12)

Pasternak's speech hinted at a special feeling of community with Bryusov when he announced that 'a sense of tragedy, the phenomenon of any great poet – and of Bryusov in his own particular way – guided me as I wrote this congratulation to him'.[31] There was a special reason for this feeling. In *Krasnaya nov'*, no. 3, 1923, Bryusov had published some poetic 'Variations on the Theme of "The Bronze Horseman"'. The work was an attempt to pick up the theme of the poet and the state, but in a conscious reworking of the material from Pasternak's own Pushkin cycle in *Themes and Variations*. At the end of his jubilee speech Bryusov responded to Pasternak's tribute with a recitation of these 'Variations', thus, to the astonishment of the audience, formally establishing a special form of dialogue with Pasternak.[32]

Bryusov's 'imitation' of Pasternak was only one special case of a widespread phenomenon in the 1920s. Many of Pasternak's younger contemporaries – some of them sharply authentic talents – registered his influence. His style, which occasionally attracted deliberate parody,[33] was recognisable by its breath-catching syntactic and metaphoric leaps and richly alliterative orchestration. (A line which Bryusov specially savoured in conversation with the young poet Tarlovsky came from 'Embarkation' ['Otplytie'], where 'The lap of dripping salt is heard' came over as a brilliant onomatopoeia: 'Slýshen lépet sóli káplyushchei'.)[34] Imitation was a sincerer form of flattery than laudatory reviews. Even young 'proletarian' poets were not immune to Pasternak's stylistic influence, despite the fact that some of his distinctive features were viewed in Marxist critiques as an obtrusive preoccupation with form at the expense of content, an abandonment of revolutionary poetics.[35]

Pasternak's manner was in fact so infectious in the early 1920s that he observed to Bryusov how some people 'write in my personal tone without even knowing it and without having seen *My Sister* – thanks to secondary, horizontal borrowings from one another'.[36] In 1923, for instance, Bobrov detected elements of Pasternakian pastiche and re-phrasing in Mandelstam's *Tristia*. Sofia Parnok in 1924 noted that Antokolsky and Tikhonov were 'sick with Pasternak (*boleyut Pasterna-kom*).' Vladimir Pozner criticised both Bryusov and Tikhonov for 'trying their hand unsuccessfully in his style'. And later in the 1920s Shklovsky observed how the poets Dementyev and Ushakov had successfully taken over Pasternak's 'laconic syntax', urban imagery and similes.[37] As Nadezhda Mandelstam later summarised:

For several years Pasternak held undivided rule over all poets and nobody escaped his influence. Akhmatova said that only Tsvetaeva emerged from this test with honour: Pasternak enriched her and she not only retained, but maybe even obtained her true voice thanks to him.[38]

The most significant factors in Pasternak's private life in 1923 were the birth of a son on 23 September, and a state of poverty and discomfort that clouded this otherwise happy event. The opening lines of *Spektorsky* later recalled those hardships:

> Once used to gouging the sonorities
> From the sweet sugar loaf of life,

331

I was now constrained to leave the path
Of know-all bloated on his rhymes.

I was in need. A son was born to us.
Childish things must needs be put aside.
And measuring my age with oblique glance,
I noticed greying hair's first signs.　　　　　　(I, 275; *SP*, 304)

The Pasternaks' son was called Evgenii, or 'Zhenya'. In the first few years he was tended by a succession of nurses. His mother meanwhile battled to continue with her painting and studies. Inevitably, cramped living space led to frayed nerves and frustration, with one room serving as dining room, living room, nursery, sleeping quarters, writer's study and artist's studio. A temporary solution was found at first by Pasternak's staying up to write at night, kept awake by cigarettes and strong tea.

In May 1924 Evgeniya took their son to visit her mother in Leningrad and then moved out to a rented holiday home at Taitsy near the Baltic coast. By this time she was in a state of nervous exhaustion and anaemic after feeding Zhenya, and the baby was also unwell. The holiday was much needed. Pasternak meanwhile stayed in Moscow 'in order to work and write my *Iliad*, *Divine Comedy* or *War and Peace*', as he told Olya Freidenberg, 'and in that way improve our affairs radically for a long time to come'.[39] The results were disappointing. He missed his family, found it hard to work in the heat of a Moscow summer, and was depressed at his inability to pay off several months of accumulated rent and income tax, in addition to raising cash to lease two rooms in Taitsy and pay for his own hoped-for holiday. Morale was also not improved by a battle with Gosizdat to secure payment of a promised advance.[40]

Amidst these worries, Pasternak's literary and social activities were a pleasant distraction. In early May he stepped in at short notice to give a poetry recital at KUBU (acronym for the Commission for the Improvement of Living Conditions of Academics), replacing Aseyev who was indisposed. He also evidently lunched frequently at KUBU, where he had an interesting encounter with Vyacheslav Ivanov (who had just left his professorship in Baku, had received an exit permit and was about to leave for exile in Italy) and also met with Maria Kudasheva, the future wife of Romain Rolland. Pasternak's letters to Evgeniya also included mention of Bely's return to Moscow, a tedious telephone conversation with Tsvetaeva's sister Anastasiya, and an enjoyable visit from the poet Pavel Antokolsky ('a real person, with a genuine talent, voice and eyes'). A more significant discovery, though, was the society of Nikolai

Tikhonov. Pasternak had met him in early 1924 through the Lef confraternity, and although Tikhonov apparently disliked *Malady Sublime*, Pasternak delighted in his energy-filled lyrical *Home Brew* (*Braga*) and saw in him 'a poet of my world and understanding'. In late June he wrote to Evgeniya announcing Tikhonov as a new member of their family: 'He has been here a couple of times to see me in the mornings. It's a joy to see such a person. He is the only one with whom I have talked about you.'[41]

Despite the tenderness of their messages,[42] Pasternak's correspondence with his wife evidenced signs of a strain over an issue that became critical in the years ahead. Evgeniya was already suspicious of her husband's rapturous correspondence with Tsvetaeva. On 20–21 May Pasternak sought to reassure her:

How can I convey to you that my friendship with Tsvetaeva is one world, large and essential, and my life with you another, still greater and essential already in its very size [...] The two worlds do not have to collide, but they frequently if not daily have occasion to quake at a score of female faces that I see precisely because of beauty's *lack of discrimination*, because of its commonplaceness, dispersal and infinity.

To add to Pasternak's troubles, he too fell ill in July with a severe form of tonsillitis, which Dr L. G. Levin diagnosed as having affected the heart muscles. All this brought creative work to a final halt. When the worst of the illness was over, Pasternak set off by train to rejoin his family. On Wednesday, 21 July, he arrived in Taitsy, where the three of them stayed on for a further six weeks.

During the holiday, although still troubled by ill health, Pasternak was able to relax in the rural setting and also visit friends and contacts in Petrograd. He called in at the offices of *Russky sovremennik* which was about to bring out *Aerial Ways* and some poems;[43] he met up with Kuzmin and Mandelstam, who introduced him to the young drama producer Piotrovsky during a visit to Lengiz publishers; and with Lengiz Pasternak was able to negotiate and sign up a new volume of prose fiction.[44]

The Mandelstams were in an even more precarious position than the Pasternaks. Despite publication of some articles and verse in the early 1920s, Mandelstam had been given to understand by colleagues in Moscow (including former fellow Acmeist Vladimir Narbut, and also Bukharin) that his verse was no longer printable. In addition, while praising his work, Bobrov had written what amounted to a damning review of Mandelstam's *Tristia* in 1923, deploring the Acmeist poetic ideals.[45] Realising that translation might well soon be his only real source of income, Mandelstam removed in the autumn of 1924 to Petrograd where he would have closer contact with possible purveyors of such work. While at Taitsy Pasternak visited the Mandelstams several times in their small flat on the Morskaya. Later he regretted having wasted the time on ordinary conversation instead of hearing Mandelstam read from his important new prose work *The Noise of Time (Shum vremeni)*.[46]

Another family in distress were the Freidenbergs. The Pasternaks' visits to them from Taitsy reinforced old family affections. But the Freidenbergs' morale was low, and they had nobody with Boris' spirit and energy. After much effort, Olya had managed to graduate in classics from the University, and had worked her dissertation on Greek hagiography into a book. With her student stipend now exhausted, her one hope of income was to obtain an academic post, for which she was required to defend her thesis and publish her researches in book form. Her dissertation was successfully passed in November of 1924 and she was singled out by scholars Frank-Kamenetsky and Marr. While in Petrograd Pasternak tried to use his 'World Literature' contacts to try and arrange for Olya to translate Frazer's *The Golden Bough*. In addition, after returning to Moscow in September he worked energetically (and without any understanding or gratitude on Olya's part) to establish openings that could lead to her academic employment and to an improved ration allocation for her. From September to December his letters insistently invited her to Moscow, where she could pursue matters further in person, and he even guaranteed her an audience with Lunacharsky. On 19 November he also sent the Freidenbergs one hundred roubles as a gift from his father in Berlin. With perverse waspishness Olya rejected the money, assuming it was meant as compensation for Boris' empty promises of assistance. In a further letter in December Olya announced that she would not be coming to Moscow. The Pasternaks were exasperated and depressed, and a further hiatus in communication with the Freidenbergs followed.

Once again relations with cousin Olya had foundered over misunderstandings and incompatibilities of character. In the midst of his own difficulties Pasternak's offers of help were often wrapped in gushingly expansive terms which elicited irritated disbelief. Olya's only excuse lay in the hardship she had to face. As she admitted to Boris, 'I am exhausted by life itself and maybe I revolted also against you by ricochet'.[47] She had no easy lot, living with an elderly and evidently tetchy mother and with her brother Sasha, who was the only potential breadwinner but was scatter-brained and unreliable. Poverty forced them to keep selling off possessions, and Olya's academic success brought neither acclaim nor material improvement. She even suspected that her novel scholastic ideas were sparking off rivalries and disapproval in certain quarters. Small wonder that her 'capacity for life [was] totally atrophied'. It was not Boris' fault for trying to offset this by his own buoyant initiatives.[48]

Living hand to mouth and without adequate housing or working space was the rule rather than the exception for writers in 1924, 'proletarians' and 'fellow travellers' alike. As a member of a still free profession Pasternak probably paid around a third of his irregular earnings in taxes, rent and rates. Publishers' fees normally made no distinction between prose and verse, and rates per printer's signature were miserly – three or four such signatures (between forty-eight and sixty-four pages) per month were usually necessary for a decent income. Not surprisingly, few authors other than journalists could both maintain this output and find an outlet for it. Any self-demanding poet was thus hopelessly disadvantaged.[49]

A further difficulty on top of all this was the remiss payment of advances and royalties. In the early summer of 1924 the Petrograd branch of Gosizdat agreed on a reprint of *My Sister Life* for 470 roubles. But failure to pay the eighty percent advance on time left the Pasternak family stranded and almost penniless at Taitsy. A special note had to be sent on 18 July, pointing out their plight, all the more painful since there were no close family or friends at hand to assist.[50]

Even when drawn up and signed, contracts were not certain to yield results. Pasternak's absence from print in 1924 surprised some of his friends. 'You are nowhere to be seen,' Tikhonov wrote to him in December. 'You are not in a single journal. When will there be a new book from you?'[51] The explanation lay not just in Pasternak's work tempo, nor in the fact that by the mid-1920s it was getting harder to publish poetry books that had no firm ideological engagement. The publishing business was altogether unreliable. The Lengiz agreement for a volume of prose signed up in summer of 1924 was cancelled by the publishers in late autumn. Perhaps it was just as well: Pasternak was aware on returning to Moscow in September that he was unlikely to produce the extra items needed, since he had 'ceased to realise what it means to write'.[52] Prior to this, negotiations with a publisher in Kharkov to bring out Pasternak's translation of Jonson's *The Alchemist* had also been cancelled. In their turn, these blows to morale and finances halted work on a translation of Shakespeare's *Hamlet*. It was a project Pasternak had had in mind for several years. Now – 'before Horatio had time to doubt whether the ghost really had appeared' – the project was shelved,[53] and it was another fifteen years before it was revived.

The only solution to these problems meant a return to the life style of the Civil War period. Again, it was a plight shared by many writers. As Pasternak jauntily remarked to the Mandelstams in a letter of 19 September, 'I have nothing to complain about. All the unpleasantness I have encountered here in Moscow I more or less foresaw'.[54] However, as a later redaction of the verse novel *Spektorsky* recorded, help was at hand:

> I was not left sitting high and dry.
> A responsive, zealous friend appeared.
> Without delay came work: to sort
> Leniniana from abroad.
>
> My employment was to gather phrases
> About Lenin. Attention never slumbered.
> Retrieving them like a deepsea diver,
> I delved my way through many a journal.
>
> My mandate offered me broad scope.
> Slitting new pages, every day
> I forced a Bosphorus of bindings
> Inaccessible to public eye.　　　　　(I, 275–4; *SP*, 304)

In fact there were two 'responsive, zealous' friends. The first was Sergei Bobrov, who because of his mathematical talents had found employment as a statistician with Gosplan (the State Planning Commission) and who now suggested that Pasternak seek work in his quarter. 'There is promise of my getting work in statistics,' Pasternak told Mandelstam in November 1924. 'I have not the faintest idea about legal disciplines, and it is being brought home to me that I am considerably more naive in theoretical matters than I imagined. So I shall have to sit down and follow various courses for a month, and I shall not count myself the complete man until I have achieved that.'[55] Meanwhile, however, a more practical suggestion came from Yakov Chernyak, who in the autumn of 1924 began working in the Party Central Committee's Lenin Institute. He arranged for Pasternak to help compile a bibliography of foreign press materials on Lenin. The work entailed sitting in the library of the People's Commissariat for Foreign Affairs (Narkomindel) and searching through Western newspapers and journals for references to be used in a bibliography that was never finally published.[56] The job was 'even pleasant in its own way', Pasternak reported to cousin Olya. Until Christmas, when he was given notice, it enabled him to browse through materials on subjects such as foreign fashions, Joyce, Proust, Satie and Joseph Conrad, which would never otherwise have come this way. Initially Pasternak worked from 10 a.m. to 4 p.m., until early October when the Jonson and Lengiz contracts were revoked. Thereafter he put in longer hours (without a completely proportionate pay rise) and usually returned home between eight and nine in the evening. Monthly earnings from this work were around 150 roubles – as he told Olya, 'three quarters of what we need, were it not for our debts'. By the autumn, Fenya the nursemaid was already owed the sum of 150 roubles over and above her current wage. More family valuables were sold off, including Boris' gold medal from school. Leonid Pasternak also helped by instructing Boris to dispose of one of his pictures; from this sale came the hundred roubles that so offended the Freidenbergs.[57]

Over and above these difficulties, there were further disappointments and troubles in the autumn of 1924. On 14 September Pasternak had attended the premier performance of his translation of *The Alchemist* at the Kommissarzhevsky Theatre in Petrograd/Leningrad. Contact with these living actors brought him genuine pleasure after the surly indiffer-ence usually encountered in publishers' offices. But the production was not a success and had only a short run. Pasternak disclaimed responsi-bility:

It is amazingly boring and stupid on the stage, despite the fact that the producer has made a farce out of it and the actors play this farce not at all badly. Probably poor Ben is to blame. My translation is good. The producer has done what he could – at least, as I see it.[58]

Apart from this disappointment and consequent financial loss, in September and October there were rumblings concerning the family's possible eviction from their home by the Moscow City Council (which at the same time had commandeered Mayakovsky's room in Vodopyany Lane, leaving him only an office apartment in Lubyansky Passage). Fortunately, the Pasternaks' fears on this score proved groundless, although enforced eviction and rehousing by the ·Council were to become a permanent feature of Moscow life. Through all this Pasternak maintained a facade of sang-froid and even confidence. To Olya Freiden-berg he admitted: 'I cannot complain of anything. It's all my fault. I should have taken a job last winter. Yet I might say that despite all the above mentioned, within myself I feel better than I can remember for a long time.'[59] The work at Narkomindel was utterly uncreative, but it was mildly interesting and distracting and it effectively used up the day. Perhaps it had the beneficial effect of a narcotic and shut out other psychological pressures. On 20 November Pasternak even sounded in contented mood:

I like my rapid, machine-like day that has been bolted together from my job and the business and occupations bound up with it, and from a lot of other bother unconnected with it and concerning the house, human relations, carrying out various tasks, and so on. I enjoy this chase as if it were some game, as though I had a part in somebody's novel and was playing an adult person perpetually rushing about, laconic, forgetful, and darting from one department to another, from one tram to another [...] I spend the day in unbroken pleasure because, I repeat, the fact that the day is filled with a thick web of simple and fleeting trifles enthralls me. This stupid feverishness is at least more like the former spiritual fever, which made me a poet, than the enforced inactivity into which I fell in the last two or three years, when I learned that individualism is a heresy, and that idealism is forbidden.[60]

Despite his claim Pasternak was not totally inactive on the creative front. He still gave public readings and strove to secure publication of completed works. In *Pravda* for 5 November 1924, for instance, he was announced to participate in an evening of modern poetry organised by the Bryusov Literary Institute to assist Petrograd/Leningrad after the floods of late September. (Pasternak had heard details of this from cousin Olya, and in early November he retailed to Mandelstam an anecdote heard from Aseyev regarding the cause of the flood: after the recent renaming of Petrograd as Leningrad, the River Neva heard that it too was to be renamed – after Rosa Luxemburg – and had sprung out of its banks!)[61] Pasternak's correspondence with Mandelstam also revealed several attempts to market his translations. Via Mandelstam he sent producer Piotrovsky his versions of Jonson and of Kleist's *Prince Friedrich of Homburg* and *The Schroffenstein Family* in the hope of their being staged in Leningrad. He asked Mandelstam to assist in placing these dramas together with an expanded *Themes and Variations* with Lengiz publishers. Alas, he overestimated Mandelstam's standing with Leningrad publishers. The only response was a suggestion (fruitless in the event) that Pasternak offer his versions of Georg Herwegh for a projected volume of Western European revolutionary verse. Meanwhile, despite the confident front presented to Olya Freidenberg, Pasternak was getting desperate: 'I need money and an outlet for my pieces as never before,' he told Mandelstam in November. 'The Institute is a skinflint. This is the second month they have not paid, and they pay more meanly than they promised.'[62]

Pasternak could not have realised that in fact Mandelstam was hard put to obtain routine translation, reviewing and editing commissions for himself. This misunderstanding caused irritation on both sides, and despite their friendly sense of common cause, there was always a certain formality in their dealings. Moreover, Mandelstam was an infrequent correspondent in contrast with Pasternak, and his failure to supply contacts in Leningrad and his use in January 1925 of Shklovsky and Arsenii Urechin (Maria Sinyakova's husband) to deliver messages to Pasternak annoyed the latter.[63] Another instance was Mandelstam's failure to respond in the spring of 1925 when Pasternak sent him extracts of his new work *Spektorsky*; Mandelstam in turn was put out by what he took to be Pasternak's lack of familiarity, or even concern, with his own works. None of this, however, undermined the two men's high regard for one another as artists. Pasternak rarely indulged in reviewing after the 1910s, but Mandelstam made several eulogistic mentions of Pasternak in the 1920s. One of these articles, entitled 'Assault' (published in *Rossiya*, no. 4 (1924), had been discussed by the two of them in Leningrad. In it Pasternak was described as a poet 'not for yesterday, nor for today, but forever'. Then came Mandelstam's assault: 'Poor poetry,' he wrote, 'shies away from under the many revolver barrels of peremptory demands directed at it [...] What monstrous ingratitude to Kuzmin, Mayakovsky, Khlebnikov, Aseyev, Vyacheslav Ivanov, Sologub, Akhmatova, Pasternak, Gumilyov and Khodasevich!'[64] Pasternak could only write back with a bashful disavowal, heaping praise on Mandelstam's own work.[65]

Pasternak's failure to write or speak out with Mandelstam's vehemence about the threat posed to literature by political ideology pointed to their basic difference in temperament. Mandelstam had early adopted an embattled position. His unmuted hostility towards official attitudes was part of a policy of confrontation – and ultimately of self-destruction. By comparison, Pasternak appeared on the surface to be supine and peaceably omnivorous. He did not lack the courage of his convictions, but it took longer to bring him to boiling point and his responses were usually oblique rather than frontal. This, as realised, could be misinterpreted. After telling Mandelstam about the débâcle of the first Lef conference in January 1925, he finished by saying: 'I shake you by the hand. From what I write to you, don't conclude that my feelings are any feebler than your own.'[66]

The year 1925, however, saw one of Pasternak's most outspoken statements about the fate of Soviet literature. Indeed, in his insinuations he went further than most other disaffected littérateurs of the time. There were two major issues that prompted him to articulate these trenchant attitudes.

On 16–17 January 1925 the First Moscow Conference of Workers of the Left Front of the Arts was held in the premises of Proletkult. Lef had been rent by schism almost since its foundation in 1923, and the journal *LEF* had been a forum for these disputes. The group's 'proletarian' theoretician, Nikolai Chuzhak, had found much to criticise in his colleagues. Specifically he had branded 'comrade genius' Mayakovsky's poem *About That* as 'lyrical rot' and as a betrayal of the 'production principles of art' announced in Lef's programme.[67] Chuzhak and Mayakovsky's verbal duel was a main feature of the January conference. Pasternak described his own impressions to Mandelstam:

Has Shklovsky told you about the Lef conference? If not, then you have missed a great deal. I have never in my life seen a spectacle more convincingly petty and comical. I was there as a guest, among the spectators, and were it not for my slight sense of offence on Mayakovsky and Aseyev's behalf everything would be fine [...] It was the enactment of a piece of absurdity – idyllic, pastoral absurdity. They all but proclaimed the polishing of brass doorknobs as art, and in the hope of such a proclamation Mayakovsky pronounced a whole speech on the uses of chalk. They seemed to me like a set of wretched old, enfeebled cavaliers rolling from one humiliation to another in honour of some lady whom they didn't know and whom nobody else wanted.[68]

Neznamov's comment à propos all this was: 'Lef as Chuzhak understood it was really an almighty bore!'[69] Pasternak on the other hand made no criticism of Chuzhak. An obvious opponent, Chuzhak was only behaving true to type. Pasternak was embarrassed at the self-compromise in which genuine artists such as Aseyev and Mayakovsky indulged. Replying to Chuzhak, Mayakovsky had tried to defend Lef's activities. One of his points actually named Pasternak and claimed it was wrong to relegate his and Petrovsky's works to the realm of 'pure lyricism':

Of course, what is interesting to us is not comrade Pasternak's lyrical outpourings [...] but his work on the construction of the phrase, the development of new syntax. By the omission of individual words a more compact mass is created which an experienced worker can apply in the language of newspapers.[70]

Doubtless, Pasternak was gratified to learn how useful his work could be when in the right hands! Mayakovsky, however, emerged with no more than a pathetic half-defence of Lef, and he himself later dissociated himself from those 'two colourless days of "conferring"'.[71] Pasternak's outrage at this capitulation and act of self-enslavement was entirely understandable. After the January 1925 conference, in a state of disarray and under fire from Voronsky's fellow-travelling *Krasnaya nov'* as well as the Russian Association of Proletarian Writers (RAPP), the journal *LEF* ceased publishing. Pasternak was one of several who did not regret its demise.[72]

Pasternak's desire to distance himself from the dismal Lef majority led him in 1925 to conclude a peculiar and almost paradoxical alliance with the Futurist 'Bogeyman of Russian Literature', Aleksei Kruchenykh. From the outset Kruchenykh had been a Cubo-Futurist *enfant terrible*. In the 1920s he remained an unreformed apologist of the movement's pre-Revolutionary extremism and had made no concession to the 'social command' and utilitarian aesthetic nominally accepted by the Lef membership. In this respect at least he had therefore retained Pasternak's sympathy. This doubtless explains why in 1925 Pasternak wrote prefaces for two of Kruchenykh's privately printed booklets: a collection of articles on Kruchenykh himself, and a book of verse, *The Calendar* (*Kalendar'*) published in 1926. *Inter alia*, Pasternak welcomed Kruchenykh's escape from the stranglehold of routine semantics and discovery of a new world of bizarre acoustic expressivity:

In places where everyone else simply names a frog, Kruchenykh, forever astonished at the staggering and shuddering of nature in the raw, sets out to galvanise the noun till he achieves the illusion that the world is growing paws.

(III, 156)

For Pasternak, Kruchenykh revealed 'a multitude of things impossible in canonic art'. If the idea of form 'containing' content were taken to its extreme, then Kruchenykh must be 'more replete with content than anyone else'; indeed, 'the world chosen by Kruchenykh is an obligatory part of any poetic world' (III, 156). With typical laconism, though, he refrained from saying whether this *was* an art replete with content; he claimed Kruchenykh's world as only *part* of the total domain of poetry; and he directly criticised Kruchenykh's polemics, which he found to be his weakest point. The flattery was thus carefully qualified, and Kruchenykh was left standing on the farthest perimeter of genuine art.

Pasternak's 'alliance' with Kruchenykh in 1925 was thus a product of the polemical moment, sincere on Pasternak's part but not of central

341

concern to him.[73] Nevertheless the two men stayed in sporadic contact throughout the 1920s and after. Deprived of any official standing in Soviet literature, Kruchenykh hung on to those who had it. His appearances on Pasternak's doorstep were charted in various memoirs and photographic records. Lev Gornung, for instance, observed his arrival in January 1926 bearing his new brochure on Esenin and reciting his own verses 'in a metallic, penetrating voice'. Pasternak usually humoured Kruchenykh and in the late 1920s contributed to his frivolous poetic rhyming contest, *Turnir poetov*. Probably Pasternak's apparent sympathy with eccentric literature led in 1926 to his attracting the attention of Aleksandr Tufanov, the Leningrad 'transmentalist' who wrote to Pasternak and sent him an outline scheme of one of his works.[74]

Despite the Lef débâcle, Pasternak's good relations with Aseyev and Mayakovsky did not suffer. In February 1925 he wrote to his younger sister Lydia à propos Josephine's expected visit to Moscow. Pasternak had arranged – presumably through Lunacharsky – that Radek provide the Soviet embassy in Berlin with authorisation for her visa. Security clearance was obtained through OGPU, and Pasternak had also written to Mirov, an embassy employee he had known in 1922–3. Pasternak told Lydia that Josephine needed only to collect her visa in Berlin and then come with all speed: 'In April Aseyev and Mayakovsky are going away (to Paris). Moscow will be empty, and I'd like her to find us all alive and kicking.'[75] In the event, Josephine's trip did not take place. Her husband was totally opposed to her visiting the USSR, and after 1926, when the first of their children was born, family responsibilities made such travel impossible.

The Russian literary scene in the first half of the 1920s was mainly divided between the orthodox 'proletarians' and the diversified community of non-party 'fellow travellers'. Proletarian critics headed by Averbakh regarded themselves as Marxist ideological watchdogs and from their journal *Na postu* regularly inveighed against unallied 'bourgeois' littérateurs.[76] Meanwhile the Lef group made their own claim to be the artistic spokesmen of the new worker state, siding with the 'proletarians' against 'bourgeois' trends yet despising their low-brow conservatism. This variety of literary programmes was a reflection of official laissez-faire on the cultural front during the New Economic Policy period, when in addition to official publications, small-scale private and cooperative ventures were permitted. Party tolerance in what was seen as a transitory political situation was designed to win over rather than antagonise potential allies among the literary intelligentsia. The 'proletarian' organisations, however, showed less patience. In May of 1924 thirty-six 'fellow travellers', including Babel, Esenin, Mandelstam and Zoshchenko, signed a letter to the Central Committee Press Section, complaining at the tone and attitude of journals like *Na postu*, and seeking assurance that their outbursts of 'proletarian' intolerance were not a reflection of official opinion.

On 18 June 1925 the Central Committee met and passed an important resolution 'On Party Policy in the Field of Literature', the text of which was printed in both *Pravda* and *Izvestiya* on 1 July. Although proletarian opinion was well represented in government and Narkompros, tolerance was still the order of the day. The Party was apparently unwilling to allow any group of writers and critics to act as self-appointed Party spokesmen, and the resolution was designed to clarify this position.

The main points of the statement can be summarised as follows. The present state of growth and cultural revolution reflect the ambivalent economic situation and continuing class struggle. Under proletarian dictatorship the stress must now be on 'peaceful organisational work' rather than on exacerbation of hostilities. A policy of tact and tolerance is needed towards 'fellow-traveller' writers, while still eradicating counter-revolution and combatting bourgeois ideology. Proletarian writers deserve support, but they in turn must support 'our' cultural heritage and must avoid 'communist presumptiousness' (*komchvanstvo*) on the one hand and capitulation on the other. Literary criticism must assist this process. The Party 'cannot at all tie itself down by supporting any one trend *in the sphere of literary form*'. The Party is there to supervise construction of a new way of life. 'All this compels one to assume that a style appropriate to the age will be created, but it will be created by other methods, and no resolution of this question has yet been noted [...] The Party must emphasise the necessity for creation of a literature aimed at a genuinely mass readership of workers and peasants...'[77]

Most proletarians and fellow-travellers took comfort from this equivocal document. Writers in tune with the Party agreed with Gorky that the resolution would have 'enormous educative significance for littérateurs' and would supply a 'powerful forward thrust to Russian artistic creativity'.[78] But the resolution also seemed to legitimise the status of non-proletarians, bringing a hope of artistic freedom and relaxation of censorship. The August–September and October issues of the magazine *Zhurnalist* for 1925 featured a series of writers' reactions to the party statement. Amid general enthusiasm, a cautious and pained response

343

came only from a few. Veresaev complained of recent censorship interference and the destruction of artistic integrity, and questioned why the ideological incongruity of such fine writers as Sologub, Voloshin and Akhmatova should condemn them to silence.[79] Andrei Sobol disliked the implication that certain writers were being treated like 'rather nice, but slightly defective children'. Ivan Novikov was concerned that party supervision and true creativity were incompatible, the magic of art lying precisely in its 'particular wilfulness'.[80] Pilnyak also complained that the resolution did not resolve discord between writers and censors and did nothing to raise deplorably low writers' fees; it existed in fact more for the benefit of the literary management than for writers.[81]

Pasternak's comment,[82] however, was a quite unique blend of superficial confidence and acid sarcasm. Welcoming this opportunity to examine the resolution in detail, he isolated three particular statements in the text: clause 1, with its remarks on 'cultural revolution'; clause 5, which emphasised the presence of a dictatorship of the proletariat; and the assumption in clause 13 that 'a style appropriate to the age will be created'. Initially an almost optimistic note seemed to sound in Pasternak's statement:

I was caught by the air of history which these statements aspire to breathe. I too desire to breathe it, and naturally I was drawn to breathe along with them [...] Behind the prophecies I seemed to hear talk about history being history completely, and myself a complete human being within it.   (III, 157)

In this respect, at least, there seemed to be a prospect of self-fulfilment in a new and challenging age. But as Pasternak rehearsed the points that caught his attention, he found each of them either untrue or inadequate. 'We are not experiencing a cultural revolution,' he retorted, but a 'cultural reaction'. And no amount of official rhetoric could alter plain facts:

The presence of a proletarian dictatorship is insufficient to have an effect upon culture. For that a real and tangible domination is required, which would speak through me without my knowledge or will – and in spite of them even. I do not feel this. And the fact that this is objectively not the case is obvious when the resolution has to call on me to resolve the themes which it has set, even if this is a more voluntary affair than it was before.   (III, 158)

Finally, concerning official confidence that a style for the epoch must inevitably emerge: 'Nothing leads one to assume that a style appropriate to it will be created. Or if you wish, one might put it thus: It has already been created, and like any statistical average it is illusory and of zero worth [...] Instead of generalisations about the epoch which posterity would be left to make, we have obliged the age itself to live in the form of an incarnated generality.' (III, 158). The resultant mediocrity had been enforced, Pasternak claimed, both by censorship and now by editorial policies. 'There is nothing for me to do. The style for the age has already been created. There is my response.' But, Pasternak maintained, the function of true art is not to render 'averages' or generalisations, and he implicitly confirmed Novikov's belief in the wilfulness of art:

The artist cannot expect good from anywhere but from his own imagination. If I thought otherwise I would say that censorship should be done away with. And the main thing is that I am convinced that art should be an extremity of its age and not its mean resultant.   (III, 159)

According to Pasternak, any art linked organically with its epoch can only appear to reflect it in historical retrospect. But the detection of this would be a task not for the present day, but for posterity. 'And that is the source of my optimism,' Pasternak wrote, forcing a major-key conclusion (III, 159). As in his comments of January 1925 about the state of lyricism, the honesty of true art was the sole guaranteee of its vitality.

The Central Committee resolution of 1925 has subsequently been recognised as a preamble to the gradual integration of Soviet Russian literature into state policy. Despite its conciliatory tone, one of its consequences was the mooting of a new Federation of Soviet Writers (FOSP). On 22 July 1925, *Isvestiya* published an appeal for the creation of such a body, proclaiming the Central Committee resolution as a 'broad basis for the unimpeded development and unification of all revolutionary literature in the USSR'. The signatories included Averbakh, Brik, Lavrenev and Lunacharsky, and they called on all writers assenting with the resolution to join the new Federation. When it was eventually set up in December 1926, it was the role of this body to prepare the way for a smothering unification of all literary schools in the 1930s.

In retrospect one can see that the grounds for Pasternak's expressed optimism in responding to the resolution were dubious. At the time, however, the moderate tone of the resolution created a sense of freedom to manoeuvre and encouraged Pasternak's belief in his ability to participate in 'history' – albeit as an eccentric element. Certainly, a new spate of writings begun by Pasternak in 1925 seemed to spring from a newly won historical awareness, or the promise of one.

An interesting aspect of Pasternak's critical response to the resolution was his choice of target. As with the Lef conference earlier that year, his main attack concentrated not on diametrical antagonists – that is, the dictatorial 'proletarians' who would readily have banished him and his ilk from literary life altogether – but on the formulators of compromise and the 'average' style. Indeed, Lunacharsky and other moderates' support for a 'renaissance of realism' in the earlier 1920s (and their sympathy with the sentiments if not the products of 'resultant' realism) sounded a threat to all writers of non-realistic 'ornamental' prose, including the Serapions, Babel, Leonov, Olesha, Pasternak, Zamyatin and others. The archetypally metaphoric genre of lyric poetry was thus even more at risk.

Pasternak's thoughts on 'averageness' and literary style set out in *Zhurnalist* tied in closely with his views on both literary characterisation and human behaviour. In the mid-1930s he ascribed his convictions to the semi-autobiographical hero of a prose fragment entitled *A Beggar Who Is Proud* (*Nadmennyi nishchii*):

Through childhood experience I had learned to regard any typicality as tanta-mount to something unnatural, believing that strictly speaking the only people who are really types are those who try to become so to the detriment of nature. Why, I thought, should one drag typicality out onto the stage when it is already theatrical enough in real life?   (III, 300; *VP*, 309–10)

Closer to the time of the Central Committee resolution, Pasternak in 1928 wrote a short, unpublished appreciation of the Swiss born poetess Lili Khorazova.* He had met her in 1926 at one of his own poetry evenings; the following year she died from typhoid. In his reflections on her work and tragic life he dwelt again on the question of mediocrity, viewed as a parasitic growth on genius. A direct analogy is discernible with what Pasternak said about the 'style appropriate to the age' vis-à-vis genuine art, which always remains at a point of extremity – and precisely

---

* Elena Georgievna Khorazova, born 1903 (Zurich), died 13 September 1927 (Moscow). Daughter of G. A. Khorazov, mathematics professor and political émigré; received an élite schooling in Switzerland. Following her father back to Russia after the Revolution, she went to Tiflis in 1919, thence to Moscow in 1922, where she married the poet Aleksandr Romm. Unable to adjust to Soviet life, she spent her last years in poverty and misery; a member of the Union of Poets (SOPO), she wrote only in German and gave an evening of readings at the Herzen House in March 1926; published translations of Russian poets in *Die Neue Zeit*; five of her lyrics appeared posthumously in *Künstlerselbsthilfe* (Berlin, 1928). She became friendly with Pasternak and was first to bring New Year greetings to the Pasternaks on the stroke of midnight at the start of 1927.

for that reason becomes a brilliant reflection of its age. All this was set out as a Pasternakian paradox:

Ordinariness is a vital quality coming from within and, strange as it may seem, it has a distinct similarity to talent. Most ordinary of all are people of genius, to whom superhumanity seems a normal moral yardstick, a daily ration of existence. And even more ordinary – indescribably, enthrallingly ordinary – is nature. Only mediocrity is extraordinary, i.e., that category of people which from time immemorial has consisted of the so-called 'interesting person'. From ancient times he has shunned ordinary deeds and has been a parasite on genius, which he has invariably distorted, not only misquoting its direct teaching but also its actual medium, which he has always understood as some form of *flattering exclusivity*. Whereas in fact genius is an extreme and vehement form of *correctness*, inspired by its own infinite quality. Mediocrity has been specially fortunate in our day, when it has seized on romanticism, anarchism and Nietzscheanism as an inventory of freedom granted to its own incorporality.

13

The epic age

O monstrous idol of the state,
Eternal outer door of freedom!
The centuries creep from their cage
And beasts prowl round the Coliseum.
The preacher lifts a fearless hand
To make a cross of benediction
And tame the panther by his faith.
From Roman circus constantly
Men step into the church of Rome,
And we too live by that same sign,
We men of mine and catacomb ...

from *Lieutenant Shmidt*

జలలలు

A view of art as an 'extremity' of its age, as an expression of vital personality in contrast to inert public dogma, and as an escape from conformist averages, was stated by Pasternak and implied in the work of several like-minded writers (Olesha, Babel and the Serapion brothers) during the 1920s. Meanwhile, converse ideas were stressed by ideologically committed authors. Novels by such writers as Fadeyev, Furmanov and Gladkov were in fact already embodying the tenets of socialist realism. A number of them (Furmanov's *Chapaev* and Fadeyev's *The Rout*, for example) contrasted the virtues of Bolshevik discipline and authority with untamed popular revolutionary 'elementalism' (as demonstrated in such works as Pilnyak's *The Naked Year*). In their work, rebellious energy was shown converted into a force of submission and restraint. This paradoxical psychological reversal had prompted Pasternak's quip to Yurkun in 1922 about 'men of the revolution' becoming counter-revolutionaries. The conversion of violent kinetic energy by the law of entropy into a static force was also an image pursued by Zamyatin in an essay on literature and revolution in 1923.[1] In the spring of 1926 Pasternak described this incongruity again in a letter to Rilke:

Anyone with a will can learn one thing from our experience of life here: that when something great occurs in *active form* it is most self-contradictory; that according to the measure of its greatness it is in reality *petty*, according to its activity – *inert*. Thus it is with our Revolution, a contradiction in its very appearance, a fragment of shifting time in the form of a fearful, motionless spectacle. And such are our own fates also – the *static* temporal *subjects* of this sinister, noble historical curiosity, tragic even in their smallest, most ridiculous aspects. But [...] what concerns poetry and the poet is a peculiar refraction of the common European light of intimacy and of the countless coalescing secrets of our contemporaries' fates – poetry's concern remains just as it was before. As ever, everything here and now depends on the favour of fortune which can provide that missing refraction if experienced deeply and at the right moment. Then everything becomes simple, absurd, unhistorical and time-fathoming, free and fatal. Then one becomes a poet once more.[2]

What Pasternak described here concerning poetic creativity was already alluded to in his response to the Central Committee resolution, whose 'closeness' he sensed because 'recently, in spite of everything I began to work, and convictions apparently long buried started to come alive in me' (III, 159). First signs of this creative release had come in January 1925, just when psychological and financial reserves seemed almost exhausted. He described it in a letter to Mandelstam:

I am living extremely modestly, not to say poorly. I feel better than ever before. Calm and confident. I have even started to scribble something. And, as I live, it appears I shall manage to shape it into something.

This time, it seemed, Pasternak had recaptured some of the impetus he felt in the years 1917–18:

This is a return to the old poetic rails of a train that once left them and for six years lay at the foot of an embankment. *Sister, Luvers* and one or two items from *Themes* were like this for me [...] Since the beginning of January I have been writing in spurts, a little at a time. It is incredibly difficult. Everything has corroded, broken up and come unscrewed. Everything is covered with hard layers of insensitivity, dullness, and settled routine. It is repulsive. But the work is far removed from the present day, just as it once was with our first initiatives and happiest achievements [...] Therein lies its splendour. It reminds me of what was forgotten. Stores of energy come to life which seemed to be exhausted.

The 'statistically average' style referred to in Pasternak's response to the Central Committee resolution was identical with what he described to Mandelstam in January 1925 as the antithesis of personal creativity:

349

The final style (the end of an age, the end of the Revolution, the end of youth, the fall of Europe) settles between its banks and gets ever shallower and ceases to function. As once before, the fate of culture in quotation marks becomes a matter of choice and goodwill [...] And I am returning to what I abandoned. Not as a name, not as a littérateur. Not as a man summoned for the final settlement. No, as a civilian, a natural human being with his mixture of joys and sorrows, withdrawn and unknown.[3]

Pasternak's new project was a fresh departure related thematically to *Three Chapters from a Tale*. It was entitled *Spektorsky*. Cast as an extended poetic narrative, or novel in verse, it excited immediate comparison with Pushkin's *Evgenii Onegin*. Pushkin had used iambic tetrameter; Pasternak used quatrains of iambic pentameter – Mayakovsky's comment to Tikhonov when he heard of this was an ironic 'Is that all that we have struggled for?' But Pasternak was aware of and resisted the temptation to fall into stereotype nineteenth-century cadence. As he later told Sergei Spassky, 'Only by Sisyphean effort did I prevent this stupid, publicly comprehensible pentameter, which had sated itself already on Fet's tragedies, from gobbling up my giblets into the bargain [...] If I had continued without giving myself a rest, an utterly unseemly champing would have set in and I would have vanished without trace in the postprandial geniality of a bloated form.'[4] Another poet, however, noted Pasternak's 'practical application of Pushkinian eidology', blending this with a 'barely perceptible stylisation'.[5]

As Pasternak told Mandelstam, the use of this genre and form in 1925 was not an arbitrary form of reminiscence, but the expression of a persisting sense of continuity and of an historical optimism which eventually proved unfounded. An explanation was also offered to Pavel Medvedev:

I was expecting some transformations in everyday life and society, as a result of which the possibility of the individual tale would be restored, that is, of a plot about individual characters, a representative model comprehensible to anyone in its personal confinement, and not in its applied breadth. I was wrong about this [...] I began in a state of some hope that the shattered homogeneity of life and its palpable manifestation would be restored in the course of years and not of decades, in my lifetime and not in some historical divination [...] Such a move would have given me strength – and its growth, accompanied by the growth of a general moral force, is the sole plot for a lyric poet.[6]

The collapse of hopes for a renewal of the framework that had sustained the nineteenth-century novel and lyric was probably a major factor in *Spektorsky*'s interrupted composition and changing conception as the

1920s wore on. As Pasternak explained in 1929, that particular part of the plot in the novel which fell in the war years and revolution was eventually rendered in prose, 'because the characteristics and formulations that are binding and self-evident in this part are beyond the power of verses' (*VP*, 477; *SP*, 671).

Some sketches for *Spektorsky* survive in the form of 'Twenty Stanzas with a Preface' ('Dvadtsat′ strof s predisloviem'), which were first published under the title 'Farewell to Romanticism' in 1928. Another extract, 'From Spektorsky's Notes' ('Iz zapisok Spektorskogo'), was preserved for many years in Lili Brik's archive, presumably after having been rejected for publication by *LEF*; it was finally printed in 1965.[7] The opening of *Spektorsky* as composed and approved in 1925, however, provided a sympathetic portrayal of a young pre-war Russian intellectual, Sergei Spektorsky. Though not made explicit, certain similarities of character and setting clearly pointed to the author's own personality and experience. Like his creator, Spektorsky was 'a natural human being with his mixture of joys and sorrows, withdrawn and unknown'. The introduction that Pasternak later added, however, suggested that the character might have some cathartic role, rather like Pushkin's Onegin:

> Through lack of habit I began 'Spektorsky',
> Dealing with a man devoid of merit [...]
> [...]
> I would give but little for my hero,
> A man I'd not have readily considered,
> But I wrote of the encasing rays of light
> In which I could observe him looming dimly. (I, 277; *SP*, 306)

And if Sergei's grip on heroism was tenuous, so too was authorial control of his self-image:

> As it is my poem hangs by a thread.
> I see no means of self-oblivion ... (I, 285, 408; *SP*, 313)

In the first four chapters that were in a publishable state in 1925–6, characterisation and plot line frequently faded amid stage-setting and impressionist depiction – as in a lyric poem, in fact. The opening pages contained an account of Spektorsky's train excursion with friends to spend the Christmas of 1912 in a snowbound woodland cottage. Amid the amusements of drinking, skiing, charades and merry-making, Sergei's *après-ski* attention focuses on Olga Bukhteyeva, the wife of an acquaintance. Their mutual attraction culminates with her as 'wearied

351

equestrienne of the mattress' in a luridly evocative love scene. (Tikhonov primly singled out this passage for its 'directness and honesty', but it was excised from the final redaction, perhaps in deference to official puritanism.) The setting, and perhaps some of the events of chapter 2, were based on Pasternak's stay in the Urals and Kama region during the war.

Chapters 3 and 4 are set in the following spring. The hero receives a surprise visit in Moscow from his sister Natasha, the wife of a provincial factory doctor. A young woman of revolutionary persuasion, she regrets missing the Mayday gathering with her husband's comrades but makes up for it by delivering a stern reprimand to her brother for his lack of concern with modern issues:

> 'Look here, you're young – and that's a plus. But you're
> So cut off from your age – and that's a minus.
>
> You have no quest in life, much to my shame.
> Which camp do you belong to? [...]   (I, 289, 414; *SP*, 318)

The published extract of chapter 4 concludes with Sergei seeing his sister off at the station and then going to give a private tutorial lesson in a run-down area of town (another detail based on Pasternak's tutoring activities while a student). On the stairs he runs into an old friend whose identification is prevented by the story's interruption at this point. (He later emerges as Sasha Baltz, a new incarnation of Schütz from the *Three Chapters from a Tale*.)[8]

Early in 1925 Pasternak sent the opening of *Spektorsky*'s manuscript to Ilya Gruzdev, who was on the editorial board of the Leningrad journal *Kovsh* (The Scoop). Gruzdev in turn showed the work to Tikhonov, who conveyed his impressions to the author some time in February or March:

Boris Leonidovich, it's very good – the love scene is quite exceptional. There have not been verses of such directness and honesty in Russian poetry for a long time. The difficulties you have set yourself with this task are great – that is apparent from the material you have already worked over, but it is worth continuing only when you struggle and have to deal with some new and opposing force [...] Your poem [...] is such a phenomenon that it will leave far behind much of what is written now [...] It is organic and therefore the demands made of it are raised very high.[9]

A more exacting reader, who neglected to report his verdict, was Mandelstam. He was sent some extracts, and when he failed to reply Pasternak wrote a prickly letter:

My dear tormentor!

What is the matter? If you do not have an opinion about *Spektorsky* or have such a low one that you do not wish to offend me, then you could write to me about the revolutionary anthology and about money. How do matters stand on this? You had better destroy the extracts I sent you; I have corrected them in many respects. The thing is altogether no longer a secret. I am handing in the first chapter to be printed.

Pasternak only half-jokingly (and erroneously) maintained Mandelstam was to blame for this premature publication through failing to help place Pasternak's translations of Herwegh and through refusing even his 'moral support in the form of some reaction'. Nevertheless, his letter ended with cordial wishes and a postscript admission that, upon correcting the typescript copy of *Spektorsky*, he found it to be 'boring and watery' – 'You can therefore abuse it as you will: it will neither harm me nor come as a surprise.'[10]

To Ilya Gruzdev Pasternak had expressed hopes of completing *Spektorsky* before releasing it for publication.[11] But work was interrupted by the need for a more lucrative short-term project, and it was not resumed for another two years. The first three chapters of *Spektorsky* appeared in *Krug*, no. 5, 1925. (In the first half of the year Krug publishers also brought out a volume of Pasternak's stories containing *Luvers*, *Apelles*, *Letters from Tula* and *Aerial Ways*.) Other extracts appeared in 1925–6 in the journals *Kovsh*, *Rossiya*, and in *Styk* (The Junction), a miscellany put out by the Moscow Poets' Workshop. (In early 1925 Pasternak complained to Gornung of being pestered over the 'phone by Anna Antonovskaya to join this latter group, which however, he refused to do.)[12]

A continuing desperate need to raise money without compromising the quality of serious artistic schemes persuaded Pasternak in the early summer of 1925 to write some children's verse. Perhaps the idea came from Mandelstam, who in 1925–6 published four such books in Leningrad. For any accomplished professional this was an easy way of producing unproblematic copy. A first poem, 'The Roundabout' ('Karusel''), was completed in early May, and with promotional help from Nikolai Chukovsky in Leningrad its pleasing naïve doggerel appeared shortly afterwards in the journal *Novy Robinzon* (The New Crusoe) and later in a separate children's edition.[13] A second poem, 'The Menagerie' ('Zverinets'), was based on a family trip to the zoo, still recalled by Pasternak's eldest son, for whom his father also improvised musical portraits of various animals at the piano. Working on the poem, however, Pasternak apparently 'got into a complete flap' and wasted an entire month. What could have gone awry in such an innocent under-taking is hard to tell. Nevertheless, even the project for such a work served its purpose in eliciting a publisher's advance, thanks to the kind offices of children's author and translator Samuil Marshak; the poem itself finally appeared in 1929. In his search for funds to house and feed his family, Pasternak also evidently tried his hand at editorial work. We have no details of this, but in a letter to Mandelstam of mid-August 1925 he expressed his pleasure in this 'clean and reliable means of income' and hoped to make editing his 'basic and constant occupation for the winter'.[14]

News of Pasternak's material plight reached other friends in Lenin-grad. The critic and children's author Kornei Chukovsky had already done much to assist Leningrad writers. Now, in July 1925, he wrote on Pasternak's behalf to Raisa Lomonosova. She was the wife of the leading rail construction expert Yurii Lomonosov, who frequently travelled abroad on business, and as a busy 'woman about literature' she had earlier that year approached Chukovsky à propos setting up a bureau to promote links between her Western literary contacts and Soviet writers. 'In Moscow there is a poet called Pasternak,' Chukovsky told her. 'In my opinion he is the best of contemporary poets. To our universal shame he is in need. We all have an obligation to help Pasternak, for Russian literature is maintained and has always been upheld by the Pasternaks of this world [...] He needs work. He is an excellent translator. Can't you send him some book for translation – verse or prose – he knows German and English.'[15] Chukovsky sent a similar letter later in July, and Lomonosova responded by sending several books, including Wilde's *De Profundis* which was promptly forwarded to Pasternak. Apart from translations, Lomonosova also suggested arranging for Pasternak to write reviews in French and English for the magazines *Nation* and *New Republic*, and even offered an advance of money from her personal reserves. From his *dacha* at Aleksandrovskoye, Pasternak wrote back to Lomonosova in August and enthusiastically agreed to translate Wilde; the proposal for articles he initially turned down owing to his inadequate knowledge of the languages concerned. Lomonosova's offer of money was also refused as 'inadmissible', although in fact over the next months she insistently rendered the Pasternaks support.[16]

Correspondence and friendship with Lomonosova were to span several decades and Pasternak came to see in her one of his most important Western contacts. (In 1926 the Lomonosovs decided not to return to Soviet Russia and spent the rest of their lives in exile, eventually settling in Britain.) Their correspondence was unusual in its pretext and tone: for once Pasternak was the embarrassed receiver of material and emotional largesse from a woman rather than its distributor. There was also sometimes a quaint contrast between the mundane content of her messages and the ecstatic elevation of his.

Before Pasternak's letter reached her, Lomonosova sent money with an anonymous courier who delivered it to the Volkhonka apartment. There it was discovered by Evgeniya on her next trip into town from Aleksandrovskoye. Where her husband might have demurred, she promptly exchanged the bills at a bank and in one morning settled four months' rent arrears and several other debts besides. Pasternak was uncertain how they could ever repay Lomonosova. Although he had translated Ben Jonson ('by a miracle in which the dictionary played a large part') he was no longer confident of his ability to cope with Wilde's English. A propos the articles, however, he told Lomonosova that he may be able to draft in linguist friends to help him. But he had no wish to embark on this immediately, as he explained:

Your idea finds me in full swing with various works planned and begun in a by no means random manner. These cannot be left now without harm even to the articles. If the publishers permit such a deferment, everything will turn out happily. I reckon on giving the articles a proper measure of vitality, interest, and a certain . . . historicism, and with this latter some of what I am so engrossed in at the moment.[17]

So far as we can tell, neither articles nor translation were ever produced. In the autumn and winter of 1925 Pasternak was absorbed by *Spektorsky* and other distractions. Meanwhile, however, after delays caused by bad weather and lack of funds, the family finally arranged a cheap summer holiday in the Moscow countryside. Pasternak described the journey in a letter of 11 June to Tikhonov, in the hope of a possible visit from him. Aleksandrovskoye was intriguingly remote. A local train from town brought one to Nemchinovka where a second train took one to Usovo, after which Aleksandrovskoye was reached by fording the river Moskva or by calling for a ferry boat.[18]

Out at their woodland dacha Pasternak read Mandelstam's newly published *Noise of Time* and Fedin's novel *Cities and Years* (*Goroda i gody*), and he discussed this very contrasted holiday reading in a letter to Mandelstam. His thoughts on the two books were clearly bound up with his own recent poetic concerns and interest in large-scale works.

The Noise of Time has afforded me rare pleasure which I have not felt for a long time. The full sound of this book, which has found happy expression for many elusive things (and many such that they were completely erased from my memory) kept me in its grip and carried me along so firmly and surely [...] Why do you not write a large novel? You have already succeeded, and all you need do is write it down. I know by my own experience that my opinion is neither unique nor original, i.e. other people think the same of your prose as I do, including Bobrov [...]

Have you read *Cities and Years*? Well done Fedin! Don't you think so? I have not managed to do anything worthwhile over the summer.[19]

Fedin's novel, which appeared the previous year, marked a partial return to the nineteenth-century epic novel tradition and dealt with a broad segment of recent Russian and European history. This emphasis doubtless appealed to Pasternak, who seemed not to be struck by another more sinister aspect of Fedin's book. The reflective, intellectual 'superfluous man' of the nineteenth-century novel was increasingly presented in Soviet literature of the 1920s as a negative and pernicious type. At the start of *Cities and Years* the intellectual Startsov is executed by the German communist Kurt Wahn in what appears as an authorial act of purgation, shedding all residue of pity for a once congenial literary hero. Just such a character had been celebrated in the opening chapters of Pasternak's *Spektorsky* however. Fedin's novel was only one of several examples demonstrating how much Spektorsky's eccentric 'privacy' ran against the grain of the times. After loss of impetus with his verse novel Pasternak lapsed again briefly into his 'swoon of many years' and, as he later told Lomonosova, succumbed to a new 'sickness of morale'.[20] He was saved, however, by a piece of shrewd professionalism: in the summer of 1925 he began planning a new work whose realisation was to improve both his mood and finances.

What Pasternak required was a lucrative large-scale project which lacked any ideological intricacies that might slow progress or hinder publication, i.e., something which could be written rapidly and with a certain honest detachment. These needs were all met by his new *poema* in several episodes entitled *The Year Nineteen Five* (*1905 god*). A seminal work for it may have been a short poem called 'January 9th' ('9-e yanvarya') printed in *Krasnaya nov'*, no. 2, 1925.

On 25 July 1925 Pasternak wrote to Chernyak with a request for help in obtaining various materials on the 1905 revolution. These included writings by Lenin, Sverchkov's *At Revolution's Dawn* (*Na zare revolyutsii*), Aiznaft's *The Strike Movement and Gapon Affair* (*Zabastovshchina i Gaponovshchina*), various works by A. Elnitsky and S. Piontkovsky, some issues of *Krasnaya letopis'* (Red Chronicle) and the journal *Byloe* (Time Past). Four months later, on 1st December, Pasternak complained to Gruzdev that he was still wading through a mass of 'pulp literature, commonplaces and trivia' as part of the background preparation for his task. The work absorbed him and he apparently saw less of his friends. Budantsev, for instance, reported in late December that he had not seen Pasternak since the summer.[21]

Once started, work on *Nineteen Five* proceeded with fluency, thanks partly to the fact that during the winter 1925–6 Pasternak was able to retreat and work next door in the room of his brother and sister-in-law. The two of them were both architects and spent the day at building sites or in their offices, and even when at home they often allowed Boris to work there in an undisturbed atmosphere.

Exhilaration at his renewed productivity restored Pasternak's morale. He later recalled:

I began recovering as I worked on the year 1905 [...] I began to work properly – i.e. as I did long ago – only very recently. I started on *1905* in a lingering state of half-sleep, surrounded by the fluff and feathers of that deep post-prandial Soviet featherbed.

The 'featherbed' of officially endorsed mediocrity, encouraged by the 1925 Central Committee resolution, formed an inauspicious background for Pasternak's work on *Nineteen Five* and on another *poema* which grew out of it entitled *Lieutenant Shmidt* (*Leitenant Shmidt*). This was explained to Raisa Lomonosova:

Until the present order of things nobody probably imagined that the purpose of the age was to serve as a plank-bed, and that for comfort it is a good idea to fill pillows and mattresses with boasting. This is especially felt now that the economic regime makes even hay an expensive and unobtainable commodity.

At the moment I am writing something in verse about Lieutenant Shmidt. I want to write it better than the low level of the ceiling demands. That is, I want to write it with my hair in the plaster moulding and my head full of bruises. And I hope that by using my head to batter my way through to the attic I shall get a good 'three plus' out of five for what I write. That is how low they are now building here.[22]

Nineteen Five was announced to the public in the first issue of the journal *Na literaturnom postu* (On Literary Guard) for the following year. In a note under the general heading 'What Writers Are Working On' Pasternak described it as 'not a *poema* but simply a chronicle of the year 1905 in versa form'. Completed episodes on the *Potemkin* mutiny,

357

'Bloody Sunday' and the December uprising 'still lack an internal link', Pasternak claimed. 'They will be printed in separate journals, after which I shall revise them and by spring put them together as a complete book.'[23] The work's relative simplicity did not, of course, eliminate all difficulty. A somewhat later note in *Na literaturnom postu*, no. 4, 1927, stated: 'I consider the epic is inspired by the times. And thus in *The Year Nineteen Five* I am moving from a lyrical way of thought to the epic, although this is very difficult.' The appearance of such an announcement in a 'proletarian' journal probably obscured the ambivalence of its tone and implication: the age might indeed make epic demands, but this could yet cause the sickness and demise of lyric poetry.

Nineteen Five did contain some personal elements in the form of authorial reminiscence, but it was not a work organically bound up with Pasternak's personality. Much of it was assembled from external sources, including the books that Chernyak was asked to supply. The effect of working from such objective raw materials was perhaps similar to translation work. By providing an obligatory narrative or factual 'semantic core', it limited the degree of metaphoric convolution and simplified Pasternak's poetic style. This was in fact Pasternak's first work in an idiom that could be apprehended by the uninitiated reader. L. Dashkov, for instance, writing in *Kniga i profsoyuzy* (Books and Trade Unions) praised this triumph of the social over the personal element, the clear style and 'lyrical pathos', and concluded that the work 'can be recommended for large workers' libraries'.[24]

The chosen theme of the 1905 revolution avoided the dilemma of trying to portray the 1917 revolution in a personally honest and at the same time acceptably Leninist light. Yet the celebration of any milestone in revolutionary prehistory almost guaranteed publication and an official accolade. Several similar works were being written at about the same time. When Pasternak started work on *Nineteen Five*, Sergei Eisenstein was shooting his film *The Battleship Potemkin*. Pasternak's friend Dmitrii Petrovsky had also written a poetic cycle on the 1905 Black Sea rebellion, centering on the *Potemkin* mutiny and Lieutenant Shmidt, and in 1926 Tikhonov had to disappoint 'a certain modest poet' by telling him that his idea for a poetic version of the Shmidt story had been preempted by Pasternak.[25] The official appeal of this subject matter was registered in the printing of several episodes of Pasternak's work in unambiguously 'proletarian' publications during 1926, such as the almanacs *High Flood* (Polovod'e) and *The Proletarian* (Proletarii), the journals *Zvezda* (The Star) and *Krasnaya niva* (Red Cornfield), as well as in *Novy mir* and *Ogonek* (The Light). *Nineteen Five* thus became an approved popular favourite. It was published four times together with *Lieutenant Shmidt* as a separate book, in 1927, 1930, 1932 and 1937, and it has appeared in most Soviet editions of Pasternak's poetic writings.[26]

Dates affixed to some subsequent printings of *Nineteen Five* suggest that most of it was finished by February of 1926. Before its final completion, though, Pasternak had run out of steam and enthusiasm. In late March he complained to his elder sister of boredom. 'This ghastly "Year 1905"! What is the point of all this? Why am I doing it?' By 30 July, even, he had still not quite completed the work or received final payment.[27]

As Pasternak announced, *Nineteen Five* is a series of striking episodes rather than an organic whole. Indeed the title on one manuscript preserved in the State Central Archive of Literature and Art (TsGALI) is not the one we know, but 'From Works on the Year 1905' ('Iz rabot o 1905 gode').[28] The main formal binding element is a continuous anapaestic pentameter, and although eventually monotonous, its triple-time gallop conveys a sense of breathless revolutionary impetus. The typographic layout (e.g., above, pp. 57–8) reinforces an impression of fleeting cinematographic images, although it originally had a more practical purpose. In a family letter to Berlin Pasternak wrote out some excerpts in regular pentameter quatrains. But, as he later explained to Lydia, the layout was altered in order to secure the 750 roubles for extracts printed in *Novy mir*, no. 2, 1926! 'This is how you obtain such money. I am breaking up the stanza so there are about ten or eleven lines in each. There is no other way. Is it my fault that proper fees are only paid after the author's death?'[29] Pasternak also commented to Lydia on the work's rhythmic monotony, promising that for the book edition the episode of the Krasnaya Presnya uprising would be rewritten in another metre.[30] However, this plan was never carried out.

Nineteen Five starts with a short apostrophe to the spirit of revolution, which is addressed variously as a 'Joan of Arc from Siberian convicts' and as a 'socialist maid' who 'struck light from the gloom of the tinder heap', and so on (I, 109; *SP*, 245). In a manuscript dated 25 October 1925 this introduction is entitled 'Ode' – another surprising concession to classical genre after an earlier acceptance of the epic.[31] Here there is none of *Malady Sublime*'s irony, however, but a frank and nostalgic loyalty to the revolutionary spirit of Pasternak's generation in 1905.

There are six further sections. 'The Fathers' recalls some history of the

Russian revolutionary movement; 'Childhood' records the 9 January massacre, combined with some youthful personal recollections of the revolution; 'Peasants and Workmen' describes a rural disturbance and the workers' uprising in Lodz; 'Mutiny' recounts the *Potemkin* episode; 'Students' describes the demonstration in Moscow at the funeral of the murdered revolutionary Bauman; and 'Moscow in December' deals with the Krasnaya Presnya rising at the end of 1905. The first two sections of main text follow on from the 'Ode'. 'The Fathers' provides a glimpse of darkness before dawn, an 'eve of disasters, political cells, and of heroes, of dynamite, daguerreotypes, hearts aflame' (I, 110; *SP*, 246). Impressions of Russia after the 1860s reforms introduce the People's Will, nihilists, and the unsound sleep of the city square – all harbingers of revolt. The effect is to present the intelligentsia as founding fathers of the revolutionary movement. Section 2 is framed by recollections of a teenage son of these fathers, one conscious enough amid school japes and music studies to register the importance of current events. 'Students' also features intelligentsia participation. Altogether, in fact, there is a tactful attempt (reinforced also by *Lieutenant Shmidt*) to rehabilitate the intelligentsia in revolutionary history[32] and thus to counterpoint the implications of *Malady Sublime*. There is little, however, of the complexity and ambivalence of the earlier *poema* or of the first chapters of *Spektorsky*. For all its technical assurance, *Nineteen Five* left the deeper problems of history and personality unprobed. Some years later, on completing *Spektorsky*, Pasternak's verdict was that here he had 'said more, and said more of substance, than I did about the 1905 revolution in my pragmatically chronistic booklet *1905*'.[33]

The public success of *Nineteen Five* only confirmed what Pasternak said in 1925 about the mediocrity of 'average' literature. As he told Tsvetaeva, 'the forces that gave rise to "1905" lie somewhere in the middle between service and hack-writing. I won't undertake to determine how far removed this is from creative literature [...] I want to publish the booklet with a dedication 'to the average reader and his guardians', or else "... to his little wooden hobby-horse".' Similarly, in 1926, to Lomonosova:

A very large tribute has been paid in this work to the commonplace and very average understanding. However, I wrote it honestly and with the best of intentions. But generally, you know, not only we but the whole world and the whole generation have caught the contagion of mediocrity.[34]

இஒஒஒ

According to dates appended on one edition, *Lieutenant Shmidt* was written in the year beginning March 1926. It was thus started before completion of *Nineteen Five* and probably grew out of it. The two works were often published under one cover as 'twins' and some reviewers treated them as part of a single opus.[35] But where *Nineteen Five* was little more than a versified chronicle, the later work was a more personal statement and is regarded as Pasternak's most successful epic composition. His deeper concern for it was evident in the many changes made at proof stage, when various episodes printed in journals were revised in the summer of 1927 for a book edition.

As with earlier works, extracts began appearing before the *poema*'s completion. As Pasternak's correspondence with Gruzdev and others in the first three months of 1926 made clear, his financial troubles were by no means over. On 19 May he also told Tsvetaeva that 'domestic circumstances force me to accept everything I have so far written of *Lieutenant Shmidt* as the complete first part of the poem, to believe firmly in part 2, and to hand over what is already written'.[36] Part 1 had in fact been handed to *Novy mir* the previous day. The continuing need to raise short-term loans and advances impeded concentration, however, and it was July before fitful work on part 2 began. Completion of part 3 was later delayed, partly owing to the shock of Rilke's death in December, and the *Novy mir* editors were clamouring before the final episode was ready in early 1927.

Lieutenant Pyotr Petrovich Shmidt was executed after leading a naval mutiny in the Russian Black Sea fleet during the 1905 revolution. After 1917 he became one of several revolutionary heroes to whom studies and memoirs were devoted. Pasternak used these in research for his epic, notably a volume of letters and other documents published in 1922, and the more recent memoirs of Shmidt's sister Anna Izbash and of various eye-witnesses of the mutiny.[37]

Pasternak treats the plot impressionistically and some details are only comprehensible with background knowledge. Typically, too, human thoughts, moods and actions are assimilated by the natural scene. As Tsvetaeva commented, the poet 'paints a picture of Lieutenant Shmidt from life, but his main character is the trees at a public meeting [...] It is always elements and not persons, just as in 'Potemkin'' it is the *sea* and not the sailors.'[38] Shmidt's story is not confined to the mutiny, though. A complete picture of the hero's character is built up, with hints of marital complexities and of an incipient affair with another girl, as well as versified extracts from Shmidt's letters. All this introduces an account of the mutiny, its failure, the trial of the hero and his co-mutineers, and his final sentence and execution in March 1906.

The contemporary critic Krasilnikov observed that both Shmidt and Spektorsky were the 'faces of one hero' and had much in common with the author himself.[39] Yet Shmidt's known real-life traits and phraseology were presented by Pasternak with surprising accuracy. Of semi-noble descent and educated, Shmidt embodied the best traditions of a group with which Pasternak still identified. He was evidently at pains to refrain from poeticising Shmidt and to divest the image of its romantic legendary adornment.[40] But the result was not everywhere appreciated; Tsvetaeva found him 'Chekhovian, Blokish, intellectual' and with surprisingly few of his creator's qualities![41] Shmidt was presented as a tragic hero, and the second part of the poem, in which the drama began, was described by Pasternak as showing the 'transformation of a man into the hero of an action in which he does not believe, his break-up and downfall'.[42] The émigré critic Svyatopolk-Mirsky registered all this in 1928:

History crystallises around the personality of Shmidt, but he is played in an utterly unheroic tonality. His letters, his personal drama emerge from the dense cosmic brew of events with a certain deliberate sparseness and weakness. Taken separately, these letters appear strangely weak – only against the background of the whole does this very weakness acquire its meaning [...] In Shmidt there dies the old intelligentsia revolution of the People's Will [...] Pasternak, a great revolutionary and transformer of Russian poetry, turns back [...] to the whole ancient tradition of Russian sacrificial revolutionariness and gives it an artistic completeness which left to itself it could not have provided.[43]

Shmidt thus does not correspond to the 'blazing revolutionary' stereotype, but resembles more the Saint-Just of Pasternak's *Dramatic Fragments*. He consents to lead the mutiny only when 'picked out from the ranks / By the very elemental wave' (I, 172; *SP*, 302). He does so fully aware of his personal sacrifice and moral duty. Not a party member, he is opposed to sectarian squabbles and to all bloodshed. His approach to revolution is a philanthropic, ethical and Christian one. In a letter to his beloved in part 3, he even paraphrases Christ's words in John 15.7:

> All commotion has ended. Standing afar,
> With all the power of my feelings I sense

> That this fate which befalls is an enviable one.
> I have lived and laid down my life for my friends.
>
> (I, 162; *SP*, 292)

The image of Golgotha is invoked at Shmidt's trial too. But the core of his concern – an involuntary and unconscious participation in history thanks to an incontravertible moral prompting – is close to what Pasternak himself enunciated shortly after completing this work. When asked along with other writers by *Na literaturnom postu* to give an assessment of the modern role of the classics, he wrote a few lines on his own view of Pushkin's significance. He claimed no longer to view Pushkin impressionistically as earlier; his understanding had expanded and was enriched by 'elements of a moral character'. 'By an artist's aesthetic, I understand his conception of the nature of art, of the role of art in history, and of his own personal *responsibility* towards it' (III, 159–60).

The ethical note sounded in *Malady Sublime* was reinforced in *Lieutenant Shmidt* by a religious element. Passivity was seen not as negative, but as a painful and positive acceptance of a tragic historical role; this poem thus served as an obvious bridge between Pasternak's early lyrical output and the ideas of his much later novel. In his speech at the trial Shmidt addresses his accusers, saying:

> I am, like you, part of the immense
> Shifting succession of the ages.
> The sentence passed I shall accept
> Without rebuke or anger.

Recalling the liberal rights recently granted to the people and then rudely flouted, he says:

> And all was once again revoked.
> Eternally and point by point
> With good intention thus they bring
> Us all to rise up in revolt.   (I, 172–3; *SP*, 302, 570)

This last quatrain was one of four that were excised from the 1927 book edition, as part of an ideological rather than artistically required revision. (Pasternak also cut out the quoted letters from his hero, and completed and honed up those sections conveying Shmidt's outward characteristics.) The statement as it stands is in quoted speech, and thus has a specific character context. On the other hand, all Shmidt's final eloquent address has the force of a general act of indictment: the trial of protestors now in progress is only part of a historical succession of revolt and suppression, a process which repeats eternally. There is a hint, too, of Pasternak's own phraseology in *Malady Sublime* in the echoed 'good intention' that paved the road to hell, and in this work to rebellion. Apart from this, the 'November Meeting' episode in part 1, section 6, provided an example of free indirect (or maybe direct) poetic speech in the stanza quoted at the head of this chapter (above, p. 348): here, the use of the word 'eternal' and the emphatic repetition of the pronoun 'we' seems to hint at a generalised relevance to post-revolutionary Russia. Pasternak's contemporaries depicted as 'men of mine and catacomb', contrasted tragically with that earlier emergence 'from catacombs' and 'blinding debouch in the forum' in the 'Spring Rain' of 1917 (above, p. 212).

In 1926 Pasternak was increasingly aware of the lyric poet's lonely stance. Some of his finest contemporaries were either expatriated, or virtually silenced like Akhmatova and Mandelstam. Pasternak's willingness to take up the epic perhaps showed more practical professionalism than those two and promoted a new bout of productivity, but the price of it was self-denial as a lyricist. The bitterness of this concession to external pressures emerged in Pasternak's letter to Lomonosova in Berlin on 10 May 1926:

They try here to pretend that I have just been a dream vision to myself and to other writers and poets, and that but for this and a few other similar dreams everyone else would be able to sleep even more like the dead, and thus much better. Actually, I myself have also been asleep, and if they had told me that I was capable of a dull but slowly ripening hatred I would not have understood what they said. I was so obliging, forgetful and tractable.

Pasternak's despair in the early months of 1926 probably explains certain fantasies he had about his own artistic and physical death. These he had confided to his sister Josephine, who wrote back on 21 April to console him.[44] But encouragement came also from a growing sense of communion with European culture, tangibly evidenced in an increasing flow of correspondence with readers and friends in the West. Lomonosova, one of the first of them, was told how the writings of Marina Tsvetaeva had been a particularly loud 'ring of the alarm-clock' that roused him.[45] It was to Tsvetaeva that Pasternak dedicated *Lieutenant Shmidt*. On 18 May 1926 he also wrote a poetic 'Dedication' ('Posvyashchenie') of fifteen lines in the form of an acrostic on Tsvetaeva's name. If the epic was a requirement of the times, this dedication was a frank and bitter comment on them. In it the passing years were likened to a forest which both sheltered the poet in its foliage and formed a setting in which he was hounded to death. This image of history viewed as a forest was to recur in several of Pasternak's lyrics of the later 1920s. (In a letter of 19 May Pasternak explained to Tsvetaeva that this dedication sprang partly from a 'sketchy, downright bad poem' written earlier that month as a concession to topicality in response to an *Izvestiya* commission for some verse on the British General Strike. His premonition that his verses would be turned down proved correct, and they would have been lost had Pasternak not copied them out for Tsvetaeva.)[46] Part 1 of *Shmidt* had appeared already in *Novy mir* when members of the editorial board identified the acrostic inscription to an émigré poetess who was now out of favour. Pasternak received a sharp rebuke from chief editor Polonsky, who in May had also had to weather a severe storm after printing Pilnyak's 'Tale of the Unextinguished Moon' with its innuendo about an official conspiracy responsible for General Frunze's recent death in hospital. Pasternak sent an effusive letter of remorse for what he saw as an innocuous private communication between poets, and cordial relations with Polonsky were repaired.[47] (Ironically, by the time the scandal erupted, Pasternak had withdrawn the dedication because of Tsvetaeva's negative view of *Lieutenant Shmidt*!)

The catacomb retreat of contemporary idealists alluded to in *Lieutenant Shmidt* was also an image type that enjoyed a certain currency in the 1920s. 'The Badger's Set' ('Barsuch'ya nora'), for instance, was the title of Mandelstam's article on Blok in 1922. With its overtones of Dostoevsky's 'underground', the image was also to find its way into various prose writings, by Zoshchenko, Pilnyak and others. Vilmont recalled a conversation of the mid-1920s with Pasternak concerning the urban intelligentsia's status vis-à-vis the state. They were, the poet maintained, 'sitting in their burrows, much more cut off from the people than was the case before the revolution'. Maintaining contact with people and breathing the air of history evidently influenced Pasternak's renewed emphasis on 'realism' (in a sense close to the traditional one) as a foundation of his aesthetics and as an increasing need in modern literature. Vilmont recalls the following statement by him:

Realism is not a movement in art, but is the very nature of art, its guard-dog, which does not allow one to swerve from a trail laid like Ariadne's thread. All one has to do is find such a ball of thread! And if we who write increasingly pass by in silence and do not talk about what is going on under our noses, then this is because of timidity – a profoundly *unartistic* timidity – because we are all far removed from events, and because of hunger...[48]

A similar emphasis emerged in another letter of May 1926 to Tsvetaeva:

I seem to be starting, still barely perceptibly, by detours, slowly and under the earth, to save and defend in a realistic dressing that idealism which one here has to keep tucked under one's coat flap.

Comparing his own imperfection with other items printed in some journals he had sent to Tsvetaeva, Pasternak noted that 'In the present, for me *difficult*, period of mastering *realism* through poetry there are always things there that are better than [...] my clumsy banalities.'[49] Perhaps in the light of events, the limits on what was proper in poetry in 1921 were beginning to shift by mid-decade.

The clarity of what one assumes to be authorial statement at certain points in *Lieutenant Shmidt* is not impaired by a factor pointed out in Yurii Levin's study of the work. By contrast with the regular monometricity of *Spektorsky* and *Nineteen Five*, which helps to highlight Pasternakian vocal intonations, *Lieutenant Shmidt* seems like an attempt to muffle or counterpoint them not merely by use of different epistolary, memoiristic and speech sources, but also by fragmentation of the poem's three parts into several subsections pointed up by changes in metre. In fact the work presents an amazing compendium of experiment in the field of strophics, metre and rhyme; there is nothing to match this spectacular prosodic laboratory elsewhere in Pasternak's œuvre.[50] Was there a gesture here towards the technical experimentation fostered by the Lef group or was this a mere escape from the monotony of *Nineteen Five*? If, as Mayakovsky later claimed, *Lieutenant Shmidt* was an 'achievement of Lef', its significance as such was hardly recognised, and by 1927 Pasternak's lyric bent was reasserting itself after the epic diversion. This was probably symbolised by an incident which Katanyan observed in the Briks' apartment: in early 1927 Pasternak arrived with a bundle of books which he deposited in Osip Brik's 'den'. 'There!' Pasternak said, apparently with the satisfied look of a student at the end of term who is able to push away the books he no longer requires. These were various editions he had borrowed concerning the year 1905 and included the letters of Shmidt.[51]

Pasternak's poems on the events of 1905 proved a general public success, and they increased his prestige in literary social circles. Yakov Chernyak, still headily enthusiastic about socialism, was apparently thrilled by the new 'social turn' in his friend's writing. In the winter of 1926–7 he frequently invited him to his Arbat home, and there Pasternak gave readings that were attended by several young writers, by Polonsky and his artist wife Kira, and also by Galina Serebryakova, the attractive wife of the important official Sokolnikov. In 1927 Pasternak also appeared at a gathering at their élite residence in Granovsky Street, bringing with him a copy of *The Year Nineteen Five*, recently published. According to Elizaveta Chernyak, Pasternak did not enjoy his visit and never returned to Serebryakova's (a reaction that doubtless pleased Elizaveta, since her memoirs betray displeasure at the attention Serebrakova received from Yakov her husband).[52]

Several critics who already admired Pasternak welcomed his apparent emergence from bourgeois lyrical domesticity into the historical arena. As Tsevetaeva later commented to Leonid Pasternak, 'The praises of the majority relate to the *theme* of 1905, that is, they are something like certificates of good conduct issued for exemplary behaviour.'[53] The implication that Pasternak had only now heeded official advice and recovered from earlier aberrations also struck Olya Freidenberg on reading a review of Pasternak's recent verse in *Pechat' i revolyutsiya* in summer 1927. Her scornful remarks about this to Pasternak found him more indulgent towards a critic who 'evidently wished me well and was forced to do so in the "terms of the age"'. In fact, Krasilnikov's article in the fifth number of the journal was a careful but sensitive and intelligent survey of Pasternak's evolution to date. A similarly positive appraisal of *Nineteen Five* by Postupalsky appeared in *Pechat' i revolyutsiya* no. 8, and there were to be several more. They included a slightly condescending but approving notice by Lezhnev, who though earlier cool especially towards Pasternak's prose eventually identified him as a key figure in modern poetry, the author not of 'epic' verse, but (even in *Nineteen Five*) of 'high tension lyricism'. Even the 'proletarian' Pertsov gave a school-masterly welcome to 'The New Pasternak' in *Na literaturnom postu*.[54] Pasternak himself, though, set greater store by positive critiques from 'the best and most independent émigrés', including Svyatopolk-Mirsky in July 1927, and from Gorky. The latter (like Lunacharsky a defective judge of all but the most straightforward verse) congratulated Pasternak in autumn 1927 on overcoming his earlier 'capricious complexity' and 'incomplete delineation of images' and welcomed this new work of 'a real poet – and a social poet, social in the best and profoundest sense of the term'. To this message Pasternak wrote a letter of carelessly rapturous response.[55]

Prior to these plaudits, however, in 1926 there were more ominous noises from certain cultural watchdogs. One of them was Lev Trotsky.

He had evidently failed to unravel Pasternak's lyrical complexities, had left him out of his survey of *Literature and Revolution* in 1923, and was now sceptical about Pasternak's recent transformation. Pasternak evidently attended a number of meetings arranged by Trotsky for poets and critics at his Glavkontsesskom (Chief Concessions Committee) offices on Dmitrovka Street.* At one such gathering which included Lef members Aseyev, Katanyan and Tretyakov, Trotsky questioned Pasternak: 'Tell me... here, you've written *Nineteen Five* and *Lieutenant Shmidt*... Is this just an offering to the age, or were you really... er, sincere?' Such was Katanyan's recollection.[57] Another chronicler recalled how on 13 March 1926 Pasternak along with Aseyev, Selvinsky and Brik visited Trotsky 'to complain that they were unable to publish their works because other journals accepted only "popular literature" [*massovaya literatura*] and rejected "experimental" works'. Following this, Trotsky held a meeting with them and other colleagues (including Abram Lezhnev, Osinsky, Polonsky and Voronsky), although nothing positive seems to have emerged either from this discussion or from other private literary gatherings arranged by Trotsky (at which those present included the above named as well as Lev Sedov, Trotsky's elder son and Adolf Ioffe, their wives, and the poet Semyon Kirsanov).[58]

The lack of outlets for lyric verse in the winter of 1925–6 even persuaded Pasternak to return to translation again. Nikolai Tikhonov had commissioned some poetic translations for a miscellany called *East and West* (*Vostok i zapad*). Lev Gornung also brought Pasternak books by the German poets Mühsam and Becher on 21 January 1926 (an occasion on which, incidentally, Gornung met Henry Lanz, Pasternak's Marburg associate who was now a resident in the USA and briefly visiting Moscow).[59] With the exception of popular celebrities like Mayakovsky and Esenin, an increasing number of poets complained after 1925 that lyric verse collections were virtually impossible to place with publishers. (There had still been only one edition of *My Sister Life* and two of *Themes and Variations*.) In February 1926 some Moscow poets tried to help themselves by founding a cooperative called 'Uzel' (The Knot) to publish their own collections. Although this association never became an important platform for him, Pasternak was a member

---

* Apart from meetings with Radek, Lunacharsky and others from Narkompros, these encounters with Trotsky were probably Pasternak's only contacts with Bolshevik leaders in this period. Ivinskaya's tale of a meeting with Stalin in the 1920s is hardly credible and is not confirmed by any other source; at most Pasternak might have observed him from a distance when he appeared in processions, platform parties and so on.[56]

(along with Anisimov, Antokolsky, Livshitz, Parnok, Petrovsky, Romm, Spassky, Shervinsky, Pyotr Zaitsev, Zenkevich, and others), and in April 1926 he was written to on Kuzmin's recommendation by the 'absurdists' Kharms and Vvedensky who complained of similar publishing problems in Leningrad.[60]

The obstacles faced by Uzel lyricists were by no means the only clouds on the horizon. On 28 December 1925 the poet Esenin had committed suicide, an event which acquired a certain symbolic significance, such that even Tsvetaeva, who never had a high opinion of him, thought to commemorate his death in a new *poema*. In January of 1926 she wrote to Pasternak asking him to send her information about the circumstances of Esenin's suicide. Via Gruzdev, Pasternak wrote to Georgii Ustinov who had seen Esenin in the last few days of his life;[61] Pasternak also enquired of Lev Gornung, who solicited help from the Leningrad poet Pavel Luknitsky. Despite Pasternak's lack of sympathy with Esenin during his lifetime, his remarks to Gornung on 1 February about his suicide included an admission that 'his death has astonished [*porazila*] me. I have a certain numb feeling, as though a noose were round my own neck [...] Yesterday Mandelstam came to see me. We talked about Esenin. He has exactly the same feeling as Tikhonov...'[62]

There were other poets, too, who were in dire straits professionally. By the mid-1920s Akhmatova, Kuzmin and Voloshin were being edged out of Soviet literature altogether. Gornung had taken a collective congratulation bearing Pasternak's signature to Kuzmin in November 1925; and Pasternak had joined in honouring the twentieth anniversary of Kuzmin's literary activities at Herzen House on Tverskoi Boulevard.[63] For the other two, a rescue operation was needed.

On 1 March 1926, at the State Academy of Arts on Prechistenka Street, a benefit evening was held for Voloshin, who had recently celebrated the thirtieth anniversary of his literary debut. The performance raised 470 roubles and was given by Pasternak's composer-pianist friend Samuil Feinberg, assisted by Bulgakov, Slyozkin and Veresaev who gave prose readings, and by the poets Antokolsky, Shervinsky and Pasternak himself (who contributed two extracts from *Nineteen Five*). Pasternak afterwards received a thanks offering of a water-colour by Voloshin, which Gornung mounted for him. Voloshin also invited Pasternak to visit him in Koktebel. Pasternak would willingly have accepted, since he could have visited nearby Sevastopol and collected some local impressions for incorporation in the Lieutenant Shmidt story. Unfortunately, shortage of money in the summer of 1926 forced him to decline, and he next saw Voloshin only the following March in Moscow.[64]

A week after the benefit concert for Voloshin, Akhmatova arrived briefly in Moscow. She too lived in awful poverty. Despite a two-month cure at a sanatorium in 1925, she was still sick with tuberculosis. Her illness reflected the hard times: other sufferers included Aseyev and the wives of both Mandelstam and Pasternak. Pasternak had not seen Akhmatova since 1924. He found her depressed, but slightly improved in health and younger looking. But she was obstinate about accepting charity and Pasternak feared to ask how she was faring. This trait of hers had prevented him and Mayakovsky from rendering assistance the previous year; eventually Pasternak was to find ways of helping Akhmatova as his own finances improved.

In connection with Pasternak's special interest in neglected contemporaries in 1925–6, it is interesting to note that in February of 1926, following conversations with his artist friend Lev Gorning, Pasternak had asked him for copies of Gumilyov's work, intending to write something on the executed Petrograd Acmeist. No such work appears to have been completed, however. Gornung's memoirs also recall other conversations with Pasternak at this time about the undeserved neglect of Kuzmin, whose 'Story of Count Caliostro' Pasternak particularly praised, and about his own neglect: Pasternak claimed he had not yet seen a single critical review of either *Spektorsky* or of the Krug edition of his *Stories* (*Rasskazy*).[65]

Although her role in Pasternak's life caused severe marital difficulties for him, Tsvetaeva was in early 1926 part of a series of circumstances which helped to alleviate his artistic crisis. In late March he first read in manuscript her new *Poem of the End* (*Poema kontsa*). It reached him by chance in a manuscript copy that had been passed from hand to hand among Moscow literati. He had read it one morning, and for the rest of the day his 'mind was still in a blur from its gripping dramatic force' (II, 344; *VP*, 481). Recording the recent agonies of Tsvetaeva's lost love for Konstantin Rodzevich, *Poem of the End* struck a painfully familiar note for Pasternak as well as entrancing him with its pace and verbal virtuosity. 'Only Scriabin, Rilke, Mayakovsky and Cohen have stirred me so,' he wrote to his sister Josephine. 'There is also a little of me in this poetry.'[66] Most importantly, however, this long-limbed lyric outpouring perhaps reminded Pasternak in a tangible way of the continuing viability of such poetry. He himself told Tsvetaeva, 'Lyrically contained,

28 Boris Pasternak with his wife Evgeniya and son (1925)

Poem of the End is right to the last step your own asserted world. Perhaps precisely because it is lyric poetry and written in the first person singular.'[67]

The impact of this poem was reinforced the very same day when a letter from Leonid Pasternak arrived and told Boris how his work had come to the favourable notice of Rilke. A short time before, Rilke had written Leonid in thanks for his fiftieth birthday congratulations and reported having seen 'some poems by him, very *beautiful* ones', in an anthology edited by Ehrenburg.[68] Pasternak never forgot that moment. He later recorded the precise setting, with evening drawing in, snow falling fitfully, and himself alone in the apartment sitting in the hallway at the still uncleared breakfast table and picking thoughtfully at cold potatoes in the frying pan, when a ring at the door announced delivery of his father's letter. 'It was the second shock of the day. I went over to the window and burst into tears. I could not have been more surprised had I been told that they were reading me in heaven' (II, 344–5; *VP*, 481).

There ensued several months of three-sided correspondence between Rilke, Pasternak and Tsvetaeva. On 12 April Pasternak wrote Rilke an impassioned letter in poetically turned and idiosyncratic German:

371

Great and most beloved poet!

I do not know where this letter would end and how it could be distinguished from real life, were I to give expression to the love, admiration and gratitude which I have felt for two decades.

I am indebted to you for the very basis of my character and the very mode of my spiritual being. They are your creations. I have words for them which one has for distant happenings that are later recognised as sources of the events that seem to arise from them. The tempestuous joy in being allowed once to make a poet's confession to you is no more commonplace for me than what I would feel towards Aeschylus or Pushkin, were this conceivable...[69]

Pasternak went on to describe his father's letter and its impact. Then followed some thoughts on Russia, on the stagnation following a dynamic revolution (above p. 349), on the well-springs of inspiration which remained untouched by this, and on his own resumption of work after years of sterility. Pasternak concluded by telling Rilke in glowing terms of Tsvetaeva and by asking him to send her the *Duino Elegies* (*Duinese Elegien*) which he himself still knew only by hearsay.

The poetic signals from Rilke and Tsvetaeva contributed significantly to Pasternak's rising morale and his awakening from what he described to Olya Freidenberg as a 'seven-year period of moral somnolence'. Other causes of this lay in an increasing stream of 'reviews and translations by foreigners, articles in the best [...] émigré press, and a multitude of great, lofty and enobling love dispersed in space and time'.[70] (Reviewing the Krug edition of Pasternak's *Stories*, Svyatopolk-Mirsky had welcomed it as a new and healthy development in Russian prose writing which had taken a wrongly ornamental path since Andrei Bely.[71] Later, in 1927, Mirsky was to identify Pasternak and Tsvetaeva as the 'most important of our living poets'.[72] While the 'Eurasian' publicist and musicologist, Suvchinsky, was overwhelmed by Pasternak's *Nineteen Five*,[73] Mirsky still preferred the lyric verse and regarded Pasternak's recent attempts to 'force himself to be like other men' as comparatively unsuccessful.[74] In a letter to Pasternak of 8 January 1927, Mirsky told him 'we have not had in Russia such a poet as you since the Golden Age, and in Europe at the moment there can only be disputation between yourself and T. S. Eliot'. Mirsky also offered payment for Pasternak's verses already published in the journal *Commerce*, enquired his view of the émigré magazine *Versty* (Versts) where part of *Nineteen Five* appeared, and announced his own work on French and English translations of *Zhenya Luvers' Childhood*.[75]

Rilke answered Pasternak's request and immediately sent Tsvetaeva his *Duino Elegies* and *Sonnets to Orpheus* (*Sonetten an Orpheus*), together with a note which she was to forward to him. Rilke's message was a heartfelt response to Pasternak's own 'direct letter which came and surrounded me as it were with the rush of beating wings', and he promised to send copies of the elegies and sonnets to Pasternak as·well. 'The receipt of this note was one of the few shocks in my life,' Pasternak later told Zelma Ruoff, and Rilke's letter remained a treasured possession throughout his life.[76] He did not respond, however, and Rilke, perplexed and saddened, could not have understood why. In fact, when Tsvetaeva's own correspondence with Rilke took flame she tormented Pasternak by keeping him in the dark about the new epistolary friendship she owed to him. Pasternak demurred further, wary of forcing himself on Rilke's attention before he had some significant new work to show which might justify such intrusion and a possible visit to Rilke. Unfortunately, it was soon too late for meetings. Rilke died in late 1926, and Pasternak could only explain in a postscript to *Safe Conduct* addressed to Rilke's departed spirit:

It was not easy to leave such a gift as your lines unanswered. But I was afraid of contenting myself with a correspondence and of settling forever only halfway down the road to meet you. But I wanted to see you [...] I comforted myself with the memory that Tsvetaeva was corresponding with you, because although I could not replace Tsvetaeva, she could replace me.   (II, 343; *VP*, 480)

The explanation was a charitable one. The tripartite correspondence was in fact bedevilled by frustrations and misunderstandings arising largely from Tsvetaeva's obsessiveness. Messages between Pasternak and Rilke initially went via Tsvetaeva in France, since Switzerland, where Rilke lived, had no postal or diplomatic link with Russia. But Pasternak quickly saw himself excluded from Tsvetaeva's relationship with Rilke as she meanwhile made one of her characteristic emotional onslaughts on the Austrian poet. Though realising he was a 'phenomenon of nature' beyond all possession, she nevertheless strove to claim him for her own.[77] In her daughter Ariadna's words, Tsvetaeva was 'highly possessive when it came to things immaterial', and she foresaw and described to Rilke his own reaction: 'All my life I have been giving myself away in poems – to all, to poets too. But always I gave too much, drowned out the possible response. The response took fright. I had preempted the entire echo.'[78] In the ten letters she sent between May and November 1926, Tsvetaeva made Rilke the object of an exquisitely fantasised love. Wayward and sensitive, Rilke meanwhile was disconcerted at her seeming deafness to hints about his failing health (he was by now fatally stricken with leukaemia). Tsvetaeva took this as a sign of indifference, even though his dedication of an elegy to her and an inscribed copy of his *Vergers* (Orchards) were evidence to the contrary. Rilke wrote cautiously in answer to her insistent messages and demands for a meeting at which, evidently, some spiritual union would be consummated between them. (For one who professed a kinship with Psyche and spiritual love, Tsvetaeva expressed her supercharged emotions in a surprisingly carnal idiom.) Finally, perplexed by her verbal excesses, Rilke gradually withdrew from their correspondence and lapsed into silence.

Possessed by a new sense of affinity with Tsvetaeva after reading *Poem of the End*, Pasternak launched his own correspondence with her onto a new level of intimacy, registered in a switch to the second person singular (although their earlier formal exchanges were not wanting in fervour). Their physical separation now seemed to intensify the electric potential between them. Their meeting in Berlin in 1922–3 was prevented when she, as a Soviet citizen, was unable to obtain a visa to travel from Czechoslovakia; a vague plan to meet up in Weimar in 1924 had come to nothing, and the physical encounter which might have brought liberation from a mutual fascination was thus denied them.[79] Meanwhile, the value of their tender 'fourth-dimensional' communion was enhanced for each of them by their increasing sense of loneliness as artists. This – despite the fact that in 1926–7 both of them enjoyed an unprecedented critical acclaim, which in Tsvetaeva's case was quickly to wane. Amid what they saw as the collapse of their cultural environment, they looked on one another as sympathetic readers and supporters. Much of their letters was taken up with the exchanges of professional littérateurs. Pasternak, for instance, had made enquiries about Esenin from Ustinov and Gornung in order to assist Tsvetaeva's plans for her *poema*, and on 20 April he mentioned further questions put to Elsa Triolet. The same month he also sent Tsvetaeva an Academy of Arts questionnaire about her life and work, with the idea of securing her inclusion in a forthcoming manual of modern authors.[80] In their correspondence Pasternak wrote her a detailed set of comments on her *Pied Piper* (*Krysolov*); in response to this came her own remarks about *Nineteen Five* and *Lieutenant Shmidt*, sections of which he copied out for her as they were completed.[81] Despite her own criticisms of *Lieutenant Shmidt* which led him to withdraw the dedication, Pasternak waxed eloquent about her own work and recounted his attempts to promote it, unsuccessfully, with the Lef group.[82]

The intensity of their correspondence in summer 1926 coincided and was probably bound up with a period of emotional crisis for Pasternak. His letters to Tsvetaeva, always exuberant, now took on some of her own febrile quality. Confessing fidelity to Evgeniya, Pasternak identified to Tsvetaeva his moral inhibitions which could only just control his 'readiness to run after any manifestation of femininity. Maybe I was born with this trait so that my character would be formed by the development of a strong, almost unfailing system of brakes.' But as the spring and summer passed, Pasternak pursued in his letters a probably quite impossible scheme to drop everything, go to Paris (assuming he could have obtained a visa) and meet up with Tsvetaeva for a joint visit to Rilke. 'Destroy me not,' he wrote to her on 20 April. 'I want to live with you, to live for a long, long time [. . .] I have an aim in life, and this aim is you [. . .] If you do not hold me back, I shall come with empty hands *only to you*.'[83] Tsvetaeva did hold him back, and indeed suggested that he should rather concern himself with the fate of her poetess friend, Sofia Parnok. This diverting tactic and her silence about her relations with Rilke only intensified Pasternak's frustration and anguish.

On 14 June visas came through for Evgeniya Pasternak and young Zhenya to visit her in-laws and take a recuperative holiday in Germany. Payment for this journey had severely taxed family finances, and with several uncompleted projects still in hand Pasternak himself planned to remain in Moscow throughout the summer in order to work. To Tsvetaeva, however, he confessed a fear of spending summer in the city with its 'heat, dust, sleeplessness, and exposure to an alien but infectious beastliness [. . .] I am afraid of falling in love. I fear the freedom. I must not now. I do not have such a grip on what I have in hand that I can lay it aside . . .'[84]

Pasternak's forebodings were realised. On 1 July he wrote Tsvetaeva an agonised letter complaining about the temptations of St Antony, describing his sufferings in terms of a cosmic sensuality: 'I lament that I could never love, neither my wife, nor you, nor myself and life if you were the only woman in the world, i.e. if you did not have millions of sisters.'[85] And on 11 July: 'I have some morbid peculiarities which can only be suppressed by lack of will. To put it briefly, they all fall directly in the area of Sigmund Freud – this is an indication of their category.' All this emotional effervescence, as Pasternak realised, was in indulgence of fantasy running counter to all real-life commitments and family loyalties:

My life, as it has formed itself, *contradicts* my inner compulsive forces. I am mindful of it and always know it, and under normal circumstances I enjoy this contradiction. On my own I am left alone with these contradictions [...] Yet if I were to submit to the effect of these forces, I would have to part immediately and forever with all those with whom I share my life [...] After such a reversal I would no longer be able to look my son in the face.

And that is what holds me back – the fear of *such* a menacing and permanent darkness.[86]

All this irritated Tsvetaeva. With her 'unquenchable hatred of Psyche for Eve', she could 'not understand carnality as such and concede[d] no rights to it'. Tsvetaeva recognised only 'fidelity born of exaltation' and had little patience with that born merely from conquering temptation.[87] Moreover, as her correspondence with Rilke revealed, she regarded *herself* as Pasternak's 'abroad' and was now jealous that his wife was in Germany and had joined his list of female foreign correspondents. In late July she wrote announcing their relations had reached an impasse.[88] It was only the death of Rilke at the end of 1926 which revived their contacts.

Pasternak's correspondence with Evgeniya and his relatives in Germany fills in the details of his solitary existence during the summer of 1926. In late June, after her and Zhenya's departure, he spring-cleaned the apartment; he collected 250 roubles from *Molodaya gvardiya* (The Young Guard) and *Ogonek* magazines, which helped to settle part of their debts to Fenya the nursemaid; he failed to get *Zhenya Luvers' Childhood* published with Gosizdat; and he took delivery of a box of chocolates from Lomonosova. There were also hospital visits to Evgeniya's mother, who was being treated by the celebrated specialist Burdenko.[89] Two years before, she had fallen and injured her spine while trying to retrieve a toy for Zhenya from the top of a wardrobe, and as a result she had developed a spinal tumour from which she was to die in 1928. The incident was later incorporated into both Pasternak's prose fragments of the 1930s and the novel, where the unhappy victim was also the hero's mother-in-law, Anna Gromeko.[90]

In July Pasternak sent Evgeniya reports of a new round of eviction orders affecting everyone in the house except themselves. Yet although they themselves were unthreatened, the incident aroused a sense of insecurity and distracted him from creative work. In August the authoress Olga Forsh called on Pasternak, bringing a copy of her recent novel. Pasternak was also visited by Ernst Rosenfeld, the son of their family friends in Berlin, who left on 11 August taking with him a hundred roubles from Boris to help cover Evgeniya's expenses. The sale of a new edition of *Sister* and *Themes* to Gosizdat for thirty kopeks a line did not clear several newly accumulated debts of between one and two hundred roubles each to brother Aleksandr, Fenya, Berta Kofman, Yakov Chernyak, and to the tailor who had sewn him a new suit for fifty-five roubles.[91] Amidst all this, hopes of a visit to Sevastopol and Koktebel to see Voloshin evaporated.

For several days Pasternak was cheered by almost daily visits from the Leningrad poet Tikhonov who recounted 'endless cavalry tales which never stopped from morning till evening'. Tikhonov was a man of very different temper and attitudes from Pasternak and resembled Petrovsky in his *élan* and rugged energy. ('Next to him my qualities acquire almost the status of virginity, surpassing even what could be called femininity,' Pasternak told Tsvetaeva.)[92] And to Evgeniya he wrote that 'the proximity of his youthful and healthy simplicity (as in a schoolboy) had a very beneficial effect on my pulse and my whole being'. Tikhonov had spent seven years at war and had tales to tell. But 'in his depiction there is nothing about the war that is terrible, nothing even dirty, just as though ten years ago it was really suitable for middle-aged children'.[93] In the long term, personality differences were to end their friendship, for in later years Tikhonov became a stereotype figure of the literary establishment. But at present his exuberant company was a welcome and healthy distraction in an otherwise distressing summer.

Overshadowing all Pasternak's correspondence with his wife in 1926 were agony and despair at their emotional estrangement. Understandably, Evgeniya had never liked the tonality of his correspondence with Tsvetaeva. In the spring of 1926 it had caused a major quarrel between them, and she had left for Germany stating she did not intend writing to her husband while she was away. Apart from a very few brief messages during a twelve-week absence, she was as good as her word. Pasternak was meanwhile abandoned to torment and despair. Apart from the few friends mentioned, he had little human contact. Unable to work as he had intended on *Lieutenant Shmidt*, he wrote Evgeniya anguished letters every day or two. Thus, on 8 July: 'I beseech you, write to me,' he implored. 'I am being destroyed by your cruelty [...] I am completely crushed by the offence that you *expertly* and lovingly cultivate towards me.' Next day too he was crushed by 'the weight of awareness that I must try and stop loving you [...] Your silence [...] has a fearfully eloquent meaning. So, at the station, without realising it, we were parting forever. I don't exist for you as I would wish to [...] I think well of you from the terrible distance which you have created.'

For weeks Pasternak contemplated the prospect that his marriage was probably over. Finally he accepted that the best thing in the short term was that Evgeniya should rest and recover her health, start painting again and perhaps accompany Leonid on a journey to Paris. He told her on 29 July that Tsvetaeva had called a halt to their correspondence, and he assured Evgeniya that he had not in any way betrayed her. Indeed, as he had already told Tsvetaeva on the 11th of that month:

I am endlessly lonely for her [i.e. Evgeniya]. Basically I love her more than anything else in the world. Parted from her, I can see her constantly as she was before our marriage was legally registered, i.e. before I knew her family and she mine.[94]

What the various correspondences of summer 1926 clearly demonstrated was a deep divide between Pasternak, whose strongest responses were as an *artist* in communion with a kindred spirit, and Evgeniya, who had more traditional and sober expectations of her husband as a *man*. In fact, the two of them lacked what Vilmont called 'spiritual closeness'. Various others close to the family, such as Lev Gornung and Elizaveta Chernyak, have provided their own basically congruent reports of this. Olya Freidenberg had a slightly different view and described their relations as follows:

Each of them was an artist and was artistically egotistical. Zhenya dreamed about Paris and imagined that marriage with Borya would save her from the earth. She was disappointed. He was used to the Tolstoyan way of noble respectability, inspired by daily routine, and to a family out of *War and Peace*. But Zhenya offered him bohemia. There was no way of seducing him with Puccini's scenario [...] His father was a painter, his mother a musical artist, and he a poet. And he knew something different: that art winds up and restrains, concentrates and crystallises the family.[95]

The Pasternaks' marital frictions had in fact started not only because of Tsvetaeva, but as a result of conflicting artistic commitments. Evgeniya had never abandoned her ambitions for professional independence as a painter. After a break in her studies at Vkhutemas following the birth of Zhenya, she had resumed again in the autumn of 1925 and eventually graduated under Mashkov in 1929 at Vkhutein.* She had therefore not taken easily to the limitations imposed by Boris' own need to work, her duties as housewife and mother, and their cramped living quarters. Differences were thus unavoidable and were no secret to their friends.

* Vkhutein – the acronymous title of Vkhutemas after 1926, which stood for 'Higher Artistic and Technical Institute'.

Vilmont recalled one of their quarrels ending in Evgeniya's departure for Leningrad, where she spent several days with her own family; some telephone exchanges led eventually to her return, however, and Boris travelled up to Bologoye in order to ride back in the train with her.[96] Although she gave some art lessons and undertook portrait commissions while studying, Evgeniya's work always took second place to Boris', which in fact provided the basic family income – this was a pattern established in his parental home and he was doubtless happy to see it continue, despite his wife's frustrations and his own occasional perform-ance of domestic chores. Akhmatova, on the poet's side, tartly commen-ted that since Evgeniya considered herself an artist Boris was obliged to cook soup for all the family. Meanwhile, Boris himself repeatedly pointed out the Budantsevs as a model family where both husband and wife pursued literary careers, which did not apparently prevent Maria Ilyina from being a paragon of wifely devotion.

In fairness to Evgeniya it must be said that she had to endure many undeserved hardships. Her fragile health was further aggravated by living conditions which affected both body and mind. There were several objective observers of their domestic discomfort, including Mandelstam. (While his wife was convalescing in Yalta he stayed in the Volkhonka flat for several nights in February and March of 1926, accommodated on the Pasternaks' 'ghastly divan'.)[97] Eventually, in order to keep Boris and his work and cigarette smoke away from the rest of the family, it was decided to divide their room by a partition. It proved hard to find the two hundred roubles for labour and materials, and during the alteration life was especially miserable. But after the autumn of 1926 this division of their quarters helped to improve the quality of life.[98]

Ideally, in 1926 it would have done the whole family good to holiday abroad and escape the pressures and hardships of Moscow life. Ever since 1923 a return visit to Berlin had been planned, and correspondence with family, Lomonosova, Tsvetaeva and others regularly mentioned hopes of spending several months in Western Europe. But Boris needed to press on with his work both for artistic and financial reasons. Moreover, the tuberculosis which Evgeniya had contracted during the hard Civil War years was becoming critical. It therefore seemed sensible that she should take Zhenya and travel to Germany independently. In mid-June the two of them left to spend the summer with Boris' relatives in Berlin and Munich. (She was actually their second Volkhonka guest that year: Stella Adelson had visited Josephine and Lydia in the spring.)

The month of July was spent with Josephine and Fedya in Munich. In August Evgeniya stayed alone at the Gasthof Schauer in Possenhofen on the Starnbergersee. (There one of her neighbours was a brother of the German author Feuchtwanger.) It was less than an hour by local train into Munich, where Zhenya was looked after by his aunt and uncle.[99] For part of the time Leonid and Rozaliya Pasternak also came down to stay in their elder daughter's home at 6, Laplacestrasse.

Evgeniya returned to Moscow by train in early October 1926. Her health was much improved, and she gave ecstatic accounts of her trips into the Bavarian Alps, boating and bathing in mountain lakes, and of her interesting new acquaintances, as well as retailing family news. In order to avoid sharing their greetings and first exchanges with other inhabitants of the communal apartment, Boris went out to Mozhaisk to join his wife and son and spend the last lap of their journey in the relative privacy of a railway compartment. Pasternak had already mentioned his differences with Evgeniya to his cousin Olya, but in a letter of 21 October he could now emphasise 'What a role is reserved for sensible goodwill at a mature age, and what a modest significance fate and chance are reduced to.'[100] Their marriage was to be further tested in the years ahead. However, in the closing months of 1926 injuries seemed to be healed, relations repaired, and happiness restored. Evgeniya later told Elizaveta Chernyak of her trip to Bavaria. There on the mountain tops she spoke of a 'lofty, full sensation, as if she could embrace and understand everything, and forgive all – even Marina Tsvetaeva'!

14

Breaches, losses, and lyric revival

'History'

When leafmould in the grove inters
The fatal squeak and crash of pines,
Then, history, your virgin forest
Of other sort before me rises.

Age-long the fine-nerved tracery sleeps.
But once or twice each hundred years
They hunt the game, arrest the poacher,
Lead away the timber thieves.

Then deafening all with snapping stems,
Above the thickets starts to rise
The awesome presence of servility,
Peg-legs and medals of the foresters,

Crashing step of human hulk.
The illumined forest wakes from trance.
Above it smiles the invalid
With lantern leer of meaty jowels.

No time to rejoice. Exchange halloos!
While we admire the fulgent red,
Gout-gripped, he's seized with ruddy flush,
Bright like a lampion – and dead.

જ⊷જ⊷જ

On 31 December 1926 Marina Tsvetaeva broke silence with a letter announcing the death of Rilke.[1] The news was a shattering blow to Pasternak. It not only dashed hopes of a personal meeting with Rilke but also severed perhaps his most vital sustaining link with Western European culture.

The next day Tsvetaeva wrote again. She enclosed the German text of her tender necrophiliac letter addressing Rilke on his own death, and she proposed new plans for a meeting with Pasternak. Pasternak did not respond. Meanwhile he heard details of Rilke's death and received words of comfort and consolation from his own father. On 12 January Tsvetaeva wrote to Pasternak again – a short covering note with a letter from Svyatopolk-Mirsky (to whom she had refused to disclose the Volkhonka address, regarding it as 'hers'!). Later in January she also sent a French newspaper cutting with an account of Rilke's funeral.[2] Finally, on 3 February, Pasternak responded, in a manner that was cordial but promised no resumption of their earlier intense exchanges:

Dear friend! I write to you by the way, and afterwards I shall lapse back into silence. But one cannot trifle even with your patience. Thick snow was falling in black tatters down the misted windows as I heard of his death. What can one say? I was ill at the news. It was as if I had been torn away and left hanging while life passed by. For a few days we did not hear or understand one another. And there was also a fierce, almost abstracted chaotic frost. Do you realise the *full* brutality with which both of us have been orphaned? Probably not. Nor is that necessary – the full blow of helplessness demeans one. Somehow everything has lost its purpose for me. Now we must live for a long time, sickeningly long – that is your duty and mine.[3]

Tsvetaeva answered by return of post on 9 February. Acknowledging his own formal note, she launched into one of her own inimitable discourses, including further details of Rilke's death and of his last words and actions. Eleven days later she sent Pasternak a copy of her poem 'Attempt at a Room' ('Popytka komnaty'). Pasternak had meanwhile mailed to her part 2 of *Lieutenant Shmidt*. The third and final part had yet to be written when news of Rilke's death came; possibly, as Pasternak later observed, this tragedy cast a shadow over his depiction of Shmidt's trial scene.[4]

In Tsvetaeva's poem Pasternak discerned some details of the previous summer's correspondence, including a dream he had had of meeting her. His account of this to her in February 1927 now revived their correspondence on a friendly but no longer impassioned note. She evidently cherished an anthroposophical fantasy about reincarnation and a future meeting with Rilke, and she also saw his death as a command to maintain her bond with Pasternak. As she told Leonid Pasternak the following year, 'Boris and I intended to travel to see Rilke together – and we have still not abandoned the idea. The path to his grave will not get overgrown, we shall be neither the first nor the last.'[5]

In the next few years both Pasternak and Tsvetaeva dedicated work to Rilke's memory. Her letter of 9 February referred to a poetic 'Letter to

Rilke' ('Pis'mo k Ril'ke') which contained impressions and details of his death; the Prague journal *Volya Rossii* (Freedom of Russia) published her prose piece 'Your Death' ('Tvoya smert'') that same year; in 1928 appeared her translated selection of Rilke's letters; and Rilkean associations and overtones were apparent in several of her subsequent writings. In the years after Rilke's death her lyrical tension seemed to slacken and she wrote more prose.[6] The same was partly true of Pasternak. He translated two of Rilke's longer poems, but his original writings did not explicitly dwell for long on Rilke's death as Tsvetaeva's did. However, the autobiographically based prose on which he started a few months later did show evidence of Rilke's artistic personality and example, with particular echoes of his *Notes of Malte Laurids Brigge (Die Aufzeichnungen des Malte Laurids Brigge)*.

At deepest level, Pasternak, Rilke and Tsvetaeva shared a congruency of artistic temper which probably explained their mutual attraction. This could be described as an acute sense of loss and transience in their lives coupled with a nostalgic straining for transcendence in their art. Tsvetaeva and Pasternak sensed this in both Rilke's early work and his masterpieces of the 1920s. Among the latter, for example, the first Duino Elegy describes the sublimest love as that which is unrequited; contemplation of great lovers and of those who die young might help reconcile us with the fact of our own transitoriness; and the Angel of Rilke's Elegies is described as 'terrible' to us through our own mortal clinging to the visible and through his angelic transformation of that visible into the invisible and eternal. The physical tragedies of Tsvetaeva's life, the death of a child, exile, penury and cultural isolation reinforced her possessiveness of non-physical things and her belief that life only had meaning when transformed through the medium of art. Similarly, as we have seen, Pasternak's biography consisted significantly of non-meetings, rejections and renunciations: the abandonment of music and philosophy, the suppression of romantic artistry, unrequited love, discovery of Tsvetaeva as a soul-mate in absentia, his loss of Rilke through silence and death, and his deprivation of Europe and the civilisation in which his personality was rooted. Perhaps, too, Rilke's example was specially valuable in the 1920s when pure lyricism was under threat and Pasternak's art was made to digest and transform the resistant subject matter of history.

Pasternak's association with Lef had continued, thanks mainly to his affection for Aseyev and Mayakovsky as individuals. But by 1927

29 Members of Lef. Front row: Pasternak, Shklovsky, Tretyakov, Mayakovsky; standing: Neznamov, Osip Brik (Moscow, November 1925)

30 Members of Lef: Standing: Boris Pasternak, Sergei Eisenstein; seated: Vladimir Mayakovsky, Lili Brik.

friendships were being strained by the hypocrisy forced on all members of Lef by their neo-Futurist utilitarian stance. In July of 1926, for instance, Pasternak had attempted to read Tsvetaeva's *Poem of the End* to some members with whom his relations were allegedly already 'shaky'. It was doubtless a provocative act on Pasternak's part and the company responded accordingly. As Pasternak recalled, 'I could not tolerate their disdain and I stopped reading on the second page. I was furious and shouted at them. It was a dreadful evening.' Shortly afterwards, though, Aseyev read Tsvetaeva's *Pied Piper* in private and was overcome. On 28 July 1926, while Mayakovsky and Lili Brik were in the Crimea, Aseyev even read some Tsvetaeva to a gathering in the Briks' apartment and there was talk of Lef's publishing *Poem of the End*. However, Pasternak implored Tsvetaeva to dismiss the idea; Mayakovsky might well be delighted in private, but he would never tolerate Tsvetaeva's work in his journal.[7] In any case, by that time the official literary press were lining up against her, and Mayakovsky had in early 1926 dismissed her 'gypsy lyricism' in the fourth issue of *Krasnaya nov'*.[8]

Pasternak's misgivings with Lef were partly a continuation of his earlier differences with Cubo-Futurism, its obsession with technical experimentation and often mindless iconoclasm. Since the Revolution these features had been reinforced. Mischievous *épatage* had turned into 'proletarian' belligerence against cultural tradition. Later, in spring of 1928, Pasternak was to recognise in the producer Meyerhold a Lef collaborator of similar persuasions to his own. In a letter he described Meyerhold as no 'prisoner of degenerate virtuosity', but as 'a vital and purposeful historian ... who cannot help loving his country and its past because each day in his work he loves part of its living future. I too understand Futurism of that sort, Futurism with a genealogy'.[9]

Until early 1927, Pasternak's and Mayakovsky's mutual affection preserved the facade and unity of Lef intact. They remained a cheery coterie of poets, critics and artistic modernists who met regularly for their 'Lefist Tuesdays' in Vodopyany Lane – and later, after April 1926, in the Briks' new apartment in Gendrikov Lane. A crisis occurred, however, when Lef resumed its publishing activities.

In January 1927 *Novy Lef* (The New Lef) began coming out with the same basic platform and contributors as before, and it was issued regularly for the next two years. Its materials, often sharply polemical, were generally of better quality than earlier; avant-garde taste and techniques were promoted, and a stance was taken against all honest left-wing writings of traditional mould. Pasternak attended the meetings in autumn 1926 when *Novy Lef* was set up, although Katanyan was the only one who later set down a brief memory of his 'improvisatory, indistinct and convoluted' contributions to the discussion: the only impression conveyed is of Pasternak's confused and apologetic misgivings.[10]

Pasternak's one contribution to *Novy Lef* was an extract from *Lieutenant Shmidt*. As he later told Lomonosova, he let Mayakovsky have this item only because 'his entreaties became a burden to me'. Allegedly Pasternak 'had no idea what there would be in the journal and what the journal would be like'. When the first issue came out he was so disenchanted that he offered to resign from Lef there and then. The others persuaded him against announcing a public breach, however, and for the time being he held his peace. But by mid-1927 several issues of the journal confirmed Pasternak's belief that *Novy Lef* was an embodiment of the 'utterly impenetrable hypocrisy and servility that have become the basis and obligatory note in our "society" and letters'.[11]

Several outsiders realised the incongruity of Pasternak's continued presence among Lefists. On 27 February 1927 Polonsky gave a sour appraisal of the new journal in *Isvestiya* and asked:

What sort of Futurist is Pasternak? Would Pasternak really approve the showbooth appearance that *Novy Lef* takes on? One can hardly believe it. In Pasternak's verse, which is remarkable for its formal virtues and inner tension, there is nothing of street and backyard vociferations, nothing of the circus or the showbooth.[12]

Polonsky followed this up with polemical blasts from *Isvestiya* and from the journal *Novy mir* during the first half of 1927. In the course of these he dismissed even Mayakovsky's early work as loud-mouthed bohemian posturing, an opinion Pasternak could not share.[13]

As Fleishman's account of this episode in Pasternak's career shows,[14] the issue that finally caused his resignation was a 'below the belt' attack on Polonsky in the fifth number of *Novy Lef*. In it, Aseyev's article 'Campaign of the Thick-Skulls' reminded readers of Polonsky's recent political error in publishing Pilnyak's 'Tale of the Unextinguished Moon' (see above, p. 365). In the cut and thrust of pre-revolutionary Futurist polemics such abuse would not have been barred, and nobody's safety or livelihood was threatened by it. But now, when censorship and official interference in literature were increasing, and when Polonsky's dismissal from chief editorship of *Novy mir* was rumoured (he was removed from office in 1928 and reinstated only after Gorky's intervention), Aseyev's attack was a mean act of denunciation. As Polonsky's friend, Pasternak was forced to dissociate himself from it, and he sent him a letter on the 1st June 1927 announcing his intention to resign from Lef. He outlined to Polonsky a further letter which he planned sending to Mayakovsky and in which he pointed out his disagreement with Polonsky's dismissal of Mayakovsky's earlier achievement:

The nonsense that imbues a large part of V. Polonsky's article in *Novy mir* cannot but be *deliberate* [...] It is not only the legitimate self-defence of a man who uses his attackers' weapons. It is a defense of all literature – of everything including *Cloud in Trousers* – against Lef methods which have never heard of such a work. All credit to you as a poet that the stupidity of Lef's theoretical positions is shown precisely by you [...] As earlier, I consider the existence of Lef a logical conundrum, and I cease to be interested in the key to it.[15]

Nevertheless, Pasternak probably still demurred before staging a public resignation. As he had told Lomonosova in mid-May, 'It will be much harder for me to give the arguments for my break with them in print. It will mean talking about what one is not meant to talk about.'[16] (A clear hint at the dangerous political implications of recent Lef polemics.) But Pasternak's wish to resign without publicity was not respected. As he later recalled, 'despite my statements that I was leaving the panel of *Lef* contributors and that I no longer belonged to their circle, they continued printing my name in the list of contributors. I wrote Mayakovsky a sharp letter that was intended to blow him up' (II, 44; *VP*, 457). The letter concerned was in fact a message dated 26 July 1927 to the whole editorial board of *Novy Lef*:

Despite my verbal statement at one of the May meetings about finally leaving Lef, my name continues to be printed in the list of contributors. Such forgetfulness is reprehensible. Your collective is perfectly aware that this was a final and categoric parting of our ways – unlike the winter's one after I had acquainted myself with the first issue, when the meeting persuaded me to refrain from breaking openly and to content myself with silent indifference to the outward illusion of participating. Kindly print the present statement in full in your journal.   Boris Pasternak[17]

This request was ignored, and the editors merely deleted Pasternak's name from subsequent issues. The journal made no response to his departure other than withdrawing Brik's article, announced earlier and entitled 'Boris Pasternak's Secret'.

Polonsky evidently registered Pasternak's defence of Mayakovsky's early work. His next article, in *Novy mir*, no. 7, 1927, moved from attacking Futurist bohemianism to a telling critique of the idea of the 'social command' in art, a command to which both Lef and 'proletarian' littérateurs had variously responded.[18]

Neither Pasternak nor the Lef membership regarded his resignation as an act of personal hostility. In the autumn of 1927 Mayakovsky presented him with a copy of his new poem *Good!* (*Khorosho!*) dedicated to him 'with friendship, affection, love, respect, comradeliness, attachment, admiration, etc. etc. etc.'[19] The feelings were mutual. Replying to a questionnaire for a projected miscellany called *Our Contemporaries* (*Nashi sovremenniki*), Pasternak listed his favourite poets in order: Tsvetaeva, Tikhonov, and then: 'Mayakovsky, whom I adore, and Aseyev, whose talent has rarely left me indifferent, have long been going through a difficult and critical phase'. Minimising his own links with Lef, Pasternak voiced a conviction that 'Mayakovsky should have been the first to leave Lef, followed by myself and Aseyev'.[20] (An interesting repetition of words addressed to Mayakovsky in March of 1917!) At Pasternak's request a meeting to discuss relations with Mayakovsky and the latter's continued loyalty to Lef was arranged in Aseyev's apartment in early April of 1928. Far from mending relations, though, it virtually put an end to their friendship. Pasternak's two autobiographies gave no details of the episode. But the report of Mayakovsky's quip about Pasternak's preference for lightning in the sky, whereas he (Mayakovsky) liked it better in an electric iron, related to this meeting and probably camouflaged what was a distressing conversation for both sides (II, 42–3; *VP*, 456). Following that contretemps, Pasternak wrote Mayakovsky a private note on 4 April 1928, describing their recent conversation as 'depressingly sterile in a life that spoils us neither with time nor unlimited means [...] Perhaps I am guilty before you with my limitations and lack of will. Perhaps, knowing you as I do, I should have loved you more warmly and actively and should have freed you against your will from this illusory and semi-conscious role as leader of a non-existent squad of men occupying a position that you have dreamed up.' Pasternak also emphasised again that his earlier letter to the Lef editorial board was not meant as a personal message to Mayakovsky: 'Had you for one moment thought that it was addressed to you, you would have *printed* it as I asked you to. *You would have done that out of pride.* But you know perfectly well that it was not you who hid it and kept quiet about it, just as it was not you that received it.' The whole business Pasternak described as 'madness, a bad dream, hocus-pocus', and he suggested waiting another year, after which relations might be repaired. He concluded:

In leaving Lef I was parting with the *last* of these useless associations, not in order to start the whole series again from the beginning. And you still persist in trying not to understand this.[21]

Pasternak's letter to Mayakovsky marked almost the end of their official and their personal dealings. It was a sign too of the imminent break-up of Lef. In early 1928 the film-maker Sergei Eisenstein resigned amidst Lef's abuse of his latest picture, *October*. Shklovsky also resigned soon after. Pasternak continued to expect that Mayakovsky would join them. Back in the summer of 1927 he had told Lomonosova:

It always seemed to me that the inborn talent of Mayakovsky would some time blow up, that it would have to explode those layers of chemically pure rubbish, dreamlike in its senselessness, in which he has voluntarily decked himself beyond recognition this last decade. In my feelings towards him I have lived only with this hope.[22]

If this were to happen, Pasternak felt sure Mayakovsky would again display those immense lyrical powers that had thrilled him in the 1910s and more recently in *About That*. In fact Mayakovsky was soon to leave Lef, but in a tragically astounding direction.

Mayakovsky's affection for Pasternak meanwhile was even more complex; it was affected by literary ideology and by the unnatural role he himself had sought to play in the 1920s. For example, although he had publicly welcomed *Lieutenant Shmidt* as an achievement of Lef, Pasternak's own memory was that Mayakovsky 'did not like *Nineteen Five* or *Lieutenant Shmidt* and regarded their writing as a mistake. He liked two books: *Over the Barriers* and *My Sister Life*' (II, 37; *VP*, 451). In the 1920s, as earlier, Mayakovsky seems privately to have valued in Pasternak precisely that lyrical quality he had expunged in himself. However, the distance between the two men after the spring of 1928 exacerbated the sense of isolation which both of them felt. In fact, after the rift with Mayakovsky, although individual friends and sympathetic colleagues remained, there was no organisation – not to mention any broader cultural setting – in which Pasternak felt at home. Even some of his official allies were now insecure. Voronsky was ousted from editorship of *Krasnaya nov'* in April 1927, mainly for refusing to promote 'proletarian' literature; accused of defeatism and Trotskyism he was then expelled from the Party in early 1928. Polonsky too was briefly removed from the *Novy mir* editorship in 1928, and though reinstated later in the year his fitness for office was disputed at government and Central Committee level. Pasternak's isolation was apparent also to friends in

Western Europe. As Tsvetaeva commented to Leonid Pasternak in Berlin: 'How little they understand him – even those that love him! "Work on the word" ... "the self-sufficient word" ... "independent life of the word"', she scoffed at the Lef phraseology. 'From his latest letters I can see that he is very lonely in his labours [...] Mayakovsky and Aseyev? I don't know the latter, but they are not people of his mould, or his breeding. Nor, most important, are they people of his spirit.'[23]

After completing the revised book versions of *Nineteen Five* and *Lieutenant Shmidt* in April 1927, Pasternak had lapsed into inactivity and morale sank again. In the preceding months, he told Lomonosova, he had been 'made healthier by concerns for my family and a position in literature which I might call loss of obscurity'. Now, overcome by inertia, he found he was a burden both to himself and to those around him.[24]

Public events had reinforced this mood. An event that depressed him was the springtime visit to Russia of the French writer Duhamel. Pasternak was not directly involved, and the fault seemingly lay with the official hosts. It was a visit contrasting sadly with Pasternak's other European associations. Duhamel 'spoke and behaved with impressive impersonality,' he told Lomonosova. 'There was nothing of the modesty and simplicity of the unknown man which I like so much. Evidently these are not in the character of our times [which ...] chase after happiness and pleasure, power, glory, and large scale.' Designed to celebrate internationalist cooperation between Soviet Russia and progressive Westerners, such visits were for Pasternak a cultural non-event, devoid of personality. 'Only the human heart [...] can become a real cultural capital.' Otherwise these events belonged to the 'astrophysical provinces' and Duhamel's speech itself was typified by a 'universal provincialism'.[25] All this lent substance to the lyricist's lament for intimacy and heartfelt experience in an age concerned with epic generalities. Pasternak's depression, aggravated by souring relations with Lef, threw a cloud over the early summer of 1927.

Pasternak once again shelved plans for a foreign visit that year. The previous October, Leonid Pasternak had written Boris and Aleksandr a tired and downcast letter:

I have become aware of a weariness – it is now high time at my age to free my brain of this oppressive concern for my family and myself. It is really time. It is one of nature's normal requirements to have somewhere to lay one's head. I think I have earned it, and yet ahead of me there is still only an empty expanse [...] of hopelessness![26]

In partial response to this pressure, as well as to his and Evgeniya's need for a break, Pasternak had promised himself a journey abroad on completing *Lieutenant Shmidt*. But by the time the book version of the two 1905 poems was safely lodged with Gosizdat, travel plans had once again receded. On 12 April 1927 he mentioned to Lomonosova a possible journey to France in the following spring, or towards the end of 1928. This, he believed, might be the occasion for spending a year abroad in order to work and escape from 'the atmosphere of our excessively extended sophism'. At the same time, though, he admitted to 'a fear that maybe in a year's time I will not be able to get abroad'.[27] The reason for not pressing ahead with travel plans lay largely with Pasternak. Permission for a trip *en famille* might of course be refused; on the other hand it was a case of 'nothing ventured, nothing gained'. On 17 May 1927 Pasternak wrote to Lomonosova as follows:

I continue to live in the hope of a trip and lengthy residence somewhere in the West. For the second year running I am putting off the realisation of this dream for another year. They say this is a bad sign. Certainly I do have a weak will – maybe none at all. From outside my reasons might seem to be empty excuses, but to me they are more than mere fabrications justifying immobility.

To what extent the inertia binding Pasternak to Moscow was a function of his own personality or of objective circumstance is a matter for speculation – at all events, this was not the first or the last example of his reluctance to intervene and oppose what seemed to be an irreversible fate.

With no alternatives in prospect, Pasternak in May 1927 took his family for a summer holiday in the Podmoskovye. The village of Mutovki was seven kilometres from the rail station of Khotkovo; it lay about sixty kilometres north of Moscow and was close to Abramtsevo, famous for its literary links with the Aksakovs and the nineteenth-century poet Tyutchev. Like many residents of the Moscow 'dacha belt', several Mutovki peasants had recently built wooden houses in traditional style which they rented out as holiday homes. The Pasternaks' landlord, Vedeneyev, owned a newly built cottage of wood and brick, which had a terrace supported on wooden beams overlooking a steep drop. 'His choice of spot makes his class consciousness suspect,' Pasternak quipped. 'For its picturesque quality it is the best place for twenty versts around.'[28]

Until mid-July they all enjoyed the natural beauties, country walks, berry picking, and other pursuits, which were graphically described in a letter to Josephine.[29] But in the third week of July came rains and cold winds. Still, there was congenial company close by. Their neighbours at Mutovki included the family of Aleksandr Pasternak and of his brother-in-law, Nikolai Vilmont. The latter's childlike, round and rubicund face and portly figure were, according to Elizaveta Chernyak, somewhat out of keeping with the stream of German philosophical discussion that flowed from him. Pasternak had a high regard for Vilmont's erudition and scholarship and during the summer used some of his influence with Polonsky to secure commissions for Vilmont's contributions to the *Large Soviet Encyclopaedia*.[30] Pasternak himself produced little during the summer; the forthcoming tenth anniversary of the October Revolution provided small stimulus. After returning to Moscow on 18 September he wrote complaining to Polonsky:

I feel all the more stupid when I realise that I have spent three and a half months in a beautiful area without any apparent benefit. What little I have done (a few poems and a short draft concerned with October, but absolutely unthematic and very feeble) I have handed to ZIF and to *Zvezda*.* [31]

During August of 1927 Pasternak corresponded briefly with the 'proletarian' poet Sergei Obradovich, one of the *ZIF* editors, and discussed a possible contribution to the first almanac issue celebrating the anniversary. Apart from some recent nature lyrics, including 'Space' ('Prostranstvo') dedicated to Vilmont, and 'Lilies of the Valley' ('Land-yshi'), there was a potentially more interesting and 'relevant' fragment of 135 lines which Pasternak also mentioned to Polonsky. Entitled 'For the October Anniversary' ('K oktyabr'skoi godovshchine'), the work had an epigraph by Tyutchev and was in three sections, dealing respectively with premonitions of revolution, the interim of summer 1917, and the October Revolution itself. Fusing human action with nature and the elements, the poem expressed Pasternak's characteristically equivocal view of October 1917: the evocation of its absolute elemental force and establishment of an 'unprecedented state' (*nebyvalyi stroi*) was devoid of any remarks or epithets approving its results. This treatment clearly disappointed Obradovich's 'heroic' expectations. The poem's length was also unsuitable and Pasternak insisted on publication in full or not at

---

* ZIF – *Zemlya i fabrika* (Land and Factory), the title of a new series of literary almanacs; *Zvezda* – a Leningrad literary monthly founded in 1924 which published many 'fellow-traveller' writings.

all.[32] Eventually some extracts only were printed in the *Oktyabr'skaya gazeta* (October Gazette) issue for 8 November 1927 and in the November number of *Zvezda*.

In a letter of 29 August 1927 Pasternak also voiced to Obradovich his thoughts on how the age of Bolshevism would be reflected in his forthcoming writings, which would include a resumption of *Spektorsky*, pursuing its plot into the revolutionary period:

In my understanding, October [i.e. the October Revolution of the year 1917] is broader than that tragic five-act structure in which an event surviving the catastrophe provides salient themes for an independent work that presents this event as a personage or as an object in its successive peripeteia.

I have come to see in October the chemical property of our air, the element and substance of our historical day. In other words, if the extracts on offer are weak, then in my view the execution of this theme would be more powerful only in something like a large prose work. October would be withdrawn into even deeper depths, and more than in the present verse. It would be aligned with the horizon and identified with nature, with the raw secret of time and its successions, in all its bitter unadorned variety. You will easily guess that what I am offering is one (and the first) of several attempts to set down for myself and assemble in one this diffuse and elusive material, for the future as it were, for that broader reworking about which I wrote above just now.

I am not intending to write any verse at all about October for the jubilee. On the other hand, my most immediate plans which are not tied down to any dates have included allowing my material, both poetic and narrative, to pass through this atmosphere. The next thing I have to do is work on the continuation of *Spektorsky*.[33]

Basically, Pasternak is again embellishing his earlier response to the Central Committee decree on literature in 1925. Although in the foreground of so much Soviet literature, the revolution and recent Russian history ought to be organically assimilated by the artist to such a degree that they no longer require explicit celebration. The root of this idea was already shown in the 'contemporary quality' of *My Sister Life*, remarked on by so many critics. In the later 1920s, however, the watchdogs of proletarian literature were requiring more than mere traces of 'historical atmosphere'. Pasternak's remarks to Obradovich were a recipe for writing of an unorthodox mould.

On returning to Moscow in September 1927, Pasternak found it hard to settle down to work. Later that month he went alone on a visit to relatives in Leningrad. He was struck there by the spacious living quarters, which contrasted with his cramped Moscow dwelling. The

Freidenbergs had rented out half of their flat to three young scholars yet still suffered none of the overcrowding familiar to Muscovites. The Margulius family had retained occupancy of the whole of their apartment. 'It reminds me of when I lived with my landlords in Lebyazhii Lane,' Pasternak told his parents.[34]

Despite his many literary contacts in Leningrad, Pasternak saw few people outside his family and did not even meet Akhmatova or Kuzmin. But he had one encounter which he described in more detail to his parents on 30 September, and to which he ascribed 'greatest and decisive significance – meaning, of course, for my heart':

My old feud with Esenin, which was imposed on me by him while he was alive, has been resolved and is over. Perhaps I am anticipating events, and it will grow again and be confirmed. But it seems to me that it is now exhausted, through that same boy (a young poet) to whom Esenin wrote verses in blood before his death. I have seen and spoken with him.

There are no other details of Pasternak's meeting with the poet Volf Erlikh. Presumably, when they met they discussed the conflicting temperaments and attitudes that had fired Esenin's and Pasternak's disagreements in the early 1920s. This posthumous reconciliation was no doubt coloured by the circumstances of Esenin's death. His physical and mental collapse and suicide in December 1925 were ostensibly the result of alcoholic and other excesses, but there was a view, which time has reinforced, that Esenin had destroyed himself in orgiastic protest against an order that left no place for rural poetic songsters.[35]

Returning to Moscow, Pasternak remained idle and depressed. On 28 October he told Lomonosova that 'for the third month I cannot work properly. Throughout October my hands have been occupied and tied up with correspondence, like a bell-ringer in his ropes.' His mood was aggravated by health problems and by a haunting 'sense of the end'. Yurii Zhivago's fatal cardiac ailment is perhaps traceable to his author's condition that was first discovered in the 1920s. After Dr Levin had diagnosed enlargement of the heart muscles back in 1924, Pasternak had the idea that he was not going to live long. Eventually this unfounded presentiment 'lost the acuteness of its dumbfounding novelty', and Pasternak reminded himself that 'mother and all the relatives on her side have had heart ailments (some nervous, some with angina) from the age of thirty'.[36] In 1925 he had voiced similar fears to his sister Josephine after hearing a false rumour of Rilke's death, and she had had to reassure her brother again in April of 1926. On top of his medical and artistic worries, Pasternak complained of 'all sorts of complications' in a letter to the Leningrad poet Sergei Spassky in mid-November 1927.[37] His final summary of the year in a December message to his parents was a vaguely gloomy one:

Unlike the early autumn, when direct prospects were still thinkable, even if they were difficult and contrary, the year now hangs in the air as an empty, shapeless and motionless puzzle. I am talking not only about myself personally, but about the mood in all those areas where one has to look ahead – consequently also therefore about the literary one.[38]

Despite this bleak outlook, Pasternak had not been entirely inactive in the final weeks of 1927. Just before the first anniversary of Rilke's death, he wrote to his Berlin relatives, mentioning plans to take remedial lessons in French. 'This is necessary,' he explained, 'because the *Nachlass* of Rilke in the sense of his poetic links and future glimmers of light connects me more with France than with Germany. There are still his friends living there, and great poets Paul Valéry, André Gide, and Léon Paul Fargue.' (Pasternak was apparently particularly touched when Fargue commissioned a special French prose translation of *My Sister Life* for himself.) The September issue of *Neue Rundschau* (New Review) had contained an article on Fargue which Pasternak asked his parents to send along with any further clippings on Rilke.[39] Prior to this, in September 1927, Polonsky who was leaving on a trip to Western Europe was charged by Pasternak to bring back a good book with biographical information on Rilke together with the Insel Verlag editions of his *Requiem* and *The Life of Mary* (*Das Marienleben*).[40] Polonsky was given no further details, but Lomonosova was told of Pasternak's intentions:

For more than anything in life (for my habits, inclinations and views on art) I am indebted to the books of R. M. Rilke. Just now my ambition is to write an article 'On the Poet', dedicated to his memory, but broader than a direct monographic discussion. I would like it to read as good belletristic prose (i.e. easily and emotionally).[41]

Once started, the project gained impetus and during the winter became more elaborate. On 3 January Pasternak described it to Spassky as 'something between an article and belletristic prose about how, in my life, life turned into art and why – a sort of autobiographical phenomenology'.[42] The February issue of the journal *Chitatel' i pisatel'* (Reader and Writer) carried a note with further details: the work was still incomplete and lacked a title, but it ran to one or one and a half signatures and was to appear in one of the spring numbers of *Zvezda*.[43] So described, the work is recognisable as the first part of Pasternak's autobiographical essay *Safe Conduct*. Its presentation of episodes from his childhood, youth and early manhood were part of an attempt in several of Pasternak's current works to establish organic links between his present self and his experience of the past. The importance of this only emerged properly in the context of that 'future without a genealogy' allegedly cultivated by Lefist Futurism, and when contrasted with official accounts of cultural history which dismissed the past and regarded October 1917 as a unique watershed or *tabula rasa*.

Part 1 of *Safe Conduct* eventually appeared in the eighth issue of *Zvezda* for 1929. It centred around reminiscences of Scriabin, the pursuit of philosophy in Moscow and the discovery of Marburg and journey there. (Subsequent parts were to deal with the Marburg and Italian experiences and Pasternak's literary debut and relations with Mayakovsky; see volume II of this study.) The parabolic relevance of all this to Pasternak's current experience in the late 1920s has been described in Lazar Fleishman's study.[44] It was also pointed out to Pasternak's parents at the time. Concerning the musical episode, for instance, he claimed to have 'described my parting from music in precisely the words that would suit my present condition. Whoever has not experienced that complexity, that all-acceptance [*vse-primirenie*] which culminates in bitter harmony, has missed out in life on his own spirituality.'[45]

Although dedicated to Rilke, *Safe Conduct* contained few explicit references to him. It recalled Pasternak's one childhood encounter with him and later discovery of his verse. But the whole aesthetics of creativity set out in the work showed a broad implicit kinship with the Austrian poet, and especially with his quasi-autobiographical *Malte Laurids Brigge*.[46] The unchartable expanse of their relationship was perhaps hinted at in the juxtaposed statements of the following passage:

The region of the subconscious in a genius is incapable of measurement. It is composed of everything that happens to his readers and that he himself is ignorant of. I am not presenting my recollections in memory of Rilke. On the contrary, I actually received them from him as a gift.   (II, 213; *VP*, 201)

While at work on the first part of *Safe Conduct*, Pasternak produced two poetic translations of Rilke's requiems 'Für eine Freundin' (in memory of the artist Paula Modersohn-Becker) and 'Für Wolf Graf von Kalckreuth' (commemorating the young poet who ended his life by suicide). The second of these, printed in *Zvezda*, no.8, 1929, contained passages faithfully translated yet showing a close textual kinship with Pasternak's original poetic writings around the turn of the decade; the 'death of the artist' – both in reality and as a literary theme – was constantly on Pasternak's mind in the later 1920s and it was to emerge in several of his writings related to this period.

The 'immeasurable' realm of the subconscious identified in *Safe Conduct* as the source of artistic inspiration itself implicitly involved Pasternak in one of the major literary debates of the 1920s, although he made no formal public contribution to it. In particular it implied a sympathy with Voronsky's controversial views that were summed up in his *Art of Viewing the World* (*Iskusstvo videt' mir*) published in 1928. A central assumption in this was that artistic expression and the images it used were not cognate with any scientific, intellectual or functional perceptions of the world, but were a means of regaining a lost privileged immediacy available to us in childhood and youth and subconsciously retained beneath a later overlay of routine worldly concerns. The relevance of this to Pasternak's earlier prose was already noted (above p. 271), and as Maguire observes, many of Voronsky's formulations were a virtual rephrasing of Proust – and the latter, recently translated, was a writer with whom Pasternak had discovered an almost frighteningly close affinity (see p. 410). Voronsky's and Pasternak's approaches inevitably made socio-political considerations an irrelevance in literature. Pasternak's *Safe Conduct*, part 1 of which appeared in 1929, thus implied a stand against both 'proletarian' and recent Lef ambitions to socialise and demystify artistic creativity.[47]

A literature created in the manner envisaged by Pasternak and by Voronsky and his sympathisers clearly could not be controlled by literary administrative dictate; it could not be probed by Marxist analytical tools, nor could it properly be charted even by its creator. Since the days of his polemics against Shershenevich in 1914, Pasternak had never believed in 'customer-supplier' or facile 'extra-literary' communications with his readership, and when such anti-élitist plebeian hobnobbing was invited again in 1928 by the journal *Chitatel' i pisatel'* he responded coolly:

By his precious inborn ability, the reader himself always understands what is happening in a book to things, persons, and to the author himself. By hammering into him our ideas on what exactly we have done and how we achieved it we don't enlighten him but render him sterile [...] Those of us who properly understand what we are doing are merely those who do very little and do it badly [...] Any appeal to the reader undeservedly debases him [...]

Probably I am fonder of the reader than I can say. I am withdrawn like he is, and [...] I do not understand any correspondence with him.[48]

Pasternak's despondent mood of 1927–8 was matched and partly caused by various new external factors. The relatively liberal and peaceful years of the New Economic Policy came to an end, and from 1928 onwards renewed class warfare, terror and hysteria begun to grip the country. The preamble came in March 1928, when Stalin framed a group of 'bourgeois specialist' engineers in the notorious Shakhty case. OGPU witch hunts began exposing sabotage in every quarter. In spring 1928, after reports that five elderly bank clerks had been arrested and sentenced to execution, the poet Mandelstam had gone round various government offices, attempting to save them, and even sent Bukharin a copy of his verse with a note stating that 'Every line in this book argues against what you are planning to do'.[49] And in the summer, following renewed calls for vigilance against supposed internal enemies, another tribunal in Moscow charged some engineers and technicians with the new crime of 'wrecking' (*vreditel'stvo*). Pasternak was filled with incredulity and abomination. On 10 May 1928 he wrote to Olya Freidenberg:

As you know, the terror has started again, without those moral foundations or justifications which they once used to find for it at the height of all the trading, careerism and unsightly 'transgression'. For a long time now they have been far from being the puritan saints that once appeared as avenging angels of judgement. And altogether there is terrible confusion. Waves come rolling past which bear no relation to the times. One cannot understand anything. Last autumn I was not expecting this, and, all told, I was not so miserable.[50]

The changing atmosphere and events of the late 1920s shook the security of several established figures on the cultural scene who had hitherto seemed on easy terms with the revolutionary order. Pasternak first used the term 'men of the revolution' in 1922 to describe Pilnyak and writers of the Serapion Brotherhood who at that time appeared more viable and compatible with the new regime than himself.[51] Another such figure was Ilya Ehrenburg, whom Pasternak described to Tsvetaeva in 1926 as 'a splendid man, successful, deft, biographically glittering, thinking easily, living and writing easily', despite the fact that he struck Pasternak as being 'absolutely no artist'.[52] A similar celebrity befriended by Pasternak was Polonsky, who had singled out Pasternak's talent and fostered his engagement with the epic genre.[53] Various such men, artists, intellectuals and administrators, had survived and flourished in the 1920s without sacrificing their decency and integrity. Psychologically different from Pasternak, they were active and assertive individuals whose idealism remained intact as they maintained working relations with the new officialdom.

It was in similar terms that Pasternak revered the author Maksim Gorky, whom he evidently came to view as chief guarantor of cultural and historical continuity in a perplexing age. A lively correspondence took place between them in late 1927: twelve letters were exchanged inside six weeks after Pasternak had in September sent the book of *Nineteen Five* and *Lieutenant Shmidt* to Gorky. In one of them Pasternak described his view of Gorky's status:

I do not know what would be left of the revolution to me, and where its *truth* would be, if you were not there in Russian history. Immediately outside yourself [...] there open up its falsehoods and vacuities, which are partly attached to it by all manner of sufferers, i.e. by a hypocritical generation, and partly transferred by a revolutionary succession that is also somewhat fictitious. Having breathed its obligatory falsehood along with everyone else these ten years, I was gradually thinking of some liberation. For this one needed to take the revolutionary theme historically like a chapter among chapters, an event among events, and then raise it to some tangible, non-sectarian, general Russian power. This was the aim I pursued in the book I sent you.[54]

It was in this sense that Pasternak could admire Gorky's recent achievement in his otherwise rambling and incomplete novel *The Life of Klim Samgin*. Its hero, not unreminiscent of Spektorsky, was another uncommitted bourgeois intellectual whose life was traced through forty years of Russian history, including two revolutions in 1905 and 1917. In a letter of 13 November 1927 Pasternak described the work as an excavation of history. 'Like some sort of Atlantis', a probing of the recent past as a 'forgotten, lost foundation of the modern world [...] a pre-revolutionary prologue under a post-revolutionary pen.'[55] Pasternak's gushing praise of Gorky's novel was doubtless part of his own ritual of exaggerated courtesy to colleagues rather than a serious value judgement. In much the same way he had heaped compliments on Fedin and Olga Forsh. Essentially this reflected only the relevance of their books to his own current thoughts on the artist's need to assimilate and 'breathe' history. In December of 1928, again, he found in his friend Spassky's recently published *Failures* (*Neudachniki*) 'a true *poetic infinity* fortified by prose [...] a mature and courageous encounter with the times'.[56] Another novel of 1927, not mentioned by Pasternak but capable of striking a kindred chord, was Olesha's *Envy*.

Surprisingly, Pasternak's reverence for Gorky was not impaired even by the sharp differences in taste which emerged during their correspondence. He had told Gorky on 13 October 1927 that thanks to his poems on 1905 his financial troubles were over and that he even found opportunity to help others in need. One such person was Marina Tsvetaeva. Pasternak hoped that Gorky might share his own enthusiasm for her sufficiently to help alleviate her fate and maybe assist her return to Russia as an author if not in person. Unfortunately, in August Gorky had been visited by Tsvetaeva's sister Anastasiya and was irritated by her scheme to use Pasternak and himself to forward advances of money from her to Marina. He had no wish to compromise himself by assisting an arrantly White-Guardist poetess (and Tsvetaeva and her husband were also scared of Parisian émigré reaction should it get about that Gorky was assisting them!).[57] Moreover, Gorky found Tsvetaeva's poetry 'vociferous, even hysterical' and concluded that 'of course she should return to Russia, but that is scarcely possible'. With regard to his own work, Pasternak had not even taken amiss Gorky's benign but patronising wishes of good health and greater simplicity on an inscribed copy of *Klim Samgin* that was sent to him in late December of 1927.[58]

Gorky's sixtieth birthday fell in 1928. The event was widely celebrated in Russia and it was announced that he was to pay a return visit to Russia after seven years as a revered pro-Bolshevik exile. The previous year Pasternak had characterised him as 'the greatest man of our confused times [...] all the elements of the confusion, so hypocritical in other combinations and in others, are in him true to the point of hugeness'.[59] Now, in a letter of 21 May 1928, he told Lomonosova:

I expect a lot of this meeting. Of important people he is maybe the only one who can provide a key to the age, a strange, half-fictitious time. Yet by his figure and fate he serves as its most brilliant justification. My main hopes rest not on his oral explanations of the inexplicable, but on the fact that this inexplicability, when gathered around Gorky [...] will become visually more comprehensible, and dead fact will maybe light up with vital obviousness.

Gorky arrived at the Belorussky Station on 31 May, and Pasternak's first proper encounter with him was at a reception in his honour at the *Krasnaya nov'* editorial offices on 9 June. Presiding was the orthodox party official Raskolnikov, replacing the now-ousted Voronsky.[60] Pasternak's speech on the occasion was not recorded in detail. Katanyan recalled it as 'out of keeping with the unctuous inanities of other speakers', and Pasternak evidently pursued the line of 'Now the master is back and will sort us out'.[61] According to another account he also talked

401

about 'certain dubious friends of literature' who desired writers to deal only with post-revolutionary history 'as though literature began only with October, and as though the Revolution is not an historical link in the chain'. Clearly, Pasternak had harped on his own recent preoccupations but had also succeeded in perplexing his audience: Katanyan remembered only a few rhetorical 'acrobatic turns over the heads of those present' and a long disappearance 'out of one window and a re-entry via the other' before the speaker managed a perfect 'three-point landing'.[62] Pasternak himself believed he had 'talked comprehensibly and not about trifles'. But soon after his speech Gorky had baffled the whole company by suddenly rising to his feet and departing without a smile. Pasternak took this personally, although his later correspondence with Gorky established that his abrupt departure was simply caused by the visitor's impatience with 'the idleness of "working" meetings'.[63] After the meeting, Aleksei Tolstoy, Nikitin, Kataev, Olesha and Pasternak evidently repaired in confusion to the Budantsevs' new apartment on the Petrovka.

Gorky's whole visit was a grave disappointment. Pasternak did not like what he heard of Polonsky's reported conversation with the veteran author on 18 June when he had apparently lumped together 'the Gladkovs and Fedins of this world' and talked dismissively of Pilnyak's literary manner. 'There is a lot of swinishness, and even more injustice in all this,' Pasternak told his wife.[64] Even prior to this, Pasternak had sent Lomonosova a dejected assessment of Gorky's visit:

His converse with the country contains the rawest truth and one can conceive of nothing to surpass it. His meetings with writers are a display of mutual incomprehension and are a failure. The self-limitation bound up with these meetings suits him ill, and this places other people in a false position.[65]

Gorky had provided no resolution to the age's contradictions, and during and after his visit his behaviour only seemed to highlight them. He had evidently interceded with the authorities on behalf of certain individuals, securing the reinstatement of Polonsky. But such interventions by him were capriciously selective – he was not going to help Tsvetaeva and was later to refuse support for Pasternak's own foreign travel application. In fact, Gorky was already upstaged by political events and in the ensuing years was probably disturbed by what he observed happening in Russia.

In 1928 Pasternak offered what was in effect a bitter commentary on the impotent and contradictory stance of Gorky in his poetic portrait of another leading Bolshevik. In a new version of *Malady Sublime*, Gorky with his 'rectilinear glance' had vanished and the eleventh issue of *Novy mir* printed two new episodes as appendices to the poem. In the second of them Lenin was now portrayed as Pasternak vividly recalled him, speaking at the Ninth Congress of Soviets in 1921. The passage concerned was cited earlier (above p. 325), but it continued with a final quatrain whose irony identified it specifically as a pronouncement of the year 1928:

> What concealed concatenation
> United year with year!
> The genius comes with a presage of bounties
> And avenges his departure with oppression.   (I, 272; *SP*, 244)

Perhaps indeed, the age was comprehensible in the context of such a historical 'concatenation'. The lines were a biting comment on the supposed 'October amnesty' at a time when its promised bounties were being systematically cancelled by the Stalinist state.

The last months of 1927 brought medical troubles to add to Pasternak's anxieties. In November he tore the ligaments of his left shoulder and spent a month in bandages, almost immobilised and in great pain. Unable to write, he spent part of the time reading *Klim Samgin*. This was the prelude to eighteen months of family illness. After Boris' recovery, young Zhenya fell ill with influenza and an inflamed calix of the kidney. Just before Christmas Pasternak went down with influenza. Then the nurse who normally looked after Zhenya fell ill and stayed away, and Praskovya Ustinova, the resident cook for both Boris and Aleksandr's families, injured her leg. For most of April 1928 Pasternak was again incapacitated first by influenza and then through inflammation of the sinuses, which caused him intense headaches. During the winter Evgeniya also spent some time in the Uzkoye sanatorium near Moscow because of her again aggravated tubercular condition. Her slight recovery was then cancelled out when she prematurely returned home, 'terrorised', so Boris believed, by the need to resume her studies. In May of 1928 she was losing weight again, although she managed to sit her examinations. Pasternak set his main hopes for her recovery on a prolonged Caucasian holiday in the summer. As a result of this, some improvement was noted. But she was far from well when her mother died in mid-November, dealing her a grievous psychological blow. To cap everything, shortly afterwards their former nurse Fenya, an old

Lurye family retainer, arrived suddenly on the doorstep, homeless, destitute and in a state of dementia. It was Evgeniya who had to see that she was cared for and admitted to hospital. At the end of all this, so Pasternak told cousin Olya, Evgeniya was little more than skin and bone. She had not painted for six months and urgently needed to recuperate in a rest-home. Eventually she went on her own for a few weeks in the Crimea in April 1929.[66]

In 1928 the question of travel and residence abroad again arose. Pasternak's mood was negative. One of several weights on his mind was a fear that 'despite all my longing to go abroad, which casts a shadow over all the joys of life here, I shall not manage to go this spring'.[67] After months of family illness, literary projects were fearfully behindhand and finances were consequently running low. There was thus little hope of affording a journey abroad. Further factors were Pasternak's increasing resignation and despair, not least with his own personality. Some of this emerged in a letter of 15 March 1928 to his sister Lydia:

Probably I am not without merits, but in general I am not a flexible type of person [...] I have always had to consolidate all my qualities with all their darker sides according to my main proclivities, because it was not a question of altering them, but only of erecting some sort of structure on this given soil, quelle qu'elle fût. [*sic*]

Comparison of himself with his father only reinforced self-doubts:

Papa was and is a living person, with all the weaknesses of a really live, ambitious, outstanding individual in his own place and time – not like me with my 'near sanctimoniousness' [...] a trait of character which has grown not out of me, but is growing into me more and more from a compound of my life, its surroundings, times, plans, etc., etc. .... And how *purely* all this has stung him! And it has left me just as *confusedly distracted*.[68]

The comings and goings of other friends between Moscow and Berlin during the 1920s were meanwhile a poor substitute for the reunions that both Pasternak and his exiled family longed for. A periodic bearer of gifts and messages was their family friend and physician Dr Levin; during the 1920s he travelled out to attend Gorky on Capri and later in Sorrento. Another regular traveller was Boris Zbarsky, now a member of the new Bolshevik scientific élite. In 1927 he reported back enthusiastically about Leonid Pasternak's Berlin exhibition and claimed he had found Boris' parents 'cheery and young-looking'. In 1928 Soviet citizens travelling abroad were permitted to take only thirty roubles' worth of hard currency (about $15) per person; the Berlin Pasternaks would therefore sometimes help subsidise a visitor's stay in order that the latter pass on an equivalent amount in roubles to Boris' family and to other relatives in Odessa and Leningrad. Both luxury items and some basic commodities figured among the gifts brought back to Moscow; they included packets of decent writing paper, chocolate, cocoa, paints for Evgeniya and a sailor-suit for Zhenya. One of the gift bearers in May 1928 was Antonina Engel. (While visiting Palestine in 1927 with his wife to collect Hebrew folk music materials, Yulii Engel had died suddenly; his wife had eventually returned to Moscow alone, via Berlin.)[69]

These visits and the delivery of messages and presents all took place against a background of increasing restrictions on Soviet citizens' contacts with the outside world. For instance, publications by émigré Russian writers could no longer be sent by post. Boris' letter of 27–8 December 1927 informed his parents that 'not a single book printed in Russian and published abroad is allowed through, and the recipient is not informed of its interception'. There were further difficulties when Leonid Pasternak in early 1928 asked Boris to send him Rilke's letters which he had left stored in the Volkhonka apartment: the Soviet embassy in Berlin was not a reliable forwarding agent; 'unfortunately Gorky is a social democrat'; and Boris risked an unpleasant interrogation by the authorities if he attempted to visit the German embassy in Moscow. A private messenger who could have taken the materials (for passing to the Rilke Archive in Germany) was Pavel Ettinger, the art historian, but in December 1928 he was refused an exit visa.[70]

By 1928 there were therefore real grounds for uncertainty about the possibility of family visits to Berlin. Pasternak made no initiatives, yet entertained their possibility while still remaining gloomy. 'I shall not see them all that soon,' he told Olya Freidenberg in a letter. 'My longing for a trip out there still continues, but it keeps getting postponed. At present I believe I shall finally manage to go next winter. But how often have I been wrong before!'[71]

The only real alternative in summer 1928 was another family holiday in the Soviet Union. Finances were at another low ebb. But the technique of raising loans and advances was by now well mastered. 'We are sitting here without money,' Pasternak told Olya on 10 May, 'but of course I'll manage to get some.' In the same letter he discussed sending

Evgeniya and Zhenya for a cheap Caucasian holiday, after which they might rent a *dacha* where Olya and her mother could come and join them.[72] The idea was not pursued, however. Instead the Pasternaks all went to the Caucasus. Evgeniya and Zhenya left Moscow on 5 June for Gelendzhik on the North Caucasian coast of the Black Sea. Pasternak remained in Moscow to work and raise further funds. In June he completed and handed to *Krasnaya nov'* the next (sixth and seventh) chapters of Spektorsky. Then, using a copy of *Over the Barriers* borrowed from Shura Shtikh, he began revising certain selected items from his two pre-revolutionary poetry collections. Most of this manuscript was handed in to Giz on 12 July. A few days later Pasternak collected his fee and, weary after several weeks of intense but fruitful exertion, set off to join his family. With him went Pasha Ustinova to help with household and child.[73]

Evgeniya had written Boris some jaundiced impressions of Gelendzhik in mid-June, complaining about the dirty sea and narrow beach with its dull grey pebbles and litter of cigarette stubs. Boris took a more favourable view and described the setting to the Polonskys who were also holidaying in the Caucasus:

Gelendzhik is not at all so bad as Zhenya [i.e. Evgeniya] represented it. The sea is fine, and by its bare and blinding expanse of mother-of-pearl with streaks of blue are scattered bathers, boats, white villas of a Greek township, white-legged sailors, Greek kiosk salesmen, boot-polishers, children from the kefir and coffee shops, the hot, innocent and uncorrupt south, idle oleanders, mimosa, peach trees, quinces... (by which time my syntax has collapsed!) And beyond it there are mountains, not all that impressive ones, but still mountains, real mountains, i.e. peaceful heaps of watchful, unchanging expanse, constantly resembling a great mass of time imagined all at once, like some 'entire lifespan' waiting to be experienced and still unlived by anyone. In a word, this is the south, just as it is supposed to be.[74]

The holiday restored all of them. A plan to join 1up with the Polonskys at Teberda in August fell through owing to Kira Polonskaya's falling ill at Kislovodsk. By way of a break, Boris and Evgeniya left Zhenya in the hands of Pasha Ustinova and went off on several days' tour of the Black Sea coast, travelling by car, train and steamer and visiting the resorts of Sochi and Tuapse.[75]

Chapter 5 of *Spektorsky* appeared in *Krasnaya nov'*'s first issue for 1928. It contained a portrait of Sashka Baltz, a character based partly (like

Schütz in *Three Chapters from a Tale*) on Pasternak's old acquaintance
Aleksandr Gavronsky. Chapters 6 and 7 were printed in *Krasnaya nov'*,
no.7, 1928, almost immediately upon their completion. They appeared
under the title 'The Courtyard' ('Dvor'); dedicated to Pilnyak, they were
some of Pasternak's favourite verses which he often recited to audiences
in the late 1920s. The new chapters showed signs of Pasternak's altering
conception of *Spektorsky*. They reflected his relationship with Tsvetaeva
and his admiration for Vera Ilyina, the poetess wife of Sergei Budantsev.
Evgenii Tager, the literary scholar, later confirmed to Evgenii Pasternak
that elements of both these women figured in the character of Maria
Ilyina, the central heroine of the work.[76]

In chapter 6 Sergei Spektorsky's encounter with Maria (like
Tsvetaeva, a professor's daughter and poetess) at the house of Baltz is
perhaps traceable to the meeting that took place in January 1918 at the
Tsetlins' home. The institute where Sergei later visits Ilyina was 'formerly a masons' lodge' (I, 298; *SP*, 326) – a clear allusion to the earlier
history of the Moscow School of Painting on Myasnitskaya. When
Tsvetaeva herself eventually read *Spektorsky*, she also recognised in the
description of Maria's dilapidated apartment some features of her own
rooms in Borisoglebsky Lane, where Pasternak had once called during
the Civil War to deliver a letter from Ehrenburg. Sergei's airy impro-
visings on the piano were evident self-portraiture by Pasternak; and
there was an element of Pasternak's own ruminations too in the note left
by Maria on her writing pad:

> ... Life has its favourites.
> It seems to me that we are not among them.
>
> Now is a time for improvising.
> But when will come the time for earnest speech?
> With hearts run dry now, when shall we rise up
> To the profession of long-buried dreams?
>
> There is no escape. As I get older
> Life's invaded by this earth's concerns.
> Free will is hounded. Meanwhile a lack of will
> Is claimed by graveyards, fields, ravines.   (I, 303; *SP*, 330)

Chapter 7 describes Sergei's separation from Maria in circumstances
perhaps symbolically relatable to Pasternak's own 'loss' of Tsvetaeva at
the time of his new family ties with Petrograd. After an urgent summons
to that city to his sick mother's bedside, Sergei departs leaving Maria no

explanation; two weeks later he returns only to find her apartment abandoned: 'dust everywhere, a sea / Of walls, demolished, and abandoned work' (I, 305; *SP*, 332).

At this point, another break in the composition and printing of *Spektorsky* occurred. Now, however, Pasternak seemed confident about the direction in which the work was developing. On 26 June 1928, as the latest chapters were completed, Pasternak wrote to the poet Mikhail Froman:

For the first time in my life I seem to have written a large piece of narrative lyric with a beginning and an ending, where everything is transformed by the movement of the tale, as in prose [...] For the first time the compositional medium [*stikhiya*] has entered my experience as an integral element, that is, I have experienced it as something instinctively simple, just like metaphor, melody, metre, or a line of verse.

In addition to the works already mentioned, Pasternak in 1928 allowed into print some of his manuscripts of much earlier vintage, among them an impressionistic *poema* fragment of 1916 entitled 'The City' ('Gorod') and two unnamed pieces headed simply 'From a Poem' ('Iz poemy'). He also reworked and published some poems from *Twin in the Stormclouds* and *Over the Barriers*. Scattered in various journals, these lyrics were by-products of his main poetic undertaking of 1928: a much altered re-edition of *Over the Barriers*, which was finally completed in the spring of 1929 and published that year. Essentially the book could be viewed as an entirely fresh piece of work. At the same time it offered a summation of Pasternak's achievement as a lyricist, containing examples of the 'epic malady' along with several sections and sequences of shorter lyrics;[77] its dedications too were designed to underline a continuing relationship with his poetic past.

The new book had the following subdivisions: 'Initial Period' (revised selections from *Twin in the Stormclouds*, dedicated to Aseyev); 'Over the Barriers' (a selection of reworkings inscribed to Mayakovsky); 'Miscellaneous Verses of the Years 1922–28'; 'Epic Motifs' (*poema* fragments of 1916–17, recent verse on the October anniversary and variants of materials from *Nineteen Five* and *Spektorsky*, dedicated to Evgeniya Pasternak); *Malady Sublime* (with the new 1928 insertions and dedicated to Anastasiya Tsvetaeva). This return by Pasternak to some of his poetic origins paralleled the concurrent review of his earlier life undertaken in *Safe Conduct*, and like the latter work it could be seen as part of a search for some personal sense of continuity spanning conflicting historical epochs. In *Over the Barriers* (1929), examples of recent original verse were set alongside early writings many of which were filtered and amended in the light of a painfully won maturity. Pasternak had recently been dismissive about the 1917 edition of *Barriers*, but it contained some qualities worth perserving which were congruent with the simplicity and seriousness described to Gorky and Olya Freidenberg as Pasternak's aim in 1928.

The new revision imparted to several poems a control and unmannered appearance which Pasternak associated specifically with Acmeist verse. In 1928 Pasternak had read Mandelstam's reworkings of some of his earlier verse in the volume of *Poems* (*Stikhotvoreniya*) published that year. It was a sobering experience, as he told Mandelstam in a letter of 24 September, for inspection of his own earlier poems revealed that 'there is nothing there but naked thematic movement, often stripped down to the point of senselessness [...] the complete opposite of your [i.e. Mandelstam's] absolute loftiness and richness of content, unshaken by changes down in the street'. And since his own poems' 'barbarian movement repels one by its poverty turned into idle pretension', Pasternak was 'dismantling these comical engines down to the last bolt and [...] assembling them into an unpretentious heap of almost immobile, stupid, school anthology documentation'.[78] Pasternak's self-deprecation and compliments to Mandelstam were characteristically exaggerated. However, now there were cogent reasons for adopting this manner, even had it not come naturally to Pasternak: by 1928 Mandelstam was increasingly the target of attack in the literary press and of administrative reprisals, and he was becoming increasingly embittered. In his September letter Pasternak was doubtless consciously trying to support and encourage him, and Mandelstam responded warmly with a copy of the *Poems* dedicated 'To dear Boris Leonidovich, with firm friendship, astonishment, and pride in him. 25 October 1928.'[79]

Quite apart from any need to cheer Mandelstam, Pasternak was in the later 1920s gravitating naturally towards a style and tone that could be related to the Petersburg Acmeists. In February 1926, for instance, he had considered writing something about Gumilyov.[80] Mention of a new quasi-Acmeist ideal pursued in *Over the Barriers* (1929) also occurred in a letter to Vladimir Pozner, to whom Pasternak admitted: 'The book is written with faith in the reader. It simply chats with him, almost despising art, i.e. without tolerating any domestic drama. In it a genial Acmeistic tone predominates.'[81] These remarks could apply equally to Pasternak's new redactions of earlier verse and to the more recent lyrics.

Nevertheless, despite the intentions, by no means all readers liked what they discovered in the new book. During the summer of 1928 Loks and one or two others who had admired the earlier Pasternak were shown some of the reworkings and were 'horrified at the adaptations'.[82] On the other hand, orthodox critical demands for simplicity were still unsatisfied; a short note in a political librarians' journal observed: 'Because of the complexity of the verses from the point of view of content and form, the reader has difficulty in picking up their meaning [...] The collection is suitable only for the very highly qualified reader.'[83] Lazar Fleishman has also emphasised the complexity of some of the adaptations and their actual reliance on the earlier versions for proper comprehension.[84] Nonetheless, Pasternak himself was convinced of his movement towards neutrality and simplicity which should not be resisted (even though its effect on his prose style was in his own view not immediately beneficial)* and which was pursued further in his verse of the 1930s.

When he began revising *Over the Barriers*, Pasternak had started already on *Safe Conduct*, which partly explains the criteria for selection and adaption of earlier texts. Despite the author's awareness of pursuing simplicity, the creative process described in the autobiographical work was still based on a metaphoric 'dislocation' of reality and a randomness of imagery that were perfectly applied in *My Sister Life* and *Themes and Variations*;[86] many of the poems under revision were still marked by the complex results of this approach. Now, however, the presence of an autobiographical link, and the elimination of episodes and whole poems lacking it were important factors. Items from *Twin in the Stormclouds* were clearly selected for their identification with the poet's early amorous biography and burgeoning artistic awareness, and their reworkings often also accented a new sense of post-revolutionary vulnerability.

Fourteen poems from the *Lirika* almanac and Pasternak's first collection were shorn of almost all their Symbolist liturgical and oracular archaism; a nocturnal garden lost its Gnostic associations, and city and snowscapes were purged of mystical overtones. Poems that depended

---

* A letter of 1929 to Vladimir Pozner, during work on *Safe Conduct* stated: 'Three years ago Proust was a complete revelation to me. I am afraid to read him (he is so close!) and I snapped the book to on the fifth page. I have left it for the future, put it aside for I know not how long. Meanwhile the danger gets less: in my prose I am approaching Boborykin, and in verse – Shchepkina-Kupernik.' Pasternak was on friendly terms with the latter, but her work and that of the prosaist Boborykin were bywords respectively for blandness and prolix monotony. Svyatopolk-Mirsky was probably the first to indicate a kinship between Pasternak and Proust in 1926.[85]

centrally on zodiacal or Doppelgänger motifs were eliminated alto-gether. Also removed were Ego-Futurist lexical trappings – especially the proliferation of Gallicism and 'barbarian' rhyme in such poems as 'The Station'. In general, revisions of metaphoric structure tended to underscore tactile and other sensory qualities through adjectival usage, at the expense of the noun-based genitive links and abstract substantives preferred by Symbolism.

In several 'Early Period' poems the lyricist's previous forlorn moods with matching meteorological accompaniment were now reinforced by a sense of exposure to a new and cruel age. The poetic 'Banquets' ('Pirshestva') of 1913 were now joined by 'heredity and death' as dining partners, and in 'Eden' ('Edem') revisited the woodland announced its own entry 'as a historical person into the family of timbertrunks' (I, 179; *SP*, 67).[87]

Thirty-one of the original forty-nine *Barriers* poems survived in the revised collection. Those omitted tended to be poems embodying 'storm and stress' romantic heroics, or anti-aesthetic Futurist grotesque. Although regrouped, the selection still conveyed a fair overall impres-sion of the 1917 collection. There were only slight concessions to ease of comprehension, and surprisingly two of the most obscure items, 'Phan-tasm', retitled as 'Possibility' ('Vozmozhnost''), and 'Ballada' were retained. The autobiographical Marburg motif was amplified by inclu-sion of a thematically related fragment 'From a Poem'. In the poem 'Marburg' itself, Ida Vysotskaya's Severyanin-esque bourgeois attributes (see the extract quoted above, p. 119) were eliminated, there was more factual motivation of the love story, and some Marburg historical associations were introduced. And although the poem was recording a poetic rebirth, in 1928 the potentiality of death was also hinted at: 'In Marburg / Some men loudly whistling fashioned crossbows / While others prepared for Trinity Fair' (I, 221; *SP*, 108). This was another of several allusions to the poet's death by hunting. One of the 'Miscell-aneous Verses', in fact, addressed the 'Strapping marksman, careful hunter' ('Roslyi strelok, ostorozhnyi okhotnik') who condemned the poet while commanding him to create: 'Let me rise above shameful death [...] Take aim. It's all over! Fire me into flight.' And at this 'sonorous parting' the poet gave thanks for the 'timidity, friendship, homeland and family' he had been forced to abandon (I, 232; *SP*, 208).[88] Thematically closely related to this was a sinister poem (not included in *Over the Barriers*) which was printed with its title removed by the censor in *Novy mir*, no. 1, 1928; it is translated at the head of this

411

chapter (p. 381). In it a revolution was presented as only one of a series of depredations in history's woodland. Once the haunt of poets, the forest grove was now invaded by the podagric, leering forestry commissioner, symbol of a stultifying officialidom. Even without its title the poem was an eloquent comment on the revolution's continuing progress of violence.[89]

The 'Miscellaneous Verses' section of *Over the Barriers* (1929) was dominated by a series of poems addressed to Akhmatova, Tsvetaeva, Meyerhold and his actress wife Zinaida Raikh, Bryusov (the jubilee poem of 1924) and a poem in memory of Larisa Reisner. Pasternak sent Akhmatova his poem to her in a letter of 6 March 1929 and requested her permission to publish it. It first appeared in *Krasnaya nov'*, no. 5, for that year, along with others to Meyerhold and Tsvetaeva. 'The last remnant of lyric feeling is alive,' Pasternak told Akhmatova, 'and it is still only burning out in me in the form of a living (and of course unpayable) debt to a few important people and friends. I have written something to you, to the Meyerholds and Mayakovsky.' In a further letter, on 6 April 1929, Pasternak also named his wife and Lomonosova as the addressees of forthcoming verse.[90] The poem to Lomonosova seems not to have been written, however, and the 'Epic Motifs' in *Over the Barriers* (1929) were the only offering to Evgeniya.

Akhmatova assented to Pasternak's poem, but was cautious about his personal view of her and her work. The poet sought to 'choose words resembling your authenticity' and based himself on an appreciation of her 'first books, where particles of attentive prose grew strong' (I, 223–4; *SP*, 199–200). But the poem was written with a restraint that Akhmatova later commended, and Acmeist values seemed to be upheld in its portraiture.[91] The poems to Akhmatova and Tsvetaeva both handled the theme of 'the poet and the age', and of 'real event' (*byl'*) as a basic substance of poetry, ideas that characterised Pasternak's own compositions of the time.

The promised Mayakovsky poem was in fact a revival of Pasternak's rueful address to him in the early 1920s and was intended as part of an attempt at dialogue with him after news of his withdrawal from Lef in September 1928. For a time Pasternak may have thought his hopes for Mayakovsky expressed in the poem and in their other recent exchanges had at least been fulfilled. But they were dashed in May of 1929 when Mayakovsky's new slogan 'To the Left of Lef' (*Levee Lefa*) emerged as part of a totally politicised programme for a new 'Revolutionary Front of Art' (Ref), in which ideological intent was placed before any consideration of content or form. Pasternak saw Mayakovsky's move as part of the tragic dénouement of his life and the collapse of his personality. Even before then, however, Raskolnikov had refused to publish Pasternak's poem in *Krasnaya nov'*, and it was also excluded from *Over the Barriers*.[92]

Pasternak's poetic address to the Meyerholds presented the actor as an emblem of artistry in general, and it continued this series of images in Pasternak's oeuvre. The interpretation it acquired in his subsequent writings was already present in this poem of 1928. In it the actor-artist was marked out for a role that involved self-sacrifice in fulfilment of a higher destiny:

> With the breath of original drama,
> Powdered and grease-painted role,
> Your whole selves are erased by persona.
> The name of this make-up is 'soul'. (I, 227; *SP*, 202)

Among the 'Miscellaneous Verses' a poem 'To Reisner's Memory' ('Pamyati Reisner') was perhaps the most unexpected item. The dedicatee was the talented daughter of a Bolshevik intelligentsia family; she had a passion for poetry and burning ambition as a 'woman of the revolution'. She and Pasternak had first met during the Civil War. In the early twenties she had been with her first husband Raskolnikov (now chief editor of *Krasnaya nov'*) as part of the Soviet diplomatic mission to Afghanistan. Her second marriage was another prominent official, Karl Radek, and during the two or three years before her premature death of typhoid on 9 February 1926 she moved freely in Moscow literary circles. Although not an intimate acquaintance, she had been on friendly terms with both Pasternak and the Mandelstams.[93] Perhaps there was something of her personality in Pasternak's portrait of Olga Bukhteyeva in the later chapters of *Spektorsky*; she embodied femininity with an ardent, pure, and now vanishing, idealism:

> You smoked there like a storm of grace.
> Scarce having bathed in its living fire,
> All mediocrity was shamed.
> All imperfection drew you ire.
>
> So sink in legend's depth, o heroine.
> This journey shall not weary your feet.
> Spread as a panoply over my thoughts:
> In your shadow my thoughts are at ease. (I, 238; *SP*, 213)

Among the papers left by Yurii Zhivago in Pasternak's novel are some notes of the mid-1920s containing observations on post-revolutionary Moscow:

The vitally formed, living language that naturally reflects the spirit of modern times is the language of the city [...] Moscow, blinded by the summer sun [...] whirls around me, turns my head and wills me to turn the heads of others by writing in its praise. For this purpose it has educated me and placed art into my hands.

The constant noise of the street day and night outside the walls is closely bound up with our modern spirit, like an overture starting with the curtain lowered, still shrouded in darkness and mystery, but already turning crimson in the glow of the footlights. Incessantly stirring and rumbling outside doors and windows, the city is a huge and boundless preamble to the life of each one of us. It is in these terms that I should like to write about the city.   (*DZh*, 500–1)

With the possible exception of the poem 'Hamlet' ('Gamlet'), the hero's notebook evidently contained no writing about the city in these terms. But one of Pasternak's poems entitled 'Space', or 'Expanse' ('Prostranstvo'), seems to hint at the spirit of Zhivago's remarks. After a summer countryside shower near Khotkovo in 1927, the poet's eye falls on the railtrack that lead towards Moscow, and the final stanzas of the poem are about the city itself – not the impressionist vision of the 1916 *poema* fragment, nor the 'ville tentaculaire' of Symbolist visions, but a city viewed as the arena of historical events. This city was to be the principal setting for Pasternak's life and work in the ensuing years, and the whole poem thus had a symbolic meaning, characterising Pasternak's career from the 1910s to the later 1920s.

> There is the city – and where can one count
> The enticements of a Muscovite congress?
> The burning wool of ill-weathers,
> Allurement of unfathomed darkness?
>
> There is the city – and just look
> How crimson it blazes at night.
> By actual event alone it's illuminated
> From within, like a lampion bright.
>
> It has closed about like a wonder in stone –
> Birth's rattling, clattering gift-offering.
> And chance's candle-stump glimmers within
> As if in a small cardboard kremlin.

From its hills it has scattered these lanterns
In order to drip, to melt down and light up
History, like the tallow
Of some candle bearing no title.   (I, 228; *SP*, 204)

At the outset, Pasternak's life and creativity had been rooted in nature, family, art, and private experience. But as the decades passed they were becoming increasingly and inescapably bound up with human affairs and history. So it was to continue . . .

Notes

The following notes are mainly bibliographical. Occasionally, however, they add points of detail and interpretation that could not be accommodated in the text or footnotes. References are given only to published or other documentary sources. Certain other information in the text has been derived from relatives and acquaintances of Pasternak, most of whom are identified and acknowledged in the preface. The following abbreviations are used in the notes:

APT	Archive of the Pasternak Trust.
Briefwechsel	Rainer Maria Rilke, Marina Zwetajewa, Boris Pasternak. *Briefwechsel*. Frankfurt, 1983.
ChPV	'Chudo poeticheskogo voploshcheniya', publ. E. B. Pasternak, *Voprosy literatury*, 9 (1972).
DLDN	'Dykhanie liriki. Iz perepiski R. M. Ril'ke, M. Tsvetaevoi i B. Pasternaka v 1926 godu', publ. K. Azadovsky, E. B. and E. V. Pasternak, *Druzhba narodov*, 6 (1987), 7 (1987), 8 (1987), 9 (1987).
DZh	*Doktor Zhivago*. Milan, 1957.
Izbr. I	*Izbrannoe*. Moscow, 1985. Volume I. *Stikhotvoreniya i poemy*.
Izbr. II	*Izbrannoe*. Moscow, 1985. Volume II. *Proza. Stikhotvoreniya*.
LOP	*Leonid Osipovich Pasternak 1862–1945*. Katalog vystavki. Moscow, 1979.
LRA	Leeds Russian Archive.
Perepiska	*Perepiska s Ol'goi Freidenberg*. New York, 1981.
Soch. I	*Sochineniya*. Ann Arbor, 1961. Volume I. *Stikhi i poemy 1912–1932*.
Soch. II	*Sochineniya*. Ann Arbor, 1961. Volume II. *Proza, 1915–1958. Povesti, rasskazy, avtobiograficheskie proizvedeniya*.
Soch. III	*Sochineniya*. Ann Arbor, 1961. Volume III. *Stikhi 1936–1959. Stikhi dlya detei. Stikhi 1912–1957, ne sobrannye v knigi avtora. Stat'i i vystupleniya*.
SP	*Stikhotvoreniya i poemy*. Moscow–Leningrad, 1965.
Vosp	Aleksandr Pasternak. *Vospominaniya*. Munich–Paderborn–Vienna–Zurich, 1983.
VP	*Vozdushnye puti. Proza raznykh let*. Moscow, 1982.
ZRL	Leonid Pasternak. *Zapisi raznykh let*. Moscow, 1975

I ORIGINS AND INFANCY

1 L. O. Pasternak, 'Vier Fragmente aus meiner Selbstbiographie', in M. Osborn, *Leonid Pasternak* (Warsaw, 1932), 44.
2 *ZRL*, 11–13, 23.
3 *Ibid.*, 15–16.
4 *Ibid.*, 17–20. *Perepiska*, 339–40.
5 *ZRL*, 22–4. See below, chapters 3 and 4.
6 *ZRL*, 24–5, 152–5.
7 *Ibid.*, 25–31.
8 S. Levitsky, 'Rose Koffman-Pasternak', in P. J. Mark (ed.), *Die Familie – La famille – The Family Pasternak* (Geneva, 1975), 11–14. E. Dagilaiskaya, 'Iz proshlogo fortepiannogo ispolnitel'stva i fortepiannoi pedagogiki v Odesse', *Masterstvo muzykal'nogo ispolnitel'stva*, vypusk 2 (Moscow, 1976), 255–6, 258–9, 264–6.
9 Levitsky, 'Rose Koffman-Pasternak', 14–20.
10 *Ibid.*, 20.
11 O. Bachmann, *Rosa Koffman: Eine biographische Skizze, nebst Auszug einiger Rezensionen* (Odessa, 1885).
12 *ZRL*, 31.
13 *Ibid.*, 31–3.
14 *Ibid.*, 34–5, 137.
15 *Ibid.*, 33, 137–8.
16 *Izbr. II*, 499. *ZRL*, 38.
17 *ZRL*, 38, 264–5. R. Salys, 'Leonid Pasternak: The Early Years', *International Programs Quarterly*, 2 nos. 2–3 (1987), 29, 31–2.
18 *ZRL*, 63.
19 *Ibid.*, 38, 52–4.
20 D. Buckman, *Leonid Pasternak: A Russian Impressionist 1862–1945* (London, 1974), 20–3. *ZRL*, 33–4, 40–51.
21 *ZRL*, 174. *ZRL*, 171–212.
22 *Ibid.*, 180. Levitsky, 'Rose Koffman-Pasternak', 22. On Leonid Pasternak's career, see also: Buckman, *Leonid Pasternak*; G. de Mallac, 'A Russian Impressionist: Leonid Osipovich Pasternak, 1862–1945', *California Slavic Studies*, 10 (1977), 87–120; Osborn, *Leonid Pasternak*; and R. Salys, 'Leonid Pasternak: The Early Years', 28–33, and 'Exhibiting in Russia at the Turn of the Century: Leonid Pasternak between 1888 and 1916', *Festschrift in Honor of Kenneth Lindsay* (Binghamton, NY, forthcoming), *passim*.
23 *Soch. II*, 1. *Izbr. II*, 224, 499. See also *Vosp.*, 12.
24 Letter of 2 May 1959, quoted in J. Proyart, *Pasternak* (Paris, 1964), 40.
25 L. Fleishman, 'K publikatsii pis'ma L. O. Pasternaka k Byaliku', *Slavica Hierosolymitana*, 1 (1977), 313.
26 *ZRL*, 38, 44. Buckman, *Leonid Pasternak*, 35.
27 *ZRL*, 44–5. *Soch. II*, 1; *VP*, 413–14.

28 *ZRL*, 51. *Soch. II*, 2; *VP*, 414. *Vosp.*, 30–2.
29 *Soch. II*, 2; *VP*, 414. See 'Nachalo prozy 1936 goda', in *VP*, esp. 305–6; esp. ch. 2 of *DZh*; 'Povest'' in *Soch. II*, 151–202; *VP*, 136–90.
30 *ZRL*, 142.
31 See 'Detstvo Lyuvers', *Soch. II*, 83–136; *VP*, 56–107; 'Nadmennyi nishchii', *Soch. II*, 295–302, *VP*, 304–12.
32 *ZRL*, 56.
33 *Soch. II*, 2–3; *VP*, 414–15.
34 *Soch. II*, 2–3; *VP*, 414–15. *Vosp.*, 21–3, 43–4.
35 *Soch. II*, 3–5; *VP*, 415–18. *Vosp.*, 22, 37–40.
36 *Soch. II*, 5–6; *VP*, 417–18. *Vosp.*, 28. *ZRL*, 192 ff.
37 B. Pasternak, *An Essay in Autobiography* (London, 1959), illustration facing p. 32; see also Buckman, *Leonid Pasternak, passim*, and *ZRL, passim*.
38 *Vosp.*, 25–7. 'Detskie risunki Borisa Pasternaka', in E. B. Pasternak, 'Boris Pasternak 1890–1960', *Den' poezii 1981* (Moscow, 1981), 159–61.
39 *Vosp.*, 27–9.
40 Letter of 17 June 1927 to M. A. Froman, *ChPV*, 163.
41 *ZRL*, 45. *Vosp.*, 16–17, 33–6, 198–201, 207.
42 *Soch. II*, 10; *VP*, 423. *Vosp.*, 26, 211–12.
43 N. S. Rodionov, *Moskva v zhizni i tvorchestve L. N. Tolstogo* (Moscow, 1954), 125.
44 Pasternak is mistaken: Gay died in early summer of 1894; see *Izbr. II*, 499.
45 *Soch. II*, 203; *VP*, 192.
46 Letter of 27 March 1950 to S. N. Durylin, *ChPV*, 168.
47 L. Pasternak-Slater, 'Boris and the Parents', in Mark (ed.), *Die Familie*, 107.
48 *Ibid.*, 110.
49 *ZRL*, 195–6. Buckman, *Leonid Pasternak*, 22. See R. Salys, 'Boris Pasternak on Leonid Pasternak and the Critics: Two Early Texts', *Russian Language Journal* (forthcoming, 1988).
50 *Vosp.*, 19–20, 204.
51 The degree of Pasternak's similarity to one parent or another is ultimately a matter of subjective surmise. An interesting and relevant statement occurred in Pasternak's letter of 15 July 1907 to his parents who were on tour in Western Europe: 'Yesterday as I went to bed I noted with displeasure the presence in me of a large dose (?) of filial feelings, and they extended specially strongly towards mama. This upset me greatly, because *parentibus presentibus* I love papa more with my mind, but *parentibus absentibus* the law of nature gains ascendancy.'
52 Fleishman, 'K publikatsii pis'ma', 316. *ZRL*, 210.
53 L. Pasternak-Slater, 'Letter to the Editor', *New York Times Book Review*, 29 October 1961, 50. On Leonid Pasternak's religiosity, see *ZRL*, 104.
54 Zh. L. Pasternak and L. L. Pasternak-Sleiter, 'Pis'mo L. O. Pasternaka k Byaliku', *Slavica Hierosolymitana*, 1 (1977), 307.
55 A. Rammelmeyer, 'Die Philipps-Universität zu Marburg in der russischen

Geistesgeschichte und schönen Literatur', *Mitteilungen. Universitätsbund Marburg*, Heft 2–3 (Marburg, 1957), 80. Letter of 2 May 1959 to J. de Proyart, quoted in Proyart, *Pasternak*, 41. On Pasternak's religious views, see G. de Mallac, 'Pasternak and Religion', *Russian Review*, 32, no. 4 (October 1973), 360–75.

56 Cf. G. de Mallac, *Boris Pasternak: His Life and Art* (Norman, OK, 1981), 31. Our own version is confirmed by both Josephine and Lydia Pasternak.

2 SCHOOL AND SCRIABIN

1 *Soch. II*, 7; *VP*, 420. *ZRL*, 56. *Vosp.*, 36–42.

2 See *Izbr. II*, 230, 499.

3 *Soch. II*, 7; *VP*, 420. *Vosp.*, 44–7.

4 *Vosp.*, 47–63.

5 *Soch. II*, 7; *VP*, 420.

6 *Soch. II*, 8; *VP*, 421. *Vosp.*, 112–16.

7 *Soch. II*, 8; *VP*, 421.

8 G. Kurlov, 'O Pasternake', *Russkaya mysl'*, no. 1288, 18 November 1958. *Soch. II*, 231; *VP*, 220, *Vosp.*, 180–1.

9 *Vosp.*, 123–7.

10 R. Payne, *The Three Worlds of Boris Pasternak* (London, 1962), 38. Kurlov, 'O Pasternake'. L. Chertkov, 'K voprosu o literaturnoi genealogii Pasternaka', in M. Aucouturier (ed.), *Boris Pasternak 1890–1960. Colloque de Cérisy-la-Salle* (Paris, 1979), 57.

11 *DZh*, 82.

12 *Vosp.* 121. *ZRL*, 66.

13 *Perepiska*, 340.

14 *Ibid.*, 348.

15 *Ibid.*, 339–42. *Soch. II*, 244.

16 *Soch. II*, 203–4; *VP*, 191–2. See also: A. von Gronicka, 'Rilke and the Pasternaks', *Germanic Review*, 27 (1952), 260–271; K. M. Azadovsky and L. Chertkov, 'Russkie vstrechi Ril'ke', in R. M. Ril'ke, *Vorpsvede, Ogyust Roden, Pis'ma, Stikhi* (Moscow, 1971), 370–71; *ZRL*, 146–50; C. J. Barnes, 'Boris Pasternak and Rainer Maria Rilke: Some Missing Links', *Forum for Modern Language Studies*, 8 no. 1 (January 1972), 62; A. Livingstone, *Lou Andreas-Salomé* (London, 1984), 107–14; Z. F. Ruoff, 'Pasternak i Ril'ke'.

17 *Soch. II*, 204; *VP*, 192. *ZRL*, 148.

18 *Vosp.*, 94–7, 142–3. *Soch. II*, 8; *VP*, 421.

19 'Detskie risunki Borisa Pasternaka', in E. B. Pasternak, 'Boris Pasternak 1890–1960', 159–61. *Soch. II*, 8–10; *VP*, 421–3. *Vosp.*, 101–2.

20 *Vosp.*, 103

21 V. Del'son, *Skryabin* (Moscow, 1971), 90–2. F. Bowers, *Scriabin* (Tokyo-Palo Alto, 1969), I, 290, 294, 320–4. *Vosp.*, 103–4.

22 Del'son, *Skryabin*, 87–8. A. N. Skryabin, 'Zapisi A. N. Skryabina', *Russkie propilei*, 6 (1919), 123–32. *Soch. II*, 9–10; *VP*, 422.

23 C. J. Barnes, 'Boris Pasternak, the Musician-Poet and Composer', *Slavica Hierosolymitana*, 1 (1977), 323, 325. Del'son, *Skryabin*, 23 ff. *Soch. II*, 11; *VP*, 424.

24 *Vosp.*, 108–10. Del'son, *Skryabin*, 160 ff. H. MacDonald, *Skryabin* (London–Oxford, 1978), 11–14.

25 *Soch. II*, 205; *VP*, 193. See ch. 11, n. 91.

26 *Vosp.*, 97–100. *Soch. II*, 10, 205; *VP*, 193, 422–3. *ZRL*, 80.

27 Pasternak's built-up shoe is visible in *Perepiska*, fig. 41. See characters of Tsvetkov in 'Detstvo Lyuvers', *Soch. II*, 105, 111, 114, 132–5, and Spektorsky in 'Tri glavy iz povesti', *VP*, 120–1.

28 Letter of 6 August 1913 to A. L. Shtikh, *ChPV*, 144.

29 *Soch. II*, 10; *VP*, 423. Barnes, 'Boris Pasternak, the Musician', 326. On Yulii Engel', see Engel'–Roginskaya, 'Yu. Engel' (Vospominaniya docheri)', in Yu. D. Engel', *Glazami sovremennika. Izbrannye stat'i o russkoi muzyke 1898–1918* (Moscow, 1971), 493–507.

30 Del'son, *Skryabin*, 92, 102–3. Bowers, *Scriabin*, II, 10 ff. *Soch. II*, 206; *VP*, 194.

31 *Soch. II*, 10–11; *VP*, 423–4. J. Pasternak, 'Three Suns', in Mark (ed.), *Die Familie*, 8. *Vosp.*, 175.

32 *Vosp.*, 176.

33 *ZRL*, 82. Yu. V. Keldysh, 'Muzykal'naya polemika', in *Russkaya khudozhestvennaya kul'tura kontsa XIX–nachala XX veka (1908–1917)* (Moscow, 1977), III, 294, 298–9. *Vosp.*, 189–92.

34 Barnes, 'Boris Pasternak, the Musician', 326–8, 330–5; 'Pasternak as Composer and Scriabin Disciple', *Tempo*, 121 (June 1977), 16–19; 'Boris Pasternak as Composer', *Performance*, 6 (April–May 1982), 12–14; and 'Poeziya i muzyka. Vtoraya stikhiya Borisa Pasternaka', *Russkaya mysl'*, 3,455–6 (10 and 17 March 1983).

35 *Soch. II*, 13; *VP*, 425–6. R. M. Plekhanova, 'Vospominaniya', in *Aleksandr Nikolaevich Skryabin 1915–1940* (Moscow–Leningrad, 1940), 65. A. Al'shvang, *Izbrannye sochineniya* (Moscow, 1964), I, 176. Del'son, *Skryabin*, 7 ff., 105.

3   REVOLUTION AND BERLIN

1 *ZRL*, 144.

2 L. O. Pasternak, letter of 24 June 1905 to P. D. Ettinger, *LOP*, [11].

3 *Nashi dni*, 3 February 1905.

4 Quoted in Ya. D. Minchenkov, *Vospominaniya o peredvizhnikakh* (Leningrad, 1963), 330.

5 *Soch. II*, 14; *VP*, 428. *ZRL*, 54. E. M. Belyutin and N. M. Moleva, *Russkaya*

khudozhestvennaya shkola vtoroi poloviny XIX–nachala XX veka (Moscow, 1967), 365.

6 *Vosp.*, 148–50.

7 *Ibid.*, 136–42.

8 *Ibid.*, 151–3.

9 *Ibid.*, 150–2.

10 *Perepiska*, figs. 17–18. L. O. Pasternak, letter of 24 June 1905 to P. D. Ettinger, *LOP*, [11]. *Vosp.*, 155–6.

11 *Vosp.*, 156–8.

12 *Ibid.*, 158–9.

13 *ZRL*, 69. *Vosp.*, 159–60.

14 *Vosp.*, 162.

15 Minchenkov, *Vospominaniya o peredvizhnikakh*, 135. *Soch. II*, 267; *VP*, 259. See also 'Dom s galereyami', *VP*, 343.

16 *ZRL*, 69–70. *Vosp.*, 161–6.

17 *Soch. II*, 14; *VP*, 427–8. Belyutin and Moleva, *Russkaya khudozhestvennaya shkola*, 281.

18 *Vosp.*, 166. *ZRL*, 67. *Vosp.*, 134–5.

19 *LOP*, [12].

20 *Vosp.*, 167–8, 170.

21 *Ibid.*, 172–3, 196–7. L. O. Pasternak, letter of 21 January 1906 to P. D. Ettinger, *LOP*, [12].

22 *ZRL*, 138, 140. L. O. Pasternak, letter of spring 1906 to P. D. Ettinger, *LOP*, [13]. *ZRL*, 70; Buckman, *Leonid Pasternak*, 51–2.

23 'Boris Pasternak v perepiske s Maksimom Gor'kim', 262. L. O. Pasternak, letter of spring 1906 to P. D. Ettinger, *LOP*, [14].

24 L. O. Pasternak, letter of spring 1906 to P. D. Ettinger, *LOP*, [13]. *ZRL*, 144–6.

25 *Soch. II*, 19; *VP*, 432. *Vosp.*, 180–6.

26 *Vosp.*,173–5.

27 *Soch. II*, 19; *VP*, 432.

28 *Vosp.*, 175. Barnes, 'Boris Pasternak, the Musician', 329.

29 *Vosp.*, 177–80.

30 *Ibid.*, 180.

31 *Ibid.*, 176, 186–8, 197.

32 *Ibid.*, 189–95. Engel'-Roginskaya, 'Yu. Engel'', 498. See also Engel', *Glazami sovremennika*, 254–6.

33 *Vosp.*, 194–5. *ZRL*, 70. Buckman, *Leonid Pasternak*, 52. *Vosp.*, 184.

4 YOUTH'S IMPRESSIONS, LITERATURE AND MUSIC

1 'Vladimir Mayakovsky. *Prostoe kak mychanie*. Petrograd 1916', in 'Kriti-cheskie pis'ma', *Literaturnaya Rossiya*, 19 March 1965. A letter of 26

February 1929 to N. N. Aseev (unpub.) also writes of multifarious and divergent talents among people of Pasternak's generation.

2 A. Akhmatova, *Sochineniya*, ed. G. P. Struve and B. A. Filippov, 2 vols. (Washington DC, 1965), I, 225.

3 See n. 1.

4 Letter of 22 August 1959 to Stephen Spender, in 'Three Letters', *Encounter* 15, no. 2 (August 1960), 5.

5 Quoted in H. Zamoyska, 'L'art et la vie chez Boris Pasternak', *Revue des études slaves*, 38 (1961), 233.

6 Letter of 20 May 1959, quoted in Proyart, *Pasternak*, 236. Cf. discussion of 'Chernyi bokal', below, pp. 202–3.

7 Proyart, *Pasternak*, 236.

8 *Vosp.*, 127–33. See below, p. 202.

9 I. Erenburg, *Lyudi, gody, zhizn'. Kniga pervaya i vtoraya* (Moscow, 1961), 600.

10 *Vosp.*, 71–83.

11 Pasternak's dating is only approximate (*Soch. II*, 18; *VP*, 431). In winter 1903–4 he was still partly disabled after his riding accident; Kommissarzhevskaya's theatre opened only in September 1904; his journey could not have been in winter 1905–6 since this coincided with the Pasternaks' departure for Berlin.

12 *Soch. II*, 14–16; *VP*, 428–9.

13 On these equestrian entertainments, see Yu. A. Dmitriev, 'Tsirk', *Russkaya khudozhestvennaya kul'tura kontsa XIX-nachala XX veka (1908–1917)*, III (Moscow, 1977), 239.

14 Del'son, *Skryabin*, 5ff. *Soch. II*, 18; *VP*, 431.

15 M. N. Stroeva, 'Moskovskii khudozhestvennyi teatr', *Russkaya khudozhestvennaya kul'tura kontsa XIX-nachala XX veka (1908–1917)*, III (Moscow, 1977), 26–8. On Pasternak and Hamsun, see E. Barksdale and D. Popp, 'Hamsun and Pasternak: the Development of Dionysian Tragedy', *Edda*, 6 (1976), 343–51.

16 *Soch. II*, 10, 208; *VP*, 196, 423. I. V. Nestyev, *Prokofiev*, trans. Florence Jonas (Stanford, CA–London, 1961), 8ff. On Feinberg, see V. Belyaev, *Samuil Evgen'evich Feinberg* (Moscow, 1927). On Dobrovein, see M. A. Dobrovein, *Stranitsy zhizni Isaya Dobroveina* (Moscow, 1972). On Glière, see *Muzykal'naya entsiklopediya*, I, 1014–16.

17 *Soch. II*, 210; *VP*, 198.

18 *Soch. II*, 10; *VP*, 423.

19 A. N. Skryabin, *Sonaty* (Moscow 1962), 91. See also A. N. Skryabin, 'Zapisi A. N. Skryabina', *Russkie propilei*, 6 (1919), 198.

20 Del'son, *Skryabin*, 127. Bowers, *Scriabin*, II, 190 ff. *Vosp.*,104.

21 *Vosp.*, 105. See also: Engel', 'A. N. Skryabin', 74–5; Engel', *Glazami sovremennika*, 244 ff.; K. Sabaneev, *Vospominaniya o Skryabine* (Moscow, 1925), 29–31.

22 *Soch. II*, 12; *VP*, 425. See also L. Fleishman, *Boris Pasternak v dvadtsatye gody* (Munich, 1981), 210–11.

23 *Soch. II*, 210; *VP*, 198.

24 Letter of 1 April 1910 to A. F. Samoilov (APT). Letter of 6 February 1915 to A. L. Shtikh (APT) (cf. similar remarks in letter of 11 July 1926 to M. I. Tsvetaeva, *DLDN*, 9 (1987), 224).

25 Letter of 27 January 1917 to K. G. Loks, *ChPV*, 155.

26 *Vosp.*, 180–3.

27 Del'son, *Skryabin*, 79–80. *Soch. II*, 210; *VP*, 198.

28 Letter of 6 February 1915 to A. L. Shtikh. Letter of 3 December 1929 to L. O. and R. I. Pasternak (APT).

29 Letter of 27 January 1917 to K. G. Loks, *ChPV*, 15.

30 *Vosp.*, 199. V. Belyaev, *Samuil Evgen'evich Feinberg*, 9. *Muzykal'naya entsiklopediya*, V, 780–1.

31 See *DZh*, ch. 2, section 20.

32 Letters of 9, 10, 11 and 14 July 1907 to L. O. and R. I. Pasternak (APT). *Perepiska*, figs. 19–20.

33 *Vosp.*, 198–9.

34 See Barnes, 'Boris Pasternak, the Musician', 329; '*Poeziya i muzyka*'. Recording of Pasternak's sonata by Annie Gicquel, Fono FSM 53210 (1981).

35 N. Vil'mont, 'Boris Pasternak. Vospominaniya i mysli', *Novyi mir*, 6 (1987), 203. *Vosp.*, 200. *Soch. II*, 12; *VP*, 425.

36 Bowers, *Scriabin*, II, 198, 211. Del'son, *Skryabin*, 130. *ZRL*, 63, 75, 95.

37 Letter of 28 May 1911 to A. L. Shtikh (APT). On *Prometheus*, see Bowers, *Scriabin*, II, 201ff; Del'son, *Skryabin*, 137–44, 398–406.

38 'Vladimir Mayakovsky. *Prostoe kak mychanie*'.

39 Del'son, *Skryabin*, 147–8, 153.

40 Del'son, *Skryabin*, 156. V. Bryusov, 'Na smert' A. N. Skryabina', *Muzyka*, 220 (1915), 281; V. Ivanov, 'Pamyati Skryabina', *Muzyka*, 220 (1915), 289.

41 Del'son, *Skryabin*, 153–4. 'Predvaritel'noe deistvie', in Skryabin, 'Zapisi', 202–47.

42 Skryabin's statement in B. A. Fokht, 'Filosofiya muzyki A. N. Skryabina' (manuscript 1941). See also Barnes, 'Boris Pasternak, the Musician', 323.

43 V. Frank, 'Realizm chetyrëkh izmerenii', *Mosty*, 2 (1959), 197. Barnes, 'Boris Pasternak, the Musician', 324–6. R. E. Peterson, 'Andrej Belyj and Nikolaj N. Vedenjapin', *Wiener Slawistischer Almanach*, 9 (1982), 111–17, proposes Bely as a partial prototype for Vedenyapin. Evgenii Pasternak has suggested that Vedenyapin also incorporates elements of S. N. Durylin. (On Durylin, see below, pp. 93, 97, 282; see also *Kratkaya literaturnaya entsiklopediya*, II, 823; Fleishman, *Boris Pasternak v dvadtsatye gody*, 228–9; *Soch. II*, 23, 219; *VP*, 206–7, 436.)

5 LITERATURE, LOVE AND CREATIVITY

1 Quoted in Barnes, 'Boris Pasternak, the Musician', 322.

2 *Soch. II*, 22–4, 212; *VP*, 200, 435–7. K. G. Loks, *Povest'*. V. Markov, *Russian Futurism: A History* (London, 1969), 229–30.

3 Yu. Anisimov, *Obitel'* (Moscow, 1913). R. M. Ril'ke, *Rasskazy o Gospode*, trans. Yu. Anisimov (Moscow, 1913); R. M. Ril'ke, *Kniga chasov*, trans. Yu. Anisimov (Moscow, 1913). On Anisimov, see B. P. Koz'min, *Pisateli sovremennoi epokhi* (Moscow, 1928), 19–20.

4 *Soch. II*, 23; *VP*, 436–7. A Gur'ev, *Bezotvetnoe* (Moscow, n.d.).

5 On Durylin, see ch. 4, n. 43.

6 Loks, *Povest'*.

7 A. Blok and A. Bely, *Perepiska* (Moscow, 1940), 243. Loks, *Povest'*.

8 Loks, *Povest'*.

9 A. Bely, *Mezhdu dvukh revolyutsii* (Moscow, 1934), 218–23, 383. *Soch. II*, 24–5; *VP*, 437–8. Fleishman, *Stat'i o Pasternake* (Bremen, 1977), 6–7. On Krakht, see Fleishman, *Stat'i*, 43; Bely, *Mezhdu dvukh revolyutsii*, 374. On Pasternak's paper, see below, pp. 149–52.

10 On Musaget, see also Bely, *Mezhdu dvukh revolyutsii, passim*; Loks, *Povest'*.

11 *Soch. II*, 24–5; *VP*, 438. Bely, *Mezhdu dvukh revolyutsii*, 392–6. On Petrovsky see R. J. Keys, 'Pis'ma Andreya Belogo k A. S. Petrovskomu i E. N. Kezel'man,' *Novyi zhurnal*, 122 (March 1976), 154–5.

12 *Soch. II*, 26–8; *VP*, 439–41.

13 *Vosp.*, 213–4. A. L. Pasternak, 'Ma mère', in Mark (ed.), *Die Familie*, 33–4.

14 On Serov and Klyuchevsky, see *ZRL*, 113–32, 152–8.

15 Ms. of *Okhrannaya gramota*. The final sentence probably refers to a habit among the Imperial family of wearing Russian folk costume.

16 *Soch. II*, 23, 220; *VP*, 436, 207–8. On Samarin, see also: *Soch. II*, 30–1; *VP*, 444–5.

17 *Soch. II*, 214, 217; *VP*, 202, 205. This episode is reflected in 'Dom s galereyami', *VP*, 339–48.

18 *ZRL*, 267. Fleishman, *Boris Pasternak v dvadtsatye gody*, 239. Proyart, 'Une amitié d'enfance', in Aucouturier (ed.), *Boris Pasternak 1890–1960*, 517. The names and identities of the Vysotsky daughters are confused in N. Berberova, *Kursiv moi. Avtobiografiya*, 2 vols. (New York, 1983), I, 233–4.

19 *Soch. II*, 231–2; *VP*, 219–20. Proyart, 'Une amitié', 518.

20 'Detstvo Lyuvers', *Soch. II*, 130–1; *VP*, 103. 'Okhrannaya gramota', *Soch. II*, 233–4; *VP*, 222. 'Povest'', *Soch. II*, 170–1; *VP*, 157–8.

21 Proyart, 'Une amitié', 517–18.

22 Letter of 23 March 1931 to R. N. Lomonosova (LRA).

23 C. J. Barnes, 'Notes on Pasternak', in *Boris Pasternak and His Times*, Berkeley Slavic Specialties (Oakland CA, in press). See also below, 228 ff.

24 *Perepiska*, 342–4.

25 *Ibid.*, 1.

26 O. M. Freidenberg, letter of 30 July 1910 (?) to B. L. Pasternak, *Perepiska*, 32.

27 *Perepiska*, 5–9, 345.

28 *Ibid.*, 8–9.

29 Letter of 23 July 1910, *Perepiska*, 9 ff. On the poem 'Zastavy', see *Izbr. II*, 507; also below, p. 112.

30 *Perepiska*, 15.

31 *Ibid.*, 15–16.

32 *Ibid.*, 12.

33 O. M. Freidenberg, letter of 25 July 1910 to B. L. Pasternak, *Perepiska*, 19–24.

34 Letter of 3 August 1910 (?), *Perepiska*, 34. The girl concerned may have been Elena Vinograd, whose family came from Irkutsk.

35 *Perepiska*, 24–39.

36 *Ibid.*, 34.

37 *Vosp.*, 253–4.

38 Letter of 17 May 1912 to Zh. L. Pasternak, 'Perepiska Borisa Pasternaka', publ. Elliott Mossman and Michel Aucouturier, *Revue des études slaves*, 53 fasc. 2 (1981), 269.

39 K. Chukovsky, 'Iz vospominanii', *Yunost'*, 8 (1965), 68.

40 See above, p. 78.

41 Letter of 28 May 1911 to A. L. Shtikh (APT). *Vosp.*, 251–2.

42 *Vosp.*, 253–6.

43 *Ibid.*, 258–9, 273–5. On this house and the Knyazhii Dvor Hotel, see E. Makedonskaya, *Ulitsa Volkhonka, 14* (Moscow, 1985), 46–55.

44 Loks, *Povest'*.

45 *Vosp.*, 256. Loks, *Povest'*.

46 M. A. Rashkovskaya, 'Poet v mire, mir v poete (Pis'ma B. L. Pasternaka k S. P. Bobrovu)', *Vstrechi s proshlym* (Moscow, 1982), 140.

47 See E. V. Pasternak, 'Pervye opyty Borisa Pasternaka', *Trudy po znakovym sistemam IV*, Uchenye zapiski Tartuskogo Gosudarstvennogo Universiteta, 236 (1969), 239–81.

48 Barnes, 'Boris Pasternak and Rainer Maria Rilke', 62.

49 L. Chertkov, *Rilke in Russland auf Grund neuer Materialien* (Vienna, 1975), 26.

50 E. V. Pasternak, 'Pervye opyty', 240–2, 277–8. G. Struve, 'Koe-chto o Pasternake i Ril'ke', in Aucouturier (ed.), *Boris Pasternak 1890–1960*, 443–4.

51 Letter of 4 February 1959 to Michel Aucouturier, quoted in M. Aucouturier, *Pasternak par lui-même* (Paris, 1963), 34.

52 E. V. Pasternak, 'Pervye opyty', 242.

53 See below, 373, 383, 396–8.

54 Letter of 31 July 1911 to A. L. Shtikh. Loks, *Povest'*. Aleksandr Gavronsky was a younger brother of philosopher and Cohen pupil Dmitry Gavronsky. On D. Gavronsky, see Fleishman, *Boris Pasternak v dvadtsatye gody*, 238. On Aleksandr Gavronsky, see below, 124, 127, 136, 284.

55 Loks, *Povest'*.

56 Letter of 23 July 1910 to O. M. Freidenberg, *Perepiska*, 9–10.

57 See also the discussion of 'Vassermanova reaktsiya', below, 000–000. A. Sinyavsky, 'Poeziya Pasternaka', in Boris Pasternak, *Stikhotvoreniya i poemy* (Moscow–Leningrad, 1965), 17ff.

58 'Zvuki Betkhovena v ulitse', E. V. Pasternak, 'Pervye opyty', 248.

59 See the discussion of 'tonal realism' in E. Mossman, 'Pasternak's Short Fiction', *Russian Literature Triquarterly*, 1 (Fall 1971), 284 ff. There is only a brief hint of Pasternak's 1911 interpretation in a later essay of 1940, 'Genrikh Kleist', which states: 'A sensitivity [*vospriimchivost'*] bordering on mediumism coloured his life with the marks of everything surrounding him.' (*VP*, 351).

60 Many of these prose extracts remain to be published; for those so far printed see: E. V. Pasternak, 'Iz rannikh prozaicheskikh opytov B. Pasternaka', *Pamyatniki kul'tury. Novye otkrytiya. Ezhegodnik 1976* (Moscow, 1977), 110–18, and 'Iz pervykh prozaicheskikh opytov Borisa Pasternaka. Publikatsiya II', in N. A. Nilsson (ed.), *Boris Pasternak. Essays* (Stockholm, 1976), 26–51; D. di Simplicio, 'Iz rannikh prozaicheskikh opytov B. Pasternaka', *Slavica Hierosolymitana*, 4 (1979), 286–93; A. Ljunggren, *Juvenilia. Boris Pasternak: 6 fragmentov o Relikvimini* (Stockholm, 1984), 3–62.

61 Cf. the dedication of *Sestra moya zhizn'* to Lermontov 'as though he were living in our midst'; see letter of 22 August 1958 to Eugene Kayden, in E. M. Kayden (trans.), Boris Pasternak, *Poems* (Ann Arbor, 1959), [ix].

62 Letter of 10 December 1959 to Renate Schweitzer, in R. Schweitzer, *Freundschaft mit Boris Pasternak* (Munich–Frankfurt–Basel, 1963), 106. See also in Barnes, 'Notes on Pasternak'.

63 See the discussion of the name 'Reliquimini' in E. V. Pasternak, 'Iz rannikh', 107, and Ljunggren, *Juvenilia*, 63ff.

64 See 'Zakaz dramy' in E. V. Pasternak, 'Iz rannikh', 113; this is discussed in A. Livingstone, 'Wherefore Poet in Destitute Times', *PN Review*, 5 no. 4 (1978), 15, and *Pasternak on Art and Creativity* (Cambridge, 1985), 24.

65 'Prezhde vsego ...', in E. V. Pasternak, 'Iz rannikh', 110.

66 See 'Uzhe temneet ...' in Ljunggren, *Juvenilia*, 21–4; similar passages are also found in 'Kogda Relikvimini vspomnilos' ...', Ljunggren, *Juvenilia*, 29.

67 Letter of 23 July 1910 to O. M. Freidenberg, *Perepiska*, 13–14.

68 'Kogda Relikvimini vspomnilos' ...', Ljunggren, *Juvenilia*, 28.

69 *Ibid.*, 29.

6 PHILOSOPHY IN MOSCOW AND MARBURG

1 Kurlov, 'O Pasternake'. *Soch. II*, 210–11; *VP*, 192.

2 *Soch. II*, 30, 217–19. *VP*, 204–7, 444. A. Bely, *Na rubezhe dvukh stoletii* (Moscow–Leningrad, 1930), 387; Loks, *Povest'*.

3 *Perepiska*, 37, 347. Loks, *Povest'*. E. V. Pasternak, 'Pervye opyty', 264. See also Fleishman, *Stat'i*, 13.

4 A. Bely, *Nachalo veka* (Moscow–Leningrad, 1933), 348–9. *Soch. II*, 219–20; *VP*, 207. F. A. Stepun, *Byvshee i nesbyvsheesya* (New York, 1956), I, 282.

5 Letter of 30 June 1912 to A. L. Shtikh. See also *Perepiska*, 349–50.

6 *Soch. II*, 220; *VP*, 207.

7 On Bergsonian elements in Pasternak, see esp. G. de Mallac, 'Zhivago versus Prometheus', *Books Abroad*, spring 1970, 227–9, and *Boris Pasternak*, 289–92.

8 Fleishman, *Stat'i*, 11.

9 *Soch. II*, 86; *VP*, 60. Letter of 23 July 1910 to O. M. Freidenburg, *Perepiska*, 14.

10 I. M. Bochenski, *Contemporary European Philosophy*, trans. D. Nicholl and K. Aschenbrenner (Berkeley and Los Angeles, 1964), 88–99. H. J. Störig, *Kleine Weltgeschichte der Philosophie* (Stuttgart, 1950), 468–75. On Cohen, see G. de Mallac, 'Pasternak and Marburg', *Russian Review*, 38, no. 4 (October 1979), 425–7, and *Boris Pasternak*, 62–5.

11 Bely, *Mezhdu dvukh revolyutsii*, 304. See also Rammelmeyer, 'Die Philipps-Universität zu Marburg in der russischen Geistesgeschichte und schönen Literatur', 76.

12 Bely, *Nachalo veka*, 350. Letter of spring 1911 to A. L. Shtikh (APT). *Soch. II*, 30, 214; *VP*, 202, 444. Mansurov was married to Mariya Fedorovna Samarina, sister of Dmitry Samarin.

13 *Soch. II*, 221–2; *VP*, 208–9. Loks, *Povest'*.

14 Letters (undated) to L. O. and R. I. Pasternak, received in Moscow on 23 and 26 April 1912 (APT); letter of 7 May 1912 to L. O. and R. I. Pasternak (from Berlin) (APT). *Soch. II*, 222–5; *VP*, 210–13.

15 *Soch. II*, 227; *VP*, 214. R. C. Williams, *Culture in Exile: Russian Emigrés in Germany 1881–1941* (Ithaca, NY, 1972), 24–5.

16 *Soch. II*, 224; *VP*, 211. Rammelmeyer, 'Die Philipps-Universität zu Marburg', 76–7. Letter of 29 May 1912 to L. O. Pasternak (APT).

17 R. M. Rilke, letter of 28 July 1909 to Gräfin Manon zu Solms, quoted in I. Schnack, *Rainer Maria Rilkes Erinnerungen an Marburg und das Hessische Land* (Marburg, n.d.), 23.

18 *Soch. II*, 226; *VP*, 213. Letter (undated) to L. O. and R. I. Pasternak, received 11 May 1912 (APT).

19 Mallac, *Boris Pasternak*, 61, corrects Pasternak's version in *Soch. II*, 227; *VP*, 215.

20 Mallac, *Boris Pasternak*, 60–1. *Soch. II*, 228–9; *VP*, 215–16.
21 *Soch. II*, 228–30; *VP*, 217–8. Mallac, *Boris Pasternak*, 59. Letter of 29 May 1912 to L. O. Pasternak (APT). Fleishman, 'Sredi filosofov (Iz kommentariev k *Okhrannoi gramote* Pasternaka)', in *Semiosis: Semiotics and the History of Culture, In honorem Georgii Lotman* (ed. Morris Halle *et al.*) (Ann Arbor, MI, 1984), 70–6.
22 Letter of 19 July 1912 to A. L. Shtikh, *ChPV*, 142.
23 Letter (undated) to L. O. and R. I. Pasternak, received 11 May 1912. Letter of 17 May 1912 to Zh. L. Pasternak (APT).
24 *Soch. II*, 230–1, 245–6; *VP*, 219, 232–3. Letter of 14 May 1912 to L. O. and R. I. Pasternak (APT).
25 Letters of 15 May, 5 June, and late June (undated) 1912 to L. O. and R. I. Pasternak (APT).
26 Letter of 11–13 July 1912 to A. L. Shtikh, quoted in *Perepiska*, 350.
27 Letter of 4 July 1912 to L. O. Pasternak. Letters of 5 July and 9 July 1912 to L. O. and R. I. Pasternak (APT).
28 Letter of 14 May 1912 to L. O. and R. I. Pasternak. Letter of 17 May 1912 to Zh. L. Pasternak. Letter of 30 June 1912 to A. L. Shtikh (APT).
29 *ChPV*, 143.
30 Letter of 30 June 1912 to A. L. Shtikh (APT).
31 See G. de Mallac, 'Pour une esthétique pasternakienne', *Problèmes soviétiques*, 7 (1964), 14–17; and 'Pasternak and Religion', *Russian Review*, 32 no. 4 (October 1973), 515–17; and *Boris Pasternak*, 349ff.
32 Quoted in J. West, *Russian Symbolism* (London, 1970), 108.
33 'O predmete i metode psikhologii', *Slavica Hierosolymitana*, 4 (1979), 282–3.
34 E. A. F. Sheikholeslami, 'Der deutsche Einfluss im Werke von Boris Pasternak', Ph.D. dissertation, University of Pennsylvania, 1973, ch. 1. S. G. Gellershtein, 'Kommentarii', in 'Boris Pasternak o predmete i metode psikhologii', *Slavica Hierosolymitana*, 4 (1979), 284–5.
35 See also the discussion of this in E. A. F. Sheikholeslami, 'Pasternak's Unpublished Essay "About the Object and Method of Psychology" and its Relation to Pasternak's Aesthetics', paper delivered to New England Slavic Conference, Amherst, MA, April 15, 1978.
36 Proyart, 'Une amitié', 518. Mallac, 'Pasternak and Marburg', 428. *Soch. II*, 231, 235; *VP*, 219, 223. A letter of late June 1912 to L. O. and R.I. Pasternak (APT) states that the Vysotsky sisters stayed five days in Marburg; cf. mention of three days in *Okhrannaya gramota*.
37 Proyart, 'Une amitié, 518'.
38 *Soch. II*, 236–9; *VP*, 224–7.
39 Letter of 18 June 1912 to A. L. Shtikh (APT).
40 Letter of late June (undated) 1912 to L. O. and R. I. Pasternak (APT).
41 Thematically related poems include: 'Iz poemy' (Ya tozhe lyubil...), *Soch. I*, 218–19; *SP*, 104–5; 'Nabroski k fantazii "Poema o blizhnem"', *SP*, 523–8;

'Elegiya 3', *SP*, 492. L. Yu. Brik, 'Chuzhie stikhi: glava iz vospominanii', in N. V. Reformatskaya (ed.), *V. Mayakovsky v vospominaniyakh sovremennikov* (Moscow, 1963), 343.

42 Letter of 11–13 July 1912 to A. L. Shtikh (APT).

43 *Soch. II*, 240–1; *VP*, 228–9.

44 *Perepiska*, 43–8.

45 Letter of 11 July 1912 to O. M. Freidenberg, *Perepiska*, 51–2.

46 Letter of 11–13 July 1912 to A. L. Shtikh, quoted in *Perepiska*, 350.

47 L. O. Pasternak, *Rembrandt i evreistvo v ego tvorchestve* (Berlin, 1923), 14–16. *ZRL*, 75, 87, 99.

48 *Soch. II*, 250; *VP*, 237.

49 Mark (ed.), *Die Familie*, 120. *LOP* [15–16]. Letter of 25 June 1912 to A. L. Shtikh (APT).

50 Letter of 16 July 1912 to A. L. Shtikh, quoted partially in *Perepiska*, 352.

51 Loks, *Povest'*. Proyart, 'Une amitié', 517–19.

52 Letter of 19 July 1912 to A. L. Shtikh, *ChPV*, 142.

53 The chronology of Pasternak's visits to Berlin and Frankfurt and Cohen's invitation is slightly confused in *Okhrannaya gramota*; his correspondence suggests our own version as more accurate. See letter of 16 July 1912 to A. L. Shtikh (APT).

54 Letter of 16 July 1912 to A. L. Shtikh (APT).

55 The barber's shop encounter with Cohen does not preclude the one described in *Okhrannaya gramota* (*Soch. II*, 248–9; *VP*, 235–6), whose location is identified in Mallac, 'Pasternak and Marburg', 429. See Mallac, 'Pasternak and Marburg', 430, and *Boris Pasternak*, 69.

56 Letter of 22 July 1912 to A. L. Shtikh (APT). Letter of 19 July 1912 to A. L. Shtikh, *ChPV*, 142–3.

57 *ChPV*, 143.

58 E. V. Pasternak, 'Pasternak i Bryusov. K istorii otnoshenii', *Russia. Rossiya*, 3 (1977), 240.

59 *ZRL*, 75–8. J. Pasternak, 'Neunzehnhundert Zwölf', *Alma Mater Philippina*, Wintersemester, 1971–2, 40–3. See also Mark (ed.), *Die Familie*, 112; A. Pyman, *The Life of Aleksandr Blok. Volume II. The Release of Harmony, 1908–1921* (Oxford, 1980), 50; *ZRL*, 80–1.

60 *Soch. II*, 249; *VP*, 237. *Perepiska*, 352–3.

61 *Soch. II*, 249–51; *VP*, 237–8.

62 *Soch. II*, 252–4; *VP*, 241–2. E. V. Pasternak, 'Pervye opyty', 258.

63 *ZRL*, 68. *Soch. II*, 254–8; *VP*, 243–6.

64 *Soch. II*, 265; *VP*, 253–4. 'Piazza San Marco', *Izbr. II*, 338–9; 'Venetsiya', *Soch. I*, 182–3, 381–2; *SP*, 70–71, 580–1.

65 *Perepiska*, 53–4.

66 *Ibid.*, 53. J. Pasternak, 'Neunzehnhundert Zwölf, 42; also in Mark (ed.), *Die Familie*, 122.

7 A LITERARY LAUNCH

1 Letter of 20 May 1927 to R. N. Lomonosova (LRA).
2 *Soch. II*, 247, 267–8; *VP*, 234–5, 258–9. *Vosp.*, 284.
3 Letter of 9 February 1913 to S. P. Bobrov, quoted in M. A. Rashkovskaya, 'Poet v mire', 143.
4 Loks, *Povest'*.
5 Fleishman, *Stat'i*, 6–8, 116–17. Concerning the date of Pasternak's paper, see *Stat'i*, 115.
6 *Soch. II*, 25–6; *VP*, 438–9. *ZRL*, 195. Georg Zimmel', 'K voprosu o metafizike smerti', *Logos*, 2 (1910), 42–9.
7 'Grozya izmeren'em chetvertym ...', in E. V. Pasternak, 'Pervye opyty', 266. On the Kleist notes, see above, 114.
8 Fleishman, *Stat'i*, 116–17.
9 C. J. Barnes, 'The Poetry of Boris Pasternak with Special Reference to the Period 1913–1917', Ph.D. dissertation, Cambridge University, 1969, 111–12. V. Asmus, 'Filosofiya i estetika russkogo simvolizma', *Literaturnoe nasledstvo*, 27–8 (1937), 42.
10 Quoted in West, *Russian Symbolism*, 78.
11 Fleishman, *Stat'i*, 117.
12 Letter of 6 August 1913 to A. L. Shtikh, *ChPV*, 145.
13 Loks, *Povest'*. *Soch. II*, 33; *VP*, 446–7. V. A. Katanyan, *Mayakovsky. Literaturnaya khronika*, 4th ed. (Moscow, 1961), 45.
14 Letter of 2 July 1913 to S. P. Bobrov (APT). Loks, *Povest'*.
15 *Lirika* (Moscow 1913), 33.
16 On *Lirika*, see Markov, *Russian Futurism*, 230–1.
17 *Perepiska*, 57.
18 There is detailed discussion of this poem in Loks, *Povest'*; see extracts in *Izbr. II*, 509.
19 *Soch. II*, 377; *SP*, 65–6, 621–2. Discussed in Barnes, 'The Poetry of Boris Pasternak', 121–3, 139–40.
20 *Soch. II*, 377, 469; *SP*, 65, 621. Concerning the link with Annensky, see D. L. Plank, *Pasternak's Lyric: A Study of Sound and Imagery* (The Hague, 1966), 65, and L. Chertkov, 'K voprosu o literaturnoi genealogii Pasternaka', in Aucouturier (ed.), 59–60. On the link with Vysotskaya, see Barnes, 'The Poetry of Boris Pasternak', 167–9.
21 *Soch. II*, 377–8; *SP*, 66, 622.
22 Letter of 17 July 1913 to A. L. Shtikh. Letter of 20 July 1913 to K. G. Loks (APT). Letter of 2 August 1913 to S. P. Bobrov, quoted in Rashkovskaya, 'Poet v mire', 143–4.
23 Letter of 2 July 1913 to S. P. Bobrov (APT).
24 Letter of 6 August to A. L. Shtikh, *ChPV*, 144–5.
25 *Soch. II*, 385; *SP*, 583–4. Discussed in Barnes, 'The Poetry of Boris Pasternak', 170–2.

26 *Soch. II*, 379–80; *SP*, 578–9. The experience underlying this poem is probably related to the 'Sashka' episode of Pasternak's *Povest'* (*Soch. II*, 172–6; *VP*, 159–63) and another unpublished student-period prose extract.

27 Letter of 2 August 1913 to S. P. Bobrov, quoted in Rashkovskaya, 'Poet v mire', 144. Pasternak later identified Blok as a source of the poem 'Serdtsa i sputniki'; see 'K kharakteristike Bloka', published with commentary by E. V. Pasternak under the title 'Pasternak o Bloke', *Blokovskii sbornik II*, Trudy vtoroi nauchnoi konferentsii, posvyashchennoi zhizni i tvorchestvu A. A. Bloka (Tartu, 1972), 448.

28 Letter of 25 December 1913 to N. V. Zavadskaya (APT). Loks, *Povest'* 'Grust' moya', *Soch. I*, 364; *SP*, 494–5. Letter of 27 September 1913 to S.P. Bobrov, quoted in Rashkovskaya, 'Poet v mire', 146. 'Liricheskii prostor', *Soch. I*, 366; *SP*, 496–7; discussed in Fleishman, 'Fragmenty "futuristicheskoi" biografii Pasternaka', *Slavica Hierosolymitana*, 4 (1979), 88–98.

29 See Barnes, 'The Poetry of Boris Pasternak', chs. 6 and 7; see also below, 410–11.

30 S. Bobrov, 'O liricheskoi teme (18 ekskursov v ee oblasti)', *Trudy i dni*, 1–2 (1913), 116–37. Letter of 14 July 1914 to A. L. Shtikh (APT).

31 Letter of 25 February 1917 to S. P. Bobrov (APT).

32 See Barnes, 'The Poetry of Boris Pasternak', 107–8, 189 ff. Loks, *Povest'*.

33 Letter of 1 July 1914 to A. L. Shtikh, *ChPV*, 146.

34 Loks, *Povest'*.

35 N. Aseev, preface to Boris Pasternak, *Bliznets v tuchakh* (Moscow, 1914), n.p.

36 Markov, *Russian Futurism*, 236–7. Two serious reviews were: M. Shaginyan, '"Bliznets v tuchakh". Stikhi Borisa Pasternaka', *Priazovsky krai* (Rostov on Don), 196 (28 July 1914), 4; and V. Shershenevich, 'Boris Pasternak. "Bliznets v tuchakh". Moskva 1914', *Svobodnyi zhurnal*, 11 (1914), 134–5. The latter, wearing his Cubo-Futurist hat and pseudonym 'Egyx', also wrote an abusive dismissal in *Pervyi zhurnal russkikh futuristov* (Moscow, 1914), 140. Other honourable but short mentions were in S. Bobrov, 'Russkaya poeziya v 1914 godu', *Sovremennik*, 1 (January 1915), 225; V. Bryusov, 'God russkoi poezii (aprel' 1913 g. – aprel' 1914 g.). Porubezhniki', *Russkaya mysl'*, no. 3, section 2 (June 1914), 17; Chelionati, 'Liriki', *Moskovskie mastera* (Moscow, 1916), 82. Among these, Bobrov actually remarked on *Bliznets'* having been virtually ignored by the critics.

37 *Soch. II*, 33; *VP*, 447.

38 L. Fleishman, 'Pervyi god "Tsentrifugi"', *Materialy XXVII nauchnoi studencheskoi konferentsii* (Tartu, 1972), 72–3.

39 Loks, *Povest'*. *Soch. II*, 36; *VP*, 450. Markov, *Russian Futurism*, 239–40.

40 Fleishman, *Stat'i*, 66. A. M. Kryukova, '"Razgovor s neizvestnym drugom" (Aseev i Pasternak)', *Literaturnoe nasledstvo*, 93 (1983), 528. Aseev, *Sobranie sochinenii*, I, 8. K. M. Aseeva, 'Iz vospominanii', in K. M. Aseeva and O. G. Petrovskaya (eds.), *Vosopominaniya o Nikolae Aseeve* (Moscow, 1980), 13.

41 *Soch. II*, 45; *VP*,460.
42 Barnes, 'The Poetry of Boris Pasternak', 211–12.
43 'Poshchechina obshchestvennomu vkusu', quoted in V. Markov (ed.), *Manifesty i programmy russkikh futuristov* (Munich, 1967), 50–1. On the history of Cubo-Futurism, see Markov, *Russian Futurism*, esp. chs. 2, 4 and 5.
44 *Soch. II*, 22; *VP*, 435. *Vosp.*, 217 ff. Katanyan, *Mayakovsky*, 40. *ZRL*, 61–2, 65–6. *LOP*, [14].
45 Katanyan, *Mayakovsky*, 59.
46 Bryusov, 'God russkoi poezii', 17. Letter of 1 July 1914 to A. L. Shtikh, *ChPV*, 146.
47 Markov, *Russian Futurism*, 135 ff. N. Khardzhiev, 'Turne kubo-futuristov 1913–1914 gg.', *Mayakovsky. Materialy i issledovaniya* (Moscow, 1940), 401–27.
48 Barnes, 'The Poetry of Boris Pasternak', 213–15. Markov, *Russian Futurism*, 172–8.
49 S. Bobrov, 'Chuzhoi golos', *Razvorochennye cherepa. Ego-futuristy IX* (Petersburg, 1913), 10. 'Gramota', *Rukonog* (Moscow, 1914), 31. On Ignat'ev, see N. Khardzhiev, 'Pamyati Ivana Ignat'eva', in N. Khardzhiev with V. Trenin, *Poeticheskaya kul'tura Mayakovskogo* (Moscow, 1970), 219–22.
50 'Turbopean', *Rukonog*, 28; reprinted in Markov, *Manifesty*, 109. S. Bobrov, 'Lira lir (Oratoriya)', *Rukonog*, 24–6. N. Aseev, 'Gudoshnaya', 'Shepot', 'Pesnya Andriya', *Rukonog*, 20–2. On Aseev and Khlebnikov, see Kryukova, 'Khlebnikov (Aseev i Khlebnikov)', *Literaturnoe nasledstvo*, 93 (1983), 506–16. Bozhidar, 'Niti', *Rukonog*, 29–30.
51 'Vassermanova reaktsiya', *Rukonog*, 37; reprinted in Markov, *Manifesty*, 116. 'Vassermanova reaktsiya' is discussed in Barnes, 'The Poetry of Boris Pasternak', ch. 10.
52 Loks, *Povest'*. N. Aseev, 'Greml'', *Sobranie sochinenii*, I, 42–3. Pasternak's *Rukonog* poems (*Soch. III*, 124–6; *SP*, 501–3) are discussed in Barnes, 'The Poetry of Boris Pasternak', ch. 10.
53 'Gramota', *Rukonog*, 31–2; reprinted in Markov, *Manifesty*, 110–11.
54 Fleishman, *Stat'i*, 68–9.
55 *Ibid.*, 69–71.
56 *Vosp.*, 217–26. *Soch. II*, 39; *VP*, 453.
57 *Soch. II*, 269–70; *VP*, 261.
58 L. Fleishman, '"Tsentrifuga" i V. Mayakovsky', *Materialy XXVII nauchnoi studencheskoi konferentsii* (Tartu, 1972), 74–5; reprinted in *Stat'i*, 70–1.
59 Fleishman, *Boris Pasternak v dvadtsatye gody*, 278.
60 Letter of 1 July 1914 to A. L. Shtikh, *ChPV*, 145.
61 Fleishman, *Stat'i*, 71. Letter of July 1914 to S. P. Bobrov, quoted in Rashkovskaya, 'Poet v mire', 147.
62 Letter of mid-July 1914 to S. P. Bobrov, quoted in Fleishman, *Stat'i*, 72. Loks, *Povest'*, also mocked the pretentiousness of 'Turbopean'.
63 Letter of mid-July 1914 to S. P. Bobrov, quoted in Fleishman, *Stat'i*, 73.

8   WARTIME IN THE URALS

1 Akhmatova, *Sochineniya*, I, 127.
2 On Baltrušaitis, see V. Dauetite, *Yurgis Baltrushaitis* (Vilnius, 1983), *passim*, and Bely, *Nachalo veka*, 380.
3 Letter of June 1914 to L. O. and R. I. Pasternak (APT). Letter of 1 June 1914 to A. L. Shtikh (APT). *Soch. II*, 274–5; *VP*, 265–6.
4 *Soch. II*, 36; *VP*, 450. Vil'mont, 'Boris Pasternak. Vospominaniya i mysli', 187.
5 *Soch. II*, 275; *VP*, 266. V. M. Zhirmunsky, 'Genrikh fon Kleist', *Russkaya mysl'*, nos. 8–9, section 2, (1914), 1–11. Letter (undated) to L. O. and R. I. Pasternak. Letter of 1 June 1914 to A. L. Shtikh (APT). Owing to the outbreak of war and ensuing delays and alterations, Pasternak's translation was not performed; on its publication, see below, 187.
6 Letter 1 (undated) of May 1914 to L. O. and R. I. Pasternak (APT). On Pasternak's response to Bryusov's review of his work, see E. V. Pasternak, 'Pasternak i Bryusov', 240–1.
7 Letter 2 (undated) of May 1914 to L. O. and R. I. Pasternak (APT). See Shershenevich, 'Boris Pasternak. "Bliznets v tuchakh"', 134–5.
8 Letter (undated) of June 1914 to L. O. and R. I. Pasternak (APT). On correspondence with Bobrov, see: Rashkovskaya, 'Poet v mire', 146–8; Fleishman, *Stat'i*, 71–4. Letters of May (undated), 1 June, 10 June, 10 July 1914 to A. L. Shtikh; letter of 1 July 1914 to A. L. Shtikh, *ChPV*, 145–7. Shtikh published verse under the pseudonym 'G. Rostovsky' in *Vtoroi sbornik Tsentrifugi* (Moscow, 1916), and a separate book of lyrics under his own name: *Stikhi* (Moscow, 1916).
9 *VP*, 119.
10 *Soch. II*, 33; *VP*, 447. See reflection of this in 'Tri glavy iz povesti', *VP*, 116–9.
11 Letter (undated) of July 1914 to L. O. and R. I. Pasternak (APT).
12 *Soch. II*, 275–6; *VP*, 266–7. *Vosp.*, 284–5.
13 Katanyan, *Mayakovsky*, 63. Mayakovsky, 'Ne babochki, a Aleksandr Makedonsky' (1914), *Polnoe sobranie sochinenii*, I, 316; 'Voina i yazyk', *Polnoe sobranie sochinenii*, I, 326.
14 See V. V. Mayakovsky (ed.), 'Traurnoe ura', *Nov'*, no. 119, 20 November, 1914. V. Pertsov, *Mayakovsky* (Moscow, 1969), 206–10.
15 G. Ivanov, 'Ispytanie ognem', *Apollon*, 8 (1914), 55. *SP*, 515, 698.
16 Loks, *Povest'*. 'Artillerist stoit u kormila ...' is discussed in P. A. Bodin, 'God, Tsar and Man: Pasternak's poem *Artillerist*', *Scottish Slavonic Review*, 6 (1986), 69–80.
17 *ZRL*, 84.
18 *SP*, 515, 585–7, 698.
19 Katanyan, *Mayakovsky*, 64. Pertsov, *Mayakovsky*, 206. *Soch. II*, 279–80; *VP*,

270–1. Loks, *Povest'*. Aseeva, 'Iz vospominanii', 15. Fleishman, 'Fragmenty', 101. On Lundberg. see *Russkii Berlin* (1983), 58–9.

20 On Listopad, see N. Baranova-Shestova, *Zhizn' L'va Shestova po perepiske i vospominaniyam sovremennikov* (Paris, 1983), I, 21, 129, 147–8 (where his name is erroneously given as 'Listopadov'). Barnes, 'Elena Vinograd'. V. Erofeev, '"Ostaetsya odno: proizvol". (Filosofiya odinochestva i literaturno-estesticheskoe kredo L'va Shestova)', *Voprosy literatury*, 10 (1975), 184.

21 Proyart, 'Une amitié', 517.

22 Kryukova, 'Razgovor', 528. *Soch. II*, 276–8; *VP*, 267–8. Aseeva, 'Iz vospominanii', 13. Loks, *Povest'*.

23 Kryukova, 'Razgovor', 528. Aseeva, 'Iz vospominanii,' 14–15.

24 *Soch. II*, 276–7; *VP*, 267–8.

25 *Soch. II*, 198–9; *SP*, 84–5, 514–16. Loks, *Povest'*. Letter of 7 June 1926 to M. I. Tsvetaeva, *DLDN*, 8 (1987), 254.

26 *Soch. II*, 34; *VP*, 447. Walter Philipp, letter of 1 April 1980 to Ann Pasternak-Slater (APT).

27 *Soch. II*, 34; *VP*, 447–8. Yu. Fedorchuk, *Moskva v kol'tse sadovykh* (Moscow, 1983), 94–5.

28 *SP*, 521–2, 591–2.

29 *Soch. II*, 34–5; *VP*, 448. *Izbr. II*, 500. Barnes, 'Biography', 52.

30 Letter of 30 April 1916 to L. O. and R. I. Pasternak (APT).

31 Letter (undated) of February 1915 to A. L. Shtikh (APT).

32 See K. D. Muratova, 'Sovremennik', in *Russkaya literatura i zhurnalistika nachala XX veka* (Moscow, 1984), 201.

33 See letter of 5 February 1921 to Maksim Gor'ky in 'Gor'ky – B. L. Pasternak', *Literaturnoe nasledstvo*, 70 (1963), 295–6. *Soch. II*, 36–7; *VP*, 450–1.

34 *Soch. II*, 34; *VP*, 448: i.e. between the earliest composed items of *Poverkh bar'erov and Sestra moya zhizn'*.

35 'Vladimir Mayakovsky. *Prostoe kak mychanie.*' On Mayakovsky and Laforgue and the 'poètes maudits', see N. Khardzhiev and V. Trenin 'Poetika rannego Mayakovskogo', in Khardzhiev and Trenin, *Poeticheskaya kul'tura Mayakovskogo*, 61–4.

36 For example, Barnes, 'The Poetry of Boris Pasternak'.

37 *Soch. I*, 198–9, 471; 209–10, 473. Letter (undated, received 29 June 1916) to S. P. Bobrov, quoted in Fleishman, 'Fragmenty', 100. On poetic coincidences between Pasternak and Bol'shakov, see 'Fragmenty', 103 ff.

38 *Soch. III*, 126–8; *SP*, 504–6. Brik, 'Chuzhie stikhi', 341.

39 B. Jangfeldt, 'Russian Futurism 1917–1919', in Nilsson (ed.), 69 ff.

40 'Materia Prima', *SP*, 513–4; 'No pochemu', *SP*, 512–13; 'Pro Domo', *SP*, 515; 'Polyarnaya shveya', *Soch. III*, 129–30; *SP*, 509–10; 'Toska', *Soch. III*, 130–2; *SP*, 507–9.

41 Letter of 16 December 1915 to D. P. Gordeev, *ChPV*, 147.
42 L. Pasternak-Slater, Introduction, in Boris Pasternak, *Fifty Poems*, trans. Lydia Pasternak-Slater (London, 1963), 15. Barnes, 'Notes on Pasternak', (forthcoming).
43 Letter of 30 December 1916 to S. P. Bobrov, quoted in Rashkovskaya, 'Poet v mire', 153.
44 R. Payne, *The Three Worlds of Boris Pasternak*, 72.
45 Mossman, 'Pasternak's Short Fiction', 288.
46 See E. B. Pasternak, 'Boris Pasternak. Istoriya odnoi kontroktavy', *Slavica Hierosolymitana*, 1 (1977), 253–4.
47 See M. Aucouturier, 'The Legend of the Poet and the Image of the Actor in the Short Stories of Pasternak', *Studies in Short Fiction*, 3 no. 2 (Winter 1966), 225–35. Barnes, 'The Poetry of Boris Pasternak', ch. 14. On Heine's impact on Pasternak, see Sheikholeslami, 'Der deutsche Einfluss', ch. 3.
48 Loks, *Povest'. Soch. II*, 35; *VP*, 449. A. Serebrov (Tikhonov), 'O Chekhove', in *Chekhov v vospominaniyakh sovremennikov* (Moscow, 1952), 468–84. Letter (undated) of January 1916 to R. I. Pasternak. Letter of 30 January 1916 to L. O. Pasternak (APT).
49 On Zinaida Grigor'evna Rezvaya-Morozova (also known as Reinboth), see H. Pitcher, *The Smiths of Moscow* (Cromer, 1984), 63–4, 125. Letter of 30 January 1916 to L. O. Pasternak. Letter of 4 March 1916 to L. O. and R. I. Pasternak. Letter (undated) to April 1916 to L. O. and R. I. Pasternak. Letter of 17 May 1916 to R. I. Pasternak (APT).
50 Letter of 17 May 1916 to R. I. Pasternak (APT).
51 Letters of 3 February, February (undated), and 4 March 1916 to L. O. and R. I. Pasternak (APT).
52 Letter of 3 April and 30 April 1916 to L. O. and R. I. Pasternak (APT).
53 Letter of 27 January 1917 to K. G. Loks, *ChPV*, 155.
54 Letter of 4 March 1916 to L. O. and R. I. Pasternak (APT).
55 Letter of 18 April 1916 to L. O. and R. I. Pasternak (APT).
56 Letters of 19 March, 3 April, and 12 April 1916 to L. O. and R. I. Pasternak (APT).
57 Fleishman, *Stat'i*, 74–6. Markov, *Russian Futurism*, 256–8, 270–4.
58 Markov, *Russian Futurism*, 258–61. Barnes, 'The Poetry of Boris Pasternak', 364–7. Fleishman, *Stat'i*, 74.
59 Cf. Pasternak's remarks in letter (undated) of October–November 1929 to V. S. Pozner, 'Iz perepiski s pisatelyami', 727. The preoccupation with Symbolist/impressionist precedent in section 1 of what is otherwise an internecine Futurist polemic suggests that this section is part of a different piece of work – perhaps a draft for an item in the uncompleted collection of articles of 1913.
60 For further discussion of 'Chernyi bokal' see Barnes, 'The Poetry of Boris Pasternak', 368–79, and Livingstone, *Pasternak on Art and Creativity*, 25–7.

61 Letter of 2 May 1916 to S. P. Bobrov, *ChPV*, 148–50.
62 Letter of 29 May 1916 to L. O. and R. I. Pasternak (APT). See 'Rudnik', *Soch. I*, 247–9; *SP*, 221–2.
63 'Ivaka', *Soch. I*, 204; *SP*, 90–1.
64 Letter of 24 June 1916 to S. P. Bobrov, quoted in Rashkovskaya, 'Poet v mire', 150.
65 Letters of 19 March and 19 June 1916 to L. O. and R. I. Pasternak (APT).
66 Letters of 22 June, 24 June, and undated (June) of 1916 to L. O. and R. I. Pasternak (APT).
67 Loks, *Povest'*. Letter of 24 September 1916 to S. P. Bobrov, extracted in Rashkovskaya, 'Poet v mire', 150.
68 Loks, *Povest'*.
69 Fleishman, *Stat'i*, 77–8. On Vermel', see also Markov, *Russian Futurism*, 285.
70 Letter of September 1916 to S. P. Bobrov, quoted in Fleishman, *Stat'i*, 79.
71 See C. J. Barnes, 'Boris Pasternak: A Review of Nikolaj Aseev's "Oksana"', *Slavica Hierosolymitana*, 1 (1977), 301–5.
72 Fleishman, 'Fragmenty', 101–2.
73 'Vladimir Mayakovsky. *Prostoe kak mychanie.*' Letter of 26 November 1916 to S. P. Bobrov, quoted in Fleishman, *Stat'i*, 80.
74 Letter (undated, received 19 September 1916) to S. P. Bobrov, quoted in Fleishman, *Stat'i*, 77. See also Rashkovskaya, 'Poet v mire'. 142.
75 Letter (undated, received 19 September 1916) to S. P. Bobrov, quoted in Fleishman, *Stat'i*, 72.
76 See Fleishman, *Stat'i*, 76.
77 Markov, *Russian Futurism*, 268–9.
78 See above, 119; *SP*, 593.
79 See poems 'Predchuvstvie', 'S rassvetom, vzvalennym za spinu ...', 'Posvyashchen'e', *SP*, 511, 514, 584. See inscription on *Poverkh bar'erov* (1929) to Kruchenykh, dated 9 December 1929, quoted *SP*, 625.
80 S. P. Bobrov, 'Kaznachei poslednei iz planet' (typescript) was preserved in the personal archives of its author and of E. F. Nikitina (Moscow). See the allusion to this article in letter to S. P. Bobrov, quoted Rashkovskaya, 'Poet v mire', 155.
81 Letter of 21 December 1917 to A. L. Shtikh (APT).
82 Letter of 7 June 1926 to M. I. Tsvetaeva, *DLDN*, 8 (1987), 254.
83 Letter of 27 January 1917 to K. G. Loks, *ChPV*, 154.
84 See below, 217, 274, on Pasternak's further interest in Swinburne. For further interpretative comment on *Poverkh bar'erov* (1917), see: Barnes, 'The Poetry of Boris Pasternak', chs. 11–13; H. Gifford, *Boris Pasternak: A Critical Study* (Cambridge, 1977), 41–7; R. Hingley, *Pasternak: A Biography* (London, 1983), 42–3, 45–9.
85 *Poverkh bar'erov* (Moscow, 1917), 69. This version is not represented in either *Soch. II* or *SP*.

9 QUIET HILLS AND REVOLUTION

1 *Soch. II*, 35; *VP*, 449. Letter of 13 October 1916 to L. O. and R. I. Pasternak and family (APT).
2 *Soch. II*, 35; *VP*, 449. Letter of 26 November 1916 to L. O. and R. I. Pasternak and family (APT).
3 Letters of 15 December 1916 and January (undated) 1917 to L. O. and R. I. Pasternak (APT).
4 Letter of October (undated) 1916 and 2 letters (undated) of December 1916 to L. O. and R. I. Pasternak (APT).
5 'Perepiska Borisa Pasternaka', 271.
6 Letter (undated) of late November 1916 to L. O. and R. I. Pasternak, 'Perepiska Borisa Pasternaka', 270.
7 Letter (undated) of November 1916 to L. O. and R. I. Pasternak. Letter of 12 January 1917 to K. G. Loks. Letter of 30 December 1916 to L. O. and R. O. Pasternak. Letter of 1 February 1917 to A. L. Shtikh (APT); cf. a similar complaining missive to S.P. Bobrov, quoted in Rashkovskaya, 'Poet v mire', 151.
8 Letter of 25 October 1916 to L. O. and R. I. Pasternak (APT). *ZRL*, 82.
9 Letter of 15 December 1916 to L. O. and R. I. Pasternak (APT).
10 Letter (undated) of late December 1916 to L. O. and R. I. Pasternak (APT).
11 *SP*, 523–4.
12 For example, 'Ulybayas', ubyvala ...', 'Uzhe v arkhiv pechali sdan ...', *SP*, 510–11, 528.
13 Letter (undated) of late December 1916 to L. O. and R. I. Pasternak (APT).
14 Letter of 13 October 1916 to L. O. and R. I. Pasternak (APT).
15 See above, 180–1.
16 Letter of 11 February 1917 to S. P. Bobrov. Several corrections were included in a letter of 5 February 1917 to A. L. Shtikh; authorial corrections were also incorporated in the texts printed in *SP*.
17 Letter of 11 February 1917 to Lydia Pasternak (APT).
18 Letter of 30 December 1916 to S. P. Bobrov.
19 Letter of 3 January 1917 to L. O. Pasternak (APT).
20 Letters of late September (undated) and 16 November 1916 to S. P. Bobrov. See publication of Pasternak's translation of Swinburne's sonnet to John Ford in M. A. Rashkovskaya and E. B. Rashkovsky, 'Sonet Suinberna v perevode Borisa Pasternaka', *Izvestiya Akademii Nauk SSSR (Seriya literatury i yazyka)*, 43 no. 6 (1984), 544–50.
21 Letter of 11 January 1917 to L. O. and R. I. Pasternak (APT). Letter of 27 January 1917 to K. G. Loks, *ChPV*, 153.
22 The ms. of 'Dva posvyashcheniya' was lost. Contents of the book of articles are identifiable from Pasternak's answers to a questionnaire of 1919; see M.

Djurčinov, 'Dva priloga za B. L. Pasternak', *Godishen zbornik na filosofskiot fakultet na Universitetot vo Skopje*, 26 (1974), 362–4.

23   Quoted in Rashkovskaya, 'Poet v mire', 154.

24   *Soch. I*, 388–90, 242–3.

25   L. Chukovskaya, *Zapiski ob Anne Akhmatovoi* (Paris, 1976), I, 77–8.

26   On 'Nabroski k fantazii "Poema o blizhnem"' and other impressionist *poemy*, see Barnes, 'The Poetry of Boris Pasternak', ch. 16. An explicit rejection of *vers libre* in which these works were largely cast is made in the 1918 ms. of 'Neskol'ko polozhenii'; see *VP*, 485.

27   Letter of 11 January 1917 to L. O. and R. I. Pasternak, quoted in E.B. Pasternak, 'O datirovke', 391. Letter of 12 January 1917 to K. G. Loks (APT).

28   Letter of 30 December 1916 to S. P. Bobrov, quoted in Rashkovskaya, 'Poet v mire', 153–4.

29   NB: photographic evidence in *Perepiska*, fig. 41, should correctly be datelined Vsevolodo-Vil'va 1916.

30   Letter of 27 January 1917 to K. G. Loks, *ChPV*, 258. 'Istoriya odnoi kontroktavy', *Slavica Hierosolymitana*, 1 (1977), 258.

31   Letter of 11 February 1917 to Lydia Pasternak; see also E. B. Pasternak, 'O datirovke', 391.

32   Rait-Kovaleva, 'Vse luchshie vospominaniya', 283–4; reprinted in Wright-Kovaleva, 'Mayakovsky and Pasternak', 128.

33   An abbreviated edition appeared in *Izvestiya Akademii Nauk SSSR (Seriya literatury i yazyka)*, 33 no. 2 (1974), 50–61. Complete edition in *Slavica Hierosolymitana*, 1 (1977), 257–92.

34   Letter (undated) of February 1917 to R. I. Pasternak (APT).

35   For Pasternak's account of the collapse of the dynasty, see *VP*, 257–8.

36   Letter of 13 February 1917 to K. G. Loks. *ChPV*, 156. Letter (undated) of February 1917 to Zh. L. Pasternak.

37   See n. 34.

38   See Fleishman, *Stat'i*, 82–4.

39   *Soch. II*, 35–6; *VP*, 449–50.

40   *Leonid Pasternak 1862–1945*, 20–2.

41   See note in *Soch. II*, 359.

42   Verses memorised by Lydia Pasternak.

43   Loks, *Povest'*; quoted also in Rashkovskaya, 'Poet v mire', 155; see also Fleishman, *Boris Pasternak v dvadtsatye gody*, 27.

44   Loks, *Povest'*.

45   *Soch. II*, 45; *VP*, 459–60.

46   Katanyan, *Mayakovsky*, 85. *Soch. II*, 280–1; *VP*, 271.

47   Quoted in J. R. Döring, *Die Lyrik Pasternaks in den Jahren 1928–1934* (Munich, 1973), 18.

48   For an account of this episode, see *Vosp.*, 286–8.

49   J. Reed, *Ten Days that Shook the World* (Harmondsworth, 1966), 40.

50 Cf. *DZh*, 148.
51 Z. A. Maslennikova, 'Portret poeta', *Literaturnaya Gruziya*, 2 (1979), 150.
52 'Svistki militsionerov' first appeared entitled 'Ulichnaya'; see *Soch. I*, 375–6. 'Vesennii dozhd''; *SP*, 635.
53 Letters of July (undated) and 28 July and 31 July 1917 to V. A. Vinograd.
54 E. A. Vinograd's recollections and impressions were recounted to E. B. and E. V. Pasternak. See also in Barnes, 'Notes on Pasternak'.
55 *SP*, 630. See also K. T. O'Connor, *'My Sister Life': The Illusion of Narrative* (Ann Arbor, forthcoming).
56 See Barnes, 'Notes on Pasternak'.
57 Tsvetaeva, 'Svetovoi liven'', *Proza* (New York, 1953). Osip Mandel'shtam, 'Zametki o poezii', *Sobranie sochinenii* (Washington–New York, 1964–9), II, 306.
58 V. S. Frank, 'Vodyanoi znak (Poeticheskoe mivovozzrenie Pasternaka)', in *Sbornik statei* (Munich, 1962), 240–52.
59 Sinyavsky, 'Poeziya Pasternaka', 14–15.
60 Letter of 25 October 1957 to D. E. Maksimov, published in Z. G. Mints, 'Pis'ma B. Pasternaka D. E. Maksimovu', *Tezisy I Vsesoyuznoi (III) konferentsii 'Tvorchestvo A. A. Bloka i russkaya kul'tura XX veka* (Tartu, 1975), 12. See similar letter of 22 August 1958 to Eugene Kayden, quoted in E. M. Kayden (trans.), Boris Pasternak, *Poems* (Ann Arbor, 1959), ix.
61 N. Mandel'shtam, *Vospominaniya* (New York, 1970), 198. A. Sinyavsky 'Odin den' s Pasternakom', in Aucouturier (ed.), *Boris Pasternak 1890–1960*, 13.
62 *Soch. II*, 283; *VP*, 274. Dating of the telephone conversation is problematic. Pasternak puts it before the Kornilov mutiny (25–30 August), which is somewhat early for the programme on 24 September (Katanyan, *Mayakovsky*, 89). On the Poets' Café, see below, ch. 10.
63 W. Wordsworth, *The Prelude*, book XI (New Haven-London, 1981), 441.
64 See Aucouturier, 'The Legend of the Poet', 225–35. See also letter of 26 March 1928 to V. E. Meierkhol'd, in V. E. Meierkhol'd, *Perepiska 1896–1939* (Moscow, 1976), 277.
65 The 'Dramaticheskie otryvki' are discussed in C. J. Barnes, 'Boris Pasternak's Revolutionary Year', *Forum for Modern Language Studies*, 11 no. 4 (October 1975), 46–60.
66 Quoted in Dauetite, *Yurgis Baltrushaitis*, 58.
67 Fleishman, *Stat'i*, 133–6. 'Dialog' is discussed in Barnes, 'Boris Pasternak's Revolutionary Year', 50–2.
68 Letter of 15 August 1922 to V. Ya. Bryusov, in E. V. Pasternak, 'Pasternak i Bryusov', 248–9.
69 See Fleishman, *Stat'i*, 39–40.
70 *Vosp.*, 291–5.

10 CIVIL WAR ACTIVITIES

1 For various impressions of the Civil War in Moscow see: *DZh*, ch. 6; *Vosp.*, 258–62.

2 E. G. Lundberg, *Zapiski pisatelya 1917–1920* (Berlin, 1922), see entries for 1918. M. I. Tsvetaeva, letter of 29 June 1922 to B. L. Pasternak, *Neizdannye pis'ma* (Paris, 1972), 267.

3 Lydia Pasternak, 'Osen' v Karzinkine', *Vspyshki magniya* (Geneva, 1974), 21–3. *Leonid Pasternak 1862–1945*, 22.

4 Pasternak probably met Rozlovsky through Lundberg, in whose memoirs he briefly appears; see Lundberg, *Zapiski pisatelya* (Leningrad, 1930), 22.

5 See *VP*, 239.

6 Letter (from Kasimov) of 18 July 1920 to A. L. Shtikh.

7 See Anna Nei (i.e. Zh. Pasternak), *Koordinaty* (Berlin, n.d.); Zh. Pasternak, *Pamyati Pedro* (Paris, 1981), and various essays and articles; Lydia Pasternak-Slater, *Before Sunrise* (London, 1971), *Vspyshki magniya*, and various translation, etc.

8 Lydia Pasternak-Slater, 'Priz Nobel de littérature 1958', in Mark (ed.), *Die Familie*, 159–60.

9 See various impressions of this episode in *DZh*, ch. 6; D. Samarin's end is recorded in 'Avtobiografichesky ocherk', *Soch. II*, 31; *VP*, 445.

10 See Barnes, 'Notes on Pasternak'. See above, 185, regarding the other source for 'Pis'ma iz Tuly'. For interpretation of this story, see below, 268–9.

11 A. Rannit, 'Neizvestnyi Boris Pasternak v sobranii Tomasa P. Uitni', *Novyi zhurnal*, 156 (1984), 9.

12 N. Aseev, 'Organizatsiya rechi (Boris Pasternak, "Temy i variatsii")', *Pechat' i revolyutsiya*, 6 (1923), 71–8.

13 *VP*, 273–4.

14 Lundberg, *Zapiski pisatelya* (Berlin, 1922), 172–6.

15 N. A. Nekrasov, *Polnoe sobranie sochinenii* (Moscow, 1948), II, 277–8.

16 F. Bryugel', 'Razgovor s Borisom Pasternakom', *Voprosy literatury*, 7 (1979), 181.

17 Letter of 6 April 1920 to D. V. Petrovsky, 'Perepiska Borisa Pasternaka', 285.

18 V. Erlich, '"Strasti razryady". Zametki o "Marburge"', in Aucouturier (ed.), *Boris Pasternak 1890–1960*, 64. V. A. Katanyan, 'Ne tol'ko vospominaniya', *Russian Literature Triquarterly*, 13 (Fall 1975), 479–82.

19 Erenburg, *Lyudi, gody, zhizn'*, I, 560–1.

20 Fleishman, *Boris Pasternak v dvadtsatye gody*, 239. Erenburg, *Lyudi, gody, zhizn'*, I, 185.

21 Katanyan, *Mayakovsky*, 94. P. Antokol'sky, 'Dve vstrechi', in Reformatskaya (ed.), *V. Mayakovsky v vospominaniyakh sovremennikov*, 148–50.

22 B. Jangfeldt, 'Russian Futurism 1917–1919', in Nilsson (ed.), *Boris Pasternak. Essays*, 106–37. S. Spassky, 'Moskva', in Reformatskaya (ed.), *V. Maya-*

kovsky v vospominaniyakh sovremennikov, 161–76. On Goltsshmidt, see L. V. Nikulin, 'Vladimir Mayakovsky', in Reformatskaya (ed.), *V. Mayakovsky v vospominaniyakh sovremennikov*, 494–5. Erenburg, *Lyudi, gody, zhizn'*, I, 395.

23 N. Mandel'shtam, *Vtoraya kniga* (Paris, 1972), 347.

24 See also *VP*, 474–6; L. Fleishman, 'Neizvestnyi avtograf B. Pasternaka', *Materialy XXVI nauchnoi studencheskoi konferentsii. Literaturovedenie. Lingvistika* (Tartu, 1971), 34–7.

25 Djurčinov, 'Dva priloga za B. L. Pasternak', 363.

26 Tsvetaeva, *Proza*, 354. V. Barsov, 'O Pasternake. Moskovskie vpechatleniya', *Grani*, 40 (1958), 102–3.

27 Vil'mont, 'Boris Pasternak. Vospominaniya i mysli', 169–72.

28 For example, 'Pasternak Speaks', Discurio record No. L7/001 (1958).

29 Wright-Kovaleva, 'Mayakovsky and Pasternak', 129.

30 Vil'mont, 'Boris Pasternak. Vospominaniya i mysli', 180, 182.

31 Aseev, 'Organizatsiya rechi'. See n. 26.

32 R. Ivnev, *U podnozhiya Mtatsmindy* (Moscow, 1973), 66.

33 Döring, *Die Lyrik Pasternaks*, 18.

34 Erenburg *Lyudi, gody, zhizn'*, I, 410.

35 *Put' osvobozhdeniya*, 4 (1917), 4.

36 On Scythianism, see S. Hoffman, 'Scythian Theory and Literature, 1917–1924', in Nilsson (ed.), *Boris Pasternak. Essays*, 138–64; A. Men'shutin and A. Sinyavsky, *Poeziya pervykh let revolyutsii* (Moscow, 1964), 64 ff.

37 Djurčinov, 'Dva priloga', 363. *Sbornik novogo iskusstva* (Khar'kov, 1919), 4–5.

38 See Fleishman, *Stat'i*, 83.

39 For other items from the Faust cycle, see 'Lyubov' Fausta', *SP*, 537–8; 'Zhizn'', *Izbr. II*, 392. N. A. Troitsky, *Boris Leonidovich Pasternak 1890–1960* (Ithaca, NY, 1969), 25–6.

40 See *Khudozhestvennoe slovo*, 1 (1920), 60. Bryusov, '[B. Pasternak. Sochineniya, t. 1]', *Literaturnoe nasledstvo*, 85 (1976), 242. On Lito, see below, 275.

41 Djurčinov, 'Dva priloga', 362.

42 Mayakovsky, *Polnoe sobranie sochinenii*, I, 192. The ms. was preserved by Lili Brik; see facsimile pages in *Russian Literature Triquarterly*, 12 (1975), 163–4. On IMO, see E. A. Dinershtein, 'Izdatel'skaya deyatel'nost' V. V. Mayakovskogo (k 75–letiyu so dnya rozhdeniya)', *Kniga issledovaniya i materialy*, sbornik XVII (Moscow, 1968), 68.

43 I. Erenburg, *Portrety russkikh poetov* (Berlin, 1922), 127.

44 Vil'mont, 'Boris Pasternak. Vospominaniya i mysli', 198.

45 Gifford, *Boris Pasternak, 72–4*.

46 See *SP*, 642.

47 See also Pasternak's 'impressionistic' characterisation of Pushkin in 'O klassikakh', *Soch. III*, 159 – relevant despite the inexact date attribution ('let 15 nazad'). Concerning Pushkin and the interpretation of this cycle, see

R. E. S. Gaigalas, 'Boris Pasternak's "Temy i variacii": A Commentary', Ph.D. dissertation, Harvard University, 1978, 38–99. (This dissertation provides the closest textual analysis of *Temy i variatsii*.) See also R. Salys, '"Izmeritel'naja edinica russkoj žizni": Puškin in the Work of Boris Pasternak', *Russian Literature*, 9 (1986), 347–92; Gifford, *Boris Pasternak*, ch. 5.

48 *DZh*, ch. 9, sections 7–8. Vil'mont, 'Boris Pasternak. Vospominaniya i mysli', 215.

49 See below, 269 ff.

50 Mayakovsky, 'Neobychainoe priklyuchenie, byvshee s Vladimirom Mayakovskim letom na dache', *Polnoe sobranie sochinenii*, II, 35–8. Pasternak visited Mayakovsky at Pushkino in summer 1920 and probably heard, or read, the poem there. See Wright-Kovaleva, 'Mayakovsky and Pasternak', 127–8.

51 Akhmatova, *Sochineniya*, I, 325. A. Voznesensky, *Akhillesovo serdtse* (Moscow, 1966), 41–2.

52 See P. Suhrcke, 'The Place of "Ja višu na pere u tvorca" in Pasternak's Work', *Slavonic and East European Journal*, 25 no. 3 (Fall 1981), 71–82.

53 O. Mandel'shtam, 'V Peterburge my soidemsya snova . . .', *Sobranie sochinenii* (Washington–New York, 1964–9), I, 85–6.

54 Djurčinov, 'Dva priloga', 363.

55 See letter of 2 August 1913 to S. P.Bobrov, quoted in Rashkovskaya, 'Poet v mire', 143–4.

56 Katanyan, *Mayakovsky*, 97–9.

57 See E. B. Pasternak, 'Boris Pasternak. Istoriya odnoi kontroktavy', 254.

58 Letter of 16 July 1918 to S. P. Bobrov, quoted in Rashkovskaya, 'Poet v mire', 156.

59 M. Tsvetaeva, letter of 29 June 1922 to B. L. Pasternak, *Neizdannye pis'ma*, 266.

60 Letter (undated) of summer 1921 to V. P. Polonsky, 'Iz perepiski s pisatelyami', 688.

61 B. Zaitsev, 'Put'', in *Sbornik statei*, 16.

62 See correspondence between Gorky and Pasternak in October 1927, 'Gor'ky – B. L. Pasternak', *Literaturnoe nasledstvo*, 70 (1963), 296–301. See also 'Predislovie Gor'kogo k povesti Pasternaka "Detstvo Lyuvers"', 'Gork'y – B. L. Pasternak', 308–10.

63 'Iz perepiski s pisatelyami', 687–8.

64 *VP*, 483.

65 Letter (undated) of summer 1921 to V. P. Polonsky, 'Iz perepiski s pisatelyami', 688.

66 Letter of 11 July 1926 to M. I. Tsvetaeva, *DLDN*, 9 (1987), 224.

67 V. Shklovsky, 'Iskusstvo kak priem', *Poetika. Sborniki po teorii poeticheskogo yazyka* (Petrograd, 1919), 101–14.

68 For example, A. Voronsky, 'Iskusstvo kak poznanie zhizni', *Krasnaya nov'*, 5 (1923), 347–84, and *Iskusstvo videt' mir* (Moscow, 1928).

69 See Barnes, 'The Poetry of Boris Pasternak', 12 ff; see especially A. Bely, 'Magiya slov', *Simvolizm* (Moscow, 1910), 429–48.

70 A. Livingstone, '"The Childhood of Luvers": An Early Story of Pasternak's', *Southern Review* (Adelaide), 1 (1963), 83–4.

71 Djurčinov, 'Dva priloga', 364.

72 *Ibid.* C. J. Barnes, 'Some Background Notes on Pasternak's Early Translations, and Two Notes by Pasternak on Hans Sachs and Ben Jonson', in *Aspects of Russia 1850–1970*, ed. William Harrison and Avril Pyman (Letchworth, 1984), 201–13. On Gosizdat and TEO, see S. Fitzpatrick, *The Commissariat of Enlightenment* (Cambridge, 1970), 131, 138.

73 The original manuscript was published in Fleishman, 'Neizvestnyi avtograf', 34–7; the *Sovremennik* version appears in *Soch. III*, 152–5, and *VP*, 109–13.

74 Djurčinov, 'Dva priloga', 364.

75 Cf. slightly erroneous account in Mallac, *Boris Pasternak*, 92, which conflates this with Pasternak's later spell of work in Narkomindel; see below, 336–7. On Tsvetaeva, see S. Karlinsky, *Marina Cvetaeva: Her Life and Art* (Berkeley, 1966), 44–5, and *Marina Tsvetaeva* (Cambridge, 1985), 78–9.

76 V. Khodasevich, *Literaturnye stat'i i vospominaniya* (New York, 1954), 349–53.

77 Letters of 6 April 1920 and 19 January 1921 to D. V. Petrovsky. N.B. the poem 'Matros v Moskve' (1919) dedicated to Petrovsky: *Soch. I*, 249–51; *SP*, 223–5.

78 'Khodataistvo v tsentral'nuyu kollegiyu Lit. otdela Narkomprosa', English translation in 'The Unpublished Letters of Boris Pasternak' (ed. and trans. Elliott Mossman), *The New York Times Magazine*, 1 January 1978. 13.

79 Erenburg, *Lyudi, gody, zhizn'*, I, 552. Tsvetaeva, *Proza*, 226. N. Mandel'shtam, *Vtoraya kniga*, 226.

80 Some echo of Pasternak's misgivings at enforced parasitism instead of paid labour was recorded in 'Uezd v tylu', *VP*, 295; his and Leonid Pasternak's attitudes were recounted to me by Aleksandr Pasternak in September 1980.

81 Letter of 18 July 1920 to A. L. Shtikh (APT).

82 Letter (undated) of July 1920 to L. O. and R. I. Pasternak (APT).

83 Letter of 19 January 1921 to D. V. Petrovsky (APT).

II BERLIN INTERLUDE

1 *ZRL*, 261–2, and figs. 115, 116, 117, 119. See also Buckman, *Leonid Pasternak*, front cover, and 65, 67. On 'Vysokaya bolezn'', see below, 321–4.

2 G. de Mallac, 'A Russian Impressionist: Leonid Osipovich Pasternak, 1862–1945', 106. Buckman, *Leonid Pasternak*, 67–8. *Vosp.*, 262–3. *ZRL*, 84.

3 Dobrovein, *Stranitsy zhizni*. *ZRL*, 82. Fitzpatrick, *The Commissariat of Enlightenment*, 132.

4 *Perepiska*, 60, 355.
5 *Vosp.*, 265. *ZRL*, 100.
6 *ZRL*, 84–6, 94. Buckman, *Leonid Pasternak*, 68.
7 *ZRL*, 84–95. Buckman, *Leonid Pasternak*, 68 ff. Mallac, 'A Russian Impressionist', 106 ff.
8 On Durylin, see ch. 4, n. 43. Struve, *Russkaya literatura*, 18.
9 Rait-Kovaleva, 'Tol'ko vospominaniya', 269. Wright-Kovaleva, 'Mayakovsky and Pasternak', 123–7. V. Bryusov, 'Vchera, segodnya i zavtra russkoi poezii', *Pechat' i revolyutsiya*, 7 (1922), 57. It is evident, for instance, that Petnikov was already familiar with *Sestra moya zhizn'* in 1920; see G. Petnikov, 'Borisu Pasternaku', *Raduga*, sbornik, book I, 1920, 12.
10 Fleishman, *Boris Pasternak v dvadtsatye gody*, 12. E. L. Mindlin, *Neobyknovennye sobesedniki* (Moscow, 1968), 90. P. N. Zaitsev, letter of 23 June 1921 to Andrei Bely, TsGALI, fond 53, t.1, ed. khr. 188. Troitsky, *Boris Leonidovich Pasternak*, 25–6.
11 *Soch. III*, 132–3; *SP*, 539. Tsvetaeva, *Neizdannye pis'ma*, 268.
12 *VP*, 114–22, 476. On Gavronsky, see ch. 5, n. 54.
13 I. G. Erenburg, 'B. Pasternak. "Sestra moya zhizn'"'. Berlin, Izd-vo Grzhebina, 1922', *Novaya russkaya kniga*, 6 (1922), 11.
14 Ya. Chernyak, 'B. Pasternak. "Sestra moya zhizn'"'. Berlin, Grzhebin, 1922', *Pechat' i revolyutsiya*, 6 (1922), 303–4.
15 A. Romm, 'B. Pasternak. "Sestra moya zhizn'"'. Berlin, Grzhebin, 1922', *Korabl'*, 1–2 (1923), 45–6.
16 Aseev, 'Pis'ma o poezii', 251.
17 Bryusov, 'Vchera, segodnya i zavtra', 57.
18 V. Pravdukhin, 'V bor'be za novoe iskusstvo', *Sibirskie ogni*, 5 (1922); reprinted in his *Literaturnaya sovremennost'* (Moscow, 1924), 156–81. A. V. Lunacharsky, undated letter to B. L. Pasternak in response to a dedication marked 1 May 1922.
19 Tsvetaeva, *Proza*, 351–71.
20 O. Mandel'shtam, *Sobranie sochinenii*, II, 306.
21 Letter of 15 August 1922 to V. Ya. Bryusov, in E. V. Pasternak, 'Pasternak i Bryusov', 247. M. Kuzmin, 'Govoryashchie', *Zhizn' iskusstva*, 31, 8–15, August 1922; reprinted in his *Uslovnosti* (Petrograd, 1923). Bely and A. Tolstoy are cited specifically because of their recent works on childhood. See also in Kuzmin's 'Pis'mo v Pekin', in his *Uslovnosti*, 164–6.
22 E. Zamyatin, 'Novaya russkaya proza', *Litsa* (New York, 1955), 203. N. Ashukin, 'Sovremennost'' v literature', *Novaya russkaya kniga*, 6 (1922), 4–6. S. Parnok, 'Pasternak i drugie', *Russkii sovremennik*, 1 (1924), 307–11.
23 See above, ch. 10, n. 62.
24 Letter of 15 August 1922 to V. Ya Bryusov, in E. V. Pasternak, 'Pasternak i Bryusov', 249.
25 Letter of 14 June 1922 to Yu. I. Yurkun, 'Pis'mo Yu. I. Yurkunu', 191–2.

26 Letter of 12 January 1922 to V. Ya. Bryusov, in E. V. Pasternak, 'Pasternak i Bryusov', 243–4.

27 On Lenin's verdict on *150,000,000*, see E. J. Brown, *Mayakovsky: A Poet in the Revolution* (Princeton, NJ, 1973), 205. L. Trotsky, *Literatura i revolyutsiya* (Moscow, 1923), ch. 4, gives only qualified approval of Futurist 'questings'.

28 See B. Jangfeldt (ed.), *V. V. Mayakovsky i L. Yu. Brik: perepiska 1915–1930* (Stockholm, 1982), 22.

29 See letter of 14 June 1922 to Yu. I. Yurkun, 'Pis'mo Yu. I. Yurkunu', 193. Aseeva, 'Iz vospominanii', 30. 'Zapiski zavsegdataya ...', *Izbr. II*, 395. R. Rait-Kovaleva, 'Misterium-Buff', *Literaturnyi sovremennik*, 4 (1940), 110. Wright-Kovaleva, 'Mayakovsky and Pasternak', 129–30.

30 L. Yu. Brik, 'Chuzhie stikhi', 342–4.

31 Erenburg, *Lyudi, gody, zhizn'*, I, 416.

32 Letter of 14 June 1922 to Yu. I. Yurkun, 'Pis'mo Yu. I. Yurkunu', 193.

33 O. G. Petrovskaya, 'Nikolai Aseev', in K. M. Aseeva and O. G. Petrovskaya (eds.), *Vospominaniya o Nikolae Aseeve* (Moscow, 1980), 55.

34 N. N. Aseev, letter of 22 May 1922 to O. G. Petrovskaya, cited by Petrovskaya, 'Nikolai Aseev', 55.

35 At Bely's lecture, when Loks and Pasternak first met. See above, 93–4; also Blok and Bely, *Perepiska*, 243; Pyman, *The Life of Aleksandr Blok*, II, 101.

36 K. Chukovsky, 'Iz dnevnika (1919–1921)', *Voprosy literatury*, 10 (1980), 309–10. Mayakovsky, 'Umer Aleksandr Blok', *Polnoe sobranie sochinenii*, XII, 22. Nikulin, 'Vladimir Mayakovsky', 496–7. S. Bobrov, 'Aleksandr Blok, "Sedoe utro. Stikhotvoreniya"', *Pechat' i revolyutsiya*, 1 (1921), 146–7, and his letter of 15 April 1967 to C. J. Barnes.

37 The 1921 date indicated by Yu. Annenkov in *Dnevnik moikh vstrech* (New York, 1966), II, 159, is probably inaccurate.

38 'Retsenziya na knigu izbrannykh stikhov Anny Akhmatovoi' (Akhmatova's *Izbrannoe* [Tashkent, 1943]), 531. On Akhmatova in 1921, see R. Timenchik, 'Khram Premudrosti Boga', *Slavica Hierosolymitana*, 5–6 (1981), 306.

39 Vil'mont, 'Boris Pasternak. Vospominaniya i mysli', 172.

40 Letter (undated) of November 1924 to O. E. Mandel'shtam, *ChPV*, 159; also 'Zametki o peresechenii', 279.

41 A. Haight, *Anna Akhmatova: A Poetic Pilgrimage* (New York–London, 1976), 58.

42 *Ibid.*, 68–74. See also 'Iz perepiski s pisatelyami', 652, 654. K. Chukovsky, 'Akhmatova i Mayakovsky', *Dom iskusstv*, 1 (1921), 23–42.

43 'Iz perepiski s pisatelyami', 654.

44 Letter of 14 June 1922 to Yu. I. Yurkun, 'Pis'mo Yu. I. Yurkunu', 189–90.

45 J. E. Malmstad, 'Mixail Kuzmin: A Chronicle of His Life and Times', in M. A. Kuzmin, *Sobranie stikhov* (Munich, 1977), III, 264–6.

46 N. Mandel'shtam, *Vtoraya kniga*, 92. Vil'mont, in 'Boris Pasternak. Vospo-

minaniya i mysli', suggests a meeting may have occurred in 1915, but there is no confirmation of this.

47 'Zametki o peresechenii', 289–90.

48 O. Mandel'shtam, 'Literaturnaya Moskva', *Rossiya*, 2 (1922), 23–4; reprinted in O. Mandel'shtam, *Sobranie sochinenii*, II, 368–73.

49 D. M. Bethea, *Khodasevich. His Life and Art* (Princeton, NJ, 1983), 187.

50 Blok, *Sobranie sochinenii*, VI, 167.

51 Letter of 14 June 1922 to Yu. I. Yurkun, 'Pis'mo Yu. I. Yurkunu', 190–1.

52 M. I. Tsvetaeva, letter of 29 June 1922 to B. L. Pasternak, in Tsvetaeva, *Neizdannye pis'ma*, 266–9. *Soch. II*, 45; *VP*, 459–60.

53 Karlinsky, *Marina Cvetaeva*, 43–51, and *Marina Tsvetaeva*, 75–114.

54 A. Efron, *Stranitsy vospominanii* (Paris, 1979), 107.

55 *Ibid.*, 107, 109.

56 *Ibid.*, 65.

57 Karlinsky, *Marina Cvetaeva*, 58.

58 See n. 52.

59 Tsvetaeva, *Proza*, 352.

60 Letter of 22 December 1921 to E. V. Lur'e, 'Perepiska Borisa Pasternaka', 277–8. On Evgeniya Lur'e, see Vil'mont, 'Boris Pasternak. Vospominaniya i mysli', 191–3.

61 Letter (undated) of December 1922 to A. L. Pasternak.

62 Letter of 16 November 1928 to O. M. Freidenberg, *Perepiska*, 116.

63 E. Chernyak, 'Pasternak'. *Perepiska*, 62–3.

64 Vil'mont, 'Boris Pasternak. Vospominaniya i mysli', 180, 183 ff.

65 L. Gornung 'Vospominaniya o Borise Pasternake' (manuscript, 1982). Fleishman, *Boris Pasternak v dvadtsatye gody*, 128.

66 Vil'mont, 'Boris Pasternak. Vospominaniya i mysli', 203–4.

67 Letter of 15 August 1922 to V. Ya. Bryusov, in E. V. Pasternak, 'Pasternak i Bryusov', 248–9.

68 Wright-Kovaleva, 'Mayakovsky and Pasternak', 129–30.

69 Letter of 14 June 1922 to Yu. I. Yurkun, 'Pis'mo Yu. I. Yurkunu', 192.

70 Letter of 15 August 1922 to V. Ya. Bryusov, in E. V. Pasternak, 'Pasternak i Bryusov', 247–8.

71 Letter of 17 January 1923 to S. P. Bobrov, quoted in Rashkovskaya, 'Poet v mire', 158.

72 Letter of 16 September 1922 to A. L. Pasternak. See Fleishman, *Boris Pasternak v dvadtsatye gody*, 24.

73 Letter of 10 January 1923 to V. P. Polonsky, 'Iz perepiski s pisatelyami', 691–2. Fleishman, *Boris Pasternak v dvadtsatye gody*, 21–3.

74 Letter of 15 August 1922 to V. Ya. Bryusov, in E. V. Pasternak, 'Pasternak i Bryusov', 245–9. Letter of 16 August 1922 to A. L. Pasternak. 'Iz perepiski s pisatelyami', 652.

75 'Otplytie', *Soch. I*, 231–2; *SP*, 207. Letter of 16 September 1922 to A. L.

Pasternak. M. Woloschin, *Die grüne Schlange. Lebenserinnerungen einer Malerin* (Frankfurt-on-Main, 1982), 361. Haight, *Anna Akhmatova*, 58.

76 Letter of 16 September 1922 to A. L. Pasternak. A. Bakhrakh, *Po pamyati, po zapisyam. Literaturnye portrety* (Paris, 1980), 63.

77 Letter of 29 December 1921 to O. M. Freidenberg, *Perepiska*, 62.

78 Erenburg, *Lyudi, gody, zhizn'*, I, 13.

79 Williams, *Culture in Exile*, 111 ff.

80 The most detailed treatment of Pasternak's Berlin period, 1922–3, is in Fleishman, *Boris Pasternak v dvadtsatye gody*, ch. 1.

81 Proyart, 'Une amitié d'enfance', 519.

82 Z. Arvatov, 'Nollendorfplattskafe', *Grani*, 41 (1959), 107.

83 N. Berberova, *Kursiv moi. Avtobiografiya* (New York, 1983), 176–7. Vil'mont, 'Boris Pasternak. Vospominaniya i mysli', 210.

84 Bakhrakh, *Po pamyati, po zapisyam*, 62. See also Fleishman, *Boris Pasternak v dvadtsatye gody*, 20.

85 Letter of 17 January 1923 to S. P. Bobrov, cited in Rashkovskaya, 'Poet v mire', 158. Erenburg, *Lyudi, gody, zhizn'*, I, 417. Katanyan, *Mayakovsky*, 171–2. V. Andreev, *Istoriya odnogo puteshestviya* (Moscow, 1974), 310–11.

86 Williams, *Culture in Exile*, 138. Berberova, *Kursiv moi*, 200. On Bely in Berlin, see Tsvetaeva, *Proza*, 314 ff.

87 Letter of 17 January 1923 to S. P. Bobrov, quoted in Rashkovskaya, 'Poet v mire', 157.

88 Aseev's negative review of Khodasevich's *Schastlivyi domik* appeared entitled 'Po moryu bumazhnomu', *Krasnaya nov'*, 4 (1922), 245–7. See letter of 17 January 1923 to S. P. Bobrov, cited in Rashkovskaya, 'Poet v mire', 158.

89 V. Sirin, review of D. Kobyakov's *Gorech'* (Paris, 1927) and *Keramika* (Paris, 1925), and of E. Shakh, *Semya na kamne* (Paris, 1927), *Rul'*, 11 May 1927.

90 Letter of 24 November 1922 to A. L. Pasternak.

91 Letter of 15 February 1923 to A. L. Pasternak. The artist Ekaterina Vasil'evna Gol'dinger was a former pupil of Leonid Pasternak. Her parents were family friends of the Pasternaks (see above, 48). Her mother, Zinaida Nikolaevna Gol'dinger, was a leading pioneer in obstetrics.

92 Letter of 10 January 1923 to V. P. Polonsky, 'Is perepiski s pisatelyami', 691–2. See also Fleishman, *Boris Pasternak v dvadtsatye gody*, 21–2.

93 Fleishman, *Boris Pasternak v dvadtsatye gody*, 28. A small bouquet of eight recent poems was prepared for publication in 1923–4 and subsequently published in M. O. Chudakova, 'Novye avtografy B. L. Pasternaka', *Zapiski otdela rukopisei*, vypusk 32 (Moscow, 1971).

94 Fleishman, *Boris Pasternak v dvadtsatye gody*, 25.

95 Akhmatova, *Sochineniya*, I, 185.

96 C. J. Barnes, 'The Original Text of "O skromnosti i smelosti"', *Slavica Hierosolymitana*, 4 (1979), 298.

97 Fleishman, *Boris Pasternak v dvadtsatye gody*, 19. *Soch. III*, 133; *SP*, 540.

98 Vil'mont, 'Boris Pasternak. Vospominaniya i mysli', 209–10.
99 V. Shklovsky, *Zhili-byli* (Moscow, 1964), 169.
100 Letter of 11 February 1923 to V. P. Polonsky, 'Iz perepiski s pisatelyami', 693.
101 S. F. Budantsev, letter of 30 January 1923 to B. L. Pasternak, quoted in Fleishman, *Boris Pasternak v dvadtsatye gody*, 24–5. On Krug, see *Kratkaya literaturnaya entsiklopediya*, III, 844–5.
102 Quoted in Katanyan, *Mayakovsky*, 172.
103 Letter of 10 January 1923 to V. P. Polonsky, 'Iz perepiski s pisatelyami', 692. Mallac, 'Pasternak and Marburg', 433, and *Boris Pasternak*, 71.
104 Letter of 15 February 1923 to A. L. Pasternak.
105 *Vosp.*, 263–70.

12 'MALADY SUBLIME'

1 Katanyan, *Mayakovsky*, 175, 184–5. Mayakovsky, *Polnoe sobranie sochinenii*, XII, 43–4, 46.
2 *LEF*, 1 (1923), 41.
3 P. M. Neznamov, 'Mayakovsky v dvadtsatykh godakh', in Reformatskaya (ed.), *V. Mayakovsky v vospominaniyakh sovremennikov*, 362. Shklovsky, *Zhili-byli*, 372.
4 Neznamov, 'Mayakovsky v dvadtsatykh godakh', 367.
5 N. Aseev, 'Organizatsiya rechi (Boris Pasternak, "Temy i variatsii"), *Pechat' i revolyutsiya*, 6 (1923), 71–8.
6 Neznamov, 'Mayakovsky v dvadtsatykh godakh', 370. *Soch. III*, 134–5; *SP*, 540–1.
7 Fleishman, 'B. Pasternak i A. Bely', 545–6. Mindlin, *Neobyknovennye sobesedniki*, 419ff. E. B. Chernyak 'Pasternak' (manuscript). On Chernyak, see 'Ya. Z. Chernyak. Nekrolog', *Literaturnoe nasledstvo*, 62 (1955), 865–7.
8 E. B. Chernyak, 'Pasternak'. M. P. Gonta, 'Betkhoven' (manuscript, 1967). On Petrovsky, see also 'Zametki o peresechenii', 293–5.
9 Ya. Chernyak, 'Iz dnevnika'.
10 Gornung, 'Vospominaniya o Borise Pasternake'.
11 Letter of 29 September 1930 to S. Spassky, 'Iz pisem B. Pasternaka k S. Spasskomu', *Voprosy literatury*, 9 (1969), 171.
12 N. S. Tikhonov, letter of 15 February 1924 to B. L. Pasternak, 'Iz perepiski s pisatelyami', 668.
13 M. I. Tsvetaeva, letter of 10 February 1923 to B. L. Pasternak, in Tsvetaeva, *Neizdannye pis'ma*, 278–9.
14 Sinyavsky, 'Poeziya Pasternaka', 40. See also Gifford, *Boris Pasternak*, 99–103.
15 *Soch. I*, 264, 391; *SP*, 236.
16 Fleishman, *Boris Pasternak v dvadtsatye gody*, 34. For discussion of 'Vysokaya bolezn'', see Fleishman, *ibid.*, 34. Ya. Chernyak, 'Iz dnevnika'.

17 Cf. Akhmatova's later description of Blok as the 'tragic tenor of the epoch', in Akhmatova, *Sochineniya*, I, 268.

18 Letter of 21 April 1924 to N. S. Tikhonov, 'Iz perepiski s pisatelyami', 669. Perhaps the result of Aseev's resolve was his 'Liricheskoe otstuplenie', in *LEF*, 2 (1924); see Aseev, *Sobranie sochinenii*, I, 386–98.

19 N. Mandel'shtam, *Vtoraya kniga*, 232–3.

20 O. Mandel'shtam, *Sobranie sochinenii*, I (2nd edn), 142.

21 Fleishman, *Boris Pasternak v dvadtsatye gody*, 230.

22 O. Mandel'shtam, *Sobranie sochinenii*, I (1964), 111–13.

23 Possibly a 'deliberate mistake' on Khodasevich's part after his earlier contretemps with Pasternak. See above, 308 and 'Boris Pasternak v perepiske s Maksimom Gor'kim', 265.

24 R. Maguire, *Red Virgin Soil: Soviet Literature in the 1920's* (Princeton, 1968), 372–4.

25 Mossman, 'Pasternak's Short Fiction', 297. Critiques that expressed reservation about 'Vozdushnye puti' included: A. Lezhnev, 'Na pravom flange', *Pechat' i revolyutsiya*, 6 (1924), 129; D. S. Mirsky, 'Boris Pasternak. Rasskazy', *Sovremennye zapiski*, 25 (1925), 544–5.

26 Ya. Chernyak, 'Iz dnevnika'.

27 On Pasternak and Bryusov's relations, see E. V. Pasternak, 'Pasternak i Bryusov', 239–65.

28 Ya. Chernyak, 'Iz dnevnika'.

29 Concerning the Bryusov jubilee, see: E. V. Pasternak, 'Pasternak i Bryusov', 250–2; Fleishman, *Boris Pasternak v dvadtsatye gody*, 34–8.

30 E. V. Pasternak, 'Pasternak i Bryusov', 242.

31 *Ibid.*, 252.

32 Fleishman, *Boris Pasternak v dvadtsatye gody*, 38.

33 For example, Nikolai Aduev i Argo, 'Seren'kii kozlik', *Rossiya*, 2 (1922), 15, and 'Kak rodilsya poet', *Rossiya*, 3 (1922), 21. Concerning Bryusov's own 'imitations' of Pasternak, see: Mochul'sky, *Valery Bryusov* (Paris, 1962), 180–1; Men'shutin and Sinyavsky, *Poeziya pervykh let revolyutsii*, 363, 367.

34 Fleishman, *Boris Pasternak v dvadtsatye gody*, 38.

35 S. Klychkov, 'Lysaya gora', *Krasnaya nov'*, 5 (1923), 385. K. Zelinsky, *Kriticheskie pis'ma. Kniga vtoraya* (Moscow, 1934), 256.

36 Letter of 15 August to V. Ya. Bryusov, in E. V. Pasternak, 'Pasternak i Bryusov', 248.

37 S. Bobrov, 'O. Mandel'shtam, "Tristia" (1923)', *Pechat' i revolyutsiya*, 4 (1923), 261. S. Parnok, 'Pasternak i drugie', *Russkii sovremennik*, 1 (1924), 311. V. Pozner, review of *Rossiya*, 1 in *Dni*, 492 (1924), 10. V. Shklovsky, *Gamburgskii schet* (Leningrad, 1928), 119.

38 N. Mandel'shtam, *Vtoraya kniga*, 514.

39 Letter of 25 July 1924 to O. M. Freidenberg, *Perepiska*, 64.

40 Letters of 16 June, 9 July, 12 July and 17 July 1924 to Evgeniya Pasternak.

41 Letter of 21 April 1924 to N. S. Tikhonov, 'Iz perepiski s pisatelyami', 669. Letter of 23 June 1924 to Evgeniya Pasternak.
42 For example, letter of 20 June 1924 to Evgeniya Pasternak, 'Perepiska Borisa Pasternaka', 278–9.
43 Letter of 2 August (?) 1924 to O. M. Freidenberg, *Perepiska*, 65.
44 'Zametki o peresechenii, 295.
45 Bobrov, 'O. Mandel'shtam. "Tristia"', 259–62.
46 'Zametki o peresechenii', 292–3.
47 O. M. Freidenberg, letter of 3 December 1924 to Evgeniya and B. L. Pasternak, *Perepiska*, 87.
48 See *Perepiska*, 66–93, concerning this episode.
49 Maguire, *Red Virgin Soil*, 384–92.
50 Fleishman, *Boris Pasternak v dvadtsatye gody*, 24.
51 N. S. Tikhonov, letter (undated) of December 1924 to B. L. Pasternak, 'Iz perepiski s pisatelyami', 671.
52 Letter of 28 September 1924 to O. M. Freidenberg, *Perepiska*, 70.
53 Letter of 2 November 1925 to O. M. Freidenberg, *Perepiska*, 77.
54 'Zametki o peresechenii', 293.
55 Letter of 19 November 1924, 'Zametki o peresechenii, 293.
56 'Iz perepiski s pisatelyami', 672.
57 Letters of 2 November 1924 to O. M. Freidenberg, and of 19 November 1924 to A. O. Freidenberg, *Perepiska*, 76–7, 80.
58 Letter of 28 September 1924 to O. M. Freidenberg, *Perepiska*, 72.
59 Letter of 2 November to O. M. Freidenberg, *Perepiska*, 78.
60 *Perepiska*, 81.
61 Letter (undated) of early November 1924 to O. E. Mandel'shtam, 'Zametki o peresechenii', 296.
62 Letter (undated) of November 1924 to O. E. Mandel'shtam, 'Zametki o peresechenii', 295–6; also in *ChPV*, 158.
63 Letter of 31 January 1925 to O. E. Mandel'shtam, *ChPV*, 159–60; 'Zametki o peresechenii', 298.
64 O. Mandel'shtam, *Sobranie sochinenii*, II, 270–1.
65 Letter (undated) of November 1924 to O. E. Mandel'shtam, *ChPV*, 159; 'Zametki o peresechenii', 297.
66 Letter of 31 January 1925 to O. E. Mandel'shtam, *ChPV*, 161; 'Zametki o peresechenii', 300.
67 Reformatskaya (ed.), *V. Mayakovsky v vospominaniyakh sovremennikov*, 662–3.
68 Letter of 31 January 1925 to O. E. Mandel'shtam, *ChPV*, 161; 'Zametki o peresechenii', 299–300.
69 Neznamov, 'Mayakovsky v dvadtsatykh godakh', 375.
70 Mayakovsky, *Polnoe sobranie sochinenii*, XII, 281–2.
71 *Ibid.*, XIII, 70.
72 Shklovsky, *Zhili-byli*, 341. Brown, *Mayakovsky: A Poet in the Revolution*,

215–16. See also coverage of this episode in Fleishman, *Boris Pasternak v dvadtsatye gody*, 40–3.

73 On Pasternak and Kruchenykh in 1925, see Fleishman, *Boris Pasternak v dvadtsatye gody*, 44–7.

74 Gornung, 'Vospominaniya o Borise Pasternake'. C. J. Barnes, 'Boris Pasternak and the Bogeyman of Russian Literature', *Russian Literature*, 6, no. 1 (January 1978), 47–68. Djurčinov, 'Edno nepoznato pismo', 435–40. A. V. Tufanov's undated letter was accompanied by a prospectus for his 'Osnovy zaumnogo mirooschchushcheniya i deklaratsiya zaumnikov'.

75 Letter of 18 February 1925 to Lydia Pasternak (APT).

76 For example, V. Pertsov, 'Vymyshlennaya figura', *Na postu*, 1 (1924), 209–24, directed against Pasternak.

77 'Chto postanovila Partiya o khudozhestvennoi literature', *Zhurnalist*, 8–9 (1925), 27–8.

78 A. M. Gor'ky, *Sobranie sochinenii*, XXIX, 432.

79 'Chto govoryat pisateli o postanovlenii Tsk RKP', *Zhurnalist*, 8–9 (1925), 30.

80 *Ibid.*, 31.

81 *Ibid.*, 10 (1925), 11–12.

82 *Ibid.*, 10–11; references are given hereafter in the text for *Soch. III*.

13 THE EPIC AGE

1 Cf. a similar image in Pasternak's account of tsarist inertia prior to the revolutionary outburst of 1917: *VP*, 257–8.

2 Letter of 12 April 1926 to R. M. Rilke, *Briefwechsel*, 76–7; also in Barnes, 'Boris Pasternak and Rainer Maria Rilke', 68–9.

3 Letter of 31 January 1925 to O. E. Mandel'shtam, *ChPV*, 160–1; 'Zametki o peresechenii', 299.

4 Letter of 3 January 1928 to S. D. Spassky, 'Iz pisem B. Pasternaka k S. Spasskomu', 167. There are no Fet tragedies of the type mentioned. Pasternak was presumably thinking of Fet's *poemy* in iambic pentameter, such as 'Talisman', 'Son poruchika Loseva', 'Dve lipki', 'Student'.

5 S. M. Gorodetsky, 'Na styke', in *Styk. Pervyi sbornik Moskovskogo tsekha poetov* (Moscow, 1925), 17.

6 Letter of 6 November 1929 to P. N. Medvedev, 'Iz perepiski s pisatelyami', 710.

7 See *Soch. I*, 243–5; *SP*, 217–19, 603–6.

8 For full details of the publication of parts of *Spektorsky*, see *Soch. I*, 481–2 and *SP*, 671.

9 N. S. Tikhonov, letter of February–March 1925 to B. L. Pasternak, 'Iz perepiski s pisatelyami', 673–4.

10 Letter (undated) of May 1925 to O. E. Mandel'shtam, 'Zametki o peresechenii', 300–1.

11 Letter (undated) of January (?) 1925 to I. A. Gruzdev, 'Iz perepiski s pisatelyami', 674.
12 Gornung, 'Vospominaniya o Borise Pasternake'.
13 See letter of 14 May 1925 to N. K. Chukovsky, 'Iz perepiski s pisatelyami', 676.
14 Letter of 16 August 1925 to O. E. Mandel'shtam, 'Zametki o peresechenii', 301–2.
15 K. I. Chukovsky, letter of 7 July 1925 to R. N. Lomonosova (LRA).
16 Letter of 17 August 1925 to R. N. Lomonosova (LRA).
17 Letter of 16 September 1925 to R. N. Lomonosova (LRA).
18 Letter of 11 June 1925 to N. S. Tikhonov, 'Iz perepiski s pisatelyami', 675.
19 Letter of August 1925 to O. E. Mandel'shtam, 'Zametki o peresechenii', 301.
20 Letter of 19 May 1926 to R. N. Lomonosova (LRA).
21 S. F. Budantsev, letter of 20 December 1925 to A. B. Kusikov, G. Nivat, 'Trois correspondents d'Aleksandr Kusikov', *Cahiers du monde russe et soviétique*, 15 nos. 1–2 (1974), 209.
22 Letter of 19 May 1926 to R. N. Lomonosova (LRA).
23 *SP*, 655–6.
24 L. Dashkov, '1905 god', *Kniga i profsoyuzy*, 10 (1927), 29.
25 D. Petrovsky, 'Boretsya more' and 'Chernomorskoe poberezh'e', *Izbrannoe* (Moscow, 1956), 11–32, 187–90. N. S. Tikhonov, letter (undated) of July 1926 to B. L. Pasternak, 'Iz perepiski s pisatelyami', 676.
26 Publication details of instalments of '1905 god' given in *Soch. I*, 453–6; *SP*, 656–60.
27 Letter of 28 March 1926 to Zh. L. Pasternak, *Briefwechsel*, 72. (References to German translations in *Briefwechsel* are given only when a Russian text is unavailable.) Letter of 30 July 1926 to M. I. Tsvetaeva, *DLDN*, (1987), 227.
28 *SP*, 656.
29 Letter (undated) of 1926 to Lydia Pasternak (APT).
30 Noted also in letter of 7 February 1926 to I. A. Gruzdev.
31 *SP*, 656.
32 B. Thomson, *The Premature Revolution* (London, 1972), 265.
33 Letter of 28 November 1929 to P. N. Medvedev, 'Iz perepiski s pisatelyami', 711.
34 Letter of 30 July 1926 to M. I. Tsvetaeva, *DLDN*, 9 (1987), 227. Letter of 12 April 1926 to R. N. Lomonosova (LRA).
35 In 'B. Pasternak, "Devyat'sot pyatyi god"', *Versty*, 3 (1928), D. S. Mirsky describes the 'majestic movement of the first parts', while in the second, 'history crystallises around the personality of Shmidt'; quoted in Fleishman, 'Iz pasternakovskoi perepiski', 539. In 1927 *Sestra moya zhizn'* and *Temy i variatsii* were published under one cover as *Dve knigi*; the pattern of twinned works continued in *Spektorsky* and *Povest'*.

36 Letter of 19 May 1926 to M. I. Tsvetaeva, 'Iz perepiski Ril'ke, Tsvetaevoi i Pasternaka', 254; *DLDN*, 7 (1987), 257.
37 Bibliography in Yu. I. Levin, 'Zametki o "Leitenante Shmidte" B. L. Pasternaka', in Nilsson (ed.), *Art, Society, Revolution*, 161.
38 Tsvetaeva, *Proza*, 409.
39 V. Krasil'nikov, 'Boris Pasternak', *Pechat' i revolyutsiya*, 5 (1927), 89–90.
40 *Briefwechsel*, 220; *DLDN*, 9 (1987), 225.
41 M. Tsvetaeva, letter of 1 July 1926 to B. L. Pasternak, in Tsvetaeva, *Neizdannye pis'ma*, 307–9; 'Iz perepiski Ril'ke, Tsvetaevoi i Pasternaka', 278.
42 Letter of 5 June 1926 to M. I. Tsvetaeva, *DLDN*, 8 (1987), 255.
43 Quoted in Fleishman, 'Iz pasternakovskoi perepiski', 539.
44 *Briefwechsel*, 284–5.
45 Letter of 19 May 1926 to R. N. Lomonosova (LRA).
46 'Iz perepiski Ril'ke, Tsvetaevoi i Pasternaka', 254–5. 'Posvyashchen'e' also in *Soch. I*, 457; *SP*, 661. 'Sobyt'e na Temze, stolbom otrubei...' in *Izbr*. II, 404.
47 See Fleishman, *Boris Pasternak v dvadtsatye gody*, 54–8, for a detailed account of this incident.
48 Vil'mont, 'Boris Pasternak. Vospominaniya i mysli', 179.
49 Letter of 23 May 1926 to M. I. Tsvetaeva, 'Iz perepiski Ril'ke, Tsvetaevoi i Pasternaka', 258–9; *DLDN*, 7 (1987), 261.
50 See Levin, 'Zametki o "Leitenante Shmidte"', 85ff.
51 Katanyan, 'O Mayakovskom i Pasternake', 503.
52 E. B. Chernyak, 'Pasternak'. G. Serebryakova, *O drugikh i o sebe* (Moscow, 1972), 262–7.
53 M. I. Tsvetaeva, letter of 5 February 1928 to L. O. Pasternak, in Tsvetaeva, *Neizdannye pis'ma*, 255–6.
54 Letter of 3 January 1928 to O. M. Freidenberg, *Perepiska*, 105. Krasil'nikov, 'Boris Pasternak', 78–91. I. Postupal'sky, 'Boris Pasternak. "Devyat'sot pyatyi god"'. Giz. M.-L. 1927', *Pechat' i revolyutsiya*, 8 (1927), 184–5. A. Lezhnev, *Literaturnye budni* (Moscow, 1929), 310–13. V. Pertsov, 'Novyi Pasternak', *Na literaturnom postu*, 2 (1927), 33–9.
55 A. M. Gor'ky, letter of 18 October 1927 to B. L. Pasternak, 'Gor'ky – B. L. Pasternak' (1963), 300. Letter of 25 October 1927 to A. M. Gor'ky, 'Gor'ky – B. L. Pasternak', 302–3.
56 O. Ivinskaya, *V plenu vremeni. Gody s Borisom Pasternakom* (Paris, 1978), 72.
57 Katanyan, 'O Mayakovskom i Pasternake', 503–4.
58 V. D. Barooshian, *Brik and Mayakovsky* (The Hague, 1978), 82. Dating of this is supplied by Fleishman in *Boris Pasternak v tridtsatye gody* (Jerusalem, 1984), 11; see also 11–14.
59 Gornung, 'Vospominaniya o Borise Pasternake'.
60 See *Knigonosha*, 8 (1926), 39. See A. Vvedensky, *Polnoe sobranie sochinenii* (Ann Arbor, 1984), II, 227.

61 P. Salys, 'Boris Pasternak: Letter to G. F. Ustinov', *Scottish Slavonic Review* (forthcoming 1989).

62 Gornung, 'Vospominaniya o Borise Pasternake'.

63 *Ibid.* See also Malmstad, 'Mixail Kuzmin: A Chronicle', 286–7.

64 Gornung, 'Vospominaniya o Borise Pasternake'. 'Pis'ma k M. A. Voloshinu i O. D. Forsh', 192–5.

65 'Iz perepiski s pisatelyami', 652–6. Gornung, 'Vospominaniya o Borise Pasternake'.

66 Letter of 28 March 1926 to Zh. L. Pasternak, *Briefwechsel*, 71.

67 Letter of 14 June 1926 to M. I. Tsvetaeva, 'Iz perepiski Ril'ke, Tsvetaevoi i Pasternaka', 273; *DLDN*, 8 (1987), 258.

68 R. M. Rilke, letter of 14 March 1926 to L. O. Pasternak, *Briefwechsel*, 60.

69 *Briefwechsel*, 75–6. On the circumstances of this correspondence, see Barnes, 'Boris Pasternak and Rainer Maria Rilke', 61ff.

70 Letter of 10 May 1926 to O. M. Freidenberg, *Perepiska*, 95–6.

71 Mirsky, 'B. Pasternak. Rasskazy' (1925), 544–5. See also a shorter note in Mirsky, 'B. Pasternak. Rasskazy' (1926), 168–9.

72 D. S. Mirsky, 'The Present State of Russian Letters', *London Mercury*, 16 no. 93 (1927), 278.

73 P. P. Suvchinsky, letter of 23 October 1927 to B. L. Pasternak, V. Kozovoi (ed.), 'Iz perepiski B. Pasternaka i P. Suvchinskogo', *Revue des études slaves*, 58 no. 4 (1986), 640.

74 Mirsky, 'The Present State of Russian Letters', 280.

75 Quoted in Fleishman, 'Iz pasternakovskoi perepiski', 535–6.

76 R. M. Rilke, letter of April (?) 1926 to B. L. Pasternak, *Briefwechsel*, 128. Letter of 12 May 1967 to Z. F. Ruoff, *ChPV*, 171.

77 M. I. Tsvetaeva, letter of 9 May 1926 to R. M. Rilke, *Briefwechsel*, 105ff. and subsequent letters.

78 Efron, *Stranitsy vospominaniya*, 109. M. I. Tsvetaeva, letter of 14 June 1926 to R. M. Rilke, *Briefwechsel*, 175. On the relationship between Rilke and Tsvetaeva, see also P. P. Brodsky, 'On Daring to be a Poet', *Germano-Slavica*, 3, no. 4 (Fall, 1980), 261–9.

79 M. I. Tsvetaeva, letter of 9 March 1923 to B. L. Pasternak, in Tsvetaeva, *Neizdannye pis'ma*, 283–90.

80 Gornung, 'Vospominaniya o Borise Pasternake'. Salys, 'Boris Pasternak: Letter to G. F. Ustinov'. Letter of 20 April 1926 to M. I. Tsvetaeva, *DLDN*, 6 (1987). 258–9. See also *Briefwechsel*, 83–7. (Letter exerpted only in 'Iz perepiski Ril'ke, Tsvetaevoi i Pasternaka', [1978], 240–1.)

81 See Pasternak's letters of 14 June and 1 July 1926, and Tsvetaeva's of 1 July 1926, *DLDN*, 8 (1987), 258–61, 262–6, 267–8; 'Iz perepiski Ril'ke, Tsvetaevoi i Pasternaka', 272–8.

82 Letter of 30–31 July 1926 to M. I. Tsvetaeva, *DLDN*, 9 (1987), 226–8.

83 Letter of 20 April 1926 to M. I. Tsvetaeva, *DLDN*, 6 (1987), 258–9.

84 Letter of 5 June 1926 to M. I. Tsvetaeva, *DLDN*, 8 (1987), 254.

85 *Ibid.*, 263.
86 *DLDN*, 9 (1987), 223–4.
87 M. I. Tsvetaeva, letter of 10 July 1926 to B. L. Pasternak, *DLDN*, 9 (1987), 221.
88 See *ibid.*, 225. On the 1926 episode of Pasternak and Tsvetaeva's relations, see also Karlinsky, *Marina Tsvetaeva*, 161–9.
89 Letters of 22, 26, and 28 June 1926 to Evgeniya Pasternak.
90 *DZh*, 63.
91 Letter of 27 July 1926 to Zh. L. Pasternak (APT). Letter of 10 August 1926 to Evgeniya Pasternak. 'Pis'ma k M. A. Voloshinu i O. D. Forsh', 195–6.
92 Letter of 11 July 1926 to M. I. Tsvetaeva, *DLDN*, 9 (1987), 224.
93 Letter of 12 August 1926 to Evgeniya Pasternak, quoted in 'Iz perepiski s pisatelyami', 666.
94 *DLDN*, 9 (1987), 224.
95 *Perepiska*, 134.
96 Vil'mont, 'Boris Pasternak. Vospominaniya i mysli', 192. Exactly how often the pilgrimage to Leningrad and Bologoe occurred is open to question.
97 O. Mandel'shtam, *Sobranie sochinenii*, III, 242.
98 Letter of 21 October 1926 to O. M. Freidenberg, *Perepiska*, 96–7.
99 Evgeniya Pasternak, letter to 9 August 1926 to R. N. Lomonosova (LRA).
100 Letter of 21 October 1926 to O. M. Freidenberg, *Perepiska*, 99–100.

14 BREACHES, LOSSES, AND LYRIC REVIVAL

1 *DLDN*, 9 (1987), 234.
2 M. I. Tsvetaeva, letter of 1 January 1927 to B. L. Pasternak, *DLDN*, 9 (1987) 234–5. See also *Briefwechsel*, 248–51; *DLDN*, 9 (1987), 236.
3 *Ibid.*, 236–7.
4 *Ibid.*, 237ff. 'O sebe i o chitatelyakh', 4.
5 *Briefwechsel*, 260–1. M. I. Tsvetaeva, letter of 5 February 1928 to L. O. Pasternak, in Tsvetaeva, *Neizdannye pis'ma*, 256.
6 *Briefwechsel*, 268. See bibliography in Karlinsky, *Marina Cvetaeva*, 291–7.
7 Letter of 30 July 1926 to M. I. Tsvetaeva, *DLDN*, 9 (1987), 226.
8 Mayakovsky, *Polnoe sobranie sochinenii*, XII, 79. Fleishman, *Boris Pasternak v dvadtsatye gody*, 54. Karlinsky, *Marina Cvetaeva*, 77–8.
9 Letter of 26 March 1928 to V. E. Meierkhol'd, in Meierkhol'd, *Perepiska*, 278–9.
10 Katanyan, 'O Mayakovskom i Pasternake', 503.
11 Letter of 19 May 1926 to R. N. Lomonosova (LRA).
12 V. P. Polonsky, 'Lef ili Blef?', *Izvestiya*, 27 February 1927.
13 V. P. Polonsky, 'Blef prodolzhaetsya', *Novyi mir*, 5 (1927), 149.
14 Fleishman, *Boris Pasternak v dvadtsatye gody*, 63ff.
15 Letter of 1 June 1927 to V. P. Polonsky, 'Iz perepiski s pisatelyami', 696.
16 Letter of 17 May 1927 to R. N. Lomonosova (LRA).

17 'Iz perepiski s pisatelyami', 697.
18 Fleishman, *Boris Pasternak v dvadtsatye gody*, 70–2.
19 Katanyan, 'O Mayakovskom i Pasternake', 507.
20 Quoted in Fleishman, *Boris Pasternak v dvadtsatye gody*, 81–2.
21 Quoted in Katanyan, 'O Mayakovskom i Pasternake', 508.
22 Letter of 17 May 1927 to R. N. Lomonosova (LRA).
23 M. I. Tsvetaeva, letter of 5 February 1928 to L. O. Pasternak, in Tsvetaeva, *Neizdannye pis'ma*, 255–6.
24 Letter of 20 May 1927 to R. N. Lomonosova (LRA).
25 Letter of 12 April 1927 to R. N. Lomonosova (LRA).
26 L. O. Pasternak, letter of 25 October 1926 to B. L. and A. L. Pasternak, *Leonid Osipovich Pasternak 1862–1945*, [19].
27 Letter of 12 April 1927 to R. N. Lomonosova (LRA).
28 Letter of 20 May 1927 to R. N. Lomonosova (LRA).
29 Letter of 13 July 1927 to Zh. L. Pasternak (APT).
30 E. Chernyak, 'Pasternak'. Letter of 1 June 1927 to V. P. Polonsky, 'Iz perepiski s pisatelyami', 696.
31 Letter of 19 September 1927 to V. P. Polonsky, 'Iz perepiski s pisatelyami', 698–9.
32 Letter of 29 August 1927 to S. A. Obradovich, 'Iz perepiski s pisatelyami', 719. 'K oktyabr'skoi godovshchine', *Soch. I*, 255–9; *SP*, 228–32.
33 Letter of 29 August 1927 to S. A. Obradovich, 'Iz perepiski s pisatelyami', 719.
34 Letter of 30 September 1927 to L. O. and R. I. Pasternak (APT). See also *Perepiska*, 101–3.
35 On Pasternak and Erlikh, see G. McVay, 'Pasternak and Other Poets: Unpublished Texts', *Journal of Russian Studies*, 47 (1984), 30.
36 Letter of 27 November 1927 to R. N. Lomonosova (LRA).
37 Zh. L. Pasternak, letter of 21 April 1926 to B. L. Pasternak, *Briefwechsel*, 284–5. Letter of 15 November 1927 to S. D. Spassky, 'Iz pisem B. Pasternaka k S. Spasskomu', 166.
38 Letter of 5 December 1927 to L. O. and R. I. Pasternak (APT).
39 Letter of 27–8 December 1927 to L. O. and R. I. Pasternak (APT).
40 Letter of 19 September 1927 to V. P. Polonsky, 'Iz perepiski s pisatelyami', 697–8.
41 Letter of 28 October 1927 to R. N. Lomonosova (LRA).
42 'Iz pisem B. Pasternaka k S. Spasskomu', 166.
43 'O sebe i o chitatelyakh', 4.
44 Fleishman, *Boris Pasternak v dvadtsatye gody*, chs. 8–11, *passim*.
45 Letter of 24 August 1928 to L. O. and R. I. Pasternak (APT).
46 This connection is explored in some detail in R. Miller-Budnitskaya, 'O filosofiii iskusstva B. Pasternaka i R. M. Ril'ke', *Zvezda*, 5 (1932), 160–8, and Livingstone, 'Ril'ke i Pasternak', in Aucouturier (ed.), *Boris Pasternak 1890–1960*, 431–40, and 'Some Affinities in the Prose of the Poets Rilke and

Pasternak', *Forum for Modern Language Studies*, 19 no. 3 (July 1983), 274–84.

47 Maguire, *Red Virgin Soil*, 218. Fleishman, *Boris Pasternak v dvadtsatye gody*, 218.

48 'O sebe i o chitatelyakh', 4–5.

49 N. Mandel'shtam, *Vospominaniya*, 120.

50 *Perepiska*, 109.

51 'Pis'mo Yu. I. Yurkunu', 190.

52 Letter of 2 July 1926 to M. I. Tsvetaeva, *DLDN*, 8 (1987), 264.

53 On Pasternak's relations with Polonsky, see: 'Iz perepiski s pisatelyami', 684–7; Fleishman, *Boris Pasternak v dvadtsatye gody*, 57–8.

54 Letter of 10 October 1927 to A. M. Gor'ky, 'Gor'ky – B. L. Pasternak', 297–8.

55 *Ibid.*, 304.

56 On Fedin, see above, 356; see letter of 1 February 1927 to O. M. Forsh, 'Pis'ma k M. A. Voloshinu i O. M. Forsh', 198. Letter of 22 December 1928 to S. D. Spassky, 'Iz pisem B. Pasternaka k S. Spasskomu', 169.

57 Letter of 13 October 1927 to A. M. Gor'ky, 'Gor'ky – B. L. Pasternak', 298–300; see also 'Boris Pasternak v perepiske s Maksimom Gor'kim', 266–7, 271ff.

58 A. M. Gor'ky, letter of 19 October 1927 to B. L. Pasternak, 'Gor'ky – B. L. Pasternak', 301–2; see also 308.

59 Letter of 12 April 1927 to R. N. Lomonosova (LRA).

60 See *Letopis' zhizni i tvorchestva A. M. Gor'kogo*, vyp. 3, 1917–1929 (Moscow, 1959), 617, 628.

61 Katanyan, 'O Mayakovskom i Pasternake', 510.

62 Quoted in Fleishman, *Boris Pasternak v dvadtsatye gody*, 89. Katanyan, 'O Mayakovskom i Pasternake', 503.

63 Letter of 18 June 1928 to Evgeniya Pasternak (on holiday at Gelendzhik). A. M. Gor'ky, letter of June (?) 1930 to B. L. Pasternak, 'Boris Pasternak v perepiske s Maksimom Gor'kim', 281. See also V.K. 'V redaktsii "Krasnoi novi"', *Chitatel' i pisatel'*, 24 (16 June 1928), 4.

64 Letter of 19 June 1928 to Evgeniya Pasternak.

65 Letter of 15 June 1928 to R. N. Lomonosova (LRA).

66 Letters of 27 November 1927 and 14 April 1928 to R. N. Lomonosova (LRA). Letter of 16 November 1928 to O. M. Freidenberg, *Perepiska*, 115–17. Letter of 3 January 1928 to S. D. Spassky, 'Iz pisem B. Pasternaka k S. Spasskomu', 166. Letter of 5 December 1927 to L. O. and R. I. Pasternak (APT).

67 Letter of 5 April 1928 to R. N. Lomonosova (LRA).

68 Letter of 16 November 1928 to O. M. Freidenberg, *Perepiska*, 117–18.

69 Letter of 19 January 1928 to L. O. Pasternak. Letter of 21 May 1928 to L. O, R. I. and Lydia Pasternak (APT). Engel'-Roginskaya, 'Yu. Engel'', 506.

70 Letter of 6 April 1928 to R. I. Pasternak. Letter of 11 December 1928 to L. O., R. I. and Lydia Pasternak (APT).
71 Letter of 20 May 1928 to O. M. Freidenberg, *Perepiska*, 111.
72 *Ibid.*, 108–9.
73 Letter of 5 June 1928 to Anna Osipovna Freidenberg, *Perepiska*, 112. Letter of 10 June 1928 to Evgeniya Pasternak. See also undated letter to Evgeniya Pasternak, 'Perepiska Borisa Pasternaka', 279.
74 Letter of (approx.) 20 July 1928 to V. P. and K. A. Polonsky, 'Iz perepiski s pisatelyami', 700.
75 See *ibid.*, 701. Postcard of 28 August 1928 to A. L. Pasternak.
76 See Hughes, 'Boris Pasternak i Marina Tsvetaeva', 290–8. Fleishman, *Boris Pasternak v dvadtsatye gody*, 162–70.
77 The form in which *Poverkh bar'erov* appears in *Soch.* and *SP* corresponds more or less to this revised 1929 edition. For general discussion of the revisions see: Barnes, 'The Poetry of Boris Pasternak', ch. 6–7; Frolovskaya, 'Nekotorye nablyudeniya nad obraznoi sistemoi stikhotvornogo tsikla B. L. Pasternaka "Poverkh bar'erov"', *Kazakhsky gosudarstvennyi universitet im. S. M. Kirova. Studencheskie nauchnye raboty. Sbornik statei*, vyp. 1, ch. 2, Filologiya, Iskusstvo (Alma-Ata, 1970), 29–48. Fleishman *Boris Pasternak v dvadtsatye gody*, ch. 5.
78 'Zametki o peresechenii', 305. Also in *ChPV*, 162.
79 'Zametki o peresechenii', 306.
80 Gornung, 'Vospominaniya o Borise Pasternake'.
81 Letter of October–November 1929 to V. S. Pozner, 'Iz perepiski s pisatelyami', 727.
82 See n. 29 above.
83 *Rekomendatel'nyi byuletten' bibliograficheskogo otdela Glavpolitprosveta*, 20 (1929), 53.
84 Fleishman, *Boris Pasternak v dvadtsatye gody*, 95.
85 Mirsky, 'B. Pasternak. Rasskazy' (1925), 544. See also J. Pasternak, 'Patior', *The London Magazine*, 4 no. 6 (September, 1964), 42–4.
86 The specific relevance of *Okhrannaya gramota* to the period and manner of *Sestra moya zhizn'* is confirmed by the poem 'Vse naklonen'ya i zalogi…', *Soch. III*, 139–40; *SP*, 555–6.
87 Barnes, 'The Poetry of Boris Pasternak', ch. 6; and 189ff. E. V. Pasternak, 'Rabota Borisa Pasternaka nad tsiklom *Nachal'naya pora*', *Russkoe i zarubezhnoe yazykoznanie*, vyp. 4 (Alma Ata, 1970), 121–41.
88 For discussion of this poem see: A. Yakobson, 'Stikhotvorenie Borisa Pasternaka "Roslyi strelok, ostorozhnyi okhotnik"', *Kontinent*, 25 (1980), 323–33; V. Vishnyak, 'Pasternak's "Roslyi strelok" and the Tradition of the Hunter and the Duck', *Irish Slavonic Studies*, 7 (1986), 53–64.
89 Cf. an eidologically related poem 'Priroda – tot zhe Rim…' by Mandel'shtam, discussed in 'Zametki o peresechenii', 284. 'Kogda smertel'nyi tresk sosny skripuchei…' is discussed in Yu. I. Levin, 'Razbor odnogo malopopu-

lyarnogo stikhotvoreniya B. Pasternaka', *Russian Literature*, 6 no. 1 (January 1978), 39–46. See *Soch. III*, 136–7; *SP*, 551–2.

90 'Iz perepiski s pisatelyami', 657–8. Following Pasternak's letter of 5 April 1928 Lomonosova had contacted Tsvetaeva and was assisting her financially; see Karlinsky, *Marina Tsvetaeva*, 174.

91 See E. Farino, 'Dva poeticheskikh portreta', in Nilsson (ed.), *Art, Society, Revolution*, 60–3.

92 See Fleishman, *Boris Pasternak v dvadtsatye gody*, 119–23, on this episode. The poem concerned (*Soch. III*, 134) is discussed above, 290.

93 See N. Mandel'shtam, *Vospominaniya*, 112–13, 115–19. See above, p. 252.

Bibliography

The following is not a complete bibliography of literature by or about Pasternak. It is confined to works specifically referred to in the text and reference notes, and in general the works listed relate to the period of Pasternak's biography up to 1928. More exhaustive documentation and literary-critical commentary on many of the topics discussed can be found in the various specialised publications indicated, particularly in the following book-length studies: Aucouturier (ed.) (1979), Barnes (1969), Fleishman (1977, 1981), Gifford (1977), Hughes (1974), Mallac (1981), Nilsson (ed.) (1976), Proyart (1964). Bibliographical lists of works by Pasternak, with full publication details, can be found in the collected editions given below.

WORKS BY BORIS PASTERNAK

Editions referred to (in order of publication)

Poverkh bar'erov. Moscow, 1917.
Doktor Zhivago. Milan, 1957.
Sochineniya, ed. G. P. Struve and B. A. Filipov, 3 vols. Ann Arbor, Michigan, 1961.
Stikhotvoreniya i poemy, ed. L. A. Ozerov. Moscow-Leningrad, 1965.
Vozdushnye puti. Proza raznykh let, ed. E. B. Pasternak and E. V. Pasternak. Moscow, 1982.
Izbrannoe v dvukh tomakh, ed. E. B. Pasternak and E. V. Pasternak. Moscow, 1985.

Works not published in collected editions

'Boris Pasternak o sebe i o chitatelyakh', *Chitatel' i pisatel'*, 4–5 (11 February 1928); reprinted in *Grani*, 53 (1963), 76–9.
'Vladimir Mayakovsky, *Prostoe kak mychanie*. Petrograd 1916'. Published together with 'Zametki perevodchika' and 'Shopen' by E. B. Pasternak, under the title 'Kriticheskie pis'ma', *Literaturnaya Rossiya*, 19 March 1965.
'Vassermanova reaktsiya'. *Rukonog*, sbornik stikhov i kritiki. Moscow, 1914, 33–8; reprinted in Markov (1967), 112–17.
'K kharakteristike Bloka', published with commentary by E. V. Pasternak under the title 'Pasternak o Bloke', *Blokovsky sbornik II*. Trudy vtoroi nauchnoi

Bibliography

konferentsii, posvyashchennoi zhizni i tvorchestvu A. A. Bloka. Tartu, 1972, 447–53.
'Retsenziya na knigu izbrannykh stikhov Anny Akhmatovoi', *Russian Literature Triquarterly*, 9 (Spring 1974), 531–2.
'Istoriya odnoi kontroktavy', *Slavica Hierosolymitana*, 1 (1977), 257–92.
'O predmete i metode psikhologii', *Slavica Hierosolymitana*, 4 (1979), 274–85.
Additional poems, prose fiction, articles, translations, etc., are contained in the following items listed in the general bibliography section: Barnes (1977, 1978, 1979, 1984), Chudakova (1971), Djurčinov (1974), Fleishman (1971, *Stat'i* 1977, 1981), Katanyan ('Ne tol'ko vospominaniya', 1975), Ljunggren (1984), E. B. Pasternak (1977, 1978, 1981), E. V. Pasternak (1969, 1972, 1976, 1977), Rannit (1984), Rashkovskaya (1984), Salys (1986), Simplicio (1979).

Correspondence

'Three Letters', publ. Stephen Spender, *Encounter*, 15 no.2 (August 1960), 3–6.
'Gor'ky – B. L. Pasternak', *Literaturnoe nasledstvo*, 70 (1963), 295–310.
'Iz pisem B. Pasternaka k S. Spasskomu', publ. V. Spasskaya, *Voprosy literatury*, 9 (1969), 165–81.
'Chudo poeticheskogo voploshcheniya', publ. E. B. Pasternak, *Voprosy literatury*, 9 (1972), 139–71.
'Pis'mo Yu.I. Yurkunu', *Glagol*, 1 (1977), 189–93.
'Iz perepiski Ril'ke, Tsvetaevoi i Pasternaka v 1926 godu', introd. L. Ozerov, publ. K. M. Azadovsky, E. B. and E. V. Pasternak, *Voprosy literatury*, 4 (1978), 233–81.
'Perepiska Borisa Pasternaka', publ. Elliott Mossman and Michel Aucouturier, *Revue des études slaves*, tome 53 fascicule 2 (1981), 267–91.
'Pis'ma k M. A. Voloshinu i O. D. Forsh', ed. E. B. and E. V. Pasternak, *Ezhegodnik rukopisnogo otdela Pushkinskogo doma 1979*. Leningrad, 1981, 191–8.
'Iz perepiski s pisatelyami', publ. E. B. and E. V. Pasternak, *Literaturnoe nasledstvo*, 93 (1983), 649–737.
Rainer Maria Rilke, Marina Zwetajewa, Boris Pasternak. *Briefwechsel*. Ed. Jewgenij Pasternak, Jelena Pasternak and Konstantin M. Asadowskij; trans. Heddy Pross-Weerth. Frankfurt, 1983.
'Boris Pasternak v perepiske s Maksimom Gor'kim', publ. E. B. and E. V. Pasternak, *Izvestiya Akademii Nauk SSSR (Seriya literatury i yazyka)*, 45 no.3 (1986), 261–83.
'Dykhanie liriki. Iz perepiski R. M. Ril'ke, M. Tsvetaevoi i B. Pasternaka v 1926 godu', publ. K. Azadovsky, E. B. and E. V. Pasternak, *Druzhba narodov*, 6 (1987), 245–62; 7 (1987), 246–62; 8 (1987), 247–68; 9 (1987), 219–46.
Additional items of correspondence are contained in the following publications listed alphabetically in the general bibliography section: Barnes (1972,

Bibliography

1981), Djurčinov (1971), Efron (1979), Fleishman (1979, 1981, 1984), Kozovoi (1986), Meierkhol'd (1976), Mints (1975), E. V. Pasternak ('Pasternak i Bryusov', 1977), Proyart (1964), Rashkovskaya (1982), Salys (1988), Schweitzer (1963), 'Zametki o peresechenii biografii...' (1981), Zamoyska (1961).

Musical works

Prelude (1906). Published in Barnes, C. J. 'Boris Pasternak, the Musician' (1977), 330–35; also Barnes, C. J. 'Pasternak as Composer' (1977), 22–5; see also under Ashkenazy, V. and Voskobojnikov, V. (1983).
Sonata for Piano, ed. N. Bogoslovsky. Moscow, 1979.
'Con moto' (1906). Published in Barnes, C. J. 'Boris Pasternak as Composer' (1982), 14.

SECONDARY WORKS

Aduev, N., i Argo. 'Seren'kii kozlik'. *Rossiya*, 2 (1922), 15.
'Kak rodilsya poet' (Anketa). *Rossiya*, 3 (1922), 21.
Akhmatova, A. *Sochineniya*, ed. G. P. Struve and B. A. Filippov, 2 vols. Washington DC: I, 1965; II, 1968.
Aleksandr Nikolaevich Skryabin 1915–1940. Sbornik k 25-letiyu so dnya smerti. Moscow-Leningrad, 1940.
Al'shvang, A. *Izbrannye sochineniya*, 2 vols. Moscow, 1964.
Andreev, V. *Istoriya odnogo puteshestviya*. Moscow, 1974.
Anisimov, Yu. *Obitel'*. Moscow, 1913.
Anisimov [translator] see also under Ril'ke.
Annenkov, Yu. *Dnevnik moikh vstrech*, 2 vols. New York, 1966.
Antokol'sky, P. 'Dve vstrechi', in Reformatskaya (ed.) (1963), 145–50.
Argo [see Aduev].
Arvatov, Z. 'Nollendorfplattskafe', *Grani*, 41 (1959), 106–22.
Aseev, N. Preface in Boris Pasternak, *Bliznets v tuchakh*. Moscow, 1914.
'Pis'ma o poezii ("Sestra moya zhizn' " Pasternaka)', *Krasnaya nov'*, 3 (1922), 248–53.
'Organizatsiya rechi (Boris Pasternak, "Temy i variatsii")', *Pechat' i revolyutsiya*, 6 (1923), 71–8.
Sobranie sochinenii, 5 vols. Moscow, 1963–4.
Aseeva, K. M. 'Iz vospominanii', in Aseeva, K. M. and Petrovskaya, O. G. (eds.) (1980), 12–34.
Aseeva, K. M. and Petrovskaya, O. G. (eds.), *Vospominaniya o Nikolae Aseeve*. Moscow, 1980.
Ashkenazy, V. and Voskobojnikov, V. 'Pasternak inedito', *Piano Time* (Milan), 7–8 (October 1983), 27–31.
Ashukin, N. 'Sovremennost' v literature', *Novaya russkaya kniga*, 6 (1922), 4–6.

Bibliography

Asmus, V. 'Filosofiya i estetika russkogo simvolizma', *Literaturnoe nasledstvo*, 27–8 (1937), 1–53.

Aucouturier, M. *Pasternak par lui-même*. Paris, 1963.

'The Legend of the Poet and the Image of the Actor in the Short Stories of Pasternak', *Studies in Short Fiction*, 3 no.2 (Winter 1966), 225–35.

Aucouturier, M. (ed.), *Boris Pasternak 1890–1960. Colloque de Cérisy-la-Salle*. Paris, 1979.

Aucouturier, M. and Mossman, M. (eds.). 'Perepiska Borisa Pasternaka', *Revue des études slaves*, tome 53 fascicule 2 (1981), 267–91.

Azadovsky, K. M., and Chertkov, L. 'Russkie vstrechi Ril'ke', in R. M. Ril'ke, *Vorpsvede, Ogyust Roden, Pis'ma, Stikhi*. Moscow, 1971, 357–85.

Azadovsky [see also under Correspondence in Works by Boris Pasternak].

Bachmann, O. *Rosa Koffman: Eine biographische Skizze, nebst Auszug einiger Rezensionen*. Odessa, 1885.

Bakhrakh, A. *Po pamyati, po zapisyam. Literaturnye portrety*. Paris, 1980.

Baranova-Shestova, N. *Zhizn' L'va Shestova po perepiske i vospominaniyam sovremennikov*, 2 vols. Paris, 1983.

Barksdale, E. and Popp, D. 'Hamsun and Pasternak: The Development of Dionysian Tragedy', *Edda*, 6 (1976), 343–51.

Barnes, C. J. 'The Poetry of Boris Pasternak with Special Reference to the Period 1913–1917'. Ph.D. dissertation, Cambridge University, 1969.

'Boris Pasternak and Rainer Maria Rilke: Some Missing Links', *Forum for Modern Language Studies*, 8 no.1 (January 1972), 61–78.

'Boris Pasternak's Revolutionary Year', *Forum for Modern Language Studies*, 11 no.4 (October 1975), 46–60.

'Boris Pasternak: A Review of Nikolaj Aseev's "Oksana" ', *Slavica Hierosolymitana*, 1 (1977), 293–305.

'Pasternak as Composer and Scriabin Disciple', *Tempo*, 121 (June 1977), 13–25.

'Pasternak, the Musician-Poet and Composer', *Slavica Hierosolymitana*, 1 (1977), 317–35.

'Boris Pasternak and the Bogeyman of Russian Literature', *Russian Literature*, 6 no.1 (January 1978), 47–68.

'Pasternak i russkaya revolyutsiya', in Aucouturier (ed.) (1979), 315–27.

'The Original Text of "O skromnosti i smelosti" ', *Slavica Hierosolymitana*, 4 (1979), 294–303.

'A Letter from Boris Pasternak to Sergei Bobrov', *Slavica Hierosolymitana*, 5–6 (1981), 523–34.

'Boris Pasternak as Composer', *Performance*, 6 (April–May 1982), 12–14.

'Biography, Autobiography and "Sister Life": Some Problems in Chronicling Pasternak's Early Years', *Irish Slavonic Studies*, 4 (1983), 48–58.

'Poeziya i muzyka. Vtoraya stikhiya Borisa Pasternaka', *Russkaya mysl'*, 3455–6 (10 and 17 March 1983).

'Some Background Notes on Pasternak's Early Translations, and Two Notes by Pasternak on Hans Sachs and Ben Jonson', in *Aspects of Russia 1850–1970: Poetry, Prose and Public Opinion*, ed. William Harrison and Avril Pyman. Letchworth, 1984, 201–13.

'Notes on Pasternak', in *Boris Pasternak and His Times*, Berkeley Slavic Specialities. Oakland, CA, forthcoming 1989.

Barnes, C. J. (ed.) *Boris Pasternak. Collected Short Prose*. New York, 1977.

Barooshian, V. D. *Brik and Mayakovsky*. The Hague, 1978.

Barsov, V. 'O Pasternake. Moskovskie vpechatleniya', *Grani*, 40 (1958), 102–16.

Belyaev, V. *Samuil Evgen'evich Feinberg*. Moscow, 1927.

Bely, A. (pseudonym of Bugaev, B.N.) *Simvolizm*. Moscow, 1910.

Na rubezhe dvukh stoletii. Moscow-Leningrad, 1930.

Nachalo veka. Moscow-Leningrad, 1933.

Mezhdu dvukh revolyutsii. Moscow, 1934.

Bely [see also under Blok].

Belyutin, E. M. and Moleva, N. M. *Russkaya khudozhestvennaya shkola vtoroi poloviny XIX-nachala XX veka*. Moscow, 1967.

Berberova, N. *Kursiv moi. Avtobiografiya*, 2 vols. New York, 1983.

Bethea, D. M. *Khodasevich. His Life and Art*. Princeton, NJ, 1983.

Blok, A. *Sobranie sochinenii*, 8 vols. Moscow-Leningrad, 1960–63.

Blok, A. and Bely, A. *Perepiska*. Moscow, 1940.

Bobrov, S. 'O liricheskoi teme', *Trudy i dni*, 1–2 (1913), 116–37.

'Russkaya poeziya v 1914 godu', *Sovremennik*, 1 (January 1915), 218–26.

'Kaznachei poslednei iz planet' (manuscript 1916).

'Aleksandr Blok, "Sedoe utro. Stikhotvoreniya". Izd. Alkonost. Peterburg, 1920', *Pechat' i revolyutsiya*, 1 (1921), 146–7.

Bochenski, I. M. *Contemporary European Philosophy*, trans. D. Nicholl and K. Aschenbrenner. Berkeley and Los Angeles, 1964.

Bodin, P. A. 'God, Tsar and Man: Pasternak's poem *Artillerist*', *Scottish Slavonic Review*, 6 (1986), 69–80.

Bowers, F. *Scriabin*, 2 vols. Tokyo-Palo Alto, 1969.

Brik, L.Yu. 'Chuzhie stikhi: glava iz vospominanii', in Reformatskaya (ed.) (1963), 328–54.

Brodsky, P. P. 'On Daring to Be a Poet: Rilke and Marina Cvetaeva', *Germano-Slavica*, 3 no.4 (Fall 1980), 261–9.

Brown, E. J. *Mayakovsky: A Poet in the Revolution*. Princeton, NJ, 1973.

Bryugel', F. (Fritz Brügel). 'Razgovor s Borisom Pasternakom', *Voprosy literatury*, 7 (1979), 179–82.

Bryusov, V. 'God russkoi poezii (aprel' 1913 g. – aprel' 1914 g.). Porubezhniki'. *Russkaya mysl'*, 6 (June 1914), section 2, 14–18.

'Na smert' A. N. Skryabina', *Muzyka*, 220 (1915), 281.

'Vchera, segodnya i zavtra russkoi poezii', *Pechat' i revolyutsiya*, 7 (1922), 38–68.

Sobranie sochinenii, 7 vols. Moscow, 1973–5.

Buckman, D. *Leonid Pasternak: A Russian Impressionist 1862–1945*. London, 1974.

Bykov, N. 'Po pravu pamyati', *Ogonek*, 24 (1987), 6–7.

Čertkov [see Chertkov].

Chelionati (pseudonym of Samuil Vermel'). 'Liriki', in *Moskovskie mastera*. Moscow, 1916, 79–83.

Chernyak, E. B. 'Pasternak' (manuscript 1962).

Chernyak, Ya. 'Iz dnevnika' (manuscript).

'B. Pasternak. "Sestra moya zhizn'"'. Berlin, Grzhebin, 1922', *Pechat' i revolyutsiya*, 6 (1922), 303–4.

Chertkov, L. *Rilke in Russland auf Grund neuer Materialien*. Vienna, 1975.

'K voprosu o literaturnoi genealogii Pasternaka', in Aucouturier (ed.) (1979), 55–62.

Chertkov [see also under Azadovsky].

'Chto govoryat pisateli o postanovlenii TsK RKP', *Zhurnalist*, 8–9 (1925), 10–11.

Chudakova, M. O. 'Novye avtografy B. L. Pasternaka', *Zapiski otdela rukopisei*, vypusk 32 (Gos. Biblioteka im. Lenina). Moscow, 1971, 208–19.

Chukovskaya, L. *Zapiski ob Anne Akhmatovoi*, I. Paris, 1976.

Chukovsky, K. 'Akhmatova i Mayakovsky', *Dom iskusstv*, 1 (1921), 23–42.

'Iz vospominanii', *Yunost'*, 8 (1965), 66–70.

'Iz dnevnika (1919–1921)', *Voprosy literatury*, 10 (1980), 284–313.

Dagilaiskaya, E. 'Iz proshlogo fortepiannogo ispolnitel'stva i fortepiannoi pedagogiki v Odesse', *Masterstvo muzykal'nogo ispolnitel'stva*, vyp. 2. Moscow, 1976, 246–88.

Dashkov, L. '1905 god'. *Kniga i profsoyuzy*, 10 (1927), 29.

Dauetite (Daujotytė), V. *Yurgis Baltrushaitis*. Vilnius, 1983.

Del'son, V. *Skryabin. Ocherki zhizni i tvorchestva*. Moscow, 1971.

Dinershtein, E. A. 'Izdatel'skaya deyatel'nost' V. V. Mayakovskogo (k 75-letiyu so dnya rozhdeniya)', *Kniga issledovaniya i materialy*, sbornik XVII. Moscow, 1968.

Djurčinov, M. 'Edno nepoznato pismo do Boris Pasternak', *Godishen zbornik na filosofskiot fakultet na Universitetot vo Skopje*, 23 (1971), 435–40.

'Dva priloga za B. L. Pasternak', *Godishen zbornik na filosofskiot fakultet na Universitetot vo Skopje*, 26 (1974), 359–65.

Dmitriev, Yu.A. 'Tsirk', in *Russkaya khudozhestvennaya kul'tura kontsa XIX-nachala XX veka (1908–1917)*, III. Moscow, 1977, 228–39.

Dobrovein, M. A. *Stranitsy zhizni Isaya Dobroveina*. Moscow, 1972.

Döring, J. R. *Die Lyrik Pasternaks in den Jahren 1928–1934*. Munich, 1973.

Efron, A. *Stranitsy vospominanii*. Paris, 1979.

Egyx (pseudonym of V. Shershenevich). 'Boris Pasternak. "Bliznets v tuchakh"', in *Futuristy. Pervyi zhurnal russkikh futuristov*. Moscow, 1914, 140–1.

Engel', Yu.D. 'A. N. Skryabin', *Muzykal'nyi sovremennik*, 4–5 (1916), 5–96.

Bibliography

Engel', Yu.D. *Glazami sovremennika. Izbrannye stat'i o russkoi muzyke 1898–1918*. Moscow, 1971.

Engel'-Roginskaya, A. 'Yu. Engel' (Vospominaniya docheri)', in Yu.D. Engel' (1971), 493–507.

Erenburg, I. G. *Portrety russkikh poetov*. Berlin, 1922.

'B. Pasternak. "Sestra moya zhizn'"'. Berlin, Izd-vo Grzhebina, 1922', *Novaya russkaya kniga*, 6 (1922), 10–12.

Lyudi, gody, zhizn', I, Kniga pervaya i vtoraya, I. Moscow, 1961.

Erlich, V. *Russian Formalism: History – Doctrine*, 3rd ed. The Hague-Paris, 1969.

'"Strasti razryady". Zametki o "Marburge"', in Aucouturier (ed.) (1979), 281–8.

Erofeev, V. '"Ostaetsya odno: proizvol". (Filosofiya odinochestva i literaturno-esteticheskoe kredo L'va Shestova)', *Voprosy literatury*, 10 (1975), 153–88.

Farino, E. 'Dva poeticheskikh portreta', in Nilsson (ed.) (1976), 52–66.

Fedorchuk, Yu. *Moskva v kol'tse sadovykh*. Moscow, 1983.

Fitzpatrick, S. *The Commissariat of Enlightenment. Soviet Organisation of Education and the Arts under Lunacharsky. October 1917–1921*. Cambridge, 1970.

Fleishman, L. 'Neizvestnyi avtograf B. Pasternaka', *Materialy XXVI nauchnoi studencheskoi konferentsii. Literaturovedenie. Lingvistika*. Tartu, 1971, 34–7.

'Pervyi god "Tsentrifugi"', *Materialy XXVII nauchnoi studencheskoi konferentsii*. Tartu, 1972, 71–3.

'"Tsentrifuga" i V. Mayakovsky', *Materialy XXVII nauchnoi studencheskoi konferentsii*. Tartu, 1972, 73–6.

'B. Pasternak i A. Bely', *Russian Literature Triquarterly*, 13 (Fall 1975), 545–51.

'K publikatsii pis'ma L. O. Pasternaka k Byaliku', *Slavica Hierosolymitana*, I (1977), 309–16.

Stat'i i Pasternake. Bremen 1977.

'Fragmenty "futuristicheskoi" biografii Pasternaka', *Slavica Hierosolymitana*, 4 (1979), 79–113.

'Iz pasternakovskoi perepiski', *Slavica Hierosolymitana*, 5–6 (1981), 535–42.

Boris Pasternak v dvadtsatye gody. Munich, 1981.

Boris Pasternak v tridtsatye gody. Jerusalem, 1984.

'Sredi filosofov (Iz kommentariev k *Okhrannoi gramote* Pasternaka)', in Morris Halle *et al.* (eds.), *Semiosis: Semiotics and the History of Culture. In honorem Georgii Lotman*. Ann Arbor, MI, 1984, 70–6.

Fokht, B. A. 'Filosofiya muzyki A. N. Skryabina' (manuscript 1941).

Frank, V. 'Realizm chetyrekh izmerenii', *Mosty* (1959), 189–209. Reprinted in his *Izbrannye stat'i*, ed. L. Schapiro. London, 1974, 62–85.

'Vodyanoi znak (Poeticheskoe mirovozzrenie Pasternaka)' in *Sbornik statei* (1962), 240–52.

Frolovskaya, T. 'Nekotorye nablyudeniya nad obraznoi sistemoi stikhotvornogo tsikla B. Pasternaka "Poverkh bar'erov"', *Kazakhsky gosudarstvennyi univer-sitet im. S. M. Kirova. Studencheskie nauchnye raboty. Sbornik statei*, vyp.1, ch.2. Filologiya, Iskusstvo. Alma-Ata, 1970, 29–48.

Gaigalas, R. E. S. 'Boris Pasternak's "Temy i variacii": A Commentary'. Ph.D. dissertation, Harvard University, 1978.

Gellershtein, S. G. 'Kommentarii', in 'Boris Pasternak o predmete i metode psikhologii', *Slavica Hierosolymitana*, 4 (1979), 274–85.

Gifford, H. *Boris Pasternak: A Critical Study.* Cambridge, 1977.

Gonta, M. P. 'Betkhoven' (manuscript 1967).

Gor'ky, A. M. *Sobranie sochinenii*, 30 vols. Moscow, 1949–56.

Gor'ky [see also under Correspondence in Works by Boris Pasternak].

Gornung, L. 'Vospominaniya o Borise Pasternake' (manuscript 1982).

Gorodetsky, S. M. 'Na styke', in *Styk. Pervyi sbornik Moskovskogo tsekha poetov.* Moscow, 1925, 13–19.

Gronicka, A. von. 'Rilke and the Pasternaks', *Germanic Review*, 27 (1952), 260–71.

Gur'ev, A. *Bezotvetnoe.* Moscow, n.d.

Haight, A. *Anna Akhmatova: A Poetic Pilgrimage.* New York-London, 1976.

Hingley, R. *Nightingale Fever: Russian Poets in Revolution.* New York, 1981.
Pasternak: A Biography. London, 1983.

Hoffmann, S. 'Scythian Theory and Literature, 1917–1924'. in Nilsson (ed.) (1979), 138–64.

Hughes, O. R. 'Boris Pasternak i Marina Tsvetaeva (k istorii druzhby)', *Vestnik RSKhD*, 100 (1971), 281–305.
The Poetic World of Boris Pasternak. Princeton-London, 1974.
'Stikhotvorenie "Marburg" i tema "vtorogo rozhdeniya". Nablyudeniya nad raznymi redaktsiyami stikhotvoreniya "Marburg"', in Aucouturier (ed.) (1979), 289–301.

Ioffe, M. 'Nachalo', *Vremya i my*, 19 (1977), 165–99; 20 (1977), 163–92.

Ivanov, G. 'Ispytanie ognem', *Apollon*, 8 (1914), 55.

Ivanov, V. 'Pamyati Skryabina', *Muzyka*, 220 (1915), 289.

Ivinskaya, O. *V plenu vremeni. Gody s Borisom Pasternakom.* Paris, 1978.

Ivnev, R. *U podnozhiya Mtatsmindy. Memuary, novelly raznykh let. Povest'.* Moscow, 1973.

Jangfeldt, B. 'Russian Futurism 1917–1919', in Nilsson (ed.) (1979), 106–37.

Jangfeldt, B. (ed.). *V. V. Mayakovsky i L.Yu. Brik: perepiska 1915–1930.* Stockholm, 1982.

Jangfeldt, B. and Nilsson, N. A. (eds.). *Vladimir Majakovskij. Memoirs and Essays.* Stockholm, 1975.

Karlinsky, S. *Marina Cvetaeva: Her Life and Art.* Berkeley, 1966.
Marina Tsvetaeva: The Woman, Her World and Her Poetry. Cambridge, 1985.

Katanyan, V. A. *Mayakovsky. Literaturnaya khronika*, 4th ed. Moscow, 1961.
'Ne tol'ko vospominaniya', *Russian Literature Triquarterly*, 13 (Fall 1975), 477–86.

'O Mayakovskom i Pasternake', *Russian Literature Triquarterly*, 13 (Fall 1975), 499–518.

Kayden, E. M. (trans.). Boris Pasternak, *Poems*. Ann Arbor, MI, 1959.

Keldysh, Yu.V. 'Muzykal'naya polemika', in *Russkaya khudozhestvennaya kul'tura kontsa XIX-nachala XX veka (1908–1917)*, III. Moscow, 1977, 288–309.

Keys, R. J. [Kiiz] 'Pis'ma Andreya Belogo k A. S. Petrovskomu i E. N. Kezel'man', *Novyi zhurnal*, 122 (March 1976), 163–72.

Khardzhiev, N. 'Mayakovsky i zhivopis'', in *Mayakovsky. Materialy i issledovaniya*, ed. V. O. Pertsov and M. I. Serebryansky. Moscow, 1940, 337–400.

'Turne kubo-futuristov 1913–1914 gg.', in Pertsov and Serebryansky (eds.) (1940), 401–27.

Khardzhiev, N. with Trenin, V. *Poeticheskaya kul'tura Mayakovskogo*. Moscow, 1970.

Khodasevich, V. *Literaturnye stat'i i vospominaniya*. New York, 1954.

Kh'yuz [see Hughes].

Klychkov, S. 'Lysaya gora', *Krasnaya nov'*, 5 (1923), 387–90.

Koz'min, B. P. *Pisateli sovremennoi epokhi*. Moscow, 1928.

Kozovoi, V. (ed.). 'Iz perepiski B. Pasternaka i P. Suvchinskogo', *Revue des études slaves*, tome 58 fascicule 4 (1986), 637–48.

Krasil'nikov, V. 'Boris Pasternak', *Pechat' i revolyutsiya*, 5 (1927), 78–91.

Kratkaya Literaturnaya Entsiklopediya, 9 vols. Moscow, 1962–75.

Kruchenykh, A. *Izbrannoe*, ed. V. Markov. Munich, 1973.

Kryukova, A. M. 'Khlebnikov (Aseev i Khlebnikov)', *Literaturnoe nasledstvo*, 93 (1983), 506–16.

'"Razgovor s neizvestnym drugom" (Aseev i Pasternak)', *Literaturnoe nasledstvo*, 93 (1983), 516–30.

Kurlov, G. 'O Pasternake', *Russkaya mysl'*, 1288 (18 November 1958).

Kuzmin, M. 'Govoryashchie', *Zhizn' iskusstva*, 31 (8–15 August 1922); reprinted in his *Uslovnosti*. Petrograd, 1923, 158–61.

Lelevich, G. 'Gippokratovo litso', *Krasnaya nov'*, 1 (1925), 295–301.

Leonid Pasternak 1862–1945, catalogue. St Andrews, 1978.

Leonid Osipovich Pasternak 1862–1945, Katalog vystavki. Moscow, 1979.

Letopis' zhizni i tvorchestva A. M. Gor'kogo, III 1917–1929. Moscow, 1959.

Levin, Yu.I. 'Zametki o "Leitenante Shmidte" B. L. Pasternaka', in Nilsson (ed.) (1976), 85–161.

'Razbor odnogo malopopulyarnogo stikhotvoreniya B. Pasternaka', *Russian Literature*, 6 no.1 (January 1978), 39–46,

Levitsky, S. 'Rose Koffmann-Pasternak', in Mark (ed.) (1975), 11–26.

Lezhnev, A. 'Na pravom flange (o zhurnalakh "Rossiya" i "Russky sovremennik")'. *Pechat' i revolyutsiya*, 6 (1924), 123–30.

'Literaturnye zametki. Otzyv o "Spektorskom"', *Pechat' i revolyutsiya*, 8 (1925), 119–23.

'Uzel (o stikhakh literaturnogo ob''edineniya "Uzel")', *Krasnaya nov'*, 8 (1926), 230–2.

'Boris Pasternak', *Krasnaya nov'*, 8 (1926), 205–19; reprinted in his *Sovremenniki*. Moscow, 1927, 32–54.

'Boris Pasternak (k vykhodu "Dvukh knig" i "1905 goda")', in his *Literaturnye budni*. Moscow, 1929, 310–13.

Lirika, Pervyi al'manakh. Moscow, 1913.

Literaturnoe Nasledstvo. 'Gor'ky i sovetskie pisateli. Neizdannaya perepiska', 70 (1963).

Livingstone, A. '"The Childhood of Luvers": An Early Story of Pasternak's', *Southern Review* (Adelaide), 1 (1963), 74–84.

'Pasternak's Early Prose', *AUMLA*, 22 (November 1964), 249–67.

'Wherefore Poet in Destitute Times', *PN Review*, 5 no.4 (1978), 14–18.

'Ril'ke i Pasternak', in Aucouturier (ed.) (1979), 431–40.

'Some Affinities in the Prose of the Poets Rilke and Pasternak', *Forum for Modern Language Studies*, 19 no.3 (July 1983), 274–84.

Lou Andreas-Salomé. London, 1984.

'Lou Andreas-Salomé and Boris Pasternak', *Blätter der Rilke-Gesellschaft*, 11–12 (1984–5), 91–99.

Pasternak on Art and Creativity. Cambridge, 1985.

Ljunggren, A. *Juvenilia. Boris Pasternak: 6 fragmentov o Relikvimini*. Stockholm, 1984.

Loks, K. G. 'B. Pasternak. "Rasskazy". Moskva, Krug, 1925', *Krasnaya nov'*, (1925), 286–7

'Povest' ob odnom desyatiletii (1907–1917)' (manuscript).

Lundberg, E. G. *Zapiski pisatelya 1917–1920*. Berlin, 1922; reprinted Leningrad, 1930.

MacDonald, H. *Skryabin*. London-Oxford, 1978.

Maguire, R. *Red Virgin Soil: Literature in the 1920's*. Princeton, 1968.

McVay, G. *Esenin: A Life*. Ann Arbor, MI, 1976.

'Pasternak and Other Poets: Unpublished Texts', *Journal of Russian Studies*, 47 (1984), 29–33.

Makedonskaya, E. *Ulitsa Volkhonka, 14*. Moscow, 1985.

Mallac, G. de. 'Pour une esthétique pasternakienne', *Problèmes soviétiques*, 7 (1964), 103–23.

'Zhivago versus Prometheus', *Books Abroad*, 44 (Spring 1970), 227–31.

'Pasternak and Religion', *Russian Review*, 32 no. 4 (October 1973), 360–75

'A Russian Impressionist: Leonid Osipovich Pasternak, 1862–1945', *California Slavic Studies*, 10 (1977), 87–120.

'Pasternak and Marburg', *Russian Review*, 38 no. 4 (October 1979), 421–33

Boris Pasternak: His Life and Art. Norman, OK, 1981.

Malmstad, J. E. 'Mixail Kuzmin: A Chronicle of His Life and Times', in Kuzmin, M.A., *Sobranie stikhov*, III. Munich, 1977, 7–319.

Mandel'shtam, N. *Vospominaniya*. New York, 1970.

Vtoraya kniga. Paris, 1972.

Mandel'shtam, O. *Sobranie sochinenii*, 3 vols. Washington-New York, 1964–9.

Sobranie sochinenii, I, 2nd edn revised and expanded. Washington, 1967.

Mark, P. J. (ed.). *Die Familie – La famille – The Family Pasternak*. Geneva, 1975.

Markov, V. *Russian Futurism: A History*. London, 1969.

Markov, V. (ed.). *Manifesty i programmy russkikh futuristov*. Munich, 1967.

Maslennikova, Z. A. 'Portret poeta. (Iz dnevnikovykh zapisei)', *Literaturnaya Gruziya*, 10–11 (1978), 267–93; 2 (1979), 132–54; 3 (1979), 137–54; 4 (1979), 137–54.

Mayakovsky, V. V. *Polnoe sobranie sochinenii*, 13 vols. Moscow, 1976.

Mayakovsky, V. V. (ed.). 'Traurnoe ura', *Nov'*, 119 (20 November 1914).

Meierkhol'd, V. E. *Perepiska 1896–1939*. Moscow, 1976.

Men'shutin, A. and Sinyavsky, A. *Poeziya pervykh let revolyutsii*. Moscow, 1964.

Meyer, A. '*Sestra moya – žizn''* von Boris Pasternak. *Analyse und Interpretation*. Munich, 1987.

Miller-Budnitskaya, R. 'O filosofii iskusstva B. Pasternaka i R. M. Ril'ke', *Zvezda*, 5 (1932), 160–8.

Minchenkov, Ya. D. *Vospominaniya o peredvizhnikakh*. Leningrad, 1963.

Mindlin, E. L. Neobyknovennye sobesedniki. Moscow, 1968.

Mints, Z. G. 'Pis'ma B. Pasternaka D. E. Maksimovu', *Tezisy I Vsesoyuznoi (III) konferentsii 'Tvorchestvo A. A. Bloka i russkaya kul'tura XX veka'*. Tartu, 1975, 11–16.

Mirsky, D. S. 'B. Pasternak. Rasskazy. "Krug". M.-L. 1925', *Sovremennye zapiski*, 25 (1925), 544–5.

'Boris Pasternak. Rasskazy. Izd. Krug. Moskva. 1925', *Blagonamerennyi*, 1 (1926), 168–9.

'The Present State of Russian Letters', *London Mercury*, 16 no. 93 (1927), 275–86.

'B. Pasternak. "Devyat'sot pyatyi god". M.-L. GIZ. 1927', *Versty*, 3 (1928), 150–4.

Mochul'sky, K. *Valery Bryusov*. Paris, 1962.

Moleva [see under Belyutin].

Mossman, E. 'Pasternak's Prose Style: Some Observations', *Russian Literature Triquarterly*, 1 (Fall 1971), 386–98.

'Pasternak's Short Fiction', *Russian Literature Triquarterly*, 2 (Winter 1972), 279–302.

Mossman [see also under Aucouturier and under Correspondence in Works by Boris Pasternak].

Muratova, K. D. 'Sovremennik', in *Russkaya literatura i zhurnalistika nachala XX veka*. Moscow, 1984, 162–201.

Muzykal'naya entsiklopediya, 6 vols. Moscow, 1973–82.

Nabokov, V. [see under Sirin]

Nei, A. (pseudonym of Josephine/Zhozefina Pasternak) *Koordinaty*. Berlin, n.d.

Nekrasov, N. A. *Polnoe sobranie sochinenii*, II. Moscow, 1948.

Nestyev, I. V. *Prokofiev*, trans. Florence Jonas. Stanford, CA-London, 1961.

Neznamov, P. M. 'Mayakovsky v dvadtsatykh godakh', in Reformatskaya (ed.) (1963), 355–91.

Nikulin, L. V. 'Vladimir Mayakovsky', in Reformatskaya (ed.) (1963), 494–511.

Nilsson, N. A. (ed.). *Boris Pasternak. Essays*. Stockholm, 1976.

Art, Society, Revolution. Russia 1917–1921. Stockholm, 1979.

Nilsson [see also under Jangfeldt].

Nivat, G. 'Trois correspondents d'Aleksandr Kusikov', *Cahiers du monde russe et soviétique*, 15 nos.1–2 (1974), 201–19.

O'Connor, K. T. 'Boris Pasternak's "Sestra moja žizn'": An Explication'. Ph.D. dissertation, Harvard University, 1972.

Pasternak's 'My Sister Life': The Illusion of Narrative. Ann Arbor, 1988.

Osborn, M. *Leonid Pasternak*. Warsaw, 1932.

Parnok, S. 'Pasternak i drugie', *Russky sovremennik*, (1924), 307–11.

Pasternak, A. 'Ma mère', in Mark (ed.) (1975), 27–42.

Vospominaniya. Munich, 1983.

Pasternak, E. B. 'Boris Pasternak. Istoriya odnoi kontroktavy', *Slavica Hierosolymitana*, 1 (1977), 251–6.

'O datirovke *Istorii odnoi kontroktavy* B. Pasternaka', *Slavica Hierosolymitana*, 3 (1978), 391.

'Boris Pasternak 1890–1960', *Den' poezii 1981*. Moscow, 1981.

[see also items listed in the first three sections of Works by Boris Pasternak]

Pasternak, E. V. 'Pervye opyty Borisa Pasternaka', *Trudy po znakovym sistemam IV*, Uchenye zapiski Tartuskogo Gosudarstvennogo Universiteta, vypusk 236 (1969), 239–81.

'Rabota Borisa Pasternaka nad tsiklom *Nachal'naya pora*', *Russkoe i zarubezhnoe yazykoznanie*, vyp. 4. Alma-Ata, 1970, 124–41.

'Iz pervykh prozaicheskikh opytov Borisa Pasternaka. Publikatsiya II', in Nilsson (ed.) (1976), 26–51.

'Iz rannikh prozaicheskikh opytov B. Pasternaka', *Pamyatniki kul'tury. Novye otkrytiya. Ezhegodnik 1976*. Moscow, 1977, 110–118.

'Pasternak i Bryusov. K istorii otnoshenii', *Russia. Rossiya*, 3 (1977), 239–65.

[See also items listed in the first three sections of Works by Boris Pasternak]

Pasternak, L. O. *Rembrandt i evreistvo v ego tvorchestve*. Berlin, 1923.

'Vier Fragmente aus meiner Selbstbiografie', in Osborn (1932).

Zapisi raznykh let. Moscow, 1975.

[see also below under: Pasternak, Zh.L., and Pasternak-Slater, L. L.]

Pasternak, J. 'Patior', *The London Magazine*, 6 (September 1964), 42–57.

'Neunzehnhundert Zwölf', *Alma Mater Philippina* (Wintersemester 1971–2), 40–3.

'Three Suns', in Mark (ed.) (1975), 7–9.

Pasternak, Zh. *Pamyati Pedro*. Paris, 1981.
[see also under Nei]
Pasternak, Zh. L. and Pasternak-Sleiter, L. L. 'Pis'mo L. O. Pasternaka k Byaliku', *Slavica Hierosolymitana*, 1 (1977), 306–8.
Pasternak-Slater, L. 'Letter to the Editor', *New York Times Book Review*, 29 October 1961.
Introduction, in Boris Pasternak, *Fifty Poems*, trans. Lydia Pasternak-Slater. London, 1963.
Before Sunrise. London, 1971.
Vspyshki magniya. Geneva, 1974.
'Boris and the Parents', in Mark (ed.) (1975), 107–15.
'Prix Nobel de littérature 1958', in Mark (ed.) (1975), 157–62.
Payne, R. *The Three Worlds of Boris Pasternak*. London, 1962.
Pertsov, V. 'Vymyshlennaya figura', *Na postu*, 1 (1924), 209–24.
'Novyi Pasternak', *Na literaturnom postu*, 2 (1927), 33–9.
Mayakovsky. Zhizn' i tvorchestvo (1893–1917). Moscow, 1969.
Peterson, R. E. 'Andrej Belyj and Nikolaj N. Vedenjapin', *Wiener Slawistischer Almanach*, 9 (1982), 111–17.
Petnikov, G. 'Borisu Pasternaku', *Raduga*, sbornik, book I, 1920, 12.
Petrovskaya, O. G. 'Nikolai Aseev', in Aseeva and Petrovskaya (eds.) (1980), 35–66.
[see also under Aseeva]
Petrovsky, D. V. *Izbrannoe*. Moscow, 1956.
Pitcher, H. *The Smiths of Moscow*. Cromer, 1984.
Plank, D. L. *Pasternak's Lyric: A Study of Sound and Imagery*. The Hague, 1966.
Plekhanova, R. M. ['Vospominaniya'], in *Aleksandr Nikolaevich Skryabin 1915–1940*. Moscow-Leningrad, (1940), 65–75.
Polikarpov, V. 'Fedor Raskol'nikov', *Ogonek*, 26 (1987), 4–7.
Polonsky, V. P. 'Lef ili Blef?', *Izvestiya*, 27 February 1927.
'Blef prodolzhaetsya', *Novyi mir*, 5 (1927), 147–67.
Popp [see under Barksdale]
Postupal'sky, I. 'Boris Pasternak. 'Devyat'sot pyatyi god'. Giz. M.-L. 1927', *Pechat' i revolyutsiya*, 8 (1927), 184–5.
Pozner, V. Review of *Rossiya*, no. 1, in *Dni*, 492 (1924), 10.
Pravdukhin, V. 'V bor'be za novoe iskusstvo', *Sibirskie ogni*, 5 (1922); reprinted in his *Literaturnaya sovremennost'*. Moscow, 1924, 130–37.
Proyart, J. *Pasternak*. Paris, 1964.
'Une amitié d'enfance', in Aucouturier (ed.) (1979), 517–20.
Put' osvobozhdeniya. Dvukhnedel'nyi istoriko-literaturno-khudozhestvennyi zhurnal, 1 (15 July 1917).
Pyman, A. *The Life of Aleksandr Blok. Volume II. The Release of Harmony, 1908–1921*. Oxford, 1980.
Raevsky-Kh'yuz/Raevsky-Hughes [see under Hughes].

Rait-Kovaleva, R. 'Misterium-Buff', *Literaturnyi sovremennik*, 4 (1940), 107–13.

Rait[-Kovaleva], R. 'Tol'ko vospominaniya', in Reformatskaya (ed.) (1963), 236–78.

'Vse luchshie vospominaniya', *Trudy po russkoi i slavyanskoi filologii. IX Literaturovedenie*. Uchenye zapiski Tartuskogo gosudarstvennogo universiteta, 184 (1966), 257–87; reprinted in Wright-Kovaleva (1967), *q.v.*.

Rammelmeyer, A. 'Die Philipps-Universität zu Marburg in der russischen Geistesgeschichte und schönen Literatur', *Mitteilungen. Universitätsbund Marburg*, Heft 2–3. Marburg, 1957, 70–81.

Rannit, A. 'Neizvestnyi Boris Pasternak v sobranii Tomasa P. Uitni', *Novyi zhurnal*, 156 (1984), 5–52.

Rashkovskaya, M. A. 'Poet v mire, mir v poete (Pis'ma B. L. Pasternaka k S. P. Bobrovu)', *Vstrechi s proshlym*. Moscow, 1982, 139–60.

Rashkovskaya, M. A., and Rashkovsky, E. B. 'Sonet Suinberna v perevode Borisa Pasternaka', *Isvestiya Akademii Nauk SSSR (Seriya literatury i yazyka)*, 43 no. 6 (1984), 544–50.

Reed, J. *Ten Days that Shook the World*. Harmondsworth, 1966.

Reformatskaya, N. V. (ed.), *V. Mayakovsky v vospominaniyakh sovremennikov*. Moscow, 1963.

Rilke [see under Correspondence in Works by Boris Pasternak].

Ril'ke, R. M. *Rasskazy o Gospode*, trans. Yu. Anisimov. Moscow, 1913.

Kniga chasov, trans. Yu. Anisimov. Moscow, 1913.

Rodionov, N. S. *Moskva v zhizni i tvorchestve L. N. Tolstogo*. Moscow, 1954.

Romm, A. 'B. Pasternak. "Sestra moya zhizn'". Berlin, Grzhebin, 1922', *Korabl'*, 1–2 (1923), 45–6.

Rukonog. Moscow, 1914.

Ruoff, Z. F. 'Pasternak i Ril'ke' (manuscript).

Russky Berlin 1921–1923, ed. L. Fleishman, M. Raeff, O. Raevsky-Hughes, N. Struve. Paris, 1983.

Sabaneev, L. *Vospominaniya o Skryabine*. Moscow, 1925.

Salys, R. '"Izmeritel'naja edinica russkoj žizni": Puškin in the Work of Boris Pasternak', *Russian Literature*, 9 (1986), 347–92.

'Leonid Pasternak: The Early Years', *International Programs Quarterly*, 2 nos 2–3 (1987), 28–33.

'Boris Pasternak: Letter to G. F. Ustinov', *Scottish Slavonic Review* (forthcoming 1989).

'P ris Pasternak on Leonid Pasternak and the Critics: Two Early Texts', *.ussian Language Journal* (forthcoming 1989).

'Exhibiting in Russia at the Turn of the Century: Leonid Pasternak between 1888 and 1916', *Festschrift in Honor of Kenneth Lindsay*. Binghamton, NY, forthcoming 1989.

Salys [see also under Gaigalas].

Sbornik statei, posvyashchennykh tvorchestvu B. L. Pasternaka. Munich, 1962.

Schnack, I. *Rainer Maria Rilkes Erinnerungen an Marburg und das Hessische Land*. Marburg, n.d.

Schwarzband, S. 'Pasternak's *Marburg*. On the Evolution of Poetic Structures', *Scottish Slavonic Review*, 8 (1987), 57–74.

Schweitzer, R. *Freundschaft mit Boris Pasternak*. Munich–Vienna–Basel, 1963.

Serebryakova, G. *O drugikh i o sebe*. Moscow, 1972.

Shaginyan, M. '"Bliznets v tuchakh". Stikhi Borisa Pasternaka', *Priazovsky krai* (Rostov on Don), 196 (28 September 1914).

Sheikholeslami, E. A. F. 'Der deutsche Einfluss im Werke von Boris Pasternak'. Ph.D. dissertation, University of Pennsylvania, 1973.

'Pasternak's Unpublished Essay "About the Object and Method of Psychology" and its Relation to Pasternak's Aesthetics', paper delivered at New England Slavic Conference, Amherst, MA, April 15, 1978.

Shershenevich, V. 'Boris Pasternak. "Bliznets v tuchakh". Moskva 1914', *Svobodnyi zhurnal*, 11 (1914), 134–5.

Shershenevich [see also under Egyx].

Shklovsky, V. 'Iskusstvo kak priem', *Poetika. Sborniki po teorii poeticheskogo yazyka*. Petrograd, 1919, 101–14.

Gamburgsky schet. Leningrad, 1928.

Zhili-byli. Moscow, 1964.

Simplicio, D. di. 'Iz rannikh prozaicheskikh opytov B. Pasternaka', *Slavica Hierosolymitana*, 4 (1979), 286–93.

Sinyavsky, A. 'Poeziya Pasternaka', in Boris Pasternak, *Stikhotvoreniya i poemy*. Moscow–Leningrad, 1965, 9–62.

'Odin den' s Pasternakom', in Aucouturier (ed.) (1979), 11–17.

Sinyavsky [see also with Men'shutin].

Sirin, V. (pseudonym of Vladimir Nabokov) Review of D. Kobyakov, *Gorech'* (Paris, 1927) and *Keramika* (Paris, 1925), and of E. Shakh, *Semya na kamne* (Paris, 1927), *Rul'*, 11 May 1927.

Skryabin, A. N. 'Zapisi A. N. Skryabina', *Russkie propilei*, 6 (1919), 120–247.

Sonaty. Moscow, 1962.

Spassky, S. 'Moskva', in Reformatskaya (ed.) (1963), 161–77.

Stepun, F. A. *Byvshee i nesbyvsheesya*, 2 vols. New York, 1956.

Störig, H. J. *Kleine Weltgeschichte der Philosophie*. Stuttgart, 1950.

Stroeva, M. N. 'Moskovsky khudozhestvenny teatr', *Russkaya khudozhestvennaya kul'tura kontsa XIX-nachala XX veka (1908–1917)*, III, Moscow, 1977, 22–64.

Struve, G. *Russkaya literatura v izgnanii*. New York, 1956.

'Koe-chto o Pasternake i Ril'ke', in Aucouturier (ed.) (1979), 441–9.

Suhrcke, P. 'The Place of "Ja višu na pere u tvorca" in Pasternak's Work', *Slavonic and East European Journal*, 25 no. 3 (Fall 1981), 71–82.

Taubman, J. A. 'Marina Tsvetaeva and Boris Pasternak: Towards the History of a Friendship', *Russian Literature Triquarterly*, 2 (Winter 1972), 303–21.

Thomson, B. *The Premature Revolution: Russian Literature and Society, 1917–1946.* London, 1972.

Timenchik, R. 'Khram Premudrosti Boga: stikhotvorenie Anny Akhmatovoi "shiroko raspakhnuty vorota..."', *Slavica Hierosolymitana,* 5–6 (1981), 297–18.

Trenin [see with Khardzhiev].

Troitsky, N. A. *Boris Leonidovich Pasternak 1890–1960. A Bibliography.* Ithaca, NY, 1969.

Trotsky, L. *Literatura i revolyutsiya.* Moscow, 1923.

Tsvetaeva, M. *Proza.* New York, 1953.

Neizdannye pis'ma. Paris, 1972.

Tsvetaeva (Zwetajewa) [see under Correspondence in Works by Boris Pasternak].

Tynyanov, Yu. 'Promezhutok', *Russky sovremennik,* 4 (1924), 209–21; reprinted in his *Arkhaisty i novatory.* Leningrad, 1929, 563–8, 579–80.

V.K. 'V redaktsii "Krasnoi novi"', *Chitatel' i pisatel',* 24 (16 June 1928).

Vermel' [see Chelionati].

Vil'mont, N. 'Boris Pasternak. Vospominaniya i mysli', *Novyi mir,* 6 (1987), 166–221.

Vishniak, V. 'Pasternak's "Roslyy strelok" and the Tradition of the Hunter and the Duck', *Irish Slavonic Studies,* 7 (1986), 53–64.

Voskobojnikov, V. 'La musica nella vita e nelle opere di Pasternak', *Rassegna sovietica,* 2 (1984), 187–98.

Voskobojnikov [see also with Ashkenazy].

Voznesensky, A. *Akhillesovo serdtse,* Moscow, 1966.

Vvedensky, A. *Polnoe sobranie sochinenii,* II. Ann Arbor, MI, 1984.

West, J. *Russian Symbolism.* London, 1970.

Williams, R. C. *Culture in Exile: Russian Émigrés in Germany, 1881–1941,* Ithaca, NY, 1972.

Woloschin, M. *Die grüne Schlange. Lebenserinnerungen einer Malerin.* Frankfurt am Main, 1982.

Wordsworth, W. *The Prelude,* book XI. New Haven–London, 1981.

Wright-Kovaleva, R. 'Mayakovsky and Pasternak: Fragments of Reminiscence', *Oxford Slavonic Papers,* 13 (1967), 108–32.

Yakobson, A. 'Stikhotvorenie Borisa Pasternaka "Roslyi strelok, ostorozhnyi okhotnik"', *Kontinent,* 25 (1980), 323–33.

Yunggren [see Ljunggren].

Zaitsev, B. 'Put'', in *Sbornik statei* (1962), 16–19.

'Zametki o peresechenii biografii Osipa Mandel'shtama i Borisa Pasternaka', *Pamyat',* 4 (1981), 283–337.

Zamoyska, H. 'L'art et la vie chez Boris Pasternak', *Revue des études slaves,* 38 (1961), 231–9.

Zamyatin, E. 'Novaya russkaya proza', *Russkoe iskusstvo,* 2–3 (1923), 57–67; reprinted in his *Litsa.* New York, 1955, 191–210.

Zelinsky, K. *Kriticheskie pis'ma. Kniga vtoraya*. Moscow, 1934.
  Na rubezhe dvukh epokh. Moscow, 1959.
Zhirmunsky, V. M. 'Genrikh fon Kleist', *Russkaya mysl'*, 8–9 (1914), section 2,
  1–11.

Index of works by Boris Pasternak

Page references are provided in each case for the Russian titles of Pasternak's works, with a cross-reference to the English titles used in the text of this book. Numerals in brackets indicate pages on which a quotation from a given work, or an allusion to it, has occurred without its being explicitly identified. Titles beginning with numerals are placed after the final alphabetical entry. Pasternak's musical compositions are listed directly after his literary works. Works by other authors which were translated by Pasternak are listed in the general index. Certain works by Pasternak are known in English by more than one title – e.g. *The Story (Povest')*, is published in George Reavey's version as *The Last Summer*; the index below provides cross-references for such alternative titles where they are in common currency. Ellipsis after an item identifies the first line of an untitled poem.

'About Myself and About Readers' *see* 'O sebe i o chitatelyakh'
'About These Verses' *see* 'Pro eti stikhi'
Aerial Ways see 'Vozdushnye puti'
'After me all call you miss . . .' *see* 'Vsled za mnoi vse zovut vas baryshnei . . .'
'Afterword' *see* 'Posleslov'e' (*Sestra moya zhizn'*)
'Afterword' *see* 'Posleslov'e' (*Okhrannaya gramota*)
'Anguish' *see* 'Toska'
'Anne Akhmatovoi', (412)
'Apassionata', 210
Apelles Mark, The see 'Apellesova cherta'
'Apellesova cherta', 193, 194–7, 200, 217, 219, 260, 269, 353
'Arctic Seamstress' *see* 'Polyarnaya shveya'
'Arising from the thunderous rhombus . . .' *see* 'Vstav iz grokhochushchego romba . . .'
'Artillerist stoit u kormila . . .', 180–1, 188, (190)
'As treasurer of the last of planets . . .' *see* 'Kak kaznachei poslednei iz planet . . .'
'As with bronze ash from braziers . . .' *see* 'Kak bronzovoi zoloi zharoven' . . .'
'Attempt to part the soul' *see* 'Popytka dushu razluchit''
Autobiographical Essay see 'Avtobiografichesky ocherk'
'Autumn. Unused to the lightnings . . .' *see* 'Osen'. Otvykli ot molnii . . .'
'Avtobiografichesky ocherk' 16, 18, 21–2, 29 (30), (32), (45–7), (50), 52, 59,

(62), (64), 75, (76), 81, 89, (92–3), (95), 96, (109), 149, (155), 156, (160), (163), 164, (170), 172, 188, 191, (192), 222, 225, (227–8), (258), (289), (290), 291, (292), (295–6), (316–17), (326), (389), (390)

'Babochka-burya', 310
'Bad Dream, A' *see* 'Durnoi son'
'Ballada', 219, 411
'Ballade' *see* 'Ballada'
'Banquets' *see* 'Pirshestva'
'Before Parting' *see* 'Pered razlukoi'
'Beggar Who Is Proud, A' *see* 'Nadmennyi nishchii'
'Beloved – o dread! When poets are in love . . .' *see* 'Lyubimaya–zhut'! Kogda lyubit poet . . .'
'Belye stikhi', 229
'Bezlyub'e', 215, 223–4, 237, 260, 328
'Black Goblet, The' *see* 'Chernyi bokal'
'Black Spring . . .' *see* 'Fevral'. Dostat' chernil i plakat' . . .'
'Blank Verses' *see* 'Belye stikhi'
Bliznets v tuchakh, 153, 159–60, 162, 177, 209, (406), 408, 410
'Blizzard, The' *see* 'Metel''
'Bol'noi sledit. Shest' dnei podryad . . .', (247)
'Break-up' *see* 'Raspad'
'Bryusovu', (330), (412)
'But they too were doomed to fade' *see* 'No i im suzhdeno bylo vytsvest' . . .'
'Butterfly Storm' *see* 'Babochka-burya'

General index

Note: the term 'trans.' after a work and author indicates Pasternak's translation of the work concerned.

483

General Index

Pachmann, Vladimir de (1848–1933), 6
Paganini, Niccolo (1782–1840), 194, 196
Palestine, 14, 27, 282, 405
Palmov, Viktor Nikandrovich
    (1888–1929), 316
Pan (Hamsun), 77
Paris, 10, 38, 120, 141, 254, 309, 342,
    375, 378
Parnok, Sofia Yakovlevna (1885–1933),
    319, 331, 369, 375
'Parting' (Tsvetaeva), 297
Pascal, Blaise (1623–62), 129
Pasternak, Aleksandr ('Shura')
    Leonidovich (1893–1982), 13, 18–24,
    26–8, 31–4, 38, 45, 50–1, 56, 58,
    63–8, 72–3, 79, 82, 84, 89, 98, 106–9,
    140, 148, 164, 169, 183–4, 186–7,
    193, 217, 236, 241–2, 244, 247, 281,
    300–1, 304, 308, 313–14, 357, 377,
    391, 393, 403; birth of 13; early life
    with Boris, 18–20; musical interests,
    21–2, 66, 66, 79, 84; schooling, 31–4,
    58, 65, 68, 107; Berlin sojourn 1906,
    64–6; relations with parents, 26, 28;
    education at Moscow University and
    School of Painting, 107, 169; in Civil
    War, 244, 247; marriage, 300, 312;
    career as architect, 314; 1924 Berlin
    journey, 314
Pasternak, Aleksandr ('Sasha'/'Indidya')
    Osipovich, 3, 39
Pasternak, Anna *see* Margulius, A. O.
Pasternak, Boris ('Borya') Leonidovich
    (1890–1960): birth and alleged
    baptism of, 12–13; infancy, 14–17, 22;
    childhood, 17–28; childhood friends,
    34, 38; schooling, 27, 31–4, 48, 55–8,
    65–8, 98; relationship with parents, 16,
    20, 23–6, 97, 106, 108, 216, 404, 418;
    Jewish status and awareness, 27–8,
    32–3, 78, 142, 313; religion 27–8, 33;
    family holidays, 38–9, 41, 45–9, 55–6,
    58, 67, 84–7, 102–3, 155; boyhood art
    interest, 19, 42–3, 45; boyhood music
    interest, 20–2, 26; musical studies,
    49–52, 67–8, 70, 77–8, 81–4, 87, 200,
    220, 397; as pianist, 21, 45, 50, 65,
    80–1, 84–5, 87–8, 93, 199–200, 318,
    353; compositions, 80–2 *see also* index
    of works by Pasternak; adolescent
    reading, 64–5, 74–7; youthful
    personality and perceptions, 26, 28,
    33–4, 46–8, 50, 69–73, 81–2; student
    and adult personality, 97, 99–100,
    102–8; *Weltgefühl* and artistic
    personality, 24, 71–2, 111–18, 122,

130–3, 136–7, 149–52, 157–8, 166–7,
202–3, 218–20, 231–4, 256, 268–9,
271–2; views of 1905 revolution, 55–7,
59–60; 1906 Berlin sojourn, 62–8; law
studies, 78, 83, 119–20; philosophy
studies, 83, 92, 119–26, 128–33,
137–8, 140–2, 148–9; tutoring, 97–9,
105, 115, 185–7, 352; childhood
literary attempts, 20; start in literature,
106–18; childhood literary attempts,
20; start in literature, 106–18; juvenilia
(prose) 16, 70, 92, 103–4, 108–10,
112, 114–18, 150–2, 194–5, 231;
(verse): 70, 73, 92, 94, 99, 106–14,
136, 142–5, 150; literary debut,
154–5; association with Lirika and
Tsentrifuga *see* Lirika; Tsentrifuga;
Rukonog; Second Tsentrifuga Miscellany;
injury and military exemption, 48–9,
177–8; adult political view, 97; in
World War I, 177–82, 185, 213–14;
sojourn in Urals, 198–205; sojourn on
Kama, 213–22; writing of *Twin in the
Stormclouds*, 155–8; *Over the Barriers*,
208–11; view of February 1917
revolution, 224–8; October revolution,
238–42, 250–3; writing of *My Sister
Life*, 228–34, 262–4; involvement in
'café culture', 255–9; Civil War
publishing, 259–63; *Themes and
Variations*, 247–50, 263–8; public
recitation, 257–8; critical response to
My Sister Life, 285–8; interest in
Petrograd culture, 75–6, 291–5; Berlin
sojourn 1922–3, 303–12; *vis à vis*
'proletarian' literature, 344–6;
involvement with Lef, 316–17,
339–41, 383–91 *see also relations with*
Mayakovsky; *Spektorsky*, 350–2, 356,
394; *Lieutenant Schmidt*, 361–6; *The
Year Nineteen Five* 356–60; prose
writings of 1930s, 16–17, 204,
213–14, 376; interest in cinema, 72,
155, 268; concern with the *poema*, 189
and n., 203, 218–19, 321–4, 408;
translation work, 142, 153, 176, 187,
217–221, 273–4, 334–5, 337–8,
353–5, 358, 368, 383, 397–8; travel
plans late 1920s, 391–2, 404–5; mood
of late 1920s, 399; family contacts late
1920s, 404–5; writing of *Safe Conduct*,
396–9; relations with women, 15–16,
76, 99–100, 271, 299, 355, 375–6;
relations with Vysotskaya, 98–100,
107, 134–5, 140–1, 155–6, 196, 219,
248, 263, 296, 306; relations with

497